SPECTRAL LOGIC
AND ITS APPLICATIONS
FOR THE DESIGN
OF DIGITAL DEVICES

SPECTRAL LOGIC AND ITS APPLICATIONS FOR THE DESIGN OF DIGITAL DEVICES

MARK G. KARPOVSKY
RADOMIR S. STANKOVIĆ
JAAKKO T. ASTOLA

WILEY-
INTERSCIENCE

A JOHN WILEY & SONS, INC., PUBLICATION

Published by John Wiley & Sons, Inc., Hoboken, New Jersey
Published simultaneously in Canada

For general information on our other products and services or for technical support, please contact our Customer Care Department within the United States at (800) 762-2974, outside the United States at (317) 572-3993, or fax (317) 572-4002.

Wiley also publishes its books in a variety of electronic formats. Some content that appears in print may not be available in electronic formats. For more information about Wiley products, visit our Web site at www.wiley.com.

Library of Congress Cataloging-in-Publication Data

Karpovsky, Mark G.
  Spectral logic and its applications for the design of digital devices / Mark G. Karpovsky, Radomir S. Stankovic, Jaakko T. Astola.
    p. cm.
  Includes bibliographical references.
  ISBN 978-0-471-73188-7 (cloth)
1. Logic design–Methodology.   2. Spectrum analysis.   3. Digital electronics–Mathematics.
4. Signal processing–Mathematics.   5. Spectral theory (Mathematics)   I. Stankovic, Radomir S., 1952–
II. Astola, Jaakko.   III. Title.
  TK7868.L6K375 2008
  621.39'5–dc22

2008002714

Printed in the United States of America

10 9 8 7 6 5 4 3 2 1

CONTENTS

PREFACE   **xv**

ACKNOWLEDGMENTS   **xxv**

LIST OF FIGURES   **xxvii**

LIST OF TABLES   **xxxiii**

ACRONYMS   **xxxix**

1. LOGIC FUNCTIONS   **1**

    1.1 Discrete Functions   2

    1.2 Tabular Representations of Discrete Functions   3

    1.3 Functional Expressions   6

    1.4 Decision Diagrams for Discrete Functions   10

        1.4.1 Decision Trees   11

        1.4.2 Decision Diagrams   13

        1.4.3 Decision Diagrams for Multiple-Valued Functions   16

    1.5 Spectral Representations of Logic Functions   16

    1.6 Fixed-polarity Reed–Muller Expressions of Logic Functions   23

    1.7 Kronecker Expressions of Logic Functions   25

    1.8 Circuit Implementation of Logic Functions   27

2. SPECTRAL TRANSFORMS FOR LOGIC FUNCTIONS   **31**

2.1   Algebraic Structures for Spectral Transforms   32

2.2   Fourier Series   34

2.3   Bases for Systems of Boolean Functions   35

    2.3.1   Basis Functions   35

    2.3.2   Walsh Functions   36

       2.3.2.1   Ordering of Walsh Functions   40

       2.3.2.2   Properties of Walsh Functions   43

       2.3.2.3   Hardware Implementations of Walsh Functions   47

    2.3.3   Haar Functions   50

       2.3.3.1   Ordering of Haar Functions   51

       2.3.3.2   Properties of Haar Functions   55

       2.3.3.3   Hardware Implementation of Haar Functions   56

       2.3.3.4   Hardware Implementation of the Inverse Haar Transform   58

2.4   Walsh Related Transforms   60

    2.4.1   Arithmetic Transform   61

    2.4.2   Arithmetic Expressions from Walsh Expansions   62

2.5   Bases for Systems of Multiple-Valued Functions   65

    2.5.1   Vilenkin–Chrestenson Functions and Their Properties   66

    2.5.2   Generalized Haar Functions   70

2.6   Properties of Discrete Walsh and Vilenkin–Chrestenson Transforms   71

2.7   Autocorrelation and Cross-Correlation Functions   79

    2.7.1   Definitions of Autocorrelation and Cross-Correlation Functions   79

    2.7.2   Relationships to the Walsh and Vilenkin–Chrestenson Transforms, the Wiener-Khinchin Theorem   80

    2.7.3   Properties of Correlation Functions   82

    2.7.4   Generalized Autocorrelation Functions   84

2.8   Harmonic Analysis over an Arbitrary Finite Abelian Group   85

    2.8.1   Definition and Properties of the Fourier Transform on Finite Abelian Groups   85

    2.8.2   Construction of Group Characters   89

    2.8.3   Fourier–Galois Transforms   94

2.9   Fourier Transform on Finite Non–Abelian Groups   97

    2.9.1   Representation of Finite Groups   98

    2.9.2   Fourier Transform on Finite Non-Abelian Groups   101

3. CALCULATION OF SPECTRAL TRANSFORMS   **106**

    3.1   Calculation of Walsh Spectra   106

       3.1.1   Matrix Interpretation of the Fast Walsh Transform   109

       3.1.2   Decision Diagram Methods for Calculation of Spectral Transforms   114

       3.1.3   Calculation of the Walsh Spectrum Through BDD   115

    3.2   Calculation of the Haar Spectrum   118

       3.2.1   FFT-Like Algorithms for the Haar Transform   118

       3.2.2   Matrix Interpretation of the Fast Haar Transform   121

       3.2.3   Calculation of the Haar Spectrum Through BDD   126

    3.3   Calculation of the Vilenkin–Chrestenson Spectrum   135

       3.3.1   Matrix Interpretation of the Fast Vilenkin–Chrestenson Transform   136

       3.3.2   Calculation of the Vilenkin–Chrestenson Transform Through Decision Diagrams   140

    3.4   Calculation of the Generalized Haar Spectrum   141

    3.5   Calculation of Autocorrelation Functions   142

       3.5.1   Matrix Notation for the Wiener–Khinchin Theorem   143

       3.5.2   Wiener–Khinchin Theorem Over Decision Diagrams   143

       3.5.3   In-place Calculation of Autocorrelation Coefficients by Decision Diagrams   148

4. SPECTRAL METHODS IN OPTIMIZATION OF DECISION DIAGRAMS   **154**

    4.1   Reduction of Sizes of Decision Diagrams   155

       4.1.1 K-Procedure for Reduction of Sizes of Decision Diagrams   156

       4.1.2   Properties of the K-Procedure   164

    4.2   Construction of Linearly Transformed Binary Decision Diagrams   169

       4.2.1   Procedure for Construction of Linearly Transformed Binary Decision Diagrams   171

       4.2.2   Modified K-Procedure   172

       4.2.3   Computing Autocorrelation by Symbolic Manipulations   172

       4.2.4   Experimental Results on the Complexity of Linearly Transformed Binary Decision Diagrams   173

    4.3   Construction of Linearly Transformed Planar BDD   177

       4.3.1   Planar Decision Diagrams   178

       4.3.2   Construction of Planar LT-BDD by Walsh Coefficients   181

       4.3.3   Upper Bounds on the Number of Nodes in Planar BDDs   185

4.3.4   Experimental Results for Complexity of Planar LT-BDDs   187

4.4   Spectral Interpretation of Decision Diagrams   188

4.4.1   Haar Spectral Transform Decision Diagrams   192

4.4.2   Haar Transform Related Decision Diagrams   197

5.   ANALYSIS AND OPTIMIZATION OF LOGIC FUNCTIONS   200

5.1   Spectral Analysis of Boolean Functions   200

5.1.1   Linear Functions   201

5.1.2   Self-Dual and Anti-Self-Dual Functions   203

5.1.3   Partially Self-Dual and Partially Anti-Self-Dual Functions   204

5.1.4   Quadratic Forms, Functions with Flat Autocorrelation   207

5.2   Analysis and Synthesis of Threshold Element Networks   212

5.2.1   Threshold Elements   212

5.2.2   Identification of Single Threshold Functions   214

5.3   Complexity of Logic Functions   222

5.3.1   Definition of Complexity of Systems of Switching Functions   222

5.3.2   Complexity and the Number of Pairs of Neighboring Minterms   225

5.3.3   Complexity Criteria for Multiple-Valued Functions   227

5.4   Serial Decomposition of Systems of Switching Functions   227

5.4.1   Spectral Methods and Complexity   227

5.4.2   Linearization Relative to the Number of Essential Variables   228

5.4.3   Linearization Relative to the Entropy-Based Complexity Criteria   231

5.4.4   Linearization Relative to the Numbers of Neighboring Pairs of Minterms   233

5.4.5   Classification of Switching Functions by Linearization   237

5.4.6   Linearization of Multiple-Valued Functions Relative to the Number of Essential Variables   239

5.4.7   Linearization for Multiple-Valued Functions Relative to the Entropy-Based Complexity Criteria   242

5.5   Parallel Decomposition of Systems of Switching Functions   244

5.5.1   Polynomial Approximation of Completely Specified Functions   244

5.5.2   Additive Approximation Procedure   249

5.5.3 Complexity Analysis of Polynomial Approximations 250

5.5.4 Approximation Methods for Multiple-Valued Functions 251

5.5.5 Estimation of the Number of Nonzero Coefficients 255

6. SPECTRAL METHODS IN SYNTHESIS OF LOGIC NETWORKS **261**

6.1 Spectral Methods of Synthesis of Combinatorial Devices 262

6.1.1 Spectral Representations of Systems of Logic Functions 262

6.1.2 Spectral Methods for the Design of Combinatorial Devices 264

6.1.3 Asymptotically Optimal Implementation of Systems of Linear Functions 266

6.1.4 Walsh and Vilenkin–Chrestenson Bases for the Design of Combinatorial Networks 270

6.1.5 Linear Transforms of Variables in Haar Expressions 272

6.1.6 Synthesis with Haar Functions 274

6.1.6.1 Minimization of the Number of Nonzero Haar Coefficients 274

6.1.6.2 Determination of Optimal Linear Transform of Variables 275

6.1.6.3 Efficiency of the Linearization Method 283

6.2 Spectral Methods for Synthesis of Incompletely Specified Functions 286

6.2.1 Synthesis of Incompletely Specified Switching Functions 286

6.2.2 Synthesis of Incompletely Specified Functions by Haar Expressions 286

6.3 Spectral Methods of Synthesis of Multiple-Valued Functions 292

6.3.1 Multiple-Valued Functions 292

6.3.2 Network Implementations of Multiple-Valued Functions 292

6.3.3 Completion of Multiple-Valued Functions 293

6.3.4 Complexity of Linear Multiple-Valued Networks 293

6.3.5 Minimization of Numbers of Nonzero Coefficients in the Generalized Haar Spectrum for Multiple-Valued Functions 295

6.4 Spectral Synthesis of Digital Functions and Sequences Generators 298

6.4.1 Function Generators 298

6.4.2 Design Criteria for Digital Function Generators 299

6.4.3 Hardware Complexity of Digital Function Generators 300

6.4.4 Bounds for the Number of Coefficients in Walsh Expansions of Analytical Functions 302

6.4.5   Implementation of Switching Functions Represented
by Haar Series   303

6.4.6   Spectral Methods for Synthesis of Sequence Generators   304

7. SPECTRAL METHODS OF SYNTHESIS OF SEQUENTIAL MACHINES   308

7.1   Realization of Finite Automata by Spectral Methods   308

7.1.1   Finite Structural Automata   308

7.1.2   Spectral Implementation of Excitation Functions   311

7.2   Assignment of States and Inputs for Completely Specified
Automata   313

7.2.1   Optimization of the Assignments for Implementation
of the Combinational Part by Using the Haar Basis   315

7.2.2   Minimization of the Number of Highest Order Nonzero
Coefficients   320

7.2.3   Minimization of the Number of Lowest Order Nonzero
Coefficients   322

7.3   State Assignment for Incompletely Specified Automata   333

7.3.1   Minimization of Higher Order Nonzero Coefficients in
Representation of Incompletely Specified Automata   333

7.3.2   Minimization of Lower Order Nonzero Coefficients in
Spectral Representation of Incompletely Specified
Automata   338

7.4   Some Special Cases of the Assignment Problem   342

7.4.1   Preliminary Remarks   342

7.4.2   Autonomous Automata   342

7.4.3   Assignment Problem for Automata with Fixed Encoding
of Inputs or Internal States   344

8. HARDWARE IMPLEMENTATION OF SPECTRAL METHODS   348

8.1   Spectral Methods of Synthesis with ROM   349

8.2   Serial Implementation of Spectral Methods   349

8.3   Sequential Haar Networks   350

8.4   Complexity of Serial Realization by Haar Series   352

8.4.1   Optimization of Sequential Spectral Networks   356

8.5   Parallel Realization of Spectral Methods of Synthesis   358

8.6   Complexity of Parallel Realization   359

8.7   Realization by Expansions over Finite Fields   362

9. **SPECTRAL METHODS OF ANALYSIS AND SYNTHESIS OF RELIABLE DEVICES** **370**

9.1   Spectral Methods for Analysis of Error Correcting Capabilities   370

    9.1.1   Errors in Combinatorial Devices   370

    9.1.2   Analysis of Error-Correcting Capabilities   371

    9.1.3   Correction of Arithmetic Errors   381

9.2   Spectral Methods for Synthesis of Reliable Digital Devices   386

    9.2.1   Reliable Systems for Transmission and Logic Processing   386

    9.2.2   Correction of Single Errors   388

    9.2.3   Correction of Burst Errors   391

    9.2.4   Correction of Errors with Different Costs   393

    9.2.5   Correction of Multiple Errors   396

9.3   Correcting Capability of Sequential Machines   399

    9.3.1   Error Models for Finite Automata   399

    9.3.2   Computing an Expected Number of Corrected Errors   400

        9.3.2.1   Simplified Calculation of Characteristic Functions   400

        9.3.2.2   Calculation of Two-Dimensional Autocorrelation Functions   404

    9.3.3   Error-Correcting Capabilities of Linear Automata   408

    9.3.4   Error-Correcting Capability of Group Automata   410

    9.3.5   Error-Correcting Capabilities of Counting Automata   411

9.4   Synthesis of Fault-Tolerant Automata with Self-Error Correction   414

    9.4.1   Fault-Tolerant Devices   414

    9.4.2   Spectral Implementation of Fault-Tolerant Automata   415

    9.4.3   Realization of Sequential Networks with Self-Error Correction   416

9.5   Comparison of Spectral and Classical Methods   419

10. **SPECTRAL METHODS FOR TESTING OF DIGITAL SYSTEMS** **422**

10.1   Testing and Diagnosis by Verification of Walsh Coefficients   423

    10.1.1   Fault Models   423

    10.1.2   Conditions for Testability   426

    10.1.3   Conditions for Fault Diagnosis   428

10.2   Functional Testing, Error Detection, and Correction by Linear Checks   430

    10.2.1   Introduction to Linear Checks   430

	10.2.2	Check Complexities of Linear Checks	431
	10.2.3	Spectral Methods for Construction of Optimal Linear Checks	434
	10.2.4	Hardware Implementations of Linear Checks	440
	10.2.5	Error-Detecting Capabilities of Linear Checks	442
	10.2.6	Detection and Correction of Errors by Systems of Orthogonal Linear Checks	446
10.3	Linear Checks for Processors	455
10.4	Linear Checks for Error Detection in Polynomial Computations	457
10.5	Construction of Optimal Linear Checks for Polynomial Computations	462
10.6	Implementations and Error-Detecting Capabilities of Linear Checks	471
10.7	Testing for Numerical Computations	474
	10.7.1	Linear Inequality Checks for Numerical Computations	474
	10.7.2	Properties of Linear Inequality Checks	475
	10.7.3	Check Complexities for Positive (Negative) Functions	479
10.8	Optimal Inequality Checks and Error-Correcting Codes	480
	10.8.1	Error Detection in Computation of Numerical Functions	483
	10.8.2	Estimations of the Probabilities of Error Detection for Inequality Checks	487
	10.8.3	Construction of Optimal Systems of Orthogonal Inequality Checks	489
	10.8.4	Error-Detecting and Error-Correcting Capabilities of Systems of Orthogonal Inequality Checks	492
10.9	Error Detection in Computer Memories by Linear Checks	498
	10.9.1	Testing of Read-Only Memories	498
	10.9.2	Correction of Single and Double Errors in ROMs by Two Orthogonal Equality Checks	499
10.10	Location of Errors in ROMs by Two Orthogonal Inequality Checks	504
10.11	Detection and Location of Errors in Random-Access Memories	507

11. EXAMPLES OF APPLICATIONS AND GENERALIZATIONS OF SPECTRAL METHODS ON LOGIC FUNCTIONS

11.	**EXAMPLES OF APPLICATIONS AND GENERALIZATIONS OF SPECTRAL METHODS ON LOGIC FUNCTIONS**	**512**
11.1	Transforms Designed for Particular Applications		513
	11.1.1	Hybrid Transforms	513
	11.1.2	Hadamard–Haar Transform	514

	11.1.3	Slant Transform	516
	11.1.4	Parameterised Transforms	518
11.2	Wavelet Transforms		521
11.3	Fibonacci Transforms		523
	11.3.1	Fibonacci p-Numbers	524
	11.3.2	Fibonacci p-Codes	525
	11.3.3	Contracted Fibonacci p-Codes	525
	11.3.4	Fibonacci–Walsh Hadamard Transform	527
	11.3.5	Fibonacci-Haar Transform	528
	11.3.6	Fibonacci SOP-Expressions	528
	11.3.7	Fibonacci Reed–Muller Expressions	529
11.4	Two-Dimensional Spectral Transforms		530
	11.4.1	Two-Dimensional Discrete Cosine Transform	534
	11.4.2	Related Applications of Spectral Methods in Image Processing	536
11.5	Application of the Walsh Transform in Broadband Radio		537

APPENDIX A   **541**

REFERENCES   **554**

INDEX   **593**

PREFACE

Spectral logic is a mathematical discipline in the area of *abstract harmonic analysis* devoted to applications in engineering, primarily electrical and computer engineering.

Abstract harmonic analysis has evolved from classical Fourier analysis by replacing the real line R, which is a particular locally compact Abelian group, by an arbitrary locally compact Abelian or compact non-Abelian group. The exponential functions, which are group characters of R, are replaced by *group characters of Abelian groups* and *group representations for non-Abelian groups*.

Spectral techniques mainly deal with signals of compact groups and in most cases *finite groups*. In this way, when using transforms defined in terms of group characters, the origins of spectral techniques can be found in classical Fourier analysis (181). Switching (Boolean) functions are an example of functions defined on a particular finite group that is the group of binary-valued n-tuples under the componentwise addition modulo 2 (EXOR). This group is known as a finite *dyadic* group.

For functions of this group, the Fourier transform is defined in terms of the discrete *Walsh functions*, which are characters of the finite dyadic groups. The origins of spectral techniques in terms of the discrete Walsh functions can be found in the theory of *Walsh analysis*, which is defined in terms of continuous Walsh functions introduced in 1923 (638) and interpreted as group characters of the infinite dyadic group in 1949 (176). Initially, Walsh functions have been defined on the interval (0, 1), which can be mapped into the infinite dyadic group.

Many important problems in analysis, design, and testing of digital devices have simple and sometimes even analytical solutions in the spectral domain whereas the solutions of these problems in the original domain are very difficult. Some of these problems will be discussed in detail in this book.

Through the group theoretic approach, various spectral transforms can be uniformly viewed as transforms on the groups. The discrete *Haar transform* is a particular spectral transform on finite dyadic groups efficiently used in computer engineering. This transform can be viewed as a discrete counterpart of the Haar transform, which is defined in terms of the Haar functions introduced in 1910 (223) as a particular set of functions defined on the interval (0, 1). Thus, the origins of spectral techniques exploiting the discrete Haar transform can be dated back to 1910 (223).

The Haar transform is an example of the so-called *local transforms* in the sense that except for the first two coefficients, all other coefficients can be calculated over a subset of function values. This is a very useful property that allows focusing on function values of subsets of their domains, and thus to study local properties of a signal modeled by the function considered. This is the main property that characterizes the *wavelets theory*, which in this respect can be viewed as an extension of Fourier analysis. The same property implies a simplified calculation of spectral coefficients, which makes the Haar transform computationally very efficient.

The *Reed–Muller transform* is another example of local transforms on finite dyadic groups. The spectral interpretation of the Reed–Muller expressions is related to the application of FFT-like algorithms for their calculations proposed by Ph.W. Besslich (60). This interpretation establishes a link between Reed–Muller expressions and spectral transforms. Thus, this interpretation permits one to consider that the mathematical foundations for the application of this particular spectral transform in switching theory and logic design were already set in 1927 (678) and 1928 (679). This transform is defined over the finite field $GF(2)$, that is, values of Reed–Muller spectral coefficients are logic values 0 and 1. Transforms with this feature are called *bit-level transforms*. *Word-level transforms* require a byte, or computer word, to represent each coefficient, since they are integers, rational numbers, or complex numbers. In other words, this classification of spectral transforms is performed with respect to the range of the basis functions in terms of which the transform is defined. Examples of word-level transforms are the discrete Walsh and Haar transforms.

The same range specified for a transform is also assumed for processed functions. The values 0 and 1 of logic functions are interpreted as integers 0 and 1 when these function are processed by word-level transforms.

The *arithmetic transform* is defined by the interpretation of the basis functions in the Reed–Muller transforms as integer-valued functions and all the calculations are performed in the field of rational numbers. Thus, the arithmetic transform is another example of word-level local transforms.

Practical applications of spectral logic in analysis and design of switching and multiple-valued (MV) functions date back to the early history of these areas (86,106,190,315,331,391,460,599).

It is believed that spectral logics developed into a separate discipline between 1970 and 1975, which is possibly best expressed by pointing out annual symposia on Walsh and other nonsinusoidal functions, with even two international meetings on that subject in 1971 and 1973. After that time, although with somewhat fluctuating interest, spectral techniques have been continuously developing, and activity in the area has been summarized at the *International Workshops on Spectral*

Techniques in Boston 1985 (282), Montreal 1986, Dortmund 1988 (382), Beijing 1990 (within the *Conference on Signal Processing*, Beijing, P.R. China, October 22–26, 1990).

In 1992, the *Workshop on Logic Design and Microprocessor Architecture* in Iizuka, Fukuoka, Japan, provided space for a tutorial discussion of spectral methods in logic design by Varma and Trachtenberg, which was further developed in a chapter (624) of a book edited afterward by Sasao (486), accompanied by a chapter on minimization of AND–EXOR expressions including fixed polarity Reed–Muller expressions (485).

Another *Workshop on Spectral Techniques* had been organized March 15–17, 1994, hosted by Beijing University of Aeronautic and Astronautics, Beijing, P.R. China and chaired by Qishang Zhang and Claudio Moraga (389), with selected papers published afterward in Reference (383). As an especially important contribution of the workshop in 1994, we mention a bibliography of papers in this areas which were published in Russian. The bibliography has been prepared by Shmerko and Mikhailov (525).

Advances in spectral methods for digital logic have often been presented at regular sessions at conferences on signal processing and circuit design, among which the *International Symposia on Multiple-Valued Logic* (ISMVL) are probably the most important for research in this area. Within the ISMVL, this activity was carefully traced and discussed, and a summary of developments in theory and practice of spectral techniques up to the late 1970s was given by Karpovsky (281), while the development in the next decade was overviewed by Moraga (380). The most recent review has been presented at the ISMVL 2001 (299).

The Workshop on Spectral Methods and Logic Design for Future Digital Systems, held on June 2–3, 2000 in Tampere, Finland, organized by Tampere International Center for Signal Processing (TICSP), within the Institute of Signal Processing at Tampere University of Technology, Tampere, Finland, was an event devoted to applications of spectral methods in logic design. It can be viewed as an additional activity in the series of annual *TICSP Workshops on Spectral Methods and Multirate Signal Processing* organized regularly by TICSP starting from 1998 to date.

In switching theory and logic design, there is apparently a renewed and considerable interest in exploiting spectral techniques after the publication of a report about applications of Walsh functions in technology mapping (655). This interest is due to requirements regarding complexity and performances of logic networks and digital devices, which in many cases cannot be met by traditional approaches.

It should be noted that renewed interest in Reed–Muller expressions is due to the publication of the paper (493) presenting a conjecture that AND–EXOR expressions require on the average a smaller number of products compared with sum-of-product (SOP) expressions. This conjecture was confirmed and experimentally verified by the same authors and many others in a series of publications. (See a discussion and References 489,491).

This renewed interest in this subject resulted in the organization of *International Workshops on Applications of Reed–Muller Expansions in Circuit Design* in Hamburg, Germany, September 16–17, 1993 and Chiba, Tokyo, Japan, August 23–25, 1995. In addition the Reed–Muller Colloquium held on, December 19, 1995, was organized at the University of Bristol, UK.

The Reed–Muller Workshops continued in Oxford, UK, September 1997; Victoria, Canada, August 20–21, 1999; Starkville, Mississippi, USA, August 10–11, 2001. In 2003, the Workshop changed its name to *Symposium on Representations and Methodology for Future Computing Technologies*, keeping the same abbreviation (RM-Workshops), and was held in Trier, Germany, March 10–11, 2003. The series of Workshops under this name has been continued on September 5-6, 2005, in Tokyo, Japan.

The series of *Workshops on Boolean Problems*, usually held in the second half of September of every second year in Freiberg, Germany, starting in October 7, 1994, also provided room for discussing various aspects of theory and practice of Reed–Muller expressions and related representations, including other spectral representations.

Besides many other interesting results, an especially important achievement of the Reed–Muller Workshops was the establishment of relationships between spectral logic and decision diagrams (DDs) as data structures for representation of large discrete functions. Decision diagram methods for calculation of spectral logic originating in Reference (104) considerably improved applicability of spectral logic, since they permit overcoming problems related to the exponential complexity of FFT algorithms in terms of both space and time.

Conversely, spectral interpretation of decision diagrams (547,550,555,569), permits a unified consideration and classification of different decision diagrams (568) and offers a way for further generalizations and optimization of decision diagram representations (166,228,549).

It should be noted that publication of a book collecting selected papers presented at the Reed–Muller Workshop in 1995, edited by Sasao and Fujita (499), was of crucial importance for the further development of both decision diagram representations and spectral logic. This research resulted in two special issues on *Spectral Techniques in Digital Logic* of the journal *Multiple Valued Logic and Soft Computing* , No. 1 and 2, 2004.

Besides the Walsh and Reed–Muller transforms, traditional approaches in spectral techniques are related to the arithmetic and Haar transforms. The conference series *Advances in Computer Systems* organized at the Technical University of Szczecin, Poland (started 1994) has acted as a forum for discussing spectral techniques, in particular arithmetic transforms, mainly owing to the previous background work in this area done in East Europe and Russia.

Publication of the monograph (353), the book chapter (266), the tutorial paper (168), and a historic overview (156) have set fundamentals for further work in this area. The importance of arithmetic expressions is further raised by showing that some classes of decision diagrams represent functions in the form of arithmetic polynomials (387,547,550,569). In Reference 99, this property is used for defining a class of decision diagrams for an efficient representation of arithmetic circuits for the purpose of their verification and related applications. The same property has recently been exploited in efficient representations of elementary numerical functions that are important from a practical point of view (501). This interest in arithmetic transforms was confirmed by the special issue of the journal *Avtomatiku i Telemekhanika* (edition in English, *Automation and Remote Control*) , No. 6, 2004 devoted to arithmetic expressions.

For the recent interest and development in Haar transforms, credit should be given to the special session on spectral techniques and decision diagrams, accompanied by another session devoted exclusively to Haar transforms within the International Conference on Informatics, Communications and Signal Processing (1st ICICS), September 9–12, 1997, in Singapore.

The organization of several workshops and preparation of related proceedings, editing of four special issues of three journals on this subject and publication in the last decade of several monographs devoted completely or in part to spectral methods in switching and multiple-valued logic, should be considered considerable support for future work in the area (8,151,323,353,379, 499,555,567,571,576,584,604,658,661, 676,675).

We believe that the present monograph will serve the same goal and be useful in further advances in theory and application of spectral methods.

Motivation

This book, in addition to the new results in representation of discrete functions by decision diagrams and calculation of spectral transforms over decision diagrams, spectral optimization of decision diagrams, spectral testing of hardware, and so on, contains almost all results from the book Karpovsky, M.G., *Finite Orthogonal Series in the Design of Digital Devices*, John Wiley, 1976, which, in turn, has been based on Reference 289. Both of these books, together with References 16,51,234, were among the very pioneering monographs in the area of applications of spectral logic in electrical and computer engineering.

While References 16,51,234 covered different areas of electrical and computer science, the book by Karpovsky was the first book devoted to application of spectral methods to digital logic and system design. At the same time, it was written to adapt classical engineering methods based on Fourier analysis and autocorrelation functions to solve problems in switching theory and logic design. Because of these two features, the book has been well accepted and has become a standard reference in the area. The book preserved this position owing to well-presented mathematical foundations as well as a slightly different approach mainly based on autocorrelation functions as the main tool, compared to other books in the area, as in References 52, 255, and 258.

Writing this book has been directly motivated by the renewed interest in spectral techniques as reviewed above and by the introduction of decision diagrams as the data structure permitting compact representation and efficient calculation with large discrete functions. Thanks to this, exponential complexity of FFT-like algorithms, which has often been considered to be the main obstacle for practical applications of spectral methods, has been overcome up to some degree and applicability of algorithms based on spectral transforms and autocorrelation functions discussed in the book has been considerably improved. Further, the advent of data structures for representation of logic functions, either binary or multiple valued, enlarged the field of application of the optimization methods in the book.

Functional testing of digital devices, irrespective of the means for their implementation, either as software, hardware, or hardware/software systems, is a very demanding task, the complexity of which is often viewed as a drawback of manufacturing procedures. Spectral methods in many cases offer analytical solutions of testing problems (both for test pattern generation and data compression of test responses) and permit efficient implementations of test procedures. For these reasons, the book contains an extensive discussion of spectral methods for testing of digital devices.

We note that in this book, we targeted hardware for the implementation of spectral techniques, but most of the presented results can easily be generalized for the case of software implementations.

Outline

In this section, we briefly present the outline of the book (Fig. P.0.1) and specify differences with the first edition.

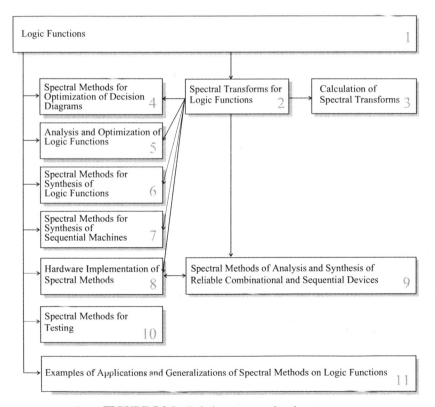

FIGURE P.0.1   Relations among the chapters.

TABLE P.0.1 Conferences and Workshops on Spectral Techniques, 1970–1999.

Year	Conference or workshop
1970	Workshop on Applications of Walsh Functions, Washington, DC, USA
1971	Workshop on Applications of Walsh Functions, Washington, DC, USA
	Proc. 1971 Symp. Theory and Applications of Walsh Functions,
	Halfield Polytechnic, Hatfield. Herts. UK.
1972	Workshop on Applications of Walsh Functions, Washington, DC, USA
1973	Workshop on Applications of Walsh Functions, Washington, DC, USA
	Symp. Walsh and Other Nonsinusoidal Functions Applications,
	Hatfield Polytechnic, England
1974	Workshop on Applications of Walsh Functions, Washington, DC, USA
1975	Symp. Walsh and Other Nonsinusoidal Functions Applications,
	Hatfield Polytechnic, England
1975	Workshop on Applications of Walsh Functions, Washington, DC, USA
1985	First Workshop on Spectral Techniques, Boston, USA
1986	Second Workshop on Spectral Techniques, Montreal, Canada
1988	Third Workshop on Spectral Techniques, Dortmund, Germany
1990	Fourth Workshop on Spectral Techniques, Beijing, P.R. China
1992	Workshop on Logic Design and Microprocessor Architecture,
	Iizuka, Fukuoka, Japan
1993	Reed–Muller Workshop, Hamburg, Germany
1994	Fifth Workshop on Spectral Techniques, Beijing, P.R. China
	First Workshop on Boolean Problems, Freiberg, Germany
	Advances in Computer Systems, Szczecin, Poland
1995	Reed–Muller Workshop, Chiba, Tokyo, Japan
	Advances in Computer Systems, Szczecin, Poland
	Reed–Muller Colloquium, University of Bristol, England, UK
1996	Second Workshop on Boolean Problems, Freiberg, Germany
	Advances in Computer Systems, Szczecin, Poland
1997	Reed–Muller Workshop, Oxford, UK
	First Int. Conf. on Information, Communication and Signal Processing,
	Singapore, *Special Session on Haar transform*
	Advances in Computer Systems, Szczecin, Poland
1998	TICSP Workshop on Transforms and Filter Banks,
	Tampere, Finland
	Third Workshop on Boolean Problems, Freiberg, Germany
	Advances in Computer Systems, Szczecin, Poland
1999	TICSP Workshop on Transforms and Filter Banks,
	Brandenburg, Germany
	Reed–Muller Workshop, Victoria, Canada

The introductory presentations in the first edition providing necessary mathematical background for discussing spectral methods are reorganized and divided into two chapters.

The first chapter contains spectral representations of discrete functions from the first edition extended by presentation of functional expressions including the Reed–

TABLE P.0.2   Conferences and Workshops on Spectral Techniques, 2000–2006.

Year	Conference or workshop
2000	Workshop on Spectral Transforms and Logic Design for Future Digital Systems, Tampere, Finland
	First Workshop on Boolean Problems, Freiberg, Germany
2001	TICSP Workshop on Spectral Methods and Multirate Signal Processing, Pula, Croatia
	Reed-Muller Workshop, Starkville, Mississippi, USA
2002	TICSP Workshop on Spectral Techniques and Multirate Signal Processing, Toulouse, France
	Fifth Workshop on Boolean Problems, Freiberg, Germany
2003	Reed-Muller Workshop, Trier, Germany
	TICSP Workshop on Spectral Methods and Multirate Signal Processing, Barcelona, Spain,
2004	TICSP Workshop on Spectral Methods and Multiratre Signal Processing, Vienna, Austria
	Sixth Workshop on Boolean Problems, Freiberg, Germany
2005	TICSP Workshop on Spectral Methods and Multirate Signal Processing, Riga, Latvia
	Reed-Muller Workshop, Tokyo, Japan
2006	TICSP Workshop on Spectral methods and Multirate Signal Processing, Florence, Italy
	Seventh Workshop on Boolean Problems, Freiberg, Germany
2007	Reed-Muller Workshop, Oslo, Norway
	TICSP Workshop on Spectral Methods and Multirate Signal Processing, Moscow, Russia

Muller expressions and their spectral interpretation, which are a basis for AND–EXOR synthesis.

The second chapter is a continuation of the overview of methods for representations of discrete functions updated by the discussion of the arithmetic expressions that are viewed as an integer-valued analog of the Reed–Muller expressions. Additional

TABLE P.0.3   Special Issues of Journals Devoted to Spectral Techniques.

Year	Journal and publisher	Issue
2002	*VLSI Design Journal*, Taylor and Francis	Vol. 14
	Spectral Techniques and Decision Diagrams	No. 1
2004	*Multiple Valued Logic and Soft Computing*, Oldcity Publisher	Vol. 10
	Spectral Techniques in Digital Logic	No. 1, No. 2
2004	*Avtomatika i Telemekhanika*, MAIK Nauka/Interperiodica, edition in English *Automation and Remote Control*, Springer	Vol. 65
	Arithmetical Logic in Control Systems	No. 6

generalizations and spectral (Fourier) transforms of finite *non-Abelian groups* are also briefly discussed.

Because of their importance, methods for efficient calculations of spectral transforms are presented in a separate chapter. Special attention has been paid to calculations of spectral transforms by decision diagrams. Methods for calculation of autocorrelation functions, which are extensively used in forthcoming chapters for analysis and synthesis of logic functions, are discussed in detail.

The new Chapter 4 presents spectral methods for optimization of decision diagrams.

Chapters 5 and 6 are updated versions of Chapters 3 and 4 in the first edition and are devoted to spectral methods for the analysis of switching and multiple-valued functions and their implementations by combinational networks.

Chapter 7 is also an updated version of Chapter 5 in the first edition and is devoted to spectral methods in the synthesis of sequential networks, with special attention paid to optimal assignment of states and related encoding problems.

Chapter 8 discusses hardware implementations of spectral methods by using memories as basic modules. It is an updated version of the corresponding chapter in the first edition of the book.

In Chapter 9, based on Chapter 6 in the first edition, we analyze error-correcting capabilities and the design of reliable digital devices by spectral logic.

Chapter 10 is a new part devoted to spectral methods for testing of digital systems. It is the first time that many results in this area are uniformly discussed and presented in a consistent way.

Chapter 11 discusses examples of various spectral transforms purposely defined to accommodate requirements in particular applications. It also describes extensions of spectral methods for different applications in image processing and broadband radio.

To conclude this section, we would like to note that, excluding classical theoretic foundations, almost all results (and possible errors) in the book belong to the authors.

MARK G. KARPOVSKY
Boston, USA
RADOMIR S. STANKOVIC
Niš, SERBIA
JAAKKO T. ASTOLA
Tampere, FINLAND

ACKNOWLEDGMENTS

Sections 2.3.2.3, 2.3.3.3, 2.3.3.4, and 11.5 were written by Dave Henderson of Coherent Logix Corp., Austin, Texas, USA.

The authors are grateful to Prof. Milena Stanković of Faculty of Electronics, Niš, Serbia; Dr. Osnat Keren of Bar Ilan University, Tel-Aviv, Israel; and Prof. Ilya Levin of Tel-Aviv University, Tel-Aviv, Israel, for useful discussions and corrections that improved the presentation in the book.

A very considerable part of this monograph was written during the stay of R.S. Stanković and M.G. Karpovsky at the Tampere International Center for Signal Processing (TICSP), Tampere University of Technology, Tampere, Finland, as a result of a long-term cooperation and joint research work. The support and facilities provided by TICSP are gratefully acknowledged.

Special thanks are due to Mrs. Pirkko Ruotsalainen, the Official for International Affairs of TICSP, for great help in many practical matters during the preparation of this book.

The authors are grateful to their families Maya and Alex Karpovsky; Milena, Stanislav, and Smiljana Stanković; Ulla, Leena, Helena, and Pekka Astola for understanding and patience.

M.G.K., R.S.S., J.T.A.

LIST OF FIGURES

P.0.1	Relations Among the Chapters.	xx
1.2.1	Step Function $\Phi(z)$ for the System in Example 1.2.2.	5
1.4.1	BDT for $m = 3$.	11
1.4.2	BDT for the Function f in Example 1.4.2.	12
1.4.3	BDD Reduction Rules.	13
1.4.4	BDD for f in Example 1.4.2.	14
1.4.5	MTBDD of f in Example 1.4.4.	15
1.4.6	SBDD of f in Example 1.4.4.	15
1.4.7	MDT for $p = 3, m = 2$.	16
1.5.1	Waveforms of Basis Functions in the Complete Disjunctive Normal Form.	19
1.5.2	Reed–Muller Matrix for $m = 3$.	21
1.5.3	Waveforms of Reed–Muller Functions for $m = 3$.	21
1.6.1	Reed–Muller Matrix for $m = 3$ and the Polarity Vector $H = (010)$.	24
1.8.1	Spectral Implementations of Logic Circuits.	28
1.8.2	Two-Level Implementation of Switching Function in Example 1.8.1.	29
1.8.3	Two-Level Implementation of f in Example 1.8.1 Though Reed-Muller Coefficients.	29
1.8.4	Simplified Two-Level Implementation of f in Example 1.8.1.	29
1.8.5	Simplified Two-Level Implementation of f in Example 1.8.1 Through Reed-Muller Coefficients.	29
2.3.1	Walsh Functions Corresponding to Definition 2.3.1 for $m = 3$.	38
2.3.2	Walsh Functions Corresponding to Definition 2.3.2 for $m = 3$.	39
2.3.3	Rademacher Functions for $m = 3$.	39
2.3.4	Generator of Walsh Functions of Order Four.	48

2.3.5   Generator of Walsh Functions of Order Four with Parity Function Implemented as a Tree of EXOR Circuits.   49

2.3.6   Generation of Walsh Function with the Fixed Index $w = (1001)$.   50

2.3.7   Generation of Walsh Function with Fixed Index $w = (1101) = 13$.   50

2.3.8   Generation of Walsh Function with Fixed Index $w = (1111) = 15$.   51

2.3.9   Haar Functions for $m = 3$.   52

2.3.10   Naturally Ordered Haar Functions for $m = 3$.   54

2.3.11   Generation of the Sign Function and the Support Function for the Haar Functions.   57

2.3.12   Generation of Specific Haar Functions for $q = 1, l = 3$.   57

2.3.13   Generation of Specific Haar Functions for $q = 2, l = 3$.   58

2.3.14   Generation of All Haar Functions for $l = 3$ by Permutation of Input Bit Inversions.   58

2.3.15   Circuit that Generates Terms in Haar Expressions (2.3.21).   59

2.3.16   Complete Inverse Haar Transform Circuit.   60

2.8.1   Spectral Transforms.   96

3.1.1   Flow-Graph of the Algorithm to Calculate the Wash Spectrum for $m = 3$.   110

3.1.2   Flow-Graph of the Algorithm for Calculation of the Walsh Spectrum with Good-Thomas Factorization for $m = 3$.   112

3.1.3   Calculation of the WHT for f Represented by the BDD in Fig. 1.4.4.   117

3.2.1   Cooley-Tukey Fast Haar Transform.   124

3.2.2   Flow-Graph of the Cooley-Tukey Fast Inverse Haar Transform.   124

3.2.3   Calculation of the Haar Spectrum in Example 3.2.1.   125

3.2.4   Fast Haar Transform for $m = 3$.   127

3.2.5   Fast Inverse Haar Transform for $m = 3$.   127

3.2.6   Calculation of the Haar Transform for $m = 3$ Through MTBDT(f).   129

3.2.7   Calculation of the Inverse Haar Transform Through MTBDT(S_f).   131

3.2.8   MTBDD for the Haar Spectrum in Example 3.2.8.   133

3.2.9   BDD for the Haar Spectrum for f in Example 1.4.2.   134

3.2.10   In-order Procedure for BDD for f in Example 3.2.9.   135

3.3.1   Vilenkin–Chrestenson FFT with Constant Geometry for $p = 3$ and $m = 2$.   138

3.3.2   Vilenkin–Chrestenson FFT for $p = 3$ and $m = 2$.   139

3.3.3   Calculation of the Vilenkin–Chrestenson Spectrum for $p = 3$ and $m = 2$ Through Multiple-Place Decision Tree.   140

3.5.1   Calculation of the Autocorrelation of $f(z_0, z_1)$.   144

3.5.2   Calculation of the Autocorrelation of $f(z_0, z_1)$ by the Fast Walsh Transform.   144

3.5.3   MTBDT and MTBDD for f in Example 3.5.2.   145

3.5.4   MTBDD for the Autocorrelation Function $B_f(\tau)$.   145

3.5.5   Calculation of the Autocorrelation Function by the Wiener-Khinchin Theorem over Decision Diagrams.   146

3.5.6   Calculation of the Autocorrelation Function B_f for f in
Example 3.5.4 by Using the Wiener–Khinchin Theorem Over
Decision Diagrams.   146

3.5.7   MTBDD for the Walsh Spectrum for f in Example 3.5.6.   149

3.5.8   Transformation of Nodes.   149

3.5.9   MTBDTs for the First Four Rows of the Autocorrelation
Matrix for $m = 3$.   150

3.5.10   MTBDDs for $f(z)$ and $f(z \oplus 3)$ in Example 3.5.7.   150

3.5.11   Calculation of the Autocorrelation Coefficient $B_f(\tau)$.   151

3.5.12   Explanation of Calculation of $B_f(1)$ for $m = 3$.   152

4.1.1   MTBDT for f.   159

4.1.2   MTBDD for f.   159

4.1.3   MTBDT for $f_{\sigma_4^{-1}}$.   161

4.1.4   MTBDT for $f_{\sigma_4^{-1}}$ with Encoded Pair of Function Values. 161

4.1.5   MTBDD($\mathbf{Q}_\sigma$) for $\sigma = \sigma_3$.   163

4.1.6   MTBDD(f_σ).   163

4.2.1   SBDD for the System of Functions in Example 4.2.1.   170

4.2.2   Shared LT-BDD for the System of Functions Derived by the
Linearization Method for $f^{(0)}$ and $f^{(1)}$ From Example 4.1.2.   171

4.2.3   LT-BDD for the Decoder for the (5, 2) Shortened Hamming Code.   174

4.3.1   BDD for the Majority Function of Five Variables.   179

4.3.2   BDD for Symmetric Functions of Three Variables.   179

4.3.3   Planar BDD for Symmetric Functions Defined on C_2^m.   180

4.3.4   Rectangular Planar BDD for $S_3(6)$.   181

4.3.5   BDD for f in Example 4.3.4.   182

4.3.6   LT-BDD for f in Example 4.3.4.   183

4.3.7   Planar MTBDD for 5xp1–1.   185

4.3.8   Decision Tree and Subtrees for Two Variables.   185

4.3.9   BDD for f in Example 4.3.6.   186

4.3.10   LT-BDD for f in Example 4.3.6.   186

4.3.11   Decision Tree for f Linearized with Respect to r Variables. 187

4.4.1   BDT and BDD for f in Example 4.4.1.   190

4.4.2   STDT for f in Example 4.4.1.   190

4.4.3   HSTDT for $m = 3$.   193

4.4.4   HSTDD for f in Example 4.4.3.   195

4.4.5   HSTDD for f_σ in Example 4.4.3.   195

4.4.6   HST for $m = 3$.   198

5.2.1   Block Diagram of a Linear Threshold Network.   217

5.2.2   Realization of the Function f in Example 5.2.4.   218

5.4.1   Matrices σ_η and T_η.   238

5.5.1   Network to Realize the Parallel Approximation of f.   245

6.1.1   Block Diagram of the Network for Spectral Implementation of
Logic Functions.   263

6.1.2   Realization of f in Example 6.1.1 From the Discrete Haar Series. 265

6.1.3   Realization of $con\,1$ from Optimized Haar Series in Example 6.1.2.   266
6.1.4   Realization of f in Example 6.1.1 from Walsh Series.   266
6.1.5   Minimal Network Realizing all Switching Functions of $m = 3$
 Variables.   268
6.1.6   Network Implementing Multiplication by σ.   270
6.1.7   Block Diagram of the Algorithm for Determination of σ_{min}.   282
6.3.1   Network Realizing Multiplication by σ in Example 6.3.2.   295
6.4.1   Design of a Sequence Generator for a Function f by Summation
 of the Finite Difference Δf.   305
6.4.2   Design of a Sequence Generator by Linear Transform of Variables.   306
7.1.1   Structure of a Moore Automaton.   311
8.3.1   Block Diagram for Implementation of Switching Functions by
 Haar Series with Single Dimensional ROM.   350
8.3.2   Block Diagram for Implementation of Switching Functions by
 Haar Series with Two-Coordinate ROM.   351
8.4.1   Block Diagram for the Implementation of the Network in
 Example 8.3.1.   354
8.5.1   Block diagram for Implementation of Switching Functions by
 Haar Series with Parallel Summation of the Coefficients.   359
8.5.2   Block Diagram of Parallel Implementation of the Network in
 Example 8.3.1.   360
9.1.1   Distribution of Correctable Errors for Majority Functions
 for $m = 3, 5, 7$.   378
9.1.2   Distribution of Correctable Errors for the Elementary Symmetric
 Switching Functions of $2k$ Variables with $k = 2, 3, 4$.   380
9.2.1   Digital System for Transmission and Processing of Information.   386
9.2.2   Linearized Digital System for Transmission and Processing.   388
9.3.1   State Diagram for the Automaton in Example 9.3.1.   402
9.3.2   Fractions of Corrected Errors $\hat{\eta}_{M,m}(l)$ with Multiplicity l for the
 Linear Automata with n Inputs and n States.   410
9.3.3   The Fraction of Corrected Errors with the Multiplicity l in the
 Input Words of the Length m, $\hat{\eta}_{M,m}(l)$, for a Counting Automaton
 with $m < n_a$.   414
9.4.1   The Fragment of a State Diagram Illustrating the "Splitting"
 Procedure for the State a_4 and the Partition $\lambda = \{\lambda_0, \lambda_1\}$,
 $\lambda_0 = \{x_0, x_1\}, \lambda_1 = \{x_2\}$ for the Finite Automaton in Example 9.4.1.   416
10.1.1   Block Diagram for Testing by Verification of a Spectral Coefficient
 $S_F(w)$.   424
10.1.2   Network from Example 10.1.2.   427
10.1.3   Networks from Example 10.1.2 with a Control Input c.   428
10.2.1   Network Implementation of the Check from Example 10.2.3.   441
10.2.2   Built-in-Self-Test Architecture for Testing by Linear Checks
 (10.12) $|T| = |C^{\perp}| = 2^{m-k}$.   442
10.2.3   Block Diagram of an n-Bit Adder.   443

10.3.1   Network Implementation of Check (10.3.1) for Basic Computer
Components.   460

10.6.1   Network Implementation of a Linear Check for a Polynomial f of
m Variables.   471

10.8.1   Function $\Delta_s |V^\perp(m, s+1)|$ for $f(y) = 10^{0.25y}$.   483

10.9.1   Correction of Double Errors $e(z) = \delta_{z,z_1} e(z_1) + \delta_{z,z_2} e(z_2)$, case 1,
Solid Dots Indicate Error Locations, Horizontal and Vertical Lines
Represent Cosets with Respect to T_1 and T_2, Respectively.   501

10.9.2   Correction of Double Error $e(z) = \delta_{z,z_1} e(z_1) + \delta_{z,z_2} e(z_2)$, Case 2,
Solid Dots Indicate Error Locations.   501

10.9.3   Block Diagram of the Algorithm for the Correction of Single and
Double Errors by Two Orthogonal Equality Checks.   503

10.10.1 Block Diagram of the Algorithm for the Location of Single
and Double Errors by Two Orthogonal Inequality Checks.   506

11.1.1   Slant Functions and Walsh Functions in Sequency Ordering for
$m = 4$.   519

11.2.1   Haar Wavelet.   521

11.2.2   Meyer, Morlet, and Mexican Hat Wavelets.   522

11.3.1   Boolean Cube and Fibonacci Cube for $m = 3$.   526

11.4.1   Two-Dimensional Walsh Functions in Sequency Ordering, $-1/2$
$\leq x, y \leq 1/2$ and $N_1, N_2 = 0, 1, \ldots, 7$.   532

11.4.2   Two-Dimensional Walsh Functions in Natural Ordering, $-1/2 \leq x,$
$y \leq 1/2$ and $N_1, N_2 = 0, 1, \ldots, 7$.   533

11.4.3   Two-Dimensional Walsh Functions in Natural Ordering, $-1/2 \leq x,$
$y \leq 1/2$ and $N_1, N_2 = 0, 1, \ldots, 7$.   533

11.4.4   Two-Dimensional Haar Functions, $-1/2 \leq x, y \leq 1/2$, and
$N_1, N_2 = 0, 1, \ldots, 7$.   534

11.4.5   Two-Dimensional Discrete Cosine Functions for (4×4) Signals.   536

LIST OF TABLES

P.0.1   Conferences and Workshops on Spectral Techniques, 1970–1999.   xxi

P.0.2   Conferences and Workshops on Spectral Techniques, 2000–2006.   xxii

P.0.3   Special Issues of Journals Devoted to Spectral Techniques.   xxii

1.2.1   Binary-Valued Input Functions of Three Variables.   4

1.2.2   Multiple-Valued Input Functions of Two Ternary Variables.   4

1.2.3   Binary-Valued Input Two-Output Functions.   4

1.2.4   Multiple-Valued Input Two-Output Functions, with $p = 2$ for z_0 and $p = 3$ for z_1.   4

1.2.5   Logic Function in Example 1.2.2.   5

1.2.6   Step Function for the System of Logic Functions in Example 1.2.2.   5

1.3.1   Logic Operations.   7

1.3.2   Characteristic Functions for $p = 3, n = 2$.   9

1.5.1   The Properties of the Reed–Muller Transform Considered as a Transform in the Boolean Algebra $(B, \vee, \wedge, -, 0, 1)$.   22

1.7.1   Assignment of Decomposition Rules and the Coefficients in Kronecker Expressions for f in Example 1.6.1   26

2.3.1   Different Orderings of Walsh Functions Represented as Products of the Rademacher Functions, $m = 3$.   43

2.5.1   Vilenkin–Chrestenson Functions for $p = 3, m = 2$.   67

2.5.2   Generalized Rademacher Functions for $p = 3, m = 2$.   67

2.5.3   Function in Example 2.5.1 and Its Vilenkin–Chrestenson Spectrum.   69

2.5.4   Generalized Haar Functions for $p = 3$ and $m = 2$.   71

2.6.1   Function $f(z)$ in Example 2.6.1, Its Spectrum in Paley Ordering by Definition 2.3.2, Linearly Transformed Function $f(\sigma \odot z)$ and the Spectrum of It.   78

2.7.1   The Function $f(z)$, the Spectrum $S(w)$ in Paley Ordering, $S^2(w)$,
        and the Autocorrelation Function $B_{2,2}^{(f,f)}(\tau)$ in Example 2.7.1.   81
2.7.2   A Function f of Two Ternary Variables z_0, z_1 and Its Autocorrelation
        Function $B_{3,3}(\tau)$.   85
2.8.1   Characters $\chi_w(z)$ for the Group C_3^2 in Example 2.8.1.   88
2.8.2   The Operation Table of the Group in Example 2.8.2.   92
2.8.3   Elements of G in Terms of Powers of Generators.   92
2.8.4   The Characters of the Group $G = C_2 \times C_3$ in Example 2.8.2.   93
2.8.5   Walsh Spectrum of the Function f Over the Real Field and $GF(3)$.   95
2.9.1   Group Operation for the Quaternion Group Q_2.   102
2.9.2   Irreducible Unitary Representations of Q_2 Over C.   102
3.1.1   Calculation of Walsh Spectrum.   107
3.1.2   Calculation of Walsh Transform Through BDDs.   119
3.2.1   Calculation of the Haar Spectrum.   120
3.5.1   Characteristics of MTBDDs and WDDs for Some Benchmark
        Functions.   147
4.1.1   Function f and f_σ.   158
4.1.2   Mapping of Function Values by σ_4^{-1}, $y = \sigma_4^{-1} \odot z$.   160
4.1.3   Mapping of Function Values by σ_3^{-1}, $y = \sigma_3^{-1} \odot z$.   162
4.1.4   Mapping of Function Values by $y = \sigma_4^{-1} \cdot \sigma_3^{-1} \odot z$.   164
4.2.1   System of Switching Functions in Example 4.2.1.   170
4.2.2   Sizes of MTBDD(f), MTBDD(f_v), and MBTDD(f_σ) for
        Benchmark and Randomly Generated Functions.   175
4.2.3   Numbers of Nonterminal Nodes in MTBDDs for Initial Ordering
        of Variables f_I, Optimal Ordering f_v, Initial Ordering with Negated
        Edges f_w, Lower-Bound Sifting with Negated Edges f_r, and
        Autocorrelation Functions f_σ.   176
4.3.1   Sizes of BDDs, BDDs with Optimal Order of Variables (BDDv),
        Planar BDD (BDDr), and Planar LT-BDDs (LT-BDD).   188
4.4.1   Function with the Minimized Haar Spectrum.   194
4.4.2   Number of Coefficients in the Haar Spectrum and the Haar-LT
        Spectrum.   196
4.4.3   Complexity of MTBDDs and LT-MTBDDs.   196
4.4.4   Complexity of MTBDDs and LT-HSTDD.   197
5.1.1   Function f in Example 5.1.1, Its Spectrum $S_f(w)$, and
        Autocorrelation Function $B_f(\tau)$.   202
5.1.2   Function f in Example 5.1.2 and Its Autocorrelation $B_f(\tau)$.   210
5.1.3   Parameters of Some Optimal Codes $N_s, b_s, \Delta_2^{(S)}$.   211
5.2.1   Functions Φ and f in Examples 5.2.1 and 5.2.2 and Their Spectral
        and Autocorrelations.   215
5.2.2   Function f in Example 5.2.4 and Its Spectrum.   218
5.2.3   Function f and the Autocorrelation Function B_f in Example 5.2.5.   221
5.4.1   Function $f = (f^{(0)}, f^{(1)})$ in Example 5.4.1, the Total
        Autocorrelation B_f, and Linearly Transformed Function
        $f_{T^{-1}} = (f_{T^{-1}}^{(0)}, f_{T^{-1}}^{(1)})$.   231

5.4.2   Function f in Example 5.4.2, Its Spectrum S_f, Autocorrelation B_f, and the Linearly Transformed Function $f_{\sigma_{\mu_1}}$.   234

5.4.3   Function $f = (f^{(0)}, f^{(1)})$ in Example 5.4.3, Its Total Autocorrelation Function B_f, and Linearly Transformed Function $f_{\sigma_\eta} = (f_{\sigma_\eta}^{(0)}, f_{\sigma_\eta}^{(1)})$.   236

5.4.4   Function f in Example 5.4.4, Its Autocorrelation B_f, and Linearly Transformed Function f_{σ_η}.   238

5.4.5   Function $f = (f^{(0)}, f^{(1)})$ in Example 5.4.5 and the Characteristic Functions.   241

5.4.6   Autocorrelation Functions for the Function $f = (f^{(0)}, f^{(1)})$ in Example 5.4.5 and Linearly Transformed Function $f_{T^{-1}} = (f_{T^{-1}}^{(0)}, f_{T^{-1}}^{(1)})$.   241

5.4.7   Function f in Example 5.4.6.   244

5.5.1   Function f in Example 5.5.1 and Its Walsh Spectrum.   249

5.5.2   Function f in Example 5.5.2, Its Spectrum, and Linear Approximation d_2.   255

5.5.3   Function $\tilde{f}_{P_\xi}(z_0)$ in Example 5.5.2.   255

6.1.1   Nonzero Haar Coefficients in the Optimized Haar Spectrum for $con1$.   265

6.1.2   Lowest Upper Bounds for $N^{(2)}(\sigma)$.   269

6.1.3   Function f in Example 6.1.5.   273

6.1.4   Functions in Example 6.1.6.   277

6.1.5   Functions in Example 6.1.6.   280

6.1.6   Initial Function f in Example 6.1.6, Linearly Transformed Function $f_{\sigma_{min}}$, and the Haar Spectra for f and $f_{\sigma_{min}}$.   281

6.1.7   Upper Bounds for $\max_{f_{m,1}} \min_\sigma L_{m-l}^H(f, \sigma)$, $l = 1, 2, \ldots, m$.   285

6.2.1   Partially Defined Function f in Example 6.2.1 and Its Optimal Completion ϕ.   288

6.2.2   The Partially Defined Function $f = f^{(3)}$ in Example 6.2.2, the Autocorrelation Functions, and Linearly Transformed Function $f_{\sigma_3}^{(3)}$.   289

6.2.3   Contracted Functions $f^{(2)}(z)$, $f^{<1>}(z)$ in Example 6.2.2, Their Autocorrelation Functions $B^{(2)}$, $B^{<1>}$, and Linearly Transformed Functions $f_{\sigma^{(2)}}^{(2)}$ and $f_{\sigma^{(1)}}^{(1)}$.   290

6.2.4   Initial Function f in Example 6.2.1, Linearly Transformed Function $f_{\sigma_{min}}$ and Their Haar Spectra.   291

6.3.1   The Partially Defined Function f in Example 6.3.1 and Its Optimal Completion.   294

6.3.2   Ternary Function $f = f^{(1)}$ in Example 6.3.3, Its Autocorrelation Functions, and the Linearly Transformed Function $f_{\sigma_1}^{(1)}$.   297

6.4.1   Function f in Example 6.4.3, Its Finite Differences, Linearly Transformed Function f_8 and Its Finite Difference Δf_8.   307

7.1.1   Next-State Function for the Automaton in Example 7.1.2.   309

7.1.2   Binary Encoded Inputs and Internal States.   310

7.1.3   Next-State Function in Example 7.1.2 Represented as a System of Switching Functions (Excitation Functions).   310

7.1.4   Function $f_T(z)$ in Example 7.1.4.   312

7.2.1	Assignment from K_5^a.	322
7.2.2	Assignment of K_5^a.	327
7.2.3	Assignment of K_4^a.	327
7.2.4	State Assignment from K_3^a.	329
7.2.5	State Assignment from K_2^x.	331
7.2.6	Input Assignment from K_1^x.	331
7.2.7	Final State Assignment.	332
7.2.8	Spectral Complexities for the Initial and Optimal Assignments.	332
7.3.1	Assignments of States and Inputs for the Automaton in Example 7.1.4.	342
7.3.2	Complexity of the Implementations.	342
8.3.1	Function f Example 8.3.1.	353
8.4.1	Nonzero Coefficients for the Function f in Example 8.3.1.	353
8.7.1	Nonzero Coefficients Over $GF(11)$ in the Expansion for f in Example 8.3.1.	364
8.7.2	Complexity of Blocks for Spectral Implementation with Calculations in R and $GF(p)$.	366
8.7.3	Total Complexity of the Implementation of the Network in Example 8.3.1.	366
9.1.1	Ternary Function f in Example 9.1.1 and Its Autocorrelation Characteristics.	374
9.1.2	Function f in Example 9.1.2 and Its Cyclic Autocorrelation Characteristics.	383
9.2.1	Function f in Example 9.2.1, Its Autocorrelation and Cross-Correlation Functions.	390
9.4.1	State Table for the Automaton in Example 9.4.2.	417
9.4.2	State Assignment for Internal States in the Automaton in Example 9.4.2.	418
9.4.3	Function $\Phi(z)$ Representing Excitation Functions of the Automaton in Example 9.4.2 and Its Haar Spectrum.	418
10.1.1	Spectrum and w-Testability Conditions for f in Example 10.1.1.	425
10.2.1	Orthogonal Checks for Some Numerical Functions ($|T_1| < |T_2|$).	448
10.3.1	Optimal Linear Equality Checks for Some Basic Hardware Components.	456
10.3.2	Optimal Linear Equality Checks for Some Basic Hardware Components (Continued).	457
10.3.3	Optimal Linear Equality Checks for Some Basic Hardware Components, $T(f)$ and d.	458
10.3.4	Linear Check Constants for Basic Instructions.	459
10.5.1	Parameters of the Optimal Checks for Polynomials of One Variable.	468
10.8.1	Optimal Inequality Checks for Some Numerical Computations for $m = 23, \epsilon = 5 \times 10^{-3}, y = 2^{-23}z, z \in \{0, 1, \ldots, 2^{23} - 1\}$.	485
10.9.1	Error-Correcting Capability of Two Checks.	504
10.9.2	Error-Correcting Capability of Two Checks for Bitwise Errors.	504

10.10.1   Error-Locating Capabilities of Two Orthogonal Inequality.   507

11.3.1   Generalized Fibonacci Numbers.   525

11.3.2   Boolean Codes, Fibonacci 1-codes, Contracted Fibonacci 1-codes, and Fibonacci Minterms for $m = 3$.   526

11.5.1   Walsh Codes for $n = 1, 2, 4$ and $k = 0, 1, \ldots n - 1$.   538

A.0.1   Switching Functions and Their Analytical Expressions.   542

A.0.2   Functions and Their Walsh Spectra.   544

A.0.3   Functions and Their Autocorrelation Functions.   547

A.0.4   Functions and Their Walsh Complexities.   550

A.0.5   Functions and Their Haar Complexities.   552

ACRONYMS

G	Finite group of order $g = \|G\|$
	(usually direct product of m groups G_i of orders $g_i = \|G_i\|$)
C_2	Cyclic group of order 2
C_2^m	Direct product of m cyclic groups C_2,
	also called the finite dyadic group of order 2^m
C_p	Cyclic group of order p
C_p^m	Direct product of m copies of C_p
χ_w	Character of G with the index w
u_w	Unitary irreducible representation of G with the index w
P	Field
C	Field of complex numbers
R	Field of real numbers
Z	Set of integers
$GF(p^m)$	Field of p-ary m-dimensional vectors
z	Variable in P
$z = (z_0, \ldots, z_{m-1})$	Componentwise representation of z on $G = \times_{i=0}^{m-1} G_i$
	$z = \sum_{i=0}^{m-1} z_i 2^{m-1-i}$
$\|z\|$	Hamming norm of z
	(number of non-zero components in the componentwise
	representation of z)
$f(z)$	Function over P in the variable $z \in G$
$f(z_0, \ldots, z_{m-1})$	Function over P of m variables $z_i \in G_i$
$f = (f^{(0)}, \ldots, f^{(k-1)})$	System of k functions
	also called a k-output function f

$f(z)$ Integer function corresponding to a k-output function f
$$f(z) = \sum_{i=0}^{k-1} 2^{m-1-i} f^{(i)}$$

$\Phi(z)$ Piecewise constant function corresponding to
a k-output function f

$W_w(z)$ Discrete Walsh function of the index w and
the argument z

$\mathbf{W}(m)$ ($2^m \times 2^m$) Walsh matrix

$C_w(z)$ Vilenkin-Chrestenson function of the index w and
the variable z

$\mathbf{C}(m)$ Vilenkin-Chestenson ($p^m \times p^m$) matrix

$H_i^{(j)}(z)$ Haar function in two parameter notation
i-index in the package j

$\mathbf{H}(m)$ ($2^m \times 2^m$) Haar matrix

$S_{f,r}(w)$ Spectrum of f with respect to the transform r
(usually written as S_f when transform r
clear from the context)

$f * g$ Logical (dyadic) convolution of f and g

$B_{f,g}(\tau)$ Logical (dyadic) correlation function of f and g

$B_f(\tau)$ Logical (dyadic) autocorrelation function of f

$\mathbf{B}_f$ Total autocorrelation for the integer function $f(z)$

Ω_f Set of points w where $S_f(w) = 0$, i.e., $\{w | S_f(w) = 0\}$

$G_I(f)$ Inertia (anti-self duality) group for f

$G_L(f)$ Linearity group for f
$$G_L(f) = \Omega_f$$

$L(f)$ (Gate) complexity for f

$\mu_i(f)$ Complexity criteria for f

$\eta_f(l)$ Fraction of errors with
the multiplicity l corrected by f

$l^{(i)}(z_0, \ldots, z_{m-1})$ Linear Boolean or p-ary function
$$i^{(i)}(z_0, \ldots, z_{m-1}) = i_0 z_{m-1} \oplus i_1 z_{m-2} \oplus \cdots \oplus i_{m-1} z_0$$

$V(m, k, d)$ Linear code (set of p-ary vectors of the length m
and minimum Hamming distance between
two vectors at least d

$V^{\perp}$ Code orthogonal to V

$\oplus$ Addition modulo p

$\ominus$ Subtraction modulo p

$\odot$ Multiplication of matrices over $GF(p)$

$\otimes$ Kronecker product

$*$ Logical (dyadic) autocorrelation

ACDD	Arithmetic transform decision diagram
BDD	Binary decision diagram
BDT	Binary decision tree
DD	Decision diagram
DT	Decision tree
FFT	Fast Fourier transform
FDD	Functional decision diagram
FNADD	Fourier decision diagram on finite non-Abelian groups
FNADT	Fourier decision tree on finite non-Abelian groups
FNAPDD	Fourier decision diagram on finite non-Abelian groups with preprocessing
FNAPDT	Fourier decision tree on finite non-Abelian groups with preprocessing
KDD	Kronecker decision diagram
mvMTDD	Matrix-valued multi-terminal decision diagram
MTBDD	Multi-terminal binary decision diagram
MTBDT	Multi-terminal binary decision tree
MDD	Multiple-place diagram
MTDD	Multi-terminal decision diagram
MTDT	Multi-terminal decision tree
nvMTDD	Number-valued multi-terminal decision diagram
PKDD	Pseudo-Kronecker decision diagram
KDD	Kronecker decision diagram
QDD	Quaternary decision diagrams
SBDD	Shared binary decision diagrams
TVFG	Two-variable function generator
WDD	Walsh decision diagram

CHAPTER 1

LOGIC FUNCTIONS

In the design of *digital devices*, many different ways are used to describe the input and output signals, and the input/output relations of the devices. The inputs and outputs are usually mathematically modeled by functions, while the input/output relations are represented by operators in some suitably selected function spaces. *Combinational* and *sequential* logic circuits alone can be viewed as particular examples of digital devices or as constitutes of their essential components.

In combinational logic circuits, the output is a (logic) function of inputs and, therefore, the input/output relations of these circuits are also represented by logic functions, or, conversely, combinational circuit *realize* (*implement*) logic functions.

In sequential circuits, the output depends also on the *internal states* of the circuit, and more sophisticated mathematical models, called *sequential machines*, are used for their representations. Combinational circuits are necessary parts of sequential circuits used to realize the *output functions* and *state functions* describing transitions between the states.

We will use several types of functions that vary with different sets as the domain and the range of the function to be able to represent the variety of the relations realized by digital devices. At the same time, representation of the same relations by functions with different domains and ranges may provide advantages in digital devices analysis, design, verification, testing, maintaining, etc.

There are also many ways to describe a function, that is, specify function values for all possible combinations of values for its variables. These specifications, establishing uniquely correspondence between the inputs and the values taken by a function, are called *representations of functions*, and could be expressed by a formula, table, graph, an ordered set of points where the function takes particular value, as cubes, or a textual-like description of links between the inputs, preselected modules (basic logic elements or equivalently, subfunctions), and the output values, as for the *netlists*.

In this chapter, we briefly review different types of functions encountered in the design of digital devices and their representations that will be used in this book.

1.1 DISCRETE FUNCTIONS

A combinational digital device has a finite number of inputs and a finite number of possible values for inputs as well as for outputs and can be represented as a *finite discrete function*

$$f : \times_{i=0}^{m-1} \mathcal{D}_i \rightarrow \times_{i=0}^{k-1} \mathcal{R}_i,$$

where $\times$ denotes the *Cartesian product* and $\mathcal{D}_i$, $i = 0, 1, \ldots, m - 1$ are finite sets.

The set R_i may be a finite or infinite, and usually, if infinite, it is either the set R of real numbers or the set C of complex numbers.

A *multioutput function* is such that $k > 1$. Thus, it is a *system of single-output functions* ($k = 1$) and can be represented as a vector $f = (f^{(0)}, \ldots, f^{(k-1)})$ of single-output functions.

Switching functions or *Boolean functions* are the basic functions in digital design and they are functions

$$f : \{0, 1\}^m \rightarrow \{0, 1\}, \tag{1.1.1}$$

that is, in this case, $\mathcal{D}_0 = \mathcal{D}_1 = \cdots = \mathcal{D}_{m-1} = \mathcal{R}_0 = \{0, 1\}$.

Often discrete functions with a finite, but nonbinary (i.e., $R_i \neq \{0, 1\}$) range, are called *multiple-valued* functions. A typical case is a function $f : Z_k \rightarrow Z_k$, where Z_k denotes the *ring of integers* (*field* if k is prime) modulo k. Definitions of rings and fields will be presented later in Section 5.1.

Whenever the domain and the range are finite sets of the cardinalities p and q, we can identify the elements with the first nonnegative integers and consider the corresponding function $f : \{0, 1, \ldots, p - 1\} \rightarrow \{0, 1, \ldots, q - 1\}$. In the case of functions of m variables and k outputs, it would be $f : \{0, 1, \ldots, p - 1\}^m \rightarrow \{0, 1, \ldots, q - 1\}^k$.

This "coding" of the domain and the range is most often done when the domain and the range or both are powers of $\{0, 1\}$, that is, an element

$$z = (z_0, z_1, \ldots, z_i, \ldots, z_{m-1}) \in \{0, 1\}^m,$$

is represented as a nonnegative integer $z \in \{0, 1, \ldots, 2^m - 1\}$ via the bijective mapping $\{0, 1\}^m \rightarrow \{Z | 0 \leq z < 2^m\}$,

$$z = \sum_{s=0}^{m-1} z_s 2^{m-1-s}.$$

When the domain $\mathcal{D}$ and the range $\mathcal{R}$ are finite sets, as for discrete functions, the number of different functions $f : \mathcal{D} \rightarrow \mathcal{R}$ is finite.

The number of discrete functions is exponential in the cardinality of the domain. Consider discrete functions $f : \mathbf{X} \rightarrow Y$. Each function is uniquely specified by a vector of its values, the length of which is $|\mathbf{X}|$ and as there are $|Y|$ choices for each component, the total number of functions is $|Y|^{|X|}$.

Example 1.1.1 *Consider $\mathcal{D}_1 = \{0, 1\}$, $\mathcal{D}_2 = \{0, 1, 2\}$, and $\mathcal{R} = \{0, 1, 2, 3\}$. The number of function $f : \mathcal{D}_1 \times \mathcal{D}_2 \rightarrow \mathcal{R}$ is $4^{2 \times 3} = 4^6$, since for each element in the set of $2 \times 3 = 6$ elements, an element out of four elements in $\mathcal{R}$ can be associated.*

Example 1.1.2 *The number of switching functions $f : \{0, 1\}^m \rightarrow \{0, 1\}$ is 2^{2^m}. Similarly, the number of ternary functions $\{0, 1, 2\}^m \rightarrow \{0, 1, 2\}$ is 3^{3^m}. For $m = 2$, there are 16 switching (two-valued) functions and 19683 ternary functions.*

1.2 TABULAR REPRESENTATIONS OF DISCRETE FUNCTIONS

Since for discrete functions, the domain $\mathcal{D}$ and the range $\mathcal{R}$ are finite, the simplest way to define a discrete function is to specify its value $f(x) \in R$ at each element $x \in \mathcal{D}$. The enumeration of function values can be presented by a table. In the case of switching and multiple-valued functions, such tables are called *truth tables*. In other cases, the term *function tables* is used.

Example 1.2.1 *Tables 1.2.1–1.2.4 show single output for $\mathcal{D} = \{0, 1\}^3$ and $\mathcal{D} = \{0, 1, 2\}^2$, and two-output functions for $\mathcal{D} = \{0, 1\}^2$ and $\mathcal{D} = \{0, 1\} \times \{0, 1, 2\}$. In these tables, the function values are shown with integer coding of the domain.*

When the order of the assignments of values to the variables is fixed, it is sufficient to present the right part of the table as a vector. In the case of switching and multiple-valued functions, these vectors are called *truth vectors*. In general, the term *function vectors* is used. Multiple-output functions are represented by separate vectors for each output.

Sometimes we want to use the rich mathematical machinery developed for real and complex-valued functions. This can be achieved by replacing logic functions by their step function equivalents defined as follows.

A k-output p-valued function

$$f : \{0, 1, \ldots, p - 1\}^m \rightarrow \{0, 1, \ldots, p - 1\}^k, \qquad (1.2.1)$$

TABLE 1.2.1 Binary-Valued Input Functions of Three Variables.

	$z_0 z_1 z_2$	$f(z)$
0.	000	$f(0)$
1.	001	$f(1)$
2.	010	$f(2)$
3.	011	$f(3)$
4.	100	$f(4)$
5.	101	$f(5)$
6.	110	$f(6)$
7.	111	$f(7)$

TABLE 1.2.2 Multiple-Valued Input Functions of Two Ternary Variables.

	$z_0 z_1$	$f(z)$
0.	00	$f(0)$
1.	01	$f(1)$
2.	02	$f(2)$
3.	10	$f(3)$
4.	11	$f(4)$
5.	12	$f(5)$
6.	20	$f(6)$
7.	21	$f(7)$
8.	22	$f(8)$

TABLE 1.2.3 Binary-Valued Input Two-Output Functions.

	$z_0 z_1$	$f(z) = (f^{(0)}, f^{(1)})$	
0.	00	$f^{(0)}(0)$	$f^{(1)}(0)$
1.	01	$f^{(0)}(1)$	$f^{(1)}(1)$
2.	10	$f^{(0)}(2)$	$f^{(1)}(2)$
3.	11	$f^{(0)}(3)$	$f^{(1)}(3)$

TABLE 1.2.4 Multiple-Valued Input Two-Output Functions, with $p = 2$ for z_0 and $p = 3$ for z_1.

	$z_0 z_1$	$f(z) = (f^{(0)}, f^{(1)})$	
0.	00	$f^{(0)}(0)$	$f^{(1)}(0)$
1.	01	$f^{(0)}(1)$	$f^{(1)}(1)$
2.	02	$f^{(0)}(2)$	$f^{(1)}(2)$
3.	10	$f^{(0)}(3)$	$f^{(1)}(3)$
4.	11	$f^{(0)}(4)$	$f^{(1)}(4)$
5.	12	$f^{(0)}(5)$	$f^{(1)}(5)$

written alternatively as the system of k single-output functions $f = (f^{(s)})$, $f^{(s)}$: $\{0, 1, \ldots, p-1\} \rightarrow \{0, 1 \ldots, p-1\}$, $s = 0, 1, \ldots, k-1$, can be represented by a step function $\Phi(z)$ of a real variable, defined on a half-open interval $[0, p^m)$ as follows.

Set

$$z = \sum_{s=0}^{m-1} z_s p^{m-1-s}, \qquad (1.2.2)$$

$$f(z) = \sum_{s=0}^{k-1} f^{(s)} p^{k-1-s}. \qquad (1.2.3)$$

and we can represent the function (1.2.1) by a discrete function $y = f(z)$, defined at the points $0, 1, \ldots, p^m - 1$ of the interval $[0, p^{m-1})$.

TABLE 1.2.5 **Logic Function in Example 1.2.2.**

z_0	z_1	z_2	$f^{(0)}$	$f^{(1)}$
0	0	0	0	0
0	0	1	1	0
0	1	0	1	0
0	1	1	0	1
1	0	0	1	0
1	0	1	0	1
1	1	0	0	1
1	1	1	1	1

TABLE 1.2.6 **Step Function for the System of Logic Functions in Example 1.2.2.**

z	$f(z)$
0	0
1	2
2	2
3	1
4	2
5	1
6	1
7	3

Finally, we complete $y = f(z)$ to a step function $\Phi(z)$ by defining

$$\Phi(z) = f(i), \quad \text{when} \quad z \in [i, i+1), \quad i = 0, 1, \ldots, p-1. \qquad (1.2.4)$$

We say that a *step function $\Phi(z)$ represents the original logic function* if $\Phi(z)$ satisfies (1.2.4) for the function $f(z)$ defined as in (1.2.1)–(1.2.3). The analysis and synthesis problems for systems of logic functions can be based on their step-function representations. Throughout the sequel, we use the same notation for the variables of the functions and the vectors of their p-ary expansions, provided no confusion can arise.

Example 1.2.2 *Let $p = 2$ and consider the system of two switching functions defined in Table 1.2.5. This table describes the operation of a one-digit adder, where $y^{(0)}$ is the sum output and $y^{(1)}$ the carry output.*

The corresponding function $f(z)$ is defined in Table 1.2.6, and the step function $\Phi(z)$ representing the system is shown in Fig. 1.2.1.

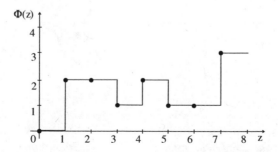

FIGURE 1.2.1   Step function $\Phi(z)$ for the system in Example 1.2.2.

1.3 FUNCTIONAL EXPRESSIONS

In switching theory, the *literal function* z^a is assigned to a binary valued variable $z \in \{0, 1\}$ as

$$z^a = \begin{cases} \overline{z}, & \text{if } a = 0, \\ z, & \text{if } a = 1, \end{cases}$$

where $\overline{z}$ is the negation of z.

In this notation, for a switching variable z_i, there is the *positive literal* z_i and the *negative literal* $\overline{z}_i$, which express logic negation of the variable, that is, $\overline{z}_i = 1 \oplus z_i$, where $\oplus$ is the logic EXOR, equivalently, addition modulo 2.

For a given number m of variables, *products* $\alpha_0 \alpha_1 \cdots \alpha_{m-1}$, where α_i is either z_i or $\overline{z}_i$ are called *minterms*.

For a given function f, minterms corresponding to the function values 0 and 1 are called 0-*minterms* and 1-*minterms*, or *false* and *true* minterms, respectively.

Similarly, *disjunctions* (i.e., logical sums) of all variables $\alpha_0 \vee \alpha_1 \vee \cdots \vee \alpha_{m-1}$, where α_i is either z_i or $\overline{z}_i$, are called *maxterms*.

Each minterm defines a function of m variables that equals 1 at exactly one element of the domain. Each maxterm defines a function that equals 0 at exactly one element of the domain. Thus, it is clear that any function can be represented as a disjunction (logic sum) of minterms, or as a conjunction (logic product) of maxterms.

Example 1.3.1   *For $m = 3$, the assignments of values for binary variables* (000), (010), *and* (111) *correspond to minterms* $\overline{z}_0 \overline{z}_1 \overline{z}_2$, $\overline{z}_0 z_1 \overline{z}_2$, *and* $z_0 z_1 z_2$.

For the functions $f^{(0)}$, $f^{(1)}$ in Table 1.2.5, 1-minterms are

$f^{(0)}$	$\overline{z}_0 \overline{z}_1 z_2,\ \overline{z}_0 z_1 \overline{z}_2,\ z_0 \overline{z}_1 \overline{z}_2,\ z_0 z_1 z_2$
$f^{(1)}$	$\overline{z}_0 z_1 z_2,\ z_0 \overline{z}_1 z_2,\ z_0 z_1 \overline{z}_2,\ z_0 z_1 z_2$

For the same functions, 0-maxterms are

$f^{(0)}$	$z_0 + z_1 + z_2,\ z_0 + \overline{z}_1 + \overline{z}_2,\ \overline{z}_0 + z_1 + \overline{z}_2,\ \overline{z}_0 + \overline{z}_1 + z_2,$
$f^{(1)}$	$z_0 + z_1 + z_2,\ z_0 + z_1 + \overline{z}_2,\ z_0 + \overline{z}_1 + z_2,\ \overline{z}_0 + z_1 + z_2$

Remark 1.3.1   *In the design of digital devices, we use mathematical machinery from many branches of mathematics where different names and different conventions exists for essentially the same mathematical structures. For instance, switching functions have properties that are found in finite fields, propositional logic, Boolean algebra, and so on. We use the conventions and notations from various branches when it is natural and there is no danger of confusion.*

Example 1.3.2   *Consider the simplest finite field $Z_2 = \{0, 1\}$ with the operations $\oplus, \cdot$ that are the addition and multiplication modulo 2. These are equivalently expressed by*

$$
\begin{array}{c|cc}
\oplus & 0 & 1 \\
\hline
0 & 0 & 1 \\
1 & 1 & 0
\end{array}
\qquad
\begin{array}{c|cc}
\cdot & 0 & 1 \\
\hline
0 & 0 & 0 \\
1 & 0 & 1
\end{array}
$$

In Boolean algebra or propositional logic, we have the same set $\{0, 1\}$ and operations $\vee, \cdot,$ and $-$ defined by

$$
\begin{array}{c|cc}
\vee & 0 & 1 \\
\hline
0 & 0 & 1 \\
1 & 1 & 1
\end{array}
\qquad
\begin{array}{c|cc}
\cdot & 0 & 1 \\
\hline
0 & 0 & 0 \\
1 & 0 & 1
\end{array}
\qquad
\begin{array}{c|c}
- & \\
\hline
0 & 1 \\
1 & 0
\end{array}
$$

It is clear that we can express any binary operation by the operations $\oplus, \cdot$ and the constant 1. For instance,

$$x \vee y = (x \oplus y) \vee xy,$$

$$\overline{x} = 1 \oplus x.$$

Table 1.3.1 shows some operators that are commonly used in logic design. For the logic addition (disjunction) OR, the symbols $+$ and $\vee$ are often used. Similarly, for the logic multiplication (conjunction) AND, symbols $\cdot, \wedge,$ or simply juxtaposition are also used.

If any operation can be expressed by the operations from a set A of operations, (e.g., $A = \{\vee, \cdot, -\}$, and $A = \{\vee, -\}$, $A = \{\cdot, -\}$), then A is called *functionally complete*. It is worth noticing that a single operation may form a functionally complete set. The example of such an operation is Sheffer stroke, $|$, defined in the tabular form as

$$
\begin{array}{c|cc}
| & 0 & 1 \\
\hline
0 & 1 & 1 \\
1 & 1 & 0
\end{array}
$$

TABLE 1.3.1   Logic Operations.

x	y	$\vee$ OR	$\oplus$ EXOR	$\downarrow$ NOR	$\cdot$ AND	$\equiv$ Equivalence	$\rightarrow$ Implication	$|$ NAND
0	0	0	0	1	0	1	1	1
0	1	1	1	0	0	0	1	1
1	0	1	1	0	0	0	0	1
1	1	1	0	1	1	1	1	0

or as the negation of the logic AND, that is, $x|y = \overline{x \wedge y}$, and therefore also called *logic NAND*. The completeness of this operation can be seen from the relations

$$\overline{x} = x|x,$$

$$x \vee y = \overline{x}|\overline{y},$$

$$x \wedge y = (x|y)|(x|y),$$

$$x \oplus y = \overline{(x+y)+xy}.$$

The operation called *logic NOR* defined as the negation of logic *OR* also forms a functionally complete set.

Definition 1.3.1 *(Complete disjunctive normal form) The complete disjunctive normal form for a switching function f is the logic OR sum of 1-minterms for f. It is also called the* Sum-of-Product *(SOP) expression for f.*

Example 1.3.3   *For the function $f(z) = (f^{(0)}, f^{(1)})$ in Table 1.2.5, the complete disjunctive normal form is*

$$f^{(0)} = \overline{z}_0\overline{z}_1z_2 \vee \overline{z}_0z_1\overline{z}_2 \vee z_0\overline{z}_1\overline{z}_2 \vee z_0z_1z_2,$$

$$f^{(1)} = \overline{z}_0z_1z_2 \vee z_0\overline{z}_1z_2 \vee z_0z_1\overline{z}_2 \vee z_0z_1z_2.$$

Notice that in Definition 1.3.1, the operation $\vee$ can be replaced by $\oplus$, since the product terms are minterms, and, thus, no two can simultaneously be equal 1. This replacement of logic operations is impossible in the reduced sum-of-product expressions where the product terms are not necessarily minterms.

Example 1.3.4   *For the function $f^{(1)}$ in Table 1.2.5, a SOP-expression is*

$$f^{(1)} = \overline{z}_0z_1z_2 \vee z_0\overline{z}_1z_2 \vee z_0z_1,$$

since $\overline{z}_2 \vee z_2 = 1$ for all the combinations of logic values 0 and 1, and therefore, $z_0z_1\overline{z}_2 \vee z_0z_1z_2$ can be reduced to z_0z_1.

From SOP expressions, *Product-of-Sum* (POS) expressions can be derived by the application of the De Morgan rules from the Boolean algebra. For more information about these and related representations of switching functions, see References 41, 395, and 491.

A single variable switching function can always be written as

$$f(z) = \overline{z}f_0 \oplus zf_1 = \overline{z}f_0 \vee zf_1, \tag{1.3.1}$$

where f_0 and f_1 are the cofactors of f with respect to the variable z, which means, $f_0 = f(z = 0)$ and $f_1 = f(z = 1)$.

This representation is called the *Shannon expansion*. A two-variable function $f(z_0, z_1)$ can be represented as a sum-of-products of variables by the recursive application of the Shannon expansion

$$f(z_0, z_1) = \overline{z}_0 f(z_0 = 0, z_1) \oplus z_0 f(z_0 = 1, z_1)$$

$$= \overline{z}_0(\overline{z}_1 f(z_0 = 0, z_1 = 0) \oplus z_1 f(z_0 = 0, z_1 = 1))$$

$$\oplus z_0(\overline{z}_1 f(z_0 = 1, z_1 = 0) \oplus z_1 f(z_0 = 1, z_1 = 1))$$

$$= \overline{z}_0\overline{z}_1 f(z_0 = 0, z_1 = 0) \oplus \overline{z}_0 z_1 f(z_0 = 0, z_1 = 1)$$

$$\oplus z_0\overline{z}_1 f(z_0 = 1, z_1 = 0) \oplus z_0 z_1 f(z_0 = 1, z_1 = 1).$$

A generalization to functions of an arbitrary number of variables is straightforward and by deleting the products corresponding to the function values 0 yields the complete disjunctive normal form.

This interpretation permits generalization of this form of functional expressions to multiple-valued logic functions. For simplicity of notation, these definitions will be introduced and explained by an example of three-valued functions.

Definition 1.3.2 *(Characteristic functions) For a multiple-valued variable z_j taking values in the set $\{0, 1 \ldots, p - 1\}$, $j = 0, \ldots, m - 1$, the characteristic functions $J_i(z_j)$, $i = 0, 1, \ldots, p - 1$ are defined as $J_i(z_j) = 1$ for $z_j = i$, and $J_i(z_j) = 0$ for $z_j \neq i$.*

Example 1.3.5 *For $p = 3$ and $m = 2$, the characteristic functions $J_i(z_j)$ are given in Table 1.3.2.*

Definition 1.3.3 *(Generalized Shannon expansion) The generalized Shannon expansion for three-valued logic functions is defined as*

$$f = J_0(z_i)f_0 + J_1(z_i)f_1 + J_2(z_i)f_2,$$

where f_i, $i = 0, 1, 2$ are the cofactors of f for $z_i \in 0, 1, 2$.

TABLE 1.3.2 Characteristic Functions for $p = 3$, $n = 2$.

$z_0 z_1$	$J_0(z_0)$	$J_1(z_0)$	$J_2(z_0)$	$J_0(z_1)$	$J_1(z_1)$	$J_2(z_1)$
00	1	0	0	1	0	0
01	1	0	0	0	1	0
02	1	0	0	0	0	1
10	0	1	0	1	0	0
11	0	1	0	0	1	0
12	0	1	0	0	0	1
20	0	0	1	1	0	0
21	0	0	1	0	1	0
22	0	0	1	0	0	1

Example 1.3.6 *For $p = 3$ and $m = 2$, expanding with respect to z_0*

$$f(z_0, z_1) = J_0(z_0)f(z_0 = 0, z_1) + J_1(z_0)f(z_0 = 1, z_1) + J_2(z_0)f(z_0 = 2, z_1).$$

After application f the generalized Shannon expansion with respect to z_1, it follows

$$
\begin{aligned}
f(z_0, z_1) = \; & J_0(z_1)(J_0(z_0)f(z_0 = 0, z_1 = 0) + J_1(z_0)f(z_0 = 1, z_1 = 0) \\
& + J_2(z_0)f(z_0 = 2, z_1 = 0)) + J_1(z_1)(J_0(x_0)f(z_0 = 0, z_1 = 1) \\
& + J_1(z_0)f(z_0 = 1, z_1 = 1) + J_2(z_0)f(z_0 = 2, z_1 = 1)) \\
& + J_2(z_1)(J_0(z_0)f(z_0 = 0, z_1 = 2) + J_1(z_0)f(z_0 = 1, z_1 = 2) \\
& + J_2(z_0)f(z_0 = 2, z_1 = 2)) \\
= \; & J_0(z_1)J_0(z_0)f(z_0 = 0, z_1 = 0) + J_0(z_1)J_1(z_0)f(z_0 = 1, z_1 = 0) \\
& + J_0(z_1)J_2(z_0)f(z_0 = 2, z_1 = 0) + J_1(z_1)J_0(z_0)f(z_0 = 0, z_1 = 1) \\
& + J_1(z_1)J_1(z_0)f(z_0 - 1, z_1 = 1) + J_1(z_1)J_2(z_0)f(z_0 = 2, z_1 = 1) \\
& + J_2(z_1)J_0(z_0)f(z_0 = 0, z_1 = 2) + J_2(z_1)J_1(z_0)f(z_0 = 1, z_1 = 2) \\
& + J_2(z_1)J_2(z_0)f(z_0 = 2, z_1 = 2)).
\end{aligned}
$$

1.4 DECISION DIAGRAMS FOR DISCRETE FUNCTIONS

All logic (switching) functions can be represented by *truth tables* or when the order of variables is fixed by *truth vectors*. However, in practical applications, the number of variables can be large (tens or even hundreds) and use and manipulation of truth vectors is impractical or impossible. The same is true also for SOP and POS representations, which may consists of a large number (millions) of terms.

If the function possesses suitable properties, it may have an alternative representation that makes it possible to determine the value of the function for any assignment of variables.

The central theme of this book is to represent the function $f(z)$ or its integer-valued equivalent $\Phi(z)$ by finding a sparse representation for $\Phi(z)$ in terms of suitably chosen basis functions. These basis functions are intimately connected with another representation called *Decision Diagrams* (555) that often lead to very compact representations and also allow efficient manipulation of functions in both direct and spectral representations.

In this section, we briefly present basic definitions from decision diagram representations of logic functions restricting the considerations to notions that will be used latter in the book. Further information about decision diagrams can be found for example in References (130, 499, and 555). For more detail about the many ways to represent logic functions, we refer for example to References (41 and 491).

We note that representations of logic functions by decision diagrams have been widely used in industry (121,491), and there are quite a few tools and the corresponding software packages for the design of devices such that their behavior is defined by decision diagrams, see Reference 661 and references therein.

1.4.1 Decision Trees

Recursive application of the Shannon decomposition (1.3.1) to all the variables in a given switching function f to derive the complete disjunctive normal form for f can be represented by a *Binary Decision Tree* (BDT)(30,76).

Example 1.4.1 *Figure 1.4.1 shows BDT representing the decomposition for three-variable switching functions f. This tree is a graphical representation of the decomposition of f with respect to all the variables by recursive application of the Shannon expansion $f = \overline{z}_i f_0 \oplus z_i f_1$, where $f_0 = f(z_i = 0)$ and $f_1 = f(z_i = 1)$.*

1. *The Shannon expansion with respect to z_0 produces*

$$f = \overline{z}_0 f_0 \oplus z_0 f_1.$$

2. *The Shannon expansion with respect to z_1 yields*

$$f_0 = \overline{z}_1 f_{00} \oplus z_1 f_{01}, \quad f_1 = \overline{z}_1 f_{10} \oplus z_1 f_{11}.$$

3. *After performing the Shannon expansion with respect to z_2,*

$$f_{00} = \overline{z}_2 f_{000} \oplus z_2 f_{001}, \quad f_{01} = \overline{z}_2 f_{010} \oplus z_2 f_{011},$$
$$f_{10} = \overline{z}_2 f_{100} \oplus z_2 f_{101}, \quad f_{11} = \overline{z}_2 f_{110} \oplus z_2 f_{111}.$$

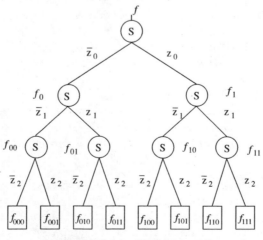

FIGURE 1.4.1 BDT for $m = 3$.

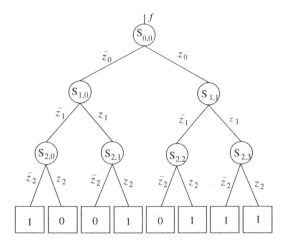

FIGURE 1.4.2   BDT for the function f in Example 1.4.2.

It follows that BDT in Fig. 1.4.1 represents f through the SOP-expression

$$f = \bar{z}_0\bar{z}_1\bar{z}_2 f_{000} \oplus \bar{z}_0\bar{z}_1 z_2 f_{001} \oplus \bar{z}_0 z_1 \bar{z}_2 f_{010} \oplus \bar{z}_0 z_1 z_2 f_{011} \qquad (1.4.1)$$

$$z_0\bar{z}_1\bar{z}_2 f_{100} \oplus z_0\bar{z}_1 z_2 f_{101} \oplus z_0 z_1 \bar{z}_3 f_{110} \oplus z_0 z_1 z_2 f_{111}.$$

If products assigned to the 0-value of f are removed from this expression, that is, products of labels at the edges along paths pointing to the constant node 0, we get the complete disjunctive form.

Example 1.4.2   *Figure 1.4.2 shows BDT for the three-variable function f given by the truth-vector $\mathbf{F} = [1, 0, 0, 1, 0, 1, 1, 1]^T$. In this figure, nodes are labeled by the symbol $S_{i,j}$, where S refers to the Shannon decomposition rule, the first index corresponds to the level in the diagram, thus, it is equal to the index of the decision variable at the level, and the second index shows the position of the node at the level. Such notation is convenient in calculations over decision diagrams, and it will be used in subsequent discussions referring to this example. In programming implementations of related algorithms, it is usually realized in the form of linked lists. When possible, the notation is simplified by using just the symbol for the decomposition rule and omitting the indices. Alternatively, a node can be labeled by the decision variable, in which case edges are labeled by values a variable can take, which in binary decision diagrams, i.e., diagrams with two outgoing edges per node, usually are logic values 0 and 1.*

BDT is a canonic representation of f in the same way as the complete disjunctive normal form is a canonic representation of f.

As can be seen from Fig.1.4.1, a BDT consists of the *root node*, internal nodes called *nonterminal nodes* and *constant nodes*. Nonterminal nodes are distributed over *levels*, each level corresponding to a variable z_i in f by starting from the root node corresponding to z_0. The nodes corresponding to ith variable form the ith level in the decision tree. Therefore, indices in the labels of nonterminal nodes show the level and the position of the node at the level, respectively. For a switching function of m variables, the number of nodes at the level i is 2^i, $i = 0, 1, \ldots, m - 1$. Since variables appear in a fixed order, such BDT is the *ordered BDT*.

Each *path* from the root node down to the constant nodes corresponds to a minterm in (1.4.1), determined as the product of labels at the edges. Alternatively, edges can be labeled by 0 and 1 instead $\bar{z}_i$ and z_i, respectively. The values of constant nodes in the BDTs are the values of the represented functions. Thus, they are elements of the truth-vector **F** of f.

1.4.2 Decision Diagrams

If in **F** there are some equal subvectors of orders 2^k, $k \leq m - 2$, then in BDT some isomorphic subtrees appear. Thanks to that, BDT can be reduced into a *Binary Decision Diagram* (BDD) (76) derived from BDT by using the *reduction rules* defined as follows.

Definition 1.4.1   *(BDD reduction rules)*

1. *If two descendent nodes of a node are identical (Fig. 1.4.3(a)), then delete the node and connect the incoming edges of the deleted node to the corresponding successor.*
2. *Share isomorphic subtrees (Fig. 1.4.3(b)).*

In a BDD, edges longer than one, that is, connecting nodes at nonsuccessive levels can appear. For example, the length of an edge connecting a node at the $(i - 1)$th level with a node at the $(i + 1)$th level is two.

Definition 1.4.2   *(Cross points) Cross point is a point where an edge longer than one crosses a level in the BDD.*

By including cross points as nodes, all the edges of the decision diagram have length equal to 1. This is convenient, since manipulations of decision diagrams are

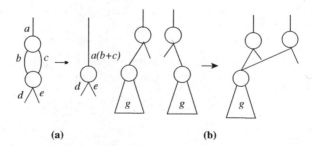

(a)   (b)

FIGURE 1.4.3   BDD reduction rules.

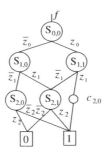

FIGURE 1.4.4   BDD for f in Example 1.4.2.

performed over the successive levels. In practical implementations, the cross points are considered as nodes with both outgoing edges pointing to the same node.

Example 1.4.3   *Figure 1.4.4 shows a BDD for f in Example 1.4.2. It is derived from the BDT in Fig. 1.4.2 in the following way. Since, both outgoing edges of the node $S_{2,3}$ point to the value 1, no decision is made in this node, and therefore, it can be deleted and the incoming edges directed toward the corresponding constant node. In this way, a path of the length 2 appears and the impact of the deleted node is represented formally by the cross point $c_{2,0}$. Subtrees rooted in the nodes $S_{2,1}$ and $S_{2,2}$ are isomorphic, and represent the same subfunction whose truth-vector is $[0, 1]$. Therefore, the subtree rooted at $S_{2,2}$ is deleted, and the incoming edge of the node $S_{2,2}$ pointed to the node $S_{2,1}$.*

To get more compact representations, *Free BDDs*, where the order of variables along different paths may be different, are also considered (56). The compactness is achieved at the price of increased complexity in constructing such diagrams and proper selecting of order of variables, and more complex algorithms for manipulation with such diagrams (195). Thus, these diagrams provide an opportunity for the trade-off between the compactness and efficiency of manipulations depending on the intended applications.

When logic functions are represented by decision diagrams, the constant nodes have values equal to 0 or 1. Often we want to represent some other discrete functions $f : \{0, 1\}^m \to R$ by a decision diagram and then the constant nodes have values from R. These decision diagrams are often called *Multiterminal Binary Decision Diagrams* (MTBDDs) (103–105).

Example 1.4.4   *Figure 1.4.5 shows a decision diagram for a function $f : \{0, 1\}^5 \to \{0, 1, 2\}$ given by the vector of function values*

$$\mathbf{F} = [0, 1, 0, 1, 0, 1, 0, 1, 1, 1, 1, 2, 1, 1, 1, 2, 1, 2, 1, 2, 1, 2, 2, 2, 1, 2, 1, 2, 1, 2, 2, 2]^T.$$

Because multioutput logic functions, that is, systems of functions, can be represented by the binary coding, these functions can be represented by a multiterminal

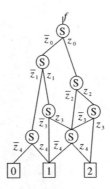

FIGURE 1.4.5   MTBDD of f in Example 1.4.4.

BDD (499). Alternatively, they can often be compactly represented by *Shared BDDs* (372). In these, each output of the multioutput function has its unique root node, but (whenever possible) "isomorphic subfunctions" are represented by a single copy of the corresponding parts of the BDDs.

Example 1.4.5   *The integer-valued function in Example 1.4.4 can be considered as the multioutput switching function $f = (f^{(0)}, f^{(1)})$, where $f^{(0)}$ and $f^{(1)}$ are given by the truth vectors*

$$\mathbf{F}^{(0)} = [0, 0, 0, 0, 0, 0, 0, 0, 0, 0, 0, 1, 0, 0, 0, 1, 0, 1, 0, 1, 0, 1, 1, 1, 0, 1, 0, 1, 0, 1, 1, 1]^T,$$

$$\mathbf{F}^{(1)} = [0, 1, 0, 1, 0, 1, 0, 1, 1, 1, 1, 0, 1, 1, 1, 0, 1, 0, 1, 0, 1, 0, 0, 0, 1, 0, 1, 0, 1, 0, 0, 0]^T.$$

These truth vectors are determined by coding the values $0, 1, 2$ in f by $0 = (0, 0), 1 = (0, 1),$ and $2 = (1, 0)$.

   Figure 1.4.6 shows SBDD, representing thus determined $f^{(1)}$ and $f^{(0)}$. The value of f is the sum $2 f^{(0)} + f^{(1)}$ of values represented by the root nodes in this SBDD.

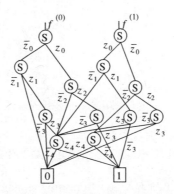

FIGURE 1.4.6   SBDD of f in Example 1.4.4.

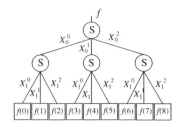

FIGURE 1.4.7 MDT for $p = 3$, $m = 2$.

1.4.3 Decision Diagrams for Multiple-Valued Functions

Extension of decision diagrams to multivalued functions and in general discrete functions is straightforward by allowing more than two outgoing edges per nodes. These decision diagrams are called *Multiple-Place Decision Diagrams* (MDDs) (534). In MDDs, edges are labeled by X_i^s, which shows that the p-valued variable X_i takes along this edge the value s, where $s \in \{0, 1, \ldots, p - 1\}$.

Example 1.4.6 *Figure 1.4.7 shows a Multiple-Place Decision Tree (MDT) for functions when $p = 3$, $m = 2$.*

The basic characteristics of decision diagrams are

1. Size—the number of nodes in the diagram.
2. Depth—the number of levels.
3. Width—the maximum number of nodes per level.
4. The number of outgoing edges per node.
5. The number of constant nodes for multiterminal diagrams.
6. The number and the complexity of interconnections.

Each of these characteristics has a strong influence to the efficiency of applications of decision diagrams. Therefore, reduction of these characteristics or at least some of them in a diagram representing a given function is a very important task and related methods are extensively discussed in the literature. An approach to find compact decision diagrams is to use various decomposition rules to assign a given function to a decision diagram. In this way, a variety of decision diagrams has been defined and a list of them can be found in Reference 555. In this respect, BDDs, MTBDDs, and MDDs can be viewed as the basic decision diagrams since they are defined by using the identity mapping to assign a function to the diagram.

1.5 SPECTRAL REPRESENTATIONS OF LOGIC FUNCTIONS

Spectral representations of discrete functions are the main theme of this book. As it will be seen in next chapters of this book, there are quite a few problems in analysis, design, testing, and diagnosis of digital devices that are much easier to solve if the logic functions describing these devices are converted to the *spectral (generalized frequency) domain*.

This situation is very similar to the application of Fourier transforms to analysis and design of analog devices. In fact, we are going to exploit the generalized Fourier transform for logic functions and to discuss analysis, design, and testing techniques based on these spectra. We note that the transition from the original domain to the spectral domain may result in a drastic reduction of the complexity of a solution.

In general, a *spectral representation* of a discrete function means that instead of representing the (vector of the) function values, we represent the (vector of the) function values after applying a suitable spectral transform to the function considered.

These representations are entirely equivalent. As long as we are able to determine all values of the function, the particular form of the representations is unimportant. However, from the practical point of view, there are very important differences. First, it may happen that the direct representation requires, for example, a large number of minterms of the full vector of the function values need to be stored while after the right *linear transform*, the corresponding *coefficient vector* would have a very simple form. Second, from the linearly transformed vector of function values, that is, vector of the coefficients, the spectrum, it may be possible to determine certain properties of the function that would be rather difficult to determine directly (spectral analysis). For instance, the transformed form may reveal particular regularities of the function that allow the use of specific types of circuits in the hardware implementations. We note that it is possible to place large numbers of powerful computing elements on a single chip and this makes the high regularity of a representation very desirable.

In this section, we briefly discuss the *spectral representations* of logic functions and their implementations. In latter chapters, a more profound exposition of these techniques based on classical Fourier analysis and abstract harmonic analysis is given.

Since we are mainly interested in representations of logic functions, we will introduce here spectral techniques by referring to the above introduced notions from switching theory, in particular, by starting from the spectral interpretation of the Shannon expansion written in the matrix form.

Recall that the *Kronecker product* of an $(m \times n)$ matrix $\mathbf{A}$ and a $(p \times q)$ matrix $\mathbf{B}$ is the $(mp \times nq)$ matrix $\mathbf{C}$

$$\mathbf{C} = \begin{bmatrix} a_{1,1}\mathbf{B} & a_{1,2}\mathbf{B} & \cdots & a_{1,n}\mathbf{B} \\ a_{2,1}\mathbf{B} & a_{2,2}\mathbf{B} & \cdots & a_{2,n}\mathbf{B} \\ \cdots & \cdots & \cdots & \cdots \\ a_{m,1}\mathbf{B} & a_{m,2}\mathbf{B} & \cdots & a_{m,n}\mathbf{B} \end{bmatrix}.$$

The Kronecker product satisfies many useful properties, such as

$$(\mathbf{A} \otimes \mathbf{B})(\mathbf{C} \otimes \mathbf{D}) = \mathbf{AC} \otimes \mathbf{BD},$$

$$(\mathbf{A} \otimes \mathbf{B})^T = \mathbf{A}^T \otimes \mathbf{B}^T,$$

and

$$(\mathbf{A} \otimes \mathbf{B})^{-1} = \mathbf{A}^{-1} \otimes \mathbf{B}^{-1},$$

if $\mathbf{A}$ and $\mathbf{B}$ are nonsingular and where $\mathbf{A}^T$ and $\mathbf{A}^{-1}$ are the transpose and the inverse matrices of $\mathbf{A}$.

Using this notation, the Shannon expansion can be compactly written for functions of m variables.

In the rest of this section and in Section 1.6, in relations with vectors and matrices, all the multiplications and additions are assumed to be modulo 2.

In the matrix notation, the Shannon expansion with respect to the variable z_i can be written as

$$f = \begin{bmatrix} \bar{z}_i & z_i \end{bmatrix} \begin{bmatrix} f(z_i = 0) \\ f(z_i = 1) \end{bmatrix} = \begin{bmatrix} \bar{z}_i & z_i \end{bmatrix} \begin{bmatrix} 1 & 0 \\ 0 & 1 \end{bmatrix} \begin{bmatrix} f(z_i = 0) \\ f(z_i = 1) \end{bmatrix}. \tag{1.5.1}$$

The vector of minterms can be expressed formally as Kronecker product of (1×2) matrices $\begin{bmatrix} \bar{z}_i & z_i \end{bmatrix}$ as follows:

$$[\,\bar{z}_0\bar{z}_1 \ \ \bar{z}_0 z_1 \ \ z_0\bar{z}_1 \ \ z_0 z_1\,] = [\,\bar{z}_0 \ z_0\,] \otimes [\,\bar{z}_1 \ z_1\,],$$

$$[\,\bar{z}_0\bar{z}_1\bar{z}_2 \ \ \bar{z}_0\bar{z}_1 z_0 \ \ \bar{z}_0 z_1\bar{z}_2 \ \cdots \ z_0 z_1 z_2\,]$$

$$= [\,\bar{z}_0 \ z_0\,] \otimes [\,\bar{z}_1 \ z_1\,] \otimes [\,\bar{z}_2 \ z_2\,],$$

and in the same way for an arbitrary number of variables.

Thus, we can write for $m = 2$,

$$f = \left(\begin{bmatrix} \bar{z}_0 & z_0 \end{bmatrix} \otimes \begin{bmatrix} \bar{z}_1 & z_1 \end{bmatrix} \right) \begin{bmatrix} f_{00} \\ f_{01} \\ f_{10} \\ f_{11} \end{bmatrix}$$

$$= \left(\begin{bmatrix} \bar{z}_0 & z_0 \end{bmatrix} \otimes \begin{bmatrix} \bar{z}_1 & z_1 \end{bmatrix} \right) \left(\begin{bmatrix} 1 & 0 \\ 0 & 1 \end{bmatrix} \otimes \begin{bmatrix} 1 & 0 \\ 0 & 1 \end{bmatrix} \right) \begin{bmatrix} f_{00} \\ f_{01} \\ f_{10} \\ f_{11} \end{bmatrix} \tag{1.5.2}$$

and for the case of m variables

$$f = \mathbf{X}(m)\mathbf{F} = \mathbf{X}(m)\mathbf{I}(m)\mathbf{F}, \tag{1.5.3}$$

where

$$\mathbf{X}(m) = \bigotimes_{i=0}^{m-1} \mathbf{X}_i(1), \quad \mathbf{X}_i(1) = \begin{bmatrix} \overline{z}_i & z_i \end{bmatrix},$$

$$\mathbf{I}(m) = \bigotimes_{i=0}^{m-1} \mathbf{I}(1) = \underbrace{\mathbf{I}(1) \otimes \cdots \otimes \mathbf{I}(1)}_{m}, \quad \mathbf{I}(1) = \begin{bmatrix} 1 & 0 \\ 0 & 1 \end{bmatrix},$$

and $\mathbf{F} = [f(0), \ldots, f(2^m - 1)]^T$ is the truth vector of f written with integer encoding of variables.

Notice that the entries of $\mathbf{X}(m)$ are minterms. We can view a minterm as a function $\{0, 1\}^m \rightarrow \{0, 1\}$ or, by using the integer encoding, as a function $\{0, 1, \ldots, 2^m - 1\} \rightarrow Z$, where Z is the set of integers. In this interpretation (1.5.3) expresses f as a *linear combination* of the basis functions which are defined by minterms. These functions are clearly linearly independent as each minterm equals 1 for exactly one value $z = \sum_{i=0}^{m-1} 2^{m-1-i} z_i$ and is zero otherwise. Thus, they form a basis and (1.5.3) is the (trivial) spectral representation of f in the Shannon basis.

Figure 1.5.1 shows the waveforms of these functions for $m = 3$.

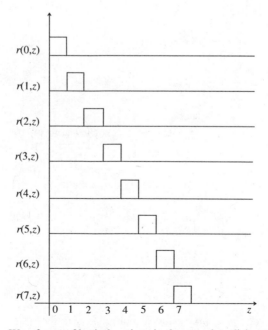

FIGURE 1.5.1   Waveforms of basis functions in the complete disjunctive normal form.

Various spectral transforms are defined by selecting different basis functions. For instance, we get the *Reed–Muller transform* if in (1.5.3) we replace the matrices $\mathbf{X}_i(1) = [\, \overline{z}_i \quad z_i \,]$ and $\mathbf{I}(1)$ with $\mathbf{X}_{R_i}(1) = [\, 1 \quad z_i \,]$ and $\mathbf{R}(1) = \begin{bmatrix} 1 & 0 \\ 1 & 1 \end{bmatrix}$, respectively. The relation obtained in this way

$$ f = \begin{bmatrix} 1 & z_i \end{bmatrix} \begin{bmatrix} 1 & 0 \\ 1 & 1 \end{bmatrix} \begin{bmatrix} f_0 \\ f_1 \end{bmatrix} \tag{1.5.4} $$

is the matrix form of the *positive Davio expansion* that can be derived from the Shannon expansion as follows:

$$ f = \overline{z}_i f_0 \oplus z_i f_1 = (1 \oplus z_i) f_0 \oplus z_i f_1 = 1 \cdot f_0 \oplus z_i (f_0 \oplus f_1). $$

The matrix $\mathbf{R}(1)$ is called the *basic Reed–Muller matrix*.

Repeated application of (1.5.4) to all the variables in f can be expressed through the Kronecker product as in the case of the Shannon expressions. In that way, for a function f defined by the vector $\mathbf{F} = [\,f(0), \ldots, f(2^m - 1)\,]^T$, the *Positive Polarity Reed–Muller (PPRM) polynomial* is given in matrix notation by

$$ f = \mathbf{X}_R(m)\mathbf{R}(m)\mathbf{F}, \tag{1.5.5} $$

where

$$ \mathbf{X}_R(m) = \bigotimes_{i=0}^{m-1} \begin{bmatrix} 1 & z_i \end{bmatrix} $$

and

$$ \mathbf{R}(m) = \bigotimes_{i=0}^{m-1} \mathbf{R}(1) = \underbrace{\mathbf{R}(1) \otimes \cdots \otimes \mathbf{R}(1)}_{m}, $$

where $\mathbf{R}(1)$ is the basic Reed–Muller matrix defined above, with calculations carried out modulo 2.

The matrix $\mathbf{R}(m)$ is called the *Reed–Muller matrix* and its columns the *Reed–Muller functions*. From (1.5.5), the *i*th Reed–Muller function is given by

$$ rm(i, z) = rm_i(i_0, \ldots, i_{m-1}; z_0, \ldots, z_{m-1}) = (z_0)^{i_0} \cdots (z_{m-1})^{i_{m-1}}, $$

where $i = \sum_{j=0}^{m-1} i_j 2^{m-1-j}$.

Notice that here $(z_i)^k$ denotes the exponentiation in the sense that $(z_i)^0 = 1$ for every z_i.

$$\mathbf{R}(3) = \begin{bmatrix} 1 & 0 & 0 & 0 & 0 & 0 & 0 & 0 \\ 1 & 1 & 0 & 0 & 0 & 0 & 0 & 0 \\ 1 & 0 & 1 & 0 & 0 & 0 & 0 & 0 \\ 1 & 1 & 1 & 1 & 0 & 0 & 0 & 0 \\ 1 & 0 & 0 & 0 & 1 & 0 & 0 & 0 \\ 1 & 1 & 0 & 0 & 1 & 1 & 0 & 0 \\ 1 & 0 & 1 & 0 & 1 & 0 & 1 & 0 \\ 1 & 1 & 1 & 1 & 1 & 1 & 1 & 1 \end{bmatrix}.$$

FIGURE 1.5.2   Reed–Muller matrix for $m = 3$.

Example 1.5.1   *Figure 1.5.2 shows the Reed–Muller matrix for $m = 3$. Figure 1.5.3 shows the waveforms of the Reed–Muller step functions for $m = 3$.*

The concepts of the sum and integral on the finite discrete structures coincide and, thus, also the concepts of the Fourier series-like representation and the Fourier-like transform. Therefore, the matrix representation of the PPRM polynomial can be alternatively considered as a spectral transform for switching functions defined in terms of the Reed–Muller functions.

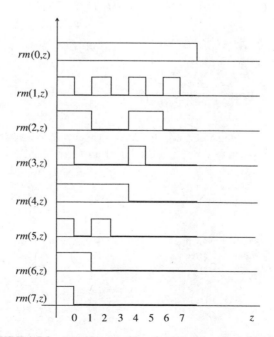

FIGURE 1.5.3   Waveforms of Reed–Muller functions for $m = 3$.

The vector $\mathbf{S}_f = [S_f(0), \ldots, S_f(2^m - 1)]^T$ defined by

$$\mathbf{S}_f = \mathbf{R}(m)\mathbf{F} \tag{1.5.6}$$

is the vector of Reed–Muller transform coefficients. We will call $\mathbf{S}_f$ the *Reed–Muller spectrum* of f. In the Russian literature, this transform is usually reported as the *conjunctive transform* (24, 27, 323).

Relation (1.5.6) together with the relation

$$f = \mathbf{X}_R(m)\mathbf{S}_f \tag{1.5.7}$$

form the Reed–Muller transform pair consisting of the direct (1.5.6) and the inverse (1.5.7) Reed–Muller transforms. Note that the basic Reed–Muller matrix is self-inverse over $GF(2)$. Thanks to the properties of the Kronecker products, the same applies to $\mathbf{R}(m)$.

Example 1.5.2   *For the three-variable function f given by the truth-vector* $\mathbf{F} = [1, 0, 0, 0, 0, 1, 1, 1,]^T$, *the Reed–Muller spectrum is calculated as*

$$\mathbf{S}_f = \mathbf{R}(3)\mathbf{F}$$
$$= [1, 1, 1, 1, 1, 0, 0, 0]^T,$$

where $\mathbf{R}(3)$ is the Reed–Muller matrix in Fig. 1.5.2. From (1.5.7), the Reed–Muller expression for f is

$$f = 1 \oplus z_0 \oplus z_1 \oplus z_2 \oplus z_1 z_2.$$

Basic properties of the Reed–Muller transform are listed in Table 1.5.1 (116). Thanks to its properties, the Reed–Muller transform can be considered as a Fourier-like transform in Boolean algebra or Boolean ring. In the subsequent chapter, the Reed–Muller transform will be derived from the Walsh (Fourier) transform.

TABLE 1.5.1   The Properties of the Reed–Muller Transform Considered as a Transform in the Boolean Algebra $(B, \vee, \wedge, -, 0, 1)$.

If $h(x) = f(x) \oplus g(x)$,	then $S_h(w) = S_f(w) \oplus S_g(w)$
If $h(x) = f(x) \vee g(x)$,	then $S_h(w) = \bigoplus_{u \vee v = w} S_f(u)S_g(v)$
If $h(x) = f(x) \wedge g(x)$,	then $S_h(w) = S_f \oplus S_g(w) \bigoplus_{u \vee v = w} R_f(u)R_g(v)$
Convolution theorem	
If $S_h(w) = S_f(w) \vee S_g(w)$,	then $h(x) = \bigoplus_{y \vee z = x} f(y)g(z)$

1.6 FIXED-POLARITY REED–MULLER EXPRESSIONS OF LOGIC FUNCTIONS

As noticed above, the Reed–Muller expressions where all the variables are represented as the positive literals are called *positive polarity Reed–Muller expressions*. A further generalization of Reed–Muller representations can be derived by taking the negative literals for variables in expanding a given function f with respect to a given basis when the basis functions can be expressed in terms of switching variables. For instance, the negative Davio expansion $f = 1 \cdot f_1 \oplus \bar{x}_i(f_0 \oplus f_1)$ is derived in this way.

The use of the negative Davio expansion together with the positive Davio expansion, permits the derivation of the *Fixed Polarity Reed–Muller (FPRM) polynomials* (487, 488, 494). In FPRMs, we perform the expansion of f by freely selecting either the positive or the negative Davio expansion for each variable in f.

These polynomials with different polarity for variables are characterized by the polarity vectors $H = (h_0, \ldots, h_{m-1})$ whose ith coordinate $h_i = 1$ shows that the corresponding variable is represented by the negative literal $\bar{x}_i$ in the polynomial representation. It follows that in the matrix notation, the use of a negative literal implies the permutation of columns in the ith basic Reed–Muller matrix in the Kronecker representation of $\mathbf{R}(m)$ (541).

In that setting, for a given polarity vector H, the FPRM polynomial is given in the matrix notation by

$$f(z_0, \ldots, z_{m-1}) = \left(\bigotimes_{i=0}^{m-1} \begin{bmatrix} 1 & z_i^{h_i} \end{bmatrix} \right) \left(\bigotimes_{i=0}^{m-1} \mathbf{R}_i^{h_i}(1) \right) \mathbf{F},$$

where

$$z_i^{h_i} = \begin{cases} z_i, & h_i = 0; \\ \bar{z}_i, & h_i = 1, \end{cases} \qquad \mathbf{R}_i^{h_i}(1) = \begin{cases} \begin{bmatrix} 1 & 0 \\ 1 & 1 \end{bmatrix}, & h_i = 0; \\ \\ \begin{bmatrix} 0 & 1 \\ 1 & 1 \end{bmatrix}, & h_i = 1. \end{cases}$$

Notice that in the usual terminology in the study of fixed-polarity expressions, see for instance Reference (489), the value of the coordinate h_i in the polarity vector means choice between the positive and the negative literals for the variable z_i and not the definition of the literal itself. In this setting, the zero polarity, that is, $h_i = 0$ for each i is called also the positive polarity.

The matrix notation permits interpretation of the coefficients in FPRMs as the spectral coefficients of fixed polarity Reed–Muller transforms defined by the transform matrices

$$\mathbf{R}_H(m) = \bigotimes_{i=0}^{m-1} \mathbf{R}_i^{h_i}(1),$$

for different choices of $H = (h_0, \ldots, h_{m-1})$.

The positive-polarity Reed–Muller transform described in the previous section (see (1.5.5)–(1.5.7)) is the special case of this transform for the polarity $H = (h_0, \ldots, h_{m-1}) = (0, 0, \ldots, 0)$.

For a given positive-polarity Reed–Muller spectrum, the Reed–Muller spectrum for the polarity $H = (h_0, \ldots, h_{m-1})$ is determined by the permutation of the $i = (i_0, \ldots, i_{m-1})$th coefficient into the $(i_0 \oplus \overline{h}_0, \ldots, i_{m-1} \oplus \overline{h}_{m-1})$th coefficient, since $\mathbf{R}_H(m)$ is derived from $\mathbf{R}(m)$ by the permutation of columns in which the ith column is shifted to the position $(i_0 \oplus h_0, \ldots, i_{m-1} \oplus h_{m-1})$. However, for a given m-variable function f, the use of different polarity Reed–Muller matrices produces 2^m different Reed–Muller spectra. The fixed polarity Reed–Muller spectrum with the minimum number of nonzero coefficients is the *minimum Reed–Muller expansion* for f. If for a given function f, there are two FPRMs with the same number of nonzero coefficients, the expression with the smaller number of literals in product terms to which the nonzero coefficients are assigned is usually selected as the minimum FPRMs.

Example 1.6.1 *Figure 1.6.1 shows the Reed–Muller transform matrix for $m = 3$ and the polarity vector $H = (0, 1, 0)$. Compared to the positive-polarity Reed–Muller matrix, that is, the Reed–Muller matrix for $H = (0, 0, 0)$ in Fig. 1.5.2, the indices of columns in $\mathbf{R}_{(010)}(3)$ are defined as $(i_0 \oplus h_0, i_1 \oplus h_1, i_2 \oplus h_2)$. Thus, $(0, 1, 2, 3, 4, 5, 6, 7) \to (2, 3, 0, 1, 6, 7, 4, 5)$. With this matrix, for f given by the truth-vector $\mathbf{F} = [1, 0, 0, 1, 0, 1, 1, 1]^T$, the Reed–Muller expansion for $H = (0, 1, 0)$ is given by*

$$f = z_2 \oplus \overline{z}_1 \oplus z_0 \oplus z_0 z_2 \oplus z_0 \overline{z}_1 z_2.$$

$$\mathbf{R}_{(010)}(3) = \begin{bmatrix} 0 & 0 & 1 & 0 & 0 & 0 & 0 & 0 \\ 0 & 0 & 1 & 1 & 0 & 0 & 0 & 0 \\ 1 & 0 & 1 & 0 & 0 & 0 & 0 & 0 \\ 1 & 1 & 1 & 1 & 0 & 0 & 0 & 0 \\ 0 & 0 & 1 & 0 & 0 & 0 & 1 & 0 \\ 0 & 0 & 1 & 1 & 0 & 0 & 1 & 1 \\ 1 & 0 & 1 & 0 & 1 & 0 & 1 & 0 \\ 1 & 1 & 1 & 1 & 1 & 1 & 1 & 1 \end{bmatrix}.$$

FIGURE 1.6.1 Reed–Muller matrix for $m = 3$ and the polarity vector $H = (010)$.

Example 1.6.2 *For f in Example 1.6.1, the Reed–Muller expansions with five product terms are derived for the polarity vectors $H = (0, 0, 0)$, $H = (0, 0, 1)$, $H = (0, 1, 0)$, $H = (1, 0, 0)$, $H = (1, 1, 1)$. Each of other three Reed–Muller expansions have six product terms. Therefore, the positive-polarity Reed–Muller expansion for f can be used as the minimal Reed–Muller expansion for f, the same as that in Example 1.6.1.*

1.7 KRONECKER EXPRESSIONS OF LOGIC FUNCTIONS

Further generalizations can be achieved by allowing to select either the Shannon, positive Davio, or negative Davio expansion for different variables in the functions that should be represented. In this way, the *Kronecker transforms* are defined, see Reference 555. The main idea is to increase the number of possible basis functions to 3^m compared to 2^m in FPRMs, and then for the given function f, select the spectrum with the fewest number of nonzero coefficients.

In matrix notation, the spectra of Kronecker transforms are calculated as

$$\mathbf{S}_f = \mathbf{K}^{-1}(m)\mathbf{F},$$

where $\mathbf{K}^{-1}(m)$ is the inverse of the Kronecker transform matrix $\mathbf{K}(m)$, determined as

$$\mathbf{K}(m) = \otimes_{i=0}^{m-1} K_i(1),$$

where $\mathbf{K}(1) \in \{\mathbf{I}_2, \mathbf{R}(1), \overline{\mathbf{R}}(1)\}$. Notice that in determination of $\mathbf{K}^{-1}$, we use the properties that $\mathbf{I}_2$ and $\mathbf{R}(1)$ are self-inverse matrices, while $\overline{\mathbf{R}}^{-1}(1) = \begin{bmatrix} 1 & 1 \\ 1 & 0 \end{bmatrix}$, which in symbolic notation corresponds to $[\, 1 \quad \overline{z}_i \,]$.

The corresponding functional expressions are determined as

$$f = \mathbf{X}(m)\mathbf{S}_f(m),$$

where

$$\mathbf{X}(m) = \bigotimes_{i=0}^{m-1} \mathbf{X}_i(1),$$

with $\mathbf{X}_i(1)$ is either $\begin{bmatrix} \overline{z}_i & z_i \end{bmatrix}$, $\begin{bmatrix} 1 & z_i \end{bmatrix}$ or $\begin{bmatrix} 1 & \overline{z}_i \end{bmatrix}$.

The following example illustrates Kronecker expressions and a possibility to trade-off between the number of nonzero coefficients and the number of literals in them by selecting different expansion rules for variables.

Example 1.7.1 *Table 1.7.1 shows coefficients in six randomly selected Kronecker expressions for the function f in Example 1.6.1. The analytical representations for*

TABLE 1.7.1   Assignment of Decomposition Rules and the Coefficients in Kronecker Expressions for f in Example 1.6.1

	Decomposition	Coefficients	Number of Coefficients
1.	S,pD,nD	$[0, 1, 1, 0, 1, 1, 0, 1]$	5
2.	pD,S,nD	$[0, 1, 1, 1, 1, 0, 0, 1]$	5
3.	pD,S,S	$[1, 0, 0, 1, 1, 1, 1, 0]$	5
4.	S,pD,S	$[1, 0, 1, 1, 0, 1, 1, 0]$	5
5.	pD,nD,nD	$[1, 1, 1, 0, 0, 1, 1, 1]$	6
6.	S,S,nD	$[0, 1, 1, 1, 1, 1, 1, 0]$	6

the first three expressions are

$$f = \overline{z}_0\overline{z}_2 \oplus \overline{z}_0 z_1 \oplus z_0 \oplus z_0\overline{z}_2 \oplus z_0 z_1\overline{z}_2,$$

$$f = \overline{z}_1\overline{z}_2 \oplus z_1 \oplus z_1\overline{z}_2 \oplus z_0\overline{z}_1 \oplus z_0 z_1\overline{z}_2,$$

$$f = \overline{z}_1\overline{z}_2 \oplus z_1 z_2 \oplus z_0\overline{z}_1\overline{z}_2 \oplus z_0\overline{z}_1 z_2 \oplus z_0 z_1\overline{z}_2.$$

For the illustration, we explain calculation of the first Kronecker expression given above.

Since in this case, the assignment of the decomposition rules or basic transforms is (S, PD, nD), the set of basic functions is defined by

$$\mathbf{X}(3) = \begin{bmatrix} \overline{z}_0 & z_0 \end{bmatrix} \otimes \begin{bmatrix} 1 & z_1 \end{bmatrix} \otimes \begin{bmatrix} 1 & \overline{z}_2 \end{bmatrix}.$$

When written as columns of a matrix, these basis functions are

$$\mathbf{K}(3) = \begin{bmatrix} 1 & 0 \\ 0 & 1 \end{bmatrix} \otimes \begin{bmatrix} 1 & 0 \\ 1 & 1 \end{bmatrix} \otimes \begin{bmatrix} 1 & 1 \\ 1 & 0 \end{bmatrix}$$

$$= \begin{bmatrix}
1 & 1 & 0 & 0 & 0 & 0 & 0 & 0 \\
1 & 0 & 0 & 0 & 0 & 0 & 0 & 0 \\
1 & 1 & 1 & 1 & 0 & 0 & 0 & 0 \\
1 & 0 & 1 & 0 & 0 & 0 & 0 & 0 \\
0 & 0 & 0 & 0 & 1 & 1 & 0 & 0 \\
0 & 0 & 0 & 0 & 1 & 0 & 0 & 0 \\
0 & 0 & 0 & 0 & 1 & 1 & 1 & 1 \\
0 & 0 & 0 & 0 & 1 & 0 & 1 & 0
\end{bmatrix}.$$

The inverse Kronecker transform is

$$\mathbf{K}^{-1}(3) = \begin{bmatrix} 1 & 0 \\ 0 & 1 \end{bmatrix} \otimes \begin{bmatrix} 1 & 0 \\ 1 & 1 \end{bmatrix} \otimes \begin{bmatrix} 0 & 1 \\ 1 & 1 \end{bmatrix}$$

$$= \begin{bmatrix} 0 & 1 & 0 & 0 & 0 & 0 & 0 & 0 \\ 1 & 1 & 0 & 0 & 0 & 0 & 0 & 0 \\ 0 & 1 & 0 & 1 & 0 & 0 & 0 & 0 \\ 1 & 1 & 1 & 1 & 0 & 0 & 0 & 0 \\ 0 & 0 & 0 & 0 & 0 & 1 & 0 & 0 \\ 0 & 0 & 0 & 0 & 1 & 1 & 0 & 0 \\ 0 & 0 & 0 & 0 & 0 & 1 & 0 & 1 \\ 0 & 0 & 0 & 0 & 1 & 1 & 1 & 1 \end{bmatrix}.$$

The Kronecker spectrum for this assignment of basic matrices is calculated as

$$\mathbf{S}_f(3) = \mathbf{K}^{-1}(3)\mathbf{F}$$
$$= [0, 1, 1, 0, 1, 1, 0, 1]^T$$

The Kronecker expression is determined as $\mathbf{X}(3)\mathbf{S}_f$, *which produces the expression shown above.*

These Kronecker expressions differ in the number of nonzero coefficients and the number of literals in product terms. Each of the expressions can be input in a minimization program and, in this case, will result in some further optimized form, which, however, will not preserve the regularity of expressions in the sense of an a priory determined way of assigning positive or negative literals to the variables.

1.8 CIRCUIT IMPLEMENTATION OF LOGIC FUNCTIONS

Devices intended for the processing of discrete information may be divided into two classes:

1. devices without memory, that is, *combinational networks*, whose output depends on the present input and
2. devices with memory, *sequential networks*, whose output and the next state are determined by the input and the internal state of the device.

In devices with memory, two blocks can be distinguished, a combinational network and the block consisting of memory elements (247,313). Therefore, we will first discuss systems of functions describing the operation of combinational networks.

The operation of a combinational network built from elements with p, $(p \geq 2)$ stable states, m p-ary inputs, and k p-ary outputs is described by a system of k p-valued logic functions of m variables. Conversely, a given system of logic functions can be implemented, that is, realized in hardware or software, by combinational networks. Design of such a network is called *synthesis of the network*. In many cases, both the synthesis procedure and the network produced are simplified if the function

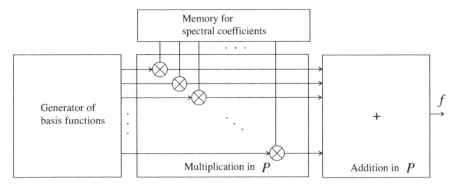

FIGURE 1.8.1 Spectral implementations of logic circuits.

realized expresses some peculiar properties. Therefore, logic functions are often first analyzed to detect their properties and classified with respect to them.

The analysis and synthesis problems may be solved with the help of Boolean algebra or the corresponding algebraic structures in binary or multiple-valued logic, respectively (247,313,633). The main shortcoming of these widely used tools, however, is that in the basic problems of the above type, they require an exhaustive examination of all alternatives (the so-called *brute-force method*). Since the number of alternatives may increase exponentially with the number m of variables, the actual use of these tools in engineering practice is limited (even when powerful computers are employed) to problems involving comparatively small number of variables.

In this book, we shall examine another approach to analysis, synthesis, and testing based on the use of *spectral expansions* of systems of logic functions. The systems will be represented by functions of a continuous variable, and the latter expanded in finite orthogonal series. The pros and cons of this "spectral" approach will be considered in Section 9.5, where it will also be compared with Boolean algebra and multiple-valued logic and recommendations will be made as to its use.

Figure 1.8.1 illustrates the basic principle of circuit implementation by spectral representations of logic functions. The network consists of a generator of basis functions, and a memory to store spectral coefficients that will be assigned to the basis functions by calculating the spectrum of the function that will be realized. The basis functions are multiplied with spectral coefficients and then added to produce the function required. The addition and multiplication are in the field P that may be a finite field or the field of real or complex numbers.

The following example explains that classical two-level implementations of switching functions can be interpreted as a particular case of spectral implementations in the same way as the disjunctive normal form is a spectral representation in terms of a particular set of basis functions. In this case, each basis function is realized by a single AND circuit providing sufficient number of inputs. Spectral coefficients are identical to function values, and those equal to zero after multiplication eliminate some of the basis functions, that is, the related AND circuits. The addition of outputs of AND circuits corresponding to the basis functions to which nonzero coefficients

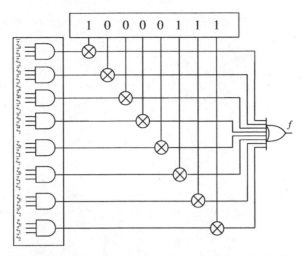

FIGURE 1.8.2 Two-level implementation of switching function in Example 1.8.1.

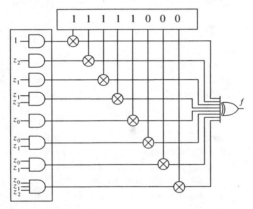

FIGURE 1.8.3 Two-level implementation of f in Example 1.8.1 though Reed–Muller coefficients.

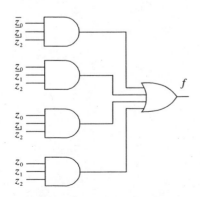

FIGURE 1.8.4 Simplified two-level implementation of f in Example 1.8.1.

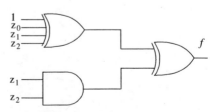

FIGURE 1.8.5 Simplified two-level implementation of f in Example 1.8.1 through Reed–Muller coefficients.

are assigned is performed by an OR or EXOR circuit with sufficiently large number of inputs.

Example 1.8.1 *Figure 1.8.2 shows a two-level implementation for the function f given by the the truth vector $\mathbf{F} = [1, 0, 0, 0, 0, 1, 1, 1]^T$. Figure 1.8.3 shows the implementation of f through the Reed–Muller expansion.*

Since in the multiplication part it trivially reduced to selection of AND circuits corresponding to 1-minterms and addition is performed by an OR or EXOR circuit, the first network is reduced as in Fig. 1.8.4. This is the implementation of the SOP-expression $f = \bar{z}_0\bar{z}_1\bar{z}_2 \vee z_0\bar{z}_1z_2 \vee z_0z_1\bar{z}_2 \vee z_0z_1z_2$. Similarly, Fig. 1.8.5 shows the implementation of f in terms of Reed–Muller coefficients and the simplified related network. This is the implementation of the positive-polarity Reed–Muller expressions $f = 1 \oplus z_0 \oplus z_1 \oplus z_2 \oplus z_1z_2$, since the Reed–Muller spectrum for f is $\mathbf{S}_f = [1, 1, 1, 1, 1, 0, 0, 0]^T$.

BIBLIOGRAPHIC NOTES

Fundamentals of theory of Boolean functions have been set in Reference 29, and developed and presented in many other publications, see References 395,410, and 491 and references therein. There are many classical textbooks and monographs discussing logic functions and their representations for applications in logic synthesis, system design, and signal processing (313,395,491). Functional expressions have been discussed in detail in References 41,499, and 661. Decision diagrams are discussed in References 130,372, and 499 and their spectral interpretations are presented in References 550,555, and 569. For fundamentals of spectral representations of discrete functions, see References 8,16,51,52,255,258,278,331,332,354,555, and 604. A detailed overview of fixed-polarity Reed–Muller expressions and their determination can be found in References 120,485,486,487, and 497. Kronecker transforms have been discussed in References 340,486, and 555. Circuit implementation of logic functions is the subject of many classical and recent books in this area (313,395,491,661).

CHAPTER 2

SPECTRAL TRANSFORMS FOR LOGIC FUNCTIONS

The subject of this chapter is the representation of systems of logic functions by orthogonal series. In the previous chapter, it has been shown that the classical Boolean representation as the sum-of-products, can be viewed as a particular Fourier series-like representation, and the same considerations can be extended to Boolean polynomial representations, that is, Reed-Muller expressions. Extensions of the same principle, achieved by changing the decomposition rules, equivalently, basis functions, lead to Fixed-polarity Reed-Muller expressions, and Kronecker expressions, for example, References 488,489,491, and 555. Coefficients $c(w)$ in these expressions are logic values, thus, $c(w) \in \{0, 1\}$ and, therefore, they are called *bit-level expressions*. In this chapter, we will discuss *word-level expressions*, which are defined in terms of basis functions borrowed from *abstract harmonic analysis on finite groups*, and having real or complex-valued (in the case of multiple-valued functions) coefficients, which are represented by computer words. These expressions will be very similar to the classical Fourier representations.

We describe the basic properties of various discrete functional transforms relating the original systems of functions to the spectral coefficients, introduce spectral and correlation characteristics of systems of logical functions, and demonstrate their use for the analysis and synthesis of digital devices. In short, the chapter sets forth the main mathematical tools to be used in the sequel. A thorough grasp of the results presented here is a prerequisite for an understanding of the subsequent chapters.

Spectral Logic and Its Applications for the Design of Digital Devices   by Mark G. Karpovsky, Radomir S. Stanković and Jaakko T. Astola
Copyright © 2008 John Wiley & Sons, Inc.

2.1 ALGEBRAIC STRUCTURES FOR SPECTRAL TRANSFORMS

To get mathematically tractable models for basis functions in terms of which various spectral transforms are defined, some algebraic structures are imposed to their domain and the range. For most of applications, it is sufficient to assume the structure of a *group*, not necessarily *Abelian*, for the domain and a *field* for the range.

Definition 2.1.1 *(Group) An algebraic structure $G = (\mathcal{G}, \circ, 0)$ with the following properties is a group.*

1. *Associative law:* $(x \circ y) \circ z = x \circ (y \circ z)$, $x, y, z \in G$.
2. *There is identity: For all $x \in G$, the unique element 0 (identity) satisfies $x \circ 0 = 0 \circ x = x$.*
3. *Inverse element: For any $x \in G$, there exists an element x^{-1} such that $x \circ x^{-1} = x^{-1} \circ x = 0$.*

The group G is *Abelian group* if for all $x, y \in G$, $x \circ y = y \circ x$.

A group that can be generated by a single element, called a *generator* of the group, is a *cyclic group*. When the group operation is assumed as multiplications, then every group element is a power of the generator.

Example 2.1.1   *The group $G = \{e = g^0, g^1, g^2, g^3, g^4, g^5\}$, where e is the identity element, is a cyclic group that is isomorphic to the group $\{0, 1, 2, 3, 4, 5\}$, since $1 + 2 = 3$ modulo 6, $2 + 5 = 1$ modulo 6, etc.*

The groups of particular interest in this book are the *finite dyadic group C_2^m*, that is, the group of m-bit binary vectors, defined as the direct product of basic cyclic groups of order 2, $C_2 = (\{0, 1\}, \oplus)$, where $\oplus$ is the addition modulo 2, (logic EXOR), and the group C_p^m, where $C_p = (\{0, 1, \ldots, p - 1\}, \oplus_p)$ with the group operation the componentwise addition modulo p.

We will also use the following notions and definitions related to the set theory and group theory.

Definition 2.1.2 *(Subset) For two sets X and Y, the set X is a subset of Y if each element of X is also an element of Y.*

The relationship of a set being a subset of another set is called inclusion *and usually written as $\subseteq$.*

If X is a subset of Y, but X is not equal to Y, then X is a proper subset *of Y, which is written as $X \subset Y$.*

Definition 2.1.3 *(Product of subsets) In a set Q, consider two subsets X and Y. The product of X and Y is defined as $XY = \{xy | x \in X, y \in Y\}$.*

Definition 2.1.4 *(Subgroup) In a group G under the operation* ∘, *a subset H of G is a subgroup is H also forms a group under the operation* ∘. *When H is a proper subset of G, then the subgroup H is a* proper subgroup.

Definition 2.1.5 *(Coset) For a subgroup H of a group G and an element x in G, the left and right* cosets *are defined, respectively, as* $xH = \{xh | h \in H\}$ *and* $Hx = \{hx | h \in H\}$.

Definition 2.1.6 *(Conjugate element) In a group G, the* conjugate element *of an element h by another element x is the element* xhx^{-1}.

Definition 2.1.7 *(Normal subgroup) A subgroup H of a group G is called a* normal subgroup *if it is invariant under conjugation, meaning that for each element* $h \in H$, *and each* $x \in G$, *the element* $xhx^{-1} \in H$.

In terms of cosets, a subgroup H is a normal subgroup if left and right cosets of H are equal, that is, $xH = Hx$.

Definition 2.1.8 *(Factor group) For a group G and its normal subgroup H, the* factor group G/H *(also called the* quotient group) *is the group of the set of all left cosets of H in G, under the operation of product of subsets, that is, the factor group is the group* $G/H = (\{xH | x \in G\}, \circ)$, *where* ∘ *is the product of subsets.*

Definition 2.1.9 *(Ring) An algebraic structure* $R = (G, +, \cdot)$ *with two operations, the addition* + *and the multiplication* ·, *is a* ring *if* $(G, +)$ *is an Abelian group, the multiplication is associative, that is, for all* $x, y, z \in g$, $(xy)z = x(yz)$, *and the distributivity is satisfied* $(x + y)z = xz + yz$.

Definition 2.1.10 *(Field) A ring* $R = (G, +, \cdot, 0)$ *is a field if* $(G \setminus \{0\}, \cdot)$ *is an Abelian group. The identity element of this multiplicative group is denoted by 1.*

In this settings, basis functions are considered as elements of a *vector space* on the group G over the field P.

Definition 2.1.11 *Given an Abelian group G with the group operation* ⊕ *and a field P with the addition* + *and multiplication denoted by* · *or juxtaposition. The pair* (G, P) *is a* linear vector space, *in short,* vector space, *if the multiplication of elements of G with elements of P, that is, the operation* $P \times G \to G$ *is defined such that the following properties hold.*

For each $x, y \in G$, *and* $\lambda, \mu \in P$,

1. $\lambda x \in G$,
2. $\lambda(x \oplus y) = \lambda x \oplus \lambda y$,
3. $(\lambda + \mu)x = \lambda x \oplus \mu x$,

4. $\lambda(\mu x) = (\lambda\mu)x$,

5. $1 \cdot x = x$, where 1 is the identity element in P.

In what follows, we will consider the vector spaces of functions defined on finite discrete groups. Spaces of particular interest in this book are $GF_2(C_2^m)$, $C(C_2^m)$, $GF_p(C_p^m)$, and $C(C_2^m)$, of functions on C_2^m and C_p^m and taking values in $GF(2)$, $GF(p)$, and C.

Definition 2.1.12 *Denote by $P(G)$ the set of all functions $f : G \to P$, where G is a finite group of order g, and P is a field. In this book P is usually the complex-field C, the real-field R, the field of rational numbers Q or a finite (Galois) field $GF(p^k)$. $P(G)$ is a vector space if*

1. *For $f, h \in P(G)$, addition of f and h, is defined by*

$$(f + h)(x) = f(x) + h(x),$$

2. *Multiplication of $f \in P(G)$ by an $\alpha \in P$ is defined as*

$$(\alpha f)(x) = \alpha f(x).$$

In these relations, the group operation on G is denoted as $\oplus$, and the addition in P as $+$.

Since the elements of $P(G)$ are vectors of the dimension g, where $g = |G|$ is the cardinality of G, it follows that the multiplication by $\alpha \in P$ can be viewed as the componentwise multiplication with constant vectors in $P(G)$.

This structure is often enriched into a *function algebra* by introducing the multiplication as

$$(f \cdot g)(x) = f(x) \cdot g(x),$$

where $f, g \in P(G)$, $x \in G$, and $f(x), g(x) \in P$.

2.2 FOURIER SERIES

In order to exploit powerful machinery of spectral methods, we first represent a multioutput function $f(z) = (f^{(0)}, \ldots, f^{(k-1)})$, where $z = (z_0, \ldots, z_{m-1})$ as an integer function $y = f(z)$, $z \in \{0, 1, \ldots, p^m - 1\}$, derived by interpreting p-ary k-tuples of values at the outputs as coordinates in the p-ary representation of integers. Then, to make another step closer to the classical Fourier analysis, y is completed to a corresponding step function $\Phi(z)$, see Section 1.2.

The next step toward application of spectral methods in analysis and synthesis of logicfunctions is to expand the step function $\Phi(z)$ representing the system of logic functions as an *orthogonal series* or *Fourier series*

$$\Phi(z) = \sum_{w=0}^{\infty} S(w)\Psi_\omega(z),\qquad(2.2.1)$$

where $\{\Psi_w(z)\}$ is a complete system of orthonormal step functions (*basis*) defined on $[0, p^m)$, that is,

$$\left(\int_0^{p^m} \Psi_w(z)\overline{\Psi_w(z)}dz\right)^{-1} \int_0^{p^m} \Psi_w(z)\overline{\Psi_r(z)}dz = \begin{cases} 1 & \text{if } w = r, \\ 0 & \text{if } w \neq r. \end{cases}\qquad(2.2.2)$$

Here and below $\overline{\Psi(z)}$ is the function complex conjugate to $\Psi(z)$.

The coefficients $S(w)$ of the series (2.2.1) are the Fourier coefficients, defined by

$$S(w) = \left(\int_0^{p^m} \Psi_w(z)\overline{\Psi_w(z)}dz\right)^{-1} \int_0^{p^m} \Phi(z)\overline{\Psi_w(z)}dz.\qquad(2.2.3)$$

The sequence of coefficients $S(0)$, $S(1)$, ... of the step function $\Phi(z)$ representing the system of logic functions, relative to the basis $\{\Psi_w(z)\}$, is called the *spectrum* of the system relative to $\{\Psi_w(z)\}$.

Thus, formulas (1.2.2), (2.2.2), (2.2.3) define a chain of one-to-one transformations:

$$\{f^{(s)}(z_0, \ldots, z_{m-1})\} \leftrightarrow f(z) \leftrightarrow \Phi(z) \leftrightarrow S(w).$$

Since there is a one-to-one correspondence between the original system of logic functions $\{f^{(s)}(z_0, \ldots, z_{m-1})\}$ and its spectrum $S(w)$, the problems of analysis and synthesis for such systems will generally be formulated and solved in terms of spectra (or in terms of correlation functions (see Section 2.7), which are double spectral transforms of the representing step function).

The solution of problems discussed clearly depends in an essential manner on the choice of the basis. The relevant questions will be considered below, for the two-valued (Boolean) logic in Section 2.3, and for the multivalued logic in Section 2.5.

2.3 BASES FOR SYSTEMS OF BOOLEAN FUNCTIONS

2.3.1 Basis Functions

As it was mentioned above, the choice of the basis is a decisive factor in the solution of analysis and synthesis problems using spectral representations of systems of logic functions. In particular, it determines the number of nonzero spectral coefficients in spectral representations, and this number in turn determines the complexity of the hardware or software *implementation* of a given system of logic functions. By an implementation of a system, we mean a device or computer program whose input and output signals stand in the relation defined by the functions of the system.

Since we are representing the initial system of p-ary logic functions of m variables by a step function $\Phi(z)$ on $(0,\ p^m)$ of *span* 1 (i.e., each "step" is of the length 1), it is natural to stipulate that the basis consist of step functions with the same span on $(0,\ p^m)$. As we will show below, it is always possible to choose a basis such that the number of nonzero terms in the series (2.2.1) representing $\Phi(z)$ is finite, in fact, at most p^m.

Another natural requirement is that each of the basis functions take on a relatively small number of values, thus simplifying hardware implementation of the system of logic functions. For example, if $p = 2$, it will be convenient to have basis functions with values $0,\ \pm1$. If this is the case, in fact, there is no need for the multiplication operation in calculation of $\Phi(z)$ by (2.2.1). Finally, it will be convenient if the values of the basis functions $\Psi(z)$ can be calculated by simple, standard, analytical procedures applied to the values of z.

We now exhibit a few bases that meet these requirements. We first consider two systems of functions (Walsh functions and Haar functions), which are exceptionally suited for spectral representations of systems of Boolean functions.

2.3.2 Walsh Functions

The *Walsh functions* have been introduced by J.L. Walsh in 1923, (638). They are an important tool in the approximation of continuous functions (151,215,523,671). A very good brief review of development in this area can be found in (635). For problems related to the approximation theory, we usually consider Walsh functions defined on the interval $(0, 1)$ and investigate properties of series formed of Walsh functions.

Walsh functions have also found applications in such fields as radar, television, electromagnetic radiation, data processing and pattern recognition, logic design, and elsewhere, (8,16,52,234,255,258,263,339,431,441,584,587,671). There are good grounds for the assertion that Walsh functions and their generalizations (Section 2.5) play a role in the analysis, synthesis and optimization of digital devices analogous to that of the exponential (or trigonometric) functions in analysis and synthesis of continuous-time (analog) devices (255,258,331,332,333, 555,576,604,610,624).

In Reference 176 it has been shown that Walsh functions can be identified as the *group characters* (defined below in Section 2.8.1), of infinite *dyadic groups*, and therefore, they can be used for the harmonic analysis of logic functions and all the functions defined over the dyadic groups C_2^m. In this book, we are interested in representation of discrete functions, logic functions and their integer encodings being a particular case, and therefore, we will use the discrete version of Walsh functions. When viewed as group characters of *finite dyadic groups*, that is, the groups $C_2^m = (\{0, 1\}^m, \oplus)$, the Walsh functions can be defined as follows.

Consider binary representations of two natural numbers $w, z \in \{0, 1, \ldots, 2^m - 1\}$, that is, $w = (w_0, \ldots, w_{m-1})$ and $z = (z_0, \ldots, z_{m-1})$, where

$$w = \sum_{s=0}^{m-1} w_s 2^s, \tag{2.3.1}$$

$$z = \sum_{s=0}^{m-1} z_s 2^s. \tag{2.3.2}$$

Definition 2.3.1 *The set of 2^m discrete Walsh functions in the Hadamard ordering of the variable z and the index w, $w, z \in \{0, 1, \ldots, 2^m - 1\}$ are defined as*

$$W_w(z) = (-1)^{\sum_{s=0}^{m-1} w_s z_s} = exp\left(\frac{2\pi}{2} i \sum_{s=0}^{m-1} w_s z_s\right), \quad i = \sqrt{-1}. \tag{2.3.3}$$

If we perform the so-called bit-reverse transform in the binary representations of w and z, that is, for

$$\overleftarrow{w} = \sum_{s=0}^{m-1} w_s 2^{m-1-s}, \tag{2.3.4}$$

$$\overleftarrow{z} = \sum_{s=0}^{m-1} z_s 2^{m-1-s}, \tag{2.3.5}$$

the definition 2.3.1 converts into the following.

Definition 2.3.2 *The discrete Walsh functions on $\{0, 1, \ldots, 2^m - 1\}$, in Paley ordering are defined by*

$$\overleftarrow{W}_w(z) = W_{\overleftarrow{w}}(z) = (-1)^{\sum_{s=0}^{m-1} w_{m-1-s} z_s} \tag{2.3.6}$$

$$= exp\left(\frac{2\pi}{2} i \sum_{s=0}^{m-1} w_{m-1-s} z_s\right), \quad i = \sqrt{-1}.$$

Thus, both definitions determine the same set of functions, the discrete Walsh functions, however, in a different order, each of them having advantages in some particular applications. Therefore, these as well as other orderings will be discussed later in more details in the Section 2.3.2.1.

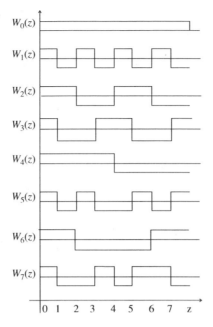

FIGURE 2.3.1 Walsh functions corresponding to Definition 2.3.1 for $m = 3$.

The discrete Walsh functions defined by either (2.3.3) or (2.3.6) are defined at the points $0, 1, \ldots, 2^m - 1$. They may be completed to step functions on the interval $[0, 2^m)$ as done above for $\Phi(z)$ in (1.2.4). This completion to a step function will be adhered to throughout the sequel for all discrete functions that are considered.

The waveforms of Walsh functions in both orderings defined by the Definitions 2.3.1 and 2.3.2 are illustrated in Figs. 2.3.1 and 2.3.2 for $m = 3$.

The subscript w of the function $W_w(z)$ is called its *index*, and the number of ones in the binary expansion of w (i.e., the quantity $\|w\| = \sum_{s=0}^{m-1} w_s$) will be called the *weight* of the index.

Consider the subset of Walsh functions with indices of the weight 1. Denote these functions by $R_s(z), s = 1, \ldots, m$. Then by (2.3.3),

$$R_s(z) = W_{2^{s-1}}(z) = (-1)^{z_{s-1}} = exp\left(\frac{2\pi}{2} i z_{s-1}\right). \tag{2.3.7}$$

Together with the first Walsh function $W_0(z) \equiv 1$, the functions $R_s(z)$ thus defined are known as the *Rademacher functions* (455). In this context, $\mathbf{W}_0(z)$ is considered as the first Rademacher function $\mathbf{R}_0 \equiv 1$. They are also called the *basic Walsh functions* or the *Walsh functions of first order*.

The first four Rademacher functions are shown in Fig. 2.3.3. Note that if we change -1 to $+1$ and $+1$ to 0, the function $R_s(z)$ is simply z_{s-1}, that is, the $(1, -1)$ encoded switching variables, viewed as trivial m variable functions $f(z_0, \ldots, z_{m-1}) = z_i$.

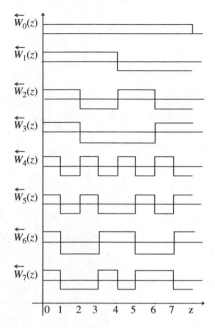

FIGURE 2.3.2   Walsh functions corresponding to Definition 2.3.2 for $m = 3$.

The following equivalent definition of the Rademacher functions is sometimes employed

$$R_s(z) = sgn(\sin 2^{s-m} \pi z),$$

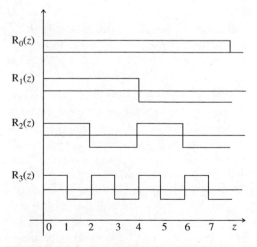

FIGURE 2.3.3   Rademacher functions for $m = 3$.

where

$$sgn(a) = \begin{cases} 1 & \text{if } a \geq 0, \\ -1 & \text{if } a < 0. \end{cases}$$

This formula illustrates the relationship of the Rademacher functions (hence also the Walsh functions) to the ordinary harmonic functions.

Any Walsh function may be expressed as a product of Rademacher functions. Indeed, by (2.3.6) and (2.3.7),

$$\overleftarrow{W}_w(z) = \prod_{s=0}^{m-1} (R_{s+1}(z))^{w_{m-1-s}}. \tag{2.3.8}$$

Thus, the set of Walsh functions is the *multiplicative closure* of the set of Rademacher functions.

2.3.2.1 *Ordering of Walsh Functions*   The relation (2.3.3) produces Walsh functions in the so-called *natural ordering* or *Hadamard ordering*. The application of the bit-reversal order of indices as in $\overleftarrow{\omega}$, (see (2.3.6), results in the *Paley ordering* of Walsh functions. However, in the original definition by J.L. Walsh (638), the Walsh functions are ordered in the *sequency order*. This ordering is in the present literature also called *Walsh ordering*.

Notice that Walsh defined the set of functions called by his name on the open interval (0, 1). The discrete Walsh functions considered above, can be viewed as the discrete counterpart of the Walsh functions derived by sampling, or as an independently defined set of functions in a different function space. However, relating the continuous and discrete Walsh functions permit to use the group theoretic approach to the interpretation of discrete Walsh functions, which is useful for generalizations to *p*-valued case.

There are other orderings of Walsh functions among $2^m!$ possible, that have proved useful in some particular applications. In the following, we briefly discuss this topic, and more information about it can be found in References 8,16,51,52,234, 235,255,258,587,592,617,663,667,669, and 683.

In Reference 638 and later in his work, Walsh has been using a two parameter notation for his functions, $f_k^{(i)}(x)$. The first parameter, written as the subscript is called *packet*, and the parameter in the parenthesis denotes the order of a particular function within the packet. Functions from a packet can be generated by compression and inversion of the functions from the previous packet. Position of a function within the packet is determined by the number of zero crossings of the function on (0, 1). Some authors (67,107) denote that number as the *sequency*, a concept resembling in some aspects the frequency in trigonometric functions. The sequency is defined by other authors (16,234) as the half of the number of zero crossings, and this definition is more widely accepted. The sequency does not satisfy certain essential and natural properties of the frequency (611).

The two parameter notation of Walsh functions is useful in some theorems in Walsh analysis. The sequency ordering of Walsh functions proved to be useful in some applications, in particular in communications and information theory (233,234). Emphasizing the resemblance between the trigonometric functions and sequency ordered Walsh functions, some authors split the set of Walsh functions into two subsets called *cal* (Cosinus WALsh) and *sal* (Sinus WALsh) functions (427)

$$W_i(z) = \text{wal}(i, z) = \begin{cases} \text{wal}(2i, z) = cal(i, z), \\ \text{wal}(2i - 1, z) = sal(i, z). \end{cases}$$

Such division of the set of Walsh functions was also suggested by J.L. Walsh himself.

Kaczmarz (271) showed that the Walsh functions can be considered as the multiplicative closure of the set of Rademacher functions (455) into a complete system. In his considerations Kaczmarz used the sequency ordering and, thus, the sequency ordered Walsh functions are somewhere called *Walsh-Kaczmarz* functions (201).

Definition of Walsh functions as the componentwise products of Rademacher functions introduced by Paley (419) proved much more convenient in some analytical considerations. For this reason, the Paley ordering is mostly used in this book for analytical definitions, while for the calculation purposes the Hadamard ordering is preferred. When the Paley ordering is used, it will be indicated by the arrow from right to the left $\leftarrow$ reminding the bit-reverse ordering of indices. This ordering of Walsh functions is also called the *dyadic order*.

Dyadic group is defined as the infinite countable direct product of the groups $C_2 = (\{0, 1\}, \oplus)$. Thus, dyadic group is the set of all sequences $\{z_i\}$, $z_i \in \{0, 1\}$, $i = 0, 1, \ldots$, under the componentwise addition modulo 2.

A correspondence between the dyadic group and the interval $(0, 1)$ can be established if for each $z \in (0, 1)$ we consider the dyadic expansion

$$z = \sum_{m=1}^{\infty} z_m 2^{-m}.$$

This mapping is unique if z does not belong to the set of dyadic rational numbers on $[0, 1)$, $\mathcal{D} = \{z \in (0, 1), z = \frac{p}{2^q}\}$, where $p \in Z$ and q is a natural number. For the dyadic rational numbers, which have two possible representations on the dyadic scale, a finite and an infinite, we will assume the finite representation.

Using this representation, it was shown by Fine (176) that the Walsh functions are characters of the dyadic group. Therefore, the Fourier analysis on dyadic group is defined in terms of the Walsh functions. In the same way, the discrete Walsh functions are characters of the finite dyadic groups on which the switching functions are defined. Therefore, the Fourier analysis for switching functions considered as a subset of complex valued functions is formulated in terms of the discrete Walsh functions.

In the case of finite groups, the *group characters* are conveniently represented by matrices. The characters of the basic dyadic group $C_2 = (\{0, 1\}, \oplus)$ are represented by the matrix

$$\mathbf{W}(1) = \begin{bmatrix} 1 & 1 \\ 1 & -1 \end{bmatrix},$$

which is called the *basic Walsh matrix*.

Since the finite dyadic group of order m is the direct product of m-cyclic groups C_2, the *characters* of C_2^m are defined by the *Walsh–Hadamard matrix*

$$\mathbf{W}(m) = \bigotimes_{i=0}^{m-1} \mathbf{W}(1),$$

whose columns can be identified with the discrete Walsh functions. The formal definition of group characters will be given in Section 2.8.

Thanks to the Kronecker product representation $\mathbf{W}(m)$ can be represented as

$$\mathbf{W}(m) = \begin{bmatrix} \mathbf{W}(m-1) & \mathbf{W}(m-1) \\ \mathbf{W}(m-1) & -\mathbf{W}(m-1) \end{bmatrix},$$

which is, as noted above, a relation characterizing the subset of so-called *Hadamard matrices* of order 2^m introduced by M.J. Hadamard (226) by a generalization of the results by J.J. Sylvester (594). Therefore, the Walsh matrix whose columns are thus ordered discrete Walsh functions is the subset of Hadamard matrices and thus ordered Walsh functions are reported as *Walsh–Hadamard functions*.

Relationship of Walsh functions to some other classes of matrices was mentioned in (201), and discussed in the contents of *circulant matrices*.

The relationships among different orderings of discrete Walsh functions have been discussed in a series of papers, for example, References 683, and 667, and references therein. These relationships were used by Zhang Qishan to develop the so-called shift-copy theory providing a broad family of the so-called bridge functions involving the discrete Walsh functions in different orderings as particular examples (674,680, 684).

The coefficients $S_f(w)$ with respect to the basic Walsh functions $W_{2^i}(z)$ express the correlation of f with the switching variables z_i. These Walsh spectral coefficients are closely related to the Chow parameters used in characterization of threshold logic functions (124). Therefore, in some applications in classification and characterization of switching functions, the Walsh functions are ordered with respect to the increasing number of component Rademacher functions. This ordering is called the *logic ordering* due to the applications mainly related to logic design and since this ordering follows the usual ordering in the set of natural numbers and is easy acceptable in everyday practice.

The four different orderings of Walsh functions mentioned above are compared in Table 2.3.1 for $m = 3$. Among the total of $2^m!$ possible orderings of discrete Walsh

TABLE 2.3.1 Different Orderings of Walsh Functions Represented As Products of the Rademacher Functions, $m = 3$.

	Ordering			
w	Sequency (Walsh)	Dyadic (Paley)	Natural (Hadamard)	Logic
0	R_0	R_0	R_0	R_0
1	R_1	R_1	R_3	R_1
2	$R_1 R_2$	R_2	R_2	R_2
3	R_2	$R_1 R_2$	$R_2 R_3$	R_3
4	$R_2 R_3$	R_3	R_1	$R_1 R_2$
5	$R_1 R_2 R_3$	$R_1 R_3$	$R_1 R_3$	$R_1 R_3$
6	$R_1 R_3$	$R_2 R_3$	$R_1 R_2$	$R_2 R_3$
7	R_3	$R_1 R_2 R_3$	$R_1 R_2 R_3$	$R_1 R_2 R_3$

functions, most of them destroy the symmetry property of the Walsh matrix, as is for example the case with the logic ordering. Therefore, the first three orderings are the most often used in applications.

2.3.2.2 *Properties of Walsh Functions*   We now consider a few properties of Walsh functions that will be used repeatedly in what follows. These properties remain valid for both orderings of Walsh functions given by Definitions 2.3.1 and 2.3.2. *Completeness and Orthogonality*

Theorem 2.3.1   *The Walsh functions form a complete orthogonal system. In particular,*

$$\sum_{z=0}^{2^m-1} W_t(z)W_w(z) = \begin{cases} 2^m, & \text{if } t = w, \\ 0, & \text{if } t \neq w. \end{cases} \tag{2.3.9}$$

Thus, if $\Phi(z)$ is a step function representing a system of switching functions of m variables and

$$\sum_{z=0}^{2^m-1} \Phi(z)W_w(z) = 0,$$

for $w = 0, 1, \ldots, 2^m - 1$, then $\Phi(z) = 0$.

Theorem 2.3.1, that can be proved by direct calculation, shows that we can use the Walsh functions as a basis for an orthogonal expansion of functions defined on 2^m points and, therefore, also step functions representing systems of Boolean functions.

Corollary 2.3.1   *For an integer* w, $0 \leq w \leq 2^m - 1$

$$\sum_{z=0}^{2^m-1} W_w(z) = \begin{cases} 2^m, & \text{if } w = 0, \\ 0, & \text{if } w \neq 0. \end{cases} \qquad (2.3.10)$$

This follows from (2.3.9) by setting $t = 0$.

Finiteness of representing series

Theorem 2.3.2   *Let* $\Phi(z)$ *be a step function representing a system of Boolean functions of m variables. Then*

$$\Phi(z) = \sum_{w=0}^{2^m-1} S(w) W_w(z), \qquad (2.3.11)$$

where

$$S(w) = 2^{-m} \sum_{z=0}^{2^m-1} \Phi(z) W_w(z). \qquad (2.3.12)$$

Theorem 2.3.2 is proved by inserting (2.3.12) into (2.3.11) and by using Theorem 2.3.1.

The expansion of (2.3.12) is the representation of $\Phi(z)$ as a *finite Walsh series*, and the numbers $S(w)$ are its *Walsh coefficients* of the *Walsh spectrum*.

It follows from Theorem 2.3.2 that the Walsh expansion of any step function representing a system of Boolean functions of m variables contains at most 2^m terms with Walsh functions with the index weight $\leq m$. Thus, if the original system of Boolean functions is defined by a sequence of 2^m values, its Walsh spectrum will also contain at most 2^m nonzero coefficients.

Example 2.3.1   *Consider a system of Boolean functions describing the operation of an adder, as in Table 1.2.5 (see Example 1.2.2). We expand the corresponding step function (see Table 1.2.6, Fig. 1.2.1) in a Walsh series. The result is*

$$\Phi(z) = 2^{-3}(12 - 2\overleftarrow{W}_1(z) - 2\overleftarrow{W}_2(z) - 2\overleftarrow{W}_4(z) - 6\overleftarrow{W}_7(z))$$
$$= 2^{-2}(6 - R_1(z) - R_2(z) - R_3(z) - 3R_1(z)R_2(z)R_3(z)).$$

Symmetry of index and variable

Theorem 2.3.3   *For any* $w, z \in \{0, 1, \ldots, 2^m - 1\}$,

$$W_w(z) = W_z(w). \qquad (2.3.13)$$

This property follows directly from the definition of Walsh functions (see Formulas (2.3.1– 2.3.6)), and has many useful consequences, for instance, in calculation of Walsh coefficients.

In matrix notation, the discrete Walsh functions (2.3.6) can be written as rows of a $(2^m \times 2^m)$ matrix $\mathbf{W}(m)$, called the *Walsh matrix*. They are particular cases of Hadamard matrices (7, 135), since the entries are ± 1.

Example 2.3.2   *For $m = 3$, the Walsh functions corresponding to Definition 2.3.1 can be represented as rows, or due to the symmetry, also columns of the matrix*

$$
\mathbf{W}(3) = \begin{bmatrix}
1 & 1 & 1 & 1 & 1 & 1 & 1 & 1 \\
1 & -1 & 1 & -1 & 1 & -1 & 1 & -1 \\
1 & 1 & -1 & -1 & 1 & 1 & -1 & -1 \\
1 & -1 & -1 & 1 & 1 & -1 & -1 & 1 \\
1 & 1 & 1 & 1 & -1 & -1 & -1 & -1 \\
1 & -1 & 1 & -1 & -1 & 1 & -1 & 1 \\
1 & 1 & -1 & -1 & -1 & -1 & 1 & 1 \\
1 & -1 & -1 & 1 & -1 & 1 & 1 & -1
\end{bmatrix}.
$$

The Walsh matrix corresponding to Definition 2.3.2 is

$$
\overleftarrow{\mathbf{W}}(3) = \begin{bmatrix}
1 & 1 & 1 & 1 & 1 & 1 & 1 & 1 \\
1 & 1 & 1 & 1 & -1 & -1 & -1 & -1 \\
1 & 1 & -1 & -1 & 1 & 1 & -1 & -1 \\
1 & 1 & -1 & -1 & -1 & -1 & 1 & 1 \\
1 & -1 & 1 & -1 & 1 & -1 & 1 & -1 \\
1 & -1 & 1 & -1 & -1 & 1 & -1 & 1 \\
1 & -1 & -1 & 1 & 1 & -1 & -1 & 1 \\
1 & -1 & -1 & 1 & -1 & 1 & 1 & -1
\end{bmatrix}.
$$

Because of the symmetry of the index and the variable of Walsh functions in Definition 2.3.2, the Walsh matrix is a symmetric matrix. A proof of this property has been given for binary encoded Walsh matrices for an arbitrary m by K.K. Nambiar in Reference 402. This property holds for various orderings of Walsh functions discussed in Section 2.3.2.1, as for instance, the dyadic, sequency, and natural ordering, however, for some orderings it can be destroyed, as for instance in the case of the so-called logic ordering, see Table 2.3.1.

From the orthogonality of Walsh functions, and symmetry of the Walsh matrix, for the orderings providing this property, it follows that the Walsh matrix is a self-inverse matrix up to the constant 2^m. Thus, the direct and the inverse discrete Walsh transform can be performed by using the same algorithm, which will be discussed in the next chapter.

Translation of variables

Theorem 2.3.4   *For any $w, z, \tau \in \{0, 1, \ldots, 2^m - 1\}$,*

$$W_w(z \oplus \tau) = W_w(z)W_w(\tau), \qquad (2.3.14)$$

where $\oplus$ is the componentwise addition modulo 2, (EXOR).

Here and below the notation $a \oplus b$ (mod p) denotes the number whose p-ary expansion is the sum modulo p of the corresponding p-ary components of a and b. Similarly, $a \ominus b$ (mod p) denotes the componentwise subtraction modulo p.

The proof of Theorem 2.3.4 follows readily from (2.3.1) to (2.3.6).

It follows from Theorems 2.3.3 and 2.3.4 that the set of Walsh functions is closed under multiplication.

Isomorphism of linear switching functions and walsh functions

A switching function $f(z_0, \ldots, z_{m-1})$ is *linear* if it may be expressed as the EXOR sum of Boolean variables, thus,

$$f(z_0, \ldots, z_{m-1}) = c_0 z_0 \oplus \cdots \oplus c_{m-1} z_{m-1}, \qquad (2.3.15)$$

where $c_s, z_s \in \{0, 1\}, s = 0, 1, \ldots, m - 1$.

The number of linear Boolean functions of m variables is 2^m. The set of linear Boolean functions is a commutative group, under $(f \oplus g)(z) = f(z) \oplus g(z)$, modulo 2. In other words, the group operation is componentwise addition modulo 2, the identity is 0, and $f^{-1} = f$ for any f.

The Walsh functions also form a group with respect to multiplication, with identity $W_0(z) = 1$, $W_w^{-1}(z) = W_w(z)$, and $(W_w \cdot W_q)(z) = W_w(z) \cdot W_q(z)$.

Two groups G_1 and G_2 are said to be *isomorphic* if there exists a one-to-one correspondence $h : a \leftrightarrow h(a), a \in G_1, h(a) \in G_2$, such that $h(a \circ b) = h(a) \circ h(b)$, where $\circ$ denotes the group operation in G_1 and G_2, as the case may be (these operations may of course be quite different).

Theorem 2.3.5   *The group of Walsh functions is isomorphic to the group of linear Boolean functions.*

Indeed, we shall show that the one-to-one correspondence

$$h(W_w(z)) = \bigoplus_{s=0}^{m-1} w_s z_s,$$

is an isomorphism. Using the symmetry and translation properties, we have

$$h(W_t(z)W_q(z)) = h(W_{t \oplus q}(z)) = \bigoplus_{s=0}^{m-1}(t_s \oplus q_s)z_s$$

$$= \bigoplus_{s=0}^{m-1} t_s z_s \oplus \bigoplus_{s=0}^{m-1} q_s z_s$$

$$= h(W_t(z)) \oplus h(W_q(z)).$$

By virtue of the isomorphism between the group of Walsh functions and the group of linear Boolean functions, it is possible to solve various problems involving linear Boolean functions and linearization of Boolean functions in terms of Walsh expansions, and, conversely, Walsh expansions may be viewed as expansions in terms of linear Boolean functions.

Example 2.3.3   *For $m = 3$, the correspondence between Walsh functions in Hadamard ordering and linear switching functions can be established as follows*

$$
\begin{array}{lcl}
1 & \leftrightarrow & [+1, +1, +1, +1, +1, +1, +1, +1] \\
z_2 & \leftrightarrow & [+1, -1, +1, -1, +1, -1, +1, -1] \\
z_1 & \leftrightarrow & [+1, +1, -1, -1, +1, +1, -1, -1] \\
z_1 \oplus z_2 & \leftrightarrow & [+1, -1, -1, +1, +1, -1, -1, +1] \\
z_0 & \leftrightarrow & [+1, +1, +1, +1, -1, -1, -1, -1] \\
z_0 \oplus z_2 & \leftrightarrow & [+1, -1, +1, -1, -1, +1, -1, +1] \\
z_0 \oplus z_1 & \leftrightarrow & [+1, +1, -1, -1, -1, -1, +1, +1] \\
z_0 \oplus z_1 \oplus z_2 & \leftrightarrow & [+1, -1, -1, +1, -1, +1, +1, -1]
\end{array}
$$

Notice that, truth vectors of linear functions can be obtained from the Walsh functions, that is, rows of the Walsh matrix, by replacing the function values $(1, -1) \rightarrow (0, 1)$.

2.3.2.3 *Hardware Implementations of Walsh Functions*   In many applications it is important to be able to generate Walsh [1] functions rapidly and economically in hardware. Examples of such applications are mobile phones, where Walsh functions are used in *Code Division Multiple Access* (CDMA) procedures in which a wide band in the spectrum is shared by many users simultaneously. The problem with this approach is, of course, that the shared signals will interfere with each other. CDMA solves this problem in part by using Walsh functions, usually called Walsh codes. Other modulation schemes such as *Orthogonal Frequency Division Multiplexing* (OFDM) and *Frequency Hopping* can also make use of the orthogonal Walsh functions.

---

[1] This section has been written by Dave Henderson of Coherent Logix Corp., Austin, Texas, USA.

The standard IS-95 CDMA from 1993, uses length 64 Walsh functions for modulation. If each transmitter is modulated by a different Walsh function, then the orthogonality of the functions provides a means of separating them at the receiver. In *Direct Sequence CDMA* the transmitted signal is multiplied by the same continuously repeating Walsh function that spreads the spectrum of the information carrying signal in a unique way, although its spectrum resembles random noise. At the receiver, many such signals are present at once and appear even more noiselike. However by multiplying the combined signals by the same Walsh function used by a specific transmitter, the desired signal is recovered.

Built In Self Test methods (BIST), discussed in Chapter 10, are another example, where circuits generating Walsh functions are required.

In both the mentioned applications, subsets of Walsh coefficients are required. Therefore, we will briefly discuss circuits derived by translating mathematical definitions of Walsh functions into logic networks using the basic logic gates.

Equation 2.3.16 was used earlier to define the Walsh functions [2] in terms of their index w and input variable z

$$W_w(z) = (-1)^{\sum_{s=0}^{m-1} w_{m-1-s} z_s} = (-1)^{\bigoplus_{s=0}^{m-1} w_{m-1-s} z_s}. \qquad (2.3.16)$$

In the right hand side of equation (2.3.16) the exponent is the sum of the bitwise product of the input, z, and the bit-reversed index, w. A bitwise product is equivalent to the AND gate. Since the sum is the exponent of -1 then the magnitude of the sum is unimportant, only whether there are an even or odd number of nonzero product bits. Digital designers will recognize this as the *parity function*.

A logic network that will generate all Walsh functions of order four is shown in Fig. 2.3.4. In order to be consistent with binary logic we can map the $\{+1, -1\}$ values of the Walsh function into $\{1, 0\}$ without any loss of generality.

The network in Fig. 2.3.4 may be expanded to generate Walsh functions of any order by adding one AND gate and one EXOR gate for each additional input bit. If

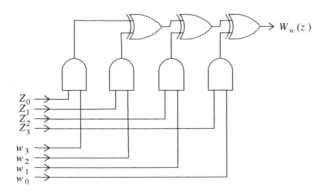

FIGURE 2.3.4   Generator of Walsh functions of order four.

[2]This section has been written by Dr. Dave Henderson of Coherent Logix Corp., Austin, Texas, USA.

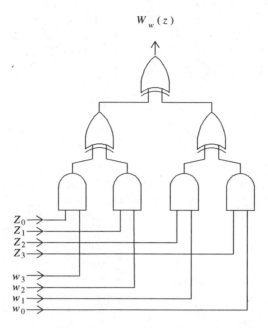

$$W_w(z)$$

FIGURE 2.3.5   Generator of Walsh functions of order four with parity function implemented as a tree of EXOR circuits.

the delay between input and output transitions becomes unacceptably long for a given application then the parity function can be implemented as tree of EXOR gates as in Fig. 2.3.5.

Current integrated circuit technology can employ this type of circuit to generate Walsh function output updated at up to several gigahertz. Some commercial circuits have stored Walsh functions in *Read-Only Memories* (ROMs) or had the ability to load new functions into *Random-Access Memory* (RAM) from an external source. However, when this circuit is employed only the function index needs to be stored. For example, in each CDMA standard IS-95 CDMA (see Chapter 11) Walsh function needs only a six bit index to completely generate it.

The complexity, expressed as the number of two-input AND and EXOR gates, of generation of $W_w(z)$ is 2^{m-1}.

This circuit generates the set of Walsh functions in Walsh–Rademacher order.

In Reference 167 it can be found a method for generating Walsh functions in different orderings in hardware. The Walsh–Rademacher ordering is the simplest to implement in hardware as described above. All of the other orderings can be derived by performing linear transformations and bit permutations on the index.

In cases where multiple Walsh functions must be generated simultaneously with fixed indices, then the circuit can be simplified by eliminating the gates associated with zeros in the index, as shown in Figs. 2.3.6–2.3.8.

In some cases, it may be practical to implement a full inverse Walsh transform at high speed by using an array of Walsh generators similar to those in Figs. 2.3.6–2.3.8.

FIGURE 2.3.6   Generation of Walsh function with the fixed index $w = (1001)$.

A minimal combinational device with m inputs $z_0, \ldots, z_m$ and 2^m outputs, $W_0(z), \ldots, W_{2^m-1}(z)$ may be constructed by the approach described in Section 5.4. This device requires $2^m - m - 1$ two-input EXOR gates.

Walsh function generators based on decision diagrams has been discussed in Reference 259.

2.3.3 Haar Functions

Each of the expansion coefficients of a function relative to the Walsh basis depends on the behavior of the function at all its points.

In some cases it is more natural to use bases in which the expansion coefficients depend only on the "local" behavior of the function, that is, on its behavior at few points which are in some sense "close together." An example is the system of Haar functions introduced in 1910 by the Hungarian mathematician Alfred Haar (233).

In the study of Haar functions and transforms, it is convenient to establish first basic terminology and review the notions that will be used before presenting definitions and providing more detailed discussions. There is not only a strong similarity and correspondence with the theory of Walsh analysis, but also some important differences.

Similarly as for the Walsh functions, we distinguish the *Haar functions* on the interval $[0, 1)$ split into 2^m subintervals, or correspondingly the interval $[0, 2^m)$, and their discrete counterpart, the *discrete Haar functions*, which can be viewed as sampled versions of the Haar functions. Conversely, the Haar functions can be interpreted as the completion of the discrete Haar functions (614, 671). In this settings, special attention has to be paid to the definition of Haar functions at the discontinuity points (234).

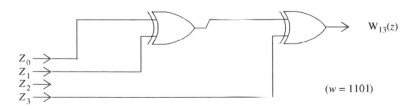

FIGURE 2.3.7   Generation of Walsh function with fixed index $w = (1101) = 13$.

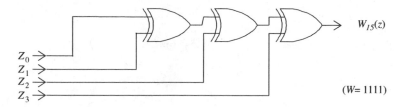

FIGURE 2.3.8   Generation of Walsh function with fixed index $w = (1111) = 15$.

In both cases, the *unnormalized* and *normalized* sets of Haar functions are used, depending on the applications. These sets differs just in the normalization factor, however, selecting between them is important for the efficiency of particular practical applications.

Similarly as the Walsh functions, the Haar functions can be ordered in different ways. In practice, two different orderings are most widely used. These are the *sequency ordering* used also by A. Haar in his initial paper (223), therefore, also called *Haar ordering*, and the *natural ordering*. Definitions of both orderings correspond to the definitions of the same orderings for the Walsh functions.

We also note that the Haar functions and their nonbinary generalizations, see Section 2.5.2, are a special case of *wavelet functions*, which are widely used in signal processing.

2.3.3.1   *Ordering of Haar Functions*   We now briefly present the basic definitions in the Haar functions theory.

Definition 2.3.3 *(Discrete Haar functions) The unnormalized discrete Haar functions $H_l^{(q)}(z)$ are defined as*

$$H_0^{(0)}(z) = 1,$$

and for $l = 0, 1, \ldots, m - 1, q = 1, 2, \ldots 2^l$,

$$H_l^{(q)}(z) = \begin{cases} 1, & \text{if } z = (2q - 2)2^{m-l-1}, \\ -1, & \text{if } z = (2q - 1)2^{m-l-1}, \\ 0, & \text{at all other points.} \end{cases} \qquad (2.3.17)$$

In this definition, it is used the same three parameter notation as in the original definition of the Haar functions (223) and the Walsh functions (638), emphasizing the splitting of functions into packages with the same number of zero crossings. As noticed above, this ordering of Haar functions originates in the work by Alfred Haar (223), and is called *sequency ordering* by the analogy with the corresponding ordering of Walsh functions or Haar ordering. In the case of Haar functions, packets are ordered by the increasing number of zero crossings. The *natural ordering* of Haar functions is also used in practice. This ordering corresponds to the natural ordering of Walsh functions and will be further discussed below.

Notice that the number of the discrete Haar functions is

$$1 + \sum_{l=0}^{m-1} 2^l = 2^m.$$

Similar to the Walsh functions, the Haar functions can be extended to the real interval $(0, 2^m)$ and this gives the definition of unnormalized Haar functions.

Definition 2.3.4 *(Haar functions in the sequency ordering) The unnormalized Haar functions are defined as $H_l^{(q)}(z)$, where the indices $l = 0, 1, \ldots, m - 1$, $q = 1, 2, \ldots, 2^l$, or $l = q = 0$, $z \in [0, 2^m)$. Thus,*

$$H_0^{(0)}(z) = 1, \tag{2.3.18}$$

$$H_l^{(q)}(z) = \begin{cases} 1, & \text{if } z \in [(2q-2)2^{m-l-1}, (2q-1)2^{m-l-1}), \\ -1, & \text{if } z \in [(2q-1)2^{m-l-1}, 2q \cdot 2^{m-l-1}), \\ 0, & \text{at all other point of } [0, 2^m). \end{cases}$$

The Haar functions for $m = 3$ are illustrated in Fig. 2.3.9. They are step functions of span 1, taking the values $0, \pm 1$.

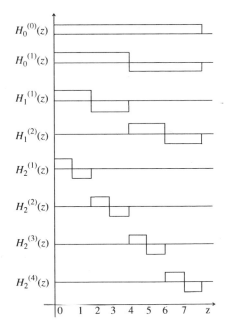

FIGURE 2.3.9   Haar functions for $m = 3$.

Similar to the Walsh functions, the matrix notation is convenient in the representation of discrete Haar functions. The Haar functions are represented as rows of the *Haar matrix*. We will later discuss the recursive structure of the Haar matrix.

Example 2.3.4 *For m* = 3, *the unnormalized discrete Haar functions in the sequency or Haar ordering is defined by the matrix*

$$
\mathbf{H}(3) = \begin{bmatrix}
1 & 1 & 1 & 1 & 1 & 1 & 1 & 1 \\
1 & 1 & 1 & 1 & -1 & -1 & -1 & -1 \\
1 & 1 & -1 & -1 & 0 & 0 & 0 & 0 \\
0 & 0 & 0 & 0 & 1 & 1 & -1 & -1 \\
1 & -1 & 0 & 0 & 0 & 0 & 0 & 0 \\
0 & 0 & 1 & -1 & 0 & 0 & 0 & 0 \\
0 & 0 & 0 & 0 & 1 & -1 & 0 & 0 \\
0 & 0 & 0 & 0 & 0 & 0 & 1 & -1
\end{bmatrix}.
$$

In certain applications, it is more natural to use normalized Haar functions, as defined in Reference 223. The following example illustrates the normalized discrete Haar functions.

Example 2.3.5 *For m* = 3, *the normalized Haar functions in the sequency ordering are defined by the matrix*

$$
\mathbf{H}(3) = \frac{1}{2\sqrt{2}} \begin{bmatrix}
1 & 1 & 1 & 1 & 1 & 1 & 1 & 1 \\
1 & 1 & 1 & 1 & -1 & -1 & -1 & -1 \\
\sqrt{2} & \sqrt{2} & -\sqrt{2} & -\sqrt{2} & 0 & 0 & 0 & 0 \\
0 & 0 & 0 & 0 & \sqrt{2} & \sqrt{2} & -\sqrt{2} & -\sqrt{2} \\
2 & -2 & 0 & 0 & 0 & 0 & 0 & 0 \\
0 & 0 & 2 & -2 & 0 & 0 & 0 & 0 \\
0 & 0 & 0 & 0 & 2 & -2 & 0 & 0 \\
0 & 0 & 0 & 0 & 0 & 0 & 2 & -2
\end{bmatrix}.
$$

In the general case, the discrete Haar functions can be represented as rows of the $2^m \times 2^m$ Haar matrices. In the matrix notation, the normalized discrete Haar functions in the sequency ordering are defined by the recurrence relation

$$
\mathbf{H}(m) = \begin{bmatrix} \mathbf{H}(m-1) \otimes \begin{bmatrix} 1 & 1 \end{bmatrix} \\ 2^{\frac{(m-2)}{2}} \begin{bmatrix} \sqrt{2} & 0 \\ 0 & \sqrt{2} \end{bmatrix} \otimes \mathbf{I}(2^{m-2}) \otimes \begin{bmatrix} 1 & -1 \end{bmatrix} \end{bmatrix} \tag{2.3.19}
$$

with

$$\mathbf{H}(1) = \begin{bmatrix} 1 & 1 \\ 1 & -1 \end{bmatrix},$$

where $\mathbf{I}(2^{m-2})$ is the $(2^{m-2} \times 2^{m-2})$ identity matrix.

The same relation defines the sequency ordered unnormalized Haar functions if all the normalization coefficients are omitted.

The sequency and naturally ordered Haar functions are related through a repeated application of the bit-reversal procedure to the binary representation of the index i denoting the ith row of the Haar matrix. For details see Reference 16.

Example 2.3.6 *The naturally ordered Haar functions for $m = 3$ are shown in Fig. 2.3.10.*

Relationships between the discrete Haar and Walsh functions and related transforms are considered in Reference 177,587 and 671.

These functions can be considered as particular examples of unitary transforms with fast algorithms called the *Identical computation family* of transforms (179,180). In this case, the discrete Haar functions in natural ordering can be generated in terms of the generalized Kronecker product of sets of matrices (179). Further advent in Haar transforms on finite Abelian groups is given in References 673 and 672. For a brief review of recent development in the Haar transforms and their applications, see Reference 559.

Definitions of unnormalized and normalized Haar functions, as well as different orderings can be extended to the generalized Haar functions, and other related functions discussed in Reference 644, see also Reference 584.

In the rest of this book, we will be mainly using unnormalized sequency ordered Haar functions defined by (2.3.18). Generalizations of these functions to p-ary ($p > 2$) case will be given in the Section 2.5.2.

$$\mathbf{H}_p(3) = \begin{bmatrix} 1 & 1 & 1 & 1 & 1 & 1 & 1 & 1 \\ 2 & -2 & 0 & 0 & 0 & 0 & 0 & 0 \\ \sqrt{2} & \sqrt{2} & -\sqrt{2} & -\sqrt{2} & 0 & 0 & 0 & 0 \\ 0 & 0 & 2 & -2 & 0 & 0 & 0 & 0 \\ 1 & 1 & 1 & 1 & -1 & -1 & -1 & -1 \\ 0 & 0 & 0 & 0 & 2 & -2 & 0 & 0 \\ 0 & 0 & 0 & 0 & \sqrt{2} & \sqrt{2} & -\sqrt{2} & -\sqrt{2} \\ 0 & 0 & 0 & 0 & 0 & 0 & 2 & -2 \end{bmatrix}.$$

FIGURE 2.3.10 Naturally Ordered Haar Functions for $m = 3$.

2.3.3.2 *Properties of Haar Functions* In this section we consider properties of the unnormalized Haar functions.
Completeness and orthogonality

Theorem 2.3.6 *The set of Haar functions is a complete orthogonal system:*

$$\sum_{z=0}^{2^m-1} H_t^{(q)}(z)H_l^{(r)}(z) = \begin{cases} 2^{m-l}, & \text{if } t = l, q = r, \\ 0, & \text{otherwise}, \end{cases} \tag{2.3.20}$$

for $l = 0, 1, \ldots, m-1$, $q = 1, 2, \ldots, 2^l$, and if $\Phi(z)$ is a step function such that

$$\sum_{z=0}^{2^m-1} \Phi(z)H_l^{(q)}(z) = 0,$$

for $l = 0, \ldots, m-1$, $q = 0, 1, \ldots, 2^l$, then $\Phi(z) \equiv 1$.

Theorem 2.3.6 shows that the Haar system is a suitable basis for expansions of step functions representing systems of Boolean functions. Like Walsh expansions, Fourier expansions in Haar functions are widely applied in numerical computations, since they yield a *uniform approximation* of continuous functions $\Phi(z)$ (223,530,639). This is an example of applications where the interval of definition is usually normalized to (0, 1), the integrals of the squared Haar functions are normalized to unity, and as the basis system the set of Haar functions for $m \to \infty$ is taken.
Finiteness of representing series.

Theorem 2.3.7 *A step function $\Phi(z)$ representing a system of switching functions of m variables, can be expressed as*

$$\Phi(z) = c_0^{(0)} H_0^{(0)}(z) + \sum_{l=0}^{m-1} \sum_{q=1}^{2^l} c_l^{(q)} H_l^{(q)}(z), \tag{2.3.21}$$

where

$$c_l^{(q)} = 2^{-m+l} \sum_{z=0}^{2^m-1} \Phi(z)H_l^{(q)}(z), \tag{2.3.22}$$

and $H_l^{(q)}(z)$ is defined by (2.3.18).

The proof follows from Theorem 2.3.6 by substitution of (2.3.22) into (2.3.21).

It follows from Theorem 2.3.7 that a step function representing a system of Boolean functions of m variables may be expanded in a series of Haar functions containing at most 2^m terms.

By (2.3.22) and (2.3.18),

$$c_{m-1}^{(q)} = 2^{-1}(\Phi(2q-2) - \Phi(2q-1)), \tag{2.3.23}$$

where $q = 1, 2, \ldots, 2^{m-1}$,

$$c_{m-2}^{(q)} = 2^{-2}(\Phi(4q-4) + \Phi(4q-3) - \Phi(4q-2) - \Phi(4q-1)), \tag{2.3.24}$$

where $q = 1, 2, \ldots, 2^{m-2}$, and

$$c_{m-l}^{(q)} = 2^{-l}\left(\sum_{s=2^{l-1}+1}^{2^l} \Phi(2^l q - s) - \sum_{s=1}^{2^{l-1}-1} \Phi(2^l q - s) \right), \tag{2.3.25}$$

where $l = 1, 2, \ldots, m-1, q-1, 2, \ldots, 2^{m-l}$.

Thus, $c_{m-1}^{(q)}$ depends on two consecutive values $\Phi(2q-2)$, and $\Phi(2q-1)$ of $\Phi(z)$, $c_{m-2}^{(q)}$ on four consecutive values $\Phi(4q-4)$, $\Phi(4q-3)$, $\Phi(4q-2)$, $\Phi(4q-1)$, and so on. In general, each of the coefficients $c_{m-l}^{(q)}$ depends on the behavior of $\Phi(z)$ on the interval $[2^l q - 2^l, 2^l q - 1)$. Thus, the expansion coefficients of $\Phi(z)$ in Haar series depend on the *local behavior* of the function, over an interval which is shorter, the higher the subscript of the coefficient. This points to the essential difference between the Walsh and Haar expansions. Every coefficient of the Walsh expansion depends on the function values over the entire interval $[0, 2^m)$. It will be shown later that this local feature of the Haar expansions considerably simplifies the selection of functions with prescribed Haar spectra out of a given class of functions.

More information about the properties of Walsh and Haar functions may be found, for example, in Reference 223,272,530, and 638.

2.3.3.3 Hardware Implementation of Haar Functions   The Haar [3] transform, or rather its inverse, has several important advantages over the Walsh transform for synthesizing logic circuits. First, the number of arithmetic operations required to compute an output for a given z is much lower. It is required at most $m + 1$ operations compared to at most 2^m operations for the Walsh transform.

Second, unlike the Walsh transform, the complexity of the Haar spectrum depends on the order of the function inputs. This order dependency can be exploited to find minimal circuits that can generate a given function (see Subsection 6.1.6.1). Third, the Haar basis functions are even simpler to generate than the Walsh functions.

The first question that might occur to anyone attempting to generate Haar functions in hardware is likely to be "how can the three function values $\{-1, 0, 1\}$ be

---

[3]This section has been written by Dave Henderson of Coherent Logix Corp., Austin, Texas, USA.

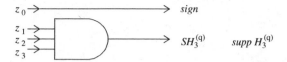

FIGURE 2.3.11 Generation of the sign function and the support function for the Haar functions.

implemented using binary logic gates that can only take on two values, $\{1, 0\}$"? The answer is simple. In synthesis only the product of Haar functions with Haar coefficients is needed, so only two of the three values are important. Multiplication by zero is quite easy to accomplish in hardware. To see this clearly, first look at the alternative definition of the Haar functions in (2.3.26),

$$H_l^{(q)}(z) = \begin{cases} R_{l-1}(z), & \text{if } z \in [(q-1)2^{m-l}, q2^{m-l}), \\ 0, & \text{at all other points of } [0, 2^m). \end{cases} \quad (2.3.26)$$

We have already seen in Section 2.3.2 that the Rademacher functions are equivalent to the bits of the circuit input. Consider the Haar functions for $m = 4$.

The logic circuit in Fig. 2.3.11 generates two functions from a four bit input value z.

The sign function is just the input z_0 mapped into R_4, $\{0, 1\} \to \{1, -1\}$. The second function we can call the support function of Haar functions. It will equal to 1 when the three bit vector $(z_3, z_2, z_1) = q$ otherwise it is zero.

The specific Haar functions are generated by the product of the sign and support functions as shown in Fig. 2.3.12 for $q = 1, l = 3$ and Fig. 2.3.13 for $q = 2, l = 3$. The circles on the inputs indicate inversion.

By repeating this circuit for all permutations of input bit inversions all of the Haar functions for $l = 3$ can be generated. For $l = 2$ bit z_0 is ignored, bit z_1 (R_3) is used as the sign, and bits (z_3, z_2) select the value of q as in Fig. 2.3.14.

For an m bit input vector $z = (z_{m-1}, \ldots, z_2, z_1)$ similar circuits can be used to generate any Haar function having $l < m$.

The Haar generator circuits of the type shown above are considerably simpler than those needed to generate Walsh functions. However, 2^m such circuits would be

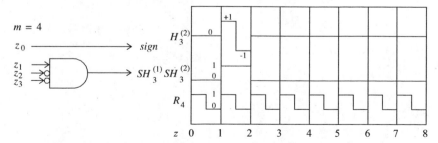

FIGURE 2.3.12 Generation of specific Haar functions for $q = 1, l = 3$.

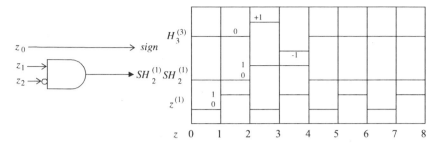

FIGURE 2.3.13 Generation of specific Haar functions for $q = 2, l = 3$.

required to generate the full set of Haar functions for an m bit input. Fortunately, we can combine these circuits with coefficient circuits as shown below to reduce the overall circuit complexity.

2.3.3.4 Hardware Implementation of the Inverse Haar Transform A
Haar [4] spectrum has a hierarchical structure consisting of multiple groups of coefficients called packages (see, Section 2.3.3.1). There are $m + 1$ packages for spectra of functions having m inputs. For considerations in this section, recall that each package has an index equal to $l + 1$ and contains 2^l coefficients. The package indexed by 0 contains the single constant coefficient $c_0^{(0)}$. This convention is useful in both hardware and software implementations of the Haar transform.

If the logic function $f(z)$ to be realized has an m-bit integer input and an k-bit integer output then the output vector will contain 2^m values. If the entire output vector is needed, then the best solution is to use the *Inverse Fast Haar Transform (IFHT)* algorithm (see, Section 3.2) since it will perform the minimum number of operations. However, in the case where the circuit is to generate a single output for each new arbitrary input, then the best approach is to compute the right side of (2.3.21) and directly sum the $m + 1$ appropriate coefficients each time a new input is presented.

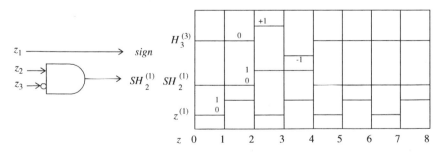

FIGURE 2.3.14 Generation of all Haar functions for $l = 3$ by permutation of input bit inversions.

[4]This section has been written by Dave Henderson of Coherent Logix Corp., Austin, Texas, USA.

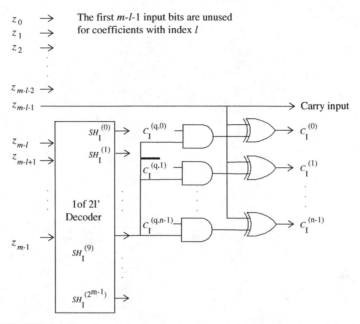

FIGURE 2.3.15   Circuit that generates terms in Haar expressions (2.3.21).

Before looking at the complete inverse transform circuit, we need a circuit to generate the coefficients from the input. Figure 2.3.15 is a schematic representation of a circuit that will generate a term of the sum in (2.3.21).

This circuit uses a subset of the input bits to generate the coefficient for the package $l + 1$. The coefficients in the package l are selected by the l most significant bits of the input. The input bits are sent to a l of 2^l decoder circuit with each output of the decoder performing the role of the support $SH_l^{(q)}$ for a Haar function. The single decoder output that is driven is followed in Fig. 2.3.15, all of the other outputs will be zero and will not affect the final result. Each nonzero bit of the coefficient $c_l^{(q)}$ is then multiplied by $SH_l^{(q)}$ and inverted if the sign bit z_{m-l-1} is equal to 1. The final outputs are terms of the sum in (2.3.21). The sign bit is also provided so that 2's compliment addition can be used.

Since the circuit must be able to generate any of the coefficients with the index l circuit following the decoder will actually be a 2^l to k encoder. Its outputs will be the k bits of the selected coefficient (plus sign). In practice, the encoder tends to be larger than the decoder, but this depends on the Haar spectrum being encoded.

Next, we can combine the circuits that generate the intermediate terms for each rank into a full inverse Haar transform circuit. An example having $m = 4$ is shown in Fig. 2.3.16. The highest rank, $l = 3$, has the largest number of inputs and will typically be the largest circuit block. The bold lines on the right indicate that these are multiple bit signals large enough to accommodate the largest encoded coefficient.

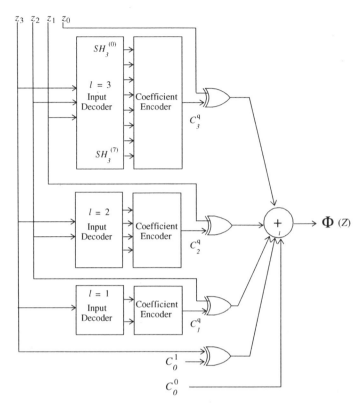

FIGURE 2.3.16   Complete inverse Haar transform circuit.

The circuit that computes the final sum is a bank of adders with five input words in this case. The type of adder is not important in producing the correct output, but it is important to the performance of the circuit. When required the adder should be optimized for the specific function. If possible a structure similar to a parallel multiplier should be used having a carry save adder for the multiple input terms and carry propagation at the last stage.

We now have a Haar function generator circuit with a simple structure that can be used as a basic building block.

2.4 WALSH RELATED TRANSFORMS

In this section, we will introduce the *Arithmetic transform* as an integer-valued counterpart of the Reed–Muller transform, see Section 1.5. In other words, the Arithmetic transform is defined with respect to the basis function used to define the Reed–Muller transform, however, with their values interpreted as integers 0 and 1 instead of logic values 0 and 1. We will show that the arithmetic transform can be derived from the Walsh transform when Walsh functions expressed in terms of switching variables whose values are interpreted as integers. In a similar way, it will be shown that the Reed–Muller transforms can be derived from the arithmetic transform by interpreting the integer values 0 and 1 as the corresponding logic values, and replacing arithmetic operations of addition, substraction, and multiplication by the addition and the multiplication modulo 2.

2.4.1 Arithmetic Transform

In the matrix notation, the *arithmetic expressions* for functions given by the vectors of function values $\mathbf{F} = [f(0), \ldots, f(2^m - 1)]^T$, are defined as

$$f = \mathbf{X}_a(m)\mathbf{S}_{a,f} = \left(\bigotimes_{i=0}^{m-1} \begin{bmatrix} 1 & z_i \end{bmatrix} \right) \mathbf{S}_{a,f}$$

with

$$\mathbf{S}_{a,f} = \mathbf{A}(m)\mathbf{F},$$

where

$$\mathbf{A}(m) = \bigotimes_{i=0}^{m-1} \mathbf{A}(1),$$

and $\mathbf{A}(1)$ is the *basic arithmetic transform matrix* given by

$$\mathbf{A}(1) = \begin{bmatrix} 1 & 0 \\ -1 & 1 \end{bmatrix}.$$

If the elements of $\mathbf{X}_a$ are interpreted as logic values 0 and 1, then this matrix is referred to as the Reed–Muller matrix or the conjunctive transform matrix (8,28). It defines a self-inverse transform in the space $GF_2(C_2^m)$ of binary-valued functions on finite dyadic group, denoted as the Reed–Muller transform, or the conjunctive transform. In this context, the arithmetic transform in $C(C_2^m)$ is denoted as the *inverse conjunctive transform* (8). For more details on arithmetic expressions, see References 8,323,349,350,351,524, and 658.

Example 2.4.1 *For $m = 3$, the arithmetic transform in $C(C_2^3)$ is defined by the matrix*

$$\mathbf{A}(3) = \begin{bmatrix} 1 & 0 & 0 & 0 & 0 & 0 & 0 & 0 \\ -1 & 1 & 0 & 0 & 0 & 0 & 0 & 0 \\ -1 & 0 & 1 & 0 & 0 & 0 & 0 & 0 \\ 1 & -1 & -1 & 1 & 0 & 0 & 0 & 0 \\ -1 & 0 & 0 & 0 & 1 & 0 & 0 & 0 \\ 1 & -1 & 0 & 0 & -1 & 1 & 0 & 0 \\ 1 & 0 & -1 & 0 & -1 & 0 & 1 & 0 \\ -1 & 1 & 1 & -1 & 1 & -1 & -1 & 1 \end{bmatrix}.$$

For the function f of $m = 3$ variables defined by $\mathbf{F} = [1, 0, 0, 0, 0, 1, 1, 1]^T$, the arithmetic spectrum is $\mathbf{S}_{a,f} = [1, -1, -1, 1, -1, 2, 2, -2]^T$. Therefore,

$$f = 1 - z_2 - z_1 + z_1 z_2 - z_0 + 2z_0 z_2 + 2z_0 z_1 - 2z_0 z_1 z_2.$$

2.4.2 Arithmetic Expressions from Walsh Expansions

Let $G = C_2^2$ and $P = C$. Each $z \in G$ can be expressed by $z = (z_0, z_1), z_0, z_1 \in \{0, 1\}$. Fourier expansions for functions $f \in C(C_2^2)$ are defined in terms of Walsh functions in the Hadamard ordering given by the columns of the Walsh matrix

$$\mathbf{W}(2) = \begin{bmatrix} 1 & 1 & 1 & 1 \\ 1 & -1 & 1 & -1 \\ 1 & 1 & -1 & -1 \\ 1 & -1 & -1 & 1 \end{bmatrix}. \tag{2.4.1}$$

The set of Walsh functions $w_i, i = 0, 1, 2, 3$ can be represented in terms of switching variables as

1. $W_0 = 1$,
2. $W_1 = 1 - 2z_1$,
3. $W_2 = 1 - 2z_0$,
4. $W_3 = (1 - 2z_0)(1 - 2z_1)$.

In symbolic notation, $\mathbf{W}(2)$ can be written as

$$\mathbf{X}(2) = \begin{bmatrix} W_0 & W_1 & W_2 & W_3 \end{bmatrix}.$$

From (2.4.1), the Walsh expression for $f \in C(C_2^2)$ is defined by

$$f = \mathbf{X}(2)\mathbf{S}_f$$
$$= \begin{bmatrix} 1 & 1 - 2z_1 & 1 - 2z_0 & (1 - 2z_0)(1 - 2z_1) \end{bmatrix} \mathbf{S}_f,$$

where $\mathbf{S}_f = [S_f(0), S_f(1), S_f(2), S_f(3)]^T$ is the vector of Walsh spectral coefficients.

With this notation, the orthogonal Walsh series expression transfers into the Walsh polynomial expressions in terms of switching variables. It is assumed that switching variables are encoded by $(0, 1)_{GF(2)} \rightarrow (0, 1)_Z$. Therefore,

$$f = 1 \cdot S_f(0) + (1 - 2z_1)S_f(1) + (1 - 2z_0)S_f(2) \qquad (2.4.2)$$
$$+ (1 - 2z_0)(1 - 2z_1)S_f(3).$$

In (2.4.2), if the multiplications are performed, then the polynomial expression for f is derived

$$f = 1 \cdot v_0 - 2z_0 v_2 - 2z_1 v_1 + 4z_0 z_1 v_3,$$

where

$$v_0 = S_f(0) + S_f(1) + S_f(2) + S_f(3),$$

$$v_1 = S_f(1) + S_f(3),$$

$$v_2 = S_f(2) + S_f(3),$$

$$v_3 = S_f(3).$$

Note that in this relation, indices of variables and coefficients are ordered in a way that corresponds to the Hadamard ordering of Walsh functions as in Definition 2.3.1.

If Walsh (Fourier) coefficients are expressed in terms of the function values for f, these polynomial representations become the arithmetic expressions for f.

In this example,

$$S_f(0) = \frac{1}{4}(f(0) + f(1) + f(2) + f(3)),$$

$$S_f(1) = \frac{1}{4}(f(0) - f(1) + f(2) - f(3)),$$

$$S_f(2) = \frac{1}{4}(f(0) + f(1) - f(2) - f(3)),$$

$$S_f(3) = \frac{1}{4}(f(0) - f(1) - f(2) + f(3)).$$

Therefore,

$$v_0 = f(0),$$

$$v_1 = \frac{1}{2}(f(0) - f(1)),$$

$$v_2 = \frac{1}{2}(f(0) - f(2)),$$

$$v_3 = \frac{1}{4}(f(0) - f(1) - f(2) + f(3)).$$

After replacement of z_i, we get the arithmetic expressions for $f \in C(C_2^m)$

$$f = 1 \cdot a_0 + z_0 a_2 + z_1 a_1 + z_0 z_1 a_3,$$

where

$$a_0 = f(0),$$

$$a_1 = f(0) - f(1),$$

$$a_2 = f(0) - f(2),$$

$$a_3 = f(0) - f(1) - f(2) + f(3).$$

If further

1. binary values 0 and 1 for variables are considered as the logic values 0 and 1,
2. the addition and subtraction in C are replaced by the addition in $GF(2)$,
3. values of coefficients are calculated modulo 2,

then, the arithmetic expressions become the Reed–Muller expressions for f.
   In this example, the Reed–Muller expression is given by

$$f = 1 \cdot r(0) \oplus r_2 z_0 \oplus z_1 r_1 \oplus r_3 z_0 z_1,$$

where $r_i \in \{0, 1\}$, are

$$r_0 = f(0),$$
$$r_1 = f(0) \oplus f(1),$$
$$r_2 = f(0) \oplus f(2),$$
$$r_3 = f(0) \oplus f(1) \oplus f(2) \oplus f(3).$$

Example 2.4.2 *For the function* f *in Example 2.4.1, the Walsh spectrum in the Hadamard ordering is* $\mathbf{S}_f = \frac{1}{8}[4, 0, 0, 0, -2, 2, 2, 2]^T$.

For $m = 3$, *the Walsh functions in the Hadamard ordering in Definition 2.3.1 can be represented as*

$$W_0(z) = 1,$$

$$W_1(z) = 1 - 2z_2,$$

$$W_2(z) = 1 - 2z_1,$$

$$W_3(z) = (1 - 2z_1)(1 - z_2),$$

$$W_4(z) = 1 - 2z_0,$$

$$W_5(z) = (1 - 2z_0)(1 - 2z_2),$$

$$W_6(z) = (1 - 2z_0)(1 - 2z_1),$$

$$W_7(z) = (1 - 2z_0)(1 - 2z_1)(1 - 2z_2).$$

Therefore, since the Walsh transform is self-inverse, when we assign the coefficients to the corresponding Walsh functions, it follows

$$f = \frac{1}{8}(4 - 2(1 - 2z_0) + 2(1 - 2z_0)(1 - 2z_2) + 2(1 - 2z_0)(1 - 2z_1)$$

$$+ 2(1 - 2z_0)(1 - 2z_1)(1 - 2z_2))$$

$$= 1 - z_0 - z_1 - z_2 + 2z_0z_1 + 2z_0z_2 + z_1z_2 - 2z_0z_1z_2,$$

which is the arithmetic expression for f.

If we reduce the coefficients modulo 2, and replace the addition and subtraction by EXOR, we get the Reed–Muller expression for f

$$f = 1 \oplus z_0 \oplus z_1 \oplus z_2 \oplus z_1z_2.$$

In should be noticed that the arithmetic and Reed–Muller expressions are defined with respect to the same set of basis functions $\{\Psi_w\} = \mathbf{X}_a$ but taking values in different fields, the field of rational numbers and $GF(2)$, respectively. Therefore, they are viewed as examples of word-level and bit-level polynomial expressions for Boolean functions, see References 499, and 555.

2.5 BASES FOR SYSTEMS OF MULTIPLE-VALUED FUNCTIONS

In this section we go over to complete systems of orthogonal functions that can be used for the analysis and synthesis of systems of p-valued logic functions. These orthogonal systems generalize the Walsh and Haar functions and do not take two or three real values, as was the case previously, but p or $p+1$ *complex values*, where $p \geq 2$ is prime.

2.5.1 Vilenkin–Chrestenson Functions and Their Properties

The generalization of Walsh functions to the p-valued case, where p is a prime, is the system of Vilenkin–Chrestenson functions (102, 626). They can be viewed as group characters of finite Abelian groups C_p^m, where $C_p = \{0, 1, \ldots, p-1\}$, and the group operation is the componentwise addition modulo p.

The Vilenkin–Chrestenson functions $\chi_w^{(p)}(z)$ are step functions defined on the interval $[0, p^m)$. Let p and m be natural numbers. The Vilenkin–Chrestenson functions $\chi_w^{(p)}(z)$, $w = 0, 1, \ldots, p^m - 1$ are first defined on integer points $z = 0, 1, \ldots, p^m - 1$ and then extended to step functions on $[0, p^m)$ by $\chi_w^{(p)}(z) = \chi_w^{(p)}(\lfloor z \rfloor)$.

For $z = 0, 1, \ldots, p^m - 1$,

$$\chi_w^{(p)}(z) = \exp\left(\frac{2\pi}{p} i \sum_{s=0}^{m-1} w_{m-1-s} z_s \right), \tag{2.5.1}$$

where $i = \sqrt{-1}$, $w_s, z_s \in \{0, 1, \ldots, p-1\}$, and

$$w = \sum_{s=0}^{m-1} w_s p^{m-1-s}, \tag{2.5.2}$$

$$z = \sum_{s=0}^{m-1} z_s p^{m-1-s}. \tag{2.5.3}$$

A comparison of formulas (2.3.6) and (2.5.1) reveals that

$$\chi_w^{(2)}(z) = \overleftarrow{W}_w(z) = W_{\overleftarrow{w}}(z), \tag{2.5.4}$$

in other words, the Vilenkin–Chrestenson system for $p = 2$ is the Walsh system.

Table 2.5.1 lists the Vilenkin–Chrestenson functions for $p = 3$, $m = 2$. Both in Tables 2.5.1 and 2.5.2, $e_1 = -\frac{1}{2}(1 - i\sqrt{3}) = \exp(2\pi i/3)$, $e_2 = \bar{e}_1 = -\frac{1}{2}(1 + i\sqrt{3}) = \exp(4\pi i/3)$, $i = \sqrt{-1}$.

Consider the subset $K_{r,s}^{(p)}(z)$ of the Vilenkin–Chrestenson system $\chi_w^{(p)}(z)$ consisting of all those functions whose subscript w is a power of p. These functions generalize the Rademacher functions:

$$K_{r,s}^{(p)}(z) = \chi_{r \cdot p^s}^{(p)}(z) = \exp\left(\frac{2\pi}{p} i \cdot r \cdot z_s \right), \quad i = \sqrt{-1}. \tag{2.5.5}$$

TABLE 2.5.1   Vilenkin–Chrestenson Functions for $p = 3, m = 2$.

$\chi_\omega^{(3)}$	0	1	2	3	4	5	6	7	8
$\chi_0^{(3)}(z)$	1	1	1	1	1	1	1	1	1
$\chi_1^{(3)}(z)$	1	1	1	e_1	e_1	e_1	e_2	e_2	e_2
$\chi_2^{(3)}(z)$	1	1	1	e_2	e_2	e_2	e_1	e_1	e_1
$\chi_3^{(3)}(z)$	1	e_1	e_2	1	e_1	e_2	1	e_1	e_2
$\chi_4^{(3)}(z)$	1	e_1	e_2	e_1	e_2	1	e_2	1	e_1
$\chi_5^{(3)}(z)$	1	e_1	e_2	e_2	1	e_1	e_1	e_2	1
$\chi_6^{(3)}(z)$	1	e_2	e_1	1	e_2	e_1	1	e_2	e_1
$\chi_7^{(3)}(z)$	1	e_2	e_1	e_1	1	e_2	e_2	e_1	1
$\chi_8^{(3)}(z)$	1	e_2	e_1	e_2	e_1	1	e_1	1	e_2

A comparison of formulas (2.3.7) and (2.5.5) shows that

$$K_{1,s}^{(2)}(z) = R_{s+1}(z), \qquad (2.5.6)$$

and so the functions $K_{r,s}^{(p)}(z)$ are known as generalized Rademacher functions. The generalized Rademacher functions for $p = 3, m = 2$ are listed in Table 2.5.2.

There is a one-to-one correspondence h between the set of values assumed by the Vilenkin–Chrestenson functions and the set $\{0, 1, \ldots, p - 1\}$. Indeed, set

$$h\left(exp\left(\frac{2\pi}{p}iq\right)\right) = q. \qquad (2.5.7)$$

Then, as is evident from (2.5.5), the mapping h takes the value of $K_{1,s}^{(p)}(z)$ onto the corresponding digit z_s of the p-ary code of z.

TABLE 2.5.2   Generalized Rademacher Functions for $p = 3, m = 2$.

$K_{r,s}^{(3)}$	0	1	2	3	4	5	6	7	8
$K_{0,0}^{(3)}$	1	1	1	1	1	1	1	1	1
$K_{1,0}^{(3)}$	1	1	1	e_1	e_1	e_1	e_2	e_2	e_2
$K_{2,0}^{(3)}$	1	1	1	e_2	e_2	e_2	e_1	e_1	e_1
$K_{1,1}^{(3)}$	1	e_1	e_2	1	e_1	e_2	1	e_1	e_2
$K_{2,1}^{(3)}$	1	e_2	e_1	1	e_2	e_1	1	e_2	e_1

The Vilenkin–Chrestenson functions may be expressed in terms of the generalized Rademacher functions. Indeed, by (2.5.5) and (2.5.1),

$$\chi_w^{(p)}(z) = \prod_{s=0}^{m-1} (K_{w_{m-1-s},s}^{(p)}(z)), \qquad (2.5.8)$$

so that the set of Vilenkin–Chrestenson functions is the multiplicative closure of the set of generalized Rademacher functions.

Formula (2.5.8) generalizes the formula (2.3.8) relating the Rademacher and Walsh functions.

We now turn to the main properties of the Vilenkin–Chrestenson functions. (The proofs are analogous to those of the properties of the Walsh functions.)

Completeness and orthogonality

Theorem 2.5.1   *The set of Vilenkin–Chrestenson functions is a complete orthogonal system:*

$$\sum_{z=0}^{p^m-1} \chi_t^{(p)}(z)\overline{\chi_q^{(p)}(z)} = \begin{cases} p^m, & \text{if } t = q, \\ 0, & \text{if } t \neq q, \end{cases} \qquad (2.5.9)$$

where $\overline{\chi_q^{(p)}(z)}$ is the complex conjugate of $\chi_q^{(p)}(z)$.

If $\Phi(z)$ is a step function representing a system of p-valued logic functions of m variables, such that

$$\sum_{z=0}^{p^m-1} \Phi(z)\overline{\chi_w^{(p)}(z)} = 0,$$

for all $w = 0, 1, \ldots, p^m - 1$, then $\Phi(z) = 0$ for all z.

It follows from (2.5.9) for $t = 0$ that

$$\sum_{z=0}^{p^m-1} \chi_w^{(p)}(z) = 0, \qquad (2.5.10)$$

for $w \neq 0$.

Finiteness of representing series

Theorem 2.5.2   *Let $\Phi(z)$ be a step function representing a system of p-valued logic functions of m variables. Then,*

$$\Phi(z) = \sum_{w=0}^{p^m-1} S(w)\chi_w^{(p)}(z), \qquad (2.5.11)$$

where

$$S(w) = p^{-m} \sum_{z=0}^{p^m-1} \Phi(z)\overline{\chi_w^{(p)}(z)}. \tag{2.5.12}$$

Example 2.5.1 *Consider the system of two ternary functions of two variables defined by Table 2.5.3 ($p = 3, m = 2$). The corresponding step function $\Phi(z)$ and its Vilenkin–Chrestenson spectrum are also given in Table 2.5.3. We have*

$$\Phi(z) = 3^{-2}\left(36 + \frac{3}{2}(1 - i\sqrt{3})\chi_4^{(3)}(z) + \left(-\frac{21}{2} - \frac{15}{2}i\sqrt{3}\right)\chi_5^{(3)}(z)\right.$$
$$\left. + \left(-\frac{21}{2} + \frac{15}{2}i\sqrt{3}\right)\chi_7^{(3)}(z) + \left(\frac{3}{2} + \frac{3}{2}i\sqrt{3}\right)\chi_8^{(3)}(z)\right).$$

Symmetry of index and variable.

Theorem 2.5.3 *For any $w, z \in \{0, 1, \ldots, p^m - 1\}$,*

$$\chi_w^{(p)}(z) = \chi_z^{(p)}(w). \tag{2.5.13}$$

TABLE 2.5.3   Function in Example 2.5.1 and Its Vilenkin–Chrestenson Spectrum.

z, w	z_0	z_1	$f^{(0)}(z)$	$f^{(1)}(z)$	$\Phi(z)$	$9S(w)$
0	0	0	0	2	2	36
1	0	1	2	2	8	0
2	0	2	0	2	2	0
3	1	0	1	0	3	0
4	1	1	0	1	1	$1.5 - 1.5i\sqrt{3}$
5	1	2	2	2	8	$-10.5 - 7.5i\sqrt{3}$
6	2	0	2	1	7	0
7	2	1	1	0	3	$-10.5 + 7.5\sqrt{3}i$
8	2	2	0	2	2	$1.5 + 1.5\sqrt{3}i$

Translation of variables

Theorem 2.5.4   *For any* $w, z, \tau \in \{0, 1, \ldots, p^m - 1\}$,

$$\chi_w^{(p)}(z \oplus \tau) = \chi_w^{(p)}(z)\chi_w^{(p)}(\tau), \qquad (2.5.14)$$

where $\oplus$ stands for the componentwise addition modulo p of p-ary representations of z and τ.

It follows from Theorems 2.5.3 and 2.5.4 that the set of Vilenkin–Chrestenson functions is closed under multiplication.

Isomorphism of the set of linear p-valued logic functions and the Vilenkin–Chrestenson system
    A p-valued logic function $f(z_0, \ldots, z_{m-1})$ is said to be *linear* if it may be expressed as

$$f(z_0, \ldots, z_{m-1}) = \bigoplus_{s=0}^{m-1} c_s z_s, \quad \text{mod } p. \qquad (2.5.15)$$

The linear functions form a commutative group of order p^m with respect to addition modulo p. The inverse of an element $\bigoplus_{s=0}^{m-1} c_s z_s$, modulo p, ($c_s \in \{0, 1, \ldots, p - 1\}$) is $\bigoplus_{s=0}^{m-1}(p - c_s)z_s$ modulo p.
    The Vilenkin–Chrestenson functions $\chi_w^{(p)}(z)$ also form a multiplicative group of order p^m.

Theorem 2.5.5   *The group of Vilenkin–Chrestenson functions is isomorphic to the group of linear p-valued logic functions. The isomorphism h is defined by*

$$h(\chi_w^{(p)}(z)) = \bigoplus_{s=0}^{m-1} w_{m-1-s} z_s, \quad \text{mod } p. \qquad (2.5.16)$$

This isomorphism is an extension of the isomorphism between the generalized Rademacher functions and the components of the p-ary expansion of the variable. It will be used in the sequel in analysis and synthesis of networks realizing systems of p-valued logic functions.

2.5.2 Generalized Haar Functions

Each expansion coefficient of a system of p-valued logic functions relative to the Vilenkin–Chrestenson basis depends on the behavior of the system over its entire interval of definition. We now define a complete system of orthogonal $(p + 1)$-valued functions, p is prime, generalizing the Haar functions, with the property that the corresponding expansion coefficients depend only on the local behavior of the original system. We refer to these functions as *generalized Haar functions* $\{M_{r,s}^{(p,q)}(z)\}$.

The generalized Haar functions $M_{r,s}^{(p)}(z)$ are defined in terms of the generalized Rademacher functions $K_{r,s}^{(p)} = \chi_{r,p^s}^{(p)}(z) = exp(2\pi r i z_s/p)$ as follows:

$$M_{0,0}^{(p,1)}(z) \equiv 1,$$

$$M_{r,s}^{(p,q)}(z) = \begin{cases} K_{r,s}^{(p)}(z), & \text{if } z \in [(q-1)p^{m-s}, qp^{m-s}), \\ 0, & \text{otherwise.} \end{cases} \qquad (2.5.17)$$

It follows from (2.5.6), (2.5.17), (2.3.18) that the generalized Haar functions for $p = 2$ are the Haar functions, $M_{1,s}^{(2,q)} = H_s^{(q)}(z)$. The values of the generalized Haar functions for $p = 3$ and $m = 2$ are given in Table 2.5.4.

The generalized Haar functions form a complete orthogonal system. Any step function representing a p-valued logic function of m variables admits an expansion in series of generalized Haar functions, containing at most p^m nonzero terms.

2.6 PROPERTIES OF DISCRETE WALSH AND VILENKIN–CHRESTENSON TRANSFORMS

Series representations
In previous sections we have shown that if the Walsh or Haar systems (for Boolean functions) and the Vilenkin–Chrestenson or generalized Haar functions (for p-valued functions) are used, the series thus obtained are finite. If the original system of logic functions is defined at p^m points, its spectrum will also take at most p^m nonzero values. Thus, the orthogonal-series representation of a system of logic functions defines a one-to-one mapping of the p^m-dimensional space of systems of logic functions

TABLE 2.5.4   Generalized Haar Functions For $p=3$ and $m=2$.

$M_{r,i}^{(3,q)}(z)$	0	1	2	3	4	5	6	7	8
$M_{0,0}^{(3,0)}(z)$	1	1	1	1	1	1	1	1	1
$M_{1,0}^{(3,1)}(z)$	1	1	1	e_1	e_1	e_1	e_2	e_2	e_2
$M_{2,0}^{(3,1)}(z)$	1	1	1	e_2	e_2	e_2	e_1	e_1	e_1
$M_{1,1}^{(3,1)}(z)$	1	e_1	e_2	0	0	0	0	0	0
$M_{1,1}^{(3,2)}(z)$	0	0	0	1	e_1	e_2	0	0	0
$M_{1,1}^{(3,3)}(z)$	0	0	0	0	0	0	1	e_1	e_2
$M_{2,1}^{(3,1)}(z)$	1	e_2	e_1	0	0	0	0	0	0
$M_{2,1}^{(3,2)}(z)$	0	0	0	1	e_2	e_1	0	0	0
$M_{2,1}^{(3,3)}(z)$	0	0	0	0	0	0	1	e_2	e_1

into the p^m-dimensional space of spectral coefficients. We shall refer to the system in question as the "original," in keeping with the terminology used in Laplace transform theory (129), and the sequence of spectral coefficients $S(0), \ldots, S(p^m - 1)$ of the expansion of the system will be called the image, transform, or spectrum of the system relative to the appropriate basis. The mapping itself will be called the *Walsh* or the *Vilenkin–Chrestenson transform*. The spectrum of the function $\Phi(z)$ relative to the basis in question will be denoted by $S_{f(z)}(w)$, where $\Phi(z) = f(\delta)$ for $z \in [\delta, \delta + 1)$, $\delta = 0, 1, \ldots, p^m - 1$.

Properties of Walsh and Vilenkin–Chrestenson expressions

In view of the fact that the Walsh and the Vilenkin–Chrestenson spectra will be used constantly in what follows as the main tool for the analysis and the synthesis of digital devices, we list the most important properties of the Walsh and the Vilenkin–Chrestenson transforms below.

Linearity

Theorem 2.6.1 *Let*

$$\Phi(z) = \sum_{q=1}^{N} a_q \Phi_q(z), \tag{2.6.1}$$

where a_q are arbitrary numbers and $\Phi_q(z)$, $(q = 1, \ldots, N)$ step functions representing systems of logic functions f_q, $(q = 1, 2, \ldots, N)$.

Then,

$$S_{f_q(z)}(w) = \sum_{q=1}^{N} a_q S_{f_q}(w). \tag{2.6.2}$$

Translation of variable in the original and in the transform domain

Theorem 2.6.2 *For every $\tau \in \{0, 1, \ldots, p^m - 1\}$*

$$S_{f(z \ominus \tau)}(w) = \overline{\chi_\tau^{(p)}(w)} S_{f(z)}(w), \quad mod\ p, \tag{2.6.3}$$

$$S_{f(z)} \chi_\tau^{(p)}(z) = S_{f(z)}(w \ominus \tau), \quad mod\ p, \tag{2.6.4}$$

where $\ominus$ stands for componentwise subtractions of p-ary representations of z and τ or w and τ.

It is worth noticing that Theorem 2.6.2 is analogous to the theorem of translation of variables in the case of the Laplace transform (129), except that here the subtraction (translation) of variables in both the original and transform domain is carried out modulo p. (The translation of z or w by an amount τ modulo p is defined by the componentwise addition (mod p) of the p-ary expansions of z (or w) and τ).

Involution property

Theorem 2.6.3 *The following relation holds for the transform of the complex conjugate of the Vilenkin–Chrestenson spectrum*

$$S_{\overline{S_f}}(z) = p^{-m} f(z). \tag{2.6.5}$$

Proof. Since,

$$\overline{S_f(w)} = p^{-m} \sum_{q=0}^{p^m-1} f(q) \chi_w^{(p)}(q),$$

it follows in view of (2.6.1), (2.6.2), (2.5.9), (2.5.13), and (2.5.14) that

$$S_{\overline{S_f}}(z) = p^{-m} \sum_{w=0}^{p^m-1} \overline{S_f(w)} \chi_z^{(p)}(w)$$

$$= p^{-m} \sum_{w=0}^{p^m-1} \left(p^{-m} \sum_{q=0}^{p^m-1} f(q) \chi_w^{(p)}(q) \right) \overline{\chi_w^{(p)}(z)}$$

$$= p^{-2m} \sum_{w=0}^{p^m-1} \sum_{q=0}^{p^m-1} f(q) \chi_w^{(p)}(q \ominus z) \quad \text{mod } p,$$

$$= p^{-2m} \sum_{q=0}^{p^m-1} f(q) \sum_{w=0}^{p^m-1} \chi_w^{(p)}(q \ominus z)$$

$$= p^{-m} f(z).$$

The involution property means that the Vilenkin–Chrestenson transform of a step function $\Phi(z)$ is the original function, up to a normalizing factor p^{-m}.

Convolution theorem

Theorem 2.6.4 *The convolution theorem for the Vilenkin–Chrestenson transform is*

$$S_{f_1 \cdot f_2}(w) = \sum_{\tau=0}^{p^m-1} S_{f_1}(\tau) S_{f_2}(w \ominus \tau), \quad \text{mod } p. \tag{2.6.6}$$

Let $\Psi(z) = \sum_{\tau=0}^{p^m-1} f_1(\tau) f_2(z \ominus \tau)$ *mod p. Then,*

$$S_\Psi(w) = p^m S_{f_1}(w) S_{f_2}(w). \tag{2.6.7}$$

Proof. By (2.6.1), (2.6.2), (2.5.9), (2.5.13), and (2.5.14),

$$S_{f_1 f_2}(w) = p^{-m} \sum_{z=0}^{p^m-1} f_1(z) f_2(z) \overline{\chi_w^{(p)}(z)}$$

$$= p^{-m} \sum_{z=0}^{p^m-1} \left(\sum_{\tau=0}^{p^m-1} S_{f_1}(\tau) \chi_\tau^{(p)}(z) \right) \left(\sum_{\alpha=0}^{p^m-1} S_{f_2}(\alpha) \chi_\alpha^{(p)}(z) \right) \overline{\chi_w^{(p)}(z)}$$

$$= p^{-m} \sum_{\tau=0}^{p^m-1} \sum_{\alpha=0}^{p^m-1} S_{f_1}(\tau) S_{f_2}(\alpha) \sum_{z=0}^{p^m-1} \chi_{\tau \oplus \alpha \ominus w}^{(p)}(z)$$

$$= p^{-m} \sum_{\tau=0}^{p^m-1} S_{f_1}(\tau) S_{f_2}(w \ominus \tau) \sum_{z=0}^{p^m-1} \chi_0^{(p)}(z)$$

$$+ p^{-m} \sum_{\alpha \neq q \ominus \tau} S_{f_1}(\tau) S_{f_2}(\alpha) \sum_{z=0}^{p^m-1} \chi_{\tau \oplus \alpha \ominus w}^{(p)}(z) \quad \text{mod } p$$

$$= \sum_{\tau=0}^{p^m-1} S_{f_1}(\tau) S_{f_2}(w \ominus \tau).$$

It follows from (2.6.7) that rather complicated operation of convolution in the original domain, corresponds to the multiplication in the spectral domain. If $\Psi = f_1 \circledast f_2$, where $\circledast$ denotes the convolution operator, then, $S_\Psi = S_{f_1} S_{f_2}$.

This convolution theorem is a particular example of the convolution theorem in Fourier analysis on groups, including the classical Fourier analysis as an example of Fourier representations on locally compact Abelian groups, see Reference 567. In the case of Abelian groups, the theorem holds also in the opposite direction, that is, the product of functions in the original domain corresponds to the convolution of their spectra. In the case of compact non-Abelian groups, just the first part of this theorem holds.

The proof of the convolution theorem (2.6.7) is analogous to the proof of (2.6.6).

Convolution Theorem (2.6.4) will be widely used in this book for spectral analysis of logic functions, spectral synthesis, and spectral testing.

Corollary 2.6.1 *Let $f(z)$ be a switching function ($p = 2$) of m variables and $S_f(w)$ its Walsh spectrum. Then,*

$$S_f(w) = \sum_{\tau=0}^{2^m-1} S_f(\tau) S_f(w \oplus \tau), \tag{2.6.8}$$

and conversely, if (2.6.8) is true, then $f(z)$ is a switching function.

Formula (2.6.8) is thus an alternative definition of switching functions. The corollary follows from Theorem 2.6.4, using the equality $f(z) = f(z)f(z)$, which is true if and only if $f(z)$ is a switching function.

Corollary 2.6.2   *Let $f(z)$ be a switching function and $S_f(w)$ its Walsh spectrum. Then,*

$$\sum_{w=0}^{2^m-1} S_f(w) \in \{0, 1\}.$$

This is verified by summing both sides of (2.6.8) over w.

Corollary 2.6.2 is useful as a check on the correctness of calculations of Walsh spectra of switching functions by means of check sums $\sum_w S_f(w)$.

Plancherel theorem

Theorem 2.6.5   *For any real-valued function $f(z)$ where $z \in C_p^m$,*

$$\sum_{z=0}^{p^m-1} f^2(z) = p^m \sum_{w=0}^{p^m-1} S_f(w)\overline{S_f(w)}, \qquad (2.6.9)$$

where $\overline{S_f(w)}$ is the complex conjugate of $S_f(w)$.

Proof. From Theorem 2.5.1 to 2.5.4, we have

$$\sum_{z=0}^{p^m-1} f^2(z) = \sum_{z=0}^{p^m-1} \left(\sum_{w=0}^{p^m-1} S_f(w)\chi_w^{(p)}(z) \right) \left(\sum_{v=0}^{p^m-1} S_f(v)\chi_v^{(p)}(z) \right)$$

$$= \sum_{z=0}^{p^m-1} \sum_{w,v=0}^{p^m-1} S_f(w)S_f(v)\chi_{w\oplus v}^{(p)}(z)$$

$$= p^m \sum_{w=0}^{p^m-1} S_f(w)\overline{S_f(w)}.$$

In classical Fourier analysis, this theorem is also called the Parseval relation or theorem.

Corollary 2.6.3   *If $f(z)$ is a switching function of m variables, that is, $f : C_2^m \to C_2$, then*

$$\|f\| = \sum_{z=0}^{2^m-1} f(z) = 2^m \sum_{w=0}^{2^m-1} S_f^2(w). \qquad (2.6.10)$$

For a function $\phi : C_p^m \rightarrow C$, where C is the field of complex numbers, the L_2-*norm* is defined as

$$\|f\|_2 = \sum_{z=0}^{p^m-1} \phi(z)\overline{\phi(z)}. \tag{2.6.11}$$

Theorem 2.6.5 states that the Vilenkin–Chrestenson and Walsh transforms for $p = 2$, are *isometric (unitary)* with respect to the L_2-norm, that is,

$$\|f\|_2 = 2^m \|S_f\|_2. \tag{2.6.12}$$

Poisson summation formula

Theorem 2.6.6 *Let V of C_p^m be a subgroup of C_p^m, and $V^\perp = \{x | x \in C_p^m, \sum_{i=0}^{m-1} x_i z_i = 0$ for all $z \in V\}$. Then, for any f defined on C_p^m,*

$$\sum_{z \in V} f(z) = |V| \sum_{\overleftarrow{w} \in V^\perp} S_f(w). \tag{2.6.13}$$

Proof. By definition of the Vilenkin–Chrestenson transform and its properties, we have

$$\sum_{z \in V} f(z) = \sum_{z \in V} \sum_{w=0}^{p^m-1} S_f(w)\chi_w^{(p)}(z)$$

$$= \sum_{w=0}^{p^m-1} S_f(w) \sum_{z \in V} \chi_w^{(p)}(z) = |V| \sum_{\overleftarrow{w} \in V^\perp} S_f(w).$$

Linear (mod p) transformation of variables

Let p be a prime, and $\sigma = (\sigma_{i,s})$, $(i, s = 0, 1, \ldots, m - 1)$ a matrix over the field $GF(p)$ of residues mod p, with nonvanishing determinant $|\sigma|_p \neq 0$ over $GF(p)$ (i.e., $\sigma_{is} \in \{0, 1, \ldots, p - 1\}$ and all the multiplication and addition operations in the calculation of $|\sigma|_p$ are performed modulo p). Let $\sigma \odot sa$ ($a \odot \sigma$) be the number whose p-ary expansion vector is the product of σ and the p-ary expansion vector of the number a (in the appropriate order), and all arithmetical operations are performed modulo p. For example,

$$\begin{bmatrix} 0 & 2 & 1 \\ 1 & 2 & 1 \\ 0 & 1 & 1 \end{bmatrix} \odot 14 = \begin{bmatrix} 0 & 2 & 1 \\ 1 & 2 & 1 \\ 0 & 1 & 0 \end{bmatrix} \odot \begin{bmatrix} 1 \\ 1 \\ 2 \end{bmatrix} = \begin{bmatrix} 1 \\ 2 \\ 1 \end{bmatrix} = 16, \quad \text{mod } 3.$$

Theorem 2.6.7 *Let* $\sigma_{i,s} \in \{0, 1, \ldots, p-1\}, i, s = 0, 1, \ldots, m-1, |\sigma|_p \neq 0$. *Then, for the Vilenkin Chrestenson transform defined by (2.5.1) to (2.5.4),*

$$S_{f(\sigma \odot z)}(w) = S_{f(z)}(\overleftarrow{w} \odot \sigma^{-1}). \tag{2.6.14}$$

The inversion of the matrix σ in (2.6.14) is again over the field of residues modulo p, and if $w = \sum_{s=0}^{m-1} w_s p^{m-1-s}$, $(w_s \in \{0, 1, \ldots, p-1\})$, then $\overleftarrow{w} = \sum_{s=0}^{m-1} w_s p^s$.

Proof. It holds,

$$\sum_{s=0}^{m-1} w_{m-1-s}(\sigma \odot z)_s = \sum_{s=0}^{m-1} w_{m-1-s} \sum_{q=0}^{m-1} \sigma_{sq} z_q = \sum_{q=0}^{m-1} z_q(\overleftarrow{w} \odot \sigma)_q$$

$$= \sum_{q=0}^{m-1} z_q(\overleftarrow{w} \odot \sigma)_{m-1-q} \quad \mod p.$$

Hence,

$$\chi_w^{(p)}(\sigma \odot z) = \chi_{\overleftarrow{w} \odot \sigma}(z) \quad \mod p. \tag{2.6.15}$$

It follows that

$$S_{f(\sigma \odot z)}(w) = \sum_{z=0}^{p^m-1} f(\sigma \odot z)\overline{\chi_w^{(p)}(z)}$$

$$= \sum_{z=0}^{p^m-1} f(\sigma \odot z)\overline{\chi_w^{(p)}(\sigma^{-1} \odot \sigma \odot z)}$$

$$= \sum_{z=0}^{p^m-1} f(\sigma \odot z)\chi_{\overleftarrow{w} \odot \sigma^{-1}}(\sigma \odot z) = S_{f(z)}(\overleftarrow{w} \odot \sigma^{-1}), \quad \mod p.$$

Corollary 2.6.4 *Let* $\sigma_{i,s} \in \{0, 1, \ldots, p-1\}, (i, s = 0, 1, \ldots m-1), |\sigma|_p \neq 0$. *Let* σ *be an orthogonal matrix, that is,*

$$\sum_{s=0}^{m-1} \sigma_{i,s}\sigma_{q,s} = \begin{cases} 0, & \text{if } i \neq q, \quad \mod p \\ 1, & \text{if } i = q. \end{cases}$$

Then,

$$S_{f(\sigma \odot z)}(w) = S_{f(z)}(\sigma \odot \overleftarrow{w}), \quad \mod p. \tag{2.6.16}$$

Formula (2.6.16) follows from (2.6.14), in view of the following identity for orthogonal matrices.

For all α,

$$\alpha \odot \sigma^{-1} = \sigma \odot \alpha, \quad \text{mod } p.$$

It follows from Theorem 2.6.7 that a nonsingular linear transformation of the variables of a function, results in a linear transformation of variables of its spectrum, and the transformation matrix for the spectrum is the inverse of that of the original transformation.

Since permutation of variables is a particular case of a linear transformation, Theorem 2.6.7 will be used when we are looking for the "optimal" order of variables, in linearization of systems of logic functions, analysis of various classes of logic functions, and so on.

Example 2.6.1   *Table 2.6.1 defines a function $f(z)$ and the function $f(\sigma \odot z)$ (mod p) for $m = 4$, $p = 2$,*

$$\sigma = \begin{bmatrix} 1 & 0 & 0 & 1 \\ 1 & 1 & 1 & 1 \\ 0 & 1 & 1 & 1 \\ 0 & 1 & 0 & 1 \end{bmatrix}, \quad \sigma^{-1} = \begin{bmatrix} 0 & 1 & 1 & 0 \\ 1 & 1 & 1 & 1 \\ 0 & 0 & 1 & 1 \\ 1 & 1 & 1 & 0 \end{bmatrix}.$$

Also shown in the table are $S_{f(z)}(w)$ and $S_{f(\sigma \odot z)}(w)$ modulo 2, illustrating Theorem 2.6.7.

TABLE 2.6.1   Function $f(z)$ in Example 2.6.1, Its Spectrum in Paley Ordering by Definition 2.3.2, Linearly Transformed Function $f(\sigma \odot z)$ and the Spectrum of It.

z, w	$\sigma \odot z$	$f(z)$	$f(\sigma \odot z)$	$16 S_{f(z)}(w)$	$16 S_{f(\sigma \odot z)}(w)$
0	0	0	0	8	8
1	15	1	0	2	0
2	6	1	0	2	−4
3	9	1	0	0	−4
4	7	0	1	−2	0
5	8	1	1	0	0
6	1	0	1	0	0
7	14	1	1	−2	0
8	12	1	0	−2	−2
9	3	0	1	−4	2
10	10	0	0	0	−2
11	5	1	1	2	2
12	11	0	1	0	2
13	4	0	0	−2	−2
14	13	1	0	2	−2
15	2	0	1	−4	2

Remark 2.6.1 *The properties of linearity, translation, and convolution considered above for Walsh and Vilenkin–Chrestenson transforms are analogs of the corresponding properties for the ordinary Laplace transform. This observation makes it possible to utilize Walsh and Vilenkin–Chrestenson functions in the analysis, synthesis, and optimization of digital of logic devices, in a role analogous to that of the exponential functions in the classical fields of electrical and computer engineering, control theory (with regard to the Laplace transform) or the theory of sampled-data control systems (discrete Laplace transform).*

2.7 AUTOCORRELATION AND CROSS-CORRELATION FUNCTIONS

In this section, we introduce the autocorrelation and cross-correlation functions, to be used subsequently for the analysis and synthesis of networks realizing logic functions. We also indicate the connection between these functions and the discrete transforms considered previously. These correlation functions are analogous to the classical correlation functions employed extensively in telecommunications, theory of stochastic processes, and so on.

2.7.1 Definitions of Autocorrelation and Cross-Correlation Functions

Consider a system of p-valued logic functions $\{f^{(s)}(z_0, \ldots, z_{m-1})\}$, where $z_q \in \{0, 1, \ldots, p-1\}, q = 0, \ldots, m-1, s = 0, \ldots, k-1$, and the corresponding integer equivalent function $f(z)$. We define the *autocorrelation function* (mod p) of the functions $\{f^{(s)}(z_0, \ldots, z_{m-1})\}$ or of the discrete function $f(z)$ by

$$B_{p,2}^{(f,f)}(\tau) = \sum_{z=0}^{p^m-1} f(z)f(z \ominus \tau), \quad \mod p, \tag{2.7.1}$$

where $z \ominus \tau$ (mod p) denotes the number whose p-ary expansion is the componentwise difference of the numbers z and τ.

It should be clear from (2.7.1) that $B_{p,2}^{(f,f)}(\tau)$ is a convolution-type transform of the original function $f(z)$, with the translation of the variable z by τ performed modulo p. The autocorrelation functions used in telecommunication systems for signal synchronization (125,330,522,407), are a special cases of (2.7.1) for $m = 1$, $p = N$, where N is the number of points at which the signal is defined, or $p = \infty$.

Now let $f_1(z)$ and $f_2(z)$ be two discrete functions, representing two systems of p-valued logic functions of m variables. We define their *cross-correlation function* (mod p) as

$$B_{p,2}^{(f_1,f_2)}(\tau) = \sum_{z=0}^{p^m-1} f_1(z)f_2(z \ominus \tau), \quad \mod p. \tag{2.7.2}$$

2.7.2 Relationships to the Walsh and Vilenkin–Chrestenson Transforms, the Wiener–Khinchin Theorem

We now determine the relationship of the correlation functions to the Walsh and Vilenkin–Chrestenson transforms discussed in Sections 2.3 and 2.5. We show that they may be expressed in terms of double transforms of the original functions, a representation similar to that of the usual correlation functions $B_{\infty,2}^{(f_1,f_2)}$ as double Laplace transforms (330) or the representation furnished by the Wiener–Khinchin theorem in the theory of stochastic processes (330).

Let f be a discrete function and S_f its Vilenkin–Chrestenson transform and S_f^{-1} the inverse Vilenkin–Chrestenson transform.

Theorem 2.7.1 *Let f_1 and f_2 be discrete functions representing two systems of functions of p-valued logic functions of m variables. Then,*

$$B_{p,2}^{(f_1,f_2)} = p^m S^{-1}(S_{f_1}\overline{S_{f_2}}), \qquad (2.7.3)$$

where $\overline{S_{f_2}}$ is the complex conjugate of S_{f_2}.

Proof. Since $f_1(z)$ and $f_2(z)$ are real functions,

$$S_{f_1}(w)\overline{S_{f_2}(w)} = p^{-2m} \sum_{z_1,z_2=0}^{p^m-1} f_1(z_1)f_2(z_2)\overline{\chi_w^{(p)}(z_1)\chi_w^{(p)}(z_2)}.$$

Hence, in view of Theorems 2.5.1, 2.5.3, 2.5.4, and 2.6.3,

$$(S^{-1}(S_{f_1}\overline{S_{f_2}}))(\tau) = \sum_{w=0}^{p^m-1} S_{f_1}(w)\overline{S_{f_2}(w)}\chi_\tau^{(p)}(w)$$

$$= p^{-2m} \sum_{w=0}^{p^m-1} \sum_{z_1,z_2=0}^{p^m-1} f_1(z_1)f_2(z_2)\overline{\chi_w^{(p)}(z_1 \ominus z_2 \ominus \tau)}$$

$$= p^{-2m} \sum_{z_1,z_2=0}^{p^m-1} f_1(z_1)f_2(z_2)\overline{\chi_w^{(p)}(z_1 \ominus z_2 \ominus \tau)}$$

$$= p^{-m} \sum_{z_1=0}^{p^m-1} f_1(z_1)f_2(z_2 \ominus \tau)$$

$$+ p^{-2m} \sum_{z_2 \neq z_1 \ominus \tau} f_1(z_1)f_2(z_2 \ominus \tau) \sum_{w=0}^{p^m-1} \chi_w^{(p)}(z_1 \ominus z_2 \ominus \tau)$$

$$= p^{-m} \sum_{z=0}^{p^m-1} f_1(z) f_2(z \ominus \tau)$$

$$= p^{-m} B_{p,2}^{(f_1, f_2)}(\tau), \quad \text{mod } p.$$

In binary case, the spectrum assumes real values, so that

$$\overline{S_{f_2}} = S_{f_2} = 2^{-m}(S_{f_2})^{-1},$$

and formula (2.7.3) then becomes

$$B_{2,2}^{(f_1, f_2)} = 2^m W(W(f_1) \cdot W(f_2)), \tag{2.7.4}$$

where W is the Walsh transform operator.

Theorem 2.7.1 is a direct analogue to the Wiener–Khinchin theorem in classical Fourier analysis and for $p = 2$ can be called the dydaic Wiener–Khinchin theorem. The theorem was published in Reference 288, for the case $p = 2$ (see Section 2.7.3) and it was in fact contained in Reference 286, and also in References 203, and 611. A generalization to arbitrary finite Abelian groups will be discussed in Section 2.8 (see Theorem 2.8.4).

Example 2.7.1 *Table 2.7.1 defines a system of two Boolean functions for $m = 3$ and the discrete function $f(z)$ representing this system. The spectrum $S_f(w)$, $S_f^2(w)$, and the autocorrelation function $B_{2,2}^{(f,f)}(\tau)$ are also shown in this table.*

It follows from Theorem 2.7.1 that the autocorrelation function is symmetric ("evenness" relation for autocorrelation functions):

$$B_{p,2}^{(f,f)}(\tau) = B_{p,2}^{(f,f)}(\overline{\tau}),$$

TABLE 2.7.1   **The Function $f(z)$, the Spectrum $S(w)$ in Paley Ordering, $S^2(w)$, and the Autocorrelation Function $B_{2,2}^{(f,f)}(\tau)$ in Example 2.7.1.**

z_0	z_1	z_2	$y^{(0)}$	$y^{(1)}$	z, w, τ	$f(z)$	$8S(w)$	$64S^2(w)$	$B_{2,2}^{(f,f)}(\tau)$
0	0	0	0	1	0	1	13	169	29
0	0	1	1	0	1	2	5	25	24
0	1	0	1	1	2	3	−3	9	22
0	1	1	1	1	3	3	−3	9	22
1	0	0	1	0	4	2	1	1	16
1	0	1	0	0	5	0	−3	9	20
1	1	0	0	1	6	1	1	1	18
1	1	1	0	1	7	1	−3	9	18

where $\tau \oplus \bar{\tau} = 0$ modulo p. This property halves the computational work needed to determine autocorrelation functions in the case $p > 2$.

We now list the basic properties of the correlation functions, which determine convolution-type transforms of the original functions. These properties are important in the study of switching functions and solving the optimization problems in their representations and circuit design.

2.7.3 Properties of Correlation Functions

Translation of variables of the original function

Theorem 2.7.2 *Let $f(z)$ and $\phi(z)$ be discrete functions corresponding to two systems of p-valued logic functions of the equal number of variables, and*

$$f_\alpha(z) = f(z \ominus \alpha), \quad \phi_\alpha(z) = \phi(z \ominus \alpha), \quad mod\ p. \tag{2.7.5}$$

Then,

$$B_{p,2}^{(f_\alpha,\phi_\alpha)}(\tau) = B_{p,2}^{(f,\phi)}(\tau). \tag{2.7.6}$$

Theorem 2.7.2 implies that the correlation functions are *invariant with respect to the translation of the variables* in the original function. It can be shown that for autocorrelation functions the converse is also true, that is, a nonnegative function is uniquely determined, up to translation of the variable, by its autocorrelation function. In the case of switching functions, translation of the variable by α is equivalent to the inversion of variables corresponding to nonzero components of the binary expansion of α. Thus, the complexity of a network realizing a switching function, relative to any basis, is completely determined by the autocorrelation function $B_{2,2}^{(f,f)}(\tau)$ (up to m inversion elements, where m is the number of variables). Thus, it can be used for solving any problem related to the minimization of networks realizing systems of switching functions.

Linearity

Theorem 2.7.3 *Let f_s, $s = 1, 2, \ldots, n$ and ϕ_q, $q = 1, 2, \ldots, l$ be discrete functions corresponding to systems of p-valued logic functions of m variables, and let c_s, $s = 1, 2, \ldots, m$ and d_q, $q = 1, 2, \ldots, l$ be arbitrary constants. Then,*

$$B_{p,2}^{\left(\sum_{s=1}^{n} c_s f_s, \sum_{q=1}^{l} d_q \phi_q\right)}(\tau) = \sum_{s=1}^{n}\sum_{q=1}^{l} c_s d_q B_{p,2}^{(f_s,\phi_q)}(\tau). \tag{2.7.7}$$

Corollary 2.7.5 *Let f be a switching function of m variables, $\sum_{z=0}^{2^m-1} f(z) = N$, and $\overline{f}$ the inversion of f, $(\overline{f} = 1 \oplus f \mod 2)$. Then,*

$$B_{2,2}^{(f,f)}(\tau) = B_{2,2}^{(\overline{f},\overline{f})}(\tau) - 2^m + 2N. \tag{2.7.8}$$

This follows from (2.7.7) in view of the equality $\overline{f} = 1 - f$.

Corollary 2.7.5 simplifies the calculation of the autocorrelation function $B_{2,2}^{f,f}(\tau)$, replacing the direct calculation by evaluation of $B_{2,2}^{(\overline{f},\overline{f})}(\tau)$ when $N > 2^{m-1}$.
Linear transformation of variables

Theorem 2.7.4 *Let $f(z)$ and $\phi(z)$ be discrete functions corresponding to two systems of p-valued logic functions of m variables, $\sigma = (\sigma_{is})$ a p-ary matrix $(i, s = 0, 1, \ldots, m - 1)$, $|\sigma|_p \neq 0$ ($|\sigma|_p$ denotes the determinant of σ over $GF(p)$), and p is a prime,*

$$f_\sigma(z) = f(\sigma \odot z), \quad \phi_\sigma(z) = \phi(\sigma \odot z), \quad \mod p.$$

Then,

$$B_{p,2}^{(f_\sigma,\phi_\sigma)}(\tau) = B_{p,2}^{(f,\phi)}(\sigma \odot \tau), \quad \mod p. \tag{2.7.9}$$

Here $\sigma \odot z$ is a vector obtained by the multiplication of the matrix σ and the vector z over $GF(p)$.

Proof. It holds

$$B_{p,2}^{(f_\sigma,\phi_\sigma)}(\tau) = \sum_{z=0}^{p^m-1} f_\sigma(z)\phi_\sigma(z \ominus \tau) = \sum_{z=0}^{p^m-1} f(\sigma \odot z)\phi(\sigma \odot (z \ominus \tau))$$

$$= \sum_{y=0}^{p^m-1} f(y)\phi(y \ominus (\sigma \odot \tau)) = B_{p,2}^{(f,\phi)}(\sigma \odot \tau), \quad \mod p.$$

For an illustration of properties of correlation functions discussed above, we provide the following example related to Corollary 2.7.1.

Example 2.7.2 *Consider the switching function of two variables $f(z_0, z_1)$ specified by the truth-vector $\mathbf{F} = [1, 0, 1, 1]^T$. The logic complement $\overline{f}(z_1, z_2)$ is defined by the truth-vector $\overline{\mathbf{F}} = [0, 1, 0, 0]^T$.*

The autocorrelation of f is calculated in matrix notation as

$$
\mathbf{B}_{2,2}^{(f,f)} =
\begin{bmatrix}
1 & 0 & 1 & 1 \\
0 & 1 & 1 & 1 \\
1 & 1 & 1 & 0 \\
1 & 1 & 1 & 0
\end{bmatrix}
\begin{bmatrix}
1 \\
0 \\
1 \\
1
\end{bmatrix}
=
\begin{bmatrix}
3 \\
2 \\
2 \\
2
\end{bmatrix}.
$$

It is obvious that in this relation, the rows of the matrix values of $f(z \oplus \tau)$ for $z = (z_1, z_2)$, $\tau = (\tau_1, \tau_2) = 0, 1, 2, 3$, and the autocorrelation function is written as the vector $\mathbf{B}_{2,2}^{(f,f)}$.

In the same way,

$$
\mathbf{B}_{2,2}^{\overline{f},\overline{f})} =
\begin{bmatrix}
0 & 1 & 0 & 0 \\
1 & 0 & 0 & 0 \\
0 & 0 & 0 & 1 \\
0 & 0 & 1 & 0
\end{bmatrix}
\begin{bmatrix}
0 \\
1 \\
0 \\
0
\end{bmatrix}
=
\begin{bmatrix}
1 \\
0 \\
0 \\
0
\end{bmatrix}.
$$

Therefore, since $m = 2$, and the number of nonzero elements in $\mathbf{F}$ is $N = 3$, it follows

$$
\mathbf{B}_{2,2}^{(f,f)} = \mathbf{B}_{2,2}^{(\overline{f},\overline{f})} - 2^m + 2N
$$

$$
=
\begin{bmatrix}
1 \\
0 \\
0 \\
0
\end{bmatrix}
-
\begin{bmatrix}
4 \\
4 \\
4 \\
4
\end{bmatrix}
+ 2
\begin{bmatrix}
3 \\
3 \\
3 \\
3
\end{bmatrix}
=
\begin{bmatrix}
3 \\
2 \\
2 \\
2
\end{bmatrix}.
$$

2.7.4 Generalized Autocorrelation Functions

We now generalize the autocorrelation functions modulo p defined by (2.7.1) and (2.7.2).

Let $f(z)$ be the discrete function representing a system of p-valued logic functions of m variables.

Consider the class $\{B_{p,q}\}$ of autocorrelation functions defined as follows

$$
B_{p,q}(\tau) = \sum_{z=0}^{p^m-1} f(z)f(z \ominus \tau) \cdots f(\underbrace{z \ominus \tau \ominus \cdots \ominus \tau}_{q-1}), \quad \text{mod } p \quad (2.7.10)
$$

Note that $B_{p,2}(\tau) = B_{p,2}^{(f,f)}(\tau)$.

TABLE 2.7.2   A Function f of Two Ternary Variables z_0, z_1 and Its Autocorrelation Function $B_{3,3}(\tau)$.

z_0	z_1	f	z, τ	$f(z)$	$B_{3,3}(\tau)$
0	0	1	0	1	6
0	1	0	1	0	0
0	2	1	2	1	0
1	0	1	3	1	0
1	1	1	4	1	6
1	2	0	5	0	0
2	0	0	6	0	0
2	1	1	7	1	0
2	2	1	8	1	6

We shall assume that $p > q$ in (2.7.10)

$$B_{p,q}(\tau) = B_{p,p}(\tau), \quad (\tau = 0, 1, \ldots, p^m - 1). \tag{2.7.11}$$

The function $B_{p,q}(\tau)$ is the cross-correlation function of q functions obtained by q successive translations (mod p) of the original function. Of this class of correlation characteristics, the most frequently used in the sequel will be $\{B_{p,p}(\tau)\}$, these functions find application in the analysis and synthesis of networks realizing systems of p-valued logic functions.

Example 2.7.3   *Table 2.7.2 defines a function f of two ternary variables $z_0, z_1 \in \{0, 1, 2\}$ and its autocorrelation function $B_{3,3}(\tau)$.*

To end this section, we note that Theorems 2.7.2–2.7.4 may be rephrased in terms of the autocorrelation characteristics $\{B_{p,q}\}$, for $q \geq 2$, under the assumption that $f_i = \phi_i$.

2.8   HARMONIC ANALYSIS OVER AN ARBITRARY FINITE ABELIAN GROUP

The preceding considerations, were focused on spectral transforms on the finite dyadic groups c_2^n, and the corresponding generalization to the cyclic groups C_p^n, for p - prime. These considerations are particular cases of a more general theory of spectral methods on *topological groups* usually called the *abstract harmonic analysis*.

2.8.1   Definition and Properties of Fourier Transform on Finite Abelian Groups

In this section we present a unified approach to the discrete transforms described above. This approach will yield more general versions of the properties of discrete transforms and correlation characteristics described in Sections 2.6 and 2.7, and also enable us to construct new discrete transforms with given properties.

Definitions and theorems

Let $G = (Z, \circ)$ be an Abelian (commutative) group, where Z is a set of N elements, $\circ$ an associative, commutative and invertible binary operation on Z.

An example of a commutative group is the set of all binary (p-ary) sequences of the length m, with the operation of componentwise addition modulo 2 (modulo p). In this case $N = 2^m$, ($N = p^m$). The most familiar infinite Abelian group is the set of all integers (including 0) with respect to the addition.

Definition 2.8.1 *Two groups $G_1 = (Z, \circ)$ and $G_2 = (Y, \Delta)$ are isomorphic if there exists a one-to-one mapping h of Z onto Y such that if $z_1 \circ z_2 = z_3$, $(z_1, z_2, z_3 \in Z)$ then*

$$h(z_1)\Delta h(z_2) = h(z_3), \quad (h(z_1), h(z_2), h(z_3) \in Y). \tag{2.8.1}$$

If the group operation is ordinary addition or multiplication, the groups are the *additive* or the *multiplicative group*, respectively.

Theorem 2.8.1 *Let $G = (Z, \circ)$, $Z = \{0, 1, \ldots, N - 1\}$, be a finite Abelian group. Then, there exists a system of orthogonal functions $\{\Psi_w^{(G)}(z)\}$, $w = 0, 1, \ldots, N - 1$, which forms a multiplicative group isomorphic to G and is a complete orthogonal basis in the space $C(G)$ of all functions from Z to the complex numbers C.*

A proof of this theorem will be presented later in this section.

It follows from Theorem 2.8.1 that any function in $C(G)$ may be expressed as a linear combination of functions $\{\Psi_w^{(G)}\}$ with the coefficients defined in the usual way as the Fourier coefficients, that is, if $f \in C(G)$, then

$$f(z) = \sum_{w=0}^{N-1} S(w)\Psi_w^{(G)}(z), \tag{2.8.2}$$

and

$$S(w) = N^{-1} \sum_{z=0}^{N-1} f(z)\overline{\Psi_w^{(G)}}(z), \tag{2.8.3}$$

where $\overline{\Psi_w^{(G)}}(z)$ is the complex conjugate of $\Psi_w^{(G)}(z)$.

The sequence $S(w)$, ($w = 0, 1, \ldots N - 1$) is known as the *Fourier transform on finite Abelian groups* or *spectrum* of f.

Theorem 2.8.1 is a generalization of Theorems 2.3.3 and 2.5.5.

Indeed, let $G = (\{0, 1\}^m, \oplus(\mathrm{mod}\ 2))$. Then, $\{\Psi_w^{(G)}(z)\} = \{W_w(z)\}$. If $G = (\{0, 1, \ldots, p - 1\}^m, \oplus(\mathrm{mod}\ p))$, we have $\{\Psi_w^{(G)}(z)\} = \{\chi_w^{(p)}(z)\}$.

Theorem 2.8.1 is also valid for some infinite groups.

For example, if $G = (\{0, \pm 1, \pm 2, \ldots\}, +)$ is the additive group of integers, then

$$\{\Psi_w^{(G)}(z)\} = \{\exp(2\pi i w z)\}, \quad i = \sqrt{-1},$$

is the system of exponential functions.

The space $C(G)$ of functions from G to the field of complex numbers contains many complete orthogonal bases. For example, if $G = (\{0, 1\}^n, \oplus (\text{mod } 2))$, we may replace the Walsh basis by the Haar basis, and so on.

It follows from Theorem 2.8.1, however, that among all these complete bases there is exactly one basis, the basis $\{\Psi_w^{(G)}(z)\}$, whose structure is identical to that of the original group G. This is one of the main reasons for the extensive use of exponential functions in the analysis of discrete-time processes. As stated, this basis forms a multiplicative group isomorphic to the additive group of integers. The theory of the discrete Laplace transform, the basic tool of the theory of sampled-data control systems, is based on this approach.

In context of considerations in this book, Theorem 2.8.1 explains the expediency of the Walsh and Vilenkin–Chrestenson bases as a tool for the analysis, synthesis, and testing of networks realizing switching and p-valued logic functions.

An immediate problem is, given a group G, how can we construct the isomorphic complete orthogonal multiplicative system $\{\Psi_w^{(G)}(z)\}$? The method described below is essentially a constructive proof of Theorem 2.8.1. Before proceeding to the construction, however, we recall a few important propositions from the theory of group characters.

Definition 2.8.2 *A mapping χ (not necessarily one-to-one) of a group $G = (Z, \circ)$ into the multiplicative group of (nonzero) complex numbers is called a homomorphism if, whenever $z_1 \circ z_2 = z_3$,*

$$\chi(z_1)\chi(z_2) = \chi(z_3), \quad (z_1, z_2, z_3 \in Z). \tag{2.8.4}$$

Definition 2.8.3 *Any homomorphism of a group G into the multiplicative group of complex numbers is known as a* character *of G.*

Let $\chi_w(z)$ denotes the wth character of G, then $\chi_0(z)$ denotes the character such that $\chi_0(z) = 1$ for any $z \in Z$, the *identity character* or the *principle character*.

Example 2.8.1 *Let $G = (\{0, 1, 2\}, \oplus (\text{mod } 3))$. Then, the function $\chi_w(z)$ defined by Table 2.8.1 is a character of G (here $e_1 = exp(2\pi i/3)$, $e_2 = exp(4\pi i/3)$, $i = \sqrt{-1}$).*

Indeed, taking, for instance, $z_1 = (0, 2)$, $z_2 = (1, 1)$, we have $z_1 \oplus z_2 = (0, 2) \oplus (1, 1) = (1, 0)$ (mod 3), and $\chi_w(z_1)\chi_w(z_2) = e_2 \cdot e_2 = e_1 = \chi_w(z_1 \oplus z_2)$ (mod 3).

Notice that this character is the Vilenkin–Chrestenson function $\chi_4^{(3)}(z)$. It will be clear from what follows that every character of this group is a Vilenkin–Chrestenson

TABLE 2.8.1   Characters $\chi_w(z)$ for the Group C_3^2 in Example 2.8.1.

z	z_0	z_1	$\chi_w(z)$
0	0	0	1
1	0	1	e_1
2	0	2	e_2
3	1	0	e_1
4	1	1	e_2
5	1	2	1
6	2	0	e_2
7	2	1	1
8	2	2	e_1

function, and every Vilenkin–Chrestenson function $\chi_w^{(p)}(z)$ is a character of $G = (\{0, 1, \ldots, p - 1\}^m, \oplus(\bmod\ p))$.

Theorem 2.8.2 *Let G be a finite Abelian group. Then, the set of all characters of G is a multiplicative group isomorphic to G.*

Theorem 2.8.2 is a corollary of Theorem 2.8.3, to be proved later in this section. From Theorem 2.8.2, the set of characters $\{\chi_w(z)\}, (w = 0, 1, \ldots, N - 1)$ of a group $G = (Z, \circ), (Z = \{0, 1, \ldots, N - 1\})$ is the complete orthogonal system whose existence is asserted in Theorem 2.8.1. In other words,

1. *Orthogonality of characters*

$$\sum_{z=0}^{N-1} \chi_w(z)\overline{\chi_s(z)} = \begin{cases} 0, & \text{if } w \neq s, \\ N, & \text{if } w = s, \end{cases} \tag{2.8.5}$$

and

2. *Completeness of characters*
   If

$$\sum_{z=0}^{N-1} f(z)\overline{\chi_w(z)} = 0, \quad w = 0, \ldots, N - 1,$$

then

$$f(z) \equiv 0, \quad z = 0, \ldots, N - 1. \tag{2.8.6}$$

Thus, whenever we are analyzing the properties of functions defined on finite groups (in particular, logic functions) or synthesizing functions of this type with prescribed properties, we may view the functions as being defined not on the original group but on its character group. This is extremely convenient, in view of the orthogonality of the characters and the fact that the group operation is now ordinary multiplication.

By the value of a function $f(z)$ on a character $\chi_w(z)$ we mean the quantity $S(w) = N^{-1} \sum_{z=0}^{N-1} f(z)\overline{\chi_w(z)}$. The numbers $S(w)$, $(w = 0, 1, \ldots, N - 1)$ form the spectrum (Fourier transform on G) of the original function. Thus, when concerned with problems of analysis, synthesis, testing, diagnosis, and optimization of digital networks, we may go over from originals to transforms, as done, for example, in automatic control theory.

2.8.2 Construction of Group Characters

We can now proceed to methods for constructing the group of characters of a given Abelian group G and describe some of the basic properties of characters. As mentioned previously, the method described below proves Theorem 2.8.2 and hence, in view of theorthogonality and completeness relations (2.8.5 and 2.8.6), also Theorem 2.8.1.

Let $G = (Z, \circ)$ be a finite Abelian group. For any $z \in Z$, the set of elements $e = z^0, z^1, z^2, \ldots$, where $z^n = \underbrace{z \circ z \circ \cdots \circ z}_{n}$, is a group. This group is known as a *cyclic subgroup* of G and z is called its *generator*.

A standard theorem of group theory states that any finite Abelian group is a direct product of cyclic subgroups. This means that there exist elements $\gamma_0, \gamma_1, \ldots, \gamma_{m-1} \in Z$ such that, for any $z \in Z$, there exist numbers $z_0, z_1, \ldots, z_{m-1}$, where $0 \le z_s \le N - 1$, $(s = 0, 1, \ldots, m - 1)$, ($N$ is the number of elements in Z), such that

$$z = \gamma_0^{z_0} \circ \gamma_1^{z_1} \circ \ldots \circ \gamma_{m-1}^{z_{m-1}}. \tag{2.8.7}$$

Note that the elements γ_s, $(s = 0, 1, \ldots, m - 1)$ are independent of z. They are known as *generators*, forming a basis of G, and m is called the dimension of G. Throughout the sequel, we shall assume that for any z the numbers z_s, $(s = 0, 1, \ldots, m - 1)$ in (2.8.7) are minimal. In that case the numbers $n_s = max_{z \in Z} z_s + 1$ will be called the orders of the appropriate subgroups.

For example, if $G = (C_p^m = \{0, 1, \ldots, p - 1\}^m, \oplus \mod p)$, then the vectors

$$(0, \ldots, 0, z_s, 0, \ldots, 0) \quad z_s = 0, 1, \ldots, p - 1,$$

form a cyclic subgroup of G of order p, with the generator defined as $\gamma_s = (0, \ldots, 0, 1, 0, \ldots, 0)$.

The group G is the direct product of all such subgroups. In this case,

$$\gamma_s^{z_s} = z_s \gamma_s, \quad 0 \le z_s \le p - 1, \tag{2.8.8}$$

and it follows from (2.8.7) that for any $z \in \{0, 1, \ldots, p - 1\}^m$ there exist numbers z_s (here z_s is simply the sth component of z) such that

$$z = \bigoplus_{s=0}^{m-1} z_s \gamma_s, \quad \text{mod } p. \tag{2.8.9}$$

Theorem 2.8.3   *Let* $G = (\{0, 1, \ldots, N - 1\}, \circ)$ *be a finite Abelian group, which is a direct product of* m *cyclic subgroups of order* n_s, $(s = 0, 1, \ldots, m - 1)$ *with generators* γ_s, *and let* $\chi_w(z)$ *be the* wth *character of* G. *Then,*

$$\chi_w(z) = exp\left(2\pi i \sum_{s=0}^{m-1} \frac{w_s z_s}{n_s}\right), \quad i = \sqrt{-1}, \tag{2.8.10}$$

where

$$z = \gamma_0^{z_0} \circ \cdots \circ \gamma_{m-1}^{z_{m-1}} \tag{2.8.11}$$
$$w = \gamma_0^{w_0} \circ \cdots \circ \gamma_{m-1}^{w_{m-1}},$$

for $(0 \leq w_s, z_s \leq n_s - 1)$. *The mapping* $h : \chi_w \rightarrow w$ *is an isomorphism of the character group of* G *onto* G.

Proof. We first show that the function $\chi_w(z)$ defined by (2.8.10 and 2.8.11) is indeed a character of G. Let $z^{(1)} \circ z^{(2)} = z^{(3)}$, where

$$z^{(q)} = \gamma_0^{z_0^{(q)}} \circ \cdots \circ \gamma_{m-1}^{z_{m-1}^{(q)}}, \quad q = 1, 2, 3.$$

Then, it follows from (2.8.11), in view of the definition of n_s, that

$$z_s^{(3)} = z_s^{(1)} \oplus z_s^{(2)}, \quad \text{mod } n_s, \quad s = 0, \ldots, m - 1, \tag{2.8.12}$$

$$\chi_w(z^{(1)} \circ z^{(2)}) = exp\left(2\pi i \sum_{s=0}^{m-1} \frac{w_s(z_s^{(1)} \oplus z_s^{(2)})}{n_s}\right)$$

$$= exp\left(2\pi i \sum_{s=0}^{m-1} \frac{w_s z_s^{(1)}}{n_s}\right) \cdot exp\left(2\pi i \sum_{s=0}^{m-1} \frac{w_s z_s^{(2)}}{n_s}\right)$$

$$= \chi_w(z^{(1)}) \cdot \chi_w(z^{(2)}), \quad \text{mod } n_s.$$

Thus, the function in question is indeed a character of G.

Now the set $\{\chi_w(z)\}$ is a multiplicative group, with

$$\chi_w^{-1}(z) = exp\left(2\pi i \sum_{s=0}^{m-1} \frac{(n_s - w_s)z_s}{n_s} \right) = \chi_{\overline{w}}(z), \quad i = \sqrt{-1},$$

where

$$\overline{w} = \gamma_0^{n_0-w_0} \circ \ldots \circ \gamma_{m-1}^{n_{m-1}-w_{m-1}}$$

and

$$\chi_w(z)\chi_w^{-1}(z) = \chi_0(z) \equiv 1.$$

We now show that the character group is isomorphic to G, under the isomorphism $h : \chi_w \to w$. Let $z, w^{(1)}, w^{(2)}, w^{(3)} \in G$, and

$$w^{(q)} = \gamma_0^{w_0^{(q)}} \circ \cdots \circ \gamma_{n-1}^{w_{m-1}^{(q)}}, \quad q = 1, 2, 3,$$

Then, if $w^{(3)} = w^{(1)} \circ w^{(2)}$, we have $w_s^{(3)} = w_s^{(1)} \oplus w_s^{(2)}$, mod n_s, $(s = 0, 1, \ldots, n_s - 1)$ and

$$\chi_{w^{(3)}}(z) = exp\left(2\pi i \sum_{s=0}^{m-1} \frac{w_s^{(3)} z_s}{n_s} \right) = exp\left(2\pi i \sum_{s=0}^{m-1} \frac{(w_s^{(1)} \oplus w_s^{(2)})z_s}{n_s} \right)$$

$$= exp\left(2\pi i \sum_{s=0}^{m-1} \frac{w_s^{(1)} z_s}{n_s} \right) \cdot exp\left(2\pi i \sum_{s=0}^{m-1} \frac{w_s^{(2)} z_s}{n_s} \right)$$

$$= \chi_{w^{(1)}}(z) \cdot \chi_{w^{(2)}}(z), \quad \text{mod } n_s.$$

Conversely, if $\chi_{w^{(3)}}(z) = \chi_{w^{(1)}}(z) \cdot \chi_{w^{(2)}}(z)$, we set $z = \gamma_s$, $(s = 0, 1, \ldots, m - 1)$, to obtain same form

$$exp\left(2\pi i \frac{w_s^{(3)}}{n_s} \right) = exp\left(\frac{2\pi}{n_s} i w_s^{(1)} \right) \cdot exp\left(\frac{2\pi}{n_s} i w_s^{(2)} \right),$$

hence it follows that $w_s^{(3)} = w_s^{(1)} \oplus w_s^{(2)}$, (mod n_s) and $w^{(3)} = w^{(1)} \circ w^{(2)}$.

Formulas (2.8.10) and (2.8.11) generate a simple procedure for constructing the characters, thus furnishing a complete multiplicative system of functions isomorphic to the original group.

In addition, these formulas yield a direct proof of Theorem 2.8.2.

If $G = (\{0, 1, \ldots, p - 1\}^m, \oplus_p)$, then $n_s = p, s = 0, 1, \ldots, m - 1, w_s, z_s$ are the components of the p-ary expansions of w, z, and the set of characters $\{\chi_w(z)\}$ is precisely the Vilenkin–Chrestenson system $\{\chi_w^{(p)}(z)\}$ (see Section 2.5). For convenience

TABLE 2.8.2   The Operation Table of the Group in Example 2.8.2.

∘	0	1	2	3	4	5
0	0	1	2	3	4	5
1	1	2	0	4	5	3
2	2	0	1	5	3	4
3	3	4	5	0	1	2
4	4	5	3	1	2	0
5	5	3	4	2	0	1

we have indexed the characters in a manner slightly different from that adopted previously for the Vilenkin–Chrestenson functions corresponding to Definition 2.3.2 for $p = 2$, and this of course does not affect the validity of the exposition.

Using Theorems 2.8.1–2.8.3, we can generalize the properties of Walsh functions (Section 2.3) and Vilenkin–Chrestenson functions (Section 2.5) to arbitrary finite commutative groups (completeness and orthogonality, finiteness of representing series, symmetry of index and variable, translation theorem, etc.). The same applies to the properties of the corresponding discrete transforms (Section 2.6, linearity, translation of original and transform, involution property, convolutions, and so on).

Example 2.8.2   *Consider the group $G = (\{0, 1, 2, 3, 4, 5\}, \circ)$, where $\circ$ is defined by Table 2.8.2 ($N = 6$, $e = 0$). We construct the characters $\chi_w^{(G)}(z)$ of G, ($z \in \{0, 1, \ldots, 5\}$). The group G contains two cyclic subgroups $G_0 = (\{0, 3\}, \circ)$ and $G_1 = (\{0, 1, 2\}, \circ)$, with generators $\gamma_0 = 3$, $\gamma_1 = 1$, respectively, and it is the direct product of these subgroups ($n_0 = 2$, $n_1 = 3$). The representation of the elements $z \in G$ in terms of powers of the generators of the cyclic groups is shown in Table 2.8.3.*

The characters $\chi_w^{(G)}(z)$ of G are, by (2.8.10),

$$\chi_w^{(G)}(z) = exp\left(2\pi i \left(\frac{w_0 z_0}{2} + \frac{w_1 z_1}{3}\right)\right), \quad i = \sqrt{-1}.$$

TABLE 2.8.3   Elements of G in Terms of Powers of Generators.

z, w	z_0, w_0	z_1, w_1
0	0	0
1	0	1
2	0	2
3	1	0
4	1	1
5	1	2

TABLE 2.8.4 The Characters of the Group $G = C_2 \times C_3$ in Example 2.8.2.

z/w	0	1	2	3	4	5
0	1	1	1	1	1	1
1	1	e_1	e_2	1	e_1	e_2
2	1	e_2	e_1	1	e_2	e_1
3	1	1	1	-1	-1	-1
4	1	e_1	e_2	-1	$-e_1$	$-e_2$
5	1	e_2	e_1	-1	$-e_2$	$-e_1$

Table 2.8.4 lists the values of these characters, $e_1 = exp(2\pi i/3)$, $e_2 = e_1^2 = exp(4\pi i/3)$.

A direct examination of Table 2.8.4 readily shows that $\chi_w^{(G)}(z) = \chi_z^{(G)}(w)$, $\sum_{z=0}^{s} \chi_w^{(G)}(z) = 0$ if $w \neq 0$, $\sum_{z=0}^{s} \chi_{w_1}^{(G)}(z)\chi_{w_2}^{(G)}(z) = 0$ if $w_1 \neq w_2$, and $\chi_w^{(G)}(z_1) \cdot \chi_w^{(G)}(z_2) = \chi_w^{(G)}(z_1 \circ z_2)$.

We can also generalize the auto- and cross-correlation functions to any group $G = (\{0, 1, \ldots, N - 1\}, \circ)$. Thus, if $f_1(z)$, $f_2(z)$ are two functions defined on the group, their cross-correlation function is defined as

$$B_{\circ,2}^{(f_1,f_2)}(\tau) = \sum_{z=0}^{N-1} f_1(z)f_2(z \circ \tau^{-1}), \qquad (2.8.13)$$

where $\tau \circ \tau^{-1} = e$ is the identity of the group.

Let $\chi(f)$ denote the generalized Fourier transform of a function f defined on $\{0, 1, \ldots, N - 1\}$, that is, the sequence of expansion coefficients of f with respect to the characters of G. We may assume that $\chi(f)$, like f is defined on $\{0, 1, \ldots, N - 1\}$. We then have the following generalization of Theorem 2.7.1 to an arbitrary finite commutative group (analog of the Wiener–Khinchin theorem (330)).

Theorem 2.8.4 Let $G = (\{0, 1, 2, \ldots, N - 1\}, \circ)$ be a finite commutative group and f_1, f_2 functions defined on $\{0, 1, \ldots, N - 1\}$. Then,

$$B_{\circ,2}^{(f_1,f_2)} = N \cdot \chi^{-1}(\chi(f_1)\overline{\chi(f_2)}), \qquad (2.8.14)$$

where χ^{-1} is the inverse Fourier transform on G.

Theorem 2.8.4 enables us to generalize to arbitrary groups the properties of the correlation functions considered in Section 2.7.

2.8.3 Fourier–Galois Transforms

We have studied discrete transforms defined by

$$f(z) = \sum_{w=0}^{N-1} S(w)\Psi_w(z), \tag{2.8.15}$$

$$S(w) = N^{-1} \sum_{z=0}^{N-1} f(z)\overline{\Psi_w(z)}, \tag{2.8.16}$$

where $\{\Psi(z)\}$ is a basis and z ranges over the elements of a finite group G, the *domain group*. The values of $f(z)$, $S(w)$, $\Psi_w(z)$ are in the field of complex numbers.

We shall now introduce transforms for which all the operations in (2.8.15 and 2.8.16) are interpreted not over the field of complex numbers but over a finite field (Galois field).

We shall denote the field with Q elements by $GF(Q)$, where Q is a prime number. The transforms thus defined will be referred to as *Walsh–Galois*, *Haar–Galois* and *Vilenkin–Chrestenson–Galois* transforms, in accordance with the choice of the basis $\{\Psi_w(z)\}$.

In the case of Vilenkin–Chrestenson–Galois transforms, as applied to p-valued logic, we have the additional condition that p be a divisor of $N - 1$.

Consider the important special case in which the field is the field $\mathcal{R}$ of residues modulo prime number Q, $\mathcal{R} = GF(Q)$. Recall that the field of residues modulo Q is the field whose elements are the numbers $0, 1, \ldots, Q - 1$, the operations of addition and multiplication being performed modulo Q. Let

$$Q > \max(\max_z f(z), p),$$

where we are dealing with p-valued logic, and p is a divisor of $Q - 1$.

We then define a discrete transform over $GF(Q)$:

$$f(z) = \bigoplus_{w=0}^{Q-1} S(w) \cdot \Psi_w(z), \quad \text{mod } Q, \tag{2.8.17}$$

$$S(w) = Q^{-1} \cdot \bigoplus_{z=0}^{Q-1} f(z) \cdot \Psi_{w^{-1}}(z), \quad \text{mod } Q, \tag{2.8.18}$$

where $w \circ w^{-1} = e$, $\circ$ denoting the operation in G.

The use of transforms over finite fields $GF(Q)$ is convenient for the design of networks realizing logic functions, since when this approach is adopted the number of p-ary digits of the code of $S(w)$ is at most $\lceil \log_p Q \rceil$, and this number may be considerably smaller than that needed for expansions over the complex field. (Here and below $\lceil a \rceil$ denotes the smallest integer $\geq a$.)

Example 2.8.3 *As an example, let us calculate the Walsh spectrum of the Boolean function defined by Table 2.8.5 over the real field, on the one hand, and over $GF(3)$ on the other (Table 2.8.5). It is clear from the table that the range of $S(w)$ for every w is decreased to* $\lceil \log_2 3 \rceil = 2$.

All the properties of the Walsh, Haar, etc. transforms remain valid for the Walsh–Galois, Haar–Galois, etc. versions.

Among many discrete transforms over finite fields, probably most important for analysis and synthesis is the special case of the Vilenkin–Chrestenson–Galois transform with the basis $\{\Psi_w(z)\} = \{\chi_w^{(p)}(z)\}$ (see Section 2.5), over the field $GF(Q^n)$ (170,171). This special case arises when $p = Q^n - 1$ and $m = 1$, and is known as the Laplace–Galois transform, used in analysis and synthesis of linear switching networks with memory described by discrete periodic time functions (with period at most $Q^n - 1$). (A linear network consists exclusively of mod p adders and flip-flops, where n is the number of flip-flops.) The use of Laplace–Galois transforms in analysis and synthesis of linear networks with memory is discussed in detail in References 170–172, and 190.

In the general case, any discrete transform may be characterized by the algebraic structure (group, field, etc.) of the variable set G of the original function and the algebraic structure of the value set R of the basis functions and the corresponding expansion coefficients. In the cases considered hitherto G is a finite commutative (Abelian)

TABLE 2.8.5   Walsh Spectrum of the Function f Over the Real Field and $GF(3)$.

z_0	z_1	z_2	z_3	z, w	$f(z)$	$16S(w)$	$S(w)(\bmod 3)$
0	0	0	0	0	1	11	2
0	0	0	1	1	0	3	0
0	0	1	0	2	1	−1	2
0	0	1	1	3	0	−1	2
0	1	0	0	4	1	−1	2
0	1	0	1	5	1	−1	2
0	1	1	0	6	1	−1	2
0	1	1	1	7	0	−1	2
1	0	0	0	8	0	−1	2
1	0	0	1	9	1	3	0
1	0	1	0	10	1	3	0
1	0	1	1	11	1	−1	2
1	1	0	0	12	1	−1	2
1	1	0	1	13	0	3	0
1	1	1	0	14	1	−1	2
1	1	1	1	15	1	3	0

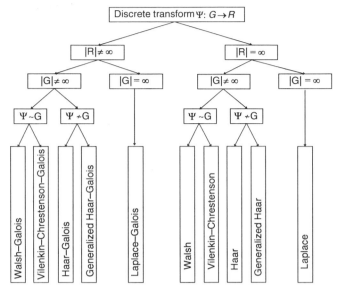

FIGURE 2.8.1   Spectral transforms.

group, while R is the field of real numbers for the Haar and Walsh transforms, the field of complex numbers for the generalized Haar transform and the Vilenkin–Chrestenson transform, and a finite (Galois) field for the Haar–Galois, Walsh–Galois, etc. transforms. For recent generalizations of the Haar transform to multiple-valued functions see Reference 580, and related discussions in Reference 555.

It is sometimes convenient to work with discrete functions defined on an infinite set G. The set G is usually the set of discrete times (sampling times) at which the behavior of the object is observed. This set is treated as the additive group of integers. If the set of values of z is the additive group G of integers and R (the field of values of the basis functions and the coefficients) is the complex field, the transform defined by the multiplicative basis isomorphic to G is the familiar discrete Laplace transform (129). Since digital devices with finite memory are described by periodic time functions, the argument group G may always be taken finite, its order coinciding with the maximum period of the functions describing the operation of the device. This explains why this book is concerned only with discrete transforms, over finite argument groups. A general classification of all discrete transforms described in this chapter is given in Fig. 2.8.1. In the figure, $|G|$, and $|R|$ denote the number of elements in G and R, respectively, $\Psi_w \sim G$ and $\Psi \not\sim G$ denote, respectively, isomorphism and nonisomorphism of the expansion basis $\{\Psi\}$ and the argument group G. As a final remark, we note that the properties of the Walsh, Vilenkin–Chrestenson, etc. transforms and the corresponding correlation characteristics are readily generalized to all the discrete transforms listed in Fig. 2.8.1.

2.9 FOURIER TRANSFORM ON FINITE NON-ABELIAN GROUPS

In this section, for the completeness of the presentation, we briefly discuss extensions of the Fourier transforms to finite non-Abelian groups, although they will not be used in further considerations in this book. Notice, however, that there are real-life signals and systems that are naturally modeled by functions and, respectively, relations between functions on non-Abelian groups. We will mention few of those related with electrical engineering practice. Some other examples of such problems are discussed in Reference 100. For these reasons we believe that spectral methods on non-Abelian groups may have in the future interesting applications in the areas discussed in this book. Therefore, in this section, we will briefly outline mathematic foundations for such a study after we first give references to some related applications.

As is noted in Reference 302, some relevant examples of such applications are a problem of pattern recognition for binary images, which may be considered as a problem of implementation of binary matrices, a problem of synthesis of rearrangeable switching networks whose outputs depend on the permutation of input terminals, a general problem of interconnecting various objects, and so on. Non-Abelian groups have found applications in linear systems theory in the approximation of a linear time-invariant system by a system whose input and output are functions defined on non-Abelian groups (301). See, also References 542, 543, and 609.

Such systems can be used for instance, as mathematical models of signal filtering. For example, in Reference 303 a general model of a suboptimal Wiener filter over a group is defined. It is shown that, with respect to some criteria, the use of non-Abelian groups may be more advantageous than the use of an Abelian group. For example, in some cases the use of the Fourier transform on various non-Abelian groups results in improved statistical performance of the filter as compared to the DFT. See, also Reference 608.

It has been pointed out in Reference 610 that in the area of logic design the non-Abelian *quaternion group* Q_2, which is used as an illustrative example in this section, may have a role equal to that played by the finite dyadic group among Abelian groups. Similarly as with the Walsh transform, that is, the Fourier transform on finite dyadic groups, the calculation of the Fourier transform on the group of quaternions does not require the multiplication. Regarding the efficiency of the fast Fourier transform on groups, it is shown 476, for sample, evaluations with different groups that in a multiprocessor environment the use of non-Abelian groups, for example quaternions, may result in many cases in optimal, fastest, performance of the FFT. Moreover, as has been shown in Reference 476, the quaternion groups as components of the direct product for G in many cases show optimal performance in the accuracy of calculation.

These performances are estimated taking into consideration the number of arithmetic operations, the number of interprocessor data transfers, and the number of communication lines operating in parallel. In this setting, it has been shown that the combination of small cyclic groups C_2 and non-Abelian quaternions Q_2 in the direct product for G results in groups exhibiting in the most cases the fastest algorithms for the computation of the Fourier transform. Therefore, such groups are a suitable finite group structure G that should be imposed on the domain of discrete signals.

In Reference 562, some aspects of the calculation complexity of FFT on such groups have been discussed.

In Reference 563, a comparison between spectral methods on finite dyadic groups C_2^m and groups defined as product of the quaternion group Q_2, C_2, and their powers has been discussed for applications in compact representations of large switching functions.

In Reference 566, the arithmetic-Haar expressions on Q_2 have been defined by combining good features of Fourier expressions on Q_2 and Haar expression on C_2^m for compact representations of large functions. These expressions directly extend to groups that are products of Q_2 and freely selected finite groups. In this case, the related transform matrices are defined the Kronecker product of arithmetic-Haar matrix on Q_2 and Fourier transforms on other groups selected as the constituents of the considered group G. Further generalizations are directly possible by combining other transforms on finite groups with the arithmetic-Haar transform. In particular, it is interesting to combine the Haar transforms of different orders with the arithmetic-Haar transform on Q_2 and their powers. In this way, a family of Haar-like transforms can be defined sharing useful properties of the Haar and the arithmetic transforms on C_2^m and the arithmetic-Haar transform on Q_2.

In Reference 557, word-level expressions with matrix-valued coefficients for representation of large switching functions have been defined by exploiting properties of Fourier series for matrix-valued functions.

In References 548, 549, 552, 553, and 554, the Fourier transform on Q_2 has been used to define compact decision diagram representations for large switching and multiple-valued functions. More details on such applications can be found in Reference 567.

2.9.1 Representation of Finite Groups

We have defined transforms for functions that have a group as the domain and a field as the range. For instance, the Walsh transform is defined for functions from the dyadic group to the real field and the discrete Fourier transform for functions from the group of integers modulo N to the complex field. In both cases, the basis of the transform was developed using group characters that can be viewed as the tool that ties together the structures of the domain and the range.

In this section, we consider functions where the domain is a *non-Abelian group* and the range a field (e.g, the complex numbers). Because a field has commutative multiplication, we cannot find a substructure within the field that would be compatible with the domain. (Such as the roots of unity that form a multiplicative group within the complex numbers).

Such a compatible structure can be found by going up in abstraction and considering linear transforms (matrices) over the field instead of elements of the field.

Therefore, generalization of Fourier transform to finite non-Abelian groups can be done in terms of group representations, and among them the irreducible *unitary repre-*

sentations are especially distinguished, which we are now going to discuss briefly. An excellent presentation of theory of group representations can be found, for instance, in Reference 246.

We will use the following notation to discuss the definition and properties of the Fourier transform on finite non-Abelian groups.

Denote by P the complex field or a finite field. Henceforth it will be assumed that:

1. $char P = 0$, or $char P$ does not divide $g = |G|$,
2. P is a so-called splitting field for G,

where $char P$ is the characteristic of P. [5] If $P = GF(Q)$, then $Q - 1$ is divisible by $char P$.

A representation of a group G on a vector space V is a correspondence between the abstract group G and a subgroup of the "concrete" group of linear transformations of V. That is, a representation is a homomorphism of G into the multiplicative group of invertible linear transformations on V, see Reference 567. In the case of finite groups, the linear transformations are usually identified with matrices. In this setting the following definition of group representations can be introduced.

Definition 2.9.1 *The general linear group $GL(n, P)$ is the group of $(n \times n)$ invertible matrices (n is a natural number) with respect to matrix multiplication, with entries in a field P that can be the field of complex numbers C or a finite field F_q, where q is power of a prime p.*

Since a matrix over a field P is invertible iff its determinant is nonzero, an alternative definition of $GL(n, P)$ is as the group of $(n \times n)$ matrices with nonzero determinant.

Definition 2.9.2 *(Group representations) A finite dimensional representation of a finite group G is a group homomorphism $R : G \to GL(n, P)$.*

The order of the matrix $\mathbf{R}_w(x)$ from $GL(n, P)$ assigned to the wth representation $R_w(x)$ is the dimension of $R_w(x)$, and is denoted by r_w.

A representation R is *unitary* if each $\mathbf{R}_w(x)$, $x \in G$, is an unitary matrix over P, and is trivial if $\mathbf{R}_w(x) = I$ for each $x \in G$, and $\mathbf{I}$ is the identity matrix.

It can be shown that in the case of *compact groups* it is sufficient to restrict the consideration just to the unitary representations without loss of generality.

Each unitary irreducible representation $\mathbf{R}_w$ for a compact group G is finite dimensional.

From two representations R_1 and R_2, it is possible to construct a larger representation R_3 by combining the matrices $\mathbf{R}_1(x)$ and $\mathbf{R}_2(x)$ assigned to them. For instance,

---

[5]If e is the identity in P, then the smallest number p for which $p \cdot e = 0$ is called the *characteristic* of P and denoted by $char P$. If $n \cdot e \neq 0$ for each $n \in N$, then $char P = 0$.

we can construct R_3 as

$$\mathbf{R}_3(x) = \begin{bmatrix} \mathbf{R}_1(x) & \mathbf{0} \\ \mathbf{0} & \mathbf{R}_2(x) \end{bmatrix},$$

where $\mathbf{0}$ is the zero matrix. Thus constructed representation R_3 is called *reducible*, since it can be decomposed into smaller representations.

A representation that does not have this block structure, and cannot be reduced to this form by a similarity transformation $\mathbf{S}^{-1}\mathbf{R}(x)\mathbf{S}$, where $\mathbf{S}$ is a given transform matrix of the corresponding order, is called an *irreducible representation* of G over the field P.

The set of all nonequivalent unitary irreducible representations for a group G forms the *dual object* Γ of G.

In the case of finite groups,

1. Every irreducible representation of a finite group G is equivalent to some unitary representation.
2. Every irreducible representation is finite dimensional.
3. The number of nonequivalent irreducible representations $\mathbf{R}_w$ of a finite non-Abelian group G of order g is equal to the number of equivalence classes of the dual object Γ of G. Denoting this number by K, it can be written

$$\sum_{w=0}^{K-1} r_w^2 = g,$$

where r_w is the dimension of R_w.

Each such equivalence class contains just one unitary representation. We shall denote the K unitary irreducible representations of G in some fixed order by $\mathbf{R}_0, \mathbf{R}_1, \ldots, \mathbf{R}_{K-1}$. We denote by $\mathbf{R}_w(z)$ the value of $\mathbf{R}_w$ at $z \in G$. Note that $\mathbf{R}_w(z)$ stands for a nonsingular r_w by r_w matrix over P, with elements $R_w^{(i,j)}(z)$, $i, j = 1, 2, \ldots, r_w$, $R_w^{(i,j)}(z) \in P$.

If the group G is representable in the form

$$G = G_1 \times \cdots \times G_m, \tag{2.9.1}$$

then its unitary irreducible representations can be obtained as the Kronecker product of the unitary irreducible representations of subgroups G_i, $i = 1, \ldots, m$ (246). Therefore, the number K of unitary irreducible representations of G can be expressed as,

$$K = \prod_{i=1}^{m} K_i, \tag{2.9.2}$$

where K_i is the number of unitary irreducible representations of the ith subgroup G_i.

Now, for a given group G of the form (2.9.1), the index w of each unitary irreducible representation $\mathbf{R}_w$ can be written as:

$$w = \sum_{i=1}^{m} b_i w_i, \quad w_i \in \{0, 1, \ldots, K_i - 1\}, \quad w \in \{0, 1, \ldots, K - 1\},$$

with

$$b_i = \begin{cases} \prod_{j=i+1}^{m} K_j, & i = 1, \ldots, m - 1, \\ 1, & i = m, \end{cases}$$

where K_j is the number of unitary irreducible representations of the subgroup G_j.

2.9.2 Fourier Transform on Finite Non-Abelian Groups

The Fourier transform on compact non-Abelian groups is defined by the so-called Peter–Weyl theorem (425). In the case of finite groups, this definition can be summarized as follows.

The functions $R_w^{(i,j)}(z)$, $w = 0, 1, \ldots, K - 1$, $i, j = 1, \ldots, r_w$ form an orthogonal system in the space $P(G)$. Therefore, the direct and the inverse Fourier transform of a function $f \in P(G)$ are respectively defined by

$$\mathbf{S}_f(w) = r_w g^{-1} \sum_{z=0}^{g-1} f(z) \mathbf{R}_w(z^{-1}), \tag{2.9.3}$$

$$f(z) = \sum_{w=0}^{K-1} Tr(\mathbf{S}_f(w) \mathbf{R}_w(z)), \tag{2.9.4}$$

where for a matrix $\mathbf{Q}$, $Tr(\mathbf{Q})$ denotes the trace of $\mathbf{Q}$, that is, the sum of elements on the main diagonal of $\mathbf{Q}$.

Here and in the sequel we shall assume, without explicitly saying so, that all arithmetical operations are carried out in the field P.

Example 2.9.1 *Let G be the Quaternion (non-Abelian) group Q_2 of order 8. This group has two generators a and b and the group identity is denoted by e. If the group operation is written as abstract multiplication, the following relations hold for the group generators: $b^2 = a^2$, $bab^{-1} = a^{-1}$, $a^4 = e$. If the following bijection V is chosen*

z	e	a	a^2	a^3	b	ab	$a^2 b$	$a^3 b$
$V(z)$	0	1	2	3	4	5	6	7

TABLE 2.9.1   Group Operation for the Quaternion Group Q_2.

○	0	1	2	3	4	5	6	7
0	0	1	2	3	4	5	6	7
1	1	2	3	0	5	6	7	4
2	2	3	0	1	6	7	4	5
3	3	0	1	2	7	4	5	6
4	4	5	6	7	2	3	0	1
5	5	6	7	4	3	0	1	2
6	6	7	4	5	0	1	2	3
7	7	4	5	6	1	2	3	0

then the full group operation is described in Table 2.9.1. All the irreducible unitary representations of Q_2 over C are given in Table 2.9.2.

The dual object Γ of Q_2, that is, the set of unitary irreducible representations of G over the field of complex numbers, is of the cardinality 5, since there are five irreducible unitary representations of this group. Four of representations are 1-dimensional and

TABLE 2.9.2   Irreducible Unitary Representations of Q_2 Over C.

x	$\mathbf{R}_0$	$\mathbf{R}_1$	$\mathbf{R}_2$	$\mathbf{R}_3$	$\mathbf{R}_4$
0	1	1	1	1	$\mathbf{I}$
1	1	-1	1	-1	$i\mathbf{A}$
2	1	1	1	1	$-\mathbf{I}$
3	1	-1	1	-1	$i\mathbf{B}$
4	1	1	-1	-1	$\mathbf{C}$
5	1	-1	-1	1	$-i\mathbf{D}$
6	1	1	-1	-1	$\mathbf{E}$
7	1	-1	-1	1	$i\mathbf{D}$
	$r_0 = 1$	$r_1 = 1$	$r_2 = 1$	$r_3 = 1$	$r_4 = 2$

$$\mathbf{I} = \begin{bmatrix} 1 & 0 \\ 0 & 1 \end{bmatrix} \qquad \mathbf{A} = \begin{bmatrix} 1 & 0 \\ 0 & -1 \end{bmatrix}$$

$$\mathbf{B} = \begin{bmatrix} -1 & 0 \\ 0 & 1 \end{bmatrix} \qquad \mathbf{C} = \begin{bmatrix} 0 & -1 \\ 1 & 0 \end{bmatrix}$$

$$\mathbf{D} = \begin{bmatrix} 0 & 1 \\ 1 & 0 \end{bmatrix} \qquad \mathbf{E} = \begin{bmatrix} 0 & 1 \\ -1 & 0 \end{bmatrix}$$

one is 2-dimensional. The Fourier transform on Q_2 is defined by the matrix

$$[\mathbf{R}]^{-1} = \frac{1}{8} \begin{bmatrix} 1 & 1 & 1 & 1 & 1 & 1 & 1 & 1 \\ 1 & -1 & 1 & -1 & 1 & -1 & 1 & -1 \\ 1 & 1 & 1 & 1 & -1 & -1 & -1 & -1 \\ 1 & -1 & 1 & -1 & -1 & 1 & -1 & 1 \\ 2\mathbf{I} & 2i\mathbf{B} & -2\mathbf{I} & 2i\mathbf{A} & 2\mathbf{E} & 2i\mathbf{D} & 2\mathbf{C} & -2i\mathbf{D} \end{bmatrix},$$

where the notation is as in Table 2.9.2. Therefore, the Fourier spectrum of a function f on Q_2 consists of five coefficients, four 1-dimensional and one 2-dimensional and can be represented as a vector

$$[\mathbf{S}_f] = \begin{bmatrix} S_f(0) & S_f(1) & S_f(2) & S_f(3) & \mathbf{S}_f(4) \end{bmatrix}^T.$$

For example, the Fourier spectrum of the function f on Q_2 given by the truth-vector $\mathbf{F} = [0\alpha 00\beta\lambda 00]^T$ is given by

$$[\mathbf{S}_f] = \begin{bmatrix} \alpha + \beta + \lambda \\ -\alpha + \beta - \lambda \\ \alpha - \beta - \lambda \\ -\alpha - \beta + \lambda \\ 2\begin{bmatrix} -i\alpha & \beta + i\lambda \\ -\beta + i\lambda & i\alpha \end{bmatrix} \end{bmatrix}.$$

Fast Fourier transform (FFT) algorithms for the calculation of Fourier transform on finite non-Abelian groups are proposed in Reference 278. Their matrix interpretation given in Reference 544 permitted extension of the method to the calculation through *Multiterminal Decision Diagrams* (MTDDs) 567. These algorithms provide an efficient way for determination of values of constant nodes in Fourier decision diagrams 567.

Theorem 2.9.1 *The main properties of the Fourier transform on finite non-Abelian groups are the following:*

1. *Linearity: For all $\alpha_1, \alpha_2 \in P$, $f_1, f_2 \in C(G)$,*

$$\mathbf{S}_{\alpha_1 f_1 + \alpha_2 f_2}(w) = \alpha_1 \mathbf{S}_{f_1}(w) + \alpha_2 \mathbf{S}_{f_2}(w).$$

2. *Right group translation: For all $\tau \in G$,*

$$\mathbf{S}_{f(z\tau)}(w) = \mathbf{R}_w(\tau)\mathbf{S}_f(w).$$

3. *Group convolution: For two functions* f_1, $f_2 \in C(G)$ *the convolution is defined by*

$$(f_1 * f_2)(\tau) = \sum_{z \in G} f_1(z) f_2(\tau^{-1} z).$$

$$r_w g^{-1} \mathbf{S}_{(f_1 * f_2)(\tau)}(w) = \mathbf{S}_{f_1}(w) \mathbf{S}_{f_2}(w).$$

It should be noted that unlike the Fourier transform on Abelian groups, a dual statement cannot be formulated since the dual object Γ does not exhibit a group structure suitable for definition of a convolution of functions on Γ.

4. *Parseval theorem: For all* f_1, $f_2 \in P(G)$,

$$\sum_{z \in G} f_1(z) \overline{f}_2(z) = g \sum_{\mathbf{R}_w \in \Gamma(G)} r_w^{-1} \mathrm{Tr}(\mathbf{S}_{f_1}(w) \mathbf{S}_{f_2}^*(w)),$$

where $\overline{f}$ denotes the complex conjugate of f, $\mathbf{S}_{f_2}^*(\cdot)$ is the conjugate transpose of $\mathbf{S}_{f_2}(\cdot)$, that is, $\mathbf{S}_{f_2}^*(\cdot) = \overline{(\mathbf{S}_{f_2}(\cdot))^T}$.

5. *The Wiener–Khinchin theorem: For two functions* f_1, $f_2 \in P(G)$, *the cross-correlation function is defined by*

$$B^{(f_1, f_2)}(\tau) = \sum_{z \in G} f_1(z) \overline{f_2(z \tau^{-1})}.$$

The autocorrelation function is the cross-correlation function for $f_1 = f_2$. Denote by $\mathbf{F}_G$ and F_G^{-1} the direct and inverse Fourier transform on G defined by (2.9.3) and (2.9.4), respectively, and by $\mathbf{F}_G^*$ the transform such that

$$(\mathbf{F}_G^*(f))(w) = \mathbf{S}_f^*(w).$$

With this notation the Wiener–Khinchin theorem on G is defined by

$$B^{(f_1, f_2)} = g F_G^{-1}(r_w^{-1} \mathbf{F}_G(f_1) \mathbf{F}_G^*(f_2)).$$

For applications of Fourier transforms on finite non-Abelian groups for problems related to logic design, we refer to Reference 567.

BIBLIOGRAPHIC NOTES

Algebraic structures for logic design are discussed in many books, see (395,491). Walsh and Haar transforms have been studied from different aspects and for different applications in References 8,51,52,151,234,235,255,258,323,555,661,671. The Vilenkin–Chrestenson transform is viewed as a generalization of the Walsh transform (378,383,611,658). For the arithmetic transform, see (266,349,658). Autocorrelation functions have been extensively used in optimization problems in logic design in References 228 and 289. For computational methods of autocorrelation functions see (558,561). Spectral transforms over finite fields are discussed in References 190,255,381,399, and 641. An excellent book for Fourier transform on groups is (479), and for abstract analysis in general (246). For Fourier analysis on non-Abelian groups, see (567).

CHAPTER 3

CALCULATION OF SPECTRAL TRANSFORMS

Efficient calculations of spectral transforms are very important for their practical applications. The efficiency is expressed in terms of

1. *Space* required to store functions that will be transformed, results of intermediate calculations, and their spectra, and
2. *Time* to perform the calculations, which is usually expressed through the number of required arithmetical operations, often reduced to the number of additions and multiplications, while the time for some auxiliary manipulations with data, as for instance various reordering, is neglected.

This chapter discusses methods for calculation of spectra and autocorrelations for different transforms and uses different data structures to represent the functions processed.

Methods presented in this chapter have been developed for calculations with a single processor.

Efficient techniques for calcuation of spectral transforms with multiprocessors and interconnection networks can be found in References (295, 304, and 475).

3.1 CALCULATION OF WALSH SPECTRA

Henceforth, Walsh spectra will be used extensively as a working tool in solution of analysis and synthesis problems for network implementations of Boolean functions.

We shall, therefore, devote some attention to methods for their efficient computation in terms of space and time.

We first consider an effective algorithm for construction of the Walsh spectrum and estimate its complexity. This algorithm is similar to the analogous algorithm used for the basis of trigonometric functions (*Fast Fourier Transform (FFT)* (75, 109)). Actually, this is the same algorithm performed over C_2^m for a transform defined with respect to a different basis, that is, instead of the discrete exponential functions, the Walsh functions are used.

Theorem 3.1.1 (36) *Let* $\Phi(z)$ *be a step function representing a system of Boolean functions of m variables, and* $S(w)$ $(w = 0, 1, \ldots, 2^m - 1)$ *its Walsh spectrum. Set*

$$
\begin{cases}
a_0(w) = \Phi(w) \\
a_0(2^{m-1} + w) = \Phi(2^{m-1} + w) & w = 0, 1, \ldots, 2^{m-1} - 1, \\
a_q(w) = a_{q-1}(2w) + a_{q-1}(2w + 1) \\
a_q(2^{m-1} + w) = a_{q-1}(2w) - a_{q-1}(2w + 1), \ q = 1, \ldots, m.
\end{cases}
\tag{3.1.1}
$$

Then, for ordering of Walsh functions defined by the Definition 2.3.2,

$$
S(w) = 2^{-m} a_m(w).
$$

Theorem 3.1.1 describes a simple algorithm for calculating the Walsh spectrum, in terms of a recursive procedure yielding the sequence $a_q(w)$.

The number of operations N_W required to calculate $S(w)$ with this algorithm is $N_W = m \cdot 2^m$, where m is the number of binary digits in the variable. A sample calculation of the spectrum is shown in Table 3.1.1.

Another method for construction of the Walsh spectrum is very convenient if m is not large.

TABLE 3.1.1   Calculation of Walsh Spectrum.

z, w	$\Phi(z)$	$a_1(w)$	$a_2(w)$	$a_3(w) = 8S(w)$
0	1	3	7	27
1	2	4	20	−5
2	0	4	−5	−13
3	4	16	0	7
4	3	−1	−1	−13
5	1	−4	−12	−5
6	7	2	3	11
7	9	−2	4	−1

Let $\mathbf{W}(m)$ be the matrix whose the wth row is $(W_w(0), W_w(1), \ldots, W_w(2^m - 1))$, $w = 0, 1, \ldots, 2^m - 1$. For example, for $m = 2$ and $m = 3$, the matrices $\mathbf{W}(2)$ and $\mathbf{W}(3)$ for the so-called Hadamard ordering determined by Definition 2.3.1 are

$$
\mathbf{W}(2) = \begin{bmatrix} 1 & 1 & 1 & 1 \\ 1 & -1 & 1 & -1 \\ 1 & 1 & -1 & -1 \\ 1 & -1 & -1 & 1 \end{bmatrix},
$$

$$
\mathbf{W}(3) = \begin{bmatrix} 1 & 1 & 1 & 1 & 1 & 1 & 1 & 1 \\ 1 & -1 & 1 & -1 & 1 & -1 & 1 & -1 \\ 1 & 1 & -1 & -1 & 1 & 1 & -1 & -1 \\ 1 & -1 & -1 & 1 & 1 & -1 & -1 & 1 \\ 1 & 1 & 1 & 1 & -1 & -1 & -1 & -1 \\ 1 & -1 & 1 & -1 & -1 & 1 & -1 & 1 \\ 1 & 1 & -1 & -1 & -1 & -1 & 1 & 1 \\ 1 & -1 & -1 & 1 & -1 & 1 & 1 & -1 \end{bmatrix}.
$$

As noticed in Section 2.8.1, matrices of this type are Hadamard matrices (36, 453), and so all the properties of Walsh functions may be phrased in terms of Hadamard matrices. For this reason, the Walsh transform is sometimes called the *Hadamard–Walsh transform* (453).

The translation of the properties of Walsh functions is as follows:

1. *Formula (2.3.9)* The scalar product of any two rows of $\mathbf{W}(m)$ is equal to 0.
2. *Formula (2.3.10)* The sum of elements of any row except the first is equal to zero.
3. *Formula (2.3.13)* $\mathbf{W}(m)$ is a symmetric matrix.
4. *Formula (2.3.14)* The element-by-element product of the zth and rth rows (columns) of $\mathbf{W}(m)$ is its $(z \oplus i)$th row (column), modulo 2.

If we express the Walsh spectrum S_f and the original function $\Phi(z)$ as vectors, $\mathbf{S} = [S(0), \ldots, S(2^m - 1)]^T$ and $\Phi = [\Phi(0), \ldots, \Phi(2^m - 1)]^T$, then, as is evident from (2.3.12), that

$$
\mathbf{S} = 2^{-m}\mathbf{W}(m)\Phi. \tag{3.1.2}
$$

For example, for the system of Boolean functions defined by Table 1.2.5 (Example 1.2.2), we have

$$\mathbf{S} = 2^{-3}\mathbf{W}(3) \begin{bmatrix} 0 \\ 2 \\ 2 \\ 1 \\ 2 \\ 1 \\ 1 \\ 3 \end{bmatrix} = \begin{bmatrix} 1.5 \\ -0.25 \\ -0.25 \\ 0.00 \\ -0.25 \\ 0.00 \\ 0.00 \\ -0.75 \end{bmatrix}.$$

It is clear from (3.1.2) that we could have defined the Walsh functions in terms of Hadamard matrices $\mathbf{W}(m)$, without taking trouble to complete the functions $f(z)$ and $W_w(z)$ to step functions. Nevertheless, our procedure is technically very convenient, since it allows us to utilize the classical theory of orthogonal series (see Section 6.4). Calculation of the Walsh spectrum by Hadamard matrices requires 2^{2m} operations of addition or subtraction for a function of m variables (2^m operations per coefficient). We now describe a matrix method for calculating the Walsh spectrum that requires only $m2^m$ operations. It is the matrix analog of Theorem 3.1.1 and defines the so-called *fast Hadamard–Walsh transform* (453).

3.1.1 Matrix Interpretation of the Fast Walsh Transform

Let

$$\mathbf{A}_m = \begin{bmatrix} 1 & 1 & 0 & 0 & 0 & \cdots & 0 & 0 & 0 \\ 0 & 0 & 1 & 1 & 0 & \cdots & 0 & 0 & 0 \\ & \vdots & & & & & & & \\ 0 & 0 & 0 & 0 & 0 & \cdots & 0 & 1 & 1 \\ 1 & -1 & 0 & 0 & 0 & \cdots & 0 & 0 & 0 \\ 0 & 0 & 1 & -1 & 0 & \cdots & 0 & 0 & 0 \\ & \vdots & & & & & & & \\ 0 & 0 & 0 & 0 & 0 & \cdots & 0 & 1 & -1 \end{bmatrix}.$$

Then by Theorem 3.1.1,

$$\mathbf{W}(m) = (\mathbf{A}_m)^m. \tag{3.1.3}$$

Together with (3.1.2), the formula (3.1.3) provides us with a matrix method of calculating the Walsh spectrum, involving m iterated multiplications of the vector Φ by the matrix $\mathbf{A}_m$, each multiplication requiring just 2^m operations of addition or subtraction, so that the total number of operations is $m2^m$, or m additions or subtractions to compute a single Walsh coefficient.

Example 3.1.1 *For $m = 3$, it follows*

$$\mathbf{W}(3) = (\mathbf{A}_3)^3,$$

where

$$\mathbf{A}_3 = \begin{bmatrix} 1 & 1 & 0 & 0 & 0 & 0 & 0 & 0 \\ 0 & 0 & 1 & 1 & 0 & 0 & 0 & 0 \\ 0 & 0 & 0 & 0 & 1 & 1 & 0 & 0 \\ 0 & 0 & 0 & 0 & 0 & 0 & 1 & 1 \\ 1 & -1 & 0 & 0 & 0 & 0 & 0 & 0 \\ 0 & 0 & 1 & -1 & 0 & 0 & 0 & 0 \\ 0 & 0 & 0 & 0 & 1 & -1 & 0 & 0 \\ 0 & 0 & 0 & 0 & 0 & 0 & 1 & -1 \end{bmatrix}.$$

Figure 3.1.1 shows the flow-graph of the algorithm derived from this factorization of the Walsh matrix. In this figure, and hereafter, solid and dotted lines denote addition and subtraction, respectively. If there are numbers at the edges, they denote the multiplicative coefficients. The absence of these coefficients means multiplication by 1.

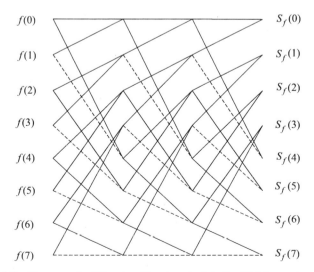

FIGURE 3.1.1   Flow-graph of the algorithm to calculate the Walsh spectrum for $m = 3$.

The representation of the Hadamard matrix $\mathbf{W}(m)$ defined by the above formula is known as matrix factorization. It can be shown that the fast Hadamard–Walsh transform defined by (3.1.3) computes the Walsh spectrum with the minimum number of addition or subtraction operations (36, 453), since this algorithm is a particular case of the fast algorithms to calculate the Fourier transform on finite groups that have this property of requiring the minimum number of arithmetic operations.

To end this section, we present another m-recursive construction of the Hadamard matrix $\mathbf{W}(m)$. It is based on the factorization (3.1.3) and described by

$$\mathbf{W}(m) = \begin{bmatrix} \mathbf{W}(m-1) & \mathbf{W}(m-1) \\ \mathbf{W}(m-1) & -\mathbf{W}(m-1) \end{bmatrix}. \tag{3.1.4}$$

The recursive procedure defined by (3.1.4) for the calculation of the spectrum is essentially the same as the fast Hadamard–Walsh transform.

Repeated application of this recursive relation permits to write the Walsh matrix $\mathbf{W}(m)$ in terms of the mth Kronecker power of the basic Walsh matrices

$$\mathbf{W}(1) = \begin{bmatrix} 1 & 1 \\ 1 & -1 \end{bmatrix}.$$

Thus,

$$\mathbf{W}(m) = \bigotimes_{i=1}^{m} \mathbf{W}(1), \tag{3.1.5}$$

where $\otimes$ denotes the Kronecker product.

Because of the properties of the Kronecker product, it follows the so-called Good–Thomas factorization of the Walsh matrix; see References 567, and 584,

$$\mathbf{W}(m) = \prod_{k=0}^{m-1} \mathbf{C}_k(m), \tag{3.1.6}$$

where

$$\mathbf{C}_k(m) = (\mathbf{I}_{m-k-1} \otimes \mathbf{W}(1) \otimes \mathbf{I}_k),$$

where $\mathbf{I}_j$ is the $(2^j \times 2^j)$ identity matrix.

Example 3.1.2 *For $m = 3$, the Walsh matrix can be represented as the product of three sparse matrices,*

$$\mathbf{W}(3) = \mathbf{C}_1(3)\mathbf{C}_2(3)\mathbf{C}_3(3),$$

where

$$\mathbf{C}_1(3) = \begin{bmatrix} \mathbf{W}(1) & & & \mathbf{0} \\ & \mathbf{W}(1) & & \\ & & \mathbf{W}(1) & \\ \mathbf{0} & & & \mathbf{W}(1) \end{bmatrix},$$

$$\mathbf{C}_2(3) = \begin{bmatrix} \mathbf{I}_2 & \mathbf{I}_2 & & \mathbf{0} \\ \mathbf{I}_2 & -\mathbf{I}_2 & & \\ & & \mathbf{I}_2 & \mathbf{I}_2 \\ \mathbf{0} & & \mathbf{I}_2 & -\mathbf{I}_2 \end{bmatrix},$$

$$\mathbf{C}_3(3) = \begin{bmatrix} \mathbf{I}_4 & \mathbf{I}_4 \\ \mathbf{I}_4 & -\mathbf{I}_4 \end{bmatrix}.$$

Figure 3.1.2 shows the flow-graph of the algorithm derived from this factorization of the Walsh matrix.

Notice that the above factorization is a particular case of a more general Good factorization for Kronecker product representable matrices where it is assumed that the transform length N is a composite number with relatively prime factors, see Reference 587. In this case, a matrix

$$\mathbf{M} = \mathbf{M}^{(1)} \otimes \mathbf{M}^{(2)} \otimes \cdots \otimes \mathbf{M}^{(r)}$$

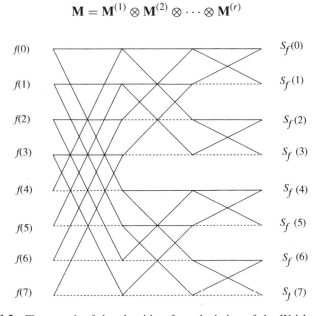

FIGURE 3.1.2 Flow-graph of the algorithm for calculation of the Walsh spectrum with Good–Thomas factorization for $m = 3$.

with entries

$$m_{k,n} = \prod_{s=1}^{r} m_{k_s,n_s}^{(s)},$$

where

$$M^{(s)} = (m_{i,j}^{(s)}),$$

for $i = 0, 1, \ldots, p_s - 1$, $j = 0, 1, \ldots, q_s - 1$, can be represented as

$$\mathbf{M} = \mathbf{A}^{(1)} \mathbf{A}^{(2)} \cdots \mathbf{A}^{(r)},$$

where

$$\mathbf{A}^{(s)} = (a_{k,n}^{(s)}),$$

and

$$a_{k,n}^{(s)} = m_{k_1,n_s}^{(s)} \delta(k_2, n_1) \delta(k_3, n_2) \cdots \delta(k_r, n_{r-1}),$$

for $0 \le k_1 < p_s, 0 \le k_2 < p_{s+1}, \ldots, 0 \le k_{r-s+1} < p_r, 0 \le k_{r-s+2} < q_1, \ldots, 0 \le k_r < q_{s-1}$, and $0 \le n_1 < p_{s+1}, 0 \le n_2 < p_{s+2}, \ldots, 0 \le n_{r-s} < p_r, 0 \le n_{r-s+1} < q_1, \ldots, 0 \le n_r < r_r$, and $\delta(i, j)$ is the Kronecker delta function taking value 1 is $i = j$, and 0, otherwise.

This factorization is a basis to derive the matrices $\mathbf{A}_m$ in (3.1.3).

For the particular case of square matrices with $p_s = q_s$, it follows

$$\mathbf{M} = \mathbf{M}^{(1)} \otimes \mathbf{M}^{(2)} \otimes \cdots \otimes \mathbf{M}^{(r)} = \mathbf{C}^{(1)} \mathbf{C}^{(2)} \cdots \mathbf{C}^{(r)},$$

where

$$\mathbf{C}^{(1)} = \mathbf{M}^{(1)} \otimes \mathbf{I}_{r_1} \otimes \cdots \otimes \mathbf{I}_{r_r}$$

$$\mathbf{C}^{(2)} = \mathbf{I}_{r_1} \otimes \mathbf{M}^{(2)} \otimes \cdots \otimes \mathbf{I}_{r_r}$$

$$\vdots$$

$$\mathbf{C}^{(r)} = \mathbf{I}_{r_1} \otimes \mathbf{I}_{r_2} \otimes \cdots \otimes \mathbf{M}^{(r)},$$

where $\mathbf{I}_{r_i}$ is the $(2^{r_i} \times 2^{r_i})$ identity matrix.

For $p_s = q_s = 2$, the above factorization for the Walsh matrix can be derived.

Remark 3.1.1 *Since the basis functions that we consider take the values $\{1, -1\}$ or $\{0, \pm 1\}$, it is sometimes convenient, when calculating the values of systems of switching functions from (2.2.1), to let switching functions take the values 1 and -1 instead*

of 0 *and* 1, *respectively, that is, to replace* $f^{(s)}(z_0, \ldots z_{m-1})$ *by* $\phi^{(s)}(z_0, \ldots, z_{m-1})$
where

$$\phi^{(s)}(z_0, \ldots, z_{m-1}) = 1 - 2f^{(s)}(z_0, \ldots, z_{m-1}).$$

It should be clear that this transformation has no effect on the validity of our results.

The encoding $\{0, 1\} \rightarrow \{1, -1\}$ in the case of Walsh representations of switching functions reduces the values of unnormalized spectral coefficients to the set of even numbers between -2^m and 2^m. Notice that not all combinations of numbers in this set can be the Walsh spectrum of a switching function, and this property has been used in characterization of particular classes of switching functions (255,258).

3.1.2 Decision Diagram Methods for Calculation of Spectral Transforms

The main disadvantage of FFT-like algorithms in application in switching theory is that calculations in FFT are performed over vectors specifying function values and intermediate results of calculations. In the case of switching functions often met in nowadays practice, the number of variables is large, even huge, and truth vectors of order 2^m, m—number of variables, are larger than it can be efficiently processed. That restricts application of FFT-like algorithms to functions of a relatively small number of variables. Therefore, alternative representations for switching functions have to be used.

FFT-like algorithms do not take into consideration particular properties that a function whose spectral transform is required may have. Decision Trees (DTs) are alternative descriptions of truth vectors. When a function has a regularity in the truth vector, due to such properties as symmetry, decomposability, and so on, decision trees can be reduced into Decision Diagrams (DDs), which are data structures that are used to represent large functions efficiently in terms of space and time. Decision trees are reduced into decision diagrams, thanks to such properties in f that are not taken into account in FFT-like algorithms. Therefore, alternative procedures for calculation of spectral transforms through decision diagrams permit processing of functions with a large number of variables on standard computer architectures; this will be briefly discussed in the next section. More information about that topic can be found in References 499, 550, 555, and 576.

Relationships between FFT and decision diagram methods

As we have seen from the previous sections, for a given function f defined on C_2^m, the spectrum with respect to a transform with Kronecker product representable transform matrix is calculated in m steps. Each step performs the transform with respect to a variable in f. The operations at the ith step are determined by the submatrix $\mathbf{K}_i(1)$, for $i = 1, \ldots, m$. In Multiterminal Binary Decision Diagrams (MTBDDs) representations, see Section 1.4, such calculation means that the spectrum is calculated through the operations defined by $\mathbf{K}_i(1)$ at each node and cross points at the ith level in the MTBDD. For transforms defined in fields different from $GF(2)$, Binary Decision Diagrams (BDDs) are considered as MTBDDs with two constant nodes showing logic values 0 and 1. It is assumed that the logic values 0 and 1 for constant nodes in BDDs are interpreted as the integers 0 and 1 in MTBDDs.

Calculation of spectral transforms can be represented by decision diagrams. In that way, decision diagrams for the spectra with respect to the considered transforms are derived.

Unlike FFT, BDDs-based calculation architectures are different for each particular function f in the same way as BDDs for different functions are different. Thanks to that, the number of processors or arithmetic operations is reduced in comparison to that required to perform FFT. Note that the number of processors is reduced even if the calculation is performed over the Binary Decision Tree (BDT) at the price of processing subfunctions sequentially. As in FFT, calculation is performed in m steps, each corresponding to a level in the BDD, thus, to a variable in f.

Compared to FFT, efficiency of decision diagrams-based calculation methods is obtained due to the following:

1. In BDDs, calculations with identical parts in the vector representing f are not repeated.
2. In BDDs, calculations are performed over subvectors represented by the subtrees in the BDDs. Thus, calculation of the spectrum is done by using vector operations.

Extensions of the method from switching to integer-valued or complex-valued functions is straightforward, thanks to MTBDDs (105) defined as a generalization of BDDs derived by allowing integer or complex numbers as the values of constant nodes. For multiple-output switching functions, calculation of the spectral transforms may be performed over

1. MTBDDs (105),
2. Shared BDDs (SBDDs) (372).

In the first case, it is assumed that a given multiple-output function with k outputs is represented by an integer-valued function derived by adding the outputs multiplied by the weighting coefficients 2^i, $i = 0, \ldots, k - 1$. In SBDDs, we use the fact that the calculated spectral transform is linear. Conversely, thanks to the linearity, the SBDDs may be used for calculation of spectral transforms for integer-valued functions. It is assumed that an integer-valued vector is represented by a multioutput switching function through the binary representations of its elements.

In what follows, we elaborate algorithms for calculation of spectral transforms considered in this monograph through decision diagrams.

3.1.3 Calculation of the Walsh Spectrum Through BDD

In this section, we consider calculation of the Walsh spectrum through BDDs as a particular example of decision diagram methods for spectral transforms. The same method can be extended to the transforms defined by transform matrices, which can be represented as the Kronecker product of some basic transform matrices. The extensions to transforms that are layer by layer Kronecker product representable matrices (663) will be discussed by the example of the Haar transform.

For a switching function f defined by a BDD or a complex-valued function on C_2^m defined by a MTBDD, the Walsh spectrum is calculated by performing operations determined by $\mathbf{W}(1)$ at each node and each cross point. The method will be explained by the following example by using the matrix notation. Note that operations are performed over decision diagrams, and matrix operations are used just for explanation of the method. It is assumed that BDT represent the vector $\mathbf{F}$ of the values for f. Similarly, subtrees in the BDT represent subvectors in $\mathbf{F}$.

Example 3.1.3 *Figure 3.1.3 shows the calculation procedure for the Walsh transform of f represented by the BDD in Fig. 1.4.4. At each node and the cross point in this BDD, we perform the same operations as specified by the basic Walsh matrix*

$$\mathbf{W}(1) = \begin{bmatrix} 1 & 1 \\ 1 & -1 \end{bmatrix},$$

the same as in FFT-like algorithms. In matrix notation, the calculation procedure can be described as follows.

The constant nodes are processed first by performing the matrix $\mathbf{W}(1)$ at the nodes and cross points at the level corresponding to z_2. Therefore, result of calculations in the nodes labeled by $S_{2,0}$, $S_{2,1}$ and the cross point $c_{2,0}$ are

$$\mathbf{W}_{S_{2,0}} = \begin{bmatrix} 1+0 \\ 1-0 \end{bmatrix} = \begin{bmatrix} 1 \\ 1 \end{bmatrix},$$

$$\mathbf{W}_{S_{2,1}} = \begin{bmatrix} 0+1 \\ 0-1 \end{bmatrix} = \begin{bmatrix} 1 \\ -1 \end{bmatrix},$$

$$\mathbf{W}_{c_{2,0}} = \begin{bmatrix} 1+1 \\ 1-1 \end{bmatrix} = \begin{bmatrix} 2 \\ 0 \end{bmatrix}.$$

Performing $\mathbf{W}(1)$ at the nodes at the level corresponding to z_1, that is, over the subvectors that point the outgoing edges of these nodes, we get

$$\mathbf{W}_{S_{1,0}} = \begin{bmatrix} \begin{bmatrix} 1 \\ 1 \end{bmatrix} + \begin{bmatrix} 1 \\ -1 \end{bmatrix} \\ \begin{bmatrix} 1 \\ 1 \end{bmatrix} - \begin{bmatrix} 1 \\ -1 \end{bmatrix} \end{bmatrix} = \begin{bmatrix} 2 \\ 0 \\ 0 \\ 2 \end{bmatrix},$$

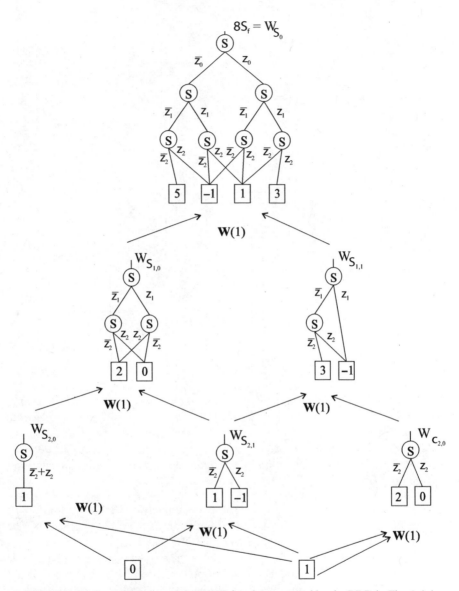

FIGURE 3.1.3   Calculation of the WHT for f represented by the BDD in Fig. 1.4.4.

$$\mathbf{W}_{S_{1,1}} = \left[\begin{array}{c} \left[\begin{array}{c} 1 \\ -1 \end{array} \right] + \left[\begin{array}{c} 2 \\ 0 \end{array} \right] \\ \left[\begin{array}{c} 1 \\ -1 \end{array} \right] - \left[\begin{array}{c} 2 \\ 0 \end{array} \right] \end{array} \right] = \left[\begin{array}{c} 3 \\ -1 \\ -1 \\ -1 \end{array} \right].$$

Performing $\mathbf{W}(1)$ *at the root node, we get the Walsh spectrum of f up to the normalization factor* 2^3 *as follows:*

$$8\mathbf{S}_f(w) = \mathbf{W}_{S_0} = \left[\begin{array}{c} \left[\begin{array}{c} 2 \\ 0 \\ 0 \\ 2 \end{array} \right] + \left[\begin{array}{c} 3 \\ -1 \\ -1 \\ -1 \end{array} \right] \\ \left[\begin{array}{c} 2 \\ 0 \\ 0 \\ 2 \end{array} \right] - \left[\begin{array}{c} 3 \\ -1 \\ -1 \\ -1 \end{array} \right] \end{array} \right] = \left[\begin{array}{c} 5 \\ -1 \\ -1 \\ 1 \\ -1 \\ 1 \\ 1 \\ 3 \end{array} \right].$$

Thus, described calculation procedure can be represented through BDDs as it is shown in Fig. 3.1.3. In this figure, the label $\bar{z}_2 + z_2$ *means that both outcoming edges point to the same constant node. It is suitable for coding in a programming language. In this respect, a notation introduced in Reference 576 for description of decision diagrams by taking into account their hierarchical and recursive structure appears very convenient.*

Table 3.1.2 taken from Reference 576 shows complexity of SBDDs for some *mcnc* benchmark functions and CPU-times for calculation of the Walsh transform. The number of inputs (In), outputs (Out), size of SBDDs, number of nonterminal nodes (ntn); constant nodes (cn), and the total of nodes (n) are shown. Calculation time is given in milliseconds. Calculations are performed on a 133 MHz Pentium PC with 32 MB of RAM. This confirms that decision diagram methods can be implemented over simple hardware, which extends the range of various applications.

3.2 CALCULATION OF THE HAAR SPECTRUM

3.2.1 FFT-Like Algorithms for the Haar Transform

We now propose an algorithm for calculation of the Haar spectrum and determine its complexity.

TABLE 3.1.2   Calculation of Walsh Transform Through BDDs.

f	In	Out	Cubes	SBDD	Ntn	cn	n	Time, ms
ex1010	10	10	1024	1079	6281	87	6368	530
ex5p	8	63	256	311	1209	82	1291	100
misex3c	14	14	305	847	9199	475	9674	1610
pdc	16	40	2810	705	10264	637	10901	7090
spla	16	16	2307	974	8270	633	8903	5160
sqrt8	8	4	40	42	144	34	178	10
t481	16	1	481	32	184	19	203	280
table3	14	14	175	941	41652	681	42333	3220
5xp1	7	10	75	88	314	49	363	20
9sym	9	1	87	33	39	4	43	10
alu4	14	8	1028	1352	6201	139	6340	1590
apex4	9	19	438	1021	4800	117	4917	370
bw	5	28	87	114	307	26	333	10
misex2	25	18	29	140	999	30	1029	140
duke2	22	29	87	946	6330	524	6854	2560
sao2	10	4	58	154	465	34	499	30

Theorem 3.2.1   (36) *Let $\Phi(z)$ be a step function representing a system of switching functions of m variables and $S_l^{(q)}$, $l = 0, 1, \ldots, m - 1$, $q = 1, 2, \ldots, 2^l$ its Haar coefficients. Set*

$$a_0(t) = \Phi(t), \qquad\qquad\qquad t = 0, 1, \ldots, 2^m - 1,$$
$$a_s(t) = a_{s-1}(2t) + a_{s-1}(2t + 1), \qquad t = 0, 1, \ldots, 2^{m-s} - 1,$$
$$a_s(2^{m-s} + t) = a_{s-1}(2t) - a_{s-1}(2t + 1), \quad s = 1, 2, \ldots, m.$$

Then,

$$c_{m-s}^{(q)} = 2^{-s} a_s(2^{m-s} - 1 + q). \tag{3.2.1}$$

Theorem 3.2.1 yields a simple algorithm calculating the Haar spectrum in sequency ordering (2.3.19) by s-recursive construction of the sequence $a_s(t)$, $s = 1, 2, \ldots, m$, $t = 0, 1, \ldots, 2^{m-s+1}$. It is apparent from a comparison of Theorems 3.1.1 and 3.2.1 that the Walsh and Haar spectra may be calculated simultaneously using the sequence $a_s(t)$.

The number of addition or subtraction operations required by this algorithm to calculate the 2^m coefficients of the Haar series is $2 \cdot 2^m - 2$. It can be shown that this is the minimum complexity for an algorithm computing the Haar spectrum.

Example 3.2.1   *Consider the system of switching functions defined by Table 1.2.5. The computation of the Haar spectrum is shown in Table 3.2.1, where $c_{m-s}^{(q)} = c(t)$ for $t = 2^{m-s} - 1 + q$. (Note that for given m, the values of s and q are uniquely determined for each t, in view of the fact that $q \in \{1, 2, \ldots, 2^{m-s}\}$, where $s \in \{1, 2, \ldots, m\}$.)*

TABLE 3.2.1 Calculation of the Haar Spectrum.

z, t	$\Phi(z)$	$a_1(t)$	$a_2(t)$	$a_3(t)$	$S_f(t)$
0	0	2	5	12	1.5
1	2	3	7	-2	-0.25
2	2	3	-1	$-$	-0.25
3	1	4	-1	$-$	-0.25
4	2	-2	$-$	$-$	-1.00
5	1	1	$-$	$-$	0.50
6	1	1	$-$	$-$	0.50
7	3	-2	$-$	$-$	-1.00

The Haar expansion of the system considered is

$$\Phi(z) = \frac{3}{2} - \frac{1}{4}H_0^{(1)}(z) - \frac{1}{4}H_1^{(1)}(z) - \frac{1}{4}H_1^{(2)}(z)$$

$$- H_2^{(1)}(z) + \frac{1}{2}H_2^{(2)}(z) + \frac{1}{2}H_2^{(3)}(z) - H_2^{(4)}(z).$$

There is an interesting relationship between the Haar functions and the Rademacher functions $R_s(z)$, $s = 1, 2, \ldots, m$. By (2.3.7) and (3.1.4), we have

$$H_l^{(q)}(z) = \begin{cases} R_{l+1}(z), & \text{if } z \in [(q-1)2^{m-l}, q2^{m-l}), \\ 0, & \text{otherwise.} \end{cases} \tag{3.2.2}$$

In view of this formula, it is fairly easy to calculate a Haar function $H_l^{(q)}(z)$ given the binary representation of its variable $(z_0, \ldots, z_{m-1})$, since (except for notation) the value of the Rademacher function $R_{l+1}(z)$ is the lth coordinate z_l in the binary representation of z (see Section 2.3.2).

Unlike the Walsh system, the Haar system is not closed under multiplication, since the product of two Haar functions need not be a Haar function. However, the Haar basis possesses a highly important advantage over the Walsh basis as regards computation of $\Phi(z)$ by serial summation of the terms of the series. This can be concluded from the following theorem.

Theorem 3.2.2 *Let $\Phi(z)$ be a step function representing a system of switching functions of m variables. Then, for any fixed $z = z^*$, $(z^* \in \{0, 1, \ldots, 2^m - 1\})$ the number of nonzero terms of the series (2.3.21) is at most $m + 1$.*

Proof. To prove Theorem 3.2.2, notice that for any fixed $z^* \in [0, 2^m)$ there are exactly $m + 1$ distinct pairs (q, l) such that $z^* \in [(q-1)2^{m-l}, q \cdot 2^{m-l})$. The assertion now follows in view of (3.2.2).

Note that the number of nonzero terms depends on the choice of z^*. For example, for $m = 3$, $z^* = 5$, we have

$$\Phi(z^*) = \Phi(5) = c_0^{(0)} - c_0^{(1)} + c_1^{(2)} - c_2^{(3)},$$

since $H_1^{(1)}(5) = H_2^{(1)}(5) = H_2^{(2)}(5) = H_2^{(4)}(5) = 0$ (see Fig. 2.3.9).

Thus, for any fixed $z = z^*$, we can express $\Phi(z^*)$ as an algebraic sum of coefficients $c_l^{(q)}$, containing exactly one coefficient with each subscript $l \neq 0$ and two with the subscript $l = 0$.

To end this section, we reemphasize the three most important features of the Walsh and Haar bases, thanks to which they find a wide application in analysis and synthesis of networks realizing systems of switching functions.

1. The expansion of any step function representing a system of Boolean functions of m variables contains at most 2^m nonzero terms.
2. The basis functions assume the values ± 1 or $0, \pm 1$.
3. The values of any basis function are calculated easily from the binary code of its variable, the calculation involving at most m elementary operations over single-digit binary numbers.

3.2.2 Matrix Interpretation of the Fast Haar Transform

Notice that unlike the Walsh matrix, the Haar matrix is not symmetric, which makes a difference in the study of fast Haar algorithms compared to the corresponding algorithms for the Walsh transform. More precisely, due to the orthogonality and symmetry, the Walsh matrix is a self-inverse matrix up to the constant 2^m. It follows that the same algorithm can be used to calculate both the direct and the inverse Walsh transform, and the difference between these two is in the multiplication by the scaling factor 2^m.

In dealing with fast calculation algorithms for the Haar transform, we study algorithms for the direct transform to calculate the Haar coefficients and the inverse Haar transform to reconstruct the signal, that is, a function representing the system of switching functions, from the spectrum. In such calculations, we use the property that, since the Haar matrix is real-valued, due to the orthogonality, the inverse Haar matrix is the transposed Haar matrix up to the normalization factors, which, however, in numerical computations can be assigned to either direct or the inverse transform matrix, or split between these two matrices equally.

The following example illustrates matrix calculations of Haar coefficients.

Example 3.2.2   *For the function f in Example 3.2.1, the normalized Haar coefficients written as a vector $\mathbf{C} = [c(0), c(1), c(2), c(3), c(4), c(5), c(6), c(7)]^T$, can be* *calculated in matrix notation as*

$$
\mathbf{C} = \frac{1}{8}
\begin{bmatrix}
1 & 1 & 1 & 1 & 1 & 1 & 1 & 1 \\
1 & 1 & 1 & 1 & -1 & -1 & -1 & -1 \\
2 & 2 & -2 & -2 & 0 & 0 & 0 & 0 \\
0 & 0 & 0 & 0 & 2 & 2 & -2 & -2 \\
4 & -4 & 0 & 0 & 0 & 0 & 0 & 0 \\
0 & 0 & 4 & -4 & 0 & 0 & 0 & 0 \\
0 & 0 & 0 & 0 & 4 & -4 & 0 & 0 \\
0 & 0 & 0 & 0 & 0 & 0 & 4 & -4
\end{bmatrix}
\begin{bmatrix}
0 \\ 2 \\ 2 \\ 1 \\ 2 \\ 1 \\ 1 \\ 3
\end{bmatrix}
=
\begin{bmatrix}
1.50 \\ -0.25 \\ -0.25 \\ -0.25 \\ -1.00 \\ 0.50 \\ 0.50 \\ -1.00
\end{bmatrix}.
$$

From this Haar spectrum, the vector of function values $\mathbf{F}$ *is reconstructed as*

$$
\mathbf{F} =
\begin{bmatrix}
1 & 1 & 1 & 0 & 1 & 0 & 0 & 0 \\
1 & 1 & 1 & 0 & -1 & 0 & 0 & 0 \\
1 & 1 & -1 & 0 & 0 & 1 & 0 & 0 \\
1 & 1 & -1 & 0 & 0 & -1 & 0 & 0 \\
1 & -1 & 0 & 1 & 0 & 0 & 1 & 0 \\
1 & -1 & 0 & 1 & 0 & 0 & -1 & 0 \\
1 & -1 & 0 & -1 & 0 & 0 & 0 & 1 \\
1 & -1 & 0 & -1 & 0 & 0 & 0 & -1
\end{bmatrix}
\begin{bmatrix}
1.50 \\ -0.25 \\ -0.25 \\ -0.25 \\ -1.00 \\ 0.50 \\ 0.50 \\ -1.00
\end{bmatrix}
=
\begin{bmatrix}
0 \\ 2 \\ 2 \\ 1 \\ 2 \\ 1 \\ 1 \\ 3
\end{bmatrix}.
$$

The discrete Haar transform is not a Kronecker product representable transform. However, the recursive structure of the Haar matrix in (2.3.19), where the Kronecker product of different submatrices appears in the upper and bottom part of the transform matrix, permits a factorization that allows definition of FFT-like algorithms for the discrete Haar transform.

For instance, the unnormalized Haar transform matrix is defined as

$$
\mathbf{H}(m) =
\begin{bmatrix}
\mathbf{H}(m-1) \otimes \begin{bmatrix} 1 & 1 \end{bmatrix} \\
\mathbf{I}_{2^{m-1}} \quad\quad \otimes \begin{bmatrix} 1 & -1 \end{bmatrix}
\end{bmatrix},
\tag{3.2.3}
$$

where $\mathbf{I}_{2^{m-1}}$ is the $(2^{m-1} \times 2^{m-1})$ identity matrix.

The inverse unnormalized Haar transform is defined as

$$
\mathbf{H}^{-1}(m) =
\begin{bmatrix}
\mathbf{H}^{-1}(m-1) \otimes \begin{bmatrix} 1 \\ 1 \end{bmatrix}, & \mathbf{I}_{2^{m-1}} \otimes \begin{bmatrix} 2^{m-1} \\ -2^{m-1} \end{bmatrix}
\end{bmatrix}.
\tag{3.2.4}
$$

The normalized Haar matrix and its inverse have the same form, and the difference with the unnormalized inverse Haar matrix is in the normalization factors, as will be illustrated below.

In the following examples, we will discuss different factorizations of the Haar matrices that lead to the definition of the corresponding fast algorithms.

Example 3.2.3 *The normalized Haar transform matrix in sequency ordering for* $m = 3$ *can be factorized as Reference 587*

$$\mathbf{H}_s(3) = \mathbf{C}_1(3)\mathbf{C}_2(3)\mathbf{C}_3(3),$$

$$\mathbf{C}_1(3) = \begin{bmatrix} 1 & 1 & 0 & 0 & 0 & 0 & 0 & 0 \\ 1 & -1 & 0 & 0 & 0 & 0 & 0 & 0 \\ 0 & 0 & \sqrt{2} & 0 & 0 & 0 & 0 & 0 \\ 0 & 0 & 0 & \sqrt{2} & 0 & 0 & 0 & 0 \\ 0 & 0 & 0 & 0 & \sqrt{2} & 0 & 0 & 0 \\ 0 & 0 & 0 & 0 & 0 & \sqrt{2} & 0 & 0 \\ 0 & 0 & 0 & 0 & 0 & 0 & \sqrt{2} & 0 \\ 0 & 0 & 0 & 0 & 0 & 0 & 0 & \sqrt{2} \end{bmatrix},$$

$$\mathbf{C}_2(3) = \begin{bmatrix} 1 & 1 & 0 & 0 & 0 & 0 & 0 & 0 \\ 0 & 0 & 1 & 1 & 0 & 0 & 0 & 0 \\ 1 & -1 & 0 & 0 & 0 & 0 & 0 & 0 \\ 0 & 0 & 1 & -1 & 0 & 0 & 0 & 0 \\ 0 & 0 & 0 & 0 & \sqrt{2} & 0 & 0 & 0 \\ 0 & 0 & 0 & 0 & 0 & \sqrt{2} & 0 & 0 \\ 0 & 0 & 0 & 0 & 0 & 0 & \sqrt{2} & 0 \\ 0 & 0 & 0 & 0 & 0 & 0 & 0 & \sqrt{2} \end{bmatrix},$$

$$\mathbf{C}_3(3) = \begin{bmatrix} 1 & 1 & 0 & 0 & 0 & 0 & 0 & 0 \\ 0 & 0 & 1 & 1 & 0 & 0 & 0 & 0 \\ 0 & 0 & 0 & 0 & 1 & 1 & 0 & 0 \\ 0 & 0 & 0 & 0 & 0 & 0 & 1 & 1 \\ 1 & -1 & 0 & 0 & 0 & 0 & 0 & 0 \\ 0 & 0 & 1 & -1 & 0 & 0 & 0 & 0 \\ 0 & 0 & 0 & 0 & 1 & -1 & 0 & 0 \\ 0 & 0 & 0 & 0 & 0 & 0 & 1 & -1 \end{bmatrix}.$$

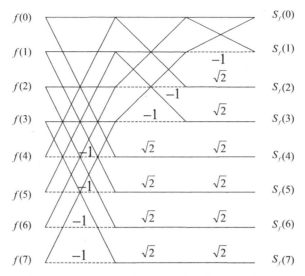

FIGURE 3.2.1   Cooley-Tukey fast Haar transform.

Figure 3.2.1 shows FFT-like algorithm for the discrete Haar transform for m = 3 based on this factorization of the Haar transform matrix. Figure 3.2.2 shows the flow-graph of the fast algorithm for the corresponding inverse Haar transform.

Notice that calculations in Example 3.2.2 can be performed by using the algorithms in these figures, however, with multiplicative factors corresponding to the

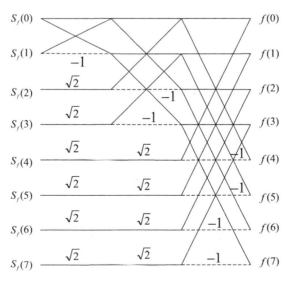

FIGURE 3.2.2   Flow-graph of the Cooley-Tukey fast inverse Haar transform.

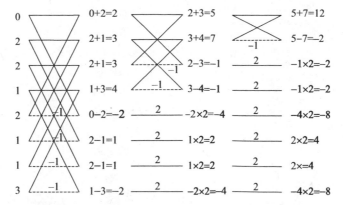

FIGURE 3.2.3   Calculation of the Haar spectrum in Example 3.2.1.

unnormalized Haar transform calculated in this example. Figure 3.2.3 illustrates the calculations of the Haar spectrum for the function f in Example 3.2.1 by using the fast algorithm. It should be noticed that the interim results after each step are equal to these in Table 3.2.1.

The Haar spectrum in natural ordering is derived from the Haar spectrum in sequency ordering by reordering of spectral coefficients (16, 52, 258, 671).

A factorization similar to that for Walsh functions in terms of the matrix A_m (see 3.1.3) yields the algorithm for the Haar transform similar to that in Fig. 3.1.1.

Example 3.2.4   *For m = 3, the Haar matrix in sequency ordering can be factorized as*

$$H_s(3) = C_1(3)C_2(3)C_3(3),$$

where

$$
C_1(3) = \begin{bmatrix}
1 & 1 & 0 & 0 & 0 & 0 & 0 & 0 \\
0 & 0 & 1 & 1 & 0 & 0 & 0 & 0 \\
0 & 0 & 0 & 0 & 1 & 1 & 0 & 0 \\
0 & 0 & 0 & 0 & 0 & 0 & 1 & 1 \\
1 & -1 & 0 & 0 & 0 & 0 & 0 & 0 \\
0 & 0 & 1 & -1 & 0 & 0 & 0 & 0 \\
0 & 0 & 0 & 0 & 1 & -1 & 0 & 0 \\
0 & 0 & 0 & 0 & 0 & 0 & 1 & -1
\end{bmatrix},
$$

$$\mathbf{C_2(3)} = \begin{bmatrix} 1 & 1 & 0 & 0 & 0 & 0 & 0 & 0 \\ 0 & 0 & 1 & 1 & 0 & 0 & 0 & 0 \\ 0 & 0 & 0 & 0 & 1 & -1 & 0 & 0 \\ 0 & 0 & 0 & 0 & 0 & 0 & 1 & -1 \\ 0 & 0 & 0 & 0 & 2 & 0 & 0 & 0 \\ 0 & 0 & 0 & 0 & 0 & 2 & 0 & 0 \\ 0 & 0 & 0 & 0 & 0 & 0 & 2 & 0 \\ 0 & 0 & 0 & 0 & 0 & 0 & 0 & 2 \end{bmatrix},$$

$$\mathbf{C_3(3)} = \begin{bmatrix} 1 & 1 & 0 & 0 & 0 & 0 & 0 & 0 \\ 1 & -1 & 0 & 0 & 0 & 0 & 0 & 0 \\ 0 & 0 & \sqrt{2} & 0 & 0 & 0 & 0 & 0 \\ 0 & 0 & 0 & \sqrt{2} & 0 & 0 & 0 & 0 \\ 0 & 0 & 0 & 0 & 1 & 0 & 0 & 0 \\ 0 & 0 & 0 & 0 & 0 & 1 & 0 & 0 \\ 0 & 0 & 0 & 0 & 0 & 0 & 1 & 0 \\ 0 & 0 & 0 & 0 & 0 & 0 & 0 & 1 \end{bmatrix}.$$

In this factorization, the scaling factor $1/8$ *is not shown, and should be performed after the calculations are done.*

Example 3.2.5 *Figure 3.2.4 shows the flow-graph of the algorithm derived from this factorization of the Haar matrix. This algorithm belongs to the class of FFT-like algorithms with constant geometry, see Reference 16. Figure 3.2.5 shows the flow-graph for the inverse Haar transform for the algorithm with constant geometry.*

3.2.3 Calculation of the Haar Spectrum Through BDD

As it was mentioned above, the Haar matrix has a recursive structure expressed by the Kronecker product over some submatrices within the Haar matrix, as it can be seen from (3.2.3) and (3.2.4). Owing to that, a procedure for calculation of the Haar spectra through BDDs can be formulated in a similar way as in the transforms with Kronecker product representable transform matrices. The difference is that in this case, processing of different nodes is done by using different rules as determined in the above-mentioned relations defining the direct and inverse Haar transform matrices.

Several methods to calculate the discrete Haar transform through BDDs have been presented in References 83, 102, 158, 228, and 600. Moreover, the number and distribution of nonzero elements in the Haar matrix allow some further savings in calculation of the Haar transform through BDDs for switching and MTBDDs for integer or complex-valued functions on C_2^m (536). The method presented in Section 3.2.3 has been introduced in References 536 and 537.

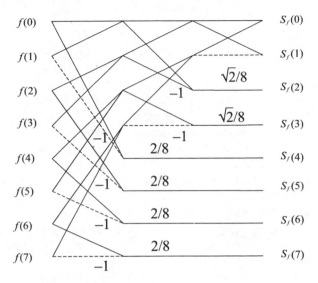

FIGURE 3.2.4   Fast Haar transform for $m = 3$.

As in other spectral transforms, we perform some calculations at each node and the cross point in the decision diagram for f. Calculations are performed over subvectors represented by subtrees rooted at the nodes that point the outgoing edges of the processed node. In *Kronecker spectral transforms*, that is, transforms with transform matrices that can be represented by the Kronecker product of transform matrices of smaller order (555), calculations at the nodes are determined by the basic transform matrices. For the Haar transform, calculations are determined by a rule derived from

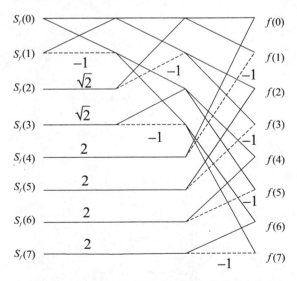

FIGURE 3.2.5   Fast inverse Haar transform for $m = 3$.

the definition of the Haar transform matrix. The method will be explained in the matrix notation.

Decision diagram methods for calculation of spectral transforms perform basic operations used in FFT and the related algorithm over decision diagrams instead of vectors used to represent the functions processed (559). These operations can be expressed as suitably defined matrix operators. In the case of Haar transform, further simplification of the algorithm can be derived by taking advantages of properties of the transform matrix, resulting in the structure of fast algorithms as in Figs. 3.2.1, 3.2.4, and 3.2.5. Except the first step for the direct transforms and the last step of the algorithms for the inverse transforms, in all other steps in these figures, calculations are performed over subsets of values that are inputs for the considered steps. This property is due to the regular structure and distribution of zero entries in the Haar transform matrices, both direct and inverse. That simplification of the fast algorithm for the Haar coefficients, compared for instance to the corresponding algorithms for the Walsh transform, can also be exploited in calculations of Haar coefficients over decision diagrams, as will be explained below.

In calculation of the Haar spectra over decision diagrams, the Haar coefficients are assigned to nonterminal nodes of the BDD representing the function whose spectrum is to be calculated. For a function f defined by a decision diagram, the procedure computes all the Haar coefficients for the natural ordering discussed in Section 2.3.3.2. It is possible to read the Haar spectrum in different orderings, by changing the way of traversing the decision diagram for f, that is, by visiting nonterminal nodes in the order corresponding to the required ordering of Haar coefficients. This can be preformed by using commonly known procedures for traversing decision diagrams widely used in the area of data representations and data structures. Therefore, in calculations over vectors, when Haar spectrum is calculated for a specified ordering, the spectrum in different ordering is determined by performing the corresponding permutation procedure. In calculation of spectra over decision diagrams, we change the way of traversing the decision diagram and read the coefficients for the required ordering.

For the description of the algorithm for calculation of Haar coefficients over decision diagrams, we need the following definition for matrix calculations and the generalized notion of decision trees and diagrams defined with respect to different spectral transforms, the *Spectral Transform Decision Trees* (STDTs) and the corresponding *Spectral Transform Decision Diagrams* (STDDs) (555).

Definition 3.2.1 *In the space $P(C_p)$, consider a $(p \times p)$ matrix $Q_p = [q_{i,j}]$, $i, j = 0, \ldots, p - 1$. For p vectors of the lengths z, that is, having z elements, $\mathbf{Y}_0, \ldots, \mathbf{Y}_{p-1}$, we define a vector of the length zp as*

$$
\mathbf{Q}_p(\mathbf{Y}_0, \ldots, \mathbf{Y}_{p-1}) =
\begin{bmatrix}
q_{0,0}\mathbf{Y}_0 + \cdots + q_{0,p-1}\mathbf{Y}_{p-1} \\
\vdots \\
q_{p-1,0}\mathbf{Y}_0 + \cdots + q_{p-1,p-1}\mathbf{Y}_{p-1}
\end{bmatrix}.
$$

Definition 3.2.2 *Consider a function f defined in k points, and the decision diagram representation of it. In a STDT for f, see Section 1.4, defined with respect to a basis*

$R = \{r_0, \dots, r_k\}$, *the leftmost nodes are nodes in the path from the root node to the constant node representing the coefficient* $S(0)$. *Thus, these nodes are connected by edges in the path corresponding to the basis function* r_0. *In the case of BDDs, MTBDDs, MDDs, and MTDDs, these are edges denoted by* 0 *in P or the corresponding literal for related variables.*

In a multiterminal binary decision diagram for a function f, MTBDD(f), each nonterminal node is a root node for a subfunction in f. For the node at the ith level, this subfunction is a cofactor of f for a particular assignment of variables $z_0, \dots, z_{i-1}$. In matrix notation, these cofactors are represented by vectors $\mathbf{Y}_0$ and $\mathbf{Y}_1$ of orders 2^{m-i}. In decision diagram methods, at each node calculations are performed over the subfunctions rooted at the nodes pointed by the outgoing edges of the considered node.

It is shown in Reference 537, from a discussion and an analysis of fast algorithms for the Haar transform, that the Haar transform in $C(C_2)$ can be calculated through MTBDT(f) by using the following algorithm.

Algorithm 3.2.1   *(Haar transform through MTBDT)*

1. *Given f by a MTBDT(f).*
2. *At each nonterminal node in MTBDD(f) perform*

$$\mathbf{Q}_2(\delta_0(z)\mathbf{Y}_0, \delta_0(z)\mathbf{Y}_1),$$

where $\delta_k(z)$ *is the Kronecker* δ *function, for* $z \in \{0, \dots, 2^i\}$, *and* $i = \{0, 1, \dots, m-1\}$ *is the number of the level that is processed in the MTBDT, and* $\mathbf{Q}_2 = \mathbf{W}(1)$.

Example 3.2.6   *Figure 3.2.6 shows calculation of the unnormalized Haar spectrum in sequency ordering over MTBDTs for* $m = 3$.

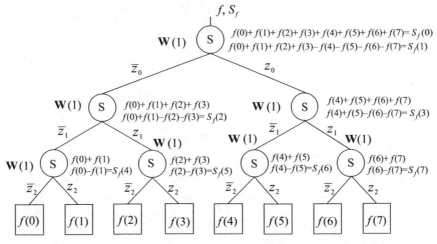

FIGURE 3.2.6   Calculation of the Haar transform for $m = 3$ through MTBDT(f).

Since from the same diagram we can read the function f and its Haar spectrum, the root node is labeled by both f and S_f. If we change the order of visiting nonterminal nodes, we can read the Haar spectrum in natural ordering.

The result of calculation at each node is stored in two fields assigned to each nonterminal node. The first field is used in further calculations, and the other field shows a particular Haar coefficient. Therefore, the MTBDD for f at the same time represent the Haar spectrum S_f of f. In a similar way, it follows that the calculation of the inverse Haar transform can be performed by using the following algorithm.

Algorithm 3.2.2 *(Inverse Haar transform through MTBDT)*

1. *Given f by a MTBDT(f).*
2. *At each non-terminal node in MTBDD(f) perform*

$$\mathbf{Q}_2(\mathbf{Y}_0, \mathbf{Y}_1),$$

where $\mathbf{Q}_2 = \mathbf{W}(1)$ for the leftmost nodes, and $\mathbf{Q}_2 = \mathbf{I}_2$ for the other nodes.

Example 3.2.7 *Figure 3.2.7 shows calculation of the unnormalized inverse Haar transform in sequence ordering over MTBDTs for $m = 3$.*

The same algorithms can be performed over MTBDDs, because the reduction of nodes does not destroy or diminish the information content in MTBDTs. In this case

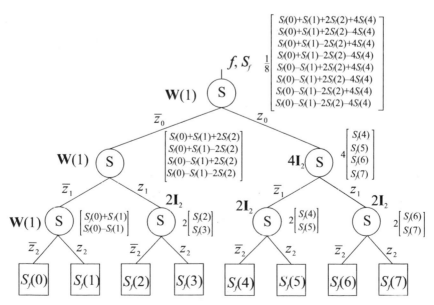

FIGURE 3.2.7 Calculation of the inverse Haar transform through MTBDT(S_f).

the impact of deleted nodes is taken into account through the cross points (569), as in other decision diagram algorithms.

Calculation procedure for the Haar spectrum through MTBDD

It follows from the properties of the Haar transform matrix that calculation over subvectors represented by subdiagrams in a decision diagram can be reduced to the processing of their first elements. In this way, a fast calculation procedure for the Haar spectrum over decision diagrams has been proposed in References 536 and 537. This procedure will be explained as follows, by using the Haar matrix in natural ordering as the direct transform matrix. Notice that both normalized and unnormalized Haar spectra can be calculated in the same way, by paying attention to the normalization factors. Since the results of all calculations are represented by decision diagrams, the Haar spectra for different ordering of the Haar functions can be read by changing the way of traversing the diagram. Moreover, the method does not require construction of a separate diagram for the Haar spectrum. Owing to the properties of the Haar matrix, resulting in the characteristic structure of the corresponding FFT-like algorithms (see Figs. 3.2.1–3.2.5), all the calculations can be performed over the decision diagram representing the given function f and attached in a file assigned to the nodes of it. In this way, the method does not require more memory than needed to store the decision diagram for the function f.

Denote by $S_{k-1,i}(0)$ and $S_{k-1,i}(1)$ the nodes and cross points such that incoming edges for these nodes and cross points are the outgoing edges of the ith node at the kth level $S_{k,i}$, denoted by $\overline{z}_i$ and z_i. The use of cross points permits to consider all the edges as edges of the length equal to 1. Thus, calculations at the kth level are performed over subvectors represented by the subtrees rooted at the nodes at $k - 1$-th level in the decision diagram.

Denote by $\mathbf{Q}_{S_{k,i}} = [q(0), \ldots, q(2^{m-k} - 1)]^T$ the subvector of the length 2^{m-k} represented by the subtree rooted at the node $S_{k,i}$. Furthermore, denote by $\mathbf{Q}_{S_{k+1,i}(0)} = [q_0(0), \ldots, q_0(2^{m-(k+1)} - 1)]^T$ the vector represented by the subtree rooted in $S_{k+1,i}(0)$. Similar, $\mathbf{Q}_{S_{k+1,i}(1)} = [q_1(0), \ldots, q_1(2^{m-(k+1)} - 1)]^T$ is the subvector rooted in $S_{k+1,i}(1)$.

For a simpler explanation, we introduce two auxiliary vectors.

Denote by $\mathbf{Z}_{S_{k+1,i}(0)} = [z_0(0), \ldots, z_0(2^{m-(k+1)} - 1)]^T$, where

$$
z_0(i) = \begin{cases} q_0(0) + q_1(0), & i = 0, \\ q_0(i), & i = 1, \ldots, 2^{m-(k+1)} - 1. \end{cases}
$$

Similarly, $\mathbf{Z}_{S_{k+1,i}(1)} = [z_1(0), \ldots, z_1(2^{m-(k+1)} - 1)]^T$, where

$$
z_1(i) = \begin{cases} \sqrt{2^{k-1}}(q_1(0) - q_1(0)), & i = 0, \\ q_1(i), & i = 1, \ldots, 2^{m-(k+1)} - 1. \end{cases}
$$

In this notation, to calculate the Haar spectrum in natural ordering through BDD for f, in each node and the cross point, we perform calculations determined by the rule

$$\mathbf{Q}_{S_{k,i}} = \mathbf{Z}_{S_{k+1,i}(0)} \diamond \mathbf{Z}_{S_{k+1,i}(1)}, \tag{3.2.5}$$

where $\diamond$ denotes concatenation of vectors. For the calculations in this section, we work with vectors written as columns, since this notation directly corresponds to the calculations performed at the nodes level by level over a decision tree, as in Figs. 3.2.6 and 3.2.7.

The method is illustrated by the following example.

Example 3.2.8 *For f discussed in Examples 1.4.2 and 1.4.3, given by the BDD in Fig. 1.4.4, the normalized Haar spectrum is calculated as follows. We first process the nodes to which z_2 is assigned by using the above rule*

$$\mathbf{Q}_{S_{2,0}} = [1 + 0] \diamond [2(1 - 0)] = \begin{bmatrix} 1 \\ 2 \end{bmatrix},$$

$$\mathbf{Q}_{S_{2,1}} = [0 + 1] \diamond [2(0 - 1)] = \begin{bmatrix} 1 \\ -2 \end{bmatrix},$$

$$\mathbf{Q}_{c_{2,0}} = [1 + 1] \diamond [2(1 - 1)] = \begin{bmatrix} 2 \\ 0 \end{bmatrix}.$$

Calculations at the nodes to which z_1 is assigned, produce

$$\mathbf{Q}_{S_{1,0}} = \begin{bmatrix} 1 + 1 \\ 2 \end{bmatrix} \diamond \begin{bmatrix} \sqrt{2}(1 - 1) \\ -2 \end{bmatrix}$$

$$= \begin{bmatrix} 2 \\ 2 \end{bmatrix} \diamond \begin{bmatrix} 0 \\ -2 \end{bmatrix} = \begin{bmatrix} 2 \\ 2 \\ 0 \\ -2 \end{bmatrix},$$

$$\mathbf{Q}_{S_{1,1}} = \begin{bmatrix} 1 + 2 \\ -2 \end{bmatrix} \diamond \begin{bmatrix} \sqrt{2}(1 - 2) \\ 0 \end{bmatrix}$$

$$= \begin{bmatrix} 3 \\ -2 \end{bmatrix} \diamond \begin{bmatrix} -\sqrt{2} \\ 0 \end{bmatrix} = \begin{bmatrix} 3 \\ -2 \\ -\sqrt{2} \\ 0 \end{bmatrix}.$$

Calculation at the root node produces the Haar spectrum for f up to the normalization factor $1/8$ as follows:

$$\mathbf{Q}_{S_0} = 8\mathbf{S}_f = = \begin{bmatrix} 2+3 \\ 2 \\ 0 \\ -2 \end{bmatrix} \diamond \begin{bmatrix} 2-3 \\ -2 \\ -\sqrt{2} \\ 0 \end{bmatrix}$$

$$= [5, 2, 0, -2, -1, -2, -\sqrt{2}, 0]^T.$$

The same spectrum is obtained when the normalized Haar matrix in natural ordering in (2.3.10) is multiplied by the truth-vector $\mathbf{F}$ of the function considered.

Figure 3.2.8 shows the MTBDD for the Haar spectrum thus calculated.

In calculation of other spectral transforms through decision diagrams, the nodes in the BDD for f are transformed into the nodes of BDD (for the Reed–Muller transform) or MTBDD (for other transforms) for the corresponding spectrum for f.

In calculation of the Haar transform, from (3.2.5), we change the value of only the first elements in the subvectors $\mathbf{Z}_{S_{k+1,i}(0)}$ and $\mathbf{Z}_{S_{k+1,i}(1)}$. The other elements remain unchanged. Therefore, we assign to each node in the decision diagram for f two fields denoted as the left and right fields.

In this way, we do not generate a MTBDD for the Haar spectrum of f (537). We determine and write during the calculations the values of spectral coefficients in the fields assigned to the nodes in the decision diagram for f. The left field contains the value that will be used in further calculations. The right field contains the value of a spectral coefficient. The position of this coefficient in the vector representing the Haar spectrum for f is determined by the labels at the edges in the path from the root node to the considered node. From thus modified decision diagram for f, the Haar spectrum is read by using the standard procedure of descending decision diagrams usually denoted in the literature as *in-order procedure* for traversing decision trees. The procedure is especially suitable for traversing binary decision trees, but can be

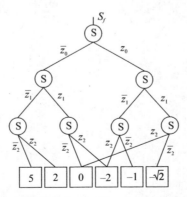

FIGURE 3.2.8   MTBDD for the Haar spectrum in Example 3.2.8.

generalized to arbitrary trees. In an in-order traversal, a node is visited after its left subtree and before its right subtree. Therefore, the procedure consists of the following steps:

1. Descend the left subtree.
2. Visit the root.
3. Descend the right subtree.

The method will be illustrated by the following example.

Example 3.2.9   *Figure 3.2.9 shows the BDD for f in Example 1.4.2 modified to represent the values of Haar coefficients for f. In that order, two fields are assigned to each nonterminal node and used as described above. Thus, in all nonterminal nodes, except the root node, the left field contains value that is used in future calculations, and the right field shows the value of the corresponding Haar spectral coefficient. In the root node, both fields, the right and the left field, show the values of spectral coefficients $S_{h,f}(0)$ and $S_{h,f}(2^{m-1})$. The index h in the coefficients denotes that the coefficients are in sequency ordering, hence it is also called the Haar ordering.*

Figure 3.2.10 explains the application of the in-order procedure to this BDD. In this figure, the gray curve shows the order of visiting nodes as specified by the in-order procedure widely used in data structures.

The coefficients $S_{h,f}(0)$ is in the left field assigned to the root node. Thus, its value is $S_{h,f}(0) = 5$. Then, we descend the left subtree and read the value of $S_{h,f}(1) = 2$.

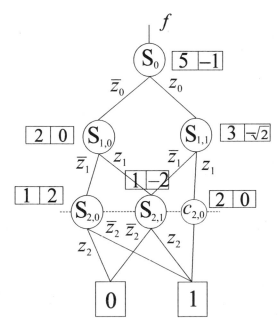

FIGURE 3.2.9   BDD for the Haar spectrum for f in Example 1.4.2.

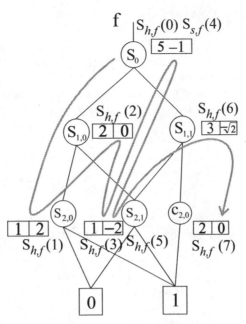

FIGURE 3.2.10   In-order procedure for BDD for f in Example 3.2.9.

We continue by traversing the left subtree, and visit the node showing the coefficient $S_{h,f}(2) = 0$. There after, we traverse the right subtree of the node $S_{1,0}$ and read the co-efficient $S_{h,f}(3) = -2$. This completes the traversal of the left subtree of the node S_0, and therefore, we visit this node and read the value of the coefficient $S_{f,h}(4) = -1$. We continue by traversing the right subtree of the root node, and thus visit the shared node $S_{2,1}$ to read the value of $S_{h,f}(5) = -2$. Since this complete the traversal of the left sub-tree of the node $S_{1,1}$, we visit this node and read $S_{h,f}(6) = -\sqrt{2}$. Finally, we traverse the right subtree and read $S_{h,f}(7) = 0$ in the right field assigned to the cross point $c_{2,0}$.

3.3 CALCULATION OF THE VILENKIN–CHRESTENSON SPECTRUM

We now examine methods for calculating the Vilenkin–Chrestenson transform. As in all other transforms, we consider calculations of the spectrum and reconstruction of the signal from it, that is, performing the direct and the inverse transforms. As in the case of the Walsh transform, due to symmetry and orthogonality of the transform matrix, the direct and the inverse Vilenkin–Chrestenson transform can be calculated by the same algorithm by exploiting the property that the inverse transform matrix is the complex conjugate of the direct transform matrix. This has very convenient implications in practical implementations. For example, in terms of the Vilenkin–Chrestenson matrix $p = 3$, which means permutation of the entries $e_1 = -\frac{1}{2}(1 - i\sqrt{3})$ and $e_2 = -\frac{1}{2}(1 + i\sqrt{3})$, since they are complex conjugate to each other. Thus, by a simple manipulation with indices of matrix entries, the same algorithm can be used to calculate the spectrum and reconstruct function values from it. The scaling factor p^{-m} can be assigned to either direct or inverse transform. In some definitions it is split between them. Notice that besides this factor, different approaches to the definitions of the Vilenkin–Chrestenson transform can be found in the literature. If the Vilenkin–Chrestenson functions are defined as columns of the Vilenkin–Chrestenson matrix, then its inverse is used to calculate the corresponding spectral coefficients, and a given function is expressed as a series in terms of these functions. Alternatively, the Vilenkin–Chrestenson matrix can be used to calculate spectral coefficients, and its inverse to reconstruct the signal from the spectrum. It should be noted that the algorithms defined below can be easily adapted to perform any of these definitions by a simple manipulation with indices of matrix entries as pointed out above.

A natural method to calculate the Vilenkin–Chrestenson transform is provided by formulas (1.2.1) and (2.2.3) for $\Psi_w(z)$.

3.3.1 Matrix Interpretation of the Fast Vilenkin–Chrestenson Transform

We proceed to a different method, generalizing the method of Section 3.1 calculating the Walsh spectrum through Hadamard matrices.

Let $\chi^{(p)}(m)$ be the $(p^m \times p^m)$ matrix whose wth row is the Vilenkin–Chrestenson function of the index w. Thus, the row w of this matrix is $(\chi_w^{(p)}(0), \chi_w^{(p)}(1), \ldots, \chi_w^{(p)}(p^m - 1))$, where $\chi_w^{(p)} = \exp\left(\frac{2\pi i}{p} \sum_{s=0}^{m-1} z_{m-1-s} w_s \right)$, $z = \sum_{s=0}^{m-1} z_s p^{m-1-s}$, $w = \sum_{s=0}^{m-1} w_s p^{m-1-s}$.

Example 3.3.1 *The matrices $\chi_1^{(3)}(m)$ and $\chi_2^{(3)}(m)$, for $m = 1$, $m = 2$, are shown below:*

$$
\chi^{(3)}(1) = \begin{bmatrix} 1 & 1 & 1 \\ 1 & e_1 & e_2 \\ 1 & e_2 & e_1 \end{bmatrix},
$$

$$
\chi^{(3)}(2) = \begin{bmatrix}
1 & 1 & 1 & 1 & 1 & 1 & 1 & 1 & 1 \\
1 & 1 & 1 & e_1 & e_1 & e_1 & e_2 & e_2 & e_2 \\
1 & 1 & 1 & e_2 & e_2 & e_2 & e_1 & e_1 & e_1 \\
1 & e_1 & e_2 & 1 & e_1 & e_2 & 1 & e_1 & e_2 \\
1 & e_1 & e_2 & e_1 & e_2 & 1 & e_2 & 1 & e_1 \\
1 & e_1 & e_2 & e_2 & 1 & e_1 & e_1 & e_2 & 1 \\
1 & e_2 & e_1 & 1 & e_2 & e_1 & 1 & e_2 & e_1 \\
1 & e_2 & e_1 & e_1 & 1 & e_2 & e_2 & e_1 & 1 \\
1 & e_2 & e_1 & e_2 & e_1 & 1 & e_1 & 1 & e_2
\end{bmatrix}.
$$

All the properties of the Vilenkin–Chrestenson functions may be rephrased in terms of the matrices $\chi^{(p)}(m)$ as was the case for the Walsh functions and Hadamard matrices (see Section 2.3.2).

Let us express the initial function and its Vilenkin–Chrestenson spectrum as vectors, $\Phi = [\Phi(0), \ldots, \Phi(p^m - 1)]^T$, $\mathbf{S}_f = [S_f(0), \ldots, S_f(p^m - 1)]^T$. Then, by (2.5.12),

$$\mathbf{S}_f = p^{-m}\overline{\chi^{(p)}(m)}\Phi, \tag{3.3.1}$$

where $\overline{\chi^{(p)}(m)}$ is the complex conjugate of $\chi^{(p)}(m)$, which is the matrix complex conjugate to $\chi_m^{(p)}$. This formula generalizes (3.1.2) and provides a simple construction of the spectrum if p and m are not too large. Calculation of the Vilenkin–Chrestenson spectrum using formula (3.3.1) requires p^{2m} addition or subtraction operations (p^m operations per coefficient).

We now exhibit another method for computing the Vilenkin–Chrestenson spectrum, generalizing the method of Theorem 3.1.1 to the p-valued case and requiring the minimum number $m \cdot p^m(p - 1)$ of operations.

Given a natural number $w = \sum_{s=0}^{m-1} w_s p^{m-1-s}$, we set $\overleftarrow{w} = \sum_{s=0}^{m-1} w_s p^s$.

If $\mathbf{A}$ is a symmetric $p^m \times p^m$ matrix, we let $\overleftarrow{\mathbf{A}}$ denote the matrix whose wth row (column) is the $\overleftarrow{w}$th row (column) of $\mathbf{A}$.

Consider the matrix

$$
\mathbf{A}_m^{(p)} =
\begin{bmatrix}
e_0^0 e_1^0 \cdots e_{p-1}^0 & 0 & 0 & \cdots & 0 \\
0 & e_0^0 e_1^0 \cdots e_{p-1}^0 & 0 & \cdots & 0 \\
0 & 0 & 0 & \cdots & e_0^0 e_1^0 \cdots e_{p-1}^0 \\
e_0^0 e_1^0 \cdots e_{p-1}^0 & 0 & 0 & \cdots & 0 \\
0 & e_0^0 e_1^0 \cdots e_{p-1}^0 & 0 & \cdots & 0 \\
0 & 0 & 0 & \cdots & e_0^0 e_1^0 \cdots e_{p-1}^0 \\
\vdots & \vdots & \vdots\ \vdots & & \vdots \\
e_0^{p-1} e_1^{p-1} \cdots e_{p-1}^{p-1} & 0 & 0 & \cdots & 0 \\
0 & e_0^{p-1} e_1^{p-1} \cdots e_{p-1}^{p-1} & 0 & \cdots & 0 \\
0 & 0 & 0 & \cdots & e_0^{p-1} e_1^{p-1} \cdots e_{p-1}^{p-1}
\end{bmatrix},
$$

where $e_q = \exp(2q\pi i/p)$, $q = 0, 1, \ldots, p - 1$. For $p = 2$, $\mathbf{A}_m^{(p)}$ is simply the matrix A_m considered in Section 3.1.

Theorem 3.3.1 *The Vilenkin–Chrestenson matrix $\chi^{(p)}(m)$ can be factorized as*

$$\chi^{(p)}(m) = (\overleftarrow{\mathbf{A}_m^{(p)}})^m. \tag{3.3.2}$$

This theorem, generalizing formula (3.1.3), defines the factorization of the matrix $\chi^{(p)}(m)$ and, together with formula (3.3.1), defines the fast Vilenkin–Chrestenson transform in Hadamard order corresponding to the same ordering of Walsh functions. Calculation of the Vilenkin–Chrestenson spectrum using this transform requires $mp^m(p-1)$ addition or subtraction operations (multiplication of Φ by $\mathbf{A}_m^{(p)}$ requires p^m operations). This is the minimum complexity of an algorithm for this purpose.

Example 3.3.2   *Figure 3.3.1 shows the flow-graph of the fast algorithm to calculate the Vilenkin–Chrestenson transform for $p = 3$ and $m = 2$ by using the factorization in Theorem 3.3.1.*

Another consequence of Theorem 3.3.1 is the following m-recursive procedure for calculating $\chi^{(p)}(m)$, expressing it as a block matrix:

$$
\overleftarrow{\chi^{(p)}(m)} =
\begin{bmatrix}
e_0^{(0)}\overleftarrow{\chi^{(p)}(m-1)} & e_1^{(0)}\overleftarrow{\chi^{(p)}(m-1)} & \cdots & e_{p-1}^{(0)}\overleftarrow{\chi^{(p)}(m-1)} \\
e_0^{(1)}\overleftarrow{\chi^{(p)}(m-1)} & e_1^{(1)}\overleftarrow{\chi^{(p)}(m-1)} & \cdots & e_{p-1}^{(1)}\overleftarrow{\chi^{(p)}(m-1)} \\
& & \vdots & \\
e_0^{(p-1)}\overleftarrow{\chi^{(p)}(m-1)} & e_1^{(p-1)}\overleftarrow{\chi^{(p)}(m-1)} & \cdots & e_{p-1}^{(p-1)}\overleftarrow{\chi^{(p)}(m-1)}
\end{bmatrix}.
$$

This formula generalizes (3.1.4) to the p-valued case and may be used to generate the Vilenkin–Chrestenson matrices in the Hadamard order.

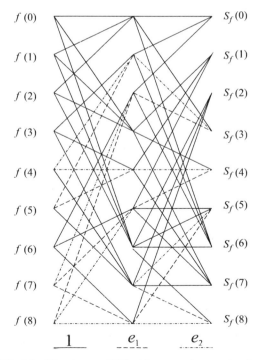

FIGURE 3.3.1   Vilenkin–Chrestenson FFT with constant geometry for $p = 3$ and $m = 2$.

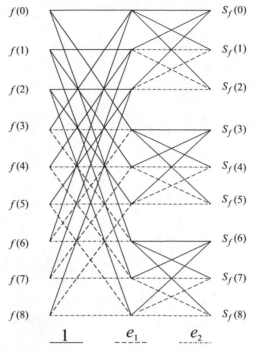

FIGURE 3.3.2   Vilenkin–Chrestenson FFT for $p = 3$ and $m = 2$.

The Good factorization can be applied to the Vilenkin–Chrestenson matrices to derive fast calculation algorithms as in the case of the Walsh transform.

Example 3.3.3   *Figure 3.3.2 shows the flow-graphs of the corresponding algorithms for $p = 3$ and $m = 2$ derived from the Good–Thomas factorization as*

$$\chi^{(3)}(2) = \mathbf{V}_1(2)\mathbf{V}_2(2),$$

where

$$\mathbf{V}_1(2) = \begin{bmatrix} 1 & 1 & 1 \\ 1 & e_2 & e_1 \\ 1 & e_1 & e_2 \end{bmatrix} \otimes \begin{bmatrix} 1 & 0 & 0 \\ 0 & 1 & 0 \\ 0 & 0 & 1 \end{bmatrix},$$

$$\mathbf{V}_2(2) = \begin{bmatrix} 1 & 0 & 0 \\ 0 & 1 & 0 \\ 0 & 0 & 1 \end{bmatrix} \otimes \begin{bmatrix} 1 & 1 & 1 \\ 1 & e_2 & e_1 \\ 1 & e_1 & e_2 \end{bmatrix}.$$

Here, as before, $\otimes$ stands for the Kronecker product. If e_1 and e_2 are permuted, the same algorithm can be used to calculate the inverse transform.

3.3.2 Calculation of the Vilenkin–Chrestenson Transform Through Decision Diagrams

Decision diagram methods for calculation of the Vilenkin–Chrestenson transform are a direct generalization of those for the Walsh transform (581). It will be explained by the following example.

Example 3.3.4   *Figure 3.3.3 shows the multiple-place decision tree for a function for $p = 3$ and $m = 2$. In this figure, the label z_i^j at an edge denotes that this edge corresponds to the value of the variable $z_i = j$.*

From the definition of the Vilenkin–Chrestenson transform, we perform at each node calculations determined by the inverse of the basic Vilenkin–Chrestenson matrix $\chi^{(3)}(1)$. Finally, at the root node, we read the Vilenkin–Chrestenson spectrum up to the normalization factor 3^2. The calculation has been performed as follows:

For the node $q_{1,0}$,

$$q_{1,0} = \begin{bmatrix} 1 & 1 & 1 \\ 1 & e_2 & e_1 \\ 1 & e_1 & e_2 \end{bmatrix} \begin{bmatrix} f(0) \\ f(1) \\ f(2) \end{bmatrix} = \begin{bmatrix} f(0) + f(1) + f(2) \\ f(0) + e_2 f(1) + e_1 f(2) \\ f(0) + e_1 f(1) + e_2 f(2) \end{bmatrix}.$$

For the node $q_{1,1}$,

$$q_{1,1} = \begin{bmatrix} 1 & 1 & 1 \\ 1 & e_2 & e_1 \\ 1 & e_1 & e_2 \end{bmatrix} \begin{bmatrix} f(3) \\ f(4) \\ f(5) \end{bmatrix} = \begin{bmatrix} f(3) + f(4) + f(5) \\ f(3) + e_2 f(4) + e_1 f(5) \\ f(3) + e_1 f(4) + e_2 f(5) \end{bmatrix}.$$

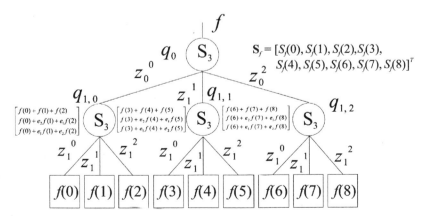

FIGURE 3.3.3   Calculation of the Vilenkin–Chrestenson spectrum for $p = 3$ and $m = 2$ through multiple-place decision tree.

For the node $q_{1,2}$,

$$q_{1,2} = \begin{bmatrix} 1 & 1 & 1 \\ 1 & e_2 & e_1 \\ 1 & e_1 & e_2 \end{bmatrix} \begin{bmatrix} f(6) \\ f(7) \\ f(8) \end{bmatrix} = \begin{bmatrix} f(6) + f(7) + f(8) \\ f(6) + e_2 f(7) + e_1 f(8) \\ f(6) + e_1 f(7) + e_2 f(8) \end{bmatrix}.$$

For the node q_0,

$$q_0 = \begin{bmatrix} 1 & 1 & 1 \\ 1 & e_2 & e_1 \\ 1 & e_1 & e_2 \end{bmatrix} \begin{bmatrix} q_{1,0} \\ q_{1,1} \\ q_{1,2} \end{bmatrix}$$

$$= \begin{bmatrix} 1 \cdot q_{1,0} + 1 \cdot q_{1,1} + 1 \cdot q_{1,2} \\ 1 \cdot q_{1,0} + e_2 \cdot q_{1,1} + e_1 \cdot q_{1,2} \\ 1 \cdot q_{1,0} + e_1 \cdot q_{1,1} + e_2 \cdot q_{1,2} \end{bmatrix}.$$

3.4 CALCULATION OF THE GENERALIZED HAAR SPECTRUM

The generalized Haar spectrum may be calculated by a procedure analogous to the fast Vilenkin–Chrestenson transform in the Hadamard ordering. This procedure is described in the next theorem, which generalizes Theorem 3.2.1.

Theorem 3.4.1   *Let $\Phi(z)$ be a step function representing a system of p-valued logic functions of m variables, and $c_{r,m-s}^{(p,q)}$ its expansion coefficients relative to the generalized Haar functions $M_{r,m-s}^{(p,q)}(z)$. Set*

$$a_0(t) = \Phi(t),$$

$$a_s(\tau p^{m-s} + t) = \sum_{\delta=0}^{p-1} e_\delta^{-\tau} a_{s-1}(pt + \delta), \tag{3.4.1}$$

where $\tau = 0, 1, \ldots, p - 1$, $s = 1, 2, \ldots, m$, and $e_\delta = \exp(2\pi\delta i/p)$, $i = \sqrt{-1}$, $\delta = 0, 1, \ldots, p - 1$. Then,

$$c_{r,m-s}^{(p,q)} = p^{-s} a_s(r(p^{m-s} - 1) + q). \tag{3.4.2}$$

As stated above, this theorem generates an algorithm calculating the generalized Haar spectrum that requires $p \cdot p^m - p$ addition and subtraction operations, which is the minimum possible number.

In Reference 580, Haar functions are generalized to the spaces of functions $f : G \to P$, where G is a finite group representable as a direct product of groups of smaller orders, and P is either a finite (Galois) field $GF(p)$ or the complex field C.

The generalization is achieved by referring to the structure of the flow-graphs of the above-mentioned fast calculation algorithms for the Haar spectra and their implementation over decision diagrams. This class of Haar functions involves the generalized Haar functions defined in Section 2.5.2 as a particular example.

3.5 CALCULATION OF AUTOCORRELATION FUNCTIONS

Autocorrelation is an important operation in signal processing and systems theory (8, 74). In particular, the autocorrelation on finite dyadic groups, denoted as dyadic autocorrelation $B^{(f,f)}(\tau) = B_f(\tau)$, defined and discussed in Section 2.7, is useful in switching theory and design of systems whose inputs and outputs are represented by functions defined in 2^m points, including switching functions as an example (278, 288, 282, 429, 433, 463, 464, 465, 467, 468, 606). Recently, some new applications of dyadic autocorrelation in spectral methods for switching functions (160), testing of logic networks (297), and optimization of decision diagrams for representation of discrete functions have been reported (468). Efficient calculation of the autocorrelation is, therefore, an important task for practical applications.

In this section, we define and discuss a method for calculation of the dyadic autocorrelation through decision diagrams, the use of which permits processing of functions of a large number of variables (561). Then, we have discussed the calculation of separate autocorrelation coefficients over decision diagrams with permuted labels of the edges. In the case of restricted memory resources, these calculations can be performed by traversing in a suitable way the decision diagram for the function whose autocorrelation coefficients are required.

In matrix notation, if a given function f and the corresponding autocorrelation function $B_f(\tau) = \sum_{z=0}^{2^m - 1} f(z) f(z \oplus \tau)$ for f are represented by vectors $\mathbf{F} = [f(0), \ldots, f(2^m - 1)]^T$ and $\mathbf{B}_f = [B_f(0), \ldots, B_f(2^m - 1)]^T$, respectively, then

$$\mathbf{B}_f = \mathbf{B}_f(m)\mathbf{F},$$

where $\mathbf{B}_f(m)$ is the dyadic autocorrelation matrix for f.

Example 3.5.1 *For $m = 3$, the dyadic autocorrelation matrix is*

$$\mathbf{B}_f(3) = \begin{bmatrix} f(0) & f(1) & f(2) & f(3) & f(4) & f(5) & f(6) & f(7) \\ f(1) & f(0) & f(3) & f(2) & f(5) & f(4) & f(7) & f(6) \\ f(2) & f(3) & f(0) & f(1) & f(6) & f(7) & f(4) & f(5) \\ f(3) & f(2) & f(1) & f(0) & f(7) & f(6) & f(5) & f(4) \\ f(4) & f(5) & f(6) & f(7) & f(0) & f(1) & f(2) & f(3) \\ f(5) & f(4) & f(7) & f(6) & f(1) & f(0) & f(3) & f(2) \\ f(6) & f(7) & f(4) & f(5) & f(2) & f(3) & f(0) & f(1) \\ f(7) & f(6) & f(5) & f(4) & f(3) & f(2) & f(1) & f(0) \end{bmatrix}.$$

The recursive structure of the autocorrelation matrix will be exploited in calculation of the autocorrelation coefficients.

Example 3.5.2 *The autocorrelation function $B_f(\tau)$ for a function f given by the vector of function values $\mathbf{F} = [0, 0, 1, 2, 3, 3, 3, 3]^T$ is calculated by the autocorrelation matrix $\mathbf{B}_f(3)$ as*

$$
\mathbf{B}_f =
\begin{bmatrix}
0 & 0 & 1 & 2 & 3 & 3 & 3 & 3 \\
0 & 0 & 2 & 1 & 3 & 3 & 3 & 3 \\
1 & 2 & 0 & 0 & 3 & 3 & 3 & 3 \\
2 & 1 & 0 & 0 & 3 & 3 & 3 & 3 \\
3 & 3 & 3 & 3 & 0 & 0 & 1 & 2 \\
3 & 3 & 3 & 3 & 0 & 0 & 2 & 1 \\
3 & 3 & 3 & 3 & 1 & 2 & 0 & 0 \\
3 & 3 & 3 & 3 & 2 & 1 & 0 & 0
\end{bmatrix}
\begin{bmatrix}
0 \\ 0 \\ 1 \\ 2 \\ 3 \\ 3 \\ 3 \\ 3
\end{bmatrix}
=
\begin{bmatrix}
41 \\ 40 \\ 36 \\ 36 \\ 18 \\ 18 \\ 18 \\ 18
\end{bmatrix}.
$$

The dyadic autocorrelation matrices are known as *circulants* on $C(2)^m$ (1). Properties of circulants on groups are studied in References 96, and 246.

3.5.1 Matrix Notation for the Wiener–Khinchin Theorem

The Wiener–Khinchin theorem, Theorem 2.7.1, states a relationship between the autocorrelation function and Walsh (Fourier) coefficients. In matrix notation, this theorem can be expressed as

$$
\mathbf{B}_f = 2^{-m}\mathbf{W}(m)(\mathbf{W}(m)\mathbf{F})^2,
$$

where $\mathbf{W}(m)$ denotes the Walsh transform matrix and $\mathbf{F}$ is the vector of function values for the given function f.

Example 3.5.3 *Figure 3.5.1 shows calculation of the autocorrelation of a function of two binary-valued variables. Figure 3.5.2 illustrates the same calculation performed by the fast Walsh transform in the Hadamard ordering.*

3.5.2 Wiener–Khinchin Theorem Over Decision Diagrams

Decision diagrams can be used to represent both functions and their autocorrelation functions, and moreover, for a function f specified by a decision diagram, the decision diagram for the autocorrelation function B_f can be constructed by performing calculations over the diagram for f.

Example 3.5.4 *Figure 3.5.3 shows a MTBDT and the corresponding MTBDD for a function f in Example 3.5.2. In this figure, we also show the cross points in the MTBDD. Figure 3.5.4 shows the MTBDD for the autocorrelation function $B_f(\tau)$.*

$$\mathbf{B}_f = \begin{bmatrix} B_f(0) \\ B_f(1) \\ B_f(2) \\ B_f(3) \end{bmatrix} = \begin{bmatrix} f(0) & f(1) & f(2) & f(3) \\ f(1) & f(0) & f(3) & f(2) \\ f(2) & f(3) & f(0) & f(1) \\ f(3) & f(2) & f(1) & f(0) \end{bmatrix} \begin{bmatrix} f(0) \\ f(1) \\ f(2) \\ f(3) \end{bmatrix}$$

$$\mathbf{B}_f = \begin{bmatrix} B_f(0) \\ B_f(1) \\ B_f(2) \\ B_f(3) \end{bmatrix} = 2^{-2} \begin{bmatrix} 1 & 1 & 1 & 1 \\ 1 & -1 & 1 & -1 \\ 1 & 1 & -1 & -1 \\ 1 & -1 & -1 & 1 \end{bmatrix} \left(\begin{bmatrix} 1 & 1 & 1 & 1 \\ 1 & -1 & 1 & -1 \\ 1 & 1 & -1 & -1 \\ 1 & -1 & -1 & 1 \end{bmatrix} \begin{bmatrix} f(0) \\ f(1) \\ f(2) \\ f(3) \end{bmatrix} \right)^2$$

FIGURE 3.5.1 Calculation of the autocorrelation of $f(z_0, z_1)$.

Figure 3.5.5 illustrates the basic principle in calculating the autocorrelation functions by the Wiener–Khinchin theorem performed over decision diagrams.

The Walsh spectrum S_f of a given function f, represented by a MTBDD, is determined by performing at each node and each cross point of the MTBDD(f) the calculations determined by $\mathbf{W}(1)$. For simplicity, we say the nodes and cross points in MTBDD(f) are processed by $\mathbf{W}(1)$. In this way, MTBDD(f) is converted into the MTBDD(S_f). Methods for construction of MTBDD(S_f) from the MTBDD(f) by performing calculations determined by $\mathbf{W}(1)$ at every node and cross points in the MTBFF(f) has been presented in Section 3.1.3.

We perform the multiplication of S_f by itself by replacing the values of constant nodes $S_f(i)$ with $S_f^2(i)$ (499). Then, the MTBDD(B_f) is determined by performing the calculations determined by $\mathbf{W}(1)$ at each node and the cross point of the resulting MTBDD(S_f^2) followed by the normalization with 2^m, since the Walsh matrix is self-inverse up to the constant 2^{-m}.

Example 3.5.5 *Figure 3.5.6 illustrates calculation of the autocorrelation function B_f by the above method for the function f in Example 3.5.4.*

Complexity of the method
   Since in calculation of the Walsh spectrum, we perform an addition and a subtraction at each node and the cross point distributed over m levels, the complexity is $O(2m \cdot size(MTBDD(f)))$. Recall that the size of a decision diagram is defined as the number of nodes in the diagram. Notice that the upper bound on the number

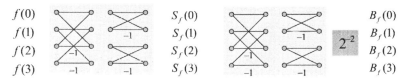

FIGURE 3.5.2 Calculation of the autocorrelation of $f(z_0, z_1)$ by the fast Walsh transform.

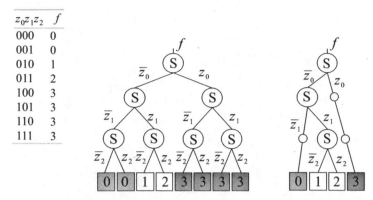

$z_0z_1z_2$	f
000	0
001	0
010	1
011	2
100	3
101	3
110	3
111	3

FIGURE 3.5.3 MTBDT and MTBDD for f in Example 3.5.2.

of cross points in a MTBDD is on the average at about 30% of the number of nonterminal nodes (499). The result of these calculations is the MTBDD(S_f). Then, we perform squaring of the values of constant nodes followed by the inverse transform. Thus, since the Walsh transform is self-inverse, the complexity of these calculations is $O(2m \cdot size(MTBDD(S_f)))$. After multiplication with the scaling factor 2^m, the MTBDD(B_f) is derived.

Notice that the size of the MTBDD for the Walsh spectrum is usually greater than that of the MTBDD for functions with a limited number of different values. Since in calculation of the autcorrelation function, MTBDD(f) is converted into a MTBDD(S_f), which in many cases has a larger size than the MTBDD(f), the space complexity of the method is $O(size(MTBDD(S_f)))$.

For an illustration, Table 3.5.1 shows the sizes of MTBDDs for few standard *mcnc* benchmark functions used in logic design (MTBDD(f)) and their Walsh spectra (MTBDD(S_f)). This table shows the number of inputs (In) of benchmark functions, number of nonterminal nodes (ntn), constant nodes (cn), size (s), and number of paths (paths) in the MTBDDs and WDDs.

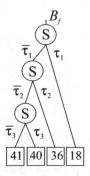

FIGURE 3.5.4 MTBDD for the autocorrelation function $B_f(\tau)$.

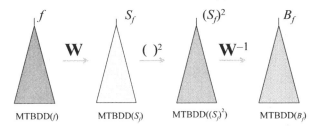

FIGURE 3.5.5 Calculation of the autocorrelation function by the Wiener–Khinchin theorem over decision diagrams.

Example 3.5.6 *For the function f represented by the MTBDD in Fig. 3.5.3, the Walsh spectrum is calculated as follows:*

We first process the cross points and the node at the level for z_2. For the left cross point, calculation is trivial since the constant node shows the value 0, the result will be the zero -valued vector of order 2. For the completeness of presentation, we also show these calculations

$$\mathbf{S}_{c-left} = \mathbf{W}(1) \circ \begin{bmatrix} 0 \\ 0 \end{bmatrix} = \begin{bmatrix} 0+0 \\ 0-0 \end{bmatrix} = \begin{bmatrix} 0 \\ 0 \end{bmatrix}.$$

For the node for z_2,

$$\mathbf{S}_{f_{z_2}} = \mathbf{W}(1) \circ \begin{bmatrix} 1 \\ 2 \end{bmatrix} = \begin{bmatrix} 1+2 \\ 1-2 \end{bmatrix} = \begin{bmatrix} 3 \\ -1 \end{bmatrix}.$$

For the right cross point,

$$\mathbf{S}_{c-right} = \mathbf{W}(1) \circ \begin{bmatrix} 3 \\ 3 \end{bmatrix} = \begin{bmatrix} 3+3 \\ 3-3 \end{bmatrix} = \begin{bmatrix} 6 \\ 0 \end{bmatrix}.$$

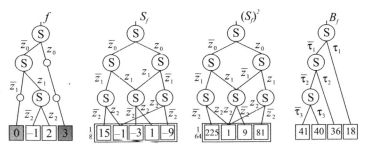

FIGURE 3.5.6 Calculation of the autocorrelation function B_f for f in Example 3.5.4 by using the Wiener–Khinchin theorem over decision diagrams.

TABLE 3.5.1 Characteristics of MTBDDs and WDDs for Some Benchmark Functions.

f	In	MTBDD(f)				MTBDD(S_f)			
		ntn	cn	s	paths	ntn	cn	s	paths
5xp1	7	127	128	255	128	41	14	55	128
9sym	9	43	3	46	125	101	30	131	224
add4	8	147	31	178	256	36	11	47	37
add5	10	387	63	450	1024	55	13	68	56
apex4	9	446	319	765	450	511	512	1023	512
bw	5	29	24	53	30	31	32	63	32
clip	9	339	33	372	498	449	170	619	464
con1	7	46	5	51	83	83	26	109	96
ex1010	10	899	178	1077	1887	1023	972	1995	1024
mul2	4	13	7	20	14	12	8	20	13
mul3	6	59	26	85	59	30	16	46	31
rd53	5	21	6	27	24	30	13	43	32
rd73	7	57	8	25	96	64	24	88	98
rd84	8	85	9	94	192	118	40	158	193
sao2	10	96	11	107	237	295	70	365	508
sqrt8	8	64	17	81	65	127	54	181	176
xor5	5	15	3	18	22	9	6	15	10
av.	8	163	495	210	298	167	112	279	201

Then, we process the node for z_1,

$$
\mathbf{S}_{f_{z_1}} = \mathbf{W}(1) \circ
\begin{bmatrix} \begin{bmatrix} 0 \\ 0 \end{bmatrix} \\ \begin{bmatrix} 3 \\ -1 \end{bmatrix} \end{bmatrix}
=
\begin{bmatrix} \begin{bmatrix} 0 \\ 0 \end{bmatrix} + \begin{bmatrix} 3 \\ -1 \end{bmatrix} \\ \begin{bmatrix} 0 \\ 0 \end{bmatrix} - \begin{bmatrix} 3 \\ -1 \end{bmatrix} \end{bmatrix}
=
\begin{bmatrix} 3 \\ -1 \\ -3 \\ 1 \end{bmatrix},
$$

where $\circ$ symbolically denotes multiplication of a matrix by a vector consisting of subvectors.

For the cross point at the level for z_1,

$$
\mathbf{S}_c = \mathbf{W}(1) \circ
\begin{bmatrix} \begin{bmatrix} 6 \\ 0 \end{bmatrix} \\ \begin{bmatrix} 6 \\ 0 \end{bmatrix} \end{bmatrix}
=
\begin{bmatrix} \begin{bmatrix} 6 \\ 0 \end{bmatrix} + \begin{bmatrix} 6 \\ 0 \end{bmatrix} \\ \begin{bmatrix} 6 \\ 0 \end{bmatrix} - \begin{bmatrix} 6 \\ 0 \end{bmatrix} \end{bmatrix}
=
\begin{bmatrix} 12 \\ 0 \\ 0 \\ 0 \end{bmatrix}.
$$

For z_0,

$$8\mathbf{S}_f = \mathbf{W}(1) \circ \begin{bmatrix} \begin{bmatrix} 3 \\ -1 \\ -3 \\ 1 \end{bmatrix} \\ \begin{bmatrix} 12 \\ 0 \\ 0 \\ 0 \end{bmatrix} \end{bmatrix} = \begin{bmatrix} \begin{bmatrix} 3 \\ -1 \\ -3 \\ 1 \end{bmatrix} + \begin{bmatrix} 12 \\ 0 \\ 0 \\ 0 \end{bmatrix} \\ \begin{bmatrix} 3 \\ -1 \\ -3 \\ 1 \end{bmatrix} - \begin{bmatrix} 12 \\ 0 \\ 0 \\ 0 \end{bmatrix} \end{bmatrix} = \begin{bmatrix} 15 \\ -1 \\ -3 \\ 1 \\ -9 \\ -1 \\ -3 \\ 1 \end{bmatrix}.$$

Thus determined vector is multiplied by $1/8$ to get the Walsh spectrum for f.

Notice that matrix calculations are used for the explanations of the method. In practice, each step of the calculation is represented by a decision diagram, which is a subdiagram in a decision diagram representing the Walsh spectrum for the function f. Figure 3.5.7 shows the MTBDD(S_f) for the Walsh spectrum, where for simplicity, the scaling factor is not shown. As specified in the Wiener–Khinchin theorem, we replace values of constant nodes by their square, and then calculate the inverse Walsh transform as explained above, since the Walsh transform is self-inverse. If in this calculation, each step is represented by a decision diagram, we get a MTBDD for the autocorrelation function B_f, as shown in Fig. 3.5.4.

3.5.3 In-place Calculation of Autocorrelation Coefficients by Decision Diagrams

We define a transformation of nodes in MTBDDs that consists of permutation of labels at the outgoing edges, as shown in Fig. 3.5.8.

The ith row of the autocorrelation matrix is the vector of function values $f(z \oplus i)$, where $\oplus$ denotes the componentwise EXOR over the binary representations for $z = (z_0, \ldots, z_{m-1})$, and $i = (i_0, \ldots, i_{m-1})$. In decision diagrams, this shift of the variable for f implies permutation of labels at the edges of some nodes in the decision diagram for f. Nodes whose edges should be permuted are located at the levels whose position within the decision diagram corresponds to the position of 1-bits in the binary representation for the row index i.

Example 3.5.7 *Figure 3.5.9 shows MTBTDs for the first four rows of the autocorrelation matrix B_f in Example 3.5.1. Figure 3.5.10 shows the decision diagrams for a three-variable switching function $f(z)$, $z = (z_0, z_1, z_2)$, given by the truth-vector $\mathbf{F} = [1, 0, 1, 1, 0, 1, 0, 1]^T$, and for $f(z \oplus 3)$, that is, for the first and the fourth row of the autocorrelation matrix for f. These diagrams differ in the order of labels at the edges of nodes at the levels for z_1 and z_2.*

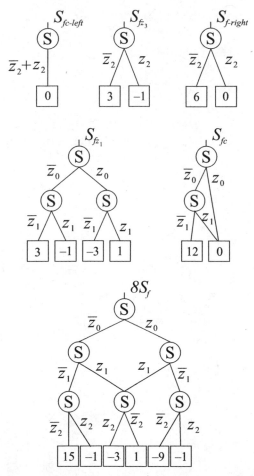

FIGURE 3.5.7   MTBDD for the Walsh spectrum for f in Example 3.5.6.

The ith autocorrelation coefficient is calculated by the multiplication of the ith row of the autocorrelation matrix $\mathbf{B}_f$ by the vector $\mathbf{F}$ of function values for f. When f and rows of $\mathbf{B}_f$ are represented by decision diagrams, it follows that the ith autocorrelation coefficient is calculated by the multiplication of the decision diagrams for $f(z)$ and $f(z \oplus i)$. This can be performed by the classical procedure for multiplication of

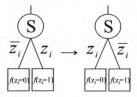

FIGURE 3.5.8   Transformation of nodes.

$$
\mathbf{B}_f =
\begin{bmatrix}
f(0) & f(1) & f(2) & f(3) & f(4) & f(5) & f(6) & f(7) \\
f(1) & f(0) & f(3) & f(2) & f(5) & f(4) & f(7) & f(6) \\
f(2) & f(3) & f(0) & f(1) & f(6) & f(7) & f(4) & f(5) \\
f(3) & f(2) & f(1) & f(0) & f(7) & f(6) & f(5) & f(4) \\
f(4) & f(5) & f(6) & f(7) & f(0) & f(1) & f(2) & f(3) \\
f(5) & f(4) & f(7) & f(6) & f(1) & f(0) & f(3) & f(2) \\
f(6) & f(7) & f(4) & f(5) & f(2) & f(3) & f(0) & f(1) \\
f(7) & f(6) & f(5) & f(4) & f(3) & f(2) & f(1) & f(0)
\end{bmatrix}
\begin{bmatrix}
f(0) \\ f(1) \\ f(2) \\ f(3) \\ f(4) \\ f(5) \\ f(6) \\ f(7)
\end{bmatrix}
$$

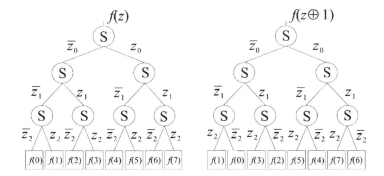

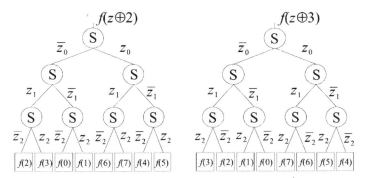

FIGURE 3.5.9   MTBDTs for the first four rows of the autocorrelation matrix for $m = 3$.

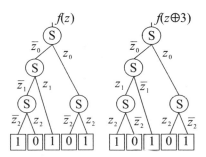

FIGURE 3.5.10   MTBDDs for $f(z)$ and $f(z \oplus 3)$ in Example 3.5.7.

decision diagrams. However, since decision diagrams for $f(z)$ and $f(z \oplus i)$ differ in labels at the edges, in practical programming implementations, calculations can be organized over a single diagram similar to calculations of FFT organized in-place (8). Therefore, complexity of calculation for this approach is proportional to the number of nodes in the decision diagram for f.

Figure 3.5.11 shows a procedure for in-place calculation of the autocorrelation function through decision diagrams with permuted labels at the edges. In this procedure, $f(z)$ is represented by a MTBDD, which is then traversed in such a way as to

```
int AUTOCORREL(*node1, *node2, level)
{
    r = level − node → level
        if (node NOT TERMINAL)
    {
            if (node → flag = 0)
            {
            if(τᵢ = 1)
            {
            pom1 = node2 → right
            pom2 = node2 → left
            }
            else
            {
            pom1 = node2 → left
            pom2 = node2 → right
            }
            i = i + 1
            a = AUTOCORREL(node1 → left, pom1)
            + AUTOCORREL(node1 → right, pom2)
            node → sub − value
            node → flag = 1
            return (2^(r−1) · a)
        }
        else
        {
        return node → sub − value
        }
    }
    else
    a = node1 → value · node2 → value
    return (2^(r−1) · a)
}
End of pseudocode.
```

FIGURE 3.5.11   Calculation of the autocorrelation coefficient $B_f(\tau)$.

multiply values of constant nodes in the MTBDD for $f(z)$ with the values of constant nodes in the MTBDD for $f(z \oplus \tau)$ and perform the addition of these values to compute $B_f(\tau) = \sum_{z=0}^{2^m-1} f(z)f(z \oplus \tau)$. The way of traversing is determined by the binary components τ_i, $i = 0, 1, \ldots, m - 1$ of τ. A flag associate to each nonterminal node to show if the node was already traversed. In this manner, the coefficient $B_f(\tau)$ is calculated. The procedure has to be repeated for each coefficient.

Complexity of in-place calculations of autocorrelation coefficients

In-place calculations are performed over the MTBDD(f) and, therefore, the space complexity, that is, the required memory, is $O(size(MTBDD(f))$. Since for each coefficient we perform a multiplication at each constant node and an addition at each nonterminal node, the number of multiplications is $O(cn)$, and the number of additions is $O(ntn)$, where cn and ntn are the number of constant and nonterminal nodes, respectively. Thus, the total complexity of in-place calculation of an autocorrelation coefficient is $O(size(MTBDD(f)))$.

Table 3.5.1 shows number of constant nodes and nonterminal nodes for several benchmark functions. The procedure is performed for each value of B_f. Thus, it is suitable for calculation of a single value of $B_f(\tau)$ for a given τ, or a small subset of values.

Example 3.5.8 *Figure 3.5.12 explains application of the procedure for calculation of the autocorrelation functions over MTBDT for a given function f for $m = 3$ and $\tau = 1 = (001)$. Recall that in this case, we should perform multiplication of $f(z)$ and $f(z \oplus 1)$, where $z = (z_0, z_1, z_2)$, $\tau = (\tau_0, \tau_1, \tau_2)$, $z_i, \tau_i \in \{0, 1\}$. Therefore,*

$$B_f(1) = \left[f(1)f(0)f(3)f(2)f(5)f(4)f(7)f(6) \right]$$
$$\times \left[f(0)f(1)f(2)f(3)f(4)f(5)f(6)f(7) \right]^T.$$

This can be done by a suitable traversing MTBDT for f. In Fig. 3.5.12 the dotted lines show the part for performing permutation of variables to transfer the MTBDD

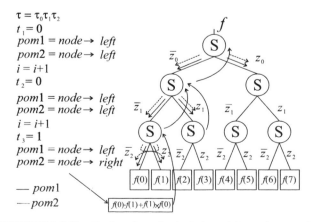

FIGURE 3.5.12   Explanation of calculation of $B_f(1)$ for $m = 3$.

for f into MTBDD for $f(z \oplus 1)$. Thus, there are two arrows, represented by dotted and solid lines, from each node to illustrate computation of the values $f(0)f(1)$ and $f(1)f(0)$ that are first two numbers in the sum determining the value of the auto-correlation coefficient $B_f(001) = f(1)f(0) + f(0)f(1) + f(3)f(2) + f(2)f(3) + f(5)f(4) + f(4)f(5) + f(7)f(6) + f(6)f(7)$. Arcs in this figure show the way of visiting nodes during traversing the decision tree.

BIBLIOGRAPHIC NOTES

Efficient calculation of spectral transforms, where the efficiency is expressed in terms of re-quired space and time to perform the computations, is of an essential importance for applications of spectral methods in practice (75). The origins of fast calculation algorithms of the Discrete Fourier Transform (DFT) can be dated back to the time of Gauss (240). In modern era, the Fast Fourier transform, as an algorithm for efficient calculation of DFT has been introduced in Reference 109, which revolutionizes practical applications of DFT. The same algorithm can be extended to Fourier and Fourier-like transforms on various groups (217). Recommend-able references in this subject are 16,52, and 555. See Reference (567) for fast algorithms for calculation of Fourier transforms on finite non-Abelian groups. Extension of FFT-like algo-rithms to calculation over decision diagrams is given in References 104 and 105. For more details see References 550 and 555. Methods for calculation of the Haar transform over deci-sion diagrams are considered in References 162,229, and 536. Methods for calculation of logic autocorrelation over decision diagrams are discussed in References 558 and 561.

CHAPTER 4

SPECTRAL METHODS IN OPTIMIZATION OF DECISION DIAGRAMS

This chapter is devoted to the minimization of basic characteristic of decision diagrams for representation of discrete functions. We will also provide a spectral interpretation of decision diagrams and based on it define decision diagrams derived from the Haar transform.

The main interest will be focused on decision diagrams for switching functions and their integer equivalent functions. In particular, we will discuss minimization of Binary Decision Diagrams (BDDs) by autocorrelation functions, minimization of planar BDDs by using Walsh coefficients, and minimization of Haar diagrams by using again the autocorrelation coefficient.

The complexity of a decision diagram is usually estimated as the number of nodes, called the *size of the BDD*. In the case of switching functions, it is enough to consider the nonterminal nodes, since the constant nodes always represent two logic values 0 and 1.

The size of a BDD is very sensitive to the order of variables, ranging from the polynomial to the exponential complexity for the same function for different orders of variables. Therefore, majority of the approaches to the reduction of sizes of BDDs is related to developing efficient algorithms for reordering of variables, see References 185 and 478. Linearly transformed BDDs (LT-BDDs) are defined by allowing linear combinations of variables (220). In this way, the number of possible transformations of variables is increased from $m!$ to $\prod_{i=0}^{m-1}(2^m - 2^i)\prod_{i=1}^{m}(2^i - 1)^{-1}$ for reordering and linear transformation of variables, respectively.

Spectral Logic and Its Applications for the Design of Digital Devices by Mark G. Karpovsky, Radomir S. Stanković and Jaakko T. Astola
Copyright © 2008 John Wiley & Sons, Inc.

Several heuristic algorithms have been proposed to determine orders or linear transformations of variables, and when integrated with widely used sifting algorithms for BDD minimization (478) they are quite efficient (see a discussion in References 364 and 365). However, a disadvantage of heuristic algorithms is that they cannot guarantee the quality of the results produced. A deterministic algorithm for construction of linearly transformed decision diagrams that exploits properties of switching functions in the original and spectral domain has been proposed in Reference 297. An algorithm for exact minimization of BDDs by linear transformation of variables has been proposed in Reference 220. The algorithm is based on sifting procedures and properties of linear transformations over the Galois field $GF(2)$. However, since the search space is very large, this method is limited to functions of a small number of variables (no more than seven variables in most cases). This may be sufficient for some applications related to Field Programmable Gate Array (FPGA) synthesis.

In this chapter, we discuss spectral methods for reduction of sizes of Multiterminal Binary Decision Diagrams (MTBDDs), construction of linearly transformed MTB-DDs, and planar MTBDDs. It will be shown that in many cases these methods provide for a simple and efficient solution of the problem.

4.1 REDUCTION OF SIZES OF DECISION DIAGRAMS

Reduction rules used to derive a decision diagram from the decision tree are adapted to the decomposition rules assigned to the nodes used in the tree (372). In a general formulation, the possibility to delete or share a node relates to the existence of isomorphic subtrees in the decision tree. Since a decision diagram is derived from the decision tree, the complexity of a decision diagram depends on the structure of the vector representing the values of constant nodes in the decision tree.

We consider the relationships among the subvectors $\mathbf{V}_k$ whose orders depend on the group on which the represented discrete function is defined. In the case of the finite dyadic group, the orders of the subvectors $\mathbf{V}_k$ are 2^k, $k = 1, \ldots, m - 1$. For discrete functions on a finite Abelian group G, the orders of $\mathbf{V}_k$ are determined by the orders of the subgroups G_i such that G can be represented as a product of G_i.

From the spectral interpretation, the complexity of a decision diagram depends on the Fourier-like spectrum of f, and thus on the transform that in turn determines the spectral decision tree (the decision tree of the spectrum).

For a given f, different transforms provide decision diagrams of different complexity. Therefore, it is important to realize to which transforms various decision diagrams defined in literature are related. It is equally important to provide definitions of decision diagrams based upon different suitably chosen transforms. For each decision tree and respectively decision diagram, there is always a class of functions for which a particular decision diagram is more suitable than any other decision diagram. Therefore, it is important to discover the connections between well known classes of decision diagrams and transform types.

4.1.1 *K*-Procedure for Reduction of Sizes of Decision Diagrams

In this section, we present a procedure for minimization of MTBDDs for systems of Boolean functions by their logic autocorrelation functions. It is assumed that a given system is represented by the integer equivalent function $f(z)$ and represented by a MTBDD, rather than by a Shared BDD (SBDD).

We note that the reduction of the size of a BDD or MTBDD is an NP-complete problem (71). The proposed procedure provides for the nearly minimal solutions in the following way. It performs minimization of the MTBDD for a given $f(z_0, \ldots, z_{m-1})$ level by level, starting from the bottom level corresponding to z_{m-1}. It guarantees the maximal number of pairs of equal values of f for input vectors that differ in the value of z_{m-1}. Thus, for each pair of equal values of f, we can reduce a node at the lowest level in the MTBDD. Then, we perform next reordering of pairs of equal values of f, and repeat the procedure at the new MTBDD for $m - 1$ variables thus produced. Under the assumption that we already minimized the width at the previous level, we get a minimum width at the present level. The width is determined by the maximum value of the total autocorrelation function for $f(z)$. This maximum value may be achieved for many different m-tuples of variables $\tau = (\tau_0, \ldots, \tau_{m-1})$. Therefore, the procedure depends on the choice of τ in the sense that for different choices of these maxima, different reduction possibilities at the upper levels may be achieved. However, this is a usual feature of nearly optimal solutions of NP-complete problems.

Unlike the method described in Reference 468, the method presented in this section can be used for both single-output and multiple-output networks, and extends the class of permutation matrices that are used in optimization of decision diagrams by ordering of variables. Therefore, the proposed method always produce MTBDDs with smaller or at most equal sizes compared to the methods using the ordering of variables.

The following procedure (K-procedure) will be used in minimization of sizes of MTBDDs for a given system $\{f^{(i)}(z_0, \ldots, z_{m-1})\}$, $i = 0, 1, \ldots, k$ of switching functions.

Procedure 4.1.1 *K-procedure*

1. *Assign to a given multioutput function $f^{(0)}, \ldots, f^{(k-1)}$, an integer equivalent function $f(z) = \sum_{i=0}^{k-1} 2^{k-i-1} f^{(i)}(z)$.*

2. *Denote by R the range of $f(z)$. For every $i \in R$, construct characteristic functions*

$$f_i(z) = \begin{cases} 1, & \text{if } f(z) = i, \\ 0, & \text{otherwise.} \end{cases}$$

3. *Calculate the autocorrelation functions B_i for each $f_i(z)$, and the total autocorrelation function $B_f = \sum_i B_i$.*

4. *Determine a* $\tau = (\tau_0, \ldots, \tau_{m-1})$, *for which* B_f *takes the maximum value, except the value* $B_f(0)$. *If there are several choices, select any of them.*

5. *Determine an* $(m \times m)$ *nonsingular over* $GF(2)$ *matrix* $\sigma = \sigma_{m-1}$ *from the requirement*

$$\sigma \odot \tau = (0, \ldots, 0, 1)^T,$$

where $\odot$ *denotes the multiplication over* $GF(2)$.

6. *Determine the function* f_σ *such that*

$$f_\sigma(\sigma \odot z) = f(z).$$

That means, reorder the components of the vector $\mathbf{F} = \mathbf{Q}_m$ *representing values of* f *by the mapping* $z = (z_0, \ldots, z_{m-1}) \to z_\sigma$, *where* $z_\sigma = \sigma^{-1} \odot z$.

7. *In the vector* $\mathbf{F}_\sigma$ *representing the values of* f_σ, *perform an encoding of pairs of adjacent values* $(f_\sigma = (z_0, \ldots, z_{m-2}, 0), f_\sigma(z_0, \ldots, z_{m-2}, 1))$ *by assigning the same symbol to the identical pairs. Denote the resulting function of* $(m - 1)$ *variables by* $\mathbf{Q}_{m-1}$.

8. *Repeat the above procedure for* $i = i - 1$ *to some* j *until all the pairs of adjacent values in* $\mathbf{Q}_j$ *are identical.*

9. *Determine MTBDD for* f_{σ_j}.

Remark 4.1.1   *The K-procedure produces the maximal number of identical pairs of values or subtrees at the positions pointed by the outgoing edges* $\bar{z}_i$ *and* z_i *for all* $i = m - 1, m - 2, \ldots, 0$.

Remark 4.1.2   *(Upper bound on the number of remaining nodes) The number of nodes in the resulting MTBDD(f_σ) is upperbounded by*

$$L \leq 2^m - 1 - \frac{1}{2} \sum_{i=1}^{r} B_{\text{max}}^{(i)},$$

where $B_{\text{max}}^{(i)}$ *is the maximum value of the total autocorrelation function at the level* i, *and* r *is the number of times the K-procedure has been applied.*

Remark 4.1.3   *For each pair of equal values of* f *at adjacent positions, which is produced by the reordering of function values determined by the K-procedure, a node at the lowest level in the MTBDD($f_{\sigma_i^{-1}}$) may be deleted. It follows that the K-procedure produces the minimal number of different nodes at lowest level in the MTBDD($f_{\sigma_i^{-1}}$). However, since the pairing of nodes at the ith level is performed by the total autocorrelation function for* Q_i, *this is not necessarily the exact minimum of nodes for the whole MTBDD(f), obtained by ordering the elements of* $\mathbf{F}$.

Remark 4.1.4 *A reordering of elements in* **F** *can be represented by the corresponding* $(2^m \times 2^m)$ *permutation matrix.*

We denote by $\mathbf{P}_{dv}$, $\mathbf{P}_{FreeBDD}$, *and* $\mathbf{P}_K$, *the set of permutation matrices used in optimization of MTBDDs by ordering of variables, in FreeBDDs where different order of variables along different paths can be used (130), and in MTBDDs for* f_σ *determined by K-procedure.*

Then,

$$\mathbf{P}_{dv} \subset \mathbf{P}_{FreeBDD} \subset \mathbf{P}_K.$$

We illustrate the K-procedure by the following example.

Example 4.1.1 *Table 4.1.1 shows a two-output function* $f^{(0)}, f^{(1)}$ *of four variables. This function is represented by the integer equivalent function* $f = 2f^{(0)} + f^{(1)}$. *In this table, there are also shown the characteristic functions* f_i, $i = 0, 1, 2, 3$, *their autocorrelation functions* B_i, *and the total autocorrelation function* B_f.

The maximum value for the total autocorrelation function B_f *for* $z \neq 0$ *is 8, which corresponds to the m-tuple* $\tau_{\max} = (1111)$.

Figure 4.1.1 shows Multiterminal Binary Decision Tree (MTBDT(f)) for f *and Fig. 4.1.2 shows the corresponding MTBDD(f).*

TABLE 4.1.1 Function f and f_σ.

	Function		Characteristic Functions				Autocorrelation Functions				
z, w	$f^{(0)}, f^{(1)}$	$f(z)$	f_0	f_1	f_2	f_3	B_0	B_1	B_2	B_3	B
0	00	0	1	0	0	0	4	4	4	4	16
1	10	2	0	0	1	0	2	0	0	2	4
2	11	3	0	0	0	1	2	2	0	0	4
3	11	3	0	0	0	1	2	2	0	0	4
4	01	1	0	1	0	0	0	0	2	2	4
5	10	2	0	0	1	0	0	0	2	2	4
6	01	1	0	1	0	0	0	0	0	0	0
7	11	3	0	0	0	1	0	0	0	0	0
8	11	3	0	0	0	1	0	0	0	0	0
9	01	1	0	1	0	0	0	0	0	0	0
10	01	1	0	1	0	0	0	0	2	2	4
11	10	2	0	0	1	0	0	0	2	2	4
12	00	0	1	0	0	0	2	2	0	0	4
13	00	0	1	0	0	0	2	2	0	0	4
14	10	2	0	0	1	0	0	2	2	0	4
15	00	0	1	0	0	0	2	2	2	2	8

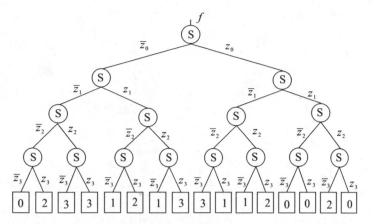

FIGURE 4.1.1 MTBDT for f.

We determine a matrix σ_4 from the requirement

$$\sigma_4 \odot \tau_{\max} = \sigma_4 \odot \begin{bmatrix} 1 \\ 1 \\ 1 \\ 1 \end{bmatrix} = \begin{bmatrix} 0 \\ 0 \\ 0 \\ 1 \end{bmatrix}.$$

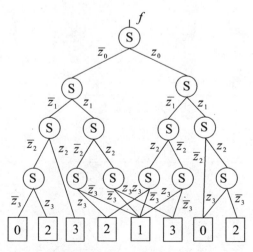

FIGURE 4.1.2 MTBDD for f.

Therefore, we can choose

$$\sigma_4 = \begin{bmatrix} 1 & 1 & 1 & 1 \\ 0 & 0 & 1 & 1 \\ 1 & 0 & 0 & 1 \\ 1 & 1 & 1 & 0 \end{bmatrix}.$$

We determine the inverse matrix for σ_4 over $GF(2)$

$$\sigma_4^{-1} = \begin{bmatrix} 1 & 0 & 1 & 1 \\ 0 & 1 & 1 & 1 \\ 1 & 1 & 0 & 1 \\ 1 & 0 & 0 & 1 \end{bmatrix}.$$

Table 4.1.2 shows the mapping of vectors of variables in f by using σ_4^{-1}. Then, we determine

$$\mathbf{F}_\sigma = [f(0), f(15), f(12), f(3), f(6), f(9), f(10),$$
$$f(5), f(11), f(4), f(7), f(8), f(13), f(2), f(1), f(14)]^T$$
$$= [0, 0, 0, 3, 1, 1, 1, 2, 2, 1, 3, 3, 0, 3, 2, 2]^T,$$

for $\sigma = \sigma_4$.
We perform the encoding $\mathbf{F}_\sigma \to \mathbf{Q}_3$ of pairs of function values in $\mathbf{F}_\sigma$ as follows:

$$\mathbf{Q}_3 = [0, 4, 1, 5, 6, 3, 4, 2]^T,$$

where $(0, 0) = 0$, $(0, 3) = 4$, $(1, 1) = 1$, $(1, 2) = 5$, $(2, 1) = 6$, $(3, 3) = 3$, $(2, 2) = 2$.

TABLE 4.1.2   Mapping of Function Values by σ_4^{-1}, $y = \sigma_4^{-1} \odot z$.

z_0	0	0	0	0	0	0	0	0	1	1	1	1	1	1	1	1
z_1	0	0	0	0	1	1	1	1	0	0	0	0	1	1	1	1
z_2	0	0	1	1	0	0	1	1	0	0	1	1	0	0	1	1
z_3	0	1	0	1	0	1	0	1	0	1	0	1	0	1	0	1
z	0	1	2	3	4	5	6	7	8	9	10	11	12	13	14	15
y_0	0	1	1	0	0	1	1	0	1	0	0	1	1	0	0	1
y_2	0	1	1	0	1	0	0	1	0	1	1	0	1	0	0	1
y_2	0	1	0	1	1	0	1	0	1	0	1	0	0	1	0	1
y_3	0	1	0	1	0	1	0	1	1	0	1	0	1	0	1	0
y	0	15	12	3	6	9	10	5	11	4	7	8	13	2	1	14

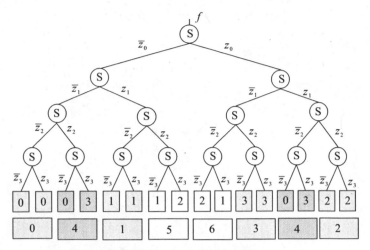

FIGURE 4.1.3   MTBDT for $f_{\sigma_4^{-1}}$.

Figure 4.1.3 shows MTBDT($f_{\sigma_4^{-1}}$) and Fig. 4.1.4 shows MTBDT(f_4^{-1}) with encoded pairs of equal values for constant nodes. We denote the characteristic functions for 0,1,2,3,4,5,6 in $\mathbf{Q}_3$ as f_i. There is a single nontrivial characteristic function f_4. It is given by

$$f_4 = [0, 1, 0, 0, 0, 0, 1, 0]^T,$$

and its autocorrelation function is given by

$$B_4 = [2, 0, 0, 0, 0, 0, 0, 2]^T.$$

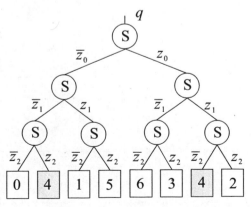

FIGURE 4.1.4   MTBDT for $f_{\sigma_4^{-1}}$ with encoded pair of function values.

Since $\max_{\tau \neq 0} B_4(\tau) = B_4(111) = 2$, *we have for* σ_3

$$\sigma_3 \odot \tau_{\max} = \sigma_3 \odot \begin{bmatrix} 1 \\ 1 \\ 1 \end{bmatrix} = \begin{bmatrix} 0 \\ 0 \\ 1 \end{bmatrix}.$$

Therefore,

$$\sigma_3 = \begin{bmatrix} 1 & 1 & 0 \\ 1 & 0 & 1 \\ 0 & 1 & 0 \end{bmatrix},$$

and

$$\sigma_3^{-1} = \begin{bmatrix} 1 & 0 & 1 \\ 0 & 0 & 1 \\ 1 & 1 & 1 \end{bmatrix}.$$

Table 4.1.3 shows the mapping of vectors of variables in $\mathbf{Q}_3$ *by using* σ_3^{-1}. *For* f *in Table 4.1.1 and* $\sigma = \sigma_3$, *we have*

$$\mathbf{Q}_\sigma = [0, 2, 4, 4, 3, 1, 6, 5]^T.$$

Figure 4.1.5 shows the corresponding MTBDD($\mathbf{Q}_\sigma$).
Therefore,

$$\mathbf{F}_\sigma = [f(0), f(15), f(1), f(14), f(12), f(3), f(13),$$
$$f(2), f(7), f(8), f(6), f(9), f(11), f(4), f(10), f(5)]^T$$
$$= [0, 0, 2, 2, 0, 3, 0, 3, 3, 3, 1, 1, 2, 1, 1, 2]^T.$$

TABLE 4.1.3   Mapping of Function Values by σ_3^{-1}, $y = \sigma_3^{-1} \odot z$.

z_0	0	0	0	0	1	1	1	1
z_1	0	0	1	1	0	0	1	1
z_2	0	1	0	1	0	1	0	1
z	0	1	2	3	4	5	6	7
y_0	0	1	0	1	1	0	1	0
y_1	0	1	0	1	0	1	0	1
y_2	0	1	1	0	1	0	0	1
y	0	7	1	6	5	2	4	3

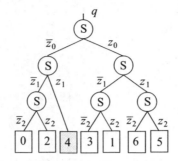

FIGURE 4.1.5   MTBDD(Q_σ) for $\sigma = \sigma_3$.

Figure 4.1.6 shows the corresponding final MTBDD(f_σ).
Note that the recursive application of σ_4^{-1} and σ_3^{-1} to f is identical to the application of a composite mapping

$$\sigma_{4,3}^{-1} = \sigma_4^{-1} \odot \sigma_{3,1}^{-1},$$

where

$$\sigma_{3,1}^{-1} = \begin{bmatrix} \sigma_3^{-1} & \mathbf{0} \\ \mathbf{0} & 1 \end{bmatrix},$$

where $\mathbf{0}$ is (3×1) zero matrix.

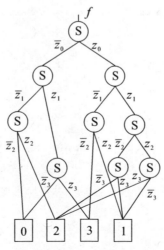

FIGURE 4.1.6   MTBDD(f_σ).

SPECTRAL METHODS IN OPTIMIZATION OF DECISION DIAGRAMS

TABLE 4.1.4 **Mapping of Function Values by** $y = \sigma_4^{-1} \cdot \sigma_3^{-1} \odot z.$

z_0	0	0	0	0	0	0	0	0	1	1	1	1	1	1	1	1
z_1	0	0	0	0	1	1	1	1	0	0	0	0	1	1	1	1
z_2	0	0	1	1	0	0	1	1	0	0	1	1	0	0	1	1
z_3	0	1	0	1	0	1	0	1	0	1	0	1	0	1	0	1
z	0	1	2	3	4	5	6	7	8	9	10	11	12	13	14	15
y_0	0	1	0	1	1	0	1	0	0	1	0	1	1	0	1	0
y_1	0	1	0	1	1	0	1	0	1	0	1	0	0	1	0	1
y_2	0	1	0	1	0	1	0	0	1	0	1	0	1	0	1	0
y_3	0	1	1	0	0	1	1	0	1	0	0	1	1	0	0	1
y	0	15	1	14	12	3	13	2	7	8	6	9	11	4	10	5

Therefore,

$$
\sigma_{4,3}^{-1} =
\begin{bmatrix}
1 & 0 & 1 & 1 \\
0 & 1 & 1 & 1 \\
1 & 1 & 0 & 1 \\
1 & 0 & 0 & 1
\end{bmatrix}
\cdot
\begin{bmatrix}
1 & 0 & 1 & 0 \\
0 & 0 & 1 & 0 \\
1 & 1 & 1 & 0 \\
0 & 0 & 0 & 1
\end{bmatrix}
=
\begin{bmatrix}
0 & 1 & 0 & 1 \\
1 & 1 & 0 & 1 \\
1 & 0 & 0 & 1 \\
1 & 0 & 1 & 1
\end{bmatrix}.
$$

*Table 4.1.4 shows the mapping of vectors of variables in f by using $\sigma_{4,3}^{-1}$. It produces the identical permutation of values in **F** as a recursive application of σ_4^{-1} and σ_3^{-1} to f, respectively.*

In this example, the size of the MTBDD(f) was reduced from 13 to 9 nonterminal nodes by using the proposed method.

4.1.2 Properties of the *K*-Procedure

Remark 4.1.5 *The K-procedure performs the decomposition of f with respect to the expansion rule*

$$
f = (\overline{z_i \oplus \cdots \oplus z_m})f_0 \oplus (z_i \oplus \cdots \oplus z_m)f_1,
$$

where f_0 and f_1 are the cofactors of f for $z_i \oplus \cdots \oplus z_m = 0$, and 1, respectively.

The following example illustrates dependency of the solutions on the choice of matrices σ and vectors τ, where the total autocorrelation functions take the maximum values, in the cases when there are several maxima in the total autocorrelation function for a given function f.

Example 4.1.2 *(Dependency on τ) Consider a four-variable Boolean function f given by the truth-vector*

$$
\mathbf{F} = [0, 0, 1, 0, 1, 0, 0, 0, 1, 0, 0, 1, 0, 1, 0, 0]^T.
$$

For this function, size(MTBDD(f)) = 9.

The maximum value of the autocorrelation function $B_f(\tau) = 14$ for the inputs $\tau = 6, 9$, and 15. For $\tau = (1111) = 15$ and

$$\sigma_4(\tau = 15) = \begin{bmatrix} 1 & 1 & 1 & 1 \\ 0 & 0 & 1 & 1 \\ 1 & 0 & 0 & 1 \\ 1 & 1 & 1 & 0 \end{bmatrix},$$

we determine

$$\sigma_4^{-1}(\tau = 15) = \begin{bmatrix} 1 & 0 & 1 & 1 \\ 0 & 1 & 1 & 1 \\ 1 & 1 & 0 & 1 \\ 1 & 0 & 0 & 1 \end{bmatrix}.$$

The components of the truth vector for f are reordered as $\mathbf{F}_\sigma = [0, 0, 0, 0, 0, 0, 0, 0, 1, 1, 0, 1, 1, 1, 0, 0]^T$.

We perform encoding of pairs of adjacent values as $\mathbf{Q}_\sigma = [0, 0, 0, 0, 1, 2, 1, 0]^T$, where $(0, 0) = 0$, $(1, 1) = 1$, and $(0, 1) = 2$. For this function, the maximum value of the total autocorrelation function $\max_\tau B_{\mathbf{Q}_\sigma(\tau)} = 6$ for the input $\tau = 2 = (010)$. For

$$\sigma_3(\tau = 2) = \begin{bmatrix} 1 & 0 & 0 \\ 0 & 0 & 1 \\ 0 & 1 & 0 \end{bmatrix},$$

it follows

$$\sigma_3^{-1}(\tau = 2) = \begin{bmatrix} 1 & 0 & 0 \\ 0 & 0 & 1 \\ 0 & 1 & 0 \end{bmatrix},$$

and the corresponding reordering is $\mathbf{Q}_\sigma = [0, 0, 0, 0, 1, 1, 2, 0]^T$, from where $\mathbf{F}_\sigma = [0, 0, 0, 0, 0, 0, 0, 0, 1, 1, 1, 1, 0, 1, 0, 0]^T$. For the resulting f_σ, it follows that $size(MTBDD(f_\sigma)) = 4$.

If for the maximum value of the autocorrelation function $B_f(\tau)$, we choose the input $\tau = 6$ instead of $\tau = 15$, then for

$$\sigma_4(\tau = 6) = \begin{bmatrix} 1 & 0 & 0 & 0 \\ 0 & 1 & 1 & 0 \\ 1 & 0 & 0 & 1 \\ 0 & 0 & 1 & 1 \end{bmatrix},$$

we determine

$$\sigma_4^{-1}(\tau = 6) = \begin{bmatrix} 1 & 0 & 0 & 0 \\ 1 & 1 & 1 & 1 \\ 1 & 0 & 1 & 1 \\ 1 & 0 & 1 & 0 \end{bmatrix}.$$

Thus, we reorder the elements of $\mathbf{F}$ for the given f as $\mathbf{F}_\sigma = [0, 0, 0, 0, 1, 1, 0, 0, 0, 0, 1, 0, 1, 1, 0, 0]^T$.

For encoding $\mathbf{Q}_\sigma = [0, 0, 1, 0, 0, 2, 1, 0]^T$, where $(0, 0)) = 0$, $(1, 1) = 1$, and $(1, 0) = 2$, the maximum values of the total autocorrelation function of $\mathbf{Q}_\sigma$ is 6 for the input $4 = (100)$.

For

$$\sigma_3(\tau = 4) = \begin{bmatrix} 0 & 0 & 1 \\ 0 & 1 & 0 \\ 1 & 0 & 0 \end{bmatrix},$$

we determine $\sigma_3^{-1}(\tau = 4) = \sigma_3(\tau = 4)$.

Therefore, the corresponding reordering is $\mathbf{Q}_\sigma = [0, 0, 1, 1, 0, 2, 0, 0]^T$, which produces $\mathbf{F}_\sigma = [0, 0, 0, 0, 1, 1, 1, 1, 1, 0, 0, 1, 0, 0, 0, 0, 0]^T$. For the resulting f_σ, we determine $size(MTBDD(f_\sigma)) = 5$.

Thus, selecting at the first step $\tau = 15$ produces smaller resulting $MTBDD(f)$ than $\tau = 6$, but for the original function $B_f(6) = B_f(15) = 14$.

Example 4.1.3 *(Dependency on σ) For the function f in the previous example, if we choose for the maximum value of $B_f(\tau)$ the assignment $\tau = 15$ and the matrix*

$$\sigma_{4,r}(\tau = 15) = \begin{bmatrix} 1 & 1 & 0 & 0 \\ 0 & 0 & 1 & 1 \\ 1 & 0 & 1 & 0 \\ 0 & 1 & 0 & 0 \end{bmatrix},$$

instead of

$$\begin{bmatrix} 1 & 1 & 1 & 1 \\ 0 & 0 & 1 & 1 \\ 1 & 0 & 0 & 1 \\ 1 & 1 & 1 & 0 \end{bmatrix}$$

as in Example 4.1.2, with the matrix

$$\sigma_{4,r}^{-1}(\tau = 15) = \begin{bmatrix} 1 & 0 & 0 & 1 \\ 0 & 0 & 0 & 1 \\ 1 & 0 & 1 & 1 \\ 1 & 1 & 1 & 1 \end{bmatrix},$$

then we obtain the reordering

$$\mathbf{F}_\sigma = [0, 0, 0, 0, 0, 0, 1, 1, 1, 1, 1, 0, 0, 0, 0, 0]^T.$$

For the encoding $\sigma(\mathbf{Q}) = [0, 0, 0, 1, 1, 2, 0, 0]^T$, *the maximum value of the total autocorrelation function is* $\max_\tau B_{\mathbf{Q}_\sigma}(\tau) = 6$ *for the input* $\tau = 7 = (111)$. *For*

$$\sigma_3(\tau = 7) = \begin{bmatrix} 1 & 1 & 0 \\ 1 & 0 & 1 \\ 0 & 1 & 0 \end{bmatrix},$$

we get

$$\sigma_3^{-1}(\tau = 7) = \begin{bmatrix} 1 & 0 & 1 \\ 0 & 0 & 1 \\ 1 & 1 & 1 \end{bmatrix},$$

which induces a reordering $\mathbf{Q}_\sigma = [0, 0, 0, 0, 2, 0, 1, 1]^T$. *From there,* $\mathbf{F}_\sigma = [0, 0, 0, 0, 0, 0, 0, 0, 1, 0, 0, 1, 1, 1, 1]^T$. *For the resulting* f_σ, $size(MTBDD(f_\sigma)) = 4$.
However, if we choose

$$\sigma_{3,r}(\tau = 7) = \begin{bmatrix} 0 & 1 & 1 \\ 1 & 1 & 0 \\ 0 & 1 & 0 \end{bmatrix},$$

and the corresponding

$$\sigma_{3,r}^{-1}(\tau = 7) = \begin{bmatrix} 0 & 1 & 1 \\ 0 & 0 & 1 \\ 1 & 0 & 1 \end{bmatrix},$$

we get the reordering $\mathbf{Q}_\sigma = [0, 0, 1, 1, 0, 0, 2, 0]^T$, *which produces the vector* $\mathbf{F}_\sigma = [0, 0, 0, 0, 1, 1, 1, 1, 0, 0, 0, 0, 1, 0, 0, 0]^T$. *For the resulting* f_σ, *size* $(MTBDD(f_\sigma)) = 5$.

The reason for the increased size is that $\sigma_{3,r}(\tau = 7)$, unlike $\sigma_3(\tau = 7)$, does not pair together sequences of four zeros in $\mathbf{Q}_\sigma$. This pairing in $MTBDD(f_\sigma)$ means assignment of identical subvectors of length 4 to the same logic value for z_0. In this case that is the negative literal $\overline{z}_0$. Owing to this fact, the subtree rooted in the node pointed by $\overline{z}_0$ in the MTBDD is reduced to a single constant node.

The presented method provides for the reduction of a number of subtrees consisting of a nonterminal node and two constant nodes, since it produces pairs of equal function values. The larger subtrees, which correspond to the equal subvectors of orders 2^i, $i > 1$, are not taken into account at this step. The method fails in the case when we choose a permutation matrix that does not provide a grouping of isomorphic smallest subtrees into a larger subtree. Example 4.1.4 illustrates this feature of the method.

Example 4.1.4   *Consider a function $f = \overline{z}_1\overline{z}_3 \vee z_1\overline{z}_2z_3 \vee z_0z_1z_3 \vee \overline{z}_0z_2\overline{z}_3$. The truth vector for f is given by $\mathbf{F} = [1, 0, 1, 0, 0, 1, 1, 0, 1, 0, 1, 0, 0, 1, 0, 1]^T$. The $size(MTBDD(f)) = 6$ for this truth vector.*

The maximum value of $B_f(\tau)$ is equal to 12, which means that we may generate six pairs of equal values for f at the adjacent places at the level z_3. The method presented in Section 4.1.1 produces MTBDDs with the size equal to 7. However, by ordering of variables it is possible to obtain the MTBDDs of sizes 5, 6, and 7 (468).

However, if we first perform encoding $\mathbf{Q} = [2, 2, 3, 2, 2, 2, 3, 3]^T$, where $(1, 0) = 2$, and $(0, 1) = 3$, and then apply the method from Section 4.1.1, we get a MTBDD of size 5, by always taking the smallest value for τ. This follows from the property that in $\mathbf{Q}$, we have five pairs denoted by 2 and three pairs denoted by 3, which permits an immediate reduction of subtrees consisting of three nonterminal nodes.

We note that the method described in Section 4.1.1 is based on an extended set of allowed permutation matrices for the inputs consisting of all nonsingular over $GF(2)$ matrices, compared to the one used in decision diagram optimization by ordering of variables. The price for such extension is minor, since the values for f can be easily determined from f_σ assigned to f. Therefore, the proposed method permits to derive efficient solutions, which cannot be achieved by the ordering of variables. In this respect, the proposed method relates to the considerations in References 56 and 185. In Reference 56, the same approach to BDDs minimization by using an extended set of permutation matrices was proposed, starting from cube representations of functions and performing transformations of cubes. However, no algorithm or heuristic for determination of a transformation for cubes has been proposed. Instead, for each given function f, a particular transformation is determined by the inspection of the characteristics of f. In Reference 185, the method in Reference 56 was extended to the method of truth-table permutation, and was further elaborated by proposing two heuristic algorithms for determination of a suitable permutation of the function values for f permitting reduction of the size of the BDD for f.

To conclude this section, we note that the method described in Section 4.1.1 results in BDDs that can be smaller than BDDs produced by methods based on ordering of variables.

Example 4.1.5 *Consider a function* $f = z_0 z_1 z_2 \vee z_1 z_2 z_3$. *The truth vector for this function is* $\mathbf{F} = [0, 0, 0, 0, 0, 0, 0, 1, 0, 0, 0, 0, 0, 0, 1, 1]^T$. *The optimization by ordering of variables can produce MTBDDs of size 5. However, the method proposed in this chapter produces a MTBDD of size 4 in the following way. The maximum value for* $B_f(\tau) = 14$ *for the inputs* $\tau = 1, 8, 9$. *For simplicity, we choose* $\tau = 1$, *which implies* $\sigma_4(\tau = 1)$ *is the identity matrix of order 4, and perform the encoding as* $\mathbf{Q} = [0, 0, 0, 2, 0, 0, 0, 1]^T$. *The maximum of the total autocorrelation function for* $\mathbf{Q}$ *is 6 and it is achieved for the input* $\tau = 4 = (100)$. *For a matrix*

$$\sigma_3(\tau = 4) = \begin{bmatrix} 0 & 0 & 1 \\ 0 & 1 & 0 \\ 1 & 0 & 0 \end{bmatrix},$$

which is self-inverse over $GF(2)$, *we get the reordering* $\mathbf{Q}_\sigma = [0, 0, 0, 0, 0, 0, 2, 1]^T$, *which produces* $\mathbf{F}_\sigma = [0, 0, 0, 0, 0, 0, 0, 0, 0, 0, 0, 0, 0, 1, 1, 1]^T$. *For this* f_σ, *size*$(MTBDD(f_\sigma)) = 4$.

4.2 CONSTRUCTION OF LINEARLY TRANSFORMED BINARY DECISION DIAGRAMS

In this section, we explain the application of the linearization method for switching functions presented above for construction of linear transformations for BDDs and SBDDs for systems of Boolean functions.

Example 4.2.1 *Figure 4.2.1 shows SBDD for the system of Boolean functions* $f^{(0)}(z)$ *and* $f^{(1)}(z)$ *defined in Table 4.2.1. This SBDD represents the given system in the form of expressions*

$$f^{(0)} = \overline{z}_0 \overline{z}_1 \overline{z}_2 z_3 \oplus \overline{z}_0 \overline{z}_1 z_2 \oplus \overline{z}_0 z_1 z_2 \oplus \overline{z}_0 z_1 \overline{z}_2 \overline{z}_3$$

$$\oplus z_0 \overline{z}_1 z_2 z_3 \oplus z_0 z_1 z_2 \overline{z}_3 \oplus z_0 \overline{z}_1 \overline{z}_2 \oplus z_0 z_1 \overline{z}_2,$$

$$f^{(1)} = \overline{z}_0 \overline{z}_1 z_2 z_3 \oplus \overline{z}_0 z_1 z_2 \overline{z}_3 \oplus z_0 \overline{z}_1 z_2 z_3 \oplus z_0 z_1 \overline{z}_2 \overline{z}_3.$$

We perform first five steps in Procedure 4.2.1 for construction of linearly transformed binary decision diagrams defined in what follows; and after the linearization, this system can be converted into the system $f_\sigma^{(0)}(y)$ *and* $f_\sigma^{(1)}(y)$, *in terms of new variables* y_i, $i = 0, 1, 2, 3$ *expressed as the linear combination of original variables* z_i, $i = 0, 1, 2, 3$. *Then, the given system can be represented by a SBDD derived from decomposition in terms of this linear combination of variables as is specified in the Step 6 for construction of LT-BDDs.*

Figure 4.2.2 shows SBDD for the system derived from the linearization method, where, in the Step 7 of Procedure 4.2.1, the labels at the edges are determined. This

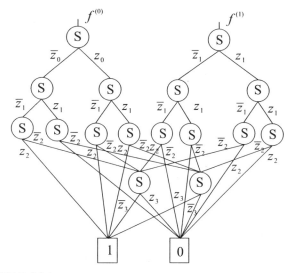

FIGURE 4.2.1   SBDD for the system of functions in Example 4.2.1.

SBDD represents the given system in the following form:

$$f^{(0)} = (z_0 \oplus z_2) \oplus (\overline{z_0 \oplus z_2})(z_1 \oplus z_3),$$
$$f^{(1)} = (z_0 \oplus z_2)(z_1 \oplus z_3).$$

**TABLE 4.2.1   System of Switching Functions in
Example 4.2.1.**

z, τ	$z_0 z_1 z_2$	$f^{(0)}$	$f^{(1)}$	$B_f(\tau)$	$f_\sigma^{(0)}$	$f_\sigma^{(1)}$
0	0000	0	0	16	0	0
1	0001	1	0	0	0	0
2	0010	1	0	0	0	0
3	0011	1	1	8	0	0
4	0100	1	0	0	1	0
5	0101	0	0	16	1	0
6	0110	1	1	8	1	0
7	0111	1	0	0	1	0
8	1000	1	0	0	1	0
9	1001	1	1	8	1	0
10	1010	0	0	16	1	0
11	1011	1	0	0	1	0
12	1100	1	1	8	1	1
13	1101	1	0	0	1	1
14	1110	1	0	0	1	1
15	1111	0	0	16	1	1

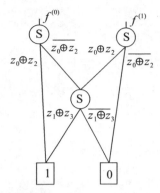

FIGURE 4.2.2 Shared LT-BDD for the system of functions derived by the linearization method for $f^{(0)}$ and $f^{(1)}$ from Example 4.1.2.

4.2.1 Procedure for Construction of Linearly Transformed Binary Decision Diagrams

The following procedure for determination of a linear transformation of variables in LT-BDD for a given function f can be formulated, as is explained by this example.

Procedure 4.2.1 *Procedure for generation of LT-BDD is as under:*

1. *Given an m-variable k-output, switching function $f = (f^{(0)}, \ldots, f^{(k-1)})$.*
2. *Represent f by the integer-valued equivalent function*

$$f(z) = \sum_{i=0}^{k-1} f^{(i)}(z) 2^{k-i-1}.$$

3. *Construct characteristic functions $f_r(z)$ for $f(z)$, where $f_r(z) = 1$ if $f(z) = r$ and $f_r(z) = 0$ for $f(z) \neq r$.*
4. *Construct a total autocorrelation function $B_f(\tau) = \sum_r B_r(\tau)$, where $B_r(\tau)$ is the autocorrelation function for $f_r(z)$ for the system $\{f_r(z)\}$.*
5. *Perform the linearization Procedure 4.1.1 (K-procedure), determine $\sigma = \sigma_{opt}$, and assign to $f(z)$ a function $f_\sigma(y)$, where $y = \sigma \odot z \ (mod\ 2)$.*
6. *Determine SBDD for $f_\sigma(y)$.*
7. *Relabel edges in SBDD($f_\sigma(y)$) by replacing each y_i with the corresponding linear combination of initial variables z_i.*

Compared to the present methods for linear transformation of decision diagrams, an advantage is that the linearization method based on autocorrelation functions provides for a deterministic algorithm, in the sense that all steps are uniquely determined.

4.2.2 Modified *K*-Procedure

Procedure 4.2.2 *(Modified K-procedure)*

1. *Compute* $\max_{\tau \neq 0} B_{f_m}(\tau) = B_m(\tau)$, *where* $f_m = f$, *and* m *is the number of variables in* f_m.
2. *Compress* f_m *into* f_{m-q} *by encoding q-tuples of successive function values in the truth vector for* f_m, *for* $q = 1, \ldots, m - 1$.
3. *Compute* $\max_i B_{f_i} = B_{f_t}$.
4. *Apply K-procedure to* f_t.

This modification of the original procedure may increase the amount of computation by the factor of 2 at the most.

4.2.3 Computing Autocorrelation by Symbolic Manipulations

We note that total autocorrelation functions and optimal LT-BDDs in many cases may be computed analytically. To illustrate this point, we consider a device implementing an error-correcting procedure based on a linear code V of length m with k-information bits (278).

A code V *correct errors* from a set $E \subset C_2^m$ iff $v_1 \oplus e_1 \neq v_2 \oplus e_2$ for any $v_1, v_2 \in V$ and $e_1, e_2 \in E$, $e_1 \neq e_2$. If V corrects l-bit errors, then E contains at least all $\sum_{i=0}^{l} \binom{m}{i}$ vectors e with $\|e\| \leq l$, where $\|e\|$ is the Hamming weight of e, that is, the number of 1 values in e.

A code V is *perfect* for a given E iff for any $z \in Z_2^m$ there exists a unique $v \in V$ and a unique $e \in E$ such that $z = v \oplus e$, $|E| = 2^{(m-k)}$.

A device implementing an error-correcting procedure based on a given V has m inputs, m outputs, and for the input z produces the output $e = f(z)$ such that there exist $v \in V$ and $z = v \oplus e$. Since V corrects a set of errors E, this e is unique.

We have Reference 278 for the total autocorrelation function for $e = f(z)$ so that

$$B_f(\tau) = \begin{cases} 2^m, & \tau \in V, \\ 0, & \tau \notin V. \end{cases}$$

If V is an (m, k) code, the K-procedure will require k steps. For the resulting optimal linear transform σ, the rows $(h_1, \ldots, h_{m-k})$ of σ form a basis of the null space for V. Thus,

$$\sigma = \begin{bmatrix} & h_1 \\ & \vdots \\ & h_{m-k} \\ \hline \mathbf{0} & \mathbf{I}_k \end{bmatrix},$$

where I_k is the $(k \times k)$ identity matrix, and the corresponding LT-BDD will have $2^{m-k} - 1$ nodes.

Example 4.2.2 *Consider* $(5, 2)$*-single-error-correcting code V (shortened* Hamming code *(278)) with the generating matrix*

$$\mathbf{G} = \begin{bmatrix} 1 & 0 & 1 & 1 & 0 \\ 0 & 1 & 1 & 0 & 1 \end{bmatrix}.$$

It is easy to check that this code can correct all single errors and two double errors, 00011 *and* 10001. *In this case,*

$$B_f(\tau) = \begin{cases} 32, & \text{if } \tau = 00000, 10110, 01101, 11011 \\ 0, & \text{otherwise}, \end{cases}$$

and

$$\sigma^{-1} = \begin{bmatrix} 1 & 1 & 1 & & 0 & 0 \\ 1 & 0 & 0 & & 1 & 0 \\ 0 & 1 & 0 & & 0 & 1 \\ \hline 0 & 0 & 0 & | & 1 & 0 \\ 0 & 0 & 0 & | & 0 & 1 \end{bmatrix}.$$

Therefore,

$$y_0 = z_0 \oplus z_1 \oplus z_2,$$
$$y_1 = z_0 \oplus z_3,$$
$$y_3 = z_1 \oplus z_4.$$

Figure 4.2.3 shows the resulting optimal BDD for the decoder for this $(5, 2)$*-single-error-correcting code.*

4.2.4 Experimental Results on the Complexity of Linearly Transformed Binary Decision Diagrams

In this section, we discuss the efficiency of linearly transformed BDDs in the light of experiments on benchmark functions used in logic design and for randomly generated multiple-output switching functions.

These results illustrate a reduction of complexities of MTBDDs, which can be obtained by linear transformations of variables.

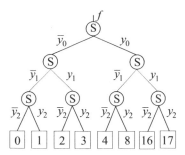

FIGURE 4.2.3   LT-BDD for the decoder for the (5, 2) shortened Hamming code.

In Table 4.2.2, we present the number of inputs (In), outputs (Out), constant nodes (cn) for the given functions, and in columns denoted by MTBDD(f) and MTBDD(f_σ), we compared the number of nonterminal nodes (ntn) whose sum with the constant nodes produces the size (s), and the width (w) of the MTBDDs for the initial ordering of variables and for LT-MTBDDs derived by the autocorrelation functions. The column MTBDD(f_v) shows the number of nonterminal nodes and width of MTBDDs for the optimal ordering of variables determined by the brute-force method estimating all possible orderings of variables. The existing methods for optimization of decision diagrams by variables ordering are heuristics and mostly produce the nearly optimal solutions. Therefore, the provided comparison is the strongest challenge for the proposed method. This table presents the results for the method using the autocorrelation functions for the smallest values for the indices τ where the autoorrelation functions take the maximum values. The other choices for τ, and subsequently σ, may produce smaller LT-MTBDDs.

However, in Table 4.2.3, we compare the number of nonterminal nodes of MTBDDs for the initial ordering of variables (MTBDD(f_I)), the optimal ordering (MTBDD(f_v)), and the initial ordering with negated edges (MTBDD(f_w)) (130, 499), the ordering determined by the lower-bound sifting method with negated edges (MTBDD(f_r)) (130, 499), and by the autocorrelation functions (MTBDD(f_σ)) for binary-valued single output randomly generated functions. In a BDD with negated edges, a subfunction f and its logic complement $\overline{f}$ are represented by the same subdiagram. It follows that by assigning negative attributes to the edges, it is not needed to represent both f and $\overline{f}$, which provides advantages in reducing complexity of BDDs as well as in computations over BDDs (371).

As it is usually the case with NP-complete problems, for some functions, the method described in Section 4.1.1 produces better solutions compared with the initial ordering and the optimal ordering of variables. However, for some functions, the MTBDDs for the optimal ordering of variables are smaller in terms of the number of nonterminal nodes, the width, or both these parameters. From these experiments, the following conclusions can be made:

1. The proposed method is very effective when the integer equivalent function $f(z)$ defined by a given multiple-output function takes a large number of different

TABLE 4.2.2 Sizes of MTBDD(f), MTBDD(f_v), and MTBDD(f_σ) for Benchmark and Randomly Generated Functions.

f	In	Out	cn	MTBDD(f)		MTBDD(f_v)		MTBDD(f_σ)	
				ntn	w	ntn	w	ntn	w
add2	4	3	7	13	6	12	6	8	3
add3	6	4	15	51	20	33	14	24	7
add4	8	5	31	113	30	78	30	64	15
add5	10	6	63	289	62	171	62	160	31
add6	12	7	127	705	126	360	126	384	63
add7	14	8	255	1665	254	741	254	896	127
ex1010	10	10	177	894	383	-	-	871	367
misex1	8		11	17	6	17	6	17	5
clip	9	5	33	339	120	141	35	159	32
t481	16	1	2	32	4	-	-	103	46
rd53	5	3	6	15	5	15	5	14	5
rd73	7	3	8	28	7	28	7	17	6
rd84	8	4	9	36	8	36	8	23	7
rd84/8	8	4	9	36	8	36	8	18	6
9sym	9	1	2	33	6	33	6	24	5
9sym/16	9	1	2	33	6	33	6	9	3
				Randomly Generated Functions					
f_2	8	1	2	75	30	68	25	66	24
f_3	8	1	2	73	28	67	23	72	27
f_6	8	1	2	58	18	58	18	69	25
f_7	8	1	2	72	28	70	26	67	23
f_8	8	3	8	174	64	167	60	168	59
f_9	8	4	16	222	95	216	90	219	94
f_{10}	8	3	5	139	56	135	54	136	54
n_1	8	2	3	84	30	77	25	80	26
n_2	8	2	3	89	29	80	26	87	27
n_3	8	2	3	91	31	85	27	50	15
n_4	8	2	3	90	31	83	24	89	28
n_5	8	2	3	82	27	76	22	77	24
n_6	8	2	2	68	25	59	18	62	19
n_7	8	2	2	72	28	64	21	63	20
n_8	8	2	2	72	29	64	22	72	28
n_9	8	2	2	73	28	69	25	68	25
n_{10}	8	2	2	118	41	111	36	115	42

values, which, however, do not repeat periodically as sequences of order 2^i, $i = 1, \ldots, m - 1$. This is the case, for example, of m-bit adders. It follows from Table 4.2.2 that for adders, transition from BDDs to LT-BDDs results in almost 50% reduction of the sizes of the corresponding decision diagrams.

For adders, the method produces the LT-MTBDDs with the optimal width, however, with the increased size in comparison to the size for the optimal

TABLE 4.2.3 Numbers of Nonterminal Nodes in MTBDDs for Initial Ordering of Variables f_I, Optimal Ordering f_v, Initial Ordering with Negated Edges f_w, Lower-Bound Sifting with Negated Edges f_r, and Autocorrelation Functions f_σ.

	MTBDD				
f	f_I	f_v	f_w	f_r	f_σ
f_1	75	68	64	62	66
f_2	73	67	67	60	72
f_6	58	58	52	51	69
f_7	72	70	64	62	67
n_1	84	77	64	62	80
n_6	68	59	63	55	62
n_7	72	64	65	60	63
n_8	72	64	65	58	72
n_9	73	69	64	62	68

ordering of variables. It should be noted that the reordering of variables does not reduce the width of the MTBDD for adders. The self-inverse matrix σ, describing the optimal ordering of variables for adders, can be derived from the values τ_i for the maximum values of the total autocorrelation functions by writing each 1-bit of τ_i in the separate row of σ, starting from the largest τ_i. For example, for 2-bit adder, the total autocorrelation function B_f takes the maximum value for $\tau_1 = 5 = (0101)$ and $\tau_2 = 10 = (1010)$. Therefore, we can select the matrix σ as a self-inverse matrix with the first two rows corresponding to binary representations for τ_2 and τ_1, and the remaining two rows as the corresponding rows of the identity matrix, that is,

$$\sigma = \begin{bmatrix} 1 & 0 & 1 & 0 \\ 0 & 1 & 0 & 1 \\ 0 & 0 & 1 & 0 \\ 0 & 0 & 0 & 1 \end{bmatrix}.$$

2. The method is less efficient when the equal values repeat as sequences of the length 2^i in the vector of function values $\mathbf{F} = [f(0), \dots, f(2^m - 1)]^T$. In a MTBDD, such sequences result in isomorphic subtrees, which permits reduction of nodes at the upper levels in the MTBDD, that is, levels with the smaller value of indices. In these cases, pairing function values at the Hamming distance 1 by the total autocorrelation function may destroy the equal sequences of the length 2^i, for $i > 1$, which results in larger MTBDDs.

As it is discussed in Reference 185, that feature is characteristic for methods using permutations of function values for multiple-output functions (permutation of components of $\mathbf{F}$) (56, 185). Since any reordering of variables is a permutation of function values, the same remark applies to optimization of

DDs by reordering of variables, in the sense that some orderings reduce, while the other increase the size of DDs.

The method is inefficient for multiple-output functions whose integer-valued equivalent functions contain few equal values. In these cases, we cannot produce large numbers of pairs of equal values resulting in a reduction of the number of nodes in the MTBDD. The examples are multipliers.

3. The method is efficient for randomly generated multiple-output functions. It should be noted that in this case the initial MTBDDs are usually large and the ordering of variables does not provide for reduction of their size.

4. An important feature of the proposed method is that, unlike widely used sifting technique (130, 478), it can be applied to the reduction of MTBDDs of symmetric functions, where the permutation of variables does not permit reduction of nodes. Symmetry implies equal sequences of the length 2^i for some large i in the function values.

First, we perform encoding of such sequences, and after this we apply the method to the function g of 2^{n-i} variables derived in this way. Then we determine g_σ for this function, and after the decoding we get f_σ for the initial function f. Table 4.2.2, in rows 11–16, illustrates the method and compares MTBDD(f) and MTBDD(f_σ) for some symmetric benchmark functions. For these benchmarks, we first perform encoding of sequences of four successive elements, and then apply the method presented in Section 4.1.1 to the MTBDDs whose constant nodes are the encoded sequences, and perform recoding before we determine the size of the MTBDD for the initial function f.

Notice that the same approach can be used to reduce the *Average path length* (APL) in decision diagrams, since $APL = m - \sum_{i=0}^{m-1} 2^{l-m} B^{(i)}$ (310, 311).

The K-procedure is presented in this chapter as a BDD minimization procedure. The basic idea is to "integrate" linear decomposition with BDD minimization. Since columns of the linearization matrix **T** form a base in the input space $\{0, 1\}^m$, the K-procedure provides for a simple method to solve the difficult problem of constructing a set of m independent vectors having high autocorrelation values and to construct a suitable base in $\{0, 1\}^m$.

We also note that the K-procedure can be very efficient for minimization of a number of literals in the sum-of-products representations for nonlinear blocks implementing the linearized functions.

4.3 CONSTRUCTION OF LINEARLY TRANSFORMED PLANAR BDD

In digital circuits, crossings of interconnections must be realized by at least two levels in the circuits connected by bias between levels. Crossings are a significant source of the delays in digital circuits. For instance, in FPGAs most of the delay occurs in interconnecting devices rather than the devices themselves (394). Therefore, the design of planar circuits, that is, circuits without crossings of interconnections, is an interesting and important task (174, 401).

In circuit synthesis, decision diagrams provide a simple mapping to technology, since a network is easily derived from a decision diagram by replacing each node with the logic element realizing the decomposition rule used to assign a given function f to the corresponding decision diagram. Planar decision diagrams, that is, decision diagrams without crossings of edges, result in planar networks.

Therefore, planar decision diagrams have been studied in several publications; see References 82,495, and 496. In particular, in Reference 495, there have been derived necessary conditions for planarity in decision diagrams of certain functions. In Reference 496, these results have been extended by completely characterizing symmetric functions with planar decision diagrams, with the motivation that such functions are an important set of functions and an indispensable part of arithmetic circuits.

In References 605 and 659, *Linear Decision Diagrams* (LDDs) that are planar by definition have been proposed as models for efficient computation of multiple-valued functions. These decision diagrams are based on the corresponding representations of logic functions by arithmetic polynomials (37).

In this section, we consider construction of linearly transformed planar binary decision diagrams by Walsh transform coefficients. The approach we are going to use will be similar to that in the previous section, but in this case, the Walsh spectrum is used instead of the logic autocorrelation to determine the optimal linear transform of input variables.

4.3.1 Planar Decision Diagrams

In this section, we define the class of planar decision diagrams and briefly discuss their properties.

Definition 4.3.1 *A binary decision diagram is planar if there are no crossings of edges connecting nonterminal nodes, under the assumption that the edges labeled by $\bar{z}_i$ and z_i emerge to the left and right of a node, respectively, constant node 0 is to the left of the constant node 1, and all edges are directed down throughout their length, which precludes arcs that extend around the root node or constant nodes.*

In planar decision diagrams that we consider, crossing of edges to constant nodes are allowed. For simplicity, in figures illustrating examples, constant nodes are repeated if there were crossing otherwise.

There are functions that due to their inherent properties have planar decision diagrams. Some classes of such functions are determined in Reference 496.

Example 4.3.1 *Figure 4.3.1 shows a BDD for the five-variable majority function f that is a planar BDD.*

It should be noticed that the planarity of a decision diagram strongly depends on the order of variables. For a given function f, nonplanar decision diagrams in some cases can be converted into planar decision diagram and vice versa by changing the order of variables.

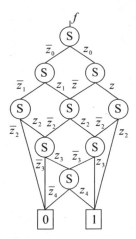

FIGURE 4.3.1   BDD for the majority function of five variables.

Notice that a planar decision diagram can be derived by the reduction of a decision tree in such a way that sharing of isomorphic subtrees is restricted to subtrees rooted at neighboring nodes at the same level in the decision tree. The planar BDDs derived in this way may not be optimal in the number of nodes and provide a simple and regular distribution of interconnections, as it can be seen from Example 4.3.5. It should be noticed that many functions with planar decision diagrams already fulfill this restriction on sharing of isomorphic subtrees. For instance, a switching function is symmetric if it does not change for any permutation of variables. Owing to this requirement, there is some regularity in the truth vectors of symmetric functions, which reflects on the regularity in the BDDs for symmetric functions corresponding to the above assumptions.

Example 4.3.2   *A symmetric function for $m = 3$ has the truth vector of the form* $\mathbf{F} = [A, V, V, W, V, W, W, K]^T$. *Figure 4.3.2 shows a planar BDD for symmetric functions of three variables.*

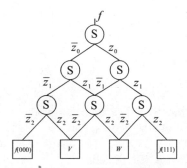

FIGURE 4.3.2   BDD for symmetric functions of three variables.

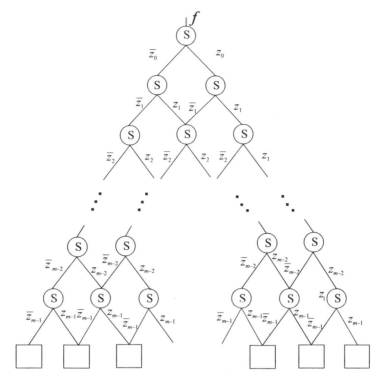

FIGURE 4.3.3   Planar BDD for symmetric functions defined on C_2^m

We note that any symmetric, not necessarily switching function of m variables $f(z_0, z_1, \ldots, z_{m-1})$, $z_i \in \{0, 1\}$, can be represented by the planar MTBDD of the form shown in Fig. 4.3.3. There are at most $m + 1$ different constant nodes in a planar MTBDD for any symmetric function $f : C_2^m \to C$.

Definition 4.3.2 *A switching function* $f(z_0, z_1, \ldots, z_{m-1})$ *is* elementary symmetric function *and denoted as* $S_i(m)$ *if*

$$f(z_0, z_1, \ldots, z_{m-1}) = S_i(m) = \begin{cases} 1, & if \ \|z\| = i \\ 0, & if \ \|z\| \neq i \end{cases}$$

for $i = 0, 1, \ldots, m - 1.$

Any symmetric switching function can be represented as OR (or EXOR) sum of at most $m + 1$ elementary symmetric functions.

The set $\{S_i(m)\}$, $i = 0, 1, \ldots, m$, is functionally closed, that is, superposition of symmetric functions is a symmetric function.

There are exactly 2^{m+1} symmetric switching functions of m variables.

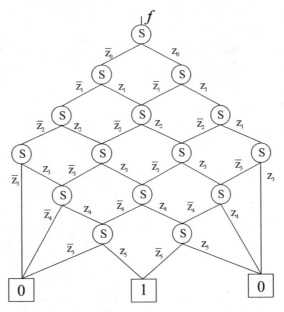

FIGURE 4.3.4   Rectangular planar BDD for $S_3(6)$.

Elementary symmetric functions can be represented by rectangular planar BDDs. The word rectangular refers to the shape of the decision diagram as it is obvious from Figure 4.3.4. We note that the size of a rectangular planar BDD for any $S_i(m)$ is upperbounded by $^1/_2 m^2$.

Example 4.3.3   *The rectangular planar BDD for $S_3(6)$ is given by Fig. 4.3.4.*

Further examples of functions with planar BDDs sharing isomorphic subtrees rooted at the neighboring nodes can be found in Reference 496.

Walsh and Haar spectra, as well as the autocorrelation functions of symmetric switching functions, are given in the Appendix A.

Owing to the correspondence between Walsh functions and linear switching functions, discussed in Section 2.3.2, the absolute values of Walsh spectral coefficients $|S_f(w)|$ express proximity of a given function f with the linear switching functions, the larger Walsh coefficients, the stronger similarity in the number of points where values for f and the corresponding linear function coincide. We exploit this property to determine optimal or near optimal linear combination of variables in planar LT-BDDs.

4.3.2 Construction of Planar LT-BDD by Walsh Coefficients

The method to construct linearly transformed BDDs by Walsh coefficients exploits the following property.

Consider a function τ defined as the EXOR sum of variables corresponding to the nonzero coordinates in the binary representation of the decimal value $w \neq 0$, where the Walsh spectral coefficients $S_f(w)$ of a given function f have the maximal value. If f is decomposed with respect to this function τ as $f = \overline{\tau} f_0 \oplus \tau f_1$, then the cofactors f_0 and f_1 tend to be simple. Therefore, it may be expected that they can be represented by MTBDDs with a small number of nodes.

The method will be introduced and illustrated by the following example.

Example 4.3.4 *Consider a four-variable function f, defined as*

$$\mathbf{F} = [0, 0, 1, 0, 1, 0, 0, 0, 1, 0, 0, 1, 0, 1, 0, 0]^T.$$

Figure 4.3.5 shows a BDD for f. The Walsh spectrum in the Hadamard ordering for this function f is

$$\mathbf{S}_f = \frac{1}{16}[5, 1, 1, 1, 1, 1, -3, 1, -1, 3, -1, -1, -1, -1, -1, -5]^T,$$

and the coefficient with the maximum absolute value for $w \neq 0$ is $S_f(w_{max}) = S_f(15) = -5/16$, and since $w_{max} = (1111)$, we get the linear function $\tau_1 = z_0 \oplus z_1 \oplus z_2 \oplus z_3$, where each z_i corresponds to the appearance of coordinate i with value 1 in the binary representation for w_{max}.

Because τ_1 is constant on cofactors, we can express them in terms of z_0, z_1, z_2 as $f_{\tau=0}(z_0, z_1, z_2) = f(z_0, z_1, z_2, \overline{z_0 \oplus z_1 \oplus z_2})$ and $f_{\tau=1}(z_0, z_1, z_2) = f(z_0, z_1, z_2, z_0 \oplus z_1 \oplus z_2)$, yielding the truth-vectors $\mathbf{F}_0 = [0, 0, 0, 0, 0, 0, 0, 0]^T$, and $\mathbf{F}_1 = [0, 1, 1, 0, 1, 1, 1, 0]^T$.

We create a node where outgoing edges point to subfunctions $\mathbf{F}_0$ and $\mathbf{F}_1$ and edges are labeled by $\overline{z_0 \oplus z_1 \oplus z_2 \oplus z_3}$ and $z_0 \oplus z_1 \oplus z_2 \oplus z_3$, respectively. Thus, this tree represents f as

$$f = \overline{(z_0 \oplus z_1 \oplus z_2 \oplus z_3)} f_0 \oplus (z_0 \oplus z_1 \oplus z_2 \oplus z_3) f_1,$$

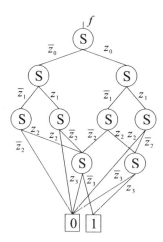

FIGURE 4.3.5 BDD for f in Example 4.3.4.

where the cofactors f_0 and f_1 are determined by the truth-vectors $\mathbf{F}_0$ and $\mathbf{F}_1$. Thus, at this step, the variable z_3 is replaced by $\tau_1 = z_0 \oplus z_1 \oplus z_2 \oplus z_3$.

Since $\mathbf{F}_0$ is a constant function 0, the edge $\overline{z_0 \oplus z_1 \oplus z_2 \oplus z_3}$ points to the constant node 0 directly. The Walsh spectrum for $\mathbf{F}_1$ is

$$\mathbf{S}_{f_1} = \frac{1}{8}[5, 1, 1, -3, -1, -1, -1, -1]^T.$$

The maximum Walsh coefficient for $\mathbf{F}_1$ is 6 for $w_{\max} = (011)$, thus we determine $\tau_2 = z_2 \oplus z_3$, and perform decomposition of f_1 into cofactors of two variables $\mathbf{F}_{1,0} = [0, 0, 1, 0]^T$ and $\mathbf{F}_{1,1} = [1, 1, 1, 1]^T$.

Thus, we have

$$f = \overline{(z_0 \oplus z_1 \oplus z_2 \oplus z_3)} \cdot 1 \oplus (z_0 \oplus z_1 \oplus z_2 \oplus z_3)$$
$$((\overline{z_1 \oplus z_2})f_{1,0} \oplus (z_1 \oplus z_2)f_{1,1}),$$

where cofactors $f_{1,0}$ and $f_{1,1}$ are determined by the truth-vectors $\mathbf{F}_{0,1}$ and $\mathbf{F}_{1,1}$.

Since $F_{1,1}$ is a constant function 1, we proceed with decomposition of $F_{1,0}$. This cofactor can be expressed by z_0 and z_1, since z_2 was the last variable in τ_2.

The Walsh spectrum of it is $\mathbf{S}_{f_{1,0}} = \frac{1}{4}[1, 1, -1, -1]^T$. Since all the coefficients in this spectrum have the same absolute value, we can choose, for example, $\tau_3 = z_0$ and we do not have to continue the decomposition.

In this way, we derive the LT-BDD for f as shown in Fig. 4.3.6. This LT-BDD represents f as $f = (z_0 \oplus z_1 \oplus z_2 \oplus z_3)((\overline{z_1 \oplus z_2})z_0\overline{z_1} \oplus (z_1 \oplus z_2))$. Thus, the proposed linearization by Walsh coefficients resulted in the reduction of a size of the BDD for f from 9 nodes for the original BDD, 7 nodes for the BDD for the optimal order of variables, to only 4 nodes for the planar LT-BDD of Fig. 4.3.6.

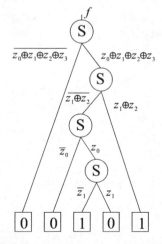

FIGURE 4.3.6 LT-BDD for f in Example 4.3.4.

Algorithm for construction of planar LT-BDD
The method presented in the example leads immediately to the following algorithm.

Algorithm 4.3.1 *(Construction of planar LT-BDD)*

1. *Given an m-variable switching function f. Calculate the Walsh spectrum in Hadamard ordering.*

2. *Find the Walsh coefficient $S_f(w_{\max})$ of the maximum absolute value, except the coefficient for $w = 0$. Declare $w = w_{\max}$ and write its binary representation, that is, $w_{\max} = (w_0, \ldots, w_{m-1})$.*

3. *Determine the linear function $\tau = \tau_1 = \bigoplus_{i=0}^{m-1} w_i z_i$.*

4. *Determine the cofactors $f_{\tau=0}$ and $f_{\tau=1}$ of f with respect to τ, where*

$$f_{\tau=0}(z_0, \ldots, z_{i_{k-1}}, z_{i_{k-1}+1}, \ldots, z_m)$$
$$= f(z_0, \ldots, z_{i_k-1}, z_{i_1} \oplus z_{i_2} \cdots \oplus z_{i_{k-1}} = 0, z_{i_k+1}, \ldots, z_m),$$
$$f_{\tau=1}(z_0, \ldots, z_{i_{k-1}}, z_{i_{k-1}+1}, \ldots, z_m)$$
$$= f(z_0, \ldots, z_{i_k-1}, z_{i_1} \oplus z_{i_2} \oplus \cdots \oplus z_{i_{k\ 1}} = 1, z_{i_k+1}, \ldots, z_m).$$

5. Create a node whose outgoing edges point to the cofactors f_0 and f_1 and label its edges by $\overline{\tau}_1$ and τ_1, respectively.

6. Repeat Steps 1–5 for cofactors f_0, f_1.

7. Share isomorphic subtrees under the restriction that they are rooted at the neighboring nodes at the same level in the decision diagrams, which guarantees planarity.

Assignment of variables to the edges in LT-BDDs can be performed by using the following algorithm, which exploits the property that when the decomposition with respect to an EXOR sum of a subset of variables $z_k \oplus z_q \oplus \cdots \oplus z_r$ is performed, then this EXOR sum is constant for a subfunction that implies that there cannot be two vectors in the domain of the subfunction that would differ just at the z_r.

Algorithm 4.3.2 *(Assignment of labels to the edges)*

1. *If at a node at the ith level for the decomposition with respect to a linear combination $z_k \oplus z_q \oplus \cdots \oplus z_r$, where $k < q < \ldots < r$, is performed, relate the variable z_r to the level i and eliminate it from the further considerations.*

2. *Repeat Step 1 to all the levels in the BDD, starting from the root node.*

We note that the planar BDDs determined by Algorithms 4.3.1 and 4.3.2 are Free BDDs (195), since they have different orderings of variables along different paths in the BDD.

Example 4.3.5 *Figure 4.3.7 shows the planar LT-BDD for the first output of the function $5xp1$, $(m = 7)$, with shown values for τ per nodes in terms of which the*

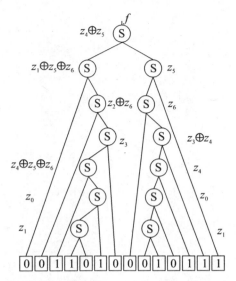

FIGURE 4.3.7   Planar MTBDD for $5xp1-1$.

decomposition has been performed. The planar BDD for this function for the initial order of variables and the planar BDD for the optimal order of variables require 14 and 11 nodes, respectively.

4.3.3 Upper Bounds on the Number of Nodes in Planar BDDs

An estimate of the number of nodes in planar BDDs constructed under restrictions assumed above can be derived from the following considerations.

Figure 4.3.8 shows a decision tree for functions of m variables, which is split into the upper part for $m - 2$ variables, and the lower part representing subfunctions of two variables. Each of these subfunctions can be any of 16 possible two-variable switching functions. Therefore, each of these subfunctions can be realized by a subtree with at most two nonterminal nodes. If all these functions are different, the number of nodes

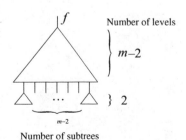

FIGURE 4.3.8   Decision tree and subtrees for two variables.

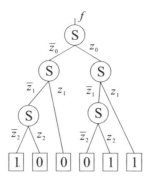

FIGURE 4.3.9 BDD for f in Example 4.3.6.

$L(m)$ in this decision diagram is

$$L(m) \leq 2^{m-2} - 1 + 2 \cdot 2^{m-2} = 2^{m-1} + 2^{m-2} - 1.$$

The most complicated functions are those in the Walsh spectrum where exists a single maximum absolute value at $w_{\text{max}} \neq 0$. In this case, for example, $L(3) = 5$ and $L(4) = 11$.

Example 4.3.6 *Figure 4.3.9 shows BDD of a function for $m = 3$ given by* $\mathbf{F} = [1, 0, 0, 0, 0, 1, 1, 1]^T$. *The Walsh spectrum of this function is* $\mathbf{S}_f = \frac{1}{8}[4, 0, 0, 0, -2, 2, 2, 2]^T$. *If we select* $w_{\text{max}} = 111$, *we determine* $\tau = z_0 \oplus z_1 \oplus z_2$. *Cofactors with respect to this* τ *are* $\mathbf{F}_0 = [1, 0, 1, 1]^T$ *and* $\mathbf{F}_1 = [0, 0, 0, 1]^T$, *and their Walsh spectra are* $\mathbf{S}_{f_0} = \frac{1}{4}[3, 1, -1, 1]^T$ *and* $\mathbf{S}_{f_1} = \frac{1}{4}[1, -1, -1, 1]^T$. *Therefore, further linearization does not reduce the number of nodes. Figure 4.3.10 shows the LT-BDD of f, and it is obvious that in this case, BDD and LT-BDD have the same form.*

With respect to the upper bounds on the number of nodes in LT-BDDs and the method proposed above, the following should be noticed.

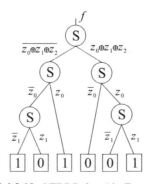

FIGURE 4.3.10 LTBDD for f in Example 4.3.6.

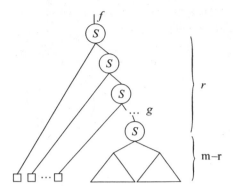

FIGURE 4.3.11   Decision tree for f linearized with respect to r variables.

A point $w = w_{max}$, where a Walsh spectrum $S_f(w)$ of a given function f has the maximum value, that is, $|S_f(w)| = 2^{-m} \sum_{z=0}^{2^m - 1} f(z)$, is called the *linearity point* for f (278). The set of all linearity points $\{w_i\}$, $i = 0, \ldots, r$, for a function f is a group, called the *linearity group* for f, with respect to the componentwise addition modulo 2 of binary representations for w_i. The linearity group contains 2^r vectors, $r = 0, 1, \ldots, m$, iff the linearization for f can be done r times in which case f can be represented as $f = \tau_1 \cdot \tau_2 \cdots \tau_r \cdot g$, where τ_i are linear functions of $z_0 - z_{m-1}$ corresponding to r linearly independent elements of the linearity group and g is a nonlinear function of at most $m - r$ variables. Owing to that, such a function f can be represented by the decision diagram in Fig.4.3.11. Decision diagrams of this form are a subset of planar decision diagrams determined by the method presented above.

4.3.4 Experimental Results for Complexity of Planar LT-BDDs

Table 4.3.1 compares the sizes of the initial BDDs, BDDs for the optimal order of variables, planar BDDs, and planar linearly transformed BDD produced by decomposition with respect to Walsh coefficients.

For BDDs and BDDs optimized by reordering of variables, sizes are determined by allowing sharing of all isomorphic subtrees; thus, these are not necessarily planar decision diagrams. It should be noticed that planar decision diagrams have larger sizes, since they may contain some redundant information, but the advantage of these decision diagrams is in avoiding crossing of edges, which may be an important feature in circuit synthesis and some other applications as explained in Reference 495. With this comparison we estimate impact of keeping decision diagrams planar and efficiency of the linearization of planar BDDs by Walsh coefficients, for example, under the restriction as in the definition of planar decision diagrams.

Each output of a multioutput benchmark function is considered as a separate single-output function $f - i$, where f is the name of the benchmark and i is the number of the output.

The experiments have been performed for small benchmarks, since we compared sizes of LT-BDDs with sizes of BDDs with optimal orders or variables, which are

TABLE 4.3.1 Sizes of BDDs, BDDs with Optimal Order of Variables (BDDv), Planar BDD (BDDr), and Planar LT-BDDs (LT-BDD).

f	n	BDD	Optimal Order BDD	Planar BDD	Planar LT-BDD
5xp1-1	7	14	11	35	13
5xp1-4	7	16	11	19	15
9sym	9	33	33	33	57
apex4-10	9	95	91	193	148
clip-1	9	37	34	67	35
clip-2	9	58	42	156	45
clip-3	9	73	32	196	51
clip-4	9	76	36	169	27
clip-5	9	36	36	36	22
con1-1	7	12	11	11	16
con1-2	7	8	7	8	8
ex1010-2	10	155	148	390	156
ex1010-8	10	154	147	377	209
rd73-3	7	16	16	16	16
rd84-1	8	32	25	54	82
rd84-2	8	25	22	169	15
rd84-4	8	19	19	22	59
sao2-1	10	46	32	75	32
sao2-2	10	48	34	85	31
squar5-1	5	5	5	6	5
z5xp1-3	7	20	14	22	12
z5xp1-6	7	15	9	21	9
av.		45	36	96	46

determined by the brute-force method examining all possible $m!$ orderings of variables. However, the method can be applied for a large number of inputs, see Chapter 3 and also References 104,267.

Notice that for applications such as FPGA synthesis, even a small gain in the number of reduced nodes count may result in a drastic simplification of the network (394).

It is worth mentioning that LT-BDD constructed by Walsh coefficients have sizes comparable to the sizes of BDDs for the optimal order of variables. This could be considered as an important feature of LT-BDDs constructed by decomposition with respect to Walsh coefficients.

For many functions planar LT-BDDs are smaller than planar BDDs.

It follows from Table 4.3.1, that on the average LT-MTBDDs are for 48% smaller than planar BDD, and for 2% and 26% larger than BDDs for initial and optimal order of variables.

4.4 SPECTRAL INTERPRETATION OF DECISION DIAGRAMS

As we have seen, decision diagrams often allow much more compact representation of discrete functions than direct enumeration of values or functional expressions.

Likewise, decision diagrams can be used to represent the spectrum of a discrete function (i.e., the discrete function whose values are the spectrum of the original function). The direct way is to compute the spectrum by using the spectral transform matrix $\mathbf{Q}$ and then represent the values by a decision diagram.

If, as is usually the case, the transform matrix is a Kronecker power of a (2×2) matrix $\mathbf{Q}(1)$, we can directly form the *spectral decision diagram* whose leaves contain the spectrum by assigning the *spectral decomposition rule* to the nodes.

Definition 4.4.1 *Consider a function* $f : \{0, 1\}^m \rightarrow P$, *where P is a field. Let*

$$\mathbf{Q}(1) = \begin{bmatrix} a & b \\ c & d \end{bmatrix},$$

with

$$\mathbf{U}(1) = \begin{bmatrix} \alpha & \beta \\ \gamma & \delta \end{bmatrix} = \mathbf{Q}^{-1},$$

be nonsingular (over P) and $\mathbf{Q}(k) = (\mathbf{Q}(1))^{\otimes k}$.
  Consider the decision tree T defined as

1. *The root of T has the value* f,
2. *If a node has the value* $g(z_k, \ldots, z_{m-1})$, $0 \leq k \leq m - 1$, *then the left child has the value*

$$g_L(z_k, \ldots z_{m-1}) = a(g(0, z_{k+1}, \ldots, z_{m-1})) + b(g(1, z_{k+1}, \ldots, z_{m-1})),$$

  and the right child has the value

$$g_R(z_k, \ldots, z_{m-1}) = c(g(0, z_{k+1}, \ldots, z_{m-1})) + d(g(1, z_{k+1}, \ldots, z_{m-1})).$$

T is called the spectral decision tree of f with respect to the transform $Q(m)$ *defined by* $\mathbf{Q}(m)$, *and the decision diagram obtained from T by the reduction rules is the spectral decision diagram of f with respect to* $Q(m)$.

Example 4.4.1 *Consider the function* $f : \{0, 1\}^2 \rightarrow Q$, *where Q is the field of rational numbers, defined by* $\mathbf{F} = [1, 0, 1, 1]^T$ *and the transform which is defined by the Kronecker powers of the matrix*

$$\mathbf{A} = \begin{bmatrix} 1 & 0 \\ 1 & -1 \end{bmatrix}.$$

Figure 4.4.1 shows the BDT and BDD for this function f, where the decomposition is the identity. Now, let the matrix defining the decomposition be $\mathbf{A}$. *Then, we have*

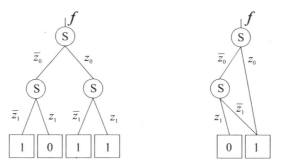

FIGURE 4.4.1   BDT and BDD for f in Example 4.4.1.

the decision tree as shown in Fig. 4.4.2, where

$$g_L(z_0, z_1) = 1 \cdot g(0, z_1) + 0 \cdot g(1, z_1),$$

$$g_R(z_0, z_1) = 1 \cdot g(0, z_1) - 1 \cdot g(1, z_1),$$

$$g_{LL}(0, z_1) = 1 \cdot g(0, 0) + 0 \cdot g(0, 1),$$

$$g_{LR}(0, z_1) = 1 \cdot g(0, 0) - 1 \cdot g(0, 1),$$

$$g_{RL}(1, z_1) = 1 \cdot (g(0, 0) - g(1, 0)) + 0 \cdot (g(0, 1) - g(1, 1)),$$

$$g_{RR}(1, z_1) = 1 \cdot (g(0, 0) - g(1, 0))) - 1 \cdot (g(0, 1) - g(1, 1)).$$

Figure 4.4.1 shows the decision tree for the function f considered in this example defined with respect to the transform determined as the Kronecker product of the matrix $\mathbf{A}$.

In this decision diagram, the constant nodes show the values of the spectrum of f in terms of the transform defined as

$$\mathbf{S}_f = (\mathbf{A} \otimes \mathbf{A})\mathbf{F} = \left(\begin{bmatrix} 1 & 0 \\ 1 & -1 \end{bmatrix} \otimes \begin{bmatrix} 1 & 0 \\ 1 & -1 \end{bmatrix} \right) \begin{bmatrix} 1 \\ 0 \\ 1 \\ 1 \end{bmatrix} = \begin{bmatrix} 1 \\ 1 \\ 0 \\ 1 \end{bmatrix}.$$

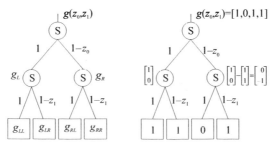

FIGURE 4.4.2   STDT for f in Example 4.4.1.

This tree can be reduced into a diagram which is the Spectral Transform Decision Diagram (STDD) with respect to the transform defined by **A**. *The reduction is performed by using the generalized BDD reduction rules, see Reference 569.*

If the matrix **A** *is selected as the arithmetic transform matrix* **A**(1) *or the Walsh transform matrix* **W**(1), *we get the Arithmetic Spectral Transform Decision Diagrams and Walsh Transform Decision Diagrams (569). In the same way, various STDDs can be defined.*

The function can be read from the spectral decision tree or diagram by descending from the leaves to the root and level by level performing the inverse operations. Thus, if the children of a node $g(x_k, \ldots, x_{m-1})$ are $g_L(x_{k+1}, \ldots, x_{m-1})$ and $g_R(x_{k+1}, \ldots, x_{m-1})$, then

$$g(x_k, \ldots, x_{m-1}) = \overline{x}_k(\alpha g_L(x_{k+1}, \ldots, x_{m-1}) + \beta g_R(x_{k+1}, \ldots, x_{m-1})$$

$$+ x_k(\gamma g_L(x_{k+1}, \ldots, x_{m-1}) + \delta g_R(x_{k+1}, \ldots, x_{m-1}))$$

$$= (\alpha \overline{x}_k + \gamma z_k)g_L + (\beta \overline{x}_k + \delta x_k)g_R.$$

Thus, over the field of rational numbers Q,

$$g(x_k, \ldots, x_{m-1}) = (\alpha(1 - x_k) + \gamma x_k)g_L + (\beta(1 - x_k))g_R$$

$$= (\alpha + (\gamma - \alpha)x_k)g_L + (\delta + (\delta - \beta)x_k)g_R.$$

Similarly, over $GF(2)$, it is

$$g(x_k, \ldots, x_{m-1}) = (\alpha + (\gamma + \alpha)x_k)g_L + (\delta + (\delta + \beta)x_k)g_R.$$

Spectral decision diagrams are useful, for instance, when the function has relatively few nonzero spectral coefficients and a compact spectral decision diagram can be obtained.

Notice that a Spectral Transform Decision Tree (STDT) represents at the same time f and the spectrum S_f for f with respect to the transform in terms of which the STDT is defined. Thus, from the same diagram both the function and its particular spectrum can be determined. When reading the spectrum, the STDD is interpreted as an MTBDD for the spectrum. Thus, from a STDD, we read the spectrum in the same way as we read f from the MTBDD. The difference in reading f from the STDD is that we do not perform the operation inverse to that used in definition of the STDD. Thus, STDDs allow a dual interpretation, as diagrams representing f or S_f, depending on the interpretation of labels at the edges.

More details on spectral interpretation of decision diagrams are given in Reference 555.

In decision trees with attributed edges, the values of coefficients may be assigned to the edges, or factorized in additive, or multiplicative, or both additive and multiplicative, parts and assigned to the edges. For more details and a discussion of that we refer to Reference 550.

As an example of STDDs, in the following section, we will discuss the Haar spectral transform decision diagrams (HSTDDs) (573).

4.4.1 Haar Spectral Transform Decision Diagrams

Above we defined spectral transform decision diagrams in a narrow sense by requiring that the decomposition rule is the same at each node. We also considered decision diagrams with two outgoing edges per node. This corresponds to a transform defined by a Kronecker power of the basic (2×2) matrix. A more general class of transforms and corresponding decision diagrams is obtained if the decomposition rule can vary from level to level (553), or even node to node. To be meaningful and useful, there needs to be a general procedure that determines the decomposition rule assigned to a particular node. Such procedures can be formulated in a uniform way for different classes of transforms, for instance, by assuming a group structure to the domain of the definition of functions that should be represented and the spectral transforms on groups point of view (553, 567).

Haar spectral transform decision diagrams (572, 580), form one such class. It is very fast to form because most of the nodes have a trivial decomposition rule, but still is able to capture essential properties of certain functions.

Definition 4.4.2 *(Haar spectral transform decision diagrams) For $f \in C(C_2^m)$, the Haar spectral transform decision tree (HSTDT) is such that at each nonterminal level of the tree, the leftmost node is decomposed using the basic Walsh matrix $\mathbf{W}(1)$ and the rest of the nodes are decomposed using the (2×2) identity matrix $\mathbf{I}(1)$.*

In HSTDDs, there are Walsh nodes performing the decomposition defined by the matrix $\mathbf{W}(1)$, and integer counterpart of Shannon nodes defined by the matrix $\mathbf{I}(1)$. Therefore, the edges are labeled by 1 and $1 - 2z_i$ as symbolic notation for the columns of $\mathbf{W}(1)$ and by $\overline{z}_i$ and z_i for the columns of $\mathbf{I}(1)$.

To have the values of the Haar transform coefficients in the constant nodes in consistent order, the variables in the edges of Walsh nodes in the diagram are written in descending order. Thus, the labels at the two edges of the leftmost node at level i are 1 and $1 - 2z_{m-i}$ by starting with the root node at the level 1. Labels of the edges of other nodes are $\overline{z}_i$ and z_i in the increasing order of indices by starting with z_0 for the root of the first subtree after a Walsh node.

This notation corresponds to the representation of Haar functions in sequency ordering in terms of binary-valued variables, as it will be discussed in Example 4.4.5.

Example 4.4.2   *Figure 4.4.3 shows a HSTDT for $m = 3$.*

Reduction of HSTDDs

The K-procedure discussed above produces the maximal number of identical values at the adjacent places in the vector of function values for a function f.

Consider the function values $f(w)$ at the points $w \geq 2^{m-1}$. In this case, we may write $w = 2^{m-1} + j$, where $j = 0, \dots, 2^{m-1} - 1$. From definition of the Haar

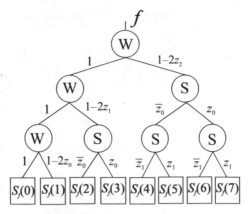

FIGURE 4.4.3   HSTDT for $m = 3$.

functions, for $w \geq 2^{m-1}$, $S_f(w) = 0$ iff $f(2j) = f(2j+1)$. It follows that in the HSTDT for f_σ determined by the K-procedure, there is a large number of constant nodes with the value 0.

Each nonzero coefficient corresponds to a term in the Haar expression for f. In a HSTDD for f, each c-path, that is, a path from the root node to a constant node showing the values $c \neq 0$, corresponds to a term in the Haar expression for f. Thus, this algorithm reduces the number of c-paths in the HSTDD for f. Moreover, HSTDD for f_σ has the minimum number of c-paths among HSTDDs for all functions generated for other possible orderings of elements in the vector $\mathbf{F}$ representing f. We denote by Q_{HSTDD} the number of c-paths in a HSTDD.

In a truth-vector $\mathbf{F}$, pairs of equal values produced by the K-procedure corresponds to subvectors of order 2 in the vector $\mathbf{F}_\sigma$ for f_σ. In MTBDDs, and thus, Haar Spectral Diagrams (HSDs), this means the possibility to reduce a node at the level corresponding to z_{m-1} whose outgoing edges point to $f(2j)$ and $f(2j+1)$. Similarly, for $w < 2^{m-1}$, $S_f(w) = 0$ if there are constant or equal subvectors of orders 2^i, $i = 2, \ldots, m-1$ in $\mathbf{F}$. Equal and constant subvectors mean possibility to share or delete nonterminal nodes at upper levels in the MTBDD(f).

Since in many cases, although not always, as shown by counterexamples in Reference 133, decision diagrams with smaller sizes have a smaller number of paths, the K-procedure can be used to reduce also the sizes of decision diagrams. Notice that, however, unlike the number of c-paths, $c \neq 0$, that depends on the number of nonzero coefficients, the size of a HSTDD depends also on the number of different nonzero coefficients and their distribution in the spectrum. Therefore, it may happen that the reordering by K-procedure although reducing the number of paths, may increase the size of the HSTDDs. Such an example are HSTDDs for adders (572).

Example 4.4.3   *(278) Table 4.4.1 shows a two-output function $f = (f^{(0)}, f^{(1)})$ of four variables. This function is represented by the integer equivalent function $f = 2f^{(0)} + f^{(1)}$. This function has the Haar spectrum with 14 nonzero coefficients. The*

TABLE 4.4.1   Function with the Minimized Haar Spectrum.

z, w	$f^{(0)}, f^{(1)}$	$f(z)$	$16S_f(w)$	$f_\sigma(z)$	$16S_{f_\sigma}(w)$
0	00	0	22	0	22
1	10	2	0	0	2
2	00	0	−5	2	−8
3	01	1	1	0	2
4	10	2	1	3	−2
5	01	1	0	3	−2
6	10	2	−2	2	2
7	11	3	1	2	0
8	11	3	−2	2	0
9	00	0	3	2	0
10	01	1	1	2	0
11	10	2	−1	0	0
12	01	1	−1	1	2
13	10	2	−1	1	2
14	10	2	−1	1	0
15	00	0	2	1	0

matrix determined by the K-procedure,

$$\sigma = \begin{bmatrix} 0 & 1 & 1 & 0 \\ 1 & 0 & 0 & 1 \\ 0 & 0 & 1 & 1 \\ 1 & 1 & 1 & 0 \end{bmatrix},$$

defines a reordering of the variables z_i, $i = 1, 2, 3, 4$ in the binary representation for $z = (z_1, z_2, z_3, z_4)$ through the relation $z_\sigma = \sigma^{-1} z$. Since

$$\sigma^{-1} = \begin{bmatrix} 1 & 0 & 0 & 1 \\ 0 & 1 & 1 & 1 \\ 1 & 1 & 1 & 1 \\ 1 & 1 & 0 & 1 \end{bmatrix},$$

the vector

$$\mathbf{F} = [f(0), f(1), f(2), f(3), f(4), f(5), f(6), f(7), f(8),$$
$$f(9), f(10), f(11), f(12), f(13), f(14), f(15)]^T,$$

where $f_\sigma(\sigma \odot z) = f(z)$, is transformed into the vector

$$\mathbf{F}_\sigma = [f(0), f(15), f(6), f(9), f(7), f(8), f(1), f(14),$$
$$f(11), f(4), f(13), f(2), f(12), f(3), f(10), f(5)]^T.$$

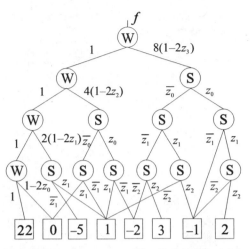

FIGURE 4.4.4   HSTDD for f in Example 4.4.3.

The matrix σ defines a function $f_{\sigma\,min}$, which has the Haar spectrum with 9 nonzero coefficients, compared to the 14 coefficients in the Haar spectrum for f.

Example 4.4.4   *Figure 4.4.4 shows HSTDD for the function f in Table 4.4.1, and Fig. 4.4.5 shows HSTDD for f_{σ}. In this example, $size(MTBDD(f)) = 18$, $size(MTBDD(f_{\sigma})) = 11$, $size(HSTDD(f)) = 22$, $size(HSTDD(f_{\sigma})) = 15$, $Q_{HSTDD(f)} = 13$, and $Q_{HSTDD(f_{\sigma})}) = 8$, since a path contains a cross point.*

Table 4.4.2 compares the number of nonzero coefficients in the Haar spectrum before and after the linear transform of variables. The savings in the number of nonzero coefficients range from 0.81% to 88.24% with the average savings of 49.48%.

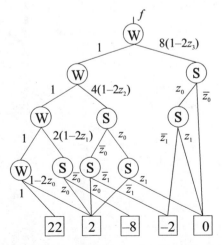

FIGURE 4.4.5   HSTDD for f_{σ} in Example 4.4.3.

TABLE 4.4.2 Number of Coefficients in the Haar Spectrum and the LT-Haar Spectrum.

f	Haar	LT-Haar	%
9sym	211	106	49.77
ex1010	989	971	1.83
misex1	32	28	12.50
rd53	32	22	31.25
rd73	128	32	75.00
rd84	265	64	75.85
xor5	17	2	88.24
add2	16	7	56.25
add3	64	29	54.69

Table 4.4.3 compares the complexity of HSTDDs before (HSTDD(f)) and after (LT-HSTDD(f)) the linear transform of variables determined by the K-procedure. It shows the number of nonterminal nodes (ntn), constant nodes (cn), whose sum is the size of the HSTDD ($s = ntn + cn$), and the width (w) of HSTDDs. We also show the number of 0-paths, c-paths and the total number of paths. The K-procedure reduced the number of c-paths and the width of HSTDDs for all the considered functions.

TABLE 4.4.3 Complexity of MTBDDs and LT-MTBDDs.

	MTBDD(f)						
f	ntn	cn	s	w	paths		
					0	c	total
9sym	33	2	35	6	72	148	220
ex1010	894	177	1071	383	190	800	990
misex1	17	11	28	6	5	13	18
rd53	15	6	21	5	1	31	32
rd73	28	8	36	7	1	127	128
rd84	36	9	45	8	1	255	256
xor5	9	2	11	2	16	16	32
add2	13	7	20	6	1	15	16
add3	41	15	66	14	1	63	64

	LT-MTBDD(f)						
f	ntn	cn	s	w	paths		
					0	c	total
9sym	24	2	26	5	27	48	75
ex1010	871	177	1048	367	180	791	971
misex1	17	11	28	5	4	14	18
rd53	17	6	23	6	1	23	24
rd73	17	7	24	6	1	31	32
rd84	23	8	41	7	1	63	64
xor5	1	2	3	1	1	1	2
add2	8	7	15	3	1	8	9
add3	24	15	39	7	1	26	27

TABLE 4.4.4   Complexity of HSTDs and LT-HSTDD.

f	ntn	cn	s	w	paths 0	paths c	paths total
					HSTDD(f)		
9sym	111	16	127	26	189	197	381
ex1010	1023	639	1662	512	35	989	1024
misex1	34	17	51	11	22	18	40
rd53	23	9	32	9	0	30	30
rd73	52	11	63	14	0	103	103
rd84	74	16	90	18	0	201	201
xor5	12	4	16	3	4	17	21
add2	4	4	8	1	0	5	5
add3	6	7	13	1	0	7	7

f	ntn	cn	s	w	paths 0	paths c	paths total
					LT-HSTDD(f)		
9sym	89	13	102	25	85	87	172
ex1010	1019	636	1655	508	53	969	1022
misex1	41	17	58	13	26	18	44
rd53	19	10	29	7	8	19	27
rd73	20	6	26	7	0	23	23
rd84	32	8	40	10	0	44	44
xor5	5	3	8	1	4	2	6
add2	6	4	10	2	4	3	7
add3	9	5	14	2	6	4	10

Table 4.4.4 compares the complexity of MTBDDs for the same set of functions before (MTBDD(f)) and after (LT-MTBDD(f)) the application of the linear transform of variables used in HSTDDs. The linear transform used in HSTDDs, reduced the number of c-paths for all the considered functions.

4.4.2 Haar Transform Related Decision Diagrams

There is apparent a renewed interest in application of the Haar transform in switching theory and logic design.

A number of publications on this subject has been published in the previous decade (299). The applications have been presented in circuit synthesis, equivalence checking, verification, and testing of logic networks (228, 229, 559, 601, 602).

Relationships between the Haar transform and related transforms, as well as the Haar transform and decision diagrams were considered; for example, in References 94,155,160,228,600, and 603.

This research activity provides rationales to study decision diagrams related to the Haar transform, as well as representation of Haar coefficients by decision diagrams.

Algorithms for calculation of Haar spectrum through decision diagrams (537, 600) overcome the exponential complexity of FFT-like algorithms for Haar wavelet

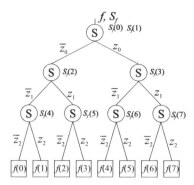

FIGURE 4.4.6   HST for $m = 3$.

transform (258, 278) and due to that extend the applications to functions with large number of variables.

The *Haar spectral diagrams* (228) have been introduced to represent Haar coefficients efficiently in terms of space and time. They are derived from assigning the Haar coefficients for a given function f to the corresponding edges in the multiterminal binary decision diagrams (105).

Example 4.4.5   *Figure 4.4.6 shows an example of the Haar spectral tree (HST) for $m = 3$. The following relation shows the correspondence among the Haar functions, labels at the edges in the multiterminal binary decision tree, and the Haar coefficients.*

$$
\begin{array}{lll}
f(0) & har(0, z) = 1 & S_f(0) \\
f(1) & har(1, z) = (1 - 2z_0) & S_f(1) \\
f(2) & har(2, z) = (1 - 2z_1)\bar{z}_0 & S_f(2) \\
f(3) & har(3, z) = (1 - 2z_1)z_0 & S_f(3) \\
f(4) & har(4, z) = (1 - 2z_2)\bar{z}_0\bar{z}_1 & S_f(4) \\
f(5) & har(5, z) = (1 - 2z_2)\bar{z}_0z_1 & S_f(5) \\
f(6) & har(6, z) = (1 - 2z_2)z_0\bar{z}_1 & S_f(6) \\
f(7) & har(7, z) = (1 - 2z_2)z_0z_1 & S_f(7)
\end{array}
$$

From this example, a Haar coefficient $S_f(w)$ is situated at the end of a subpath consisting of edges denoted by variables used in symbolic description of the corresponding Haar function $har(w, z)$ with respect to which this Haar coefficient is calculated.

A good feature of HSDs is that the same diagram can represent both f and the Haar spectrum of f, which means that the size of the diagram to represent the Haar spectrum is not larger than the size of the diagram for f. Thus, HSDs are actually MTBDDs, or BDDs, with the Haar coefficients assigned to the edges. It follows that they do not exploit properties of the Haar spectra to possibly get reduced representations for f.

BIBLIOGRAPHIC NOTES

Complexity of decision diagrams is discussed in many books in this area, see References, 130,366,372,499, and 555. The optimization by reordering of variables using the sifting algorithm is discussed in References 130,185,478, and 661. The application of autocorrelation functions in optimization of decision diagrams is explored in References 297,467, and 468. Planar decision diagrams have been discussed in References 82,495, and 496. Construction of planar BDD by using Walsh coefficients is discussed in Reference 298. For spectral interpretation of decision diagrams, see References 547,550,555, and 569.

An XML (Extensible Markup Language) environment for description of various classes of decision diagrams has been developed in Reference 586, and methods for automatic generation of VHDL descriptions of circuits derived from such representations of decision diagrams are presented in Reference 585.

CHAPTER 5

ANALYSIS AND OPTIMIZATION OF LOGIC FUNCTIONS

In this chapter, we study spectral methods for solving the decision problems for some important classes of logical functions[1] and also develop spectral methods for solving optimization problems in the algebra of logic (including the linearization and approximation of systems of logical functions). We will also present in this chapter spectral methods for serial and parallel decomposition of combinatorial networks.

A special section will be devoted to the analysis of spectral complexity of Boolean functions, deriving bounds for the number of nonzero coefficients in their orthogonal expansions. The main tool throughout the chapter will be the Walsh transform, since this is a transform defined in terms of two-valued ± 1 functions.

It is assumed that, when appropriate, the logic values 0 and 1 are also interpreted as the corresponding integers. In this sense, the Walsh transform is compatible with the switching functions to which it is applied.

5.1 SPECTRAL ANALYSIS OF BOOLEAN FUNCTIONS

The problem of the analysis of Boolean functions (BF), or switching functions, is to decide whether a given function belongs to some standard class (linear, self-dual,

---

[1]The decision problem for a class of functions is to devise a procedure (or algorithm) whereby, given any function, determine ("recognize") whether or not it is a member of the class (the rigorous definition is formulated in the framework of mathematical logic).

Spectral Logic and Its Applications for the Design of Digital Devices   by Mark G. Karpovsky, Radomir S. Stanković and Jaakko T. Astola
Copyright © 2008 John Wiley & Sons, Inc.

threshold, among other functions). In other words, we determine whether a given function possesses any of the properties characterizing these classes of switching functions. The reason for the importance of the corresponding decision problems is that standard methods of network synthesis are available for the standard classes of switching functions, and these "special-purpose" methods are usually incomparably more efficient than universal methods. Thus, the synthesis stage of network design is frequently preceded by the analysis of an appropriate system of switching functions.

Below, we evolve decision procedures for some important classes of switching functions using their Walsh spectra and the autocorrelation functions. (Tables of spectra and autocorrelation functions of several classes of switching functions widely used in engineering practice are given in the Appendix A.)

The analysis methods described in this section may be generalized to many-valued logic functions by using the Vilenkin–Chrestenson transforms and the appropriate autocorrelation functions.

All the switching functions considered in this section will be assumed to be completely specified. If $f(z) = f(z_0, \ldots, z_{m-1})$, we denote its Walsh spectrum in Paley ordering by $S_f(w)$ or $S_f(w_0, \ldots, w_{m-1})$, where

$$w = \sum_{i=0}^{m-1} w_i 2^{m-1-i}, \quad S_f(w) = 2^{-m} \sum_{z=0}^{2^m-1} (-1)^{\sum_{i=0}^{m-1} w_i z_{m-1-i}} f(z),$$

where $w_i \in \{0, 1\}$. Notice that in consideration of methods in this chapter, we will use this definition of Walsh spectrum. We denote the autocorrelation function by $B_f(\tau)$ or $B_f(\tau_0, \ldots, \tau_{m-1})$, where by (2.7.1) for $p = 2$,

$$B_f(\tau) = \sum_{z=0}^{2^m-1} f(z)f(z \oplus \tau) \mod 2,$$

and $\tau = \sum_{i=0}^{m-1} \tau_i 2^{m-1-i}, \tau \in \{0, 1\}$.

5.1.1 Linear Functions

A switching function $f(z_0, \ldots, z_{m-1})$ is *linear* iff there exist numbers $c_i \in \{0, 1\}$, $(i = 0, 1, \ldots, m - 1)$ such that

$$f(z_0, \ldots, z_{m-1}) = \bigoplus_{i=0}^{m-1} c_i z_i, \quad \mod 2. \tag{5.1.1}$$

The class of linear functions is closed under superposition: the superposition of any two linear switching functions is again a linear switching function. Any linear switching functions of m variables can be realized by a network of at most $m - 1$ two-input mod 2 adders, that is, two-input EXOR circuits. Any k linear switching functions of m variables may be realized by a network using a number of EXORs of the order $mk/\log_2 m$.

Theorem 5.1.1 *Let $f(z) = \bigoplus_{s=0}^{m-1} c_s z_s$ (mod 2). Then,*

$$S(w) = \begin{cases} \frac{1}{2}, & if\ w = 0, \\ -\frac{1}{2}, & if\ w = \overleftarrow{c}, \\ 0, & otherwise, \end{cases} \tag{5.1.2}$$

where $\overleftarrow{c} = \sum_{s=0}^{m-1} c_s 2^s$ and

$$B(\tau) = 2^{m-2}(W_{\overleftarrow{c}}(\tau) + 1). \tag{5.1.3}$$

Proof. By the definition of Walsh functions,

$$\bigoplus_{s=0}^{m-1} c_s z_s = \frac{1}{2}(1 - W_{\overleftarrow{c}}(z)).$$

Hence, using (2.3.5), (2.3.9), and (2.3.10), we obtain (5.1.2). Formula (5.1.3) is derived from (5.1.2) using Theorem 2.7.1.

The converse is also valid in the sense that if either of the conditions (5.1.2) or (5.1.3) holds, the function $f(z)$ may be expressed in the form (5.1.1).

Thus, to decide whether a function is linear, we need to calculate only its spectrum. If the spectrum contains only one nonzero point $w = \overleftarrow{c}$ (apart from the point $w = 0$), the switching function is linear and has the form $\bigoplus_{s=0}^{m-1} c_s z_s$ (mod 2).

Example 5.1.1 *Consider the switching function defined in Table 5.1.1. Since*

TABLE 5.1.1 Function f in Example 5.1.1, Its Spectrum $S_f(w)$, and Autocorrelation Function $B_f(\tau)$.

z_0, z_1, z_2	$f(z)$	w, τ	$S_f(w)$	$B_f(\tau)$
000	0	0	0.5	4
001	1	1	0	0
010	1	2	0	0
011	0	3	0	4
100	1	4	0	0
101	0	5	0	4
110	0	6	0	4
111	1	7	-0.5	0

$$S(w) = \begin{cases} \frac{1}{2}, & \text{if } w = 0, \\ -\frac{1}{2}, & \text{if } w = 7, \\ 0, & \text{otherwise,} \end{cases}$$

it follows that $f(z)$ is linear and $c = \overleftarrow{c} = 7$ and $f(z_0, z_1, z_2) = z_0 \oplus z_1 \oplus z_2$.

5.1.2 Self-Dual and Anti-Self-Dual Functions

A switching function is *self-dual (anti-self-dual)* iff

$$f(z_0, \ldots, z_{m-1}) = \overline{f(\overline{z}_0, \ldots, \overline{z}_{m-1})}, \tag{5.1.4}$$

$$f(z_0, \ldots, z_{m-1}) = f(\overline{z}_0, \ldots, \overline{z}_{m-1}). \tag{5.1.5}$$

The bar over a function or a variable denotes inversion, that is, $\overline{z} = 1 - z = 1 \oplus z$ (mod 2).

The class of self-dual switching functions is closed under superposition. Since self-duality and anti-self-duality are invariant with respect to translation of variables, these classes may be characterized in terms of autocorrelation functions.

Theorem 5.1.2 *A switching function $f(z) = f(z_0, \ldots, z_{m-1})$ is self-dual and anti-self-dual iff,*

$$B_f(2^m - 1) = \sum_{z=0}^{2^m-1} f(z) - 2^{m-1}, \tag{5.1.6}$$

and

$$B_f(2^m - 1) = \sum_{z=0}^{2^m-1} f(z), \tag{5.1.7}$$

respectively.

Proof. To prove (5.1.6) observe that if the condition (5.1.4) holds then $f(z) = \overline{f}(\overline{z})$ and $\overline{f}(z) = 1 - f(z)$, where $\overline{z} = (\overline{z}_0, \ldots, \overline{z}_{m-1})$ and $f(z)f(\overline{z}) = 0$, $\overline{f}(z)\overline{f}(\overline{z}) = 0$ for all $z \in \{0, 1, \ldots, 2^m - 1\}$. Then,

$$\sum_{z=0}^{2^m-1} f(z)f(\overline{z}) + \sum_{z=0}^{2^m-1} \overline{f}(z)\overline{f}(\overline{z}) = 2 \sum_{z=0}^{2^m-1} f(z)f(\overline{z}) + 2^m - 2 \sum_{z=0}^{2^m-1} f(z) = 0$$

and

$$B_f(2^m - 1) = \sum_{z=0}^{2^m-1} f(z)f(\overline{z}) = \sum_{z=0}^{2^m-1} f(z) - 2^{m-1}.$$

Conversely, by (5.1.6)

$$2B_f(2^m - 1) + 2^m - 2\sum_{z=0}^{2^m-1} f(z) = \sum_{z=0}^{2^m-1} f(z)f(\overline{z}) + \sum_{z=0}^{2^m-1} \overline{f}(z)\overline{f}(\overline{z}) = 0$$

and $f(z)f(\overline{z}) = 0$, $\overline{f}(z)\overline{f}(\overline{z}) = 0$. Hence $f(z) = \overline{f}(\overline{z})$. The proof of (5.1.7) is similar.

We have thus reduced the verification of (anti-)self-duality to calculation of the autocorrelation function at the point $2^m - 1$.

For example, for the switching function in Example 5.1.1, $(m = 3)$, we have $B_f(7) = 0$ so that it is self-dual.

5.1.3 Partially Self-Dual and Partially Anti-Self-Dual Functions

A switching function $f(z_0, \ldots, z_{m-1})$ is said to be *partially self-dual* and *partially anti-self-dual* iff there exists $\alpha = \sum_{s=0}^{m-1} \alpha_s 2^{m-1-s}$ such that

$$f(z_0, \ldots, z_{m-1}) = \overline{f}(z_0^{\alpha_0}, \ldots, z_{m-1}^{\alpha_{m-1}}) \tag{5.1.8}$$

and

$$f(z_0, \ldots, z_{m-1}) = f(z_0^{\alpha_0}, \ldots, z_{m-1}^{\alpha_{m-1}}), \tag{5.1.9}$$

respectively, where

$$z_s^{\alpha_s} = \begin{cases} z_s, & \text{if } \alpha_s = 1, \\ \overline{z}_s, & \text{if } \alpha_s = 0. \end{cases}$$

A switching function satisfying (5.1.8) or (5.1.9) will also be called α-*(anti)-self-dual*, where $\overline{\alpha} = \sum_{s=0}^{m-1} \overline{\alpha}_s 2^{m-1-s}$ and $\overline{\alpha}_s = 1 - \alpha_s$. (According to this definition, a switching function is (anti-) self-dual if it is $(2^m - 1)$-(anti-)self-dual.)

For the same function $f(z)$, there may be several numbers $\alpha_1, \alpha_2, \ldots, \alpha_g$ such that $f(z)$ is α_s-self-dual $(s = 1, 2, \ldots, g)$ and $\beta_1, \beta_2, \ldots, \beta_h$ such that $f(z)$ is β_s-anti-self-dual $(s = 1, 2, \ldots, h)$.

Note that any switching function is 0-anti-self-dual, and if $f(z)$ is both β_s-anti-self-dual and β_q-anti self dual, then it is also $(\beta_s \oplus \beta_g)$-anti-self-dual. Indeed, in that case it follows from (5.1.9) that $f(z) = f(z \oplus \beta_s) = f(z \oplus \beta_q)$, and $f(z) = f(z \oplus \beta_s \oplus \beta_q)$ (mod 2) for every $z \in \{0, 1, \ldots, 2^m - 1\}$.

We call β an *(anti-)self-duality point* for $f(z)$ iff $f(z)$ is β-(anti-)self-dual. The set of anti-self-duality points for any switching function is a group, and the number of such points (the order of the group) is a power of 2. The group of anti-self-duality points will be called the *anti-self-duality group* or the *inertia group*.

If $f(z_0, \ldots, z_{m-1})$ is 2^s-anti-self-dual, then it is independent of z_s.

Theorem 5.1.3 *A function* $f(z) = f(z_0, \ldots, z_{m-1})$ *has self-duality points* α_1, $\ldots, \alpha_g$ *and anti-self-duality points* $\beta_1, \ldots, \beta_h$ *iff*

$$B_f(\alpha_s) = \sum_{z=0}^{2^m-1} f(z) - 2^{m-1},$$

for $s = 1, \ldots, g$, *and*

$$B_f(\beta_q) = \sum_{z=0}^{2^m-1} f(z), \qquad (5.1.10)$$

for $q = 1, \ldots, h$, *where* $1 \leq g + h \leq 2^m$.

Theorem 5.1.3 is a generalization of Theorem 5.1.2 (in the latter $\alpha = 2^m - 1$ or $\beta = 2^m - 1$), and the proof is analogous.

Corollary 5.1.1 *For any switching function* $f(z)$, *the number of points at which the autocorrelation function takes the value* $\sum_{z=0}^{2^m-1} f(z)$ *is a power of 2, and the corresponding autocorrelation assignments form a group.*

Corollary 5.1.1 generates a simple procedure for checking the validity of a calculation of the autocorrelation function of a switching function $f(z)$. Thus, if $\sum_z f(z) = 2^{m-1}$, the zeros of the autocorrelation function defines the self-duality points. In any case, the set of all τ such that $B_f(\tau) = \sum_{z=0}^{2^m-1} f(z)$ defines the anti-self-duality points.

As an example of analysis for partial anti-self-duality, let us consider a switching function that is a characteristic function of a linear code.

A *linear (m, k)-code* **V** is defined by a generating matrix

$$\begin{bmatrix} \mathbf{V}_1 \\ \mathbf{V}_2 \\ \vdots \\ \mathbf{V}_k \end{bmatrix},$$

where $\mathbf{V}_s = [V_s(0), \ldots, V_s(m-1)]$ is a binary vector of the length m. The code **V** is the set of all linear combinations $\bigoplus_{s=1}^{k} c_s \mathbf{V}_s$ (mod 2), where $c_s \in \{0, 1\}$.

The *characteristic function* $f_V(z)$ of **V** is defined by

$$f_V(z) = \begin{cases} 1, & \text{if } z \in \mathbf{V}, \\ 0, & \text{if } z \notin \mathbf{V}. \end{cases} \tag{5.1.11}$$

Theorem 5.1.4 *A function $f(z)$ is the characteristic function of a linear (m, k)-code* **V** *iff*

$$S(w) = 2^{-m} \prod_{r=1}^{k} (W_{V_r}(w) + 1), \tag{5.1.12}$$

where

$$V_r = \sum_{q=0}^{m-1} V_r(q) 2^q,$$

or iff

$$B(\tau) = \begin{cases} 2^k, & \text{if } \tau \in \mathbf{V}, \\ 0, & \text{if } \tau \neq \mathbf{V}. \end{cases} \tag{5.1.13}$$

Proof. We prove (5.1.12) by induction on k.

If $k = 1$, we have

$$f_V(z) = \begin{cases} 1, & \text{if } z = 0, V_1, \\ 0, & \text{otherwise,} \end{cases}$$

and $S(w) = 2^{-m}(W_{\overleftarrow{V}_1}(w) + 1)$.

Now let $f_{V_1, \dots, V_{k-1}}(z)$ be the characteristic function of the code with generating matrix

$$\begin{bmatrix} \mathbf{V}_1 \\ \mathbf{V}_2 \\ \vdots \\ \mathbf{V}_{k-1} \end{bmatrix},$$

$S_{V_1, \dots, V_{k-1}}(w)$ its spectrum, and f_{V_k} the characteristic function of the code whose generating matrix is V_k. Let

$$S_{V_1, \dots, V_{k-1}}(w) = 2^{-m} \prod_{r=0}^{k-1} (W_{V_r}(w) + 1).$$

Since $f_V(z)$ is the characteristic function of the code with generating matrix

$$\begin{bmatrix} \mathbf{V}_1 \\ \mathbf{V}_2 \\ \vdots \\ \mathbf{V}_k \end{bmatrix},$$

iff

$$f_V(z) = f_{V_1,\ldots,V_k}(z) = \sum_{\tau=0}^{2^m-1} f_{V_k}(\tau) f_{V_1,\ldots,V_{k-1}}(z \oplus \tau), \quad \text{mod } 2,$$

it follows by the convolution theorem for the original function (2.6.7) that (5.1.12) is true.

To prove (5.1.13), we note that a linear (m, k)-code is a group with respect to the addition modulo 2, and $f_V(z)$ is the characteristic function of an (m, k)-code $\mathbf{V}$ iff $\sum_{z=0}^{2^m-1} f_V(z) = 2^k$, and if $f_V(z) = 1$, then

$$f_V(z) = \begin{cases} f_V(z \oplus \tau), & \text{if } \tau \in V, \\ \overline{f}_V(z \oplus \tau), & \text{otherwise,} \end{cases} \quad \text{mod } 2.$$

Thus the vectors τ of the code are anti-self-duality points for $f_V(z)$.

5.1.4 Quadratic Forms, Functions with Flat Autocorrelation

A switching function $f(z_0, \ldots, z_{m-1})$ is called a *quadratic form* iff there exists c_{qs}, $\alpha_q \in \{0, 1\}$, such that

$$f(z_0, \ldots, z_{m-1}) = \bigoplus_{q,s=0,q<s}^{m-1} c_{qs}(z_q)^{\alpha_q}(z_s)^{\alpha_s}. \tag{5.1.14}$$

The design of a network realizing a quadratic form (c_{qs}) requires at most $L_{\text{AND}} = \sum_{s=0}^{m-1}\sum_{q=0}^{s-1} c_{qs}$ two-input AND gates (logical multiplication) and $L_{\text{EXOR}} = L_{\text{AND}} - 1$ two-input mod 2 adders, that is, EXOR circuits.

A quadratic form in $m = 2s$ variables is said to be *nonrepetitive* if each of its variables z_q appears in (5.1.14) exactly once.

An example of a nonrepetitive quadratic form is

$$f_s(z) = \bigoplus_{q=0}^{s-1} z_q z_{q+s},$$

with calculations modulo 2 and $m = 2s$.

The function may also be expressed as

$$\bigoplus_{q=0}^{s-1} z_q z_{q+s} = \frac{1}{2}\left(1 - (-1)^{\bigoplus_{q=0}^{s-1} z_q z_{q+s}}\right) = \frac{1}{2}(1 - W_{a(z)}(b(z))), \quad (5.1.15)$$

where

$$a(z) = \sum_{q=0}^{s-1} z_q 2^q,$$

$$b(z) = \sum_{q=0}^{s-1} z_{q+s} 2^{s-1-q}.$$

Any nonrepetitive quadratic form in $m = 2s$ variables may be realized by a network of s two-input AND gates and $s - 1$ two-input EXOR circuits.

Theorem 5.1.5   *If a switching function is a nonrepetitive quadratic form in $m = 2s$ variables, then its autocorrelation function $B_s(\tau)$ satisfies the condition*

$$B_s(\tau) = \begin{cases} 2^{2s-1} - 2^{s-1}, & \text{for } \tau = 0, \\ 2^{2s-2} - 2^{s-1}, & \text{for } \tau \neq 0. \end{cases} \quad (5.1.16)$$

We first prove the following lemma.

Lemma 5.1.1   *Let $\phi_1(z) = \bigoplus_{q=0}^{s-1} a_q z_q$ and $\phi_2(z) = \bigoplus_{q=0}^{s-1} b_q z_q$, $a \neq b$, and $a, b \neq 0$. Then, for any $\tau \in \{0, 1, \dots, 2^s - 1\}$,*

$$B_{\phi_1,\phi_2}(\tau) = \sum_{z=0}^{2^s-1} \phi_1(z)\phi_2(z \oplus \tau) = B_{\phi_1,\overline{\phi_2}}(\tau) = 2^{s-2}. \quad (5.1.17)$$

The equality $B_{\phi_1,\phi_2}(\tau) = 2^{s-2}$ follows from Theorem 5.1.1 and formula (2.7.4). For the other equality, we have

$$B_{\phi_1,\overline{\phi_2}}(\tau) = \sum_{z=0}^{2^s-1} \phi_1(z)(1 - \phi_2(z \oplus \tau)) = \sum_{z=0}^{2^s-1} \phi_1(z) - B_{\phi_1,\phi_2}(\tau)$$

$$= 2^{s-1} - 2^{s-2} = 2^{s-2}.$$

Proof of Theorem 5.1.5   We first show that if $f_s(z) = \bigoplus_{q=0}^{s-1} z_q z_{q+s}$ is a nonrepetitive quadratic form, its autocorrelation function $B_s(\tau)$ satisfies (5.1.16). Consider the function

$$Q(z_0, \ldots, z_{s-1}, \tau) = \sum_{z_s, \ldots, z_{2s-1} \in \{0,1\}} \left(\bigoplus_{q=0}^{s-1} z_q z_{q+s} \right) \left(\bigoplus_{q=0}^{s-1} (z_q \oplus \tau_q)(z_{q+s} \oplus \tau_{q+s}) \right).$$

Let $a(z) = \sum_{q=0}^{s-1} z_q 2^q \neq 0$, $\tau = 0$. Then, for any $z_0, \ldots, z_{s-1}$,

$$Q(z_0, \ldots, z_{s-1}, \tau) = \sum_{z_s, \ldots, z_{2s-1} \in \{0,1\}} \left(\bigoplus_{q=0}^{s-1} z_q z_{q+s} \right)^2$$

$$= \sum_{z_s, \ldots, z_{2s-1} \in \{0,1\}} \bigoplus_{q=0}^{s-1} z_q z_{q+s} = 2^{s-1}.$$

Let $a(z) \neq 0$, $\tau \neq 0$. Then, for any $z_0, \ldots, z_{s-1}$, by Lemma 5.1.1,

$$Q(z_0, \ldots, z_{s-1}, \tau) = 2^{s-2}.$$

Thus,

$$Q(z_0, \ldots, z_{s-1}, \tau) = \begin{cases} 2^{s-1}, & \text{if } a(z) \neq 0, \tau = 0, \\ 2^{s-2}, & \text{if } a(z) \neq 0, \tau \neq 0, \\ 0, & \text{if } a(z) = 0. \end{cases} \tag{5.1.18}$$

Next, we have

$$B_s(\tau) = \sum_{z=0}^{2s-1} f_s(z) f_s(z \oplus \tau) = \sum_{z_0, \ldots, z_{s-1} \in \{0,1\}} Q(z_0, \ldots, z_{s-1}, \tau). \tag{5.1.19}$$

Formula (5.1.16) now follows from (5.1.18), (5.1.19).

Thus, formula (5.1.16) holds for $f_s(z)$. Now, any nonrepetitive form of $2s$ variables may be obtained from $f_s(z)$ by a suitable permutation and translation of the variables. The translation leaves the autocorrelation function invariant. A permutation is equivalent to a linear transformation of the variables (with the transformation matrix containing exactly one unit in each row and column). A linear transformation of the variables in $f_s(z)$ induces the same linear transformation of the variables in the autocorrelation function (see Theorem 2.7.4), but since $B_s(\tau) = const.$ ($\tau \neq 0$) (see 5.1.19)), it follows that $B_s(\tau)$ is invariant under linear transformations. Thus any nonrepetitive quadratic form has the autocorrelation function (5.1.16).

Example 5.1.2 *Table 5.1.2 defines the switching function $f(z) = z_0 z_3 \oplus z_1 z_2$, whose autocorrelation is $B_f(\tau) = 2$ for $\tau \neq 0$.*

TABLE 5.1.2 Function f in Example 5.1.2 and Its Autocorrelation $B_f(\tau)$.

z, τ	$f(z)$	$B_f(\tau)$
0	0	6
1	0	2
2	0	2
3	0	2
4	0	2
5	0	2
6	1	2
7	1	2
8	0	2
9	1	2
10	0	2
11	1	2
12	0	2
13	1	2
14	1	2
15	0	2

It is a useful observation that nonrepetitive quadratic forms are switching functions with the "best" correlation characteristics in the following sense.

For a function specified in N points, of the correlation functions involved in transmission of synchronizing signals,

$$B_{\infty,2}(\tau) = \sum_{z=0}^{N-1} f(z)f(z-\tau),$$

$$B_{N,2}(\tau) = \sum_{z=0}^{N-1} f(z)f(z \ominus \tau),$$

where calculation is modulo N, is specified for a given N and signal power (number of 1 values) $\sum_{z=0}^{N-1} f(z)$ by $\Delta_\infty = B_{\infty,2}(0) - \max_{\tau \neq 0} B_{\infty,2}(\tau)$ or $\Delta_N = B_{N,2}(0) - \max_{\tau \neq 0} B_{N,2}(\tau)$, respectively. These quantities determine the error-correcting capability in transmission of synchronizing signals using $f(z)$ (330, 522). Determination of the best synchronizing codes $f(z)$, maximizing Δ_∞ or Δ_N for given "length" N and "power" $\sum_{z=0}^{N-1} f(z)$, is a highly important and difficult problem. From this standpoint, the best quality is that of a switching function with $B_{\infty,2}(\tau) = const.$ ($\tau \neq 0$) or $B_{N,2}(\tau) = const.$ ($t \neq 0$) (if such a switching function exists). A function whose autocorrelation function is "most nearly" a constant for $\tau \neq 0$ is closest to a pseudorandom sequence of the given length.

With these remarks in mind, let us consider the autocorrelation functions $B_s(\tau)$ ($s = 1, 2, \ldots$) of nonrepetitive quadratic forms in $m = 2s$ variables. By Theorem 5.1.5, we have

$$B_s(\tau) = 2^{2s-2} - 2^{s-1} = const., \quad \tau \neq 0,$$

and

$$\Delta_{2,s} = B_s(0) - \max_{\tau \neq 0} B_s(\tau) = 2^{2s-2}.$$

Now the quadratic form $f_s(z) = \bigoplus_{i=0}^{s-1} z_i z_{i+s}$ satisfies the condition $f_s(z) = 0$ for $0 \leq z < 2^s$ and, if a zero value of $f_s(z)$ corresponds to the absence of a signal at the transmitter output (passive zero codes (522)), we may assume that the transmitted code is of length $2^{2s} - 2^s$.

Thus, if we define an (N, b, Δ_2)-code to be a code of the length N such that $B(0) = b$ and $\Delta_2 = B_f(0) - \max_{\tau \neq 0} B_f(\tau)$, then the nonrepetitive quadratic forms in $2s$ variables constitute the class of optimal $(2^s(2^s - 1), 2^{s-1}(2^s - 1), 2^{2s-2})$-codes.

Some of these optimal codes are shown in Table 5.1.3. Note that codes defined by nonrepetitive quadratic forms have the same number of 0 and 1 values.

We note that nonrepetitive quadratic forms with a flat autocorrelation are known as *bent functions* (474). These functions are widely used in coding theory, see for example, (347, 438). For instance, in this settings, they can be viewed as a coset of the first order Reed–Muller code with the largest minimum weight (88, 89, 347). Thus, a bent function has a maximum distance from a linear functions and, therefore, due to its maximum nonlinearity, such functions are widely exploited in cryptography, see References 213, 666.

In particular, bent functions are used for design of substitution boxes (S-boxes) in secure block ciphers in *Advanced Cryptography Standard* (374).

Theorem 5.1.5 can be generalized for the Q-ary case when f is a mapping from $GF(Q^{2s})$ onto $GF(Q)$, $Q = p^t$, where p is a prime and t an integer.

In this case, $z_j \in GF(Q)$ and all the additions and the multiplications in the definition of the nonrepetitive quadratic form are in $GF(Q)$.

In this case, we have the following generalization of Theorem 5.1.5.

For a Q-ary nonrepetitive quadratic form $f(z) = \bigoplus_{q=0}^{s-1} z_q z_{s+q}$, $z_q, z_{s+q} \in GF(Q)$, we can define the total autocorrelation function $B_f(\tau)$ for the quadratic

TABLE 5.1.3 Parameters of Some Optimal Codes N_s, b_s, $\Delta_2^{(S)}$.

s	Code length N_s	No. of 1-values b_s	$\Delta_2^{(s)}$
1	2	1	1
2	12	6	4
3	56	28	16
4	240	120	64
5	992	496	256

form $f(z)$ as

$$B_f(\tau) = \sum_i \sum_z f_i(z) f_i(z \oplus \tau), \tag{5.1.20}$$

where $z, \tau \in GF(Q)$, $\oplus$ stands for the addition in $GF(Q)$, and $f_i(z)$ is the characteristic function of $f(z)$, that is, $f_i(z) = 1$ iff $f(z) = i$.

Then, by using the approach similar to that used in the proof of Theorem 2.3.5 [294], it is possible to show that for Q-ary nonrepetitive quadratic form $\bigoplus_{j=0}^{s-1} z_j z_{s+j}$, we have

$$B_f(\tau) = Q^{2s-1}. \tag{5.1.21}$$

Applications of nonrepetitive quadratic forms for construction of optimal robust error-detecting codes with equal error-correcting probabilities for all errors can be found in Reference 293, and applications for the design of optimal compressors for test responses can be found in References 291, 292, and 400. Notice that in this case, $Q = 2^t$.

In the case of compression of test responses by Q-ary ($Q = 32^t$) quadratic forms, z_j is the t-bit response of a device-under-test and $f(z) = \sum_{q=0}^{s-1} z_q z_{s+q}$ is the compressed response (signature) of the device, to be verified for testing. For these quadratic compressors, all errors have the same probability 2^t of being masked (*aliasing probability*) in the process of compression of test responses (284,292).

We note also that nonrepetitive quadratic forms are special cases of perfect nonlinear functions that are widely used in cryptography (91,114,412). These functions are also closely related to difference sets and balanced combinatorial designs (66).

5.2 ANALYSIS AND SYNTHESIS OF THRESHOLD ELEMENT NETWORKS

5.2.1 Threshold Elements

Threshold elements (TE) have been used quite widely in digital data-processing systems. Nowadays, they are related to the artificial neural networks, see Reference 21 and references therein.

By a threshold element with weights $d_0, d_1, \ldots, d_{m-1}$ and the threshold T we mean an element realizing the function

$$f(z_0, \ldots, z_{m-1}) = sign\left(\sum_{s=0}^{m-1} d_s z_s - T\right), \tag{5.2.1}$$

where[2]

$$sign(z) = \begin{cases} 0, & \text{if } z \le 0, \\ 1, & \text{if } z > 0. \end{cases} \tag{5.2.2}$$

The numbers $d_0, d_1, \ldots, d_{m-1}$, and T in (5.2.1) are assumed to be integers.

The class $\Pi(m)$ of switching functions of m variables for which there exist d_s and T satisfying (5.2.1) is called the class of *single-threshold switching functions*. It is quite difficult to determine whether a given function $f(z_0, \ldots, z_{m-1})$ belongs to the class $\Pi(m)$. For instance, no analytical methods are available for this purpose. Tables have been constructed (124,649,650) that enable to determine whether a switching function is in $\Pi(m)$ according to $m + 1$ certain characteristics of the function and to solve the so-called threshold synthesis problem to determine weights d_s ($s = \{0, 1, \ldots, m - 1\}$) and the threshold T for a given single-threshold switching function that minimize the quantity $T + \sum_{s=0}^{m-1} d_s$.

There are fairly sophisticated methods for the synthesis of networks with a single threshold element. The situation is more difficult for threshold networks realizing functions not in $\Pi(m)$, and the problem of synthesis of threshold element networks in which the number of inputs of threshold elements exceeds the number of variables of the function realized by the entire network is especially complex.

In view of this situation, we propose in this section a spectral characterization of $\Pi(m)$. We pay special attention to spectral methods for synthesis of threshold element networks realizing both completely and partially specified switching functions.

Several papers in this area have been related to the properties of threshold elements and the links to neural networks with extensions to multiple-valued logic (21,22,376,384,593). Recent achievements in circuit implementation of threshold logic are reviewed in Reference 53. An algorithm for efficient threshold logic synthesis aimed at delay minimization has been proposed in Reference 677, see also Reference 417. Realization of large logic circuits by programmable threshold logic gate arrays has been discussed in Reference 309.

In this section, we discuss the spectral approaches to the threshold logic synthesis.

Thanks to the isomorphism between the variables z_s and the Rademacher functions $R_{s+1}(z)$, we may view the representation of a switching function in $\Pi(m)$ in the form (5.2.1) as its expansion in an orthogonal series of Walsh functions. In this interpretation, we consider series containing $m + 1$ terms. To calculate the value of the switching functions, we need the sign of the sum of the series; that is, it suffices to consider the sign digit of the adder computing the sum. Thus, the spectral analysis and synthesis methods developed in the preceding sections may be utilized for this narrow class $\Pi(m)$ of switching functions.

---

[2]The reader is warned that we are using two different "sign" functions (see the definition of $sign(\sigma)$ in the footnote on page 6).

5.2.2 Identification of Single Threshold Functions

We now define the concept of k-*monotonicity*, $k = 1, \ldots, m$, which proves very useful for the identification of single-threshold functions and the synthesis of threshold element networks.

Two switching function f_1, and f_2 of m variables are said to be *comparable* if

$$f_1(z_0, \ldots, z_{m-1}) \leq f_2(z_0, \ldots, z_{m-1}) \tag{5.2.3}$$

or

$$f_1(z_0, \ldots, z_{m-1}) \geq f_2(z_0, \ldots, z_{m-1}), \tag{5.2.4}$$

for all $(z_0, \ldots, z_{m-1})$.

Fix k $(1 \leq k \leq m)$ variables of a function $f(z_0, \ldots, z_{m-1})$. The function f is said to be k-*comparable* if any two switching functions obtained by substituting the constants 0, 1 for the fixed k variables are comparable and this property is independent of which k variables are fixed and how. The function f is said to be n-*monotone* $(1 \leq n \leq m)$ if it is k-comparable for all $k - 1, 2, \ldots, n$. An m-monotone function will be called *completely monotone*.

Theorem 5.2.1 *(649) If $f(z_0, \ldots, z_{m-1})$ is $\lfloor m/2 \rfloor$-monotone, it is completely monotone. ($\lfloor a \rfloor$ denotes the largest integer $\leq a$.)*

The next theorem establishes the connection between the monotonicity and the concept of a single-threshold function.

Theorem 5.2.2 *(649) If $f \in \Pi(m)$, then f is completely monotone; if $m \leq 6$ and f is completely monotone, then $f \in \Pi(m)$.*

A completely monotone switching function that is not single threshold was constructed by Moore (649) for $m = 12$. We now discuss the use of spectral methods for the identification of 1, 2-monotone functions, leading to corresponding necessary conditions for a switching function to be single threshold. Denote

$$\Pi_f(q) = \sum_{\|z\|=q} f(z), \tag{5.2.5}$$

$$\Pi_s(q) = 2^m \sum_{\|w\|=q} \|S(w)\|, \tag{5.2.6}$$

$$\Pi_B(q) = \sum_{\|\tau\|=q} B(\tau), \quad q = 0, 1, \ldots, m, \tag{5.2.7}$$

where $\|z\|$, $\|w\|$, $\|\tau\|$ denote the number of 1 values in the binary expansions of the numbers z, w, and τ, and $S(w)$ is the spectrum and $B_f(\tau)$ the autocorrelation function of $f(z)$.

Theorem 5.2.3 *A function* $f(z_0, \ldots, z_{m-1})$ *is 1-monotone iff*

$$\sum_{q=0}^{m-1} \Pi_f(q)(m - q) = \frac{1}{2}\Pi_B(1), \tag{5.2.8}$$

or

$$\Pi_s(1) + \Pi_B(1) = m\Pi_B(0). \tag{5.2.9}$$

Thus, either of the conditions (5.2.8) or (5.2.9) may be used to check whether a given switching function is 1-monotone.

Example 5.2.1 *Table 5.2.1 defines a switching function* $f(z_0, z_1, z_2, z_3)$ *for which* $\Pi_f(0) = \Pi_f(1) = 0$, $\Pi_f(2) = 3$, $\Pi_f(3) = 4$, $\Pi_f(4) = 1$, $\Pi_B(0) = 8$, $\Pi_B(1) = 20$, *and* $\Pi_s(1) = 12$. *Since both conditions (5.2.8) and (5.2.9) are satisfied,* f *is 1-monotone.*

Theorem 5.2.4 *A* 1-*monotone function* $f(z_0, \ldots, z_{m-1})$ *is 2-monotone iff*

$$2^m \sum_{p=1}^{m-1} (m - p)|S(2^{i_p})| + \Pi_B(2) = \binom{m}{2} \Pi_B(0), \tag{5.2.10}$$

TABLE 5.2.1 Functions Φ and f in Examples 5.2.1 and 5.2.2 and Their Spectral and Autocorrelations.

z, w, τ	$f(z)$	$16S(w)$	$B(\tau)$	$\phi(z)$	$16S(w)$	$B(\tau)$
0	0	8	8	0	5	5
1	0	−4	6	0	−3	2
2	0	−4	6	0	−3	2
3	0	0	4	0	1	2
4	0	−2	4	0	−3	2
5	0	−2	4	0	1	2
6	1	2	4	0	1	2
7	1	2	4	1	1	0
8	0	−2	4	0	−3	2
9	1	2	4	0	1	2
10	0	−2	4	0	1	2
11	1	2	4	1	1	0
12	1	0	2	0	1	2
13	1	0	2	1	1	0
14	1	0	2	1	1	0
15	1	0	2	1	−3	0

where $i_1, i_2, \ldots, i_{m-1} \in \{0, 1, \ldots, m - 1\}$ are defined by the condition

$$|S(2^{i_1})| \leq |S(^{i_2})| \leq \cdots \leq |S(2^{i_{m-1}})|. \tag{5.2.11}$$

We thus have a condition (5.2.10) providing a check on the 2-monotonicity of a switching function.

Example 5.2.2 *Turning again to the function $f(z_0, z_1, z_2, z_3)$ in Table 5.2.1, we have $2^4 S(2^0) = -4$, $2^4 S(2^1) = -4$, $2^4 S(2^2) = -2$, $2^4 S(2^3) = -2$, $\Pi_B(0) = 8$, $\Pi_B(2) = 22$. Thus, $i_1 = 0$, $i_2 = 1$, $i_3 = 2$, and*

$$2^4 \sum_{p=1}^{3}(4 - p)|S(2^{i_p})| + \Pi_B(2) = 12 + 8 + 2 + 22 = 44$$

and

$$\binom{4}{2} \Pi_B(0) = 48.$$

Thus, the condition (5.2.10) is not satisfied, and f is not 2-monotone; hence, it is not a single-threshold function.

Example 5.2.3 *The function $\phi(z_0, \ldots, z_3)$ defined in Table 5.2.1 has $\Pi_s(1) = 12$, $\Pi_B(1) = 8$, $\Pi_B(0) = 5$, and thus (5.2.9) holds and ϕ is 1-monotone. Furthermore, $2^4 S(2^0) = 2^4 S(2^1) = 2^4 S(2^2) = 2^4 S(2^3) = -3$; $\Pi_B(2) = 12$; $i_1 = 0$, $i_2 = 1$, $i_3 = 2$, $i_4 = 3$, and*

$$2^4 \sum_{p=1}^{3}(4 - p)|S(2^{i_p})| + \Pi_B(2) = 9 + 6 + 3 + 12 = 30,$$

and

$$\binom{4}{2} \Pi_B(0) = 30.$$

Thus, the condition (5.2.10) is satisfied and so ϕ is 2-monotone. But in this case, $\lfloor m/2 \rfloor = 2$, and so, by Theorems 5.2.1 and 5.2.2, ϕ is a single-threshold function.

It is a laborious matter to check k-monotonicity when $k \geq 3$; in practice, therefore, tables of monotone functions are often used (124,649), according to which a switching function may be identified as being in class $\Pi(m)$ on the basis of the $m + 1$ characteristics $S(0), S(2^0), \ldots, S(2^{m-1})$ (these characteristics are often called Chow parameters (101)). The tables also provide values of integers d_s and T that minimize $\sum_{s=0}^{m-1} d_s + T$ (see (5.2.1)). If $(S(0), a_0, a_1, \ldots, a_{m-1})$, where $a_i = S(2^i)$

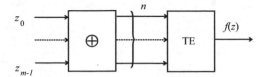

FIGURE 5.2.1 Block diagram of a linear threshold network.

for $i = 0, \ldots, m - 1$, conform to these tables so that the corresponding switching function is single threshold, we write $(S(0), a_0, a_1 \ldots, a_{m-1}) \in \Pi$.

Since the fraction of switching functions of m variables, which are single-threshold switching function, tends to zero quite rapidly as $m \to \infty$ [649], it is important to consider the analysis and synthesis of networks containing one threshold element and additional equipment, and also networks of several threshold elements.

Let us consider the class of linear-threshold networks consisting of a linear block of EXOR circuits and one threshold element (see Fig. 5.2.1).

Theorem 5.2.5 *Any switching function may be realized by a linear-threshold network.*

Proof. The assertion follows from the fact that any switching function may be represented by a finite series of Walsh functions and from the isomorphism between the multiplicative group of Walsh functions and the group of linear switching functions.

The number n of inputs for the threshold element may exceed the number m of variables of the switching functions. We now consider the important special case $n = m$.

Theorem 5.2.6 *A switching function may be realized by a linear-threshold network in which the number of threshold element inputs is equal to the number m of variables of the switching function iff there exist $w_0, \ldots, w_{m-1}$, such that $(S(0), S(w_0), S(w_1), \ldots, S(w_{m-1})) \in \Pi$ and the matrix (w) whose rows are the binary expansions of the numbers w_i, $(i = 0, 1, \ldots, m - 1)$ is nonsingular over $GF(2)$; that is, the determinant over $GF(2)$ is $|w|_2 \neq 0$.*

Note that in this case the linear block $\oplus$ in Fig. 5.2.1 computes the product of $(z_0, \ldots, z_{m-1})$ by the matrix $[\overleftarrow{w}]$ (where $\overleftarrow{w} = \sum_{s=0}^{m-1} w_i^{(s)} 2^s$ if $w_i = \sum_{s=0}^{m-1} w_i^{(s)} 2^{m-1-s}$), $w_i^{(s)} \in \{0, 1\}$.

The proof of Theorem 5.2.6 is based on the Theorem 2.6.7 for the case $p = 2$.

Example 5.2.4 *Consider the function $f(z_0, z_1, z_2)$ defined by Table 5.2.2 and its Walsh spectrum $S(w)$. Setting $w_0 = 1$, $w_2 = 2$, $w_2 = 7$, we have*

TABLE 5.2.2   Function f in Example 5.2.4 and Its Spectrum.

z, w	$f(z)$	$8S(w)$
0	0	5
1	1	1
2	1	-1
3	1	-1
4	1	-1
5	0	-1
6	0	1
7	1	-3

$(S(0), S(1), S(2), S(7)) \in \Pi$ *and*

$$|w|_2 = \begin{vmatrix} 0 & 0 & 1 \\ 0 & 1 & 0 \\ 1 & 1 & 1 \end{vmatrix}_2 = 1.$$

Thus, $f(z_0, z_1, z_2)$ can be realized by a linear-threshold network with $n = m = 3$ (see Fig. 5.2.2), with weights $d_1 = 1$, $d_2 = 1$, $d_3 = 2$, and the threshold $T = 1$.

Since not every switching function is realizable by a linear-threshold network with $n \leq m$, we are naturally interested in upper bounds for the number n of threshold element inputs for an arbitrary switching function $f(z)$. The results presented below are relevant to both completely and incompletely specified switching functions.

Let $B_{(f_0, f_0)}$, $B_{(f_1, f_1)}$ denote the autocorrelation functions of the characteristic functions of occurrence of 0 and 1, respectively, in the original function f and $B_{(f_0, f_1)}$ their cross-correlation function. By the characteristic function, we mean the switching function $f_i(z)$ such that $f_i(z) = 1$ iff $f(z) = i$. It is clear that for incompletely specified functions $f \neq f_1$, $\overline{f} \neq f_0$ (where $\overline{f}(z)$ is undefined if $f(z)$ is undefined) and for any z we have $f_0(z) + f_1(z) \leq 1$. If $f(z)$ is completely specified, however, then $f = f_1$ and $B^{(f_1, f_1)}(\tau) = B_f(\tau)$.

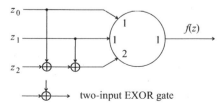

FIGURE 5.2.2   Realization of the function f in Example 5.2.4.

Theorem 5.2.7 *Any switching function f defined at $N(f)$ points is realizable by a linear-threshold network with n threshold element inputs, where*

$$n \leq N(f) - \max \left\{ \frac{1}{2} \max_{\tau \neq 0}(B_{(f_0, f_0)}(\tau) + B_{(f_1, f_1)}(\tau)), \right. \tag{5.2.12}$$

$$\left. \max_{\tau \neq 0} B_{(f_0, f_1)}(\tau) \right\}.$$

For the proof, we need two lemmas, that are also of an independent interest.

Lemma 5.2.1 *Let f be a switching function that is not defined at $d(f)$ points. Then, there exists a completion $\tilde{f}$ of f such that*

$$\overline{L^W}(\tilde{f}) \geq d(f), \tag{5.2.13}$$

where $\overline{L^W}(\tilde{f})$ is the number of zero coefficients in the Walsh expansion of $\tilde{f}$.

The proof follows easily from the linear independence of the rows of the Walsh matrix and from (3.1.2).

Lemma 5.2.2 *Let f be a switching function undefined at $d(f)$ points. Suppose that there are $d_1(f) + d_0(f)$ points $p_1, \ldots, p_{d_1(f)}, q_1, \ldots, q_{d_0(f)}$ at which f is defined, such that*

$$f(2p_j) \neq f(2p_j + 1), (j = 1, \ldots, d_1(f)), \tag{5.2.14}$$

$$f(2q_s) = f(2q_s + 1), (s = 1, \ldots, d_0(f)). \tag{5.2.15}$$

Then there exists a function $\phi(z)$ such that, if $f(z^*)$ is defined,

$$sign(\phi(z^*)) = f(z^*), \tag{5.2.16}$$

$$\overline{L^W}(\phi) \geq d(f) + \max\{d_1(f), d_0(f)\}. \tag{5.2.17}$$

Proof. We shall prove that there exists a function $\phi = \phi_1$ satisfying (5.2.16), such that

$$\overline{L^W}(\phi_1) \geq d(f) + d_1(f). \tag{5.2.18}$$

(The proof that there exists a function ϕ_0 satisfying (5.2.16) such that $\overline{L^W}(\phi_0) \geq d(f) + d_0(f)$ is similar.)

We first note that for any $\phi(z)$,

$$\overline{L^W}(\phi(z)) = \overline{L^W}(\phi(2z) + \phi(2z + 1)) + \overline{L^W}(\phi(2z) - \phi(2z + 1)). \tag{5.2.19}$$

This follows from the factorization (3.1.3) of the Walsh matrix or from Theorem 3.1.1.

We now see that for any $y_1, \ldots, y_{d_1(f)}$ there exists $\phi_1(z)$ such that, if $f(z^*)$ is defined,

$$
\begin{cases}
sign(\phi_1(z^*)) = f(z^*), \\
\phi_1(2p_j) + \phi_1(2p_j + 1) = y_j, \quad j = 1, \ldots, d_1(f),
\end{cases}
\tag{5.2.20}
$$

and $\phi_1(z^*) = f(z^*)$ if $z^* \neq 2p_j, 2p_j + 1$ for $j = 1, \ldots, d_1(f)$. In view of (5.2.20), we may assume that the function $\phi_1(2z) + \phi_1(2z + 1)$ is not defined at the points p_j, $j = 1, \ldots, d_1(f)$, and hence, by Lemma 5.2.1,

$$
\overline{L^W}(\phi_1(2z) + \phi_1(2z + 1)) = d_1(f).
\tag{5.2.21}
$$

Now, the functions $\phi(2z) + \phi(2z + 1)$ and $\phi(2z) - \phi(2z + 1)$ are also not defined at no less than $d(f)$ points where $f(2z)$ or $f(2z + 1)$ is not defined. Hence, again by using Lemma 5.2.1 and (5.2.19), we obtain (5.2.18).

Proof of Theorem 5.2.7. We first note that

$$
n \leq 2^m - \overline{L^W}(f).
\tag{5.2.22}
$$

This follows from the isomorphism of the group of linear switching functions and the group of Walsh functions.

In addition, for any switching function $f(z)$, there always exist linear transformations σ_1 and σ_0 of z such that, if we define a switching function $f_{\sigma_1}(z)$ and $f_{\sigma_0}(z)$ by

$$
f_{\sigma_1}(\sigma_1 \odot z) = f_{\sigma_0}(\sigma_0 \odot z) = f(z), \quad \mathrm{mod}\ 2,
$$

then the number of points z such that $f_{\sigma_1}(2z) \neq f_{\sigma_1}(2z + 1)$ and $f_{\sigma_0}(2z) = f_{\sigma_0}(2z + 1)$ is equal to $\max_{\tau \neq 0} B_{(f_0, f_0)}(\tau)$ and $\frac{1}{2}\max_{\tau \neq 0}(B_{(f_0, f_1)})(\tau) + B_{(f_1, f_1)}(\tau)$, respectively.

In view of Theorem 2.7.4, the matrices σ_1 and σ_0 may be found from the conditions

$$
\sigma_1 \odot \tau_1 = 1,
\tag{5.2.23}
$$

$$
\sigma_0 \odot \tau_0 = 1,
$$

with calculations modulo 2, where

$$
\max_{\tau \neq 0}(B_{(f_0, f_1)}(\tau) + B_{(f_1, f_1)}(\tau)) = B_{(f_0, f_0)}(\tau_0) + B_{(f_1, f_1)}(\tau_0).
$$

TABLE 5.2.3 Function f and the Autocorrelation Function B_f in Example 5.2.5.

z, τ	$f(z)$	$B_f(\tau)$
0	0	5
1	0	4
2	1	2
3	1	2
4	1	2
5	1	2
6	0	4
7	1	4

Since $\overline{L^W}(f(\sigma \odot z)) = \overline{L^W}(f(z))$ for any σ (see Theorem 2.6.7) and $N(f) = 2^m - d(f)$, formula (5.2.12) now follows from (5.2.22) and Lemma 5.2.2.

Corollary 5.2.1 *For any completely specified switching function f of m variables,*

$$n \le 2^m - \max \left\{ 2^{m-1} - B_f(0) + \max_{\tau \ne 0} B_f(\tau), \, B_f(0) - \min_{\tau \ne 0} B_f(\tau) \right\} \quad (5.2.24)$$

This follows from (5.1.2) with $N(f) = 2^m$ by using the fact that

$$B_{(f_0, f_0)}(\tau) = 2^m - 2B_f(0) + B_f(\tau), \quad (5.2.25)$$

$$B_{(f_0, f_1)}(\tau) = B_f(0) - B_f(\tau). \quad (5.2.26)$$

Example 5.2.5 *Table 5.2.3 defines a completely specified switching function $f(z_0, z_1, z_2)$ and the corresponding $B(\tau)$. It is clear from the table and from (5.2.24) that*

$$n \le 2^3 - \max \left\{ 4 - 5 + \max_{\tau \ne 0} B_f(\tau), \, 5 - \min_{\tau \ne 0} B_f(\tau) \right\} = 5.$$

Remark 5.2.1 *Thanks to the isomorphism between the linear switching function f and the Walsh functions (Theorem 2.3.5), formulas (5.2.12) and (5.2.24) yield upper bounds for the number of nonzero coefficients in the Walsh expansions of the completions of partially defined switching function f.*

To conclude this section, we point out that the spectral methods considered above may also be used in synthesis and analysis of networks of many-valued threshold elements, as described in References 21, 22, 23, 376, and 405.

5.3 COMPLEXITY OF LOGIC FUNCTIONS

In the following sections, we shall be studying some optimization problems for logic functions and spectral methods for their solution. Before solving an optimization problem, we must have criteria for the complexity of systems of logic functions. This section is therefore devoted to some basic results in regard to complexity of logic functions. Most of the discussion is devoted to binary logic. The reader should note that although this section is essentially auxiliary in nature, it is necessary for a good understanding of the subsequent sections.

5.3.1 Definition of Complexity of Systems of Switching Functions

The complexity of a system of logic functions is defined as the sum of complexities of the individual functions. The latter concept will now be defined.

By the *complexity* $L(f)$ of a switching function $f(z_0, \ldots, z_{m-1})$, we mean the minimum number of two- and one-input elements necessary for a network realizing f; that is, $L(f)$ is the complexity of a minimal implementation of f.

It is clear that complexity in terms of two-input elements does not necessarily imply such implementation of logic functions. It is rather related to equivalent networks consisting of these basic elements that can be derived from various implementations of switching functions by different technological platforms. Thus, reduction to equivalent networks of simplest two-input elements permits a uniform comparison of different possible implementations and makes complexity analysis independent on technological issues.

Yablonskii (652) has conjectured that the labor involved in determining the exact value of $L(f)$ is roughly of the same order of magnitude as that required to construct a minimal network for f by the brute-force method. Since this conjecture seems highly reasonable, the theory of network complexity (342,519,526) deals mainly with asymptotic ($m \to \infty$) estimates for the complexity of functions in various classes. Shannon was the first to point out that although almost all functions admit only the most complex network implementation, the functions actually used in practice are quite simple (519). Since the exact complexity of a switching functions is generally impossible to determine, there have been introduced special functionals on the set of switching functions, known as *complexity criteria*. These criteria actually provide an upper bound for the complexity, and the level curves of each criterion induce a classification of functions according to their complexity.

To be precise, a *complexity criterion* on the set of switching functions is a functional $\pi(f)$ with the following property.

There exists a monotone real-valued function $\theta_\pi(t)$ such that, for any sequence of functions $f_m(z_0, \ldots, z_{m-1})$, $m = 1, 2, \ldots$, for which

$$\lim_{m \to \infty} \pi(f_m)/m \log_2 m = \infty,$$

the following two conditions are satisfied:

1. Any function f of m variables such that $\pi(f) \le \pi(f_m)$ has complexity

$$L(f) \lesssim Q_\pi(\pi(f_m)), \tag{5.3.1}$$

(we write $\alpha_m \lesssim \beta_m$ if $\lim_{m \to \infty} \alpha_m / \beta_m \le 1$, and $\alpha_m \sim \beta_m$ if $\alpha_m \lesssim \beta_m$ and $\beta_m \lesssim \alpha_m$).

2. For almost all such functions,

$$L(f) \lesssim Q_\pi(\pi(f_m)), \tag{5.3.2}$$

that is, the fraction of functions f not satisfying this condition tends to zero as $m \to \infty$. (Henceforth, we shall use this terminology freely. We say that a proposition A holds for *almost all* switching functions of m variables iff the fraction of functions of m variables for which A holds tends to 1 as $m \to \infty$.)

The function $Q_\pi(t)$ of the definition enables us to estimate the actual complexity of a switching function in terms of the criterion, and $Q_\pi(\pi(f_m))$ will be called the complexity of f_m relative to π or the π-*complexity* of f_m.

To facilitate the comparison of criteria, it is convenient to normalize them in such a way that $Q_\pi(t)$ is the same for all criteria π. We set

$$Q_\pi(t) = \frac{t}{\log_2 t}, \tag{5.3.3}$$

since, under quite broad assumptions, the asymptotic estimates for complexity will have the form $\pi(f_m)/\log_2 \pi(f_m)$ [526].

Note that the values of complexity criteria are independent of the choice of the basis system of elements participating in the design of the network.

An example of a very simple complexity criterion is 2^m, where m is the number of variables on which the switching function depends essentially. Denote this criterion by $\zeta(f)$.

The choice of this functional as a criterion is justified by the following proposition (first proved by Shannon and Lupanov (342,519)). For almost all switching functions of m variables, the complexity $L(m)$ of a minimal network realizing the switching function satisfies the asymptotic estimate

$$L(m) \sim \frac{2^m}{m}. \tag{5.3.4}$$

We now present another important sequence of complexity criteria.

If $\sum_{i=0}^{k-1} t_i = 1$, for $0 \le t_i \le 1$, then the *entropy function* is defined as $H(t_0, t_1, \ldots, t_{k-1}) = -\sum_{i=0}^{k-1} t_i \log_2 t_i$, (where $0 \log_2 0 = 0$ by convention). Then,

$$0 \le H(t_0, t_1, \ldots, t_{k-1}) \le \log_2 k. \tag{5.3.5}$$

We can represent the function $f_m(z_0, \ldots, z_{m-1})$ by a vector of length 2^m of function values $\mathbf{F} = [f_m(0, 0, \ldots, 0), f_m((0, 0, \ldots, 1), \ldots, f_m(1, 1, \ldots, 1)]^T$. Divide this vector into 2^{m-r} nonoverlapping subvectors of the length 2^r. Set $p_i(f_m) = l_i(f_m)/2^{m-r}$, where $l_i(f_m)$ is the number of distinct subvectors of the ith type in f_m. Now define a functional

$$\mu_r(f_m(z_0, \ldots, z_{m-1})) = \begin{cases} 2^{m-r} H(p_0, p_1, \ldots, p_{R-1}), & \text{if } r \leq m, \\ 0, & \text{if } r > m, \end{cases} \quad (5.3.6)$$

where $R = 2^{2^r}$.

The values of the functionals $\mu_r (r = 0, 1, \ldots)$ are obtained by substituting constants for $m - r$ variables of the original function in all possible ways. Thus the values of μ_1, are defined by substituting constants in all possible ways for $m - 1$ variables; each such substitution determines a pair of assignments of the original function whose variables differ in only one position, and μ_1 is defined by the entropy function of the frequencies with which the various pairs appear.

It is evident that the values of the criteria μ_r depend on the order of the variables. If the order of the variables of f_m is T, let us denote $\mu_r(f_m)$ by $\mu_r^T(f_m)$ and

$$\hat{\mu}_r(f_m) = \min_T \mu_r^T(f_m). \quad (5.3.7)$$

Theorem 5.3.1 *(526) The functionals μ_r and $\hat{\mu}_r$ are complexity criteria. Moreover, for every r, $\hat{\mu}_r$ is stronger than $\hat{\mu}_{r-1}$, in the sense that $\hat{\mu}_r$ gives a sharper upper bound than $\hat{\mu}_{r-1}$.*

Theorem 5.3.1 shows that the "power" of the criterion $\hat{\mu}_r$ increases with increasing r, but on the contrary it becomes more difficult to calculate, since to calculate $\hat{\mu}_r$ the total of $\binom{m}{m-r} \cdot 2^m$ operations are required to examine $\binom{m}{m-r} = \binom{m}{r}$ different arrangements of the $m - r$ variables, and the complexity of each alternative is 2^m.

Example 5.3.1 *Let $f_m(z_0, \ldots, z_{m-1})$ be a sequence of functionally separable switching functions, that is, functions of the form*

$$f_m(z_0, \ldots, z_{m-1}) = F_m(z_0, \ldots, z_{m-r-1}, g_m(z_{m-r}, \ldots, z_{m-1})), \quad (5.3.8)$$

where F_m and g_m are switching functions.

Let us calculate $\mu_r(f_m)$. Substitution of constants for $z_0, \ldots, z_{m-r-1}$ yields a total of four functions: $1, 0, g_m, \overline{g}_m$, and thus the 2^r-component subvectors in the representation of f_m may have only four forms, whose frequencies we denote by p_0, p_1, p_2, p_3. Then, by (5.3.6),

$$\mu_r(f_m) = 2^{m-r} H(p_0, p_1, p_2, p_3) \leq 2^{m-r+1},$$

whence, in view of (5.3.3),

$$L(f_m) \lesssim \frac{2^{m-r+1}}{m-r+1}, \qquad (5.3.9)$$

and this bound is asymptotically the best possible (526).

The properties of the criteria $\hat{\mu}_r$ ($r = 0, 1, \ldots$) yield information on the structure of the most complex functions. In particular, the most complex switching functions have approximately the same number of zeros and ones, and substitution of constants for $m - r$ arbitrary variables in the most complex switching function of m variables yields all switching functions of r variables; moreover, the number of such switching functions of each type are approximately the same.

5.3.2 Complexity and the Number of Pairs of Neighboring Minterms

The next complexity criterion that we consider is quite widely used in practice. We first recall a few simple definitions from switching algebra.

We call z^* a *minterm* of a switching function $f(z)$ if $f(z^*) = 1$, and a *maxterm* for $f(z)$ if $f(z^*) = 0$. Minterms (maxterms) z_1^* and z_2^* are said to *match* if $z_1^* \oplus z_2^* = 2^i$ (mod 2).

A switching function $\phi(z) = \prod_{s=1}^{q} (z_{i_s})^{\alpha i}$, ($q \leq m$, $z^\alpha = z$ if $\alpha = 1$, $z^\alpha = \bar{z} = 1 - z$ if $\alpha = 0$) is called a *prime implicant* of a function $f(z_0, z_1, \ldots, z_{m-1})$ if $\phi(z) = 1$ always implies $f(z) = 1$; the integer q will be called the *length* of $\phi(z)$. We shall also say that the prime implicant $\phi(z)$ *covers* minterms $\sum_z \phi(z)$ of $f(z)$ (a maxterm z^* is *covered* by $\phi(z)$ if $\phi(z^*) = 1$).

A set of prime implicants $\phi_1(z), \ldots, \phi_l(z)$ of a switching function $f(z)$ will be called a *minimal complete set of implicants* if any minterm of $f(z)$ is covered by at least one implicant $\phi_i(z)$ and the sum of lengths of $\phi_1(z), \ldots, \phi_l(z)$ is minimal. The disjunction (logical sum) of all prime implicants in a minimal complete set is the *minimal disjunctive form* of $f(z)$, which in turn determines an economical implementation of $f(z)$ (224, 247).

The construction of minimal complete sets of implicants is among the most important and difficult problems in the theory of network synthesis (78,110,111,224,239,247,265,325,373,362,490).

We now introduce another complexity criterion for $f(z) = f(z_0, \ldots, z_{m-1})$. Let $\tilde{\eta}(f)$ denote the number of unordered pairs of matching minterms or maxterms in $f(z)$, that is,

$$\tilde{\eta}(f) = \sum_{\|\tau\|=1} \sum_{z=0}^{2^m-1} (f(z)f(z \oplus \tau) + \bar{f}(z)\bar{f}(z \oplus \tau)) \mod 2, \qquad (5.3.10)$$

where $\|\tau\|$ is the number of 1-values in the binary expansion of τ. From now on, we shall compare the complexity of pairs of switching functions (f_1, f_2) such that

$$\sum_{z=0}^{2^m-1} f_1(z) = \sum_{z=0}^{2^m-1} f_2(z).$$

Therefore, if $\sum_{z=0}^{2^m-1} f(z)$ is known, the number

$$\sum_{\|\tau\|=1} \sum_{z=0}^{2^m-1} \overline{f}(z)\overline{f}(z \oplus \tau)$$

of matching maxterms may easily be calculated in terms of the number

$$\sum_{\|\tau\|=1} \sum_{=0}^{2^m-1} f(z)f(z \oplus \tau)$$

of matching minterms. Indeed, we have

$$\sum_{\|\tau\|=1} \sum_{z=0}^{2^m-1} \overline{f}(z)\overline{f}(z \oplus \tau) = \sum_{\|\tau\|=1} \sum_{z=0}^{2^m-1} (1 - f(z))(1 - f(z \oplus \tau))$$

$$= \sum_{\|\tau\|=1} \sum_{z=0}^{2^m-1} (1 - f(z) - f(z \oplus \tau) + f(z)f(z \oplus \tau))$$

$$= 2^m - 2\|f\| + \sum_{\|\tau\|=1} \sum_{z=0}^{2^m-1} f(z)f(z \oplus \tau).$$

We may thus characterize the complexity of a switching function by the quantity $\eta(f)$, defined as the number of pairs of matching constituents of unity:

$$\eta(f) = \sum_{\|\tau\|=1} \sum_{z=0}^{2^m-1} f(z)f(z \oplus \tau). \qquad (5.3.11)$$

An experimental check of this criterion shows that in most cases it provides a quite satisfactory estimate of the complexity of network implementations of $f(z)$. In particular, it can be shown, see Reference 288, that the number of nonoverlapping pairs of minterms in $f(z)$ (for which $\|f\| = 2^{m-1}$) is equal to $\frac{1}{4}(2^{m+1}\eta(f)/m)^{1/2}$ for almost all $f(z)$ that depend on m variables. Consequently, at least $\frac{1}{2}(2^{m+1}\eta(f)/m)^{1/2}$ minterms are covered by $\frac{1}{4}(2^{m+1}\eta(f)/m)^{1/2}$ prime implicants of the length $m - 1$.

Remark 5.3.1   *It would be more appropriate to call the criterion η (and its generalizations to multivalued logic, see 5.3.3) not the complexity but the* simplicity *of the switching functions, since for almost all switching functions a decrease in $\eta(f)$ implies an increase in the complexity of the minimal implementation for f. We shall nevertheless continue to use the term "complexity," since the only important factor for our purposes is the monotonicity of the complexity of the minimal implementation of f as a function of $\eta(f)$.*

The specific complexity criteria ξ, $\hat{\mu}_r$, for $r = 0, 1, \ldots$, and η were selected in view of the fact that, on the one hand, they are used quite frequently, and on the other hand they provide a good illustration of the effective use of spectral methods in optimization problems.

5.3.3 Complexity Criteria for Multiple-Valued Functions

The complexity criteria $\xi(f)$, $\hat{\mu}(f)$ $(r = 0, 1, \ldots)$, and $\eta(f)$ considered above are readily generalized to multiple-valued logic functions. We shall do this for $\eta(f)$.

If $f(z) = f(z_0, \ldots, z_{m-1})$ is a p-valued logical function, we define its complexity $\eta(f)$ to be the number of sets $\{y_1, \ldots, y_p\}$ such that

$$\begin{cases} f(y_1) = f(y_2) = \cdots = f(y_p), \\ y_2 \ominus y_1 = y_3 \ominus y_2 = \cdots = y_p \ominus y_{p-1} = p^s \quad \bmod p, \end{cases}$$

that is, the p-ary expansions of the numbers $y_i \ominus y_{i+1} \pmod p$, $(i = 1, 2, \ldots, p-1)$ have the form $(\underbrace{0, \ldots, 0}_{s}, 1, 0, \ldots, 0)$.

5.4 SERIAL DECOMPOSITION OF SYSTEMS OF SWITCHING FUNCTIONS

5.4.1 Spectral Methods and Complexity

In this section, we discuss spectral methods for solving certain optimization problems related to the design of switching networks. We shall use the languages of spectral and correlation characteristics. In contrast to the methods of classical algebra of logic, the solutions will be analytical, in the sense that the calculation of the final result does not require an exhaustive search of all possible alternatives (in other words, the number of elementary operations will not be an exponential but only a linear or at most quadratic function of the number of points at which the system of functions is defined).

The topic studied in this section and the next is *linearization of logic functions*, that is, the problem of representing a given system of logic functions as the superposition of a system of linear functions and a residual nonlinear part of minimal complexity. Any such representation determines the design of a network realizing the original system as a serial connection of two blocks, a linear and a nonlinear. For a system of p-valued logical functions, the linear block consists of mod p ($p \geq 2$) adders and networks implementing multiplication by constants.

We shall show that the complexity of the linear block increases asymptotically no faster than $m^2 / \log_p m$ as $m \to \infty$, where m is the number of variables, whereas the complexity of the nonlinear block is almost always an exponentially increasing function of m (see (5.3.4)). For this reason, the complexity of the linear block may be ignored in linearization problems.

Throughout this section and in Section 5.4.6, we shall assume that all systems of functions defining the behavior of the device to be designed are completely specified. This section is devoted to the case of greatest practical importance switching functions $p = 2$. We employ the complexity criteria ξ, $\hat{\mu}$, η introduced in Section 5.3.

Recall that the complexity of a system of functions is the sum of complexities of the switching function occurring therein.

A rigorous formulation of the *linearization problem* is as follows. Consider a system of switching function $f(z) = \{f^{(i)}(z_0, \ldots, z_{m-1})\}$ for $i = 0, 1, \ldots, k - 1$. Let Θ denote the class of all nonsingular (mod 2) ($m \times m$) matrices and α any one of our complexity criteria. Problem: Given α, devise an algorithm that, for any $f(z)$, computes a matrix $\sigma \in \Theta$ that minimizes $\alpha(f_\sigma)$, where f_σ is defined by

$$f_\sigma(\sigma \odot z) = f(z), \quad \text{mod } 2. \tag{5.4.1}$$

We shall refer to this as the linearization problem relative to α. In Section 5.4.2 to 5.4.4, we will consider the linearization problems relative to the criteria ζ, $\hat{\mu}$, and η.

5.4.2 Linearization Relative to the Number of Essential Variables

We first consider the linearization problem for the most easily calculated criterion ξ, which means the criterion taking into account the number of essential variables in a nonlinear part.

Recall that $\xi(\phi) = 2^m$, where ϕ is a switching function depending essentially on exactly m of its variables (ϕ is said to *depend essentially on* z_i if

$$\phi(z_0, \ldots, z_{i-1}, 0, z_{i+1}, \ldots, z_{m-1}) \neq \phi(z_0, \ldots, z_{i-1}, 1, z_{i+1}, \ldots, z_{m-1})$$

for some $z_0, \ldots, z_{i-1}, z_{i+1}, \ldots, z_{m-1}$.

Let $f(z) = \{f^{(i)}(z_0, \ldots, z_{m-1})\}$, $i = 0, 1, \ldots, k - 1$ be a system of switching functions depending on all their variables. Set

$$B(\tau) = \sum_{i=0}^{k-1} B_i(\tau) = \sum_{i=0}^{k-1} \sum_{z=0}^{2^m-1} f^{(i)}(z) f^{(i)}(z \oplus \tau), \quad \text{mod } 2.$$

To determine a matrix σ_ξ minimizing $\xi(f_\sigma)$ (see (5.4.1)), we shall use the *total autocorrelation functions* $B_f(\tau)$ thus defined.

Note that for any τ we have $B_f(\tau) \leq B_f(0)$.

Let $G_I(f)$ denote the set of all values τ such that $B(\tau) = B_f(0) = \sum_{i=0}^{k-1} \sum_{z=0}^{2^m-1} f^{(i)}(z)$.

It is clear that $G_I(f)$ is a group (with respect to $\oplus$ (mod 2)), which, in accordance with Section 5.1.3, we call the *inertia group* of the system f.

Let $\tau_0, \tau_1, \ldots, \tau_{a(f)-1}$ be an arbitrary basis of $G_I(f)$ (i.e., a maximal set of elements of $G_I(f)$ linearly independent modulo 2).

Theorem 5.4.1 *Let T be an arbitrary $(m \times m)$ nonsingular binary matrix $(T \in \Theta)$ whose set of columns includes a basis of the inertia group $G_I(f)$ of the system $\{f^{(i)}(z_0, \ldots, z_{m-1})\}$ $(i = 0, \ldots, k-1)$ of switching functions that depend essentially on all their variables. Then,*

$$\min_{\sigma \in \Theta} \xi(f_\sigma) = \xi(f_{\sigma_\xi}) = k2^{m-a(f)}, \tag{5.4.2}$$

and

$$\sigma_\xi \odot T = \mathbf{I}_m = \begin{pmatrix} 1 & & & \\ & 1 & & \mathbf{0} \\ & & \ddots & \\ \mathbf{0} & & & 1 \end{pmatrix} \quad mod\ 2, \tag{5.4.3}$$

that is, $\sigma_\xi = T^{-1} \quad mod\ 2$.

Proof. The proof falls into two parts.

1. We first prove that $\xi(f_{T^{-1}}) = k \cdot 2^{m-a(f)}$.
   Let $B_\sigma(\tau)$ be the total autocorrelation function of the system f_σ (see (5.4.1)). Then, by Theorem 2.7.4, if $\{\tau_s\}$ is a basis element of $G_I(f)$,

   $$B_{T^{-1}}(T^{-1} \otimes \tau_s) = B_f(\tau_s) = \sum_{i=0}^{k-1} \sum_{z=0}^{2^m-1} f^{(i)}(z),$$

   for $s = 0, 1, \ldots, a(f) - 1$.
   But, by the definition of T, the binary expansion of $T^{-1} \odot \tau_s$ (mod 2) contains exactly one 1; hence, it follows that $f^{(i)}(z)$ $(i = 0, 1, \ldots, k-1)$ is independent of $a(f)$ variables, that is,

   $$\xi(f_{T^{-1}}^{(i)}) = 2^{m-a(f)},$$

   $$\xi(f_{T^{-1}}) = \sum_{i=0}^{k-1} \xi(f_{T^{-1}}^{(i)}) = k2^{m-a(f)}.$$

2. We now prove that there is no $\sigma \in \Theta$ such that

$$\xi(f_\sigma) < k2^{m-a(f)}.$$

Indeed, were σ a matrix satisfying this condition, there would exist $\beta_0, \beta_1, \ldots, \beta_{a(f)-1+\Delta}$ ($\Delta \geq 1$) such that $B_\sigma(\beta_s) = \sum_{i=0}^{k-1} \sum_{z=0}^{2^m-1} f^{(i)}(z)$ and the binary expansion of β_s contains exactly one 1, for $s = 0, 1, \ldots, a(f) - 1 + \Delta$. Next, since $\sigma^{-1} \odot \beta_s \neq \sigma^{-1} \odot \beta_q \pmod 2$, $(s \neq q)$ and

$$B(\sigma^{-1} \odot \beta_s) = B_\sigma(\beta_s) = \sum_{i=0}^{K-1} \sum_{i=0}^{2^m-1} f^{(i)}(z) \quad \text{mod } 2,$$

for $s = 0, 1, \ldots, a(f) - 1 + \Delta$, it follows that the system $\{\sigma^{-1} \odot \beta_0, \ldots, \sigma^{-1} \odot \beta_{a(f)-1+\Delta}\}$ is linearly dependent (since $\sigma^{-1} \odot \beta_s \in G_I(f)$ and the basis of $G_I(f)$ contains exactly $a(f)$ elements). But since $\sigma^{-1} \in \Theta$, this contradicts the assumption that $\{\beta_0, \beta_1, \ldots, \beta_{a(f)-1+\Delta}\}$ are linearly independent.

Theorem 5.4.1 provides a procedure for determining a ξ-optimal linear transformation σ_ξ of the variables of a system of switching functions and also an estimate for the ξ-complexity of the nonlinear part corresponding to σ_ξ, (see (5.4.2)). To settle these questions, we need to only construct an arbitrary basis of the inertia group $G_I(f)$ of the system.

Example 5.4.1 *Table 5.4.1 defines a system $f^{(0)}$, $f^{(1)}$ ($m = 4$, $k = 2$), and also its total autocorrelation function $B_f(\tau)$. It follows from the table that*

$$G_I(f) = \{(0, 0, 0, 0), (0, 1, 0, 1), (1, 0, 1, 0), (1, 1, 1, 1)\}.$$

As a basis, we take $\tau_0 = (0, 1, 0, 1)$, $\tau_1 = (1, 0, 1, 0)$, $(a(f) = 2)$. Now set

$$T = \begin{bmatrix} 1 & 0 & 0 & 1 \\ 0 & 1 & 1 & 0 \\ 0 & 0 & 0 & 1 \\ 0 & 0 & 1 & 0 \end{bmatrix}.$$

Then,

$$\sigma_\xi = T^{-1} = \begin{bmatrix} 1 & 0 & 1 & 0 \\ 0 & 1 & 0 & 1 \\ 0 & 0 & 0 & 1 \\ 0 & 0 & 1 & 0 \end{bmatrix}.$$

TABLE 5.4.1 Function $f = (f^{(0)}, f^{(1)})$ in Example 5.4.1, the Total Autocorrelation B_f, and Linearly Transformed Function $f_{T^{-1}} = (f_{T^{-1}}^{(0)}, f_{T^{-1}}^{(1)})$.

z, τ	$z_0 z_1 z_2 z_3$	$f^{(0)}$	$f^{(1)}$	B_f	$f_{T^{-1}}^{(0)}$	$f_{T^{-1}}^{(1)}$
0	0000	0	0	16	0	0
1	0001	1	0	8	0	0
2	0010	1	0	8	0	0
3	0011	1	1	8	0	0
4	0100	1	0	8	1	0
5	0101	0	0	16	1	0
6	0110	1	1	8	1	0
7	0111	1	0	8	1	0
8	1000	1	0	8	1	0
9	1001	1	1	8	1	0
10	1010	0	0	16	1	0
11	1011	1	0	8	1	0
12	1100	1	1	8	1	1
13	1101	1	0	8	1	1
14	1110	1	0	8	1	1
15	1111	0	0	16	1	1

The functions $f_{T^{-1}}^{(0)}$ and $f_{T^{-1}}^{(1)}$ are shown in Table 5.4.1, from where it is evident that $f_{T^{-1}}^{(0)}$ and $f_{T^{-1}}^{(1)}$ do not depend essentially on z_2, z_3. Consequently, by (5.4.2),

$$\xi(f_{\sigma_\xi}) = \xi(f_{T^{-1}}^{(0)}) + \xi(f_{T^{-1}}^{(1)}) = 4 + 4 = 8.$$

5.4.3 Linearization Relative to the Entropy-Based Complexity Criteria

We now consider linearization with respect to the criteria $\hat{\mu}$. Recall that for a switching function $f(z_0, \ldots, z_{m-1})$

$$\mu_r(f) = \begin{cases} 2^{m-r} H(p_0, \ldots, p_{R-1}), & \text{if } r \le m, \\ 0, & \text{if } r > m, \end{cases} \tag{5.4.4}$$

where $R = 2^{2^m}$, $H(p_0, \ldots, p_{R-1}) = -\sum_{i=0}^{R-1} p_i \log_2 p_i$, and $p_i = l_i 2^{-m+r}$ ($0 \log_2 0 = 0$), with l_i the number of subvectors of length 2^r of the ith type in the vector $\mathbf{F} = [f(0), \ldots, f(2^m - 1)]^T$ of function values f. The criterion $\hat{\mu}_r(f)$ is then defined as the minimum of $\mu_r(f)$ over all possible orders of the binary variables z_i of f.

Since $\hat{\mu}_0$ depends on the number of 1 values in the truth vector of each function, which remains invariant under any nonsingular linear transformation, it follows from

(5.4.1) that for any σ

$$\hat{\mu}_0(f_\sigma) = \hat{\mu}_0(f),$$

and the linearization problem relative to $\hat{\mu}_0$ is trivial.

We, therefore, proceed to the linearization problem for $\hat{\mu}_1$, the most simply evaluated criterion for which the problem is not trivial. Denote the corresponding optimal linear transformation by σ_{μ_1}

$$\hat{\mu}_1(f_{\sigma_{\mu_1}}) = \min_{\sigma \in \Theta} \hat{\mu}_1(f_\sigma).$$

Let $\{f = (f^{(i)}(z_0, \ldots, z_{m-1}))\}$ $(i = 0, 1, \ldots, k - 1)$ be a given system and $S_i(\tau)$, $B_i(\tau)$ the Walsh spectrum and the autocorrelation function of it, respectively. We set $S_f(w) = \sum_{i=0}^{k-1} S_i(w)$, and $B_f(\tau) = \sum_{i=0}^{k-1} B_i(\tau)$

Theorem 5.4.2 *Let*

$$\max_{w \neq 0} |S_f(w)| = |S_f(w')|, \quad \min_{\tau \neq 0} B_f(\tau) = B_f(\tau'), \tag{5.4.5}$$

and

$$\left.\begin{array}{c} (00, \cdots, 01) \odot \tilde{\sigma} = \overleftarrow{w}' \\[2mm] \tilde{\sigma} \odot \tau' = \begin{bmatrix} 0 \\ 0 \\ \vdots \\ 0 \\ 1 \end{bmatrix} \end{array}\right\} \quad mod \ 2, \tag{5.4.6}$$

where $\overleftarrow{\alpha} = (\alpha_{m-1}, \ldots, \alpha_0)$ *if* $\alpha = (\alpha_0, \ldots, \alpha_{m-1})$. *Then,* $\sigma_{\mu_1} = \tilde{\sigma}$.

Proof. By the definitions of $\hat{\mu}_1$, $S_f(w)$ and $B_f(\tau)$,

$$\hat{\mu}_1(f) = \sum_{i=0}^{k-1} \hat{\mu}_1(f^{(i)}) = 2^{m-1} H(p_0, p_1, p_2, p_3), \tag{5.4.7}$$

where

$$\begin{aligned} p_0 &= 1 - 2^{-m+1} B_f(0) + 2^{-m} B_f(1), \\ p_1 &= 2^{-m}(B_f(0) - B_f(1) - 2^m S_f(2^{m-1})), \\ p_2 &= 2^{-m}(B_f(0) - B_f(1) + 2^m S_f(2^{m-1})), \\ p_3 &= 2^{-m} B_f(1). \end{aligned} \tag{5.4.8}$$

In view of (5.4.7) and (5.4.8), we may express $\hat{\mu}_1(f)$ as

$$\hat{\mu}_1(f) = \Theta(B_f(1), S(2^{m-1}), B_f(0), m) \tag{5.4.9}$$

and by Theorems 2.6.7 and 2.7.4,

$$\hat{\mu}_1(f_\sigma) = \sum_{i=0}^{k-1} \hat{\mu}(f_\sigma^{(i)}) = \Theta(B_f(\sigma \odot 1), S_f(\overleftarrow{2^{m-1}} \odot \sigma^{-1}), B_f(0), m).$$

The functional Θ is minimized by the matrix σ defined in (5.4.6). The value $\hat{\mu}(f_{\sigma_{\mu_1}})$ is determined by substituting $B_f(\tau')$ for $B_f(1)$ and $S_f(w')$ for $S_f(2^{m-1})$ in (5.4.7) and (5.4.8), where τ' and w' are defined in (5.4.5).

Example 5.4.2 *Table 5.4.2 defines a switching function $f(z_0, z_1, z_2, z_3)$ and the corresponding $S(w)$, $B(\tau)$.*
For this function, $\mu_1(f) = \hat{\mu}_1(f) = 8H(3/8, 2/8, 3/8) = 12.4$.
It follows from the table that $w' = 7$, $\tau' = 14$. Then, by (5.4.6),

$$\sigma_{\mu_1} = \begin{bmatrix} 1 & 1 & 0 & 0 \\ 0 & 1 & 1 & 0 \\ 0 & 0 & 0 & 1 \\ 1 & 1 & 1 & 0 \end{bmatrix}.$$

The function $f_{\sigma_{\mu_1}}(z)$, where $f_{\sigma_{\mu_1}}(\sigma_{\mu_1} \odot z) = f(z)$ (mod 2), is also given in Table 5.4.2.
We have $\mu_1(f_{\sigma_{\mu_1}}) = \hat{\mu}_1(f_{\sigma_{\mu_1}}) = 8H(7/8, 1/8) \simeq 4.4$. Thus linearization brings about a decrease in μ_1 by a factor of 3.3 and in $\hat{\mu}_1$ by a factor of 2.8.

5.4.4 Linearization Relative to the Numbers of Neighboring Pairs of Minterms

We now proceed to the linearization relative to the criterion η (see Section 5.3.2) that takes into account the merging of adjacent minterms and maxterms. Recall that the criterion $\eta(f)$ for a switching function $f^{(i)}(z_0, \ldots, z_{m-1})$ is defined by

$$\eta(f^{(i)}) = \sum_{\|\tau\|=1} \sum_{z=0}^{2^m-1} f^{(i)}(z) f^{(i)}(z \oplus \tau) \quad \text{mod } 2, \tag{5.4.10}$$

where $\|\tau\|$ is the number of 1 values in the binary expansion of τ.

Given a system of switching functions $f(z) = \{f^{(0)}(z), \ldots, f^{(k-1)}(z)\}$, we wish to find a linear transformation matrix σ_η such that

$$\max_{\sigma \in \Theta} \eta(f_\sigma) = \eta(f_{\sigma_\eta}), \tag{5.4.11}$$

where f_σ is defined as before by

$$f_\sigma(\sigma \odot z) = f(z) \mod 2,$$

and Θ is the class of all $(m \times m)$ nonsingular binary matrices ($\sigma \in \Theta$ iff $|\sigma|_2 = 1$).

Let $T = (\tau_{qs})$, where $\tau_{qs} \in \{0, 1\}$, $(q, s = 0, 1, \ldots, m-1)$, $B_i(\tau)$ be the autocorrelation function of $f = \{f^{(i)}(z)\}$, and $B_f(\tau) = \sum_{s=0}^{k-1} B_i(\tau)$. Set

$$B_f(T) = \sum_{s=0}^{k-1} B_f \left(\sum_{q=0}^{m-1} \tau_{q,s} 2^{m-1-q} \right). \tag{5.4.12}$$

Theorem 5.4.3   *Let*

$$\max_{T \in \Theta} B_f(T) = B_f(T_\eta). \tag{5.4.13}$$

TABLE 5.4.2   Function f in Example 5.4.2, Its Spectrum S_f, Autocorrelation B_f, and the Linearly Transformed Function $f_{\sigma_{\mu_1}}$.

z, w, τ	$f(z)$	$16S_f(w)$	$B_f(\tau)$	$f_{\sigma_{\mu_1}}(z)$
0	1	8	8	1
1	1	2	6	0
2	0	-2	2	1
3	0	0	2	0
4	1	2	2	1
5	0	0	2	0
6	1	0	6	1
7	1	6	6	0
8	0	0	2	1
9	0	2	2	0
10	0	-2	6	1
11	1	0	6	0
12	1	2	6	0
13	1	0	6	1
14	0	0	0	1
15	0	-2	2	0

Then,

$$\sigma_\eta \odot T_\eta = \mathbf{I}_m = \begin{bmatrix} 1 & & & \\ & 1 & & \mathbf{0} \\ & & & \\ \mathbf{0} & & \ddots & \\ & & & 1 \end{bmatrix} \quad mod\ 2. \qquad (5.4.14)$$

Proof. For any function $f_\sigma^{(i)}(z)$ with ($\sigma \in \Theta$), where $f_\sigma^{(i)}(\sigma \odot z) = f^{(i)}(z)$, let $B_{\sigma,i}(\tau)$ denote the autocorrelation function and $B_\sigma(\tau) = \sum_{i=0}^{k-1} B_{\sigma,i}(\tau)$. Then, by Theorem 2.7.4,

$$B_\sigma(\sigma \odot \tau) = B_f(\tau). \qquad (5.4.15)$$

In addition, by the definition of η (see (5.4.10)), we see that for any f_σ,

$$\eta(f_\sigma) = B_\sigma(\mathbf{I}_m). \qquad (5.4.16)$$

In view of (5.4.11)–(5.4.14), formulas (5.4.15) and (5.4.16) imply that

$$\max_{\sigma \in \Theta} \eta(f_\sigma) = \max_{\sigma \in \Theta} B_\sigma(\mathbf{I}_m) = \max_{\sigma \in \Theta} B_\sigma(\sigma \odot \sigma^{-1})$$

$$= \max_{\sigma \in \Theta} B(\sigma^{-1}) = \max_{T \in \Theta} B(T)$$

$$= B(T_\eta) = B_{\sigma_\eta}(\sigma_\eta \odot T_\eta) = B_{\sigma_\eta}(\mathbf{I}_m)$$

$$= \eta(f_{\sigma_\eta}) \quad \mod 2.$$

Theorem 5.4.3 generates a simple procedure for determining the η-optimal linear transformation σ_η.

We first calculate the autocorrelation function $B(\tau) = \sum_{i=0}^{m-1} B_i(\tau)$ and then find m linearly independent vectors over $GF(2)$ such that the sum of $B_f(\tau)$ over them is maximal.

These m vectors may be found recursively as follows.

Supposing that we already have s vectors, $1 \leq s \leq m - 1, \tau_0, \tau_1, \ldots, \tau_{s-1}$ we find τ_s from the condition

$$B(\tau_s) = \max_{\tau \notin Q_s} B(\tau), \qquad (5.4.17)$$

where Q_s is the set of all linear combinations (mod 2) of the binary vectors $\tau_0, \tau_1, \ldots, \tau_{s-1}$. It can be shown (288) that the vectors $\tau_0, \tau_1, \ldots, \tau_{m-1}$ thus determined are columns of the matrix T_η, defined by (5.4.13). The η-optimal matrix σ_η is now determined from (5.4.14).

Example 5.4.3 *Table 5.4.3 shows a system $f^{(0)}(z)$, $f^{(1)}(z)$ for $m = 4$ and the functions $B_0(\tau)$, $B_1(\tau)$, and $B(\tau) = B_0(\tau) + B_1(\tau)$. We have $\eta(f) = \eta(f^{(0)}) + \eta(f^{(1)}) = 3 + 1 = 4$. Using the procedure described above, we have from (5.4.13) that*

$$
T_\eta = \begin{bmatrix} 1 & 1 & 0 & 0 \\ 0 & 0 & 0 & 1 \\ 0 & 0 & 1 & 0 \\ 0 & 1 & 1 & 1 \end{bmatrix}, \quad \sigma_\eta = \begin{bmatrix} 1 & 1 & 1 & 1 \\ 0 & 1 & 1 & 1 \\ 0 & 0 & 1 & 0 \\ 0 & 1 & 0 & 0 \end{bmatrix}.
$$

The functions $f_{\sigma_\eta}^{(0)}$ and $f_{\sigma_\eta}^{(1)}(z)$ are shown in Table 5.4.3.

For this example, we have $\eta(f_{\sigma_\eta}) = \eta(f_{\sigma_\eta}^{(0)}) + \eta(f_{\sigma_\eta}^{(1)}) = 4 + 4 = 8$, and the η-optimal linear transformation doubles the number of matching pairs of minterms.

Using the autocorrelation function $B_f(\tau)$, we can estimate the criteria $\eta(f)$ and $\eta(f_{\sigma_\eta})$.

The quantity $\frac{1}{2} B_f(\tau_s)$, where τ_s is determined by the above procedure, is equal to the number of pairs of minterms for f_{σ_η}, which are matched in the sth variable. For example, if

$$
B_f(\tau_0) = B_f(\tau_1) = \cdots = B_f(\tau_s) = \sum_{i=0}^{k-1} \sum_{z=0}^{2^m-1} f^{(i)}(z), \qquad (5.4.18)
$$

TABLE 5.4.3 Function $f = (f^{(0)}, f^{(1)})$ in Example 5.4.3, Its Total Autocorrelation Function B_f, and Linearly Transformed Function $f_{\sigma_\eta} = (f_{\sigma_\eta}^{(0)}, f_{\sigma_\eta}^{(1)})$.

z, τ	$f^{(0)}(z)$	$f^{(1)}(z)$	$B_0(\tau)$	$B_1(\tau)$	$B(\tau)$	$f_{\sigma_\tau}^{(0)}(z)$	$f_{\sigma_\eta}^{(1)}(z)$
0	0	0	5	5	10	0	0
1	0	0	2	0	2	0	1
2	1	1	0	0	0	1	0
3	1	0	2	2	4	1	0
4	0	0	2	0	2	0	0
5	0	1	2	2	4	0	0
6	1	0	0	2	2	0	0
7	0	0	0	2	2	0	0
8	1	0	2	2	4	1	0
9	0	0	2	2	4	0	1
10	0	0	2	0	2	1	1
11	1	1	2	2	4	0	1
12	0	0	0	2	2	0	0
13	0	1	2	0	2	0	0
14	0	1	2	2	4	1	1
15	0	0	0	2	2	0	0

it can be shown that as $m \to \infty$ the complexity $L(f_{\sigma_\eta})$ of a minimal network realizing f_{σ_η} satisfies the asymptotic estimate

$$L(f_{\sigma_\eta}) \sim \frac{k2^{m-s-1}}{m-s-1}. \tag{5.4.19}$$

5.4.5 Classification of Switching Functions by Linearization

The linearization procedure of this section may be utilized in spectral analysis of switching functions to identify certain important classes of functions.

As an example, consider the class of *partially linear* switching functions.

Definition 5.4.1 *A switching function $f(z) = f(z_0, \ldots, z_{m-1})$ is said to be partially linear iff*

$$f(z_0, \ldots, z_{m-1}) = \phi(z_0, \ldots, z_{m-b-1}, l(z_{m-b}, \ldots, z_{m-1})), \tag{5.4.20}$$

where $l(z_{m-b}, \ldots, z_{m-1}) = \bigoplus_{i=m-b}^{m-1} c_i z_i, c_i \in \{0, 1\}, (mod \ 2)$.

It is apparent that when a function f has been identified as partially linear, the design of a network implementation for it becomes much simpler.

Given a switching function f, let $G_I(f)$ denotes the group of inertia points, that is, $\beta \in G_I(f)$ iff $f(z) = f(z \oplus \beta), (mod \ 2)$ (see Section 5.1.3).

Set $a(f) = \log_2 |G_I(f)|$, where $|G_I(f)|$ is the order of the group $G_I(f)$.

We assume throughout that f essentially depends on all its variables z_i, for $i = 0, 1, \ldots, m-1$.

Theorem 5.4.4 *The function $f(z_0, \ldots, z_{m-1})$ satisfies (5.4.20) iff*

$$a(f) = b - 1, \tag{5.4.21}$$

and if $\beta = (\beta_0, \ldots, \beta_{m-1}) \in G_I(f)$, then $\beta_i = 0, i = 0, \ldots, m - b - 1$.

Proof. If f satisfies (5.4.20) (or, conversely, (5.4.21)), the matrices σ_η and T_η ($\sigma_\eta \odot T_\eta = \mathbf{I}_m$ (mod 2)) have the form shown in Fig. 5.4.1.

The $a(f)$ last columns of T_η are $a(f)$ linearly independent vectors in $G_I(f)$, and the function ϕ in (5.4.20) is defined by

$$\phi(z) = f_{\sigma_\eta}(z). \tag{5.4.22}$$

From Theorem 5.4.4, we see, setting $b = m$, that f is a linear function of all its variables iff $a(f) = m - 1$.

Example 5.4.4 *Table 5.4.4 defines a function $f(z)$ and its autocorrelation function $B(\tau), (m = 4)$.*

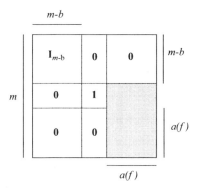

FIGURE 5.4.1   Matrices σ_η and T_η.

It follows from this table that $B(0) = B(3) = \sum_{z=0}^{15} f(z) = 8$, *and so by Theorem 5.1.3,* $G_I(f) = \{(0,0,0,0), (0,0,1,1)\}$, $f(z) = f(z \oplus (0,0,1,1))$ *(mod 2),* $a(f) = 1$. *The assumptions of Theorem 5.4.4 hold with* $b = 2$, *and we have*

$$
T_\eta = \left[
\begin{array}{ccc}
\mathbf{I}_2 & \mid & \mathbf{0} \\
\text{---} & \text{---} & \text{---} \\
\mathbf{0} & \mid & \begin{array}{cc} 1 & 1 \\ 0 & 1 \end{array}
\end{array}
\right],
$$

and $\sigma_\eta = T_\eta$.

TABLE 5.4.4   Function f in Example 5.4.4, Its Autocorrelation B_f, and Linearly Transformed Function f_{σ_η}.

z, τ	$f(z)$	$B_f(\tau)$	$f_{\sigma_\eta}(z)$
0	0	8	0
1	1	0	0
2	1	0	1
3	0	8	1
4	0	4	0
5	1	4	0
6	1	4	1
7	0	4	1
8	0	4	0
9	1	4	0
10	1	4	1
11	0	4	1
12	1	4	1
13	0	4	1
14	0	4	0
15	1	4	0

The switching function $f_{\sigma_\eta}(z)$ (where $f_{\sigma_\eta}(\sigma_\eta \odot z) = f(z) \pmod{2}$) is also shown in Table 5.4.4.

Again by using the table, we see that

$$f(z) = f_{\sigma_\eta}(z_0, z_1, z_2 \oplus z_3) = z_0 z_1 \oplus z_2 \oplus z_3, \quad mod\ 2.$$

Thus, an identification procedure for partially linear functions may be based on the inertia group $G_I(f)$ or, in other words, on the autocorrelation function $B(\tau)$ (since $\beta \in G_I(f)$ iff $B(\beta) = \sum_z f(z)$; see Theorem 5.1.3).

To end this section, we note that the linearization methods considered above are also useful in connection with other problems related to optimal ordering of the variables in switching functions or linearization of systems of switching functions (see Reference 207).

5.4.6 Linearization of Multiple-Valued Functions Relative to the Number of Essential Variables

We first generalize the linearization method of Section 5.4.2 (criterion ξ based on the minimization of the number of essential variables for a nonlinear part) to systems of p-valued logic functions $p \geq 2$, where p is a prime.

Let $f(z_0, \ldots, z_{m-1})$ be a p-valued logic function. We shall say that f *depends inessentialy* on the variable z_i if for any fixed $z_0, \ldots, z_{i-1}, z_{i+1}, \ldots, z_{m-1}$,

$$f(z_0, \ldots, z_{i-1}, r, z_{i+1}, \ldots, z_{m-1}) = f(z_0, \ldots, z_{i-1}, s, z_{i+1}, \ldots, z_{m-1}),$$

for all $r, s \in \{0, 1, \ldots, p-1\}$.

If n is the number of p-ary variables on which f depends essentially, we set $\xi(f) = p^n$.

For a system of functions $f = (f^{(0)}, \ldots, f^{(k-1)})$, we have

$$\xi(f) = \sum_{i=0}^{k-1} \xi(f^{(i)}).$$

Consider a system

$$f(z) = (f^{(i)}(z_0, \ldots, z_{m-1})), \quad i = 0, 1, \ldots, k-1, z_i \in \{0, 1, \ldots, p-1\},$$

which depend essentially on all their variables. Let Θ_p be the set of all $(m \times m)$ p-ary matrices that are nonsingular modulo p. In other words, $\sigma = (\sigma_{ij}) \in \Theta_p$ iff $|\sigma|_p \neq 0$, where $|\sigma|_p$ is the determinant of σ over $GF(p)$, $\sigma_{ij} \in \{0, 1, \ldots, p-1\}$.

The problem is to devise an algorithm computing a matrix $\sigma = \sigma_\xi \in \Theta_p$ that, for each $f(z)$, minimizes $\xi(f_\sigma)$, where

$$f_\sigma(\sigma \odot z) = f(z), \quad mod\ p. \tag{5.4.23}$$

For each of the original logic function $f^{(i)}(z)$, we define a system of characteristic functions

$$f_t^{(i)}(z) = \begin{cases} 1, & \text{if } f^{(i)}(z) = t, \\ 0, & \text{if } f^{(i)}(z) \neq t. \end{cases} \tag{5.4.24}$$

Autocorrelation functions modulo p

$$B_t^{(i)}(\tau) = \sum_{z=0}^{p^m-1} f_t^{(i)}(z) f_t^{(i)}(z \ominus \tau) \quad \text{mod } p, \tag{5.4.25}$$

where $\ominus$ stands for the subtraction modulo p, and the total autocorrelation function

$$B_{p,2}(\tau) = \sum_{t=0}^{p-1} \sum_{i=0}^{k-1} B_t^{(i)}(\tau). \tag{5.4.26}$$

We now define $\tau_s \in G_I(f)$ iff

$$B_{p,2}(\tau_s) = B_{p,2}(0) = k \cdot p^m. \tag{5.4.27}$$

The set $G_I(f)$ is a group with respect to the addition modulo p, which we call the *inertia group* of the initial system of logic functions. The motivation for the usage of this term is that, as follows from (5.4.24)–(5.4.27), if $\tau \in G_I(f)$, then $f(z) = f(z \oplus \tau)$, mod p (see also Section 5.1).

Let $a(f)$ be the number of elements in any basis of $G_I(f)$. The generalized version of Theorem 5.4.1 to p-valued functions is stated as follows.

Theorem 5.4.5 *Let T be an arbitrary nonsingular matrix $(T \in \Theta_p)$ whose set columns include a basis of the inertia group of a system of k p-valued $(p \geq 2)$ logic functions $f(z)$, which depend essentially on all their m variables. Then,*

$$\min_{\sigma \in \Theta_p} \xi(f_\sigma) = \xi(f_{\sigma_\xi}) = k \cdot p^{m-a(f)}, \tag{5.4.28}$$

$$\sigma_\xi \odot T = \mathbf{I}_m = \begin{bmatrix} 1 & & & \\ & 1 & & \mathbf{0} \\ & & \ddots & \\ \mathbf{0} & & & 1 \end{bmatrix}, \quad \text{mod } p. \tag{5.4.29}$$

The proof is analogous to that of the Theorem 5.4.1. The difference is that for p-valued functions we must replace each function by its system of characteristic functions (5.4.24), and the variables are now translated into not modulo 2 but modulo p in the formula for the autocorrelation functions $B_{p,2}(\tau)$.

TABLE 5.4.5 Function $f = (f^{(0)}, f^{(1)})$ in Example 5.4.5 and the Characteristic Functions.

z, τ	$z_0 z_1$	$f^{(0)}$	$f^{(1)}$	$f_0^{(0)}$	$f_2^{(0)}$	$f_1^{(1)}$	$f_2^{(1)}$
0	00	0	1	1	0	1	0
1	01	2	2	0	1	0	1
2	02	2	1	0	1	1	0
3	10	2	1	0	1	1	0
4	11	0	1	1	0	1	0
5	12	2	2	0	1	0	1
6	20	2	2	0	1	0	1
7	21	2	1	0	1	1	0
8	22	0	1	1	0	1	0

Example 5.4.5 *Table 5.4.5 defines a system $f = (f^{(0)}, f^{(1)})$ with $p = 3, k = 2, m = 2$. The table also shows the nonvanishing characteristic functions $f_0^{(0)}, f_1^{(0)}, f_1^{(1)}, f_2^{(1)}$. Table 5.4.6 shows the autocorrelations $B_0^{(0)}, B_2^{(0)}, B_1^{(1)}, B_2^{(1)}$ for the characteristic functions and the total autocorrelation function $B_{3,2}$.*

An examination of the table shows that

$$G_I(f) = \{(0, 0), (1, 1), (2, 2)\}.$$

The basis for $G_I(f)$ will be $\tau_0 = (1, 1), (a(f) = 1)$. Now, set $T = \begin{bmatrix} 1 & 1 \\ 0 & 1 \end{bmatrix}$. Then,

$$\sigma_\xi \odot T^{-1} = \begin{bmatrix} 1 & 2 \\ 0 & 1 \end{bmatrix}, \ (mod\ 3).$$

The functions $f_{T-1}^{(0)}, f_{T-1}^{(1)}$ are also shown in Table 5.4.6, and from which it follows that they depend inessentially on z_1. Therefore, by (5.4.24), $\xi(f(\sigma_\xi)) = \xi(f_{T-1}^{(0)}) + \xi(f_{T-1}^{(1)}) = 3 + 3 = 6$.

TABLE 5.4.6 Autocorrelation Functions for the Function $f = (f^{(0)}, f^{(1)})$ in Example 5.4.5 and Linearly Transformed Function $f_{T-1} = (f_{T-1}^{(0)}, f_{T-1}^{(1)})$.

z, τ	$z_0 z_1$	$B_0^{(0)}$	$B_2^{(0)}$	$B_1^{(1)}$	$B_1^{(2)}$	$B_{3,2}$	$f_{T-1}^{(0)}$	$f_{T-1}^{(1)}$
0	00	3	6	6	3	18	0	1
1	01	0	3	3	0	6	0	1
2	02	0	3	3	0	6	0	1
3	10	0	3	3	0	6	2	1
4	11	3	6	6	3	18	2	1
5	12	0	3	3	0	6	2	1
6	20	0	3	3	0	6	2	2
7	21	0	3	3	0	6	2	2
8	22	3	6	6	3	18	2	2

Remark 5.4.1 *By using the inertia group concept, it is possible to generalize Theorem 5.4.4 (decision procedure for partially linear logic functions) to p-valued logic.*

5.4.7 Linearization for Multiple-Valued Functions Relative to the Entropy-Based Complexity Criteria

In this section, we generalize the linearization methods discussed in Section 5.4 (the criterion η) to p-valued logic functions.

Recall (see Section 5.3.3) that in this case, the criterion η for a function $f^{(i)}(z)$ is defined as the number of sets of p vectors $y_1, y_2, \ldots, y_p$ such that

$$\begin{cases} f^{(i)}(y_1) = f^{(i)}(y_2) = \cdots = f^{(i)}(y_p), \\ y_2 \ominus y_1 = y_3 \ominus y_2 = \cdots = y_p \ominus y_{p-1} = p^s, \quad \text{mod } p. \end{cases} \tag{5.4.30}$$

As usual, the complexity of a system of functions is the sum of complexities of the individual functions.

The linearization problem relative to η is to find a matrix $\sigma = \sigma_\eta$ such that

$$\eta(f_{\sigma_\eta}) = \max_{\sigma \in \Theta_p} \eta(f_\sigma), \tag{5.4.31}$$

where $\sigma = (\sigma_{q,s})$, $\sigma_{q,s} \in \{0, 1, \ldots, p-1\}$.

As before, we construct the system of characteristic functions $\{f_t^{(i)}(z)\}$, but now, instead of the functions $B_{2,2}(\tau)$, we construct a class of autocorrelation functions

$$B_{p,p}(\tau) = \sum_{t=0}^{p-1} B_t(\tau) \tag{5.4.32}$$

$$= \sum_{t=0}^{p-1} \sum_{i,z} f_t^{(i)}(z) f_t^{(i)}(z \ominus \tau) \cdots f_t^{(i)}(z \ominus \overbrace{\tau \ominus \cdots \ominus \tau}^{p-1}),$$

with calculations modulo p.

In analogy to the case of switching functions ($p = 2$), the algorithm computing σ_η makes use of functions $B_{p,p}(\tau)$.

Let $T = [\tau_{q,s}]$ ($\tau_{q,s} \in \{0, 1, \ldots, p-1\}$, $q, s = 0, 1, \ldots, m-1$). We set

$$B_{p,p}(T) = \sum_{s=0}^{m-1} B_{p,p} \left(\sum_{q=0}^{m-1} \tau_{q,s} p^{m-1-q} \right). \tag{5.4.33}$$

Theorem 5.4.6 *Let*

$$\max_{T \in \Theta_p} B_{p,p}(T_\eta) = B_{p,p}(T_\eta). \tag{5.4.34}$$

Then,

$$\sigma_\eta \odot T_\eta = \mathbf{I}_m = \begin{bmatrix} 1 & & & \\ & 1 & & 0 \\ & & \ddots & \\ 0 & & & 1 \end{bmatrix}, \quad mod \ p. \quad (5.4.35)$$

Proof. First, by the definitions of $\eta(f)$, $B_{p,p}$, σ_η, and T_η, we have

$$\eta(f) = B_{p,p}(\mathbf{I}_m)$$

$$\eta(f_{\sigma_\eta}) = B_{p,p}(T_\eta).$$

Second, the analog of Theorem 2.7.4 for the function $B_{p,p}(\tau)$ is true. If $f(z)$ corresponds to $B_{p,p}(\tau)$, then $f(\sigma \odot z)$, where $\sigma = [\sigma_{i,j}]$ $\sigma_{i,j} \in \{0, 1, \ldots, p-1\}$, $\sigma \in \Theta_p$, corresponds to $B_{p,p}(\sigma \odot \tau)$ (mod p). These two remarks directly yield Theorem 5.4.6.

Theorem 5.4.6 generalizes Theorem 5.4.3 to p-valued logic.

The matrix T_η may be determined from $B_{p,p}(\tau)$ by a recursive procedure analogous to that described in Section 5.4.4.

It is readily seen from (5.4.32) that

$$B_{p,p}(\tau) = B_{p,p}(\overline{\tau}), \quad (5.4.36)$$

where $\tau \oplus \overline{\tau} = (0, \ldots, 0)$ (mod p). This remark yields a substantial simplification of the construction of $B_{p,p}(\tau)$.

Example 5.4.6 *Table 5.4.7 defines a ternary logic function of two variables ($p = 3$, $m = 2$, $k = 1$) and also gives the autocorrelation functions $B_0(\tau)$, $B_1(\tau)$, the characteristic functions f_0, f_1, ($f_2(z) = 0$), and the function $B_{3,3}(\tau)$. We have $\eta(f) = 0$.*

By using the table and formulas (5.4.34)–(5.4.35), we see that

$$T_\eta = \begin{bmatrix} 1 & 1 \\ 0 & 1 \end{bmatrix}, \quad \sigma_\eta = \begin{bmatrix} 1 & 2 \\ 0 & 1 \end{bmatrix},$$

and $\eta(f_{\sigma_\eta}) = 3$.

The linearization procedures considered here may be extended to systems of incompletely specified switching functions or many-valued logic functions. Linearization methods employing other complexity criteria have been considered in Reference 277, which also describes a generalization of the procedures to nonprime p.

TABLE 5.4.7   Function f in Example 5.4.6.

z, τ	$f(z)$	$B_0(\tau)$	$B_1(\tau)$	$B_{3,3}(\tau)$	$f_{\sigma_\eta}(z)$
0	1	3	6	9	1
1	0	0	0	0	1
2	1	0	0	0	1
3	1	0	0	0	1
4	1	0	6	6	1
5	0	0	0	0	1
6	0	0	0	0	0
7	1	0	0	0	0
8	1	0	6	6	0

5.5 PARALLEL DECOMPOSITION OF SYSTEMS OF SWITCHING FUNCTIONS

The linearization methods discussed above are related to serial connections of linear and nonlinear blocks, minimizing the complexity of a nonlinear part.

In this section, we shall discuss structures in which the linear and nonlinear blocks are connected in parallel and the minimized functional will again be the complexity of the nonlinear part.

Another difference between this and the preceding sections is that whereas previously our main tools were the correlation functions, the methods of polynomial approximation to be considered here illustrate the effective use of spectral characteristics in optimization problems.

We shall measure the complexity of a given completely specified switching function $f(z_0, \ldots, z_{m-1})$ (depending essentially on all its variables) in terms of the simplest criterion $\xi(f) = 2^n$, where $n \le m$ and n is the number of essential variables in f (see Section 5.3). As before, we will use the Paley ordering of Walsh spectra.

In this context, we shall use the term "linear function" not only for a linear function proper but also for its inversion; in other words, $l_i(z)$ is a linear function iff

$$l_i(z) = \bigoplus_{s=0}^{m-1} l_i^{(s)} z_s \oplus l_i^{(m)} \quad \text{mod } 2, \tag{5.5.1}$$

where $l_i^{(s)} \in \{0, 1\}$, $s = 0, 1, \ldots, m$.

5.5.1 Polynomial Approximation of Completely Specified Functions

We can now state the problem of *polynomial approximation* for a completely specified switching functions.

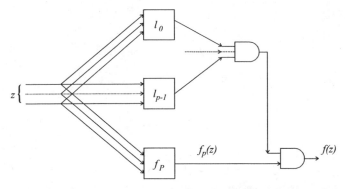

FIGURE 5.5.1 Network to realize the parallel approximation of f.

We say that a switching function f is *approximated* by a product of q linear functions $l_0, \ldots, l_{q-1}$ if

$$f(z) = f_P(z) \cdot \prod_{i=0}^{q-1} l_i(z). \tag{5.5.2}$$

The function $P(z) = \prod_{i=0}^{q-1} l_i(z)$ is a polynomial of degree q, which we shall call a *polynomial approximation* of f.

If f has a polynomial approximation $P(z) = \prod_{i=0}^{q-1} l_i(z)$, it may be realized by a network of the type shown in Fig. 5.5.1.

Notice that for a given f and a given polynomial approximation $P(z)$, there may exist several functions f_P satisfying (5.5.2). Let $\mathcal{F}_P$ denote the set of all such functions, and

$$\min_{f_P \in \mathcal{F}_P} \xi(f_P) = \xi(\tilde{f}_P). \tag{5.5.3}$$

Denote the set of all approximations $P(z)$ of f by π_f.

We shall say that an approximation $P(z) = P_\xi(z)$ is *optimal* for f if it minimizes the complexity of the residual part f_P

$$\min_{P(z) \in \pi_f} \xi(\tilde{f}_P) = \xi(\tilde{f}_{P_\xi}). \tag{5.5.4}$$

The problem is thus to determine an optimal approximation $P_\xi(z)$ for a given function f from the condition (5.5.4).

If $f(z) = f(z_0, \ldots, z_{m-1})$, we shall call $l_i = (l_i^{(0)}, \ldots, l_i^{(m-1)})$, $(l_i^{(s)} \in \{0, 1\}, s = 0, \ldots, m-1)$ a *linearity point* if

$$l_i(z) = \bigoplus_{s=0}^{m-1} l_i^{(s)} z_s \oplus l_i^{(m)}, \quad \text{mod } 2,$$

is an approximation of f, for some $l_i^m \in \{0, 1\}$.

Theorem 5.5.1   *A switching function $f(z_0, \ldots, z_{m-1})$ has linearity points $l_0, l_1, \ldots, l_{Q(f)-1}$ iff*

$$|S_f(\overleftarrow{l_i})| = 2^{-m} \sum_{z=0}^{2^m-1} f(z), \quad i = 0, 1, \ldots, Q(f) - 1, \tag{5.5.5}$$

where S_f is the Walsh spectrum in Paley ordering of f and $\overleftarrow{l} = \sum_{s=0}^{m-1} l_i^{(s)} 2^s$, for $l = \sum_{s=0}^{m-1} l_i^{(s)} 2^{m-1-s}$.

Proof. Notice that $l_i(z)$ is an approximation of f iff for any fixed z^* such that $f(z^*) = 1$, it is always true that $l_i(z^*) = 1 \oplus l_i^{(m)}$, $W_{\overleftarrow{l_i}}(z^*) = (-1)^{1 \oplus l_i^{(m)}}$. Consequently, $|S_f (\overleftarrow{l_1})| = 2^{-m} \sum_{z=0}^{2^m-1} f(z)$.

Corollary 5.5.1   *The set of linearity points of an arbitrary switching function is a group relative to the addition modulo 2.*

Proof. We first note that $l(z) = 0$ is a linearity point for any switching function, since $1 \oplus l(z) = 1$ is an approximation of any switching function and if $f(z) = l_i(z) f_{l_i}(z) = l_j(z) f_{l_j}(z)$, then for any fixed z^* it follows from $f(z^*) = 1$ that

$$W_{\overleftarrow{l_i \oplus l_j}}(z^*) = W_{\overleftarrow{l_i} \oplus \overleftarrow{l_j}}(z^*) = W_{\overleftarrow{l_i}}(z^*) W_{\overleftarrow{l_j}}(z^*) = (-1)^{l_i^{(m)} + l_j^{(m)}}, \quad \text{mod } 2,$$

and so $|S_f(\overleftarrow{l_i \oplus l_j})| = 2^{-m} \sum_z f(z)$. Hence, it follows by Theorem 5.5.1 that $l_i \oplus l_j$ is a linearity point for f.

Corollary 5.5.2   *The number of points at which the Walsh spectrum of an arbitrary switching function $f(z_0, \ldots, z_{m-1})$ assumes its maximum absolute value $2^{-m} \sum_z f(z)$ is always a power of 2.*

This corollary, which follows from Theorem 5.5.1 and Corollary 5.5.1, yields yet another simple method for checking the validity of a calculation of spectra.

Comparing Theorem 5.5.1 and Corollary 5.5.1 with Theorem 5.1.3 and Corollary 5.1.1, we see that while the maximum absolute value of the spectrum of a switching function determines its linearity group, the maximum values of the autocorrelation function define its inertia (anti-self-duality) group.

Now let $l_0, l_1, \ldots, l_{Q(f)-1}$ be an arbitrary basis (maximal linearly independent set of vectors over $GF(2)$) of the group of linearity points of f.

Denote

$$\log_2 \xi(\tilde{f}_{P_\xi}) = \xi(f). \tag{5.5.6}$$

Theorem 5.5.2   *For any $f(z_0, \ldots, z_{m-1})$ with a linearity group containing $2^{q(f)}$ vectors,*

$$P_\xi(z) = \prod_{i=0}^{q(f)-1} \left(\bigoplus_{s=0}^{m-1} l_i^{(s)} z_s \oplus sign(S_f(\overleftarrow{l_i})) \right), \quad mod\ 2, \qquad (5.5.7)$$

where

$$sign(x) = \begin{cases} 1, & if\ x > 0, \\ 0, & if\ x \le 0, \end{cases}$$

and

$$n(f) \le m - q(f). \qquad (5.5.8)$$

Proof.   The fact that

$$P_\xi(z) = \prod_{i=0}^{q(f)-1} \left(\bigoplus_{s=0}^{m-1} l_i^{(s)} z_s \oplus sign(S_f(\overleftarrow{l_i})) \right), \quad mod\ 2,$$

is an approximation of f follows from the definition of $l_0, \ldots, l_{q(f)-1}$, Theorem 5.5.1 and Corollary 5.5.1 in view of the fact that if $sign(S_f(\overleftarrow{l_i})) = 0$ $(sign(S_f(\overleftarrow{l_i})) = 1)$, then $f(z^*) = 1$ always implies $W_{\underset{l_i}{\leftarrow}}(z^*) = -1$, (or $W_{\underset{l_i}{\leftarrow}}(z^*) = 1$) and

$$l_i(z) = \bigoplus_{i=0}^{m-1} l_i^{(s)} z_s, \quad (\text{or}\ \ 1 \oplus l_i(z)), \quad mod\ 2,$$

is an approximation of f.
   Now, if $\hat{P}(z) \in \pi_f$, and

$$\hat{P}(z) = \prod_{i=0}^{\hat{q}-1} \left(\bigoplus_{s=0}^{m-1} \hat{l}_i^{(s)} z_s \oplus \hat{l}_i^{(m)} \right), \quad mod\ 2,$$

where $\hat{l}_i^{(s)} \in \{0, 1\}$, $i = 0, 1, \ldots, \hat{q} - 1$, $s = 0, 1, \ldots, m$, then the vectors $\hat{l}_i = (\hat{l}_i^{(0)}, \ldots, \hat{l}_i^{(m-1)})$, $(i = 0, 1, \ldots, q - 1)$ belong to a subgroup of the group of linearity points. Since $l_0, l_1, \ldots, l_{q(f)-1}$ form a basis for this group, it follows that for any z^* if $P_\xi(z^*) = 1$, then necessarily $\hat{P}(z^*) = 1$ and so $\xi(\tilde{f}_{P_\xi}) \le \xi(\hat{f}_P)$. Thus the polynomial $P_\xi(z)$ defined by (5.5.6) is an optimal approximation.

We now prove (5.5.8). Consider a system of $q(f)$ linearly independent equations in m variables $z_0, \ldots, z_{m-1}$,

$$\bigoplus_{s=0}^{m-1} l_i^{(s)} z_s \oplus sign(S_f(\overleftarrow{l_i})) = 1. \tag{5.5.9}$$

There always exist $s_0, s_1, \ldots, s_{q(f)-1}$ such that $\sum_{i=0}^{q(f)-1} l_i^{(s_r)} > 0$, $r = 0, 1, \ldots, \eta(f) - 1$, since $l_0, l_1, \ldots l_{q(f)-1}$ are linearly independent. Then, by (5.5.9)

$$z_s = g_{s_r}(z_0, z_1, \ldots, z_{m-1}), \quad (r = 0, 1, \ldots, q(f) - 1), \tag{5.5.10}$$

where g_{s_r} are linear functions and each of which is independent of $z_{s_0}, \ldots, z_{s_{q(f)-1}}$. Now, if $f(z) = P_\xi(z) f_{P_\xi}(z)$, substitution of g_{s_r} for $z_{s_r}, (r = 0, \ldots, q(f) - 1)$ in $f_{P_\xi}(z)$ yields a function $f'_{P_\xi}(z)$ that does not depend on z_{s_r} and if $P(z^*) = 1$ for some z^* (i.e., all the equations of system (5.5.9) are satisfied), then $f'_{P_\xi}(z^*) = f_{P_\xi}(z^*)$. Hence $f'_{P_\xi} \in \pi_f$ and

$$n(f) = \min_{P(z) \in \pi_f} \log_2 \xi(\tilde{f}_P) \leq \log_2 \xi(f'_{P_\xi}) \leq m - q(f).$$

Theorems 5.5.1 and 5.5.2 yield a simple procedure for determining the optimal polynomial approximation $P_\xi(z)$ and estimating the complexity of the nonlinear part. We calculate the spectrum S_f of the function f, construct the group of linearity points l_i for which $|S_f(\overleftarrow{l_i})| = 2^m \sum_z f(z)$, and select an arbitrary basis of this group. An upper bound for the complexity $n(f)$ of the nonlinear part of f may even be established without finding a basis, as $n(f)$ depends on the number m of variables of f and on the number $q(f)$, which is equal to the binary logarithm of the number of elements in the group of linearity points of f.

Example 5.5.1   *Table 5.5.1 defines a switching function $f(z)$ and its spectrum $S_f(w)$, for $m = 4$. The table shows that $|S_f(0)| = |S_f(2)| = |S_f(8)| = |S_f(10)| = 2^{-m} \sum_z f(z) = 3$. The group of linearity points contains the vectors $(0, 0, 0, 0), (0, 1, 0, 0), (0, 0, 0, 1), (0, 1, 0, 1)$ $(q(f) = 2)$. As the basis, we take $l_0 = (0, 0, 0, 1), l_1 = (0, 1, 0, 1)$. Since $sign(S_f(\overleftarrow{l_0})) = sign(S_f(8)) = 0$ and $sign(S_f(\overleftarrow{l_1})) = sign(S_f(10)) = 0$, the optimal approximation is $P_\xi(z) = (z_1 \oplus z_3)z_3 = z_3 \oplus z_1 z_3$ and by (5.5.8), we have $n(f) \leq 2$. The nonlinear part $\tilde{f}_{P_\xi}(z)$ (where $f(z) = P_\xi(z \tilde{f}_{P_i}(z))$ in this example is $\tilde{f}_{P_i}(z) = z_0 \vee z_2$. Finally,*

$$f(z) = (z_3 \oplus z_1 z_3)(z_0 \vee z_2).$$

TABLE 5.5.1   Function f in Example 5.5.1 and Its Walsh Spectrum.

z, w	$f(z)$	$16S_f(w)$
0	0	3
1	0	−1
2	0	3
3	1	−1
4	0	−1
5	0	−1
6	0	−1
7	0	−1
8	0	−3
9	1	1
10	0	−3
11	1	1
12	0	1
13	0	1
14	0	1
15	0	1

5.5.2 Additive Approximation Procedure

In this section, we generalize the approximation procedure of the preceding section. Hitherto we have been studying multiplicative approximations

$$f(z) = f_P(z) \prod_{i=0}^{q-1} l_i(z). \tag{5.5.11}$$

We now consider *additive approximations*, with logical product replaced throughout by the logic sum

$$f(z) = f_P(z) \vee \bigvee_{i=0}^{q-1} l_i(z), \tag{5.5.12}$$

$$P(z) = \bigvee_{i=0}^{q-1} l_i(z). \tag{5.5.13}$$

As before, we say that an approximation $P(z) = P_\xi(z)$ is optimal if it minimizes $\xi(f_P)$ (see (5.5.4) and (5.5.6)).

The physical implementation of an additive approximation is described by the same block diagram as in Fig. 5.5.1, except that the logic multiplication elements (AND gates) are replaced throughout by logic adders (OR gates).

The optimal additive approximation may be determined by using De Morgan laws (247)

$$1 \oplus \prod_{i=0}^{q-1} a_i = \bigvee_{i=0}^{q-1} (1 \oplus a_i), \quad \mod 2, \tag{5.5.14}$$

where $a_i \in \{0, 1\}$.

Applying (5.5.14) and (5.5.11), we obtain a simple rule for the additive approximation as follows. If $\prod_{i=0}^{q-1} l_i(z)$ is the optimal multiplicative approximation to f, then $\bigvee_{i=0}^{q-1} (1 \oplus l_i(z))$ is the optimal additive approximation to $f = 1 \oplus f$.

Since $f(z) = f(z_0, \ldots, z_{m-1})$ has a nontrivial multiplicative approximation if $\sum_z f(z) \leq 2^{m-1}$, and a nontrivial additive approximation exists if $\sum_z f(z) \geq 2^{m-1}$, it is clear that these two types of approximation complement each other in a natural way.

The above approximation procedures may also be generalized to systems of switching functions. We call $P(z)$ an *approximation of the system* $f^{(i)}(z), i = 0, 1, \ldots, k - 1$ if each $f^{(i)}(z)$ may be expressed as

$$f^{(i)}(z) = f_P^{(i)}(z)P(z), \quad i = 0, 1, \ldots, k - 1. \tag{5.5.15}$$

An *optimal approximation* is the approximation that minimizes the quantity

$$\xi(f) = \sum_{i=0}^{k-1} \xi(f^{(i)}).$$

The solution of the optimal approximation problem for a system of switching functions is entirely analogous to the case of a single switching function, except that the linearity group is the set of vectors that are linearly points simultaneously for all switching functions in the system.

5.5.3 Complexity Analysis of Polynomial Approximations

We conclude this section with a discussion of the relationships between the optimal approximation problems just considered and the problem of minimizing the complexity of devices realizing systems of switching functions.

Let f be a system of k switching functions of m variables and P_ξ a ξ-optimal polynomial approximation of f.

Let $L(f)$ denote the complexity of a minimal network realizing the system f, that is, the minimum number of required single- and two-input gates.

Theorem 5.5.3   *As $m \to \infty$,*

$$L(f) \lesssim \frac{k2^{n(f)}}{n(f)} + \frac{2^m}{\log_2 m}. \tag{5.5.16}$$

Proof. By Theorem 5.5.2, $P_\xi(z)$ is a product of $q(f)$ linear functions of m variables, and so it can be realized by linear networks computing these functions and AND gates computing their product. The complexity of the multiplication network is at most $q(f) - 1$ AND gates. Since $q(f) \lesssim m$, it follows, in view of the complexity estimate $m^2/\log_2 m$, $(m \to \infty)$ for the linear network with m inputs (see Section 6.1.3), that the complexity $L(P_\xi)$ satisfies the estimate

$$L(P_\xi) \lesssim \frac{m^2}{\log_2 m}. \tag{5.5.17}$$

We can now use the Shannon–Lupanov estimate (5.3.4) for the complexity $L(\tilde{f}_{P_\xi})$ of the system$\tilde{f}_{P_\xi}$ of k switching functions of $n(f) = \log_2 \xi(\tilde{f}_{P_\xi})$ variables

$$L(\tilde{f}_{P_\xi}) \lesssim \frac{k \cdot 2^{\xi(f)}}{\xi(f)}. \tag{5.5.18}$$

By using the relation

$$L(f) \leq L(P_\xi) + L(\hat{f}_{P_\xi}), \tag{5.5.19}$$

we now deduce the desired estimate from (5.5.17) and (2.8.17).

Theorem 5.5.3 is valid for both multiplicative and additive approximations. It provides a good illustration of how important is to know the complexity $\xi(f)$ of the nonlinear part to estimate the complexity in terms of the number of logic elements required for a minimal implementation of f.

For example, if $k = 1, \xi(f) = 0$ (f is a product or the logic sum of linear functions), it follows from Theorem 5.5.3 that $L(f) \lesssim m^2/\log_2 m$.

If $\eta(f) = m$, (i.e., $q(f) = 0$, $P_\xi(z) = 1$, and there is no linear part), the estimate of Theorem 5.5.3 coincides with the Shannon–Lupanov estimate (5.3.4), and if $q(f) \geq 1$, it is more precise.

5.5.4 Approximation Methods for Multiple-Valued Functions

The above polynomial approximation methods will now be generalized to p-valued logical functions.

As before, the criterion for the complexity of a completely specified p-valued logical function $f(z_0, z_1, \ldots, z_{m-1})$, depending essentially on all its m variables, will be $\xi(f) = p^m$.

Let $l_r(z)$ be a linear p-valued logic function,

$$l_r(z) = \bigoplus_{s=0}^{m-1} l_r^{(s)} z_s, \quad \text{mod } p, \quad l_r^{(s)} \in \{0, 1, \ldots, p-1\}. \tag{5.5.20}$$

Let $d_t(l_r)$ denote the tth characteristic function of $l_r(z)$, that is,

$$d_t(l_r(z)) = \begin{cases} 1, & \text{if } l_r(z) = t, \\ 0, & \text{otherwise,} \end{cases} \tag{5.5.21}$$

where $t = 0, 1, \ldots, p-1$.

In the case $p = 2$, we have $t \in \{0, 1\}$ in (5.5.21), and

$$d_0(l_r(z)) = 1 \oplus l_r(z), \quad d_1(l_r(z)) = l_r(z), \quad \text{mod } 2, \tag{5.5.22}$$

so that the characteristic functions thus defined generalize those defined by (5.5.1) for $p = 2$.

We shall say that f is *approximated* by a product of q linear functions $l_0, \ldots, l_{q-1}$ iff there exist $t_0, \ldots, t_{q-1} \in \{0, 1, \ldots, p-1\}$ such that

$$f(z) = f_P(z) \prod_{r=0}^{q-1} d_{t_r}(l_r(z)). \tag{5.5.23}$$

We then call $P(z) = \prod_{r=0}^{q-1} d_{t_r}(l_r(z))$ a *polynomial approximation* for f.

Let $\mathcal{F}_P$ denote the set of functions f_P satisfying (5.5.23) for given f and $P(z)$, and set

$$\min_{f_P \in \mathcal{F}_P} \xi(f_P) = \xi(\tilde{f}_P). \tag{5.5.24}$$

An approximation $P(z) = P_\xi(z)$ is said to be *optimal* if

$$\min_{P(z) \in \pi_f} \xi(\tilde{f}_P) = \xi(\tilde{f}_{P_\xi}), \tag{5.5.25}$$

where π_f is the set of all polynomial approximations of f. In other words, as before, an optimal approximation minimizes the ξ-complexity of the nonlinear part f_P.

A vector $l_r = (l_r^{(0)}, \ldots, l_r^{(m-1)})$, $l_r^{(s)} \in \{0, 1, \ldots, p-1\}$, $s = 0, \ldots, m-1$ will be called a *linearity point* for a p-valued logical function $f(z) = f(z_0, \ldots, z_{m-1})$ if $l_r(z) = \bigoplus_{s=0}^{m-1} l_r^{(s)} z_s$ (mod p) approximates $f(z)$; that is, there exist $t_r \in \{0, 1, \ldots, p-1\}$ such that

$$f(z) = d_{t_r}(l_r(z)) f_P(z). \tag{5.5.26}$$

Theorem 5.5.4   *A p-valued logical function $f(z) = f(z_0, \ldots, z_{m-1})$ may be expressed as*

$$f(z) = d_{l_r}(l_r(z)) f_P(z), \tag{5.5.27}$$

where $l_r(z) = \bigoplus_{s=0}^{m-1} l_r^{(s)} z_s$, (mod p), iff

$$S_f(\overleftarrow{1}_r) = p^{-m} \sum_{z=0}^{p^m-1} f(z) \exp\left(\frac{2\pi}{p} i \sum_{s=0}^{m-1} l_r^{(s)} z_s\right) = p^{-m} \overline{e}_{t_r} \sum_{z=0}^{p^m-1} f(z)$$

is the spectral coefficient for $l_r = \sum_{s=0}^{m-1} l_r^{(s)} 2^s$ in the expansion of $f(z)$ in terms of Vilenkin–Chrestenson functions $\chi_w^{(p)}(z)$ and $\overline{e}_{t_r} = \exp(-2\pi i t_r/p)$, $(i = \sqrt{-1})$.

Proof. We first note that (5.5.26) holds iff for any fixed z^*, $f(z^*) \neq 0$ implies $l_r(z^*) = t_r$. Furthermore, by virtue of the isomorphism of the linear p-valued logical functions and the Vilenkin–Chrestenson functions (Theorem 2.5.5),

$$\chi_{\overleftarrow{l}_r}(z^*) = \exp\left(\frac{2\pi}{p} i t_r\right) = e_{t_r},$$

and therefore

$$S_f(\overleftarrow{1}_r) = p^{-m} \sum_{z=0}^{p^m-1} f(z) \overline{\chi_{\overleftarrow{1}(z)}} = p^{-m} \overline{e}_{t_r} \sum_{z=0}^{p^m-1} f(z),$$

proving (5.5.27).

Setting $p = 2$ in Theorem 5.5.4, we obtain Theorem 5.5.1 (since $|e_{t_r}| = 1$ for any $t_r \in \{0, 1\}$).

Theorem 5.5.4 thus states that l_r is a linearity point of $f(z)$ iff

$$|S_f(\overleftarrow{l}_r)| = p^{-m} \sum_{z=0}^{p^m-1} f(z). \tag{5.5.28}$$

In analogy with the Corollary 5.5.1, the set of linearity points of any p-valued logic function is a group with respect to componentwise addition modulo p. This also follows from Theorem 5.5.4.

Hence, the following corollary can be stated.

Corollary 5.5.3   *The number of points at which the Vilenkin–Chrestenson spectrum of an arbitrary p-valued logic function $f(z_0, \ldots, z_{m-1})$ (where p is a prime) is of the absolute value $p^{-m} \sum_z f(z)$ is always an integral power of p.*

Corollary 5.5.3 is a generalization of Corollary 5.5.2 and provides a check on calculations of Vilenkin–Chrestenson spectra.

When $p > 2$, the calculation of spectra may be simplified by using the identity

$$S_f(\overline{w}) = \overline{S}_f(w), \quad w \oplus \overline{w} = 0, \quad \mod p, \tag{5.5.29}$$

and $\overline{S}_f(w)$ is complex conjugate of $S_f(w)$, which follows from $\chi_{\overline{w}}^{(p)}(z) = \overline{\chi_w^{(p)}(z)}$, (mod p). This halves the complexity of computation of Vilenkin–Chrestenson spectra.

We can now prove the main result related to polynomial approximations of p-valued logical functions, generalizing Theorem 5.5.2.

Theorem 5.5.5   *Let $f(z) = f(z_0, \ldots, z_{m-1})$ be a p-valued logic function, and $l_0, l_1, \ldots, l_{q(f)-1}$ a basis of its linearity group. Let*

$$S_f(\overleftarrow{l}_r) = p^{-m}\overline{e}_{t_r} \sum_{z=0}^{p^m-1} f(z),$$

where S_f is the Vilenkin–Chrestenson spectrum of the function f and $\overline{e}_{l_r} = \exp(-2\pi i t_r/p)$. Then, an optimal polynomial approximation $P_\xi(z)$ and the complexity $\xi(f) = \log_p \xi(\tilde{f}_{P_\xi})$ of the nonlinear part of f satisfy the conditions

$$P_\xi(z) = \prod_{r=0}^{q(f)-1} d_{t_r} \left(\bigoplus_{s=0}^{m-1} l_r^{(s)} z_s \right), \quad \mod p, \tag{5.5.30}$$

$$\xi(f) \le m - q(f). \tag{5.5.31}$$

Proof.   Analogous to that of Theorem 5.5.2, except that in proving (5.5.31,) it should be considered instead of (5.5.9) the system

$$\bigoplus_{s=0}^{m-1} l_r^{(s)} z_s = t_r, \quad r = 0, 1, \ldots, q(f) - 1, \quad \mod p \tag{5.5.32}$$

of $q(f)$ linearly independent linear equations over $GF(p)$ in m variables z_i, $i = 0, \ldots, m - 1$.

Example 5.5.2   *Table 5.5.2 defines a ternary logic function of two variables ($p = 3$, $m = 2$) and its Vilenkin–Chrestenson spectrum (using the notation $e_1 = \exp(2\pi i/3)$, $e_2 = \overline{e}_1 = \exp(4\pi i/3)$). The linearity group consists of the points $\{(0, 0), (1, 2), (2, 1)\}$, and its basis consists of the single vector $(1, 2)$ and $q(f) = 1$. By Theorem 5.5.4, in view of the relation*

$$S_f(\overleftarrow{5}) = S_f(7) = 3^{-2}\overline{e}_2 \cdot 5,$$

TABLE 5.5.2 Function f in Example 5.5.2, Its Spectrum, and Linear Approximation d_2.

n	z, w	$z_0 z_1$	$f(z)$	$9S_f(w)$	$d_2(z)$
0	0	0	0	5	0
1	0	1	2	$-e_2$	1
2	0	2	0	$-e_1$	0
3	1	0	0	$-e_1$	0
4	1	1	0	-1	0
5	1	2	1	$5e_2$	1
6	2	0	2	$-e_2$	1
7	2	1	0	$5e_1$	0
8	2	2	0	-1	0

we find by Theorem 5.5.5 that the optimal approximation is

$$P_\xi(z) = d_2(z_0 \oplus 2z_1), \quad mod\ 3,$$

and $\xi(f) \leq 1$. The function $d_2(z_0 \oplus 2z_1)$ (mod 3) is also shown in Table 5.5.2.

It is evident from Table 5.5.2 that a function $\tilde{f}_{P_\xi}(z)$ such that $f(z) = d_2(z_0 \oplus 2z_1)\tilde{f}_{P_{xi}}(z)$ is the function of a single variable z_0 ($\xi(f) = 1$) defined by Table 5.5.3.

Remark 5.5.1   *The procedure for the optimization of polynomial approximations may be generalized to systems of p-valued logical functions. In this case, a linearity point of the system is defined as a vector that is a linearity point for each function in the system. Further generalizations to systems of functions defined on arbitrary finite commutative groups may be found in Reference 277.*

5.5.5 Estimation on the Numbers of Nonzero Coefficients

In this section, we consider bounds for the spectral complexity of several important classes of completely specified switching functions. As it will be shown later, these bounds enable the complexity of networks realizing functions from these classes to be estimated by spectral methods. In addition, a comparison of the bounds for Walsh and Haar bases is frequently an aid to more rational choice of a basis system.

The *spectral complexity* of a switching function f relative to the Walsh (Haar) basis, denoted by $L^W(f)$ and $L^H(f)$, is defined as the number of nonzero coefficients in the Walsh (Haar) expansion of f.

TABLE 5.5.3   Function $\tilde{f}_{P_\xi}(z_0)$ in Example 5.5.2.

z_0	$\tilde{f}_{P_\xi}(z_0)$
0	2
1	1
2	2

As will be shown later (see Sections 6.1.1–6.1.5), the spectral complexity of a switching function determines the complexity of a network implementing f or equivalently, the necessary memory size the function f is being computed by the corresponding program.

In Appendix A, the reader may find the Walsh transforms, autocorrelation functions, and bounds for the Walsh and Haar spectral complexities for 21 important classes of switching functions. Next section (Section 5.5.5) is in fact a commentary on Appendix A.

Appendix A employs the following notation.

For any $z \in \{0, 1, \ldots, 2^m - 1\}$, $z = \sum_{i=0}^{m-1} z_i 2^{m-1-i}$, $z_i \in \{0, 1\})$, we put

$$\overleftarrow{z} = \sum_{i=0}^{m-1} z_i 2^i, \quad \|z\| = \sum_{i=0}^{m-1} z_i.$$

In Appendix A, the Walsh and Haar spectra are in Paley ordering.

For determination of bounds for the spectral complexity, we begin with a few considerations that enable us to extend the applicability of the bounds for spectral complexity given in the Appendix A.

Theorem 5.5.6 *Let $f(z)$ be a switching function of m variables and σ a nonsingular matrix over $GF(2)$. Then,*

$$L^W(\overline{f}(z)) = L^W(1 \oplus f(z)) = L^W(f(z)), \quad mod\ 2, \tag{5.5.33}$$

$$L^H(\overline{f}(z)) = L^H(1 \oplus f(z)) = L^H(f(z)), \quad mod\ 2, \tag{5.5.34}$$

$$L^W(f(z \oplus \tau)) = L^W(f(z)), \quad mod\ 2, \tag{5.5.35}$$

$$L^H(f(z \oplus \tau)) = L^H(f(z)), \quad mod\ 2, \tag{5.5.36}$$

$$L^W(f(\sigma \odot z)) = L^W(f(z)), \quad mod\ 2, \tag{5.5.37}$$

where $\tau \in \{0, 1, \ldots, 2^m - 1\}$.

Theorem 5.5.6, in effect, states that the bounds for the Walsh and Haar spectral complexities are invariant under inversion of functions and translation (inversion) of variables. The Walsh complexity is also invariant under linear transformations of the variable, but the Haar complexity is not, and in particular, it depends on the order of variables of the function. The bounds given in Appendix A for the Haar spectral complexity refer to the optimal order of variables (i.e., the order that minimizes the complexity).

Theorem 5.5.6 implies a certain duality principle for the spectral complexities L^W and L^H.

We first note that any switching function may be built up from its variables by superposition of the following operations: disjunction $\vee$ (logical addition, OR), conjunction (logic multiplication, AND), negation $'$, and addition modulo 2, $\oplus$.

(This set of operations is, of course, redundant, and it is sufficient, for example, to take the disjunction or the conjunction together with negation.)

Corollary 5.5.4 *Let $f^*(z)$ be the switching function of m variables derived from a switching function $f(z)$ by interchanging the disjunction and conjunction operations in any representation of $f(z)$ in terms of the disjunction, conjunction, negation, and addition modulo 2. Then,*

$$L^W(f^*(z)) = L^W(f(z)), \quad L^H(f^*(z)) = L^H(f(z)). \tag{5.5.38}$$

The proof of (5.5.38) is based on the De Morgan laws (5.5.14) and formulas (5.5.33), (5.5.34), (5.5.36), (5.5.37) with $\tau = 2^m - 1$.

By virtue of the *duality principle* (5.5.38), it is possible to considerably expand the range of application of the spectral complexity bounds listed in the Appendix A. For example, according to this principle, the switching function $\bigoplus_{i=0}^{k-1}(z_i \vee z_{i+k})$ has the same spectral complexity as the nonrepetitive quadratic form $\bigoplus_{i=0}^{k-1} z_i z_{i+k}$ (mod 2), that is (see Appendix A),

$$L^W \left(\bigoplus_{i=1}^{k-1}(z_i \vee z_{i+k}) \right) = 2^{2k}, \quad \text{mod } 2 \tag{5.5.39}$$

$$L^H \left(\bigoplus_{i=0}^{k-1}(z_i \vee z_{i+k}) \right) = \frac{1}{3}(2^{2k} - 1) + k + 1, \quad \text{mod } 2.$$

An analysis of rows 2 through 5 of the Appendix A shows that the spectral complexity of conjunction or disjunction increases with the number of variables, exponentially for the Walsh basis and linearly for the Haar basis. For these functions, therefore, the Haar basis is far more efficient.

On the contrary, for linear functions (Appendix A, 6), quadratic forms $\bigoplus_{i,q=0}^{m-1} c_i d_q z_i z_q, c_i, d_q \in \{0, 1\}$, which are products of two linear functions (Appendix A, 4) and k-ary forms (i.e., products of k linear functions of m variables, $k << m$; see Appendix A, 5), the use of Walsh functions is more efficient, since the Walsh complexity is an exponential function of k and the Haar complexity an exponential function of m.

We now look more closely into complexity bounds of products of linear functions. Let A be a $(k \times m)$ binary matrix $\mathbf{A} = [a_{i,s}], i = 1, 2, \ldots, k, s = 0, 1, \ldots, m - 1$ whose rows are linearly independent over $GF(2)$.

A function $f(z_0, \ldots, z_{m-1})$ is called a k-ary form of m variables if

$$f(z_0, \ldots, z_{m-1}) = \prod_{i=1}^{k} \bigoplus_{s=0}^{m-1} a_{i,s} z_s = \bigoplus_{s_1,\ldots,s_k=0}^{m-1} a_{i,s_i} z_{s_i}, \quad \text{mod } 2. \tag{5.5.40}$$

Example 5.5.3 *Let*

$$
A = \begin{bmatrix} 1 & 1 & 0 & 0 & 0 & 0 \\ 0 & 0 & 1 & 1 & 0 & 0 \\ 0 & 1 & 0 & 0 & 1 & 1 \end{bmatrix},
$$

where $k = 3$, $m = 6$. Then,

$$
f(z) = f(z_0, \ldots, z_5) = (z_0 \oplus z_1)(z_2 \oplus z_3)(z_1 \oplus z_4 \oplus z_5), \quad mod\ 2.
$$

For the function $f(z)$ defined by (5.5.40), we set

$$
f_r(z) = \frac{f(z)}{\bigoplus_{s=0}^{m-1} a_{r,s} z_s} = \prod_{i=1, i \neq r}^{k} \bigoplus_{s=0}^{m-1} a_{i,s} z_s, \quad mod\ 2. \tag{5.5.41}
$$

In addition, let $f_r(z_{s_1} = \alpha_{s_1}, z_{s_2} = \alpha_{s_2}, \ldots, z_{s_t} = \alpha_{s_t})$ denote the subfunction of $f_r(z)$ obtained from $f_r(z)$ by fixing $z_{s_1} = \alpha_{s_1}, z_{s_2} = \alpha_{s_2}, \ldots, z_{s_t} = \alpha_{s_t}$, $(1 \leq t \leq m)$.

Example 5.5.4 *In the above example, for instance,*

$$
f_2(z) = (z_0 \oplus z_1)(z_1 \oplus z_4 \oplus z_5),
$$

$$
f_2(z_1 = 0) = z_0(z_4 \oplus z_5), \quad mod\ 2.
$$

Theorem 5.5.7 *Let $f(z) = \prod_{i=1}^{k} \bigoplus_{s=0}^{m-1} a_{i,s} z_s$, (mod 2) be a k-ary form, $\min_{1 \leq i \leq k} \sum_{s=0}^{m-1} a_{i,s} = \sum_{s=0}^{m-1} a_{q,s}$, and $\{s_1, s_2, \ldots, s_t\}$ all the column indices of the matrix $[a_{i,s}]$ such that $a_{q,s_1} = a_{q,s_2} = \cdots = a_{q,s_t} = 1$. Then,*

$$
L^W(f) = 2^k, \tag{5.5.42}
$$

$$
L^H(f) \leq L^H(f_q(z_{s_1} = 0, z_{s_2} = 0, \ldots, z_{s_t} = 0)) 2^{\sum_{s=0}^{m-1} a_{q,s} - 1} + 1.
$$

Formula (5.5.42) may be proved by induction on the number k of factors in the k-ary form. The proof of (5.5.42) also involves the convolution theorem (Theorem 2.6.4).

Formula (5.5.42) generates a $(k - 1)$-step recursive procedure for computing a bound for $L^H(f)$, since it essentially reduces the estimation of the complexity of a k-ary form f to the same problem for a $(k - 1)$-ary form f_q (which generally depends on fewer variables than f).

The following example illustrates this procedure.

Example 5.5.5 *We estimate $L^H(f)$ for the function f of Example 5.5.3. In this case, $m = 6$ and*

$$\min_{1 \leq i \leq 3} \sum_{s=0}^{5} a_{i,s} = \sum_{s=0}^{5} a_{1,s} = 2, q = 1, s_1 = 0, s_2 = 1.$$

By (5.5.43),

$$L^H(f) \leq L^H(f_1(z_0 = 0, z_1 = 0))2^1 + 1,$$

where

$$f_1(z_0 = 0, z_1 = 0) = (z_2 \oplus z_3)(z_4 \oplus z_5), \quad mod\ 2.$$

Proceeding in the same way for $L^H(f_1(z_0 = 0, z_1 = 0))$, we get

$$L^H(f_1(z_0 = 0, z_1 = 0)) \leq L^H(f_{1,2}(z_0 = 0, z_1 = 0, z_2 = 0, z_3 = 0))2 + 1,$$

where

$$f_{1,2}(z_0 = 0, z_1 = 0, z_2 = 0, z_3 = 0) = z_4 \oplus z_5, \quad mod\ 2, \quad L^H(z_4 \oplus z_5) = 3.$$

Finally, therefore,

$$L^H(f) \leq 2(2 \cdot 3 + 1) + 1 = 15.$$

Rows 16 to 18 of the Appendix A give the Walsh transforms, the autocorrelation functions, and the spectral Walsh and Haar complexities for the signs of the elementary trigonometric functions $sign \sin(2^{-k}\pi z)$, $sign \cos(2^{-k}\pi z)$, $sign \tan(2^{-k}\pi z) = sign \cot(2^{-k}\pi z)$ for $z \in [0, 2^m)$. The sign functions are viewed as step functions representing switching functions and (see (1.2.4)) are assumed to be right continuous—that is to say, $f(z + 0) = f(z)$ or $\lim_{\epsilon \to 0} f(z + \epsilon) = f(z)$, $(\epsilon > 0)$.

Rows 16 and 18 illustrate the relationship of the trigonometric functions to the Walsh functions.

Rows 19 to 21 list the transforms, autocorrelation functions, and complexities of the unit step and impulse functions widely used in automatic control, and also of the sign functions for the logarithm. These are again step functions representing switching functions. In all these cases, the Haar basis is usually more convenient than the Walsh basis, since the Haar complexity is a linear function of the number of variables and the Walsh complexity an exponential function.

The notation for the transforms in rows 20 and 21 employs *integral Walsh functions* $I_w(y) = \sum_{z=0}^{y-1} W_w(z)$, $w = 0, 1, \ldots, 2^m - 1$. These may be viewed as *piecewise-linear* functions, they are linearly independent and therefore, after orthogonalization, may be utilized as a basis for the expansion of systems of logic functions of continuous functions. In that case, it is convenient to represent a system of logic functions not by a step function $\Phi(z)$ but by the corresponding piecewise-linear function. Similar considerations apply to integral Haar functions or Schauder functions $I_i^{(j)}(y) = \sum_{z=0}^{y-1} H_i^{(j)}(z)$ (511).

BIBLIOGRAPHIC NOTES

Classical references for spectral methods in analysis of properties of switching functions are References 255,258,278,282,331,332,333,385,658. Threshold functions and related logic gates are discussed in References 23 and 376. An excellent monograph on this subject with generalizations and links to neural networks is Reference 21. Reference publications for complexity of logic functions are Refernces 342,343,519, see also discussions in References 278,491. Linearization of switching functions has been discussed in References 277,301, and 378.

CHAPTER 6

SPECTRAL METHODS IN SYNTHESIS OF LOGIC NETWORKS

The present chapter is devoted to methods for the design of combinational digital devices realizing systems of logical functions. These methods are based on the orthogonal series expansions of logic functions, with various spectral transforms and correlation functions as the main tools.

All the methods described in this chapter for the design of digital devices realizing systems of logic functions are also applicable to the construction of algorithms for software implementations of logic functions. In other words, spectral methods may be interpreted from both network and programming standpoint. The synthesis methods are illustrated by network interpretations.

As it has been noticed in Reference 299, there is apparent a renewed and considerable interest in spectral techniques after the publication of a report about applications of Walsh functions to technology mapping (655). This interest is due to the development of technology of digital circuits imposing requirements and strong demands regarding complexity and performances of logic networks and digital devices in general, which cannot be met by traditional approaches.

In the last decade, spectral method for synthesis, including testing, has been discussed in a considerable number of publications, see References 37, 54, 57, 98, 204, 228, 283, 295, 297, 318, 319, 345, 346, 356, 385, 434, 458, 475, 481, 497, 600, 602, 604, 656, and 657.

Spectral Logic and Its Applications for the Design of Digital Devices   by Mark G. Karpovsky, Radomir S. Stanković and Jaakko T. Astola
Copyright © 2008 John Wiley & Sons, Inc.

6.1 SPECTRAL METHODS OF SYNTHESIS OF COMBINATORIAL DEVICES

6.1.1 Spectral Representations of Systems of Logic Functions

Before describing the design procedure, we briefly review the finite orthogonal series representations of systems of p-ary ($p \geq 2$) logic functions described in previous chapters.

Given a system of logic functions

$$y^{(s)}(z) = y^{(s)}(z_0, \ldots, z_{m-1}), \tag{6.1.1}$$

for $s = 0, \ldots, k - 1$, and $y^{(s)}(z)$, $z_i \in \{0, \ldots, p - 1\}$, we define the discrete function $y = f(z)$ corresponding to the system by

$$f(z) = \sum_{s=0}^{k-1} p^{k-1-s} y^{(s)}(z_0, \ldots, z_{m-1}), \tag{6.1.2}$$

where

$$z = \sum_{i=0}^{m-1} z_s p^{m-1-i}. \tag{6.1.3}$$

The function $f(z)$ is defined at all integer points of the half-open interval $[0, p^m)$. We complete $f(z)$ to a step function $\Phi(z)$ by setting

$$\Phi(z) = f(\delta), \quad \text{for } z \in [\delta, \delta + 1). \tag{6.1.4}$$

This step function represents the system (6.1.1).

Let $\{\Psi_w(z)\}$ be a complete system of orthogonal functions. Expand $\Phi(z)$ in a series in terms of $\{\Psi_w(z)\}$,

$$\Phi(z) = \sum_{w=0}^{p^m-1} S(w)\Psi_w(z), \tag{6.1.5}$$

where the Fourier coefficients $S(w)$ are defined by

$$S(w) = \left(\sum_{z=0}^{p^m-1} \Psi_w(z)\overline{\Psi_w(z)} \right)^{-1} \sum_{z=0}^{p^m-1} \Phi(z)\overline{\Psi_w(z)}. \tag{6.1.6}$$

From (6.1.5), we can set up a block diagram of a device realizing system (6.1.1), as illustrated in Fig. 6.1.1. The main blocks are as follows:

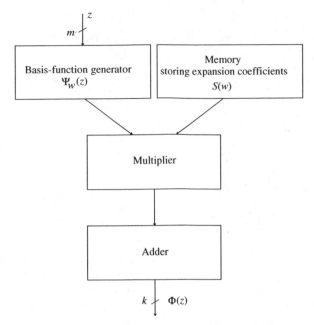

FIGURE 6.1.1   Block diagram of the network for spectral implementation of logic functions.

First, we have a basis-function generator with the input z and its output $\Psi_w(z)$ for $w = 0, 1, 2, \ldots, p^m - 1$. The memory stores the values of spectral coefficients $S_f(w)$. These data are fed to a multiplier that computes the products of $\Psi_w(z)$ and $S(w)$, and the sum of the series (6.1.5) is computed by an adder-accumulator.

At the end of the summation process, the adder outputs the value of the step function $\Phi(z)$ representing the original system of logic functions.

The block diagram in Fig. 6.1.1 will be used constantly in what follows, in connection with all spectral methods of synthesis to be described. The complexity and computing time of physical implementation of blocks may of course vary depending on the technological platform used.

The reader should note that according to this method of synthesis, the networks realizing the individual functions of the initial system are minimized jointly. Indeed, each component of the device represented by the block diagram participates in the computation of each function, since the step function $\Phi(z)$ is defined by all the functions in the system. This points to the expediency of spectral methods in synthesis of multioutput functions with a large number of outputs.

Although we have included a multiplier in the block diagram, in the case of most practical importance, namely, implementation of systems of switching functions ($p = 2$) using the Walsh and Haar bases, the multiplier becomes superfluous, since the basis functions then take on values $-1, +1$, or $0, \pm 1$, so that they merely play the role of signs to be ascribed to the coefficients $S(w)$ in the adder.

6.1.2 Spectral Methods for the Design of Combinatorial Devices

The spectral methods with which we are concerned may be classified according to the following three parameters:

1. The basis $\{\Psi_w(z)\}$ used, as for instance, Walsh or Haar when $p = 2$, and Vilenkin–Chrestenson or generalized Haar when $p > 2$.
2. The field over which the arithmetical operations involved in calculating by formulas (6.1.5) and (6.1.6) are implemented (complex numbers or residues modulo Q and for expansions over the field of residues modulo Q, the discrete transforms over Galois fields are used, and the adder and multiplier must of course implement the appropriate operations modulo Q).
3. Parallel or serial summation of terms in series (6.1.5).

The main topic here is the choice of the basis $\{\Psi_w(z)\}$. We will also discuss various approaches to the optimization of the implementations for the given basis.

The question as to which basis is more effective in regard to some given system of logic functions must be settled in each individual case. The aim here is to provide some signposts indicating the comparative efficiency of a particular basis or another for certain classes of logic functions.

Before presenting discussions of particular bases, we present the following illustrative examples:

Example 6.1.1 *Consider the function $f(z_0, z_1, z_2)$ defined by the truth-vector $\mathbf{F} = [1, 0, 1, 1, 0, 0, 1, 0]^T$. The nonnormalized Haar spectrum in sequency ordering for f is $\mathbf{S}_f = \frac{1}{8}[4, 2, -1, -1, 1, 0, 0, 1]^T$. Therefore, this function f can be represented as the discrete Haar series*

$$f(z) = \frac{1}{8}(4 + 2H_0^{(1)}(z) - H_1^{(1)}(z) - H_1^{(2)}(z) + H_2^{(1)}(z) + H_2^{(4)}(z)),$$

where $z = (z_0, z_1, z_2)$ and Haar functions $H_w(x)$ are rows of the Haar matrix $\mathbf{H}(3)$.

Since the Haar functions can be expressed in terms of switching variables as in Example 4.4.5, the Haar series for the function f is

$$f(z) = \frac{1}{8}(6 - 4z_0 - 2\bar{z}_0 + 4z_1\bar{z}_0 + \bar{z}_1\bar{z}_0 + z_1z_0 - 2z_2\bar{z}_1\bar{z}_0 - 2z_2z_1z_0).$$

Figure 6.1.2 shows an implementation of f from this Haar series representation in terms of switching variables. Thus, as mentioned above, the Haar functions generator and the multiplier array is avoided, and the multiplication reduced to the weight coefficients at the inputs of the adder.

We note that in the case of implementation of one switching function, the adder with weighted inputs can be replaced with the threshold element.

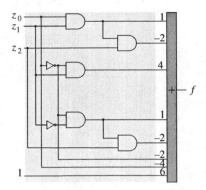

FIGURE 6.1.2   Realization of f in Example 6.1.1 from the discrete Haar series.

In the case of implementation of logic functions by the Haar series, complexity of the implementation depends on the ordering of input variables. The same holds for the implementations in terms of other local transforms as discussed in Section 2.4.

Example 6.1.2   *(169) For the benchmark function con1 of seven variables, the Haar spectrum has 38 nonzero coefficients. If coordinates w_i in binary representations of the indices w of Haar functions are permuted as $(0, 1, 2, 3, 4, 5, 6) \rightarrow (2, 3, 6, 1, 0, 5, 4)$, the number of nonzero coefficients reduces from 38 to 12. Table 6.1.1 shows the values and the position of nonzero coefficients in the vector $\mathbf{S}_f$ representing the Haar spectrum for con1 after optimization by permutation of coordinates of indices. Figure 6.1.3 shows the block diagram for the implementation of con1 by this optimized Haar series. In this figure har(w, i) is the wth row of the Haar matrix $\mathbf{H}(7)$, that is the corresponding Haar function of seven variables.*

This example illustrates that reordering of basis functions (or equivalently, reordering of variables in the input $(z_0, \ldots, z_{m-1})$) may be used as an approach to the optimization of the network or software implementations of switching functions, and often it can reduce the amount of required hardware or software resources. The method used in the above example has been extended to multiple-valued functions in Reference 560.

We will discuss the techniques for optimal ordering of variables of implementations by the Haar series in Sections 6.1.5 – 6.1.6.2.

Example 6.1.3   *For the function f in Example 6.1.1, the Walsh spectrum in the Hadamard ordering is $\mathbf{S}_f = \frac{1}{8}[4, 2, -2, 0, 2, 0, 0, 2]^T$.*

TABLE 6.1.1   **Nonzero Haar Coefficients in the Optimized Haar Spectrum for *con*1.**

i	0	1	3	6	7	12	13	24	35	43	114	115
S_f	148	-20	-12	-12	-16	-4	-8	-4	-4	-4	2	2

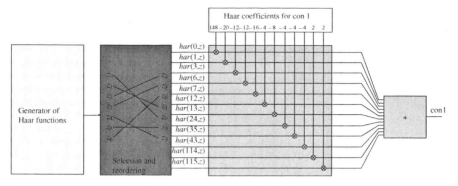

FIGURE 6.1.3 Realization of *con*1 from the optimized Haar series in Example 6.1.2.

Since the Walsh functions in the Hadamard ordering can be expressed in terms of switching variables as shown in Example 2.4.2, the function f can be expressed as

$$f(z) = 1 - z_2 - z_0 + z_1 z_2 + z_0 z_2 + z_0 z_1 - 2 z_0 z_1 z_2.$$

Figure 6.1.4 shows the implementation of f from this Walsh expression in terms of switching variables.

6.1.3 Asymptotically Optimal Implementation of Systems of Linear Functions

When using a linear transformation of the variables, we may represent the block diagram of a device realizing the relevant system of switching functions as a serial connection of two blocks, the first (σ) implementing the linear transformation of variables, the second of the type shown in Fig. 6.1.1, realizing the function $f_\sigma(z)$, where

$$f_\sigma(\sigma \odot z) = f(z), \quad \text{mod } 2.$$

The linear σ-block may be constructed from EXOR gates.

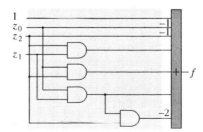

FIGURE 6.1.4 Realization of f in Example 6.1.1 from Walsh series.

Before proceeding to methods for determination of σ_{min}, we estimate the complexity of the block implementing multiplication by an arbitrary matrix σ, in terms of the number $N^{(2)}(\sigma)$ of two-input EXOR gates.

It is obvious that if $\sum_{i=1}^{m} \sigma_{i,s} = \sum_{s=1}^{m} \sigma_{i,s} = 1$, then $N^{(2)}(\sigma) = 0$, since then multiplication by σ is simply permutation of the components of z.

An upper bound for $N^{(2)}(\sigma)$ in the general case is given by the following theorem:

Theorem 6.1.1 *For any $\sigma = (\sigma_{i,s})$, $\sigma_{i,s} \in \{0, 1\}$, $s = 0, 1, \ldots, m - 1$,*

$$N^{(2)}(\sigma) \leq \min_{a \in \{1,2,\ldots,m\}} \left(\left(2^{\lceil m/a \rceil} - \left\lfloor \frac{m}{a} \right\rfloor - 1 \right) res_a(m) \right. \tag{6.1.7}$$
$$\left. + \left(2^{\lceil m/a \rceil} - \left\lfloor \frac{m}{a} \right\rfloor - 1 \right) (a - res_a(m)) + (a - 1)m \right),$$

where $res_a(m)$ denotes the remainder upon division of m by a, and $\lfloor x \rfloor$ ($\lceil x \rceil$) is the largest (smallest) integer $\leq x$ ($\geq x$).

For the proof, we need the following lemma, which is also of an independent interest.

Lemma 6.1.1 *Let $L_{\oplus}^{(2)}(n)$ be the minimal number of two-input EXOR gates necessary to implement all linear switching functions of n variables, that is, functions of the form $\bigoplus_{i=0}^{n-1} c_i z_i$, $(c_i \in \{0, 1\})$ (mod 2). Then,*

$$L_{\oplus}^{(2)}(n) = 2^n - n - 1. \tag{6.1.8}$$

Proof. Realization of $n + 1$ functions $0, z_0, \ldots, z_{n-1}$ requires no hardware. Let $R^{(2)}(n)$ be the number of linear switching functions of n variables that depend essentially on more than one variable. Then, $R^{(2)}(n) \leq L_{\oplus}^{(2)}(n)$ and, since $R^{(2)}(n) = 2^n - n - 1$,

$$L_{\oplus}^{(2)}(n) \geq 2^n - n - 1. \tag{6.1.9}$$

We now prove by induction on n that

$$L_{\oplus}^{(2)}(n) \leq 2^n - n - 1. \tag{6.1.10}$$

Suppose we have a network realizing all linear switching functions of $n - 1$ variables $z_0, \ldots, z_{n-2}$.

We can obtain all functions depending on the nth variable, with the exception of the function z_{n-1}, by connecting one more EXOR circuit to each output of the appropriate network. Since the number of such functions is $2^{n-1} - 1$, we have

$$L_{\oplus}^{(2)}(n) \leq L_{\oplus}^{(2)}(n - 1) + 2^{n-1} - 1. \tag{6.1.11}$$

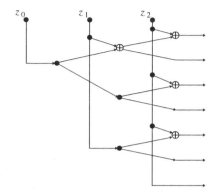

FIGURE 6.1.5 Minimal network realizing all switching functions of $m = 3$ variables.

Hence, (6.1.10) is true for all n. The assertion now follows from (6.1.9) and (6.1.10). Lemma 6.1.1 is readily generalized to linear p-valued logic functions ($p \geq 2$).

If $L_{\oplus}^{(p)}(n)$ is the minimal number of two-input mod p adders necessary to implement all linear p-valued logic functions, then

$$L_{\oplus}^{(p)} = p^n - n - 1. \tag{6.1.12}$$

Figure 6.1.5 illustrates a minimal network realizing all linear switching functions of three variables (except the identically zero function) in accordance with the proof of Lemma 6.1.1.

The method thus provided for synthesis of minimal linear networks enables us to synthesize minimal generators for the Walsh or Vilenkin–Chrestenson functions, in view of the isomorphism between the linear logic function and the Walsh or Vilenkin–Chrestenson functions.

Proof of Theorem 6.1.1. We first observe that for any natural numbers a and m, $a \leq m$,

$$m = \left\lfloor \frac{m}{a} \right\rfloor (a - res_a(m)) + \left\lceil \frac{m}{a} \right\rceil res_a(m), \tag{6.1.13}$$

where $res_a(m)$ is the residue of m modulo a.

In accordance with this formula, we partition the $(m \times m)$ matrix σ into a submatrices of which each of the first $a - res_a(m)$ containing $\lfloor m/a \rfloor$ columns of σ, and each of the remaining $res_a(m)$ containing $\lceil m/a \rceil$ columns of σ.

A network realizing multiplication by σ may now be constructed from a networks multiplying by each of the submatrices, in series with a network summing their outputs modulo 2.

Each of the submatrix networks implements a linear switching function of $\lfloor m/a \rfloor$ or $\lceil m/a \rceil$ variables, respectively, so that the corresponding complexities are $L_{\oplus}^{(2)}(\lfloor m/a \rfloor)$

or $L_\oplus^{(2)}(\lceil m/a \rceil)$. Summation of the outputs of these networks requires at most $(a-1)m$ EXOR gates.

Thus, by Lemma 6.1.1, for any matrix σ,

$$N^{(2)}(\sigma) \le L_\oplus^{(2)}\left(\left\lfloor \frac{m}{a} \right\rfloor\right)(a - res_a(m)) \tag{6.1.14}$$

$$+ L_\oplus^{(2)}\left(\left\lceil \frac{m}{a} \right\rceil\right) res_a(m) + (a-1)m$$

$$= \left(2^{\lfloor m/a \rfloor} - \left\lfloor \frac{m}{a} \right\rfloor - 1\right)(a - res_a(m))$$

$$+ \left(2^{\lceil m/a \rceil} - \left\lceil \frac{m}{a} \right\rceil - 1\right) res_a(m) + (a-1)m.$$

Since a may be selected arbitrarily, this implies the conclusion of our theorem.

Table 6.1.2 lists lowest upper bounds $\tilde{N}^{(2)}$ for $N^{(2)}(\sigma)$ as given by (6.1.7), and the corresponding values of $a = a_{opt}$.

A fairly sharp approximation to the bound $\tilde{N}^{(2)}$ is given by

$$\tilde{N}^{(2)} \cong \frac{2m^2}{\log_2 m} - 2m - \frac{m}{\log_2 m}. \tag{6.1.15}$$

This estimate follows from Theorem 6.1.1 by setting $a = \lceil m/\log_2 m \rceil$.

It can be shown that the bound (6.1.7) is asymptotically optimal ($m \to \infty$) for almost all matrices σ (i.e., the number of linear transformation matrices σ for which this bound is larger than $N_\sigma^{(2)}$ specified in (6.1.7) tends to zero as $m \to \infty$).

The asymptotically optimal value of the parameter a is

$$Q_{opt} = \left\lfloor \frac{m}{\log_2 m - \log_2 \log_2 m} \right\rfloor, \tag{6.1.16}$$

and for any σ

$$N^{(2)}(\sigma) \sim \frac{m^2}{\log_2 m}. \tag{6.1.17}$$

TABLE 6.1.2 Lowest Upper Bounds for $N^{(2)}(\sigma)$.

m	1	2	3	4	5	6	7	8	9	10
a_{opt}	1	1	1	2	2	2	3	3	3	3
$\tilde{N}^{(2)}$	0	1	4	6	10	14	20	25	30	39

m	11	12	13	14	15	16	17	18	19	20
a_{opt}	4	4	4	4	5	5	5	5	5	5
$\tilde{N}^{(2)}$	46	52	62	72	80	91	102	113	124	135

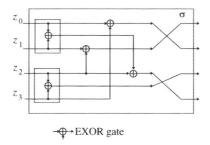

→⊕→ EXOR gate

FIGURE 6.1.6 Network implementing multiplication by σ.

In other words, the ratio of the number of two-input mod 2 adders (EXOR gates) needed for a best implementation of any $(m \times m)$ matrix σ and $m^2 / \log_2 m$ tends to unity as $m \to \infty$, for almost all matrices σ.

Example 6.1.4 *Figure 6.1.6 illustrates a network implementing multiplication by*

$$\sigma = \begin{bmatrix} 0 & 1 & 1 & 0 \\ 1 & 0 & 0 & 1 \\ 0 & 0 & 1 & 1 \\ 1 & 1 & 1 & 0 \end{bmatrix},$$

in accordance with the proof of Theorem 6.1.1. Here $m = 4$ and, as is evident from Table 6.1.2, $a_{opt} = 2$.

Theorem 6.1.1 may also be generalized to matrices σ with elements in $\{0, 1, \ldots, p - 1\}$, and also to the case of rectangular matrices σ. In these cases again the resulting estimate is asymptotically optimal for almost all matrices σ.

6.1.4 Walsh and Vilenkin–Chrestenson Bases for the Design of Combinatorial Networks

When using the Walsh or Vilenkin–Chrestenson bases, each coefficient in (6.1.5) depends on the values of the system at all points of specification, that is, on the "global" behavior of $\Phi(z)$. As we know, this is not the case for the Haar basis. For example, in the case of the Haar basis (and the situation for the generalized Haar basis is similar), the two "leading" coefficients $(c_0^{(0)}, c_0^{(1)})$ (see (2.3.25)) depend on the "global" behavior of $\Phi(z)$. Each of the next two coefficients $(c_1^{(1)}, c_1^{(2)})$ depends on the values of $\Phi(z)$ on one half of the interval and the relevant interval is further contracted as proceeding along the series, until finally each of the $2^m - 1$ lowest-order coefficients $(c_{m-1}^{(1)}, \ldots, c_{m-1}^{2^{m-1}})$ (see (2.3.23)) is determined by the values of $\Phi(z)$ at the corresponding two "neighboring" assignments. Thus, the coefficients of the Haar expansion of $\Phi(z)$ depend essentially on the "local" behavior of $\Phi(z)$.

Consequently, the use of the Walsh or Vilenkin–Chrestenson basis should be recommended when the original system of logic functions is from a class whose defining properties relate to the behavior of each function at all points of specification. The following theorem is an illustration of this statement.

Theorem 6.1.2 *Let $f(z) = f(z_0, \ldots, z_{m-1})$ be a switching function with 2^q anti-self-duality points.[1] Then,*

$$L^W(f) \le 2^{m-q}, \tag{6.1.18}$$

where $L^W(f)$ is the number of nonzero coefficients in the Walsh expansion of f.

Proof. Let $\beta_1, \ldots, \beta_q$ be anti-self-duality points that are linearly independent over $GF(2)$. Then,

$$f(z) = f(z \oplus \beta_1) = \cdots = f(z \oplus \beta_q), (\text{mod } 2),$$

and, if $S_f(w)$ is the spectrum of f, it follows from the translation theorem (Theorem 2.6.2) that

$$S_f(w) = W_{\beta_1}(w)S(w) = \cdots = W_{\beta_q}(w)S_f(w).$$

Hence, if $S(w) \ne 0$, then $W_{\beta_1}(w) = \cdots = W_{\beta_q}(w) = 1$. Using the linear independence of $\beta_1, \ldots, \beta_q$, we see that the number of distinct w-values satisfying this relation is 2^{m-q}, proving (6.1.18).

According to Theorem 6.1.2, the use of the Walsh basis is advisable when the number of anti-self-duality points of the functions is greater than 1.

By contrast, Haar functions are more convenient when the defining properties of the relevant class of logic functions are "local," that is, depend on the values of the function at a few points. An example is the class of systems of logic functions represented by step functions $\Phi(z)$ with a small number $V(\Phi)$ of discontinuities, where

$$V(\Phi) = \sum_{z=0}^{p^m-1} sign|\Phi(z+1) - \Phi(z)|. \tag{6.1.19}$$

The important factor here is that, as shown by the following theorem, $V(\Phi)$ determines an upper bound for the number $L^H(\Phi)$ of nonzero coefficients in the Haar expression for $\Phi(z)$.

---

[1]For the definition of anti-self-duality points and the proof that the number of such points is a power of 2, see Section 5.1.

Theorem 6.1.3   *Let* $\Phi(z)$ *be a step function representing a system of p-valued logic functions of m variables. Then,*

$$L^H(\Phi) \leq V(\Phi)(p-1)(m-1) + p. \tag{6.1.20}$$

Proof. The proof is by induction on $V(\Phi)$, an increase by 1 in the number of discontinuities implies an increase by at most $(p-1)(m-1)$ in the number of nonzero coefficients for functions that take nonzero values just in a part of the interval of their definition. The second term in (6.1.20) is due to the p coefficients of the basis functions that are not equal to zero at any point of the interval.

For example, if $p = 2$, and

$$\Phi(z) = \begin{cases} 1, & \text{if } z \geq a, \\ 0, & \text{otherwise,} \end{cases}$$

($\Phi(z)$ represents a single-threshold function, see Section 5.2, then $V(\Phi) = 1$ and by Theorem 6.1.3, we have $L^H(\Phi) \leq m + 1$ for any a. By contrast, the number L^W of nonzero coefficients of the Walsh expansion of this function $\Phi(z)$ depends on a and may reach as much as 2^m so that for these functions the Haar basis is clearly preferable.

In Section 6.4.6, we describe a method for minimization of $V(\Phi)$ by means of a special linear transformation of variables, thus, minimizing the upper bound for the complexity $L^H(\Phi)$ of the Haar expressions.

The Appendix A lists bounds for L^W and L^H for 22 important classes of Switching functions (see the comments on the Appendix A in Section 5.5.5). The results presented in the Appendix A and in Section 5.5.5 may also be used when selecting bases for various classes of switching functions.

6.1.5 Linear Transforms of Variables in Haar Expressions

We now consider another important feature of Haar expressions related to their behavior under linear transformation of variables in the initial system of given logic functions.

Let σ be some permutation of the vector of variables $z = (z_0, \ldots, z_{m-1})$. The image of z under this permutation σ will be denoted by

$$\sigma \odot z = (z_{\sigma(0)}, \ldots, z_{\sigma(m-1)}).$$

The discrete function $y = f_\sigma(z)$ corresponding to the permuted system of logic functions is (see (6.1.1), (6.1.2)),

$$y = f_\sigma(z) = \sum_{s=0}^{k-1} p^{k-1-s} y^{(s)}(z_{\sigma_0}, \ldots, z_{\sigma_{m-1}}), \tag{6.1.21}$$

where

$$z = \sum_{s=0}^{m-1} z_{\sigma(s)} 2^{m-1-s}. \qquad (6.1.22)$$

The function $f(z)$ defined by (6.1.2) and (6.1.3) represents the original system (6.1.1) for the identity permutation $\sigma(s) = s$, for $s = 0, 1, \ldots, m - 1$.

The step-function completion of $f_\sigma(z)$, (see Section 6.1.5) will be denoted by $\Phi_\sigma(z)$. We say that $\Phi_\sigma(z)$ *represents the given system for the permutation* σ.

Letting σ vary over different permutations and expanding the corresponding functions $\Phi_\sigma(z)$ in series as (6.1.5), we can generally obtain different spectral coefficients and, therefore, implementations of different complexity.

Since implementation of a permutation requires no special hardware, we have a problem of construction of the optimal permutation, which minimizes the number L^H of nonzero coefficients, since L^H determines the size of the most complex component of the block diagram in Fig. 6.1.1, the memory block to store the coefficients.

It follows from Theorem 2.6.7 that when the Walsh and the Vilenkin–Chrestenson bases are used, the number of nonzero spectral coefficients is independent of permutations of the variables. The situation is quite different for the Haar transform, as it has been already demonstrated by Example 6.1.2. In this example, reordering of coordinates in binary representation of indices of Haar functions, equivalently rows of the Haar matrices, has been discussed. Notice that reordering of coordinates in binary representation of indices of columns in the Haar matrix corresponds to the reordering of variables in the functions processed.

Example 6.1.5 *Consider the function $f(z_0, z_1, z_2)$ defined in Table 6.1.3, In this table, there are also shown the discrete functions $f(z)$ and $f_\sigma(z)$ for $\sigma \odot z = (z_0, z_2, z_1)$. It follows that $L^H = 5$ for $\Phi(z)$, but $L^H = 3$ for $\Phi_\sigma(z)$.*

This illustrates the dependence of L^H on permutations of components in the vector of variables $(z_0, \ldots, z_{m-1})$. In the following, we present an analytical solution of the problem of the optimal permutation of variables (i.e., minimizing L^H) for the Haar bases, in the case of completely specified logic functions. The case of incompletely specified logic functions will be discussed in Sections 6.2 and 6.3. Permutations of

TABLE 6.1.3 Function f in Example 6.1.5.

z_0, z_1, z_2	z	$f(z_0, z_1, z_2)$	$f(z)$	$f_\sigma(z)$	$8S_f$	$8S_{f_\sigma}$
000	0	0	0	0	4	4
001	1	1	1	0	0	0
010	2	0	0	1	0	-2
011	3	1	1	1	0	2
100	4	1	1	1	-1	0
101	5	0	0	1	-1	0
110	6	1	1	0	1	0
111	7	0	0	0	1	0

variables thus considerably enhance the advantage of Haar bases over Walsh and Vilenkin–Chrestenson bases as tools for the synthesis of network implementations of systems of logic functions.

6.1.6 Synthesis with Haar Functions

The Haar bases have other advantages in regard to the implementation in Fig. 6.1.1.

It was shown in Sections 2.3.3 and 2.5.2 that when calculating $\Phi(z^*)$ for any fixed z^*, the number of nonzero terms of the series is at most $((p-1)m+1)$ for the generalized Haar functions $((m+1)$ for the ordinary Haar functions). Thus, the number of additions performed in summation of the series is at most $((p-1)m+1)$ for the generalized Haar functions, whereas the corresponding figure for the Vilenkin–Chrestenson functions may reach p^m. The advantages of using Haar bases in the synthesis of logical networks are thus evident. In the sequel, therefore, our discussions of spectral methods for synthesis will be concerned for the most part with the Haar bases and the generalized Haar functions. The Walsh and Vilenkin–Chrestenson expansions will usually be used as an intermediate, but important auxiliary tool.

6.1.6.1 Minimization of the Number of Nonzero Haar Coefficients We

showed in Section 6.1.5 that the number L^H of nonzero coefficients, and hence also the complexity of the realizing network, depends on the ordering of variables when Haar bases are employed, whereas the corresponding figure for the Walsh and Vilenkin–Chrestenson bases is independent of the order. An immediate goal is, therefore, to find the optimal order of variables in a system of completely specified switching functions, minimizing L^H. Any ordering of variables for a system of switching functions of m variables may be described by an $(m \times m)$ matrix $\sigma = [\sigma_{i,s}]$, where $\sigma_{i,s} \in \{0, 1\}$ and $\sum_{i=1}^m \sigma_{i,s} = \sum_{s=1}^m \sigma_{i,s} = 1$, that is, each row (column) of σ contains exactly one 1. Then the argument vector z_σ defined by the matrix is obtained by multiplying $z = (z_0, \ldots, z_{m-1})$ by σ, that is,

$$z_\sigma = \sigma \odot z, \quad \text{mod } 2. \tag{6.1.23}$$

For example, if

$$\sigma = \begin{bmatrix} 1 & 0 & 0 \\ 0 & 0 & 1 \\ 0 & 1 & 0 \end{bmatrix}, \quad m = 3,$$

then $z_\sigma = \sigma \odot z = (z_0, z_2, z_1)$.

To indicate the dependence of L^H on σ, we shall write $L^H(\sigma)$.

We may thus state the problem of the optimal ordering of variables for the Haar basis as finding a matrix σ minimizing $L^H(\sigma)$. In Section 6.1.6.2 we shall solve a more general problem, in which σ may be any nonsingular binary matrix.

For example, if

$$\sigma = \sigma^* = \begin{bmatrix} 0 & 1 & 1 & 0 \\ 1 & 0 & 0 & 1 \\ 0 & 0 & 1 & 1 \\ 1 & 1 & 1 & 0 \end{bmatrix}, \quad m = 4,$$

then

$$z_{\sigma^*} = (z_1 \oplus z_2, z_0 \oplus z_3, z_2 \oplus z_3, z_0 \oplus z_1 \oplus z_2), \quad (\text{mod } 2).$$

Recall that σ is *nonsingular* if its determinant $|\sigma|_2$ over the field $GF(2)$ is different from 0. Let Θ denote the class of all nonsingular $(m \times m)$ matrices. The generalized optimization problem may be formulated as finding a nonsingular matrix $\sigma_{min} \in \Theta$, such that

$$\min_{\sigma \in \Theta} L^H(\sigma) = L^H(\sigma_{min}). \tag{6.1.24}$$

6.1.6.2 Determination of Optimal Linear Transform of Variables
We can now tackle the main problem of finding a nonsingular matrix σ_{min} that minimizes the number $L^H(\sigma)$ of Haar expansion coefficients.

Since the upper bound for the complexity of the block realizing σ is of the order of $m^2/\log_2 m$, while the complexity of the entire network is in general an exponential function of m, minimization of the whole network should be approached via minimization of only the nonlinear part of the network, in terms of the number of nonzero coefficients $L^H(\sigma)$.

The definition and properties of the Haar basis were considered in detail in Section 2.3. Recall that the expansion coefficients of a discrete function $f_\sigma(z)$ in terms of the Haar basis are defined by

$$c_{m-1}^{(q)} = 2^{-1}(f_\sigma(2q - 2) - f_\sigma(2q - 1)), \quad q = 1, \ldots, 2^{m-1}, \tag{6.1.25}$$

$$\vdots$$

$$c_{m-l}^{(q)} = 2^{-l} \left(\sum_{i=2^{l-1}+1}^{2^l} f_\sigma(2^l q - i) - \sum_{i=1}^{2^{l-1}} f_\sigma(2^l q - i) \right),$$

$$q = 1, \ldots, 2^{m-l},$$

where

$$f_\sigma(z_\sigma) = f(z), \tag{6.1.26}$$

$$z_\sigma = \sigma \odot z, \quad \text{mod } 2.$$

Let $L_{m-l}^H(\sigma)$ denote the number of nonzero coefficients with subscript $m - l$. Then it follows from (6.1.25) and (6.1.26) that for any σ

$$0 \le L_{m-1}^H(\sigma) \le 2^{m-1}, \tag{6.1.27}$$

$$\vdots$$

$$0 \le L_{m-l}^H(\sigma) \le 2^{m-l},$$

for $l = 1, \ldots, m - 1$, and

$$L^H(\sigma) = \sum_{l=1}^{m-1} L_{m-l}^H(\sigma) \le 2^m. \tag{6.1.28}$$

Thus, our search for $\sigma_{\min}$ may be organized recursively along the following lines: Let $\Theta_m = \Theta$ be the class of all nonsingular matrices over $GF(2)$.

1. Find the class $\Theta_{m-1} \subseteq \Theta_m$ of matrices σ such that

$$L_{m-1}^H(\sigma_{m-1}) = \min_{\sigma \in \Theta_m} L_{m-1}^H(\sigma), \tag{6.1.29}$$

   where σ_{m-1} is an arbitrary matrix in Θ_{m-1}
2. Find the class $\Theta_{m-2} \subseteq \Theta_{m-1}$ such that

$$L_{m-2}^H(\sigma_{m-2}) = \min_{\sigma \in \Theta_{m-1}} L_{m-2}^H(\sigma), \tag{6.1.30}$$

   where σ_{m-2} is an arbitrary matrix in Θ_{m-2}.
3. Find the class $\Theta_{m-l} \subseteq \Theta_{m-l+1}, l = 1, 2, \ldots, m - 1$, such that

$$L_{m-l}^H(\sigma_{m-l}) = \min_{\sigma \in \Theta_{m-l+1}} L_{m-l}^H(\sigma), \tag{6.1.31}$$

   where σ_{m-l} is an arbitrary matrix in Θ_{m-l}.

We may now take any matrix in Θ_1 as $\sigma_{\min}$. This matrix makes $L_{m-1}^H(\sigma)$ assume its absolute minimum, while the numbers $L_{m-l}^H(\sigma), l = 2, \ldots, m - 1$, take certain local minima.

Determination of Θ_{m-1}

We now consider how to find the class of matrices Θ_{m-1} minimizing $L_{m-1}^H(\sigma)$. First let $\sigma = \mathbf{I}_m$ be the identity matrix of order m, and denote the function $f(z)$ corresponding to the given system of k switching functions of m variables by $f^{(m-1)}(z)$.

TABLE 6.1.4   Functions in Example 6.1.6.

$z_0z_1z_2z_3$	$y^{(0)}y^{(1)}$	z, τ	$f^{(3)}(z)$	$f_i^{(3)}(z)$	$B_i^{(3)}(z)$	$B^{(3)}(\tau)$	$f_{\sigma_3}^{(3)}(z)$
0000	00	0	0	1000	4444	16	0
0001	10	1	2	0010	2002	4	0
0010	11	2	3	0001	2200	4	0
0011	11	3	3	0001	2200	4	3
0100	01	4	1	0100	0022	4	1
0101	10	5	2	0010	0022	4	1
0110	01	6	1	0100	0000	0	1
0111	11	7	3	0001	0000	0	2
1000	11	8	3	0001	0000	0	2
1001	01	9	1	0100	0000	0	1
1010	01	10	1	0100	0022	4	3
1011	10	11	2	0010	0022	4	3
1100	00	12	0	1000	2200	4	0
1101	00	13	0	1000	2200	4	3
1110	10	14	2	0010	0220	4	2
1111	00	15	0	1000	2222	8	2

Then, we define the characteristic functions $f_i^{(m-1)}(z)$ for $i = 0, 1, \ldots, 2^k - 1$ by

$$f_i^{(m-1)}(z) = \begin{cases} 1, & \text{if } f^{(m-1)}(z) = i, \\ 0, & \text{if } f^{(m-1)}(z) \neq i. \end{cases} \qquad (6.1.32)$$

Example 6.1.6   *Table 6.1.4 defines a system of two switching functions* $y^{(0)}, y^{(1)}$ *of four variables, showing also the discrete function* $f^{(m-1)}(z)$ *and the system of characteristic functions* $\{f_i^{(m-1)}(z)\}$, $i = 0, 1, 2, 3$. *For each characteristic function* $f_i^{(m-1)}(z)$, *we have an autocorrelation function* $B_i^{(m-1)}(\tau)$ *defined as*

$$B_i^{(m-1)}(\tau) = \sum_{z=0}^{2^m-1} f_i^{(m-1)}(z) f_i^{(m-1)}(z \oplus \tau), \quad mod\ 2. \qquad (6.1.33)$$

Table 6.1.4 shows the corresponding functions for the example, the functions $f^{(3)}(z)$, $f_i^{(3)}(z)$, *the autocorrelation functions* $B_i^{(3)}(z)$, *for* $i = 0, 1, 2, 3$, *and the total autocorrelation function* $B^{(3)}(z) = \sum_{i=0}^{3} B_i^{(3)}(\tau)$. *Notice that this table also shows* $f_{\sigma_3}^{(3)}(z)$ *that will be determined later in Example 6.1.7. (The properties of the autocorrelation functions and their relationship to double Walsh transforms were considered in Section 2.7.)*

The desired class Θ_{m-1} is determined by the following theorem.

Theorem 6.1.4 *Let*

$$B^{(m-1)}(\tau) = \sum_{i=0}^{2^k-1} B_i^{(m-1)}(\tau).$$

Then, Θ_{m-1} is the set of all matrices σ_{m-1} such that

$$\sigma_{m-1} \odot \tau_{m-1} = \begin{bmatrix} 0 \\ \vdots \\ 0 \\ 1 \end{bmatrix}, \quad mod\ 2, \qquad (6.1.34)$$

where

$$\max_{\tau \neq 0} B^{(m-1)}(\tau) = B^{(m-1)}(\tau_{m-1}). \qquad (6.1.35)$$

Proof. Let $\overline{L_{m-1}^H}(\sigma)$ denote the number of vanishing (equal to 0) coefficients with the subscript $(m-1)$ $(L_{m-1}^H(\sigma) = 2^{m-1} - L_{m-1}^H(\sigma))$.

Setting $f_\sigma^{(m-1)}(\sigma \odot z) = f^{(m-1)}(z)$, we denote the characteristic functions of $f_\sigma^{(m-1)}(z)$ by $f_{i,\sigma}^{(m-1)}(z)$, and the corresponding autocorrelation functions by $B_{i,\sigma}^{(m-1)}(\tau)$.

Then, by (6.1.25), $\overline{L_{m-1}^H}$ is equal to the number of pairs of identical values of $f_\sigma^{(m-1)}(z)$ at points of the type $z = 2s$, $z = 2s + 1$ $(s = 0, 1, \ldots, 2^{m-1} - 1)$, that is, the number of pairs of 1 values for all functions $f_{i,\sigma}^{(m-1)}(z)$ at points $z = 2s, z = 2s + 1$ $(i = 0, 1, \ldots, 2^k - 1)$. Thus the required number is $\frac{1}{2} \sum_{i=0}^{2^k-1} B_{i,\sigma}^{(m-1)}(1)$.

In view of Theorem 2.7.4, this implies Theorem 6.1.4.

It follows from Theorem 6.1.4 that to determine Θ_{m-1}, it is sufficient to find the maximum of the total autocorrelation function $B^{(m-1)}(\tau) = \sum_{i=0}^{2^k-1} B_i^{(m-1)}(\tau)$.

Example 6.1.7 *Going back to Example 6.1.6, we find the function $B^{(3)}(\tau) = \sum_{i=0}^3 B_i^{(3)}(\tau)$, as specified in Table 6.1.4, we have that τ_{m-1} is $\tau_3 = 15$, and by Theorem 6.1.4 we can select*

$$\sigma_{m-1} = \sigma_3 = \begin{bmatrix} 1 & 1 & 1 & 1 \\ 0 & 0 & 1 & 1 \\ 1 & 0 & 0 & 1 \\ 1 & 1 & 1 & 0 \end{bmatrix}.$$

The function $f_{\sigma_3}^{(3)}(z)$ is shown in Table 6.1.4. For this example, we have $L_3^H(\mathbf{I}_4) = 6$, and $L_3^H(\sigma_3) = 4$.

Determination of classes of Θ_i

We now determine the classes $\Theta_{m-2} \supseteq \Theta_{m-3} \supseteq \cdots \supseteq \Theta_1$.

To determine Θ_{m-2}, we construct the function $f_{\sigma_{m-1}}^{(m-1)}(z)$ for $f^{(m-1)}(z)$ (see (6.1.26)), hence obtaining the "contracted" function $f^{(m-2)}(z)$ defined at 2^{m-1} points

$$f^{(m-2)}(z) = f_{\sigma_{m-1}}^{(m-1)}(2z) + f_{\sigma_{m-1}}^{(m-1)}(2z+1). \tag{6.1.36}$$

We now apply the algorithmic procedure that was used for the determination of the matrix Q_{m-1} to $f^{(m-2)}(z)$, and denote the resulting $(m-1) \times (m-1)$ matrix by $\sigma^{(m-2)}$.

Theorem 6.1.5 Θ_{m-2} *is the set of all matrices σ_{m-2} such that*

$$\sigma^{(m-2)} = \begin{bmatrix} \sigma^{(m-2)} & \vdots & \mathbf{0} \\ \cdots & \cdots & \cdots \\ \mathbf{0} & \vdots & 1 \end{bmatrix} \odot \sigma_{m-1}, \quad mod\ 2, \tag{6.1.37}$$

where $\sigma_{m-1} \in \Theta_{m-1}$.

Proof. It follows from (6.1.37) that the last $((m-1)\text{th})$ components of the vectors $\sigma_{m-2} \odot z$ and $\sigma_{m-1} \odot z$, (mod 2) are the same for any z, and so

$$L_{m-1}^{H}(\sigma_{m-2}) = L_{m-1}^{H}(\sigma_{m-1}^{(q)}).$$

In addition, by (6.1.26) and (6.1.36) all the coefficients $c_{m-l}^{(q)}$, $(l > 1)$ of the functions $f_{\sigma_{m-1}}^{(m-1)}$ and $f^{(m-2)}$ coincide.

The construction of the classes $\Theta_{m-3}, \Theta_{m-4}, \ldots, \Theta_1$ is analogous. The final result is

$$\sigma_{\min} = \begin{bmatrix} \sigma^{(1)} & \mathbf{0} \\ \mathbf{0} & \mathbf{I}_{m-2} \end{bmatrix} \odot \cdots \odot \begin{bmatrix} \sigma^{(m-2)} & \mathbf{0} \\ \mathbf{0} & \mathbf{I}_1 \end{bmatrix} \odot \sigma_{m-1}, \tag{6.1.38}$$

with calculations modulo 2.

Example 6.1.8 *Continuing discussion of Example 6.1.6, we construct the classes $\Theta_{m-2} = \Theta_2, \Theta_1$. The "contracted" function $f^{(m-2)}(z) = f^{(2)}(z)$, the total autocorrelation function $B^{(2)}(\tau)$ for $f^{(2)}(z)$, and the transformed function $f_{\sigma_2}^{(2)}(z)$ are given*

TABLE 6.1.5   Functions in Example 6.1.6.

z, τ	$f^{(2)}(z)$	$B^{(2)}(\tau)$	$f^{(2)}_{\sigma_2}(z)$	$f^{(1)}(z)$	$B^{(1)}(\tau)$	$f^{(1)}_{\sigma_1}(z)$
0	0	8	0	2	4	2
1	3	0	2	6	0	10
2	2	4	3	6	0	6
3	3	0	3	10	2	6
4	3	0	3	-	-	-
5	6	4	3	-	-	-
6	3	0	6	-	-	-
7	4	4	4	-	-	-

in Table 6.1.5. We have

$$\sigma^{(m-2)} = \sigma^{(2)} = \begin{bmatrix} 1 & 0 & 0 \\ 0 & 0 & 1 \\ 0 & 1 & 0 \end{bmatrix}.$$

The functions $f^{(1)}(z)$, $B^{(1)}(\tau)$, and $f^{(1)}_{\sigma^{(1)}}(z)$ are also shown in Table 6.1.5. We have

$$\sigma^{(m-3)} = \sigma^{(1)} = \begin{bmatrix} 1 & 1 \\ 0 & 1 \end{bmatrix}.$$

Finally, by using (6.1.38), we see that the minimizing matrix is

$$\sigma_{\min} = \begin{bmatrix} 1 & 1 & 0 & 0 \\ 0 & 1 & 0 & 0 \\ 0 & 0 & 1 & 0 \\ 0 & 0 & 0 & 1 \end{bmatrix} \odot \begin{bmatrix} 1 & 0 & 0 & 0 \\ 0 & 0 & 1 & 0 \\ 0 & 1 & 0 & 0 \\ 0 & 0 & 0 & 1 \end{bmatrix} \odot \begin{bmatrix} 1 & 1 & 1 & 1 \\ 0 & 0 & 1 & 1 \\ 1 & 0 & 0 & 1 \\ 1 & 1 & 1 & 0 \end{bmatrix}$$

$$= \begin{bmatrix} 0 & 1 & 1 & 0 \\ 1 & 0 & 0 & 1 \\ 0 & 0 & 1 & 1 \\ 1 & 1 & 1 & 0 \end{bmatrix}, \quad mod\ 2.$$

A network implementation of $\sigma_{\min}$ is shown in Fig. 6.1.6.

Table 6.1.6 gives the values of the original function $f(z)$, its Haar spectrum $S_f(w) = c_l^{(q)}$, where $w = 2^l + q - 1$ (note that q and l are uniquely determined by this condition for any given w), and also $f_{\sigma_{\min}}(z)$ and the corresponding Haar spectrum $S_{\sigma_{\min}}(w)$.

It is evident from the table that in this example the linear transformation $\sigma_{\min}$ yields a savings of approximately 45% in the number of nonzero spectral coefficients.

**TABLE 6.1.6 Initial Function f in Example 6.1.6,
Linearly Transformed Function $f_{\sigma_{min}}$, and the
Haar Spectra for f and $f_{\sigma_{min}}$.**

z, w	$f(z)$	$16S_f(w)$	$f_{\sigma_{min}}(z)$	$16S_{f_{\sigma_{min}}}(w)$
0	0	24	0	24
1	2	6	0	0
2	3	2	1	−16
3	3	10	1	0
4	1	−16	3	−8
5	2	−4	3	8
6	1	4	2	0
7	3	−8	2	0
8	3	−16	2	0
9	1	0	1	0
10	1	−8	0	0
11	2	−16	3	0
12	0	16	0	8
13	0	−8	3	−24
14	2	0	1	−24
15	0	16	2	−8

Figure 6.1.7 is a block diagram of the algorithm for determination of the optimal linear transformation σ_{min}, relative to the Haar basis and a system of completely specified switching functions. The notation $a = b$ used in the figure signifies assignment of the value b to the variable a.

The above algorithm for computation of σ_{min} involves $m - 1$ iterations of the maximization procedure for finding a maximum of the total autocorrelation function

$$B^{(m-l)}(\tau) = \sum_i \sum_z f_i^{(m-l)}(z) f_i^{(m-l)}(z \oplus \tau), \quad \bmod 2, \quad l = 1, \ldots, m - 1.$$

Instead, we can use $m - 1$ iterations of the procedure for finding a maximum for the *total cross-correlation functions*

$$A^{(m-l)}(\tau) = \sum_{i \neq s} \sum_z f_i^{(m-l)}(z) f_s^{(m-l)}(z \oplus \tau), \quad \bmod 2, \quad l = 1, \ldots, m - 1.$$

This follows from the following theorem.

Theorem 6.1.6   *Let $\{f^{(i)}(z)\}$ be a system of discrete functions, $f_i(z) \in \{0, 1\}$, $z \in \{0, 1, \ldots, p^m - 1\}$, $i = 0, 1, \ldots, p^k - 1$, and*

$$B(\tau) = \sum_i \sum_z f_i(z) f_i(z \ominus \tau), \quad \bmod p,$$

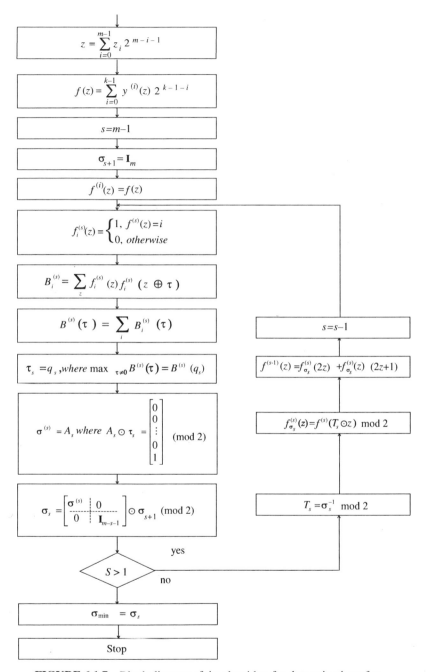

FIGURE 6.1.7   Block diagram of the algorithm for determination of σ_{min}.

$$A(\tau) = \sum_{i \neq s} \sum_z f_i(z) f_s(z \ominus \tau), \quad mod\ p.$$

Then,

$$B(\tau) + A(\tau) = p^m. \tag{6.1.39}$$

The reason that we have been using the autocorrelation functions $B^{(m-l)}(\tau)$ throughout, rather than the cross-correlation functions $A^{(m-l)}(\tau)$, is that the former are easier to calculate.

It is worth noting that the same remark as to the possible use of cross-correlation functions applies to the linearization algorithm in Section 5.4.3, which also made use of the total autocorrelation function.

6.1.6.3 *Efficiency of the Linearization Method*   A good efficiency criterion for the method of linear transformations of variables is the maximal number of nonzero coefficients for an arbitrary system of k completely specified switching functions of m variables, assuming the best choice of the linear transformation σ.

Theorem 6.1.7   *Let $\{f_{m,k}\}$ be the set of all discrete functions corresponding to systems of k completely specified switching function of m variables, and $L_{m-l}^H(f, \sigma)$ the number of nonzero Haar coefficients with subscript $m-l$ for a discrete function $f \in \{f_{m,k}\}$ with variables transformed by σ. Then*

$$\max_{f_{m,k}} \min_{\sigma} L_0^H(f, \sigma) \leq 2, \tag{6.1.40}$$

$$\max_{f_{m,k}} \min_{\sigma} L_{m-l}^H(f, \sigma) \leq 2^{m-l} - \lceil \frac{\lfloor d \rfloor \lfloor d - 1 \rfloor}{2d} \rceil, \tag{6.1.41}$$

where

$$d = \frac{2^{m-l+1}}{2^{k+l-1} - 2^{l-1} + 1}, \quad l = 1, \dots, m-1. \tag{6.1.42}$$

Proof.   Formula (6.1.40) follows from the definition of $L_0^H(f, \sigma)$. The proof of (6.1.41) will require more effort.

Let $f^{(m-l)}$ be the function produced at the lth iteration of the algorithm (see Fig. 6.1.7), $\{f_i^{(m-l)}\}$ its system of characteristic functions, and $\{B_i^{(m-l)}\}$ the corresponding system of autocorrelation functions. Then, by Theorems 6.1.4 and 6.1.5,

$$\min_{f_{m,k}} \min_{\sigma} L_{m-l}^H(f, \sigma) = 2^{m-l} - \min_{f_{m,k}} \max_{\tau \neq 0} \frac{1}{2} \sum_{i=0}^{2^{k+l-1}-2^{l-1}} B_i^{(m-l)}(\tau). \tag{6.1.43}$$

We proceed to estimate the min–max term on the right side of (6.1.43). Denote

$$\sum_{z=0}^{2^{m-l+1}-1} f_i^{(m-l)}(z) = N_i.\tag{6.1.44}$$

Then,

$$\sum_{i=0}^{2^{k+l-1}-2^{l-1}} N_i = 2^{m-l+1},\tag{6.1.45}$$

and

$$\frac{1}{2}\sum_{\tau=1}^{2^{m-l+1}-1} B_i^{(m-l)}(\tau) = \binom{N_i}{2}, \quad i = 0,\ldots,2^{k+l-1}-2^{l-1}.\tag{6.1.46}$$

Since $f^{(m-l)}$ and $f_i^{(m-l)}$ are defined at 2^{m-l+1} points and the number of characteristic functions $f_i^{(m-l)}$ is $2^{k+l-1}-2^{l-1}$, it follows that

$$\min_{f_{m,k}}\max_{\tau\neq 0}\frac{1}{2}\sum_{i=0}^{2^{k+l-1}-2^{l-1}} B_i^{(m-l)}(\tau) \geq \min_{f_{m,k}}\left\lceil\frac{\sum_{i=0}^{2^{k+l-1}-2^{l-1}}\binom{N_i}{2}}{2^{m-l+1}}\right\rceil$$

$$\geq \left\lceil\frac{1}{d}\binom{[d]}{2}\right\rceil = \left\lceil\frac{\lfloor d\rfloor\lfloor d-1\rfloor}{2d}\right\rceil,\tag{6.1.47}$$

where

$$d = \frac{2^{m-l+1}}{2^{k+l-1}-2^{l-1}+1}.$$

The formula (6.1.41) now follows from (6.1.47) and (6.1.43).

In practical computations, the bound (6.1.41) may be simplified as follows, provided $k \ll m$ (so that $\lfloor d\rfloor \gg 1$)

$$\left\lceil\frac{\lfloor d\rfloor\lfloor d-1\rfloor}{2d}\right\rceil \geq \left\lceil\frac{(\lfloor d\rfloor-1)\lfloor d\rfloor}{2(\lfloor d\rfloor+1)}\right\rceil\tag{6.1.48}$$

$$= \left\lceil\frac{\lfloor d\rfloor}{2}+\sum_{i=0}^{\infty}(-1)^{i+1}\frac{1}{\lfloor d\rfloor^i}\right\rceil\tag{6.1.49}$$

$$\geq \left\lceil\frac{\lfloor d\rfloor}{2}-1\right\rceil \geq \left\lceil\frac{d-3}{2}\right\rceil.$$

This inequality yields the coarser estimate

$$\max_{f_{m,k}} \min_{\sigma} L^H_{m-l}(f, \sigma) \leq 2^{m-l} - \left\lceil \frac{d-3}{2} \right\rceil. \tag{6.1.50}$$

We now estimate the number $L^H_{m-l}(\sigma)$ of nonzero coefficients for the case of a single switching function($k = 1$).

Corollary 6.1.1 *For a single-output switching function f,*

$$\max_{f_{m,1}} \min_{\sigma} L^H_{m-l}(f, \sigma) \leq 2^m - \lceil 0.36 \cdot 2^m \rceil + \lceil 1.5(m-1) \rceil. \tag{6.1.51}$$

Proof. It follows from (6.1.50), in view of (6.1.28), that

$$\max_{f_{m,1}} \min_{\sigma} \sum_{l=1}^{m} L^H_{m-1}(\sigma) \leq 2^m - \sum_{l=1}^{m-1} \left\lceil \frac{1}{2} \left(\frac{2^{m-l+1}}{2^{l-1}+1} - 3 \right) \right\rceil$$

$$\leq 2^m + \left\lceil \frac{3}{2}(m-1) \right\rceil$$

$$- \left(\left\lceil \frac{1}{4} \cdot 2^m \right\rceil + \left\lceil \frac{1}{12} \cdot 2^m \right\rceil + \left\lceil \frac{1}{40} \cdot 2^m \right\rceil + \left\lceil \frac{1}{144} \cdot 2^m \right\rceil \right)$$

$$\leq 2^m - \lceil 0.36 \cdot 2^m \rceil + \lceil 1.5(m-1) \rceil.$$

Table 6.1.7 lists upper bounds for $\max_{f_{m,1}} \min_{\sigma} L^H_{m-l}$, for $l = 1, 2, \ldots, m$ in the case of a single switching function f, $m = 2, 3, \ldots, 10$. It is also given in the table the upper bound $\tilde{L}^H$ of $\max_{f_{m,1}} \min_{\sigma} \sum_{l=1}^{m} L^H_{m-l}(f, \sigma)$, for $l = 1, 2, \ldots, m$.

TABLE 6.1.7 **Upper Bounds for $\max_{f_{m,1}} \min_{\sigma} L^H_{m-l}$**
$(f, \sigma), l = 1, 2, \ldots, m.$

$l \backslash m$	2	3	4	5	6	7	8	9	10
1	1	2	4	8	16	32	64	128	256
2	2	2	3	6	11	22	43	86	171
3	0	2	2	4	7	13	26	52	103
4	0	0	2	2	4	8	15	29	57
5	0	0	0	2	2	4	8	16	31
6	0	0	0	0	2	2	4	8	16
7	0	0	0	0	0	2	2	4	8
8	0	0	0	0	0	0	2	2	4
9	0	0	0	0	0	0	0	2	2
10	0	0	0	0	0	0	0	0	2
$\tilde{L}^H$	3	6	11	22	42	83	164	327	650

It follows from Theorem 6.1.7 that in the case $k = 1$, the use of linear transformations reduces the upper bound for the number of nonzero coefficients with subscript $m - 1$ by about one half, while by (6.1.51) the total number of nonzero coefficients is reduced by about one third.

In this case, then, introduction of a linear block σ, requiring a number of two-input mod 2 adders of the order of $m^2 / \log_2 m$ (see Section 6.1.3), produces a savings of at least $\lceil 0.36 \cdot 2^m \rceil - \lceil 1.5(m - 1) \rceil$ multibit storage cells for the coefficients.

6.2 SPECTRAL METHODS FOR SYNTHESIS OF INCOMPLETELY SPECIFIED FUNCTIONS

6.2.1 Synthesis of Incompletely Specified Switching Functions

The design of networks realizing systems of incompletely specified switching functions is one of the most important and difficult problems of modern digital network design theory. Some recent results in this area, supporting this statement and illustrating different approaches to the problem, are presented, for instance, in References 120, 264, 337, 338, 492, 500, 532, 640, and 687.

The added difficulty, in comparison with the analogous problem for completely specified functions, is that here the optimal completions of the functions involved should be determined.

In this section we shall show how to determine an optimal completion of a system and an optimal linear transformation of its variables, in the sense that the number of nonzero Haar expansion coefficients is minimized.

Before proceeding to the solution of these problems, we shall estimate the degree to which networks may be simplified if the function to be realized is allowed to be incompletely specified.

Theorem 6.2.1 *Let $\{\Psi_w(z)\}$, $z \in [0, p^m)$, be a complete orthogonal system of step functions, and $f(z)$ a function defined at N points $y_0, \ldots, y_{N-1} \in \{0, 1, \ldots, p^m - 1\}$. Then there exists a completion of $f(z)$ to $[0, p^m)$ such that the number of nonzero coefficients in its expansion in terms of the basis $\{\Psi_w(z)\}$ is at most N.*

In the case of the Walsh basis, this is simply Lemma 5.2.1. In regard to the Haar basis, we shall develop an algorithm computing the desired completion in Section 6.2.2.

6.2.2 Synthesis of Incompletely Specified Functions by Haar Expressions

We consider the optimal completion problem for a system of switching functions in the case of the Haar basis.

If L_{m-l}^H is the number of nonzero coefficients $c_{m-l}^{(q)}$, $q = 1, 2, \ldots, 2^m - 1$, then $0 \le L_{m-l}^H \le 2^{m-l}$ (where m, as usual, is the number of variables).

The optimal completion may therefore be sought by the following recursive procedure. The procedure will produce completion classes $K_{m-1} \supseteq K_{m-2} \supseteq \cdots \supseteq K_0$, where $K_{m-l}, l = 1, 2, \ldots, m$ is the set of all completions in K_{m-l+1}, which minimize L_{m-l}^H (K_m is the set of all completions of the system).

Suppose that we have a system of k incompletely specified switching functions of m variables

$$y^{(s)} = y^{(s)}(z_0, z_1, \ldots, z_{m-1}), \quad s = 0, 1, \ldots, k - 1. \tag{6.2.1}$$

Notice that all the functions in this system are assumed to be undefined at exactly the same points. We represent the system (6.2.1) by a discrete function $y = f(z)$, where

$$z = \sum_{s=0}^{m-1} z_s 2^{m-1-s},$$

$$y = \sum_{s=0}^{k-1} y^{(s)} 2^{k-1-s}.$$

Then K_{m-1} will be the class of all completions such that the number of distinct z for which

$$f(2z - 2) = f(2z - 1), \tag{6.2.2}$$

is maximum.

The class $K_{m-2} \subseteq K_{m-1}$ is the set of all completions in K_{m-1} such that the number of distinct z for which

$$f(4z - 4) + f(4z - 3) = f(4z - 2) + f(4z - 1), \tag{6.2.3}$$

is maximum.

The definition of $K_{m-3} \supseteq K_{m-4} \supseteq \cdots \supseteq K_1 \supseteq K_0$ is similar.

Then, any completion in class K_0 will meet these requirements. The essential point here is that determination of a completion in K_0 does not require an exhaustive search. Thus, given a system of incompletely specified switching functions, with their variables in a selected order, we can construct a completion corresponding to an absolute minimum of L_{m-1}^H and certain relative minima for L_{m-l}^H, for $l = 2, 3, \ldots, m$.

Example 6.2.1   *Consider the switching function f of four variables defined in Table 6.2.1, where the asterisk $*$ stands for undefined values. The classes K_3, K_2, $K_1 = K_0$ are shown in the table. Here $a_1, a_2, a_3, a_4, a_5 \in \{0, 1\}$, $a_6 \in \{a_2, a_3\}$, $a_7 \in \{a_4, a_5\}$, and $a_8 \in \{a_6, a_1\}$. There are two functions in K_0, one of which (ϕ) is shown in Table 6.2.1.*

TABLE 6.2.1 Partially Defined Function f in Example 6.2.1 and Its Optimal Completion ϕ.

$z_0 z_1 z_2 z_3$	f	K_3	K_2	$K_1 = K_0$	$\phi \in K_0$
0000	1	1	1	1	1
0001	0	0	0	0	0
0010	*	0	0	0	0
0011	0	0	0	0	0
0100	*	a_1	0	0	0
0101	*	a_1	0	0	0
0110	0	0	0	0	0
0111	1	1	1	1	1
1000	*	a_2	a_6	a_8	0
1001	*	a_2	a_6	a_8	0
1010	*	a_3	a_6	a_8	0
1011	*	a_3	a_6	a_8	0
1100	*	a_4	a_7	a_8	0
1101	*	a_4	a_7	a_8	0
1110	*	a_5	a_7	a_8	0
1111	*	a_5	a_7	a_8	0

The next task is to look for an optimal linear transformation of variables $\sigma_{\min}$. For any σ, we retain the same method of completion as before.

To determine $\sigma_{\min}$, we use the algorithm in Fig. 6.1.7, except that the characteristic functions $f_i^{(m-1)}(z)$ will now be defined not by (6.1.32), but as

$$f_i^{(m-1)}(z) = \begin{cases} 1, & \text{if } f^{(m-1)}(z) = i, \text{ or } f^{(m-1)}(z) = *, \\ 0, & \text{otherwise,} \end{cases} \tag{6.2.4}$$

and

$$f_*^{(m-1)}(z) = \begin{cases} 1, & \text{if } f^{(m-1)}(z) = *, \\ 0, & \text{otherwise,} \end{cases} \tag{6.2.5}$$

the function $\sum_{i=0}^{2^k-1} B_i^{(m-1)}(\tau)$ in (6.1.35) is replaced by

$$\sum_{i=0}^{2^k-1} (B_i^{(m-1)}(\tau) - B_*^{(m-1)}(\tau)) + B_*^{(m-1)}(\tau)$$

$$= \sum_{i=0}^{2^k-1} B_i^{(m-1)}(\tau) - (2^k - 1)B_*^{(m-1)}(\tau),$$

where $B_*^{(m-1)}(\tau)$ is the autocorrelation function of $f_*^{(m-1)}(z)$, and in (6.1.36) we set

$$a + * = 2a, \qquad (6.2.6)$$

$$* + * = *.$$

We note that for weakly specified functions, it follows from (6.2.4) and (6.2.5) that

$$\sum_{z=0}^{2^m-1} f_i^{(m-1)}(z) \gg 2^{m-1},$$

and, therefore, it is convenient to calculate $B_i^{(m-1)}(\tau)$ with the aid of Corollary 2.7.1, according to which one can use the inverse function

$$\overline{f_i^{(m-1)}}(z) = 1 - f_i^{(m-1)}(z),$$

for $i = 0, 1, \ldots, 2^k - 1, *$.

Example 6.2.2 *Let us find the classes* $\Theta_{m-1} = \Theta_3, \Theta_2, \Theta_1$ *and the matrix* $\sigma_{\min}$ *for the switching function in Example 6.2.1.*

Table 6.2.2 presents the original incompletely specified switching function $f^{(3)}(z)$; *its inverse characteristic functions* $\overline{f_*^{(3)}}(z)$; $\overline{f_0^{(3)}}(z)$, *and* $\overline{f_1^{(3)}}(z)$; *the autocorrelation*

TABLE 6.2.2 The Partially Defined Function $f = f^{(3)}$ **in Example 6.2.2, the Autocorrelation Functions, and Linearly Transformed Function** $f_{\sigma_3}^{(3)}$.

$z_0z_1z_2z_3$	z, τ	$f^{(3)}$	$\overline{f_*^{(3)}}(z)$	$\overline{f_0^{(3)}}$	$\overline{f_1^{(3)}}$	$B_*^{(3)}$	$B_0^{(3)}$	$B_1^{(3)}$	$B^{(3)}$	$f_{\sigma_3}^{(3)}$
0000	0	1	1	1	0	11	14	13	16	1
0001	1	0	1	0	1	10	12	10	12	*
0010	2	*	0	0	0	8	12	12	16	0
0011	3	0	1	0	1	8	12	10	14	0
0100	4	*	0	0	0	8	12	10	14	0
0101	5	*	0	0	0	8	12	12	16	0
0110	6	0	1	0	1	10	12	10	12	*
0111	7	1	1	1	0	10	14	12	16	1
1000	8	*	0	0	0	6	12	10	16	*
1001	9	*	0	0	0	6	12	10	16	*
1010	10	*	0	0	0	6	12	10	16	*
1011	11	*	0	0	0	6	12	10	16	*
1100	12	*	0	0	0	6	12	10	16	*
1101	13	*	0	0	0	6	12	10	16	*
1110	14	*	0	0	0	6	12	10	16	*
1111	15	*	0	0	0	6	12	10	16	*

functions $B_*^{(3)}(\tau)$, $B_0^{(3)}(\tau)$, and $B_1^{(3)}(\tau)$ (constructed by using Corollary 2.7.1); and the function $B_0^{(3)}(\tau) + B_1^{(3)}(\tau) - B_*^{(3)}(\tau)$. From Table 6.2.2, we can set $\tau_{m-1} = \tau_3 = 2$, and by Theorem 6.1.4,

$$\sigma_3 = \begin{bmatrix} 1 & 0 & 0 & 0 \\ 0 & 1 & 0 & 0 \\ 0 & 0 & 0 & 1 \\ 0 & 0 & 1 & 0 \end{bmatrix}.$$

The function $f_{\sigma_3}^{(3)}(z)$ defined by

$$f_{\sigma_3}^{(3)}(\sigma_3 \odot z) = f^{(3)}(z), \quad mod\ 2,$$

is shown in Table 6.2.2. With the completion defined as above, this gives $L_3^H(\sigma_3) = 0$, whereas for the original function $L_3^H(\mathbf{I}_4) = 2$.

Table 6.2.3 shows the "contracted" function $f^{(2)}(z)$ constructed by (6.1.36) and (6.2.6), and the function

$$B^{(2)}(\tau) = \sum_{i=0}^{3} B_i^{(2)}(\tau) - 3B_*^{(2)}(\tau) = B_0^{(2)}(\tau) + B_2^{(2)}(\tau) - B_*^{(2)}(\tau),$$

since $B_1^{(2)}(\tau) = B_3^{(2)}(\tau) = B_*^{(2)}(\tau)$.

Table 6.2.3 yields $\tau_2 = 4$, and by Theorem 6.1.4

$$\sigma^{(2)} = \begin{bmatrix} 0 & 0 & 1 \\ 0 & 1 & 0 \\ 1 & 0 & 0 \end{bmatrix}.$$

TABLE 6.2.3 Contracted Functions $f^{(2)}(z)$, $f^{<1>}(z)$ in Example 6.2.2, Their Autocorrelation Functions $B^{(2)}$, $B^{<1>}$, and Linearly Transformed Functions $f_{\sigma^{(2)}}^{(2)}$ and $f_{\sigma^{(1)}}^{(1)}$.

z, τ	$f^{(2)}(z)$	$B^{(2)}(\tau)$	$f_{\sigma^{(2)}}^{(2)}(\tau)$	$f^{(1)}(z)$	$B^{(1)}(\tau)$	$f_{\sigma^{(1)}}^{(1)}(z)$
0	2	8	2	4	4	4
1	0	4	*	0	0	4
2	0	4	0	0	0	0
3	2	8	*	4	4	0
4	*	8	0	-	-	-
5	*	8	*	-	-	-
6	*	8	2	-	-	-
7	*	8	*	-	-	-

The function $f_{\sigma^{(2)}}^{(2)}(z)$, the "contracted" function $f^{(1)}(z)$, the corresponding $B^{(1)}(\tau) = B_0^{(1)}(\tau) + B_4^{(1)}(\tau)$ and $f_{\sigma^{(1)}}^{(1)}(z)$ are also shown in Table 6.2.3. It is assumed that $\tau = 3$ and $\sigma^{(1)} = \begin{bmatrix} 1 & 1 \\ 0 & 1 \end{bmatrix}$.

The final result, using (6.1.31), is

$$
\sigma_{\min} = \begin{bmatrix} 1 & 1 & 0 & 0 \\ 0 & 1 & 0 & 0 \\ 0 & 0 & 1 & 0 \\ 0 & 0 & 0 & 1 \end{bmatrix} \odot \begin{bmatrix} 0 & 0 & 1 & 0 \\ 0 & 1 & 0 & 0 \\ 1 & 0 & 0 & 0 \\ 0 & 0 & 0 & 1 \end{bmatrix} \odot \begin{bmatrix} 1 & 0 & 0 & 0 \\ 0 & 1 & 0 & 0 \\ 0 & 0 & 0 & 1 \\ 0 & 0 & 1 & 0 \end{bmatrix}
$$

$$
= \begin{bmatrix} 0 & 1 & 0 & 1 \\ 0 & 1 & 0 & 0 \\ 1 & 0 & 0 & 0 \\ 0 & 0 & 1 & 0 \end{bmatrix}, \quad mod \ 2.
$$

Realization of the $\sigma_{\min}$-block requires one two-input EXOR gate. The results for this example are summarized in Table 6.2.4, which presents the original function $f(z)$, the function $f_{\sigma_{\min}}(z)$, and the Haar spectra of their optimal completions $\phi(z)$ and $\phi_{\min}(z)$, with $S_f(w) = c_l^{(q)}$, $(w = 2^l + q - 1)$.

TABLE 6.2.4 Initial Function f in Example 6.2.1, Linearly Transformed Function $f_{\sigma_{min}}$ and Their Haar Spectra.

z, τ	f	ϕ	$8S_f(w)$	$f_{\sigma_{min}}$	$\phi_{\sigma_{min}}$	$8S_{f_{\sigma_{min}}}(w)$
0000	1	1	1	1	1	4
0001	0	0	1	*	1	4
0010	*	0	0	*	1	0
0011	0	0	0	*	1	0
0100	*	0	2	*	1	0
0101	*	0	-2	1	1	0
0110	0	0	0	*	1	0
0111	1	1	0	*	1	0
1000	*	0	4	0	0	0
1001	*	0	0	0	0	0
1010	*	0	0	*	0	0
1011	*	0	-4	*	0	0
1100	*	0	0	*	0	0
1101	*	0	0	0	0	0
1110	*	0	0	*	0	0
1111	*	0	0	*	0	0

The data in Table 6.2.4 show that whereas the optimal completion of $f(z)$ gives $L^H = L^H(I_4) = 6$, the result after optimal rearrangement of the variables is $L^H(\sigma_{\min}) = 2$.

6.3 SPECTRAL METHODS OF SYNTHESIS OF MULTIPLE-VALUED FUNCTIONS

6.3.1 Multiple-Valued Functions

Recent years have seen considerable progress in the development of economical multistable elements, see Reference 661 and references therein. Several examples of various particular implementations of multiple-valued logic circuits and different related technologies are discussed References in 26, 46, 79, 81, 113, 205, 230, 312, 404, 521, 633, 636, and 660.

As a result, there is a need to formalize the problem of network synthesis for components of this type. The problem turns out to be far more complex than its analog for binary elements, in view of the fact that the methods of multiple-valued switching logic (205, 312, 633) are noneffective from the practical standpoint, and indeed sometimes quite unsuitable for the synthesis of networks from multistable elements.

In this section, we discuss spectral methods for the solution of this problem. They yield fairly simple, but approximate results.

6.3.2 Network Implementations of Multiple-Valued Functions

Networks based on p-stable elements are described by systems of p-valued logic functions.

In the framework of spectral methods, we proceed as in the two-valued case, expanding the step function representing a given system in a series of generalized Haar functions $\{M_{r,m-l}^{(p,q)}(z)\}$. These are step functions, defined on $[0, p^m)$ and taking on at most $p + 1$ complex values from the set $\{0, \exp(2\pi i q/p)\}$ ($q = 0, 1, \ldots, p - 1, i = \sqrt{-1}$). The properties of these functions and methods for calculating the generalized Haar spectrum were considered in Section 2.5. As before, we shall measure the complexity by the number L^M of nonzero series coefficients. If the original system depends on m variables, then $L^M \le p^m$.

We shall assume throughout this section that p is a prime.

The use of spectral methods in multiple-valued logic raises the following two problems:

1. The optimal completion of the original system of partially defined p-valued logic functions (the solution of this problem will be given in Section 6.3.3).
2. Choice of the optimal order of variables or, in more general terms, the optimal linear transformation of variables (the solution of this problem will be presented in Section 6.3.4 and 6.3.5).

6.3.3 Completion of Multiple-Valued Functions

Let L_{m-l}^M denote the number of nonzero coefficients $c_{r,m-l}^{(p,q)}$, $r = 0, 1, \ldots, p-1$, and $q = 1, 2, \ldots p^{m-l}$. Then,

$$0 \le L_{m-l}^M < (p-1)p^{m-l}. \tag{6.3.1}$$

We shall assume that the functions of the original system are undefined at the same points.

In view of (6.3.1), we shall use the following m-step procedure to find an optimal completion. We first determine the class K_{m-1} of completions minimizing L_{m-1}^M, the subclass $K_{m-2} \subseteq K_{m-1}$ of completions minimizing L_{m-2}^M, and so on, obtaining classes $K_{m-3} \supseteq K_{m-4} \supseteq \cdots \supseteq K_0$. Any member of K_0 may be taken as the optimal completion.

It follows from the definition of the system $\{M_{r,m-l}^{(p,q)}(z)\}$ that the expansion coefficients $c_{r,m-1}^{(p,q)}$, $r = 0, 1, \ldots, p-1$ of a discrete function $f(z)$ are equal to 0 iff

$$f(pq - p) = f(pq - (p-1)) = \cdots = f(pq - 1). \tag{6.3.2}$$

This condition defines the class K_{m-1}, which will consist of all completions for which the number of distinct numbers q satisfying (6.3.2) is a maximum. The class K_{m-2} will then be the set of all completions in K_{m-1} for which the number of distinct q is such that

$$\sum_{i=1}^{p} f(p^2q - i) = \sum_{i=1}^{p} f(p^2q - p - i) = \cdots = \sum_{i=1}^{p} f(p^2q - p(p-1) - i),$$

is a maximum.

The construction of the remaining classes $K_{m-3} \supseteq K_{m-4} \supseteq \cdots \supseteq K_0$ is analogous.

This completion method is a generalization of the method discussed in Section 6.2 for switching functions to p-valued logic. In view of (6.3.1), the method guarantees an absolute minimum for L_{m-1}^M and certain local minima for L_{m-l}^M, $(l > 1)$.

Example 6.3.1 *We start with a partially defined ternary logical function of two variables (Table 6.3.1). The classes K_1 and K_0 are shown in Table 6.3.1, where $(a_1, a_2 \in \{0, 1, 2\})$. The optimal completion reduces the number of nonzero spectral coefficients to 3.*

6.3.4 Complexity of Linear Multiple-Valued Networks

We now turn to the problem of optimal choice of the order of variables. As in Sections 6.1.6.1 and 6.2, we deal with a more general problem, that is, the optimal linear transformation of variables.

TABLE 6.3.1 The Partially Defined Function f in Example 6.3.1 and Its Optimal Completion.

$z_0 z_1$	f	K_1	K_0
00	1	1	1
01	*	a_1	0
02	2	2	2
10	1	1	1
11	1	1	1
12	*	1	1
20	*	a_2	1
21	*	a_2	1
22	*	a_2	1

Any linear transformation of a p-ary argument, vector $z = (z_0, \ldots, z_{m-1})$ is defined by a nonsingular matrix $\sigma = [\sigma_{i,j}]$, where $\sigma_{i,j} \in \{0, 1, \ldots, p-1\}$ and the determinant $|\sigma|_p \neq 0$ over the field $GF(p)$ of residues modulo p.

Example 6.3.2   *For example, if $p = 3$ and*

$$\sigma = \begin{bmatrix} 1 & 0 & 0 \\ 2 & 1 & 0 \\ 1 & 1 & 1 \end{bmatrix},$$

then,

$$z_\sigma = \sigma \odot z = (z_0, 2z_0 \oplus z_1, z_0 \oplus z_1 \oplus z_2), \quad mod\ 3.$$

Multiplication by the matrix σ requires a special block, which may be implemented with modulo p adders and networks realizing multiplication mod p by the constants $1, 2, \ldots, p-1$.

A network implementing multiplication by the matrix shown above is illustrated in Fig. 6.3.1.

Let $N^{(p)}(\sigma)$ denote the minimum number of two-input adders and multipliers by constants modulo p in network implementing the matrix σ.

Theorem 6.3.1   *For any $\sigma = [\sigma_{i,j}]$, where $\sigma_{i,j} \in \{0, 1, \ldots, p-1\}$, $i, j = 1, 2, \ldots, m$,*

$$N^{(p)}(\sigma) \leq \min_{a \in \{1,\ldots,m\}} \left(\left(p^{\lfloor m/a \rfloor} - \left\lfloor \frac{m}{a} \right\rfloor - 1 \right) (a - res_a(m)) \right. \tag{6.3.3}$$
$$\left. + \left(p^{\lceil m/a \rceil} - \left\lceil \frac{m}{a} \right\rceil - 1 \right) res_a(m) + (a-1)m \right),$$

where $res_a(m)$ denotes the remainder upon division of m by a.

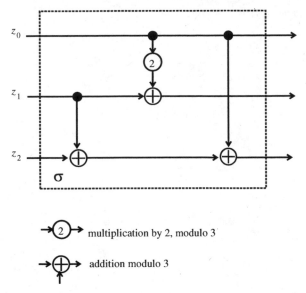

→②→ multiplication by 2, modulo 3

→⊕→ addition modulo 3

FIGURE 6.3.1   Network realizing multiplication by σ in Example 6.3.2.

This theorem is a generalization of Theorem 6.1.1 and its proof employs an analogous construction.

The asymptotic behavior of $N^{(p)}(\sigma)$ as $m \to \infty$ is described for almost all σ by

$$N^{(p)}(\sigma) \sim \frac{m^2}{\log_2 m}. \tag{6.3.4}$$

It follows from Theorem 6.3.1 and formula (6.3.4) that if the network realizing a system of p-valued logical functions is designed as a serial connection of two blocks, a linear block implementing the optimal linear transformation $\sigma_{\min}$, and a nonlinear block using spectral methods to realize the appropriate system of functions of the variables $\sigma_{\min} \odot z \pmod{p}$, then the complexity of the linear part may be neglected, since it increases with m more slowly than m^2, whereas the complexity of the nonlinear block is generally an exponential function of m.

6.3.5 Minimization of Numbers of Nonzero Coefficients in the Generalized Haar Spectrum for Multiple-Valued Functions

We now proceed to the construction of an optimal linear transformation $\sigma_{\min}$. This will be done by an $(m-1)$-step procedure, yielding a sequence of classes $\Theta_{m-1} \supseteq \Theta_{m-2} \supseteq \cdots \supseteq \Theta_1$, where Θ_{m-l} is the set of all matrices in Θ_{m-l+1}, that minimize L^M_{m-l}, (Θ_m is the set of all nonsingular matrices over $GF(p)$).

The construction of Θ_{m-1} is as follows. By starting with the system $f(z) = f^{(m-1)}(z)$ of k incompletely specified p-valued logic functions of m variables, we construct the characteristic functions

$$f_i^{(m-1)}(z) = \begin{cases} 1, & \text{if } f^{(m-1)}(z) = i, \text{ or } f^{(m-1)}(z) = *, \\ 0, & \text{otherwise}, \end{cases} \tag{6.3.5}$$

$$f_*^{(m-1)}(z) = \begin{cases} 1, & \text{if } f^{(m-1)}(z) = *, \\ 0, & \text{otherwise}, \end{cases} \tag{6.3.6}$$

for $i = 0, 1, \ldots, p^k - 1$.

Now define the function $B_i^{(m-1)}(\tau)$ by

$$B_i^{(m-1)}(\tau) = \sum_{z=0}^{p^m-1} f_i^{(m-1)}(z) f_i^{(m-1)}(z \ominus \tau) \cdots f_i^{(m-1)}(z \ominus \overbrace{\tau \ominus \cdots \ominus \tau}^{p-1}). \tag{6.3.7}$$

This is the autocorrelation function of p functions obtained by successive translation modulo p of the variable of the characteristic function $f_i^{(m-1)}(z)$, and it coincides with our previous autocorrelation function when $p = 2$.

Theorem 6.3.2   *The class Θ_{m-1} is the set of all nonsingular matrices σ_{m-1} over $GF(p)$ such that*

$$\sigma_{m-1} \odot \tau_{m-1} = \begin{bmatrix} 0 \\ 0 \\ \vdots \\ 0 \\ 1 \end{bmatrix}, \quad \mod p, \tag{6.3.8}$$

where

$$\max_{\tau \neq 0} \left(\sum_{i=0}^{p^k-1} (B_i^{(m-1)}(\tau) - B_*^{(m-1)}(\tau)) + B_*^{(m-1)}(\tau) \right) \tag{6.3.9}$$

$$= \sum_{i=0}^{p^k-1} (B_i^{(m-1)}(\tau_{m-1}) - B_*^{(m-1)}(\tau_{m-1})) + B_*^{(m-1)}(\tau_{m-1}).$$

This is actually a generalization of Theorem 6.1.4 to systems of partially defined p-valued functions.

Example 6.3.3   *Consider the ternary logical function $f(z_0, z_1) = f^{(1)}(z)$ of two variables defined by Table 6.3.2. The table also gives the system of characteristic*

TABLE 6.3.2 Ternary Function $f = f^{(1)}$ in Example 6.3.3, Its Autocorrelation Functions, and the Linearly Transformed Function $f^{(1)}_{\sigma_1}$.

z_0, z_1	z, τ	$f^{(1)}$	$f^{(1)}_0$	$f^{(1)}_1$	$f^{(1)}_2$	$B^{(1)}_0$	$B^{(1)}_1$	$B^{(1)}_2$	$B^{(1)}$	$f^{(1)}_{\sigma_1}$
00	0	1	0	1	0	2	5	2	9	1
01	1	2	0	0	1	0	0	0	0	0
02	2	1	0	1	0	0	0	0	0	2
10	3	1	0	1	0	0	3	0	3	0
11	4	1	0	1	0	0	0	0	0	1
12	5	2	0	0	1	0	3	0	3	2
20	6	1	0	1	0	0	3	0	3	1
21	7	0	1	0	0	0	3	0	3	1
22	8	0	1	0	0	0	0	0	0	1

functions $f^{(1)}_i(z)$, autocorrelation functions $B^{(1)}_i(\tau)$, $(i = 0, 1, 2)$, and the function $B^{(1)} = \sum_{i=0}^{2} B^{(1)}_i(\tau)$.

Thus, we have

$$\tau_1 = \begin{pmatrix} 2 \\ 1 \end{pmatrix}.$$

By Theorem 6.3.2,

$$\sigma_{\min} = \sigma_1 = \begin{bmatrix} 1 & 1 \\ 1 & 2 \end{bmatrix}.$$

The function $f^{(1)}_{\sigma_1}(z)$ defined by $f^{(1)}_{\sigma_1}(\sigma \odot z) = f^{(1)}(z) \pmod 3$ is shown in the table, where $B^{(1)} = \sum_{i=0}^{2} B^{(1)}_i$. It follows that whereas $L^M = 9$ for the original system $f(z)$, the transformed system $f^{<1>}_{\sigma_1}(z)$ gives $L^M = 5$.

In this section we will discuss construction of linear transformations that minimize the number L^M_{m-l}, $l = 2, 3, \ldots, m - 1$ of spectral coefficients.

We outline a recursive procedure constructing the classes $\Theta_{m-2} \supseteq \cdots \supseteq \Theta_1$, which is a generalization of the similar procedure for the two-valued case.

To construct Θ_{m-2}, we start with the function $f^{(m-1)}(z)$, defining a function $f^{(m-1)}_{\sigma_{m-1}}(z)$ by

$$f^{(m-1)}_{\sigma_{m-1}}(\sigma_{m-1} \odot z) = f^{(m-1)}(z), \quad \bmod p.$$

We define the "contracted" function $f^{(m-2)}(z)$ at $p^{(m-1)}$ points by

$$f^{(m-2)}(z) = \begin{cases} \sum_{s=0}^{p-1} f_{\sigma_{m-1}}^{(m-1)}(pz+s), & \text{if } f_{\sigma_{m-1}}^{(m-1)}(pz+s), s = 0, \ldots, p-1, \\ & \text{is completely specified,} \\ \\ pa, & \text{if } f_{\sigma_{m-1}}^{(m-1)}(pz+s) \in \{*, a\}, \\ & a, s = 0, \ldots, p-1, \\ \\ *, & \text{otherwise.} \end{cases} \quad (6.3.10)$$

The application of the algorithm from Section 6.3.5 to the function $f^{(m-2)}(z)$ produces an $(m-1) \times (m-1)$ matrix $\sigma^{(m-2)}$.

The construction of $\sigma^{(m-3)}, \sigma^{(m-4)}, \ldots, \sigma^{(1)}$ is analogous.

Finally, we define $\sigma_{\min}$ by

$$\sigma_{\min} = \begin{bmatrix} \sigma^{(1)} & \vdots & \mathbf{0} \\ \cdots & \cdots & \cdots \\ \mathbf{0} & \vdots & \mathbf{I}_{m-2} \end{bmatrix} \odot \begin{bmatrix} \sigma^{(2)} & \vdots & \mathbf{0} \\ \cdots & \cdots & \cdots \\ \mathbf{0} & \vdots & \mathbf{I}_{m-3} \end{bmatrix} \quad (6.3.11)$$

$$\odot \cdots \odot \begin{bmatrix} \sigma^{(m-2)} & \vdots & \mathbf{0} \\ \cdots & \cdots & \cdots \\ \mathbf{0} & \vdots & \mathbf{I}_1 \end{bmatrix} \odot \sigma_{m-1}, \quad \text{mod } p.$$

Remark 6.3.1 *The algorithms we have described for determination of an optimal linear transformation and an optimal completion in multiple-valued logic are almost identical with the appropriate algorithms for systems of binary switching functions. This is yet another demonstration that the algorithms provided by spectral methods of synthesis are independent of the "arity" of the logic.*

6.4 SPECTRAL SYNTHESIS OF DIGITAL FUNCTIONS AND SEQUENCES GENERATORS

6.4.1 Function Generators

When devising complex systems of automatic control, signal processing, and measurement, there is the need to design devices that reproduce given functions. This involves designing digital generators of continuous functions of one or more variables (208–210). When the input of such a device is the m-bit binary code of the variable z, the output is the value of the required function $f(z)$, or rather its k-bit code. A *Digital Function Generator* (DFG) may be designed with the aid of any method for the synthesis of m input k output functions realized by an (m, k)-terminal combinational logic network. However, the functions produced by a DFG are not continuous functions, but functions derived from continuous functions by quantization; thus, a more detailed study of DFG design is indispensable. In this section, we consider spectral methods to this end and establish a few estimates.

6.4.2 Design Criteria for Digital Function Generators

Throughout this section we assume that $f(z)$, $\Phi(z)$, as well as the Walsh and Haar functions, are defined on the closed interval $[0, 1]$.

The principal technical parameters of a DFG are the accuracy with which it reproduces the given function, its speed, and the amount of hardware required. The *accuracy* is estimated by the distance ϵ between the object function $f(z)$ and the approximating function $\Phi(z)$ produced at the output. There are various definitions of this "distance" between two functions. For instance, the *uniform distance* ϵ_c is defined by

$$\epsilon_c = \max_{z \in (0,1)} |f(z) - \Phi(z)|, \tag{6.4.1}$$

and the *mean-square distance* (or L_2 distance) is defined by

$$\epsilon_2 = \left(\int_0^1 (f(z) - \Phi(z))^2 dz \right)^{1/2}. \tag{6.4.2}$$

The *speed* of the DFG is estimated by the quantity $1/t_{\text{DFG}}$, where t_{DFG} is the time interval elapsing from application of the code of z at the input to production of the function value at the output.

The *complexity* is measured, as usual, by the number L_{DFG} of logic elements (from some complete basis system) necessary for implementation of the DFG.

In most cases, the given parameters for design of a DFG are the required accuracy ϵ and the admissible value-generation time t_{DFG}. Analyzing the various methods of synthesis, one selects the optimal solution—that minimizing the hardware complexity L_{DFG} of the DFG.

The reader should note that the spectral methods considered in this book for the synthesis of combinational networks in many cases are more efficient than the classical methods. The reasons are as follows:

First, the spectral approach greatly increases the likelihood that the synthesis method actually selected will yield a device answering most completely to the demands. To this end the basis systems should be sought not only among the systems studied in our book (Walsh functions, Haar functions, and their many-valued analogs), but also among the systems obtained, say, by integrating them ($\{ \int_0^z W_w(z) dz \}$ (208)), *Schauder functions* (511)), as well as the Reed–Muller functions, arithmetic transform, and so on.

Second, the DFGs designed by spectral methods are multiphase devices—the value of the function is produced only after several arithmetic operations have been performed. The decrease in speed nevertheless makes it possible to reduce the necessary hardware; in other words, to make use of the available time t_{DFG}, which is fixed in advance. Indeed, L_{DFG} is determined largely by the size of the memory device in which the coefficients are stored (combinatorial network may be regarded as a memory holding codes of the function values). As we shall show later in this section, when spectral methods are used, the number of expansion coefficients to be stored is often much smaller than the number of function values to be computed. This is the case for a quite broad range of continuous functions. All this implies a reduction in the complexity of a DFG.

Finally, spectral methods are applicable in cases where the variables and functions involve a large number of digits, where classical methods for synthesis of combination networks demand a prohibitive amount of labor. This is because the functions to be produced by DFG are generally specified in analytical form, and the techniques for analysis of the errors arising in approximation of these functions by series are independent of the length of the variable or function-value codes (see Sections 6.4.3–6.4.5).

6.4.3 Hardware Complexity of Digital Function Generators

The hardware complexity L_{DFG} will be measured by the number L of nonzero coefficients stored in the memory. This number depends on the form of $f(z)$, the accuracy of reproduction ϵ, the type of approximation (uniform or mean-square), and also on the selected basis. We now proceed to estimate L_{DFG} as a function of these parameters.

To approximate $f(z)$ by a finite Walsh or Haar series, we must first approximate $f(z)$ by a step function $\Phi(z)$.

(Throughout this section we shall adopt the approximation in the uniform norm (6.4.1), since this is customary in the theory of function generators.)

Let $\{\Phi(z)\}^n$ be the set of step functions with at most n discontinuities of the first kind (272).

Theorem 6.4.1 *For any differentiable function $f(z)$ defined on $[0, 1]$ and any arbitrarily small $\epsilon > 0$, there exists $\Phi(z) \in \{\Phi(z)\}^n$, such that*

$$\max_{z \in [0,1]} |\Phi(z) - f(z)| \le \epsilon,$$

provided

$$n \ge \left\lceil \frac{\max_{z \in [0,1]} |f'(z)|}{2\epsilon} \right\rceil, \tag{6.4.3}$$

where $f'(z)$ is the derivative of $f(z)$ with respect to z.

Proof. The required step function $\Phi(z) \in \{\Phi(z)\}$ may be constructed as follows:

Divide the interval $[0, 1]$ into n subintervals of equal length, where n satisfies (6.4.3), by points $z_0 = 0, y_1, \ldots, y_n = 1$, and set

$$\Phi(y) = \frac{1}{2}(f_1(y_i) + f(y_{i+1})), \tag{6.4.4}$$

for $y_i \le y < y_{i+1}, i = 0, 1, \ldots, n - 1$ and $\max_{y \in [0,1]} |\Phi(y) - f(y)| \le \epsilon$.

Corollary 6.4.1 *Denote*

$$m = \lceil \log_2 \max_{z \in [0,1]} |f'(z)| - \log_2 \epsilon - 1 \rceil. \tag{6.4.5}$$

Then for any differentiable function $f(z)$, $(z \in [0, 1])$, there exists

$$\Phi(z) = \sum_{w=0}^{2^m-1} S(w)W_w(z) = c_0^{(0)} + \sum_{l=0}^{m-1}\sum_{q=1}^{2^l} c_l^{(q)} H_l^{(q)}(z),$$

such that $\max_{z \in [0,1]} |f(z) - \Phi(z)| \le \epsilon$, *that is,* $L^W, L^H \le 2^m$, *where* L^W (L^H) *is the number of nonzero coefficients in the Walsh (Haar) expansion of $\Phi(z)$.*

Proof. The assertion follows from Theorem 6.4.1 (with the interval divided into $2^m \ge n$ parts) and the fact that any left-continuous step function $\Phi(z)$ with discontinuities at the points $i/2^m$, $(i = 0, 1, \ldots, 2^m - 1)$ has a Walsh (Haar) expansion containing at most 2^m terms.

Example 6.4.1 *Suppose we wish to design a function generator for $f(z) = \arctan z$, $(z \in [0, 1])$ with accuracy $\epsilon = \pi/180$ radians, with $m = 20$ and $k = 20$. The number L^W (L^H) of nonzero coefficients in the Walsh (Haar) expansion of $f(z)$ is calculated as follows:*
  Calculate m by (6.4.5), noticing that

$$\max_{z \in [0,1]} (\arctan z)' = (1 + z^2)^{-1}|_{z=0} = 1, \quad m = \lceil 1 - \log_2 \frac{\pi}{180} - 1 \rceil = 6,$$

and so $L^W, L^H \le 64$.

In this example it is not taken into consideration that there is an additional error δ in the values of $f(z)$, due to the fact that the number k of binary digits of the function at the generator output is finite. It is clear that this error does not exceed one half of the lowest order digit, that is, the last significant bit. In other words, assuming that the maximum of $f(z)$ is normalized to 1, we have

$$\delta \le 2^{-k-1}. \tag{6.4.6}$$

To summarize, the uniform error $\tilde{e}$ in reproduction of a function $f(z)$ by a DFG is

$$\tilde{\epsilon} \leq \epsilon + \delta, \tag{6.4.7}$$

where ϵ is the error in approximation of $f(z)$ by a step function $\Phi(z)$, and δ is the error due to the finite accuracy of computation of $\Phi(z)$. Thus, when calculating the complexities L^W (L^H) as in Corollary 6.4.1, the error in (6.4.5) should be taken equal to $\epsilon = \tilde{\epsilon} - \delta$, where $\tilde{\epsilon}$ s is the prescribed uniform error.

6.4.4 Bounds for the Number of Coefficients in Walsh Expansions of Analytical Functions

Sharper bounds for L^W may be established by the approximation of $f(z)$ by a power series, such as the Taylor series.

Recall that the weight $\|w\|$ of the index of the Walsh function $W_m(z)$ is the number of 1 values in the binary expansion of w.

Theorem 6.4.2 *For any function $f(z)$, $z \in [0, 1]$, having a continuous qth derivative $f^{(q)}(z)$, the coefficients $S(w)$ of its expansion in a series of Walsh functions with index weight q ($\|w\| = q$) satisfy the inequality*

$$|S(w)| \leq (2^{(q^2+3q)})^{-1/2} |\max_{z \in [0,1]} f^{(q)}(z)|, \tag{6.4.8}$$

where $f^{(q)}(z)$ denotes the qth derivative of $f(z)$.

Proof. By Taylor formula,

$$f(z) = \sum_{s=0}^{q-1} (s!)^{-1} f^{(s)}\left(\frac{1}{2}\right)\left(z - \frac{1}{2}\right)^s + (q!)^{-1} f^{(q)}(\theta(z))\left(z - \frac{1}{2}\right)^q, \tag{6.4.9}$$

$$\tag{6.4.10}$$

where $0 \leq \theta(z) \leq 1$.

The binomial $(z - \frac{1}{2})^s$ may be represented as a Walsh series (441)

$$\left(z - \frac{1}{2}\right)^s = \left(-\sum_{i=1}^{\infty} 2^{-i-1} R_i(z)\right)^s, \tag{6.4.11}$$

where $R_i(z)$ are the Rademacher functions and $R_i(z) = W_{2^{i-1}}(z)$.

It follows that the nonzero coefficients $D(w)$ in the Walsh spectrum of $(z - \frac{1}{2})^q$ have indices with the weight at most q, and the maximum absolute value of these coefficients is given by

$$\max_{\|w\|=q} |D(w)| = 2^{-\sum_{i=1}^{q}(i+1)} \cdot q! = (2^{(q^2+3q)})^{-1/2} \cdot q!. \qquad (6.4.12)$$

Substituting (6.4.11) for $(z - \frac{1}{2})^s$ in (6.4.9), we obtain

$$f(z) = \sum_{s=0}^{q-1} (s!)^{-1} f^{(s)} \left(\frac{1}{2}\right) \left(-\sum_{i=0}^{\infty} 2^{-i+1} R_i(z)\right)^s \qquad (6.4.13)$$

$$+ f^{(q)}(\theta(z))(q!)^{-1} \left(-\sum_{i=1}^{\infty} 2^{-i-1} R_i(z)\right)^q,$$

where $0 \le \theta(z) \le 1$.

It follows that the nonzero coefficients with the index weight q in the spectrum of $f(z)$ are determined only by the second term, and by (6.4.12),

$$\max_{\|w\|=q} |S(w)| = (2^{(q^2+3q)})^{-1/2} | \max_{z \in [0,1]} f^{(q)}(z)|.$$

Other estimates based on power series may be found in Reference 441.

Example 6.4.2 *Let us estimate the maximum coefficient with the index weight* 10 *for* $f(z) = \sin 2\pi z, (z \in [0, 1])$.
We have

$$\max_{z \in [0,1]} |\sin^{(10)} 2\pi z| = (2\pi)^{10}.$$

Thus, by (6.4.8),

$$\max_{\|w\|=10} |S(w)| \le 2^{-65} \cdot (2\pi)^{10} < 2 \cdot 10^{-10}.$$

Theorem 6.4.2 and Example 6.4.2 illustrate the rapid convergence of Walsh series and the advantage of using the Walsh basis in designing DFG for smooth functions.

6.4.5 Implementation of Switching Functions Represented by Haar Series

We now consider the same problem for the number L^H of nonzero Haar coefficients.
Let $0 < \alpha \le 1$. We say that $f(z)$ *is in the class* $H_\alpha(A)$ if, for any $z_1 z_2 \in [0, 1]$,

$$|f(z_1) - f(z_2)| \le A(z_1 - z_2)^\alpha, \qquad (6.4.14)$$

where $A > 0$. We call $H_\alpha(A)$ the *Lipschitz class of order α with constant A*.

Theorem 6.4.3 *(530) If $f(z) \in H_\alpha(A)$, then*

$$L^H \leq 2^{\lceil \log_2((\alpha+1)\epsilon^{-1}A)^{1/\alpha} \rceil}. \tag{6.4.15}$$

These bounds for the number of nonzero Haar coefficients may be lowered if the number m of digits in the code of the variable z is fixed in advance.

Let $f(z)$ be approximated with prescribed accuracy ϵ by a step function $\Phi(z) \in \{\Phi(z)\}^n$, where $\Phi(z)$ has discontinuities at points of the form $i \cdot 2^m$, $i = 0, 1, \ldots, 2^m - 1$.

Then, by Theorem 6.1.2,

$$L^H \leq n(m - 1) + 2. \tag{6.4.16}$$

This bound is useful when $n < 2^m/m$.

The above results demonstrate that in the design of function generators for analytic functions, the use of Walsh functions is generally preferable to that of Haar functions, as far as the memory size necessary for storing the coefficients is concerned. The underlying reason is that, unlike the Haar coefficients, each of the Walsh coefficients depends on the behavior of $f(z)$ throughout its interval of definition, since it is a global transform in that respect.

Methods for DFG design, estimates of the accuracy of reproduction for some other bases, related to the Walsh and Haar bases, and also methods for the design of DFG computing functions of several variables, were considered in References 208–210.

From the hardware point of view, DFGs designed on the basis of expansion in orthogonal series are described by the same block diagrams as devices realizing systems of logic functions by spectral methods and details will be given in the following chapters.

6.4.6 Spectral Methods for Synthesis of Sequence Generators

We now consider spectral methods for the synthesis of an important special class of DFG, which we call *Sequence Generators* (SG).

A sequence generator generates a function $y = f(z)$ defined at points $(0, 1, \ldots, M - 1)$, that is, when the binary codes of the numbers $(0, 1, \ldots, M - 1)$ are applied at its input in this order, the corresponding output is the sequence $f(0), f(1), \ldots, f(M - 1)$.

Thus, the characteristic feature of a signal generator is that the sequence of input vectors z is fixed in advance. This generally simplifies implementation of the sequence generators in comparison with digital function generators. In the majority of sequence generators, the variable z is the time. All our spectral methods of synthesis may be applied to the design of sequence generators, and the estimates for the convergence of the series representing $f(z)$ remain valid.

We now proceed to some special methods for the synthesis of sequence generators, which frequently yield substantial reductions in the required hardware.

We shall assume that the complexity of a sequence generator is a monotone increasing function of the number L_f of nonzero values of $f(z)$. There are several reasons for this choice of the complexity criterion. If the network implementation of the sequence generator is an (m, k)-terminal combinatorial logic network, it is clear that with decreasing L_f the number of zero values of the corresponding switching functions will increase, and so, as shown in Section 5.3, the complexity of a minimal network realizing the system will decrease (see the criterion $\mu_0(f)$ for the complexity of switching functions discussed in Section 5.3.1.

If a sequence generator is realized by spectral methods, a decrease in L_f implies a decrease in the absolute values of the expansion coefficients of $f(z)$, thus leading to a reduction in the complexity of the coefficient-storage block.

Denote

$$\Delta f(z) = f(z) - f(z \ominus 1), \quad \bmod M. \tag{6.4.17}$$

Then

$$f(z) = \sum_{s=1}^{z} \Delta f(z) + f(0), \quad z \in \{1, 2, \ldots, M-1\}. \tag{6.4.18}$$

This representation determines a method for designing SG, in terms of the first order finite differences $\Delta f(z)$ of $f(z)$, as illustrated in Fig. 6.4.1.

In this figure, the symbol $\Delta f(z)$ denotes an SG computing the function $\Delta f(z)$, and Σ is an adder-accumulator whose initial state is $f(0)$. For smooth functions, $L_{\Delta f} \ll L_f$, and this method of SG design turns out to be highly effective. An SG implementing the function $\Delta f(z)$ may in turn be designed by the same method, as a result of which $f(z)$ will be represented in terms of higher order finite differences.

Another method for designing sequence generators is related to the linearization of $f(z)$ with respect to the above criterion.

Let $0 < \sigma < M$, and express $f(z)$ as

$$f_\sigma(\sigma \odot z) = f(z), \quad \bmod M, \tag{6.4.19}$$

where f_σ is a discrete function defined at the points $0, 1, \ldots, M - 1$. Thus, for each $\sigma \in \{1, 2, \ldots, M - 1\}$ we have a linear transformation of variables modulo M. We

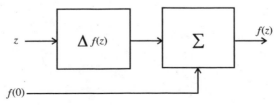

FIGURE 6.4.1 Design of a sequence generator for a function f by summation of the finite difference Δf.

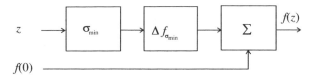

FIGURE 6.4.2 Design of a sequence generator by linear transform of variables.

consider transformations that are nonsingular modulo M, so that the equation

$$\sigma \odot z = 1, \quad \mathrm{mod} \ M, \tag{6.4.20}$$

is solvable for any $z \in \{1, 2, \ldots, M - 1\}$. The number σ generates a nonsingular transformation iff σ and M are relatively prime.

Denote the set of nonsingular transformations modulo M by Θ_M. (The number of elements in this set is $\phi(M)$, where ϕ is Euler function (329).)

The linearization problem for a sequence generator realizing $f(z)$ is to find a number $\sigma_{\min} \in \Theta_M$ such that

$$L_{\Delta f_{\sigma_{\min}}} = \min_{\sigma \in \Theta_M} L_{\Delta f_\sigma}, \tag{6.4.21}$$

where f_σ, $f_{\sigma_{\min}}$ are defined as in (6.4.19).

An sequence generator designed by linearization of $f(z)$ is illustrated in Fig. 6.4.2.

The transformation $\sigma_{\min}$ itself can be determined by analyzing the appropriate correlation functions.

Let $\{f(z)\}$ be the system of characteristic functions of $f(z)$,

$$f_i(z) = \begin{cases} 1, & f(z) = i, \\ 0, & \text{otherwise.} \end{cases} \tag{6.4.22}$$

The cyclic autocorrelation functions (mod M) of $f_i(z)$ are defined by

$$B_{M,i}(\tau) = \sum_{z=0}^{M-1} f_i(z) f_i(z \ominus \tau), \quad \mathrm{mod} \ M. \tag{6.4.23}$$

It is evident from (6.4.23) and Theorem 2.7.1 that if M is a prime, the functions $B_{M,i}(\tau)$ may be expressed as double Vilenkin–Chrestenson transforms $\chi^{(M)}$ of $f_i(z)$ (see Section 2.7).

Theorem 6.4.4 *Let*

$$\max_{\tau \in \Theta_M} \sum_i B_{M,i}(\tau) = \sum_i B_{M,i}(\tau_M). \tag{6.4.24}$$

TABLE 6.4.1 Function f in Example 6.4.3, Its Finite Differences, Linearly Transformed Function f_8 and Its Finite Difference Δf_8.

z, τ	f	Δf	$B_{11,0}$	$B_{11,1}$	$B_{11,0} + B_{11,1}$	f_8	Δf_8
0	1	0	5	6	11	1	1
1	0	1	2	3	5	1	0
2	1	1	0	1	1	1	0
3	1	0	3	4	7	1	0
4	0	1	4	5	9	1	0
5	0	0	1	2	3	1	0
6	1	1	1	2	3	0	1
7	1	0	4	5	9	0	0
8	0	1	3	4	7	0	0
9	0	0	0	1	1	0	0
10	1	1	2	3	5	0	0

Then,

$$\sigma_{\min} \odot \tau_M = 1, \quad mod\ M. \tag{6.4.25}$$

The proof is based on Theorem 2.7.4 for the case $m = 1$, $p = M$.

Thus, to find an optimal nonsingular linear transformation modulo M for a sequence generator, we need to determine the maximum value of the total cyclic autocorrelation function $\sum_i B_{M,i}(\tau)$ over all τ relatively prime to M.

Example 6.4.3 *Let $M = 11$ and define $f(z)$ as in Table 6.4.1. Also given in the table are $\Delta f(z)$, $L_{\Delta f} = 6$, and the correlations $B_{11,0}(\tau)$, $B_{11,1}(\tau)$, $B_{11,0}(\tau) + B_{11,1}(\tau)$ for $\Delta f(z)$.*

We thus obtain $\tau_M = \tau_{11} = 7$, and by (6.4.25), $\sigma_{\min} = 8$. The functions $f_8(z)$ and $\Delta f_8(z)$ also shown in the table. The result is $L_{\Delta f_8} = 2$.

Remark 6.4.1 *The linearization method of this section is essentially equivalent to minimization of the number of discontinuities of $f(z)$. It may be used in implementation of $f(z)$ by expansion in the Haar series, since the number L^H of nonzero coefficients is then determined by the number of discontinuities (see (6.4.16)). The method is useful in the implementation of logical functions by threshold element networks (3, 53, 92, 134, 418, 470, 471, 588, 589), and in many other cases.*

BIBLIOGRAPHIC NOTES

Recommendable references about spectral methods for synthesis of logic networks are 37, 54, 57, 228, 255, 257, 258, 297, 318, 345, 346, 604, 610, 624, 656, and 657. First university textbook on this subject is Reference 379, while the first research monograph is Reference 289.

CHAPTER 7

SPECTRAL METHODS OF SYNTHESIS OF SEQUENTIAL MACHINES

In the previous chapters we discussed the elements of the theory of discrete transforms and methods for their application to the analysis, synthesis, and optimization of digital devices implementing logical functions (combinational networks). In this chapter we consider their application to the synthesis of digital devices with memory.

In particular, we will investigate the problem of constructing optimal state assignments for input signals and internal states for Haar based implementations of sequential devices by the corresponding finite automata.

7.1 REALIZATION OF FINITE AUTOMATA BY SPECTRAL METHODS

7.1.1 Finite Structural Automata

A *Finite Automaton* (FA) or a *state transition machine* is a model of the operation of a digital device with memory.

The operation of any device may be modeled at two levels, *abstract* and *structural*. The appropriate mathematical models are respectively known as *abstract automata* and *structural finite automata*.

An abstract finite automaton is defined as a set of six objects

$$M = \{X, A, Y, a_0, \phi(x, a), g(a)\},$$

Spectral Logic and Its Applications for the Design of Digital Devices by Mark G. Karpovsky, Radomir S. Stanković and Jaakko T. Astola
Copyright © 2008 John Wiley & Sons, Inc.

TABLE 7.1.1   Next-State Function for the Automaton in Example 7.1.2.

	x_0	x_1	x_2	x_3
a_0	a_0	a_0	a_3	a_3
a_1	a_2	a_2	a_2	a_0
a_2	a_1	a_3	a_0	a_3
a_3	a_3	a_1	a_1	a_1

where X is the (finite) set of *input signals*, A the (finite) set of *internal states*, Y the (finite) set of *output signals*, a_0 the *initial state*, $\phi(x, a)$ the *next-state function*, and $g(a)$ the *output function* ($x \in X$, $a \in A$, $a_0 \in A$, and $\phi(x, a) \in A$, $g(a) \in Y$ for any (a, x).[1]

It is clear from this definition that an abstract finite automaton is essentially a formal description of the operational algorithm of the digital device in question. The synthesis of a digital device usually begins with the construction of an abstract finite automaton describing its operation. The abstract finite automaton may be defined by a *state table* or a *state diagram*. The state table is a matrix whose element $a_{q,r}$ is the state into which the automaton goes from the state a_q when the input signal x_r is applied ($a_q, a_{q,r} \in A$, $x_r \in X$). In other words, $a_{q,r} = \phi(x_r, a_q)$.

The state diagram is a labeled directed graph whose vertices represent the states of the automaton and the corresponding output signals. A vertex a_s is connected to a vertex a_q by a directed edge labeled x_r iff $a_s = \phi(x_r, a_q)$.

Example 7.1.1   *Table 7.1.1 is the state table of an automaton with the states $A = \{a_0, a_1, a_2, a_3\}$, and the inputs $X = \{x_0, x_1, x_2, x_3\}$.*

When the operation of a digital device has been simulated by a model at the abstract level, it is possible to determine the structural model of it. Here the operational algorithm of the device is modeled by a structural finite automaton.

A *structural finite automaton* describing the operation of a digital device based on p-ary elements is an abstract finite automaton whose input signals, states, and output signals are p-ary vectors, so that the next-state and output functions are essentially systems of p-valued logic functions.

The transition from the abstract finite automaton to the structural finite automaton is known as a *state-input assignment* or simply *assignment* and also *state encoding*, simply *encoding*.

When the assignment is determined, the synthesis of the automaton amounts to the implementation of the system of logic functions defined by the next-state and output functions.

Throughout this chapter we shall limit the discussion to automata based on binary elements.

---

[1]This is the *Moore model* of an abstract automaton (247). If the *Mealy model* (247) is used instead, no essential changes are needed in the spectral methods developed below.

TABLE 7.1.2 Binary Encoded Inputs and Internal States.

a_q	Code of a_q	x_r	Code of x_r
a_0	00	x_0	00
a_1	01	x_1	01
a_2	10	x_2	10
a_3	11	x_3	11

Example 7.1.2 *Suppose that the states and inputs of the abstract automaton in Example 7.1.1 are assigned binary codes as shown in Table 7.1.2. Then the truth table for the system of Boolean functions corresponding to the next-state function is shown in Table 7.1.3. (Here x_s, a_s denote the sth components of the input signal and state, respectively.)*

The implementation of a finite automaton means the design of a digital device whose behavior is modeled by the automaton considered.

The structural finite automaton may be realized as shown in the block diagram in Fig. 7.1.1, where $x(t)$, $a(t)$, and $y(t)$ denote the input signal, the state, and the output signal, respectively, at time t. Blocks ϕ and g are combinational networks described by systems of switching functions corresponding to the next-state and output functions. Thus, implementation of the finite automaton for a given state-input assignment, reduces to implementation of the combinational networks ϕ and g.

TABLE 7.1.3 Next-State Function in Example 7.1.2 Represented as a System of Switching Functions (Excitation Functions).

$x_0 x_1$	$a_0 a_1$	$\phi(x, a)$
00	00	00
00	01	10
00	10	01
00	11	11
01	00	00
01	01	10
01	10	11
01	11	01
10	00	11
10	01	10
10	10	00
10	11	01
11	00	11
11	01	00
11	10	11
11	11	01

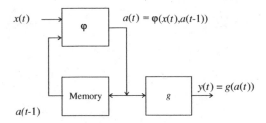

FIGURE 7.1.1   Structure of a Moore automaton.

Throughout this chapter we will assume that outputs are equal to internal states, that is, $y(t) = g(a(t)) = a(t)$. Whenever this condition is not satisfied, the output-function block g may be implemented by the methods of the previous chapters.

Switching functions realized by the next-state function block are called *excitation functions*.

7.1.2 Spectral Implementation of Excitation Functions

The methods discussed in the previous chapter may be employed to realize the excitation functions by expanding them in orthogonal series. The adder accumulator computing the sums of these series will then fulfill the function of a memory.

For a fixed state-input assignment, the implementation of a system of excitation functions is equal to the problem of realizing a system of completely or incompletely specified switching functions. We assume that the number of states is $n_a = 2^n$, and the number of input signals is $n_x = 2^c$.

As usual in spectral methods for implementation of switching functions, we first represent the system by a step function $\Phi(z)$.

This is done as follows. Set

$$z_s = \begin{cases} x_s(t), & \text{for } s = 0, 1, \ldots, \log_2 n_x - 1; \\ a_s - \log_2 n_x(t-1), & \text{for } s = \log_2 n_x, \log_2 n_x + 1, \ldots, m-1, \end{cases} \quad (7.1.1)$$

where $m = \log_2 n_a + \log_2 n_x$,

$$z = \sum_{s=0}^{m-1} z_s 2^{m-1-s}. \quad (7.1.2)$$

Then the next-state function $\phi(x(t), a(t-1))$ defines a discrete function $\tilde{a} = f(z)$.

Example 7.1.3   *Table 7.1.4 defines the function $\tilde{a} = f(z)$ for the Example 7.1.2.*

We complete $f(z)$ to a step function $\Phi(z)$ representing the system of excitation functions

$$\Phi(z) = f(\delta), \quad \delta \leq z < \delta + 1. \quad (7.1.3)$$

TABLE 7.1.4   Function $f_T(z)$ in Example 7.1.4.

z	0	1	2	3	4	5	6	7	8	9	10	11	12	13	14	15
$f(z)$	0	2	1	3	0	2	3	1	3	2	0	1	3	0	3	0
$f_T(z)$	0	2	3	2	0	2	3	0	1	3	0	1	3	1	3	0

We now expand $\Phi(z)$ in an orthogonal series

$$\Phi(z) = \sum_{q=0}^{n_a n_x - 1} c_q \Psi_q(z), \qquad (7.1.4)$$

where

$$c_q = \left(\sum_{z=0}^{n_a n_x - 1} \Psi_q(z)\overline{\Psi_q(z)} \right)^{-1} \cdot \sum_{q=0}^{n_a n_x - 1} \Phi(z)\overline{\Psi_q(z)}, \qquad (7.1.5)$$

and $\{\Psi_q(z)\}$ is a complete system of orthogonal (basis) step functions.

Formula (7.1.4) defines a physical implementation of the finite automaton as a network consisting of a function generator for the basis functions $\Psi_q(z)$, the coefficient block c_q and the adder.

The step function $\Phi(z)$ representing a system of excitation functions may be constructed in various ways, depending on the choice of the order of variables $x_0, x_1, \ldots, x_{\log_2 n_x - 1}, a_0, a_1, \ldots, a_{\log_2 n_a - 1}$.

Let $T = (T_0, T_1, \ldots, T_{m-1})$, where $m = \log_2 n_a + \log_2 n_x$, be a permutation of the numbers $0, 1, \ldots, m - 1$. Set

$$z_s = \begin{cases} x_s(t), & \text{for } s = 0, 1, \ldots, \log_2 n_x - 1, \\ a_{s - \log_2 n_x}(t-1), & \text{for } s = \log_2 n_x, \log_2 n_x + 1, \ldots, m - 1. \end{cases}$$

If $\Phi_T(z)$ is the step function representing the system of excitation functions with order of variables T, then z is determined by

$$z = \sum_{s=0}^{m-1} z_{T_s} 2^{m-1-s}, \qquad (7.1.6)$$

$\tilde{a}$ is defined by (7.1.1 and from (7.1.1) and (7.1.6), the next-state function $\phi(x(t), a(t-1))$ is defined by $\tilde{a} = f_T(z)$, and $\Phi(z)$ is the completion of $f_T(z)$ defined as in (7.1.3).

The function $\Phi(z)$ defined by (7.1.6) corresponds to the identity permutation $(0, 1, \ldots, m - 1)$.

Example 7.1.4   *Consider the assignment in Table 7.1.2 for the automaton in Example 7.1.1. Let $T = (2, 1, 0, 3)$, $(m = 4)$ is the permutation of the vector (x_0, x_1, a_0, a_1).*

Then, $z_0 = x_0$, $z_1 = x_1$, $z_2 = a_0$, $z_3 = a_1$, and by (7.1.6),

$$z = a_0 2^3 + x_1 2^2 + x_0 2^1 + a_1 2^0.$$

The corresponding function $f_T(z)$ is shown in Table 7.1.4.

The problem of optimizing the order of variables so as to minimize the number of nonzero coefficients in (7.1.4) for a given basis $\{\Psi_q(z)\}$ (and hence also minimize the complexity of the combinational part of the automaton) is inextricably bound up with the state-input assignment problem. Both these problems will be discussed in Sections 7.2 and 7.3.

When the excitation functions are being realized by expansion in orthogonal series, we can utilize all the spectral methods of synthesis described in the previous chapters, optimizing the linear transformation (minimizing the number of nonzero terms in the series) (see Subsection 6.1.6.1), optimizing the completion of the excitation functions (see Sections 6.2 and 7.3), summation of series over finite fields (see Section 2.8), and so on.

To end this section, we list the main distinguishing features and advantages of spectral methods for the implementation of finite automata:

1. The structure of the digital device is fixed in advance, the single parameter to be minimized is the number of nonzero coefficients in the expansion of the step function representing the system of excitation functions (see Sections 6.1.1 and 6.1.5).
2. For a fixed assignment, minimization of the number of nonzero coefficients and optimization of the completion of the excitation functions may be accomplished by techniques, which almost completely avoid the brute-force approach (see Sections 6.1.6.1–6.1.6.3, and 6.2).
3. It is relatively easy to determine asymptotically optimal assignments for abstract finite automata and asymptotically optimal completions of the next-state function for incompletely specified finite automata (see Sections 7.2 and 7.3).
4. Sequential networks designed by spectral methods provide for a simple organization of error detection and/or correction using arithmetic error-detecting and/or -correcting codes (see Section 9.4).

A more detailed comparison of spectral and classical methods of synthesis will be carried out in Section 9.5.

7.2 ASSIGNMENT OF STATES AND INPUTS FOR COMPLETELY SPECIFIED AUTOMATA

The optimization of state-input assignments is a very important problem in theory and practice of finite automata, as regards the complexity, reliability, etc. of the device.

To represent R states, we need a binary code with at least $\lceil \log_2 R \rceil$ bits. Such a code is the *minimum length code*.

It was shown in the last section that, for a given assignment, implementation of an automaton reduces to the implementation of a system of switching functions representing the next-state and output functions of the automaton. The disadvantage of classical methods of Boolean algebra for the state-assignment problem is that the system of switching functions describing the combinational part for a given assignment does not readily yield information concerning the complexity, reliability, etc. of the corresponding network implementation. The situation is further complicated if the finite automaton to be synthesized is incompletely specified, that is, the next-state function is undefined for certain input signal-internal state pairs.

Because of these complicating factors, classical solutions of the assignment problem always involve some measure of brute force. The number of alternatives to be checked generally increases exponentially with the number of states or inputs of the automaton. This situation is apparently intrinsic in nature, thus limiting application of the classical methods to relatively simple devices. A complete survey of existing methods for solving the assignment problem by classical methods may be found, for example, in Reference 231. For these methods see also References 40, 236, 484, and 645.

Because of the importance of selecting a good assignment, this problem is a subject of continuous study, and there are many efforts to solve it by using a variety of approaches (123,375). Recently, genetic algorithms have been used as a tool to address this problem, see References 32 and 34.

The traditional approaches to encoding of states have been intended primarily to reduce the number of flip-flops required at the price of the complexity of the combinational logic (194,654). Different technologies may force other optimality criteria and related state encodings.

The so-called 1-*hot bit encoding* where the code words for each state have a single 1 bit, provides for fast sequential networks. Notice that since the number of bits is equal to the number of states, this assignment necessarily implies more flip-flops for the memory part than optimal minimum length encoding (491). This results in wasting of area, which, however does not effect the performances much in *Field Programmable Gate Arrays* (FPGA) (41) based sequential networks, since FPGAs usually have more flip-flops than function generators. Therefore, in most FPGAs synthesis tools for implementations of sequential networks, this encoding is usually used by default to improve the speed of the networks produced, see Reference 148.

Some variants of this approach are also discussed and adapted to different implementations of the combinational part of the sequential network. For example, in Reference 473, it is proposed the encoding where exactly half of the state variables are equal to 1. The method is intended for *Programmable Logic Array* (PLA) (491,41), implementations of the combinational logic.

We note that this balanced encoding may be useful for protection of some devices against attacks based on measuring of power consumption, since balanced encoding makes the power consumption less data dependent. We also note that the balanced encoding provides for detection of *all unidirectional errors* by verification that exactly half of the state variables are equal to 1.

In Reference 623, it has been proposed a method for determination of good state assignment by using partition theory and spectral translation techniques. The method is adapted for implementation of the combinational part of the sequential machines by PLAs.

Low power state assignment (97,140,616), and easy testable implementations (44,45,126), are among the most important design criteria.

There are algorithms adapted for implementations of particular classes of finite automata, as for instance, incompletely specified automata (33,423), or asynchronous automata (403,502,620). In the case of asynchronous automata, state assignment takes into account avoiding of critical races and logic hazards (619,620). Various algorithms has been developed to ensure such encoding see References 188,189, and 619.

There are several synthesis tools for sequential networks including various algorithms for state encoding, to provide references for just few of them (122,127, 131,516,629). A rule based system developed in Reference 503 includes a solution to the state assignment problem.

A parallel implementation of classical state assignment algorithms, also implemented in the mentioned synthesis tools, can reduce time and memory implementation requirements without compromising with the quality of solutions produced, see References 47 and 238.

By contrast to classical and many other present methods performed in the Boolean domain, as we will see in Sections 7.2–7.4, the spectral approach to the implementation of the combinational part of an automaton yields highly simple assignment algorithms computing asymptotically optimal orderings of variables in the excitation functions for almost all finite automata (i.e., the fraction of automata for which the state assignment is not optimal tends to zero very fast as the number of states tends to infinity).

We measure the complexity of the combinational part by the number of nonzero expansion terms.

The basis system will again be the Haar basis (see Section 2.3). For the sake of convenience, we restrict ourselves here and in Section 7.3 to the Haar expansions over the field of real numbers. However, the method described here for optimal assignments, optimal ordering of variables of the excitation functions and optimal completion of the state table carries over practically unchanged to the Haar–Galois expansions (see Section 6.3).

7.2.1 Optimization of the Assignments for Implementation of the Combinational Part by Using the Haar Basis

We proceed to the first two of the last-mentioned problems,

1. the optimization of the state-input assignment, and

2. the optimization of the order of variables in the excitation functions, for implementation of the combinational part of a completely specified finite automata by using the Haar basis.

We have already discussed the main properties of the Haar system $\{H_l^{(q)}(z)\}$, the reasons for choosing it as a basis, and efficient computational procedures for the expansion coefficients $c_l^{(q)}$ (see Section 2.3).

Let L_l, for $l = 0, 1, \ldots, m - 1$ denote the number of nonzero coefficients $c_l^{(q)}$, $(q = 1, 2, \ldots, 2^l)$ with subscript l in the expansion of $\Phi_T(z)$.

Then, $0 \le L_l \le 2^l$, and so our first task is to determine the set of assignments minimizing the number L_{m-1} of nonzero coefficients $c_{m-1}^{(q)}$. We shall then look for the subset of assignments minimizing L_{m-2} for the optimal L_{m-1}, and so on.

Arbitrary assignments will be represented by two functions $K^a(q)$ and $K^x(r)$, $(q = 0, 2, \ldots, n_a - 1, r = 0, 1, \ldots, n_x - 1)$, where $K^a(q)$ $(K^x(r))$ is the number whose binary expansion is the code vector of the state a_q (input signal x_r) in the assignment. In other words,

$$K^a(q) = \sum_{s=0}^{\log_2 n_a - 1} a_{q,s} 2^{\log_2 n_a - 1 - s}, \tag{7.2.1}$$

$$K^x(r) = \sum_{s=0}^{\log_2 n_x - 1} x_{r,s} 2^{\log_2 n_x - 1 - s}, \tag{7.2.2}$$

where $a_{q,s}$, $(x_{r,s})$ is the sth component of the binary code of the state a_q (input signal x_r).

Denote the inverse functions of the assignments $K^a(q)$, $K^x(r)$ by $(K^a)^{-1}(q)$ and $(K^x)^{-1}(r)$, respectively. To be precise, $(K^a)^{-1}(q) = \lambda$, $((K^x)^{-1}(q) = \lambda)$ iff the code of the state a_λ (input signal x_λ) is the binary expansion of the number q. For example, if the state a_4 is encoded by 011, then $K^a(4) = 3$ $((K^a)^{-1}(3) = 4)$.

We now consider how to determine the set of assignments minimizing L_{m-1}.

We shall assume that the original abstract automaton is defined by a state matrix $\mathbf{A}_{m-1} = [a_{q,r}]$ $(q = 0, 1, \ldots, n_a - 1, n_a = 2^n, r = 0, 1, \ldots, n_x - 1, n_x = 2^c)$, where $a_{q,r}$ is the state into which the automaton goes from a_q upon application of the input signal x_r.

We need *distance functions* on the set of rows and columns, respectively, of the next-state matrix. The distance $\rho_{m-1}^a(q, s)$ $(\rho_{m-1}^x(q, s))$ between rows (columns) q and s of the state matrix is defined as follows

$$\rho_{m-1}^a(q, s) = \sum_{r=0}^{n_x - 1} \delta(a_{q,r}, a_{s,r}), \tag{7.2.3}$$

$$\rho^x_{m-1}(q, s) = \sum_{r=0}^{n_a-1} \delta(a_{r,q}, a_{r,s}). \qquad (7.2.4)$$

where

$$\delta(a_{\alpha,\beta}, a_{\gamma,\delta}) = \begin{cases} 1, & \text{if } a_{\alpha,\beta} \neq a_{\gamma,\delta}, \\ 0, & \text{if } a_{\alpha,\beta} = a_{\gamma,\delta}. \end{cases} \qquad (7.2.5)$$

Using formulas (7.2.3–7.2.5), we construct $(n_a \times n_a)$ and $(n_x \times n_x)$ *distance matrices* $[\rho^a(q, s)]$ and $[\rho^x(q, s)]$, respectively, given the next-state matrix of the automaton.[2]

Theorem 7.2.1 *Given an automaton $A_{m-1} = [a_{q,r}]$ and an assignment of states and inputs $(K^a(q), K^x(r))$. Then,*

$$L_{m-1} = \min(L^a_{m-1}, L^x_{m-1}),$$

where

$$L^x_{m-1} = \sum_{s=1}^{n_x/2} \rho^x_{m-1}((K^x)^{-1}(2s - 2), (K^x)^{-1}(2s - 1)), \qquad (7.2.6)$$

$$L^a_{m-1} = \sum_{i=1}^{n_a/2} \rho^a_{m-1}((K^a)^{-1}(2i - 2), (K^a)^{-1}(2i - 1)).$$

Proof. Define a function $\hat{\phi}(\lambda, \beta)$ by setting $\hat{\phi}(\lambda, \beta) = t$ iff there exist $q, t \in \{0, 1, \ldots, n_a - 1\}$ and $r \in \{0, 1, \ldots, n_x - 1\}$ such that

$$\begin{cases} K^a(q) = \lambda, \ K^x(r) = \beta, \ K^a(t) = t, \\ \phi(x_r, a_q) = a_t. \end{cases}$$

Then depending on the selected order of variables of $\hat{\phi}$, we have

$$L_{m-1} = L^a_{m-1} = \sum_{\beta=0}^{n_x-1} \sum_{i=1}^{n_a/2} sign|\hat{\phi}(2i - 2, \beta) - \hat{\phi}(2i - 1, \beta)|,$$

---

[2] The distance thus defined on the state matrix satisfies the usual axioms for a metric, and it is a generalization of the Hamming metric (55).

or

$$L_{m-1} = L_{m-1}^x = \sum_{\lambda=0}^{n_a-1} \sum_{s=1}^{n_x/2} sign|\hat{\phi}(\lambda, 2s-2) - \hat{\phi}(\lambda, 2s-1)|.$$

We first consider the case $L_{m-1} = L_{m-1}^a$. Set

$$q' = (K^a)^{-1}(2i-2),$$
$$q'' = (K^a)^{-1}(2i-1),$$
$$r = (K^x)^{-1}(\beta),$$

for $i \in \{1, 2 \dots, n_a/2\}, q', q'' \in \{0, 1, \dots, n_a - 1\}, r, \beta \in \{0, 1, \dots, n_x - 1\}$.
Then,

$$sign|\hat{\phi}(2i-2, \beta) - \hat{\phi}(2i-1, \beta)| = 1$$

iff

$$\phi(x_r, a_{q'}) \neq \phi(x_r, a_{q''}),$$

or, in view of (7.2.5), iff

$$\delta(a_{q',r}, a_{q'',r}) = 1.$$

Hence, by (7.2.4),

$$\sum_{\beta=0}^{n_x-1} sign|\hat{\phi}(2i-2, \beta) - \hat{\phi}(2i-1, \beta)|$$

$$= \sum_{r=0}^{n_x-1} \rho(a_{q',\ r}, a_{q'',r})$$

$$= \delta_{m-1}^a(q', q'') = \rho_{m-1}^a((K^a)^{-1}(2i-2), (K^a)^{-1}(2i-1)).$$

Consequently,

$$L_{m-1}^a = \sum_{i=1}^{n_a/2} \sum_{\beta=0}^{n_x-1} sign|\hat{\phi}(2i-2, \beta) - \hat{\phi}(2i-1, \beta)|,$$

$$= \sum_{i=1}^{n_a/2} \rho_{m-1}^a((K^a)^{-1}(2i-2), (K^a)^{-1}(2i-1)).$$

The proof of the equality

$$L_{m-1}^x = \sum_{s=1}^{n_x/2} \rho_{m-1}^x((K^x)^{-1}(2s-2), (K^x)^{-1}(2s-1)),$$

is analogous, completing the proof.

Example 7.2.1 *Consider the automaton with the next-state matrix*

$$\mathbf{A}_{m-1} = [a_{q,r}] = \mathbf{A}_5 = \begin{bmatrix} a_0 & a_4 & a_0 & a_6 & a_4 & a_0 & a_2 & a_0 \\ a_1 & a_0 & a_2 & a_3 & a_0 & a_2 & a_3 & a_2 \\ a_5 & a_1 & a_7 & a_6 & a_7 & a_5 & a_6 & a_6 \\ a_0 & a_3 & a_0 & a_6 & a_3 & a_0 & a_7 & a_0 \\ a_1 & a_0 & a_2 & a_3 & a_4 & a_2 & a_3 & a_2 \\ a_0 & a_3 & a_0 & a_4 & a_3 & a_0 & a_4 & a_0 \\ a_0 & a_6 & a_0 & a_4 & a_6 & a_0 & a_4 & a_0 \\ a_5 & a_2 & a_7 & a_6 & a_2 & a_5 & a_6 & a_6 \end{bmatrix}.$$

Then

$$[\rho_5^a(q, s)] = \begin{bmatrix} 0 & 8 & 7 & 2^* & 7 & 4 & 4 & 8 \\ 8 & 0 & 8 & 8 & 1^* & 8 & 8 & 8 \\ 7 & 8 & 0 & 7 & 8 & 8 & 8 & 2^* \\ 2^* & 8 & 7 & 0 & 8 & 2 & 4 & 7 \\ 7 & 1^* & 8 & 8 & 0 & 8 & 8 & 8 \\ 4 & 8 & 8 & 2 & 8 & 0 & 2^* & 8 \\ 4 & 8 & 8 & 4 & 8 & 2^* & 0 & 8 \\ 8 & 8 & 2^* & 7 & 8 & 8 & 8 & 0 \end{bmatrix}$$

and

$$[\rho_5^x(q, s)] = \begin{bmatrix} 0 & 8 & 4 & 8 & 8 & 2^* & 8 & 4 \\ 8 & 0 & 8 & 8 & 1^* & 8 & 8 & 8 \\ 4 & 8 & 0 & 8 & 8 & 2 & 8 & 2^* \\ 8 & 8 & 8 & 0 & 8 & 8 & 2^* & 6 \\ 8 & 1^* & 8 & 8 & 0 & 8 & 8 & 8 \\ 2^* & 8 & 2 & 8 & 8 & 0 & 8 & 2 \\ 8 & 8 & 8 & 2^* & 8 & 8 & 0 & 6 \\ 4 & 8 & 2^* & 6 & 8 & 2 & 6 & 0 \end{bmatrix}$$

By Theorem 7.2.1, the assignment $K^a(q) = q$, $K^x(q) = q$ gives $L_{m-1} = L_5 = min(31, 30) = 30$. (As we shall show below, the optimal assignment for this example gives $L_{m-1} = 7$.)

It follows from Theorem 7.2.1 that the optimal assignment for L_{m-1} minimizes one of the quantities L^a_{m-1}, L^x_{m-1}.

To find an optimal assignment, we first determine the class of assignments $K^a_{m-1} = \{K^a(q)\}$ minimizing L^a_{m-1} and then the class of assignments $K^x_{m-1} = \{K^x(q)\}$ minimizing L^x_{m-1}. The class of assignments K_{m-1}, minimizing L_{m-1}, is then either K^a_{m-1} or K^x_{m-1}, depending on whether $L^a_{m-1} \leq L^x_{m-1}$ or $L^a_{m-1} > L^x_{m-1}$.

If z_{T_s} is the sth variable of the excitation function (see Section 7.1.2) for the required optimal order T of variables, we set

$$z_{T_{m-1}} = \begin{cases} x_{\log_2 n_x - 1} & \text{if } L^x_{m-1} < L^a_{m-1}, \\ a_{\log_2 n_a - 1} & \text{if } L^a_{m-1} \leq L^x_{m-1}, \end{cases} \tag{7.2.7}$$

where x_i and a_i are ith components in the binary representations of $x(t)$ and $a(t-1)$.

7.2.2 Minimization of the Number of Highest Order Nonzero Coefficients

In order to determine the classes K^a_{m-1} and K^x_{m-1} minimizing, respectively,

$$L^a_{m-1} = \sum_{i=1}^{n_a/2} \rho^a_{m-1}((K^a)^{-1}(2i-2), (K^a)^{-1}(2i-1))$$

and

$$L^x_{m-1} = \sum_{i=1}^{n_x/2} \rho^a_{m-1}((K^x)^{-1}(2q-2), (K^x)^{-1}(2q-1))$$

it suffices to partition the set of rows (columns) of the next-state matrix into disjoint pairs in such a way that the sum of distances (7.2.3) ((7.2.4)) within the pairs is minimized. If these pairs are $\{i_0, i_1\}, \ldots, \{i_{n_a-2}, i_{n_a-1}\}$ and $\{g_0, g_1\} \ldots, \{g_{n_x-2}, g_{n_x-1}\}$, then the required class of assignments is the set of all assignments such that

$$\begin{cases} (K^a)^{-1}(2\alpha) = i_{2q}, \\ (K^a)^{-1}(2\alpha + 1) = i_{2q+1}, \end{cases}$$

or

$$\begin{cases} (K^a)^{-1}(2\alpha) = i_{2q+1} \\ (K^a)^{-1}(2\alpha + 1) = i_{2q}, \end{cases} \tag{7.2.8}$$

for $\alpha = 0, 1, \ldots, n_a/2 - 1$, and $q = 0, 1, \ldots, n_a/2 - 1$ and

$$\begin{cases} (K^x)^{-1}(2\alpha) = g_{2s}, \\ (K^x)^{-1}(2\alpha + 1) = g_{2s+1}, \end{cases}$$

or

$$\begin{cases} (K^x)^{-1}(2\alpha) = g_{2s+1} \\ (K^x)^{-1}(2\alpha + 1) = g_{2q}, \end{cases}$$

for $\alpha = 0, 1, \ldots, n_x/2 - 1$, and $s = 0, 1, \ldots, n_x/2 - 1$.

It follows from (7.2.8) that K^a_{m-1} (K^x_{m-1}) is the set of all assignments for which the states (input signals) from the same pair are assigned binary codes differing in the least significant bit.

The above constructions of K^a_{m-1}, (K^x_{m-1}) may be formulated in terms of the matrix $[\rho^a_{m-1}(q, s)]$ $([\rho^x_{m-1}(q, s)])$ as follows.

We want to find n_a (n_x) elements of the matrix, for instance,

$$\rho^a_{m-1}(q_0, s_0), \rho^a_{m-1}(q_1, s_1), \ldots, \rho^a_{m-1}(q_{n_a-1}, s_{n_a-1}),$$
$$(\rho^x_{m-1}(q_0, s_0), \rho^x_{m-1}(q_1, s_1), \ldots, \rho^x_{m-1}(q_{n_x-1}, s_{n_x-1})),$$

where $q_i \neq s_i$, such that each row and column of the matrix contains exactly one of the selected elements. The elements are symmetrically situated around the principal diagonal, and their sum is a minimum. We call any set of matrix elements satisfying these conditions a *minimal symmetric matching* of the matrix.

It is apparent from Theorem 7.2.1 that half the sum of elements of a minimal symmetric matching for the matrix $[\rho^a_{m-1}(q, s)]$ $([\rho^x_{m-1}(q, s)])$ gives L^a_{m-1}, (L^x_{m-1}). The minimal symmetric matching of a matrix is relatively easy to determine, for instance, by using the *Hungarian* algorithm (137, 321, 322, 390, 632). Notice that to ensure that the minimal matching is symmetric, we will use a slightly modified version of the Hungarian algorithm.

Example 7.2.2 *Resuming the discussion of Example 7.2.1, we find the class of assignments $K_{m-1} = K_5$ minimizing L_{m-1}. To determine K^a_5, we find a minimal symmetric matching for $[\rho^a_5(q, s)]$, which in this case is*

$$\{\rho^a_5(0, 3), \rho^a_5(1, 4), \rho^a_5(2, 7), \rho^a_5(5, 6)\}.$$

*In view of the symmetry, we shall henceforth specify matchings in terms of elements above the principal diagonal, elements appearing in the matching are denoted by * in the matrix $[\rho^a_5(q, s)]$.*

TABLE 7.2.1 Assignment from K_5^a.

q	0	1	2	3	4	5	6	7
$K^a(q)$	0	2	4	1	3	6	7	5

The states are thus partitioned into pairs

$$\{a_0, a_3\}, \{a_1, a_4\}, \{a_2, a_7\}, \{a_5, a_6\}.$$

The class K_5^a is the set of all assignments in which states from the same pair are assigned codes differing only in the lowest order digit $a_{\log_2 n_a - 1}$. For example, the assignment in Table 7.2.1 is in K_5^a.
Half the sum of the "intrapair" distances is

$$\rho_5^a(0, 3) + \rho_5^a(1, 4) + \rho_5^a(2, 7) + \rho_5^a(3, 6) = 7,$$

and so $L_5^a = 7$.
Similarly, to determine K_5^x we find a minimal symmetric matching for $[\rho_5^x(q, s)]$ as

$$\{\rho_5^x(0, 5), \rho_5^x(1, 4), \rho_5^x(2, 7), \rho_5^x(3, 6)\}.$$

The input signals are divided into pairs

$$\{x_0, x_5\}, \{x_1, x_4\}, \{x_2, x_7\}, \{x_3, x_6\}$$

and

$$L_5^x = \rho_5^x(0, 5) + \rho_5^x(1, 4) + \rho_5^x(2, 7) + \rho_5^x(3, 5) = 7,$$

Since $L_5^a = L_5^x = 7$, we may take, say $K_5 = K_5^a$. Thus, whereas the original assignment, for Example, 7.2.1 gave $L_{m-1} = L_5 = 30$, any assignment in class K_5 gives $L_5 = 7$.

7.2.3 Minimization of the Number of Lowest Order Nonzero Coefficients

Continuing the procedure, we must now determine the classes of assignments $K_{m-2} \supseteq K_{m-3} \supseteq \cdots \supseteq K_0$, where K_{m-s} is the set of all assignments in K_{m-s+1} for which L_{m-s} assumes a local minimum, preserving the previously attained value of L_{m-s+1}. Along with the classes K_{m-s} ($s = 1, 2, \ldots, m$) we determine the order T (see Section 7.1.2) of variables in the excitation functions of the automaton.
We now outline the construction of $K_{m-2} \subseteq K_{m-1}$ assuming that $L_{m-1}^a \leq L_{m-1}^x$, so that $K_{m-1} = K_{m-1}^a$.

Construct the $(n_a/2 \times n_x)$ matrix $\mathbf{A}_{m-2} = \mathbf{A}^a_{m-2} = [b_{qr}]$ whose (q, r)th element is the (unordered) pair

$$b_{q,r} = \{a_{i_{2q},r}, a_{i_{2q+1},r}\}, \tag{7.2.9}$$

where $q = 0, 1, \ldots, n_a/2 - 1, r = 0, 1, \ldots, n_x - 1$, and let

$$\{\{i_0, i_1\}, \ldots, \{i_{n_a-2}, i_{n_a-1}\}\},$$

is the partition into pairs of the rows of $\mathbf{A}_{m-1}$, determined by a minimal matching for the matrix $[\rho^a_{m-1}(q, s)]$.

Thus, to the qth row of $\mathbf{A}_{m-2} = \mathbf{A}^a_{m-2}$ corresponds the pair of rows i_{2q}, i_{2q+1} of the state matrix $\mathbf{A}_{m-1}$.

Example 7.2.3 *In the case of Example 7.2.1 and partition* $\{a_0, a_3\}, \{a_1, a_4\}, \{a_2, a_7\},$ $\{a_5, a_6\}$,

$$\mathbf{A}_{m-2} = \mathbf{A}_4 =$$

$$\begin{bmatrix} \{a_0, a_0\}, \{a_4, a_3\}, \{a_0, a_0\}, \{a_6, a_6\}, \{a_4, a_3\}, \{a_0, a_0\}, \{a_7, a_7\}, \{a_0, a_0\} \\ \{a_1, a_1\}, \{a_0, a_0\}, \{a_2, a_2\}, \{a_3, a_3\}, \{a_0, a_4\}, \{a_2, a_2\}, \{a_3, a_3\}, \{a_2, a_2\} \\ \{a_5, a_5\}, \{a_1, a_2\}, \{a_7, a_7\}, \{a_6, a_6\}, \{a_1, a_2\}, \{a_5, a_5\}, \{a_6, a_6\}, \{a_6, a_6\} \\ \{a_0, a_0\}, \{a_3, a_6\}, \{a_0, a_0\}, \{a_4, a_4\}, \{a_3, a_6\}, \{a_0, a_0\}, \{a_4, a_4\}, \{a_0, a_0\} \end{bmatrix}.$$

As in (7.2.3–7.2.5), we define distances $\rho^a_{m-2}(q, s)$ and $\rho^x_{m-2}(q, s)$ for $\mathbf{A}_{m-2} = [b_{i,j}]$ on the rows and columns, respectively,

$$\rho^a_{m-2}(q, s) = \sum_{r=0}^{n_x-1} \delta(b_{q,r}, b_{s,r}), \quad q, s \in 0, 1, \ldots, n_a/2 - 1, \tag{7.2.10}$$

$$\rho^x_{m-2}(q, s) = \sum_{r=0}^{n_a/2-1} \delta(b_{r,q}, b_{r,s}), \quad q, s \in 0, 1, \ldots, n_x - 1, \tag{7.2.11}$$

where

$$\delta(b_{\alpha,\beta}, b_{\gamma,\delta}) = \begin{cases} 1, & \text{if } b_{\alpha,\beta} \neq b_{\gamma,\delta}; \\ 0, & \text{if } b_{\alpha,\beta} = b_{\gamma,\delta}. \end{cases} \tag{7.2.12}$$

Notice that the equality of elements of $\mathbf{A}_{m-2}$ is equality of unordered pairs.

Example 7.2.4 *In Example 7.2.1,*

$$[\rho_4^a(q, s)] = \begin{bmatrix} 0 & 8 & 7 & 4^* \\ 8 & 0 & 8^* & 8 \\ 7 & 8^* & 0 & 8 \\ 4^* & 8 & 8 & 0 \end{bmatrix}$$

and

$$[\rho_4^x(q, s)] = \begin{bmatrix} 0 & 4 & 2 & 4 & 4 & 1^* & 4 & 2 \\ 4 & 0 & 4 & 4 & 1^* & 4 & 4 & 4 \\ 2 & 4 & 0 & 4 & 4 & 1 & 4 & 1^* \\ 4 & 4 & 4 & 0 & 4 & 4 & 1^* & 3 \\ 4 & 1^* & 4 & 4 & 0 & 4 & 4 & 4 \\ 1^* & 4 & 1 & 4 & 4 & 0 & 4 & 1 \\ 4 & 4 & 4 & 1^* & 4 & 4 & 0 & 4 \\ 2 & 4 & 1^* & 3 & 4 & 1 & 4 & 0 \end{bmatrix}.$$

If $L_{m-1}^a > L_{m-1}^x$, so that $K_{m-1} = K_{m-1}^x$, we define $\mathbf{A}_{m-2}$ as $\mathbf{A}_{m-2}^x$ instead of $\mathbf{A}_{m-2}^a$, (this is an $(n_a \times n_x/2)$ matrix, derived from $\mathbf{A}_{m-1}$ in the same way as $\mathbf{A}_{m-2}^a$). The procedure is then analogous except that in formulas (7.2.9–7.2.12) the optimal matching $\{i_{2q}, i_{2q+1}\}$, $q = 0, 1, \ldots, n_a/2 - 1$ on $[\rho_{m-1}^a]$ is replaced by an optimal matching on $[\rho_{m-1}^x]$, i.e., $\{g_{2q}, g_{2q+1}\}$, $q = 0, 1, \ldots, n_x/2 - 1$.

Any state (input) assignment in the class K_{m-2}^a (K_{m-2}^x) may be defined, as in (7.2.1), by a function $K_{m-2}^a(q)$ ($K_{m-2}^x(q)$)

$$K_{m-2}^a(q) = \sum_{s=0}^{\log_2 n_a - 2} a_{i_{2q},s} \cdot 2^{\log_2 n_a - 2 - s}$$

$$= \sum_{s=0}^{\log_2 n_a - 2} a_{i_{2q+1},s} 2^{\log_2 n_a - 2 - s}, \tag{7.2.13}$$

$$q = 0, \ldots \frac{1}{2} n_a - 1$$

and

$$K_{m-2}^x(q) = \sum_{s=0}^{\log_2 n_x - 2} x_{g_{2q},s} \cdot 2^{\log_2 n_x - 2 - s}$$

$$= \sum_{s=0}^{\log_2 n_x - 2} x_{g_{2q+1},s} 2^{\log_2 n_x - 2 - s}, \tag{7.2.14}$$

$$q = 0, \ldots, \frac{1}{2} n_x - 1.$$

It follows from these formulas that for fixed q the value of $K_{m-1}^a(q)$ $(K_{m-1}^x(q))$ may be regarded as the number whose binary expansion is determined by the first $\log_2 n_a - 1$ $(\log_2 n_x - 1)$ components of states $a_{i_{2q}}, a_{i_{2q+1}}$ (input signals $\{x_{g_{2q}}, x_{g_{2q+1}}\}$).

Since the pair of states $\{a_{i_{2q}}, a_{i_{2q+1}}\}$ (input signals $\{x_{g_{2q}}, x_{g_{2q+1}}\}$) corresponds to the qth row of $\mathbf{A}_{m-2}^a$ (qth column of $\mathbf{A}_{m-2}^x$), we may assume $K_{m-2}^a(q)$ $(K_{m-2}^x(q))$ defines the number corresponding to the qth row of $\mathbf{A}_{m-2}^a$ (the qth column of $\mathbf{A}_{m-2}^x$) in the given assignment.

The inverse functions for $K_{m-2}^a(q)$, $K_{m-2}^x(q)$ will be denoted by $(K_{m-2}^a)^{-1}(q)$ and $(K_{m-2}^x)^{-1}(q)$, respectively. These functions define, respectively the row of $\mathbf{A}_{m-2}^a$ and the column of $\mathbf{A}_{m-2}^x$ which the assignment associates with the number q.

For example, if states a_{i_2} and a_{i_3} are assigned codes (110) and (111), respectively, then $K_{m-2}^a(1) = 3$ and $(K_{m-2}^a)^{-1}(3) = 1$.

Theorem 7.2.2 *For almost all automata with the assignment in K_{m-1}*

$$
L_{m-2} \sim \min \left(\sum_{q=1}^{n_a/4} \rho_{m-2}^a((K_{m-2}^a)^{-1}(2q-2), (K_{m-2}^a)^{-1}(2q-1)), \right.
$$

$$(7.2.15)$$

$$
\left. \sum_{q=1}^{n_x/4} \rho_{m-2}^x((K_{m-2}^x)^{-1}(2q-2)), (K_{m-2}^x)^{-1}(2q-1) \right),
$$

for $m = \log_2 n_a + \log_2 n_x$, as $n = \log_2 n_a \to \infty$ and $\log_2 n_x \to \infty$.

Proof. The proof is analogous to that of Theorem 7.2.1. The new point is the use of the limit relation

$$
\rho(b_{\alpha,\beta}, b_{\gamma,\rho}) = \lim_{n_a \to \infty} P\left(\sum_{a_q \in b_{\alpha,\beta}} K^a(q) \neq \sum_{a_q \in b_{\gamma,\rho}} K^a(q) \right),
$$

where $\rho(b_{\alpha,\beta}, b_{\gamma,\rho})$ is defined by (7.2.12) and

$$
P\left(\sum_{a_q \in b_{\alpha,\beta}} K^a(q) \neq \sum_{a_q \in b_{\gamma,\rho}} K^a(q) \right)
$$

is the fraction of assignments $K^a(q)$ for the automaton such that the sum of the numbers corresponding to codes of states in the set $b_{\alpha,\beta}$ is not equal to the analogous sum for the set $b_{\gamma,\delta}$.

Theorem 7.2.2 provides a fairly simple procedure for estimating L_{m-2} in terms of the matrix $\mathbf{A}_{m-2}$, with the right-hand side of (7.2.15) as a bound for L_{m-2}.

Example 7.2.5   *In Example 7.2.1, for an assignment in $K_5 = K_5^a$, analysis of the matrices $[\rho_4^a(q, s)]$ and $[\rho_4^x(q, s)]$ by Theorem 7.2.2 with $K_4^a(q) = q$, $K_4^x(q) = q$ gives $L_4 \leq 16$. We shall see later that by optimizing the assignment we can lower the bound for L_4 to 4.*

It follows from Theorem 7.2.2 that for almost all automata the asymptotically optimal assignment in class K_{m-2} (minimizing L_{m-2}) minimizes at least one of the quantities

$$L_{m-2}^a = \sum_{q=1}^{n_a/4} \rho_{m-2}^a((K_{m-2}^a)^{-1}(2q - 2), (K_{m-2}^a)^{-1}(2q - 1)),$$

or

$$L_{m-2}^x = \sum_{q=1}^{n_x/4} \rho_{m-2}^x((K_{m-2}^x)^{-1}(2q - 2), (K_{m-2}^x)^{-1}(2q - 1)).$$

To determine K_{m-2}, we first find the class K_{m-2}^a of assignments minimizing L_{m-2}^a and the class K_{m-2}^x of assignments minimizing L_{m-2}^x, and then set

$$K_{m-2} = \begin{cases} K_{m-2}^a, & \text{if } L_{m-2}^a \leq L_{m-2}^x, \\ K_{m-2}^x, & \text{if } L_{m-2}^x < L_{m-2}^a. \end{cases} \tag{7.2.16}$$

If $K_{m-1} = K_{m-1}^a$, we put

$$z_{T_{m-2}} = \begin{cases} a_{\log_2 n_a - 2}, & \text{if } L_{m-2}^a \leq L_{m-2}^x, \\ x_{\log_2 n_x - 1}, & \text{if } L_{m-2}^x < L_{m-2}^a, \end{cases} \tag{7.2.17}$$

and if $K_{m-1} = K_{m-1}^x$,

$$z_{T_{m-2}} = \begin{cases} a_{\log_2 n_a - 1}, & \text{if } L_{m-2}^a \leq L_{m-2}^x, \\ x_{\log_2 n_x - 2}, & \text{if } L_{m-2}^x < L_{m-2}^a. \end{cases} \tag{7.2.18}$$

A comparison of Theorems 7.2.1 and 7.2.2 shows that the procedures for K_{m-2} and K_{m-1}, are entirely analogous, amounting to the determination of a minimal symmetric matching, except that now this is done for the matrices $[\rho_{m-2}^a(q, s)]$ and $[\rho_{m-2}^x]$.

As in (7.2.9), the minimum of these matchings defines the class K_{m-2}. For example, if $\{i_0, i_1\}, \ldots, \{i_{n_a/2-2}, i_{n_a/2-1}\}$ is the partition of the rows of $\mathbf{A}_{m-2}^a$ into pairs corresponding to the computed minimal matching on $[\rho_{m-2}^a(q, s)]$, then K_{m-2}^a is the

TABLE 7.2.2   Assignment of K_5^a.

q	0	1	2	3	4	5	6	7
$K^a(q)$	0	4	6	1	5	2	3	7

set of all assignments in K_{m-1} for which

$$\begin{cases} (K_{m-2}^a)^{-1}(2\alpha) = i_{2q}, \\ (K_{m-2}^a)^{-1}(2\alpha + 1) = i_{2q+1}, \end{cases} \tag{7.2.19}$$

or

$$\begin{cases} (K_{m-2}^a)^{-1}(2\alpha) = i_{2q+1}, \\ (K_{m-2}^a)^{-1}(2\alpha + 1) = i_{2q}. \end{cases} \tag{7.2.20}$$

Example 7.2.6   *Returning to Example 7.2.1 considered above, we now compute $K_{m-2} = K_4$. To this end, we need a minimal symmetric matching for $[\rho_4^{(a)}(q, s)]$. This is found to be $\{\rho_4^a(0, 3), \rho_4^a(1, 2)\}$ (the elements participating in the matching are denoted by * in the matrix $[\rho_4^a(q, s)]$).*

The rows of $[\rho_4^a(q, s)]$ are divided into pairs $\{0, 3\}, \{1, 2\}$. The class K_4^a is the set of assignments in which the codes of states in the same pair may differ in the second bit (in order of significance).

For example, K_4^a will contain the assignment from K_5^a shown in Table 7.2.2. We have $L_4^a = \rho_4^a(0, 3) + \rho_4^a(1, 2) = 12$.

To find K_4^x, we construct a minimal matching for $[\rho_4^x(q, s)]$, as

$$\{\rho_4^x(0, 5), \rho_4^x(1, 4), \rho_4^x(2, 7), \rho_4^x(3, 6)\}.$$

Then,

$$L_4^x = \rho_4^x(0, 5) + \rho_4^x(1, 4) + \rho_4^x(2, 7) + \rho_4^x(3, 6) = 4.$$

Consequently, $K_{m-2} = K_4 = K_4^x$, and $L_4 = L_4^x = 4$ (instead of 16 in the original assignment) and, since $K_5 = K_5^a$ and $K_4 = K_4^x$, we have $z_{T_5} = a_2, z_{T_4} = x_2$. An example of an assignment from the class $K_4 = K_4^x$ is given in Table 7.2.3.

The classes $K_{m-3}, K_{m-4}, \ldots, K_0$ may be constructed in the same way as K_{m-1} and K_{m-2}, together with the order of variables for the excitation functions.

A general outline of the procedure is as follows.

TABLE 7.2.3   Assignment of K_4^a.

q	0	1	2	3	4	5	6	7
$K^a(q)$	0	2	4	6	3	1	7	5

The initial data for computation of the class K_{m-t}, is the matrix $\mathbf{A}_{m-(t-1)}$ determined at the $(t-1)$th iteration, which defines the class $K^a_{m-(t-1)}$, $(K^x_{m-(t-1)})$ and the minimal symmetric matching for $[\rho^a_{m-(t-1)}(q, s)]$ $([\rho^x_{m-(t-1)}(q, s)]$. The tth iteration of the algorithm consists of the following operations:

1. By using $\mathbf{A}_{m-(t-1)}$, construct the matrix $\mathbf{A}^a_{m-t}$, $(\mathbf{A}^x_{m-t})$ as in (7.2.9).
2. Construct the distance matrices $[\rho^a_{m-t}(q, s)]$ and $[\rho^x_{m-t}(q, s)]$ for $\mathbf{A}^a_{m-t}$ and $\mathbf{A}^x_{m-t}$ as in (7.2.10–7.2.12).
3. Employing the Hungarian algorithm, determine minimal symmetric matchings for the matrices $[\rho^a_{m-t}(q, s)]$ and $[\rho^x_{m-t}(q, s)]$.
4. If the sum of elements of the matching for $[\rho^a_{m-t}(q, s)]$ is less or equal (greater) the analogous sum for $[\rho^x_{m-t}(q, s)]$, set $K_{m-t} = K^a_{m-t}$ $(K_{m-t} = K^x_{m-t})$. The construction of K_{m-t} is analogous to (7.2.8).
5. Suppose that the set of variables of the excitation functions determined in the previous $(t-1)$ iterations, that is, in computation of the assignments $K_{m-1}, K_{m-2}, \ldots, K_{m-(t-1)}$,

$$\{z_{T_{m-1}}, z_{T_{m-2}}, \ldots, z_{T_{m-(t-1)}}\},$$

contains the components $a_{\log_2 n_a - 1}, a_{\log_2 n_a - 2}, \ldots, a_{\log_2 n_a - \gamma}$ and $x_{\log_2 n_x - 1}, x_{\log_2 n_x - 2}, \ldots, x_{\log_2 n_x - (t-1-\gamma)}$. Then, assuming that the sum of elements of the matching for $[\rho^a_{m-t}(q, s)]$ is less or equal (greater) than the sum for $[\rho^a_{m-t}(q, s)]$, we set

$$z_{T_{m-t}} = a_{\log_2 n_a - \gamma - 1},$$

and, respectively when greater,

$$z_{T_{m-t}} = x_{\log_2 n_x - (t-1-\gamma)-1} = x_{\log_2 n_x - t + \gamma}.$$

Example 7.2.7 *We now construct the classes $K_{m-3} = K_3, K_2, K_1, K_0$ for the above example, and find the final state-input assignment and order of variables in the excitation functions.*

We have already seen that from the first iteration $K_5 = K^a_5$, $z_{T_5} = a_2$, $L_5 = 7$. The second iteration gave $K_4 = K^x_4$, $z_{T_4} = x_2$, $L_4 \leq 4$.

Third iteration. *In the previous section, it has been determined the matrix $\mathbf{A}_{m-2} = \mathbf{A}_4$. We have $K_4 = K^x_4$ and the minimal symmetric matching for $[\rho^x_4(q, s)]$ is $\{\rho^x_4(0, 5), \rho^x_4(1, 4), \rho^x_4(2, 7), \rho^x_4(3, 6)\}$.*

1. *By using $\mathbf{A}_4$ and the above matching, we construct $\mathbf{A}_3^x$*

$$\mathbf{A}_3^x = \begin{bmatrix} \{a_0, a_0, a_0, a_0\} & \{a_4, a_3, a_4, a_3\} & \{a_0, a_0, a_0, a_0\} & \{a_6, a_6, a_7, a_7\} \\ \{a_1, a_1, a_2, a_2\} & \{a_0, a_0, a_0, a_4\} & \{a_2, a_2, a_2, a_2\} & \{a_3, a_3, a_3, a_3\} \\ \{a_5, a_5, a_5, a_5\} & \{a_1, a_2, a_1, a_2\} & \{a_7, a_7, a_6, a_6\} & \{a_6, a_6, a_6, a_6\} \\ \{a_0, a_0, a_0, a_0\} & \{a_3, a_6, a_3, a_6\} & \{a_0, a_0, a_0, a_0\} & \{a_4, a_4, a_4, a_4\} \end{bmatrix}.$$

2. *The distance matrices $[\rho_3^a(q, s)]$ and $[\rho_3^x(q, s)]$ for $q, s = 0, 1, 2, 3$ are*

$$[\rho_3^a(q, s)] = \begin{bmatrix} 0 & 4 & 4 & 2^* \\ 4 & 0 & 4^* & 4 \\ 4 & 4^* & 0 & 4 \\ 2^* & 4 & 4 & 0 \end{bmatrix},$$

$$[\rho_3^x(q, s)] = \begin{bmatrix} 0 & 4 & 2^* & 4 \\ 4 & 0 & 4 & 4^* \\ 2^* & 4 & 0 & 4 \\ 4 & 4^* & 4 & 0 \end{bmatrix}.$$

3. *Minimal symmetric matchings for $[\rho_3^x(q, s)]$ and $[\rho_3^x(q, s)]$ are, respectively,*

$$\{\rho_3^a(0, 3), \rho_3^a(1, 2)\}$$

and

$$\{\rho_3^x(0, 2), \rho_3^x(1, 3)\},$$

which gives $L_3 \leq 6$.

4. *Since the sum of elements in the matchings are equal, we set, for instance, $K_3 = K_3^a$. Since K_5 is the set of assignments in which states in the same pair $\{a_0, a_3\}$ $\{a_1, a_4\}$, $\{a_2, a_7\}$, $\{a_5, a_6\}$ have codes that differ in the least significant bit, we see that K_3^a is the set of assignments in which the codes of states in the 4-tuples $\{a_0, a_3, a_5, a_6\}$, $\{a_1, a_4, a_2, a_7\}$, differ in the second digit. For example, K_3^a will contain the state assignment in Table 7.2.4.*

5. *Since $K_3 = K_3^a$, $z_{T_5} = a_2$, $z_{T_4} = x_2$, it follows that $z_{T_3} = a_1$.*

Fourth iteration.

TABLE 7.2.4   State Assignment from K_3^a.

q	0	1	2	3	4	5	6	7
$K^a(q)$	0	4	6	1	5	2	3	7

1. The matrix $\mathbf{A}_2^a$ *is*

$$\mathbf{A}_2^a = \begin{bmatrix} k_{00} & k_{01} & k_{02} & k_{03} \\ k_{10} & k_{11} & k_{12} & k_{13} \end{bmatrix},$$

where

$$k_{00} = \{a_0, a_0, a_0, a_0, a_0, a_0, a_0, a_0\},$$
$$k_{01} = \{a_4, a_3, a_4, a_3, a_3, a_6, a_3, a_6\},$$
$$k_{02} = \{a_0, a_0, a_0, a_0, a_0, a_0, a_0, a_0\},$$
$$k_{03} = \{a_6, a_6, a_7, a_7, a_4, a_4, a_4, a_4\},$$
$$k_{10} = \{a_1, a_1, a_2, a_2, a_5, a_5, a_5, a_5\},$$
$$k_{11} = \{a_0, a_0, a_0, a_4, a_3, a_6, a_3, a_6\},$$
$$k_{12} = \{a_2, a_2, a_2, a_2, a_7, a_7, a_6, a_6\},$$
$$k_{13} = \{a_3, a_3, a_3, a_3, a_6, a_6, a_6, a_6\},$$

2. Then,

$$[\rho_2^a(q, s)] = \begin{bmatrix} 0 & 4^* \\ 4^* & 0 \end{bmatrix},$$

$$[\rho_2^x(q, s)] = \begin{bmatrix} 0 & 2 & 1^* & 2 \\ 2 & 0 & 2 & 2^* \\ 1^* & 2 & 0 & 2 \\ 2 & 2^* & 2 & 0 \end{bmatrix}.$$

3. Minimal matching are $\{\rho_2^a(0, 1)\}$ *and* $\{\rho_2^x(0, 2), \rho_2^x(1, 3)\}$.

4. For now we have $K_2 = K_2^x$, *and* $L_2 \leq 3$. *The class* $K_4 = K_4^x$ *is the set of assignments in which the codes of input signals in each of the pairs* $\{x_0, x_5\}$, $\{x_1, x_4\}$, $\{x_2, x_7\}$, $\{x_3, x_6\}$, *differ in the least significant digit, and since the matching on* $\{\rho_2^x(q, s)\}$ *is* $\{\rho_2^x(0, 2), \rho_2^x(1, 3)\}$, *it follows that* K_2^x *is the set of assignments in which the codes on inputs signals in each of the 4-tuples* $\{x_0, x_5, x_2, x_7\}$ *and* $\{x_1, x_4, x_3, x_6\}$ *differ in their second digits. For example,* K_2 *contains the assignment in Table 7.2.5*

5. Since $K_2 = K_2^x$, $z_{T_5} = a_2$, $z_{T_4} = x_2$, $z_{T_3} = a_1$, *we have* $z_{T_2} = x_1$.

Fifth iteration.

TABLE 7.2.5   State Assignment from K_2^x.

q	0	1	2	3	4	5	6	7
$K^x(q)$	0	4	2	6	5	1	7	3

1. The matrix $\mathbf{A}_1^x$ is

$$\mathbf{A}_1^x = \begin{bmatrix} k_{00} & k_{01} \\ k_{10} & k_{11} \end{bmatrix},$$

where

$$k_{00} = \{a_0, a_0, a_0, a_0, a_0, a_0, a_0, a_0, a_0, a_0, a_0, a_0, a_0, a_0, a_0, a_0\},$$

$$k_{01} = \{a_4, a_3, a_4, a_3, a_3, a_6, a_3, a_6, a_6, a_6, a_7, a_7, a_4, a_4, a_4, a_4\},$$

$$k_{10} = \{a_1, a_1, a_2, a_2, a_5, a_5, a_5, a_5, a_2, a_2, a_2, a_2, a_7, a_7, a_6, a_6\},$$

$$k_{11} = \{a_0, a_0, a_0, a_4, a_3, a_6, a_3, a_6, a_3, a_3, a_3, a_3, a_6, a_6, a_6, a_6\},$$

2. The distance matrices are

$$[\rho_1^a(q, s)] = \begin{bmatrix} 0 & 2^* \\ 2^* & 0 \end{bmatrix}$$

and

$$[\rho_1^x(q, s)] = \begin{bmatrix} 0 & 2^* \\ 2^* & 0 \end{bmatrix}.$$

3. Minimal matchings are $\{\rho_1^a(0, 1)\}$ and $\{\rho_1^x(0, 1)\}$.

4. We set $K_1 = K_1^x$, and $L_1 \leq 2$. For example, K_1^x contains the input assignments shown in Table 7.2.6.

5. We have $z_{T_1} = x_0$.

Sixth iteration.

TABLE 7.2.6   Input Assignment from K_1^x.

q	0	1	2	3	4	5	6	7
$K^x(q)$	0	4	2	6	5	1	7	3

TABLE 7.2.7   Final State Assignment.

q	0	1	2	3	4	5	6	7
$K^x(q)$	0	4	2	6	5	1	7	3
$K^a(q)$	0	4	6	1	5	2	3	7

1. *The matrix* $\mathbf{A}_0^x$ *is*

$$\mathbf{A}_0^x = \begin{bmatrix} k_0 \\ k_1 \end{bmatrix},$$

where

$$k_0 = \{a_0, a_0, a_0, a_0, a_0, a_0, a_0, a_0, a_0, a_0, a_0, a_0, a_0, a_0, a_0, a_0,$$
$$a_4, a_3, a_4, a_3, a_3, a_6, a_3, a_6, a_6, a_6, a_7, a_7, a_4, a_4, a_4, a_4\}$$
$$k_1 = \{a_1, a_1, a_2, a_2, a_5, a_5, a_5, a_5, a_2, a_2, a_2, a_2, a_7, a_7, a_6, a_6,$$
$$a_0, a_0, a_0, a_4, a_3, a_6, a_3, a_6, a_3, a_3, a_3, a_3, a_6, a_6, a_6, a_6\}$$

2. *The distance matrix is*

$$[\rho_0^a(q, s)] = \begin{bmatrix} 0 & 1^* \\ 1^* & 0 \end{bmatrix}.$$

3. *Minimal matching is* $\{\rho_0^a(0, 1)\}$.
4. *We have* $K_0 = K_0^a$ *and* $L_0 \leq L_0^a + 1 = 2$.
5. *Therefore,* $z_{T_0} = a_0$.

To summarize, the final state-input assignment is shown in Table 7.2.7. The order of variables for the excitation functions is $z = (a_0, x_0, x_1, a_1, x_2, a_2)$, defined by the permutation $T = (3, 0, 1, 4, 2, 5)$.

The complexity bounds L (giving the number of nonzero coefficients in the initial and optimal assignments) are shown in Table 7.2.8.

It is evident that optimal choice of the state-input assignment and optimal ordering of variables in the excitation functions have reduced the complexity of the automaton to about 2/5 of its original value.

TABLE 7.2.8   Spectral Complexities for the Initial and Optimal Assignments.

l		0	1	2	3	4	5
L_l	Initial assignment	2	2	4	4	14	30
	Optimal assignment	2	2	3	5	4	7

The above method may be generalized for implementation of automata based on multistable elements by using expansions of the excitation functions in series of generalized Haar functions (see Section 2.5). In addition, if the numbers of states and input signals are not powers of 2, the automaton in question may be treated as an incompletely specified automaton with $2^{\lceil \log_2 n_a \rceil}$ states and $2^{\lceil \log_2 n_x \rceil}$ input signals. The assignment problem for incompletely specified automata will be considered in the next section.

To conclude this section, we note that in order to establish sharper bounds for the expected values of $L_{m-2}, L_{m-3}, \ldots, L_0$ during the implementation of the algorithm, should proceed as follows.

To define distances between the rows (columns) of the appropriate matrices $\mathbf{A}_{m-2}, \mathbf{A}_{m-3}, \ldots, \mathbf{A}_0$, put the distance $\rho(c_{\alpha,\beta}, c_{\gamma,\delta})$ between elements $c_{\alpha,\beta}$ and $c_{\gamma,\delta}$ of the matrix $\mathbf{A}_{m-t}$ ($t = 2, 3, \ldots, m$) (recall that each element of $\mathbf{A}_{m-t}$ is a set of 2^{t-1} elements) equal to

$$\rho(c_{\alpha,\beta}, c_{\gamma,\delta}) = P\left(\sum_{a_q \in c_{\alpha,\beta}} K^a(q) \neq \sum_{a_q \in c_{\gamma,\delta}} K^a(q) \right), \qquad (7.2.21)$$

The right-hand side of this expression is the fraction of assignments $K^a(q)$ for which the sum of numbers corresponding to codes of states in $c_{\alpha,\beta}$ is not equal to the analogous sum for $c_{\gamma,\delta}$. It can be shown that

$$\lim_{\log_2 n_a \to \infty} P\left(\sum_{a_q \in c_{\alpha,\beta}} K^a(q) \neq \sum_{a_q \in c_{\gamma,\delta}} K^a(q) \right) \qquad (7.2.22)$$

$$= \begin{cases} 1, & \text{if } c_{\alpha,\beta} \neq c_{\gamma,\delta}, \\ 0, & \text{if } c_{\alpha,\beta} = c_{\gamma,\delta}, \end{cases}$$

The quantity on the left side of (7.2.22) tends to unity ($c_{\alpha,\beta} \neq c_{\gamma,\delta}$) as $\log_2 n_a \to \infty$, and does so very fast. Thus, for as low a value as $\log_2 n_a = 4$ the deviation from one is at most 0.1. This justifies the use of a formula of type (7.2.12) in the definition of $\rho(c_{\alpha,\beta}, c_{\gamma,\delta})$, instead of the more accurate (7.2.21).

7.3 STATE ASSIGNMENT FOR INCOMPLETELY SPECIFIED AUTOMATA

7.3.1 Minimization of Higher Order Nonzero Coefficients in Representation of Incompletely Specified Automata

The state-input assignment problem for incompletely specified finite automata is even more complicated than for completely specified. Besides the difficulties outlined in

Section 7.2, we are faced here with the complex problem of optimal completion of the state table. At present, there seem to be no really effective assignment procedures for optimal design of incompletely specified finite automata, as far as the classical approach is concerned.

When spectral methods are employed, however, one can construct a fairly simple and effective completion and assignment algorithm, producing optimal results for almost all incompletely specified automata. The method of completion, as we shall see, is analogous to the completion of incompletely specified logical functions in the framework of spectral methods (see Section 6.2). As before, we shall adopt the Haar functions as our basis system, measuring the complexity of implementation in terms of the number L of nonzero expansion coefficients.

The following example illustrates construction of assignments for incompletely specified automata. We first construct K_{m-1}.

Example 7.3.1 *Consider an incompletely specified automaton with the state matrix* $\tilde{\mathbf{A}}_{m-1} = [\tilde{a}_{q,r}], (q = 0, 1, \ldots, n_a - 1, r = 0, 1, \ldots, n_x - 1)$. *By using the matrix* $\tilde{\mathbf{A}}_{m-1}$ *of the original automaton, we construct an equivalent[3] automaton with the state matrix* $\mathbf{A}_{m-1} = [a_{q,r}] (q = 0, 1, \ldots, 2^{\lceil \log_2 n_a \rceil} - 1, r = 0, 1, \ldots, 2^{\lceil \log_2 n_x \rceil} - 1)$, *where*

$$
a_{q,r} = \begin{cases} \tilde{a}_{q,r}, & \text{if } 0 \leq q \leq n_a - 1 \text{ and } 0 \leq r \leq n_x - 1, \\ -, & \text{otherwise}. \end{cases} \tag{7.3.1}
$$

In this relation, the symbol $-$ *stands for undefined elements of the state matrix* $\mathbf{A}_{m-1}$.
Let

$$
\tilde{\mathbf{A}}_{m-1} = \tilde{A}_5 = \begin{bmatrix} a_0 & - & a_3 & a_6 & a_4 & - & a_7 \\ a_1 & a_0 & a_2 & a_3 & a_0 & a_2 & - \\ - & a_1 & a_7 & - & a_1 & a_5 & a_6 \\ a_0 & - & a_0 & a_6 & a_3 & - & a_7 \\ a_1 & a_0 & a_2 & a_3 & a_4 & - & - \\ a_0 & a_3 & - & a_4 & a_3 & a_0 & - \end{bmatrix},
$$

where $n_a = 6$ *and* $n_x = 7$.

---

[3]Two automata A and A' are *equivalent* as they define the same mapping of the set of input words, that is, strings of input signals, into the set of output words, which means, strings of output signals.

Then,

$$
\mathbf{A}_{m-1} = \mathbf{A}_5 =
\begin{bmatrix}
a_0 & - & a_3 & a_6 & a_4 & - & a_7 & - \\
a_1 & a_0 & a_2 & a_3 & a_0 & a_2 & - & - \\
- & a_1 & a_7 & - & a_1 & a_5 & a_6 & - \\
a_0 & - & a_0 & a_6 & a_3 & - & a_7 & - \\
a_1 & a_0 & a_2 & a_3 & a_4 & - & - & - \\
a_0 & a_3 & - & a_4 & a_3 & a_0 & - & - \\
- & - & - & - & - & - & - & - \\
- & - & - & - & - & - & - & -
\end{bmatrix}.
$$

We now apply to $\mathbf{A}_{m-1}$ the method in Section 7.2 for the optimal assignment and optimization of the order T of variables in the excitation functions. As before, we minimize the numbers $L_{m-1}, L_{m-2}, \ldots, L_0$, consecutively, Now, however, we simultaneously construct a completion of $\mathbf{A}_{m-1}$, which is optimal for almost all automata.

The first iteration of the algorithm constructs matrices $[\rho^a_{m-1}(q, s)]$ and $[\rho^x_{m-1}(q, s)]$ for $\mathbf{A}_{m-1}$ by (7.2.3) and (7.2.4). Formula (7.2.5) is now replaced by

$$
\rho(a_{\alpha,\beta}, a_{\gamma,\rho}) =
\begin{cases}
1, & \text{if } a_{\alpha,\beta} \neq a_{\gamma,\delta} \text{ provided } a_{\alpha,\beta}, a_{\gamma,\delta} \text{ are defined,} \\
0, & \text{otherwise.}
\end{cases}
\tag{7.3.2}
$$

Example 7.3.2   *In Example 7.3.1,*

$$
[\rho^a_5(q, s)] =
\begin{bmatrix}
0 & 4 & 3 & 2 & 3 & 2 & 0^* & 0 \\
4 & 0 & 3 & 4 & 1^* & 5 & 0 & 0 \\
3 & 3 & 0 & 3 & 3 & 3 & 0 & 0^* \\
2 & 4 & 3 & 0 & 4 & 1^* & 0 & 0 \\
3 & 1^* & 3 & 4 & 0 & 4 & 0 & 0 \\
2 & 5 & 3 & 1^* & 4 & 0 & 0 & 0 \\
0^* & 0 & 0 & 0 & 0 & 0 & 0 & 0 \\
0 & 0 & 0^* & 0 & 0 & 0 & 0 & 0
\end{bmatrix}
$$

and

$$[\rho_5^x(q, s)] = \begin{bmatrix} 0 & 3 & 3 & 4 & 5 & 1^* & 2 & 0 \\ 3 & 0 & 3 & 3 & 1^* & 3 & 1 & 0 \\ 3 & 3 & 0 & 4 & 5 & 1 & 3 & 0^* \\ 4 & 3 & 4 & 0 & 5 & 2 & 2^* & 0 \\ 5 & 1^* & 5 & 5 & 0 & 3 & 3 & 0 \\ 1^* & 3 & 1 & 2 & 3 & 0 & 1 & 0 \\ 2 & 1 & 3 & 2^* & 3 & 1 & 0 & 0 \\ 0 & 0 & 0^* & 0 & 0 & 0 & 0 & 0 \end{bmatrix}.$$

We now find minimal symmetric matchings for $[\rho_{m-1}^a(q, s)]$ and $[\rho_{m-1}^x(q, s)]$. In the example, these are

$$\{\rho_5^a(0, 6), \rho_5^a(1, 4), \rho_5^a(2, 7), \rho_5^a(3, 5)\}$$

and

$$\{\rho_5^x(0, 5), \rho_5^x(1, 4), \rho_5^x(2, 7), \rho_5^x(3, 6)\}.$$

The matchings on $[\rho_{m-1}^a(q, s)]$ and $[\rho_{m-1}^x(q, s)]$ define partitions of the sets of states and input signals (and also the sets of rows and columns of the matrices $[\rho_{m-1}^a(q, s)]$ and $[\rho_{m-1}^x(q, s)]$) into disjoint pairs. In this example, these partitions are

$$\{\{a_0, a_6\}, \{a_1, a_4\}, \{a_2, a_7\}, \{a_3, a_5\}\}$$

and

$$\{\{x_0, x_5\}, \{x_1, x_4\}, \{x_2, x_7\}, \{x_3, x_6\}\}.$$

As in the completely specified case, the sum of elements of the matching on $[\rho_{m-1}^a(q, s)]$ or $[\rho_{m-1}^x(q, s)]$ determines L_{m-1}, if the binary codes of states or inputs in each pair differ in the last significant digit. We thus choose a minimal matching.

Example 7.3.3 *For the Example 7.3.1, the minimal matching is defined for $[\rho_{m-1}^a(q, s)] = [\rho_5^a(q, s)]$, and so*

$$L_5 = L_5^a = \rho_5^a(0, 6) + \rho_5^a(1, 4) + \rho_5^a(2, 7) + \rho_5^a(3, 5) = 2.$$

Since $L_5 = L_5^a$, it follows that

$$z_{T_{m-1}} = z_{T_5} = a_{\lceil \log_2 n_a \rceil - 1} = a_2.$$

For a given minimal matching, we construct a class of completions minimizing L_{m-1}.

It follows from (7.3.2) that

$$\rho(a_{\alpha,\beta}, -) = 0, \tag{7.3.3}$$

for any $a_{\alpha,\beta}$.

Therefore, we complete $\mathbf{A}_{m-1}$ to $\mathbf{A}'_{m-1} = [a'_{p,r}]$ as follows. If $L_{m-1} = L^a_{m-1}$ ($L_{m-1} = L^x_{m-1}$) and $\{\{i_0, i_1\}, \ldots, \{i_{n-2}, i_{n-1}\}\}$ is the partition of rows (columns) into pairs corresponding to the selected matching, we set $a'_{i_{2q},r} = a'_{i_{2q+1},r}$ if $a_{i_{2q}} = -$ or $a_{i_{2q+1},r} = -$, $(a'_{r,i_{2q}} = a'_{r,i_{2q+1}}$ if $a_{r,i_{2q}} = -$ or $a_{r,i_{2q+1}} = -)$.

The matrix $\mathbf{A}_{m-1}$ defines a class of completions minimizing L_{m-1}.

Example 7.3.4 *For the Example 7.3.1, we have $L_5 = L^a_5$ and*

$$
\mathbf{A}'_5 =
\begin{bmatrix}
a_0 & -1 & a_3 & a_6 & a_4 & -2 & a_7 & -3 \\
a_1 & a_0 & a_2 & a_3 & a_0 & a_2 & -4 & -5 \\
-6 & a_1 & a_7 & -7 & a_1 & a_5 & a_6 & -8 \\
a_0 & \mathbf{a_3} & a_0 & a_6 & a_3 & \mathbf{a_0} & a_7 & -9 \\
a_1 & a_0 & a_2 & a_3 & a_4 & \mathbf{a_2} & -4 & -5 \\
a_0 & a_3 & \mathbf{a_0} & a_4 & a_3 & a_0 & \mathbf{a_7} & -9 \\
\mathbf{a_0} & -1 & \mathbf{a_3} & a_6 & \mathbf{a_4} & -2 & \mathbf{a_7} & -3 \\
-6 & \mathbf{a_1} & \mathbf{a_7} & -7 & \mathbf{a_1} & \mathbf{a_5} & \mathbf{a_6} & -8
\end{bmatrix},
$$

where $-_i$ are undefined values (generally distinct)[4] and the completed elements of $\mathbf{A}'_5$ are indicated by the bold type.

Note that in this method the fictitious states (input signals) introduced in order to bring the number of states (input signals) up to $2^{\lceil \log_2 n_a \rceil}$ $(2^{\lceil \log_2 n_x \rceil})$ are equivalent[5] to the states (input signals) paired with them in the selected partition.

Example 7.3.5 *The fictitious states a_6 and a_7 in the above example are equivalent to a_0 and a_2, respectively. Thus, the first iteration of the algorithm produces a class of assignments K_{m-1} and completions minimizing L_{m-1}.*

---

[4] In other words, in any completion the matrix entries $-_i$, may be replaced by arbitrary states, with the restriction that bars with equal subscripts i must be replaced by the same state.

[5] States a_p and a_q of an automaton A are equivalent if $\phi(x, a_p) = \phi(x, a_q)$ for any input x, where ϕ is the next-state function of A.

7.3.2 Minimization of Lower Order Nonzero Coefficients in Spectral Representation of Incompletely Specified Automata

The second iteration constructs a class of assignments and completions minimizing L_{m-2}. First, by using the matrix A'_{m-1} and the optimal matching, we construct a matrix $\mathbf{A}^a_{m-2}$ or $\mathbf{A}^x_{m-2}$ as in (7.2.9).

Example 7.3.6   *For the Example 7.3.1, we have,*

$$\mathbf{A}_{m-2} = \mathbf{A}_4 = \mathbf{A}^a_4,$$

where $\mathbf{A}_4$ is the matrix

$$\begin{bmatrix} \{a_0, a_0\}, \{-1, -1\}, \{a_3, a_3\}, \{a_6, a_6\}, \{a_4, a_4\}, \{-2, -2\}, \{a_7, a_7\}, \{-3, -3\} \\ \{a_1, a_1\}, \{a_0, a_0\}, \{a_2, a_2\}, \{a_3, a_3\}, \{a_0, a_4\}, \{a_2, a_2\}, \{-4, -4\}, \{-5, -5\} \\ \{-6, -6\}, \{a_1, a_1\}, \{a_7, a_7\}, \{-7, -7\}, \{a_1, a_1\}, \{a_5, a_5\}, \{a_6, a_6\}, \{-8, -8\} \\ \{a_0, a_0\}, \{a_3, a_3\}, \{a_0, a_0\}, \{a_6, a_4\}, \{a_3, a_3\}, \{a_0, a_0\}, \{a_7, a_7\}, \{-9, -9\} \end{bmatrix}.$$

The next step is to construct the distance matrices $[\rho^a_{m-2}(q, s)]$ and $[\rho^x_{m-2}(q, s)]$ for $\mathbf{A}_{m-2}$, by using formulas (7.2.10–7.2.12), the latter formula being modified in the same way as (7.3.2)

$$\rho(b_{\alpha,\beta}, b_{\gamma,\delta}) = \begin{cases} 1, & \text{if } b_{\alpha,\beta} \neq b_{\gamma,\delta} \text{ provided } b_{\alpha,\beta} \text{ and } b_{\gamma,\delta} \text{ are defined,} \\ 0, & \text{otherwise,} \end{cases} \quad (7.3.4)$$

where $b_{\alpha,\beta}, b_{\gamma,\delta}$ are elements of $\mathbf{A}_{m-2}$.

Example 7.3.7   *In the example, $\mathbf{A}_{m-2} = \mathbf{A}^a_4$ and the distance matrices are*

$$[\rho^a_4(q, s)] = \begin{bmatrix} 0 & 4 & 3 & 3^* \\ 4 & 0 & 4^* & 6 \\ 3 & 4^* & 0 & 5 \\ 3^* & 6 & 5 & 0 \end{bmatrix},$$

$$
[\rho_4^x(q,s)] = \begin{bmatrix}
0 & 2 & 2 & 3 & 3 & 1^* & 2 & 0 \\
2 & 0 & 3 & 2 & 1^* & 3 & 2 & 0 \\
2 & 3 & 0 & 3 & 4 & 1 & 3 & 0^* \\
3 & 2 & 3 & 0 & 3 & 2 & 2^* & 0 \\
3 & 1^* & 4 & 3 & 0 & 3 & 3 & 0 \\
1^* & 3 & 1 & 2 & 3 & 0 & 2 & 0 \\
2 & 2 & 3 & 2^* & 3 & 2 & 0 & 0 \\
0 & 0 & 0^* & 0 & 0 & 0 & 0 & 0
\end{bmatrix}.
$$

The minimal matchings are indicated by *, *and* $L_4 \le L_4^x = 4$, $z_{T_4} = x_2$.

We now construct a class of completions minimizing L_{m-2}. The construction of a completion $\mathbf{A}'_{m-2} = [b'_{p,q}]$ of $\mathbf{A}_{m-2} = [b_{p,q}]$, using the optimal partition of the set of rows (columns) of $\mathbf{A}_{m-2}$ into pairs, is analogous to the construction of $\mathbf{A}'_{m-1}$, in the first iteration.

Example 7.3.8   *For Example 7.3.1,* $L_4 \le L_4^x$, *the partition of columns is determined as* $\{\{0, 5\}, \{1, 4\}, \{2, 7\}, \{3, 6\}\}$, *and*

$$
\mathbf{A}'_{m-2} = \mathbf{A}'_4 =
$$

$$
\begin{bmatrix}
\{a_0, a_0\}, \{a_4, a_4\}, \{a_3, a_3\}, \{a_6, a_6\}, \{a_4, a_4\}, \{a_0, a_0\}, \{a_7, a_7\}, \{a_3, a_3\} \\
\{a_1, a_1\}, \{a_0, a_0\}, \{a_2, a_2\}, \{a_3, a_3\}, \{a_0, a_4\}, \{a_2, a_2\}, \{a_3, a_3\}, \{a_2, a_2\} \\
\{a_5, a_5\}, \{a_1, a_1\}, \{a_7, a_7\}, \{a_6, a_6\}, \{a_1, a_1\}, \{a_5, a_5\}, \{a_6, a_6\}, \{a_7, a_7\} \\
\{a_0, a_0\}, \{a_3, a_3\}, \{a_0, a_0\}, \{a_6, a_4\}, \{a_3, a_3\}, \{a_0, a_0\}, \{a_7, a_7\}, \{a_0, a_0\}
\end{bmatrix}.
$$

For this example, then, all undefined states become defined in the second iteration of the algorithm. The final, completely specified state matrix is

$$
\mathbf{A}'_5 = \begin{bmatrix}
a_0 & \mathbf{a_4} & a_3 & a_6 & a_4 & \mathbf{a_0} & a_7 & \mathbf{a_3} \\
a_1 & a_0 & a_2 & a_3 & a_0 & a_2 & \mathbf{a_3} & \mathbf{a_2} \\
\mathbf{a_5} & a_1 & a_7 & \mathbf{a_6} & a_1 & a_5 & a_6 & \mathbf{a_7} \\
a_0 & a_3 & a_0 & a_6 & a_3 & a_0 & a_7 & \mathbf{a_0} \\
a_1 & a_0 & a_2 & a_3 & a_4 & a_2 & \mathbf{a_3} & \mathbf{a_2} \\
a_0 & a_3 & \mathbf{a_0} & a_4 & a_3 & a_0 & \mathbf{a_7} & \mathbf{a_0} \\
a_0 & \mathbf{a_4} & a_3 & a_6 & a_4 & \mathbf{a_0} & a_7 & \mathbf{a_3} \\
\mathbf{a_5} & a_1 & a_7 & \mathbf{a_6} & a_1 & a_5 & a_6 & \mathbf{a_7}
\end{bmatrix}.
$$

The elements defined in the second iteration are in bold.

The procedure for assignments minimizing $L_{m-3}, L_{m-4}, \ldots, L_0$ is analogous. We illustrate using the same example as before.

Example 7.3.9 Third iteration.

$$A_3 = A_3^x = \begin{bmatrix} \{a_0, a_0, a_0, a_0\} & \{a_4, a_4, a_4, a_4\} & \{a_3, a_3, a_3, a_3\} & \{a_6, a_6, a_7, a_7\} \\ \{a_1, a_1, a_1, a_1\} & \{a_0, a_0, a_0, a_4\} & \{a_2, a_2, a_2, a_2\} & \{a_3, a_3, a_3, a_3\} \\ \{a_5, a_5, a_5, a_5\} & \{a_1, a_1, a_1, a_1\} & \{a_7, a_7, a_7, a_7\} & \{a_6, a_6, a_6, a_6\} \\ \{a_0, a_0, a_0, a_0\} & \{a_3, a_3, a_3, a_3\} & \{a_0, a_0, a_0, a_0\} & \{a_6, a_4, a_7, a_7\} \end{bmatrix},$$

$$[\rho_3^a(q, s)] = \begin{bmatrix} 0 & 4 & 4 & 3^* \\ 4 & 0 & 4^* & 4 \\ 4 & 4^* & 0 & 4 \\ 3^* & 4 & 4 & 0 \end{bmatrix},$$

$$[\rho_3^x(q, s)] = \begin{bmatrix} 0 & 4 & 3^* & 4 \\ 4 & 0 & 4 & 4^* \\ 3^* & 4 & 0 & 4 \\ 4 & 4^* & 4 & 0 \end{bmatrix}.$$

Therefore, $L_3 \leq L_3^x = 7$ and $z_{T_3} = x_1$.

Fourth iteration.

$$A_2 = A_2^x = \begin{bmatrix} \{a_0, a_0, a_0, a_0, a_3, a_3, a_3, a_3\} & \{a_4, a_4, a_4, a_4, a_6, a_6, a_7, a_7\} \\ \{a_1, a_1, a_2, a_2, a_2, a_2, a_2, a_2\} & \{a_0, a_0, a_0, a_4, a_3, a_3, a_3, a_3\} \\ \{a_5, a_5, a_5, a_5, a_7, a_7, a_7, a_7\} & \{a_1, a_1, a_1, a_1, a_6, a_6, a_6, a_6\} \\ \{a_0, a_0, a_0, a_0, a_0, a_0, a_0, a_0\} & \{a_3, a_3, a_3, a_3, a_6, a_4, a_7, a_7\} \end{bmatrix},$$

$$[\rho_2^a(q, s)] = \begin{bmatrix} 0 & 2 & 2 & 2^* \\ 2 & 0 & 2^* & 2 \\ 2 & 2^* & 0 & 2 \\ 2^* & 2 & 2 & 0 \end{bmatrix},$$

$$[\rho_2^x(q, s)] = \begin{bmatrix} 0 & 4^* \\ 4^* & 0 \end{bmatrix},$$

and $L_2 \leq L_2^a = 4$, $z_{T_2} = a_1$.

Fifth iteration.

The matrix $\mathbf{A}_1 = \mathbf{A}_1^a$ *is*

$$\mathbf{A}_1^a = \begin{bmatrix} k_{00} & k_{01} \\ k_{10} & k_{11} \end{bmatrix},$$

where

$$k_{00} = \{a_0, a_0, a_0, a_0, a_3, a_3, a_3, a_3, a_0, a_0, a_0, a_0, a_0, a_0, a_0, a_0\},$$
$$k_{01} = \{a_4, a_4, a_4, a_4, a_6, a_6, a_7, a_7, a_3, a_3, a_3, a_3, a_6, a_4, a_7, a_7\},$$
$$k_{10} = \{a_1, a_1, a_2, a_2, a_2, a_2, a_2, a_2, a_5, a_5, a_5, a_5, a_7, a_7, a_7, a_7\},$$
$$k_{11} = \{a_0, a_0, a_0, a_4, a_3, a_3, a_3, a_3, a_1, a_1, a_1, a_1, a_6, a_6, a_6, a_6\}.$$

The distance matrices are

$$[\rho_1^1(q, s)] = \begin{bmatrix} 0 & 2^* \\ 2^* & 0 \end{bmatrix},$$

$$[\rho_1^x(q, s)] = \begin{bmatrix} 0 & 2^* \\ 2^* & 0 \end{bmatrix},$$

and $L_1 \leq L_1^a = 2$, $z_{T_1} = a_0$.

Sixth iteration.

The matrix $\mathbf{A}_0$ *is*

$$\mathbf{A}_0^a = \begin{bmatrix} k_0 & k_1 \end{bmatrix},$$

where

$$k_0 = \{a_0, a_0, a_0, a_0, a_3, a_3, a_3, a_3, a_0, a_0, a_0, a_0, a_0, a_0, a_0, a_0$$
$$a_1, a_1, a_2, a_2, a_2, a_2, a_2, a_2, a_5, a_5, a_5, a_5, a_7, a_7, a_7, a_7\},$$
$$k_1 = \{a_4, a_4, a_4, a_4, a_6, a_6, a_7, a_7, a_3, a_3, a_3, a_3, a_6, a_4, a_7, a_7$$
$$a_0, a_0, a_0, a_4, a_3, a_3, a_3, a_3, a_1, a_1, a_1, a_1, a_6, a_6, a_6, a_6\}.$$

TABLE 7.3.1 Assignments of States and Inputs for the Automaton in Example 7.1.4.

q	0	1	2	3	4	5	6	7
$K^a(q)$	0	4	6	2	5	3	1	7
$K^x(q)$	0	4	2	6	5	1	7	3

The distance matrix is

$$[\rho_0^x(q, s)] = \begin{bmatrix} 0 & 1^* \\ 1^* & 0 \end{bmatrix}$$

and $L_0 \leq L_0^x + 1 = 2$, $z_{T_0} = x_0$.

In our example, therefore, the argument vector of the excitation functions is $z = (x_0, a_0, a_1, x_1, x_2, a_2)$. *Tables 7.3.1 and 7.3.2 provide the assignments and complexity bounds.*

The above method of completion and assignment for incompletely specified finite automata, like its counterpart (Section 7.2) for completely specified finite automata, is asymptotically optimal for almost all automata. Indeed, even for comparatively low values of $n = \log_2 n_a$ the probability p that the completion and assignment will be optimal is close to one (thus, if $n = 4$ we have $p > 0.9$).

7.4 SOME SPECIAL CASES OF THE ASSIGNMENT PROBLEM

7.4.1 Preliminary Remarks

The solutions of the assignment problem presented in Section 7.2 and 7.3 can be applied to any automaton. In this section, we discuss a few important special classes of automata whose specific features yield simplifications of the general algorithms. The special classes considered in this section are autonomous automata and automata for which a fixed state (or input) assignment is given in advance. All the notation used in Sections 7.2 and 7.3 will be retained.

7.4.2 Autonomous Automata

The next state of an *autonomous automaton* is determined by the previous state, and its state matrix $\mathbf{A}_{m-1} = [a_{q,r}]$ reduces to a single column $[a_q, 1]$. The algorithms in Sections 7.2 and 7.3 are substantially simplified when applied to autonomous automata. First and foremost, there is no need to construct the function $K^x(q)$, the matrices $\mathbf{A}_{m-t}^x$, or $[\rho_{m-t}^x(q, s)]$, $(t = 1, \ldots, m)$. Further, $z_{m-i} = a_{m-i}$. Moreover, for

TABLE 7.3.2 Complexity of the Implementations.

l	0	1	2	3	4	5
L_t	2	2	4	7	4	2

any t we have $\rho_{m-1}^a(q, s) \in \{0, 1\}$ for any q, s, and all the matrices $\mathbf{A}_{m-t}^a$ are single columns.

We now establish a bound on the number of nonzero expansion coefficients for autonomous automata.

Let $\phi^{-1}(a_i)$, $(i = 0, 1, \ldots, n_a - 1)$, denote the set of states such that if $a_j \in \phi^{-1}(a_i)$, then $\phi(a_j) = a_i$, where ϕ is the next-state function of the automaton. In other words, $a_{j,1} = a_i$ in the matrix $\mathbf{A}_{m-1} = [a_{q,1}]$. Let $|\phi^{-1}(a_i)|$ denote the number of elements in $\phi^{-1}(a_i)$.

Theorem 7.4.1 *Consider an autonomous automaton with n_a states whose next-state function is undefined at n_- points. Then*

$$L = \sum_{t=1}^{m} L_{m-t} \le n_a - n_- - \sum_{t=1}^{\lceil \log_2 n_a \rceil} \sum_{i=0}^{n_a-1} \lfloor 2^{-t}|\phi^{-1}(a_i)|\rfloor, \qquad (7.4.1)$$

$$m = \lceil \log_2 n_a \rceil,$$

Proof. Notice that if $\sum_{i=0}^{n_a-1} \lfloor 2^{-t}|\phi^{-1}(a_i)|\rfloor = t$, then the matrix $[\rho_{m-t}^a(q, s)]$ contains t elements $\rho_{m-1}^a(q_i, s_i)$ $(i = 1, 2, \ldots, t)$ above the principal diagonal such that $\rho_{m-t}^a(q_i, s_i) = 0$, $q_i \neq q_j$, $s_i \neq s_j$, $(i \neq j, i, j = 1, 2, \ldots, t)$. Consequently, the elements (q_i, s_i) $(i = 1, \ldots, \delta)$ must be in minimal symmetric matrix for $[\rho_{m-t}^a](q, s)]$, (since $\rho_{m-t}^a(q, s) \in \{0, 1\}$ for any $q, s \in \{0, 1, \ldots, n_a - 1\}$), and the number of coefficients $c_{m-t}^{(l)}$, $(l = 1, 2, \ldots, 2^{m-t})$ equal to zero is at least t. Hence, summing over t and using the fact that the next-state function is defined at $n_a - n_-$, points and Theorem 6.2.1, we obtain (7.4.1).

Example 7.4.1 *Consider an autonomous automaton with the state matrix*

$$\mathbf{A}_{m-1} = [a_0, a_1, a_1, a_2, -, a_1, a_2, -, a_1]^T,$$

where $-$ stands for undefined value of the next-state function ϕ. We have $n_a = 9$, $n_- = 2$, $\phi^{-1}(a_0) = a_0$, $\phi^{-1}(a_1) = \{a_1, a_2, a_5, a_8\}$, $\phi^{-1}(a_2) = \{a_3, a_6\}$, $\phi^{-1}(a_3) = \phi^{-1}(a_4) = \phi^{-1}(a_5) = \phi^{-1}(a_6) = \phi^{-1}(a_7) = \phi^{-1}(a_8) = \emptyset$, where $\emptyset$ is the symbol for the empty set. Then,

$$\sum_{i=0}^{8} \left\lfloor \frac{1}{2}|\phi^{-1}(a_i)| \right\rfloor = 3,$$

$$\sum_{i=0}^{8} \left\lfloor \frac{1}{4}|\phi^{-1}(a_i)| \right\rfloor = 1,$$

$$\sum_{i=0}^{8} \left\lfloor 2^{-t}|\phi^{-1}(a_i)| \right\rfloor = 0,$$

for $t > 2$. Thus, by Theorem 7.4.1, we have $L \le 3$.

Therefore, Theorem 7.4.1 yields a bound on the spectral complexity of autonomous automata, directly in terms of the next-state function and there is no need to construct the matrices $[\rho^a_{m-t}(q, s)]$ to estimate the spectral complexity.

The state assignment problem for autonomous automata is reduced to determination of minimal symmetric matchings for the matrices $[\rho^a_{m-t}(q, s)]$. The construction of these matrices is analogous to that described in Sections 7.2 and 7.3, facilitated by the fact that here all the elements are zeros and ones. The problem of a minimal symmetric matching for a matrix of zeros and ones is known as the *matching problem*. Efficient algorithms for its solution, based on a modification of the Hungarian algorithm, may be found, for example, in References 136, 137, and 250.

7.4.3 Assignment Problem for Automata with Fixed Encoding of Inputs or Internal States

We now consider the assignment problem for automata whose input signals or internal states have preassigned codes that are fixed before the synthesis.

Assume that an assignment $K^x(q)$ of input signals ($K^a(q)$ of states) is fixed. The problem is to determine the order of variables in the excitation functions and a state assignment $K^a(q)$ (the input assignment $K^x(q)$). The algorithm is again a simplified version of the general procedure.

If $K^x(q)$ is fixed, we set

$$K^x(q) = K^x_{m-1}(q) = \sum_{i=0}^{\lceil \log_2 n_x \rceil - 1} x_{q,i} 2^{\lceil \log_2 n_x \rceil - i - 1}, \qquad (7.4.2)$$

$$K^x_{m-s}(q) = \sum_{i=0}^{\lceil \log_2 n_x \rceil - s - i - 1} x_{q,i} 2^{\lceil \log_2 n_x \rceil - s - i - 1}. \qquad (7.4.3)$$

If the state assignment $K^a(q)$ is fixed, we construct similar functions $K^a_{m-s}(q)$. The inverse functions to $K^x_{m-s}(q)$ and $K^a_{m-s}(q)$ will be denoted by $(K^x_{m-s})^{-1}(q)$ and $(K^a_{m-s})^{-1}(q)$, respectively.

Now suppose that the tth iteration has produced a $(2^{\lceil \log_2 n_x \rceil - g} \times 2^{\lceil \log_2 n_a \rceil - d})$ matrix $\mathbf{A}_{m-t}$, where $g + d = t - 1$, $m = \lceil \log_2 n_a \rceil + \lceil \log_2 n_x \rceil$.

Then, if the assignment $K^x(q)$ (or $K^a(q)$) is fixed, we define a minimal symmetric matching for $[\rho^a_{m-t}(q, s)]$ (or $[\rho^x_{m-t}(q, s)]$) to be

$$\{\rho^x_{m-t}((K^x_{m-1-d})^{-1}(2q - 2), (K^x_{m-1-d})^{-1}(2q - 1))\}, \quad q = 1, \ldots, 2^{\lceil \log_2 n_x \rceil - d - 1},$$

and similar,

$$\{\rho^a_{m-t}((K^a_{m-1-g})^{-1}(2q - 2), (K^a_{m-1-g})^{-1}(2q - 1))\}, \quad q = 1, \ldots, 2^{\lceil \log_2 n_a \rceil - g - 1}.$$

Thus, in this type of automaton there is no need to construct the matrices $[\rho^a_{m-t}(q, s)]$, $([\rho^x_{m-t}q, s)])$ for all $t = 1, 2, \ldots, m$ or to search for minimal symmetric matchings on these matrices.

Remark 7.4.1   *In many cases it is convenient to change the notation for the input signals (states) of the original automaton before actually beginning the assignment procedure, in such a way that the fixed assignment has the form $K^x(q) = q$ (or $K^a(q) = q$). This merely involves a suitable permutation of the columns (rows) of the state matrix $\mathbf{A}_{m-1}$ and clearly has no effect on the final result.*

If the fixed assignment is $K^a(q)$, we replace the states $a_{q,s}$ in the original matrix $\mathbf{A}_{m-1}$ by the values of their codes. The elements $b_{r,s}$ of $\mathbf{A}_{m-t}$, were defined as sets of 2^{t-1} elements of $\mathbf{A}_{m-1}$, (see (7.2.9)). Since $K^a(q)$ is given, we can replace the sets $b_{r,s}$ by the corresponding numbers $\sum_{a_q \in b_{r,s}} K^a(q)$. Thus, the elements of the matrices $\mathbf{A}_{m-t}$ are no longer sets but numbers, and this simplifies the construction of the matrices $[\rho^x_{m-t}(q, s)]$.

In addition, it can be shown that the resulting values of L_{m-t} ($t = 2, 3, \ldots, m$) are not only asymptotically optimal (see Theorem 7.2.2), but exact minima with respect to all assignments that give L_{m-t+1} the previously determined minimal value.

Example 7.4.2   *Consider the automaton with $K^a(q) = q$, for $q = 0, 1, 2, 3$ defined by the next-state matrix*

$$\mathbf{A}_3 = \begin{bmatrix} 0 & 2 & 0 & 3 \\ 0 & 3 & 1 & 3 \\ 2 & 2 & 2 & 0 \\ 3 & 1 & 3 & 1 \end{bmatrix},$$

where $m = 4$. Here $n_a = n_x = 4$ and the element $a_{i,j}$ of $\mathbf{A}_3$ is s if the input signal x_j converts the automaton from a state assigned the code of the number i into the state assigned the code of s.

We determine an assignment $K^x(q)$ and an optimal ordering T of the variables of the excitation functions for this automaton.

First iteration. *The matrix $[\rho^x_3(q, s)]$ is*

$$[\rho^x_3(q, s)] = \begin{bmatrix} 0 & 3 & 1^* & 4 \\ 3 & 0 & 3 & 2^* \\ 1^* & 3 & 0 & 4 \\ 4 & 2^* & 4 & 0 \end{bmatrix}.$$

The minimal matching for $[\rho^x_3(q, s)]$ is $\{\rho^x_3(0, 2), \rho^x_3(1, 3)\}$.
As a minimal matching for $[\rho^a_3(q, s)]$ we take $\{\rho^a_3(0, 1), \rho^a_3(2, 3)\}$.
Then, $L^x_3 = 3$, $L^a_3 = 6$, $L^x_3 < L^a_3$, $z_{T_3} = x_1$.

The input signals x_0, x_2 and x_1, x_3 are assigned codes that differ in the least significant bit x_1.

Second iteration. *The matrix* $\mathbf{A}_{m-2} = A_2 = A_2^x$ *is*

$$
\mathbf{A}_2 = \mathbf{A}_2^x =
\begin{bmatrix}
0 & 5 \\
1 & 6 \\
4 & 2 \\
6 & 2
\end{bmatrix}.
$$

Then

$$
[\rho_2^x(q, s)] =
\begin{bmatrix}
0 & 4^* \\
4^* & 0
\end{bmatrix}.
$$

The minimal matching for $[\rho_2^x q, s)]$ *is* $\{\rho_2^x(0, 1)\}$.
As the minimal matching for $[\rho_2^a(q, s)]$ *we take* $\{\rho_2^a(0, 1), \rho_2^a(2, 3)\}$.
Then, $L_2^x = 4$, $L_2^a = 3$, $L_2^a < L_2^x$, $z_{T_2} = a_1$.

Third iteration. $\mathbf{A}_{m-3} = \mathbf{A}_1 = \mathbf{A}_1^a = \begin{bmatrix} 1 & 11 \\ 10 & 4 \end{bmatrix}$. *Then,*

$$
[\rho_1^x(q, s)] =
\begin{bmatrix}
0 & 2^* \\
2^* & 0
\end{bmatrix}.
$$

The minimal matching for $[\rho_1^a(q, s)]$ *is* $\{\rho_1^x(0, 1)\}$ *and that for* $[\rho_1^x(q, s)]$ *is* $\{\rho_1^x(0, 1)\}$, $L_1^x = L_1^a = 2$. *We set* $z_{T_1} = a_0$.

Fourth iteration. *We have* $\mathbf{A}_0 = \mathbf{A}_0^a = \begin{bmatrix} 11 & 15 \end{bmatrix}$, *then* $[\rho_0^x(q, s)] = \begin{bmatrix} 0 & 1^* \\ 1^* & 0 \end{bmatrix}$, *and*

$L_0 = L_0^x + 1 = 2$, $z_{T_0} = z_0$.
In this example, then, the result is $L_3 = 3$, $L_2 = 3$, $L_1 = 2$, $L_0 = 2$, $K^x(0) = 0$, $K^x(1) = 2$, $K^x(2) = 1$, $K^x(3) = 3$. *The optimal order of variables is* (x_0, a_0, a_1, x_1).

To conclude this chapter, we again state that the algorithms presented here provide for computationally very efficient and asymptotically optimal methods for problems of state assignment for inputs and internal states and ordering of variables for excitation functions for the case when the sequential networks implementing partially and completely defined automata are based on the Haar expansions of excitation functions.

We note that solutions of these problems for the classical approaches based on minimization of excitation functions require exponential complexity. This is the major advantage of spectral methods of synthesis of sequential networks over the traditional methods.

BIBLIOGRAPHIC NOTES

Classical references for automata theory and implementations are 247,313, and 395. Recently published books discussing also this subject are 41,491, and 620. For details on design asynchronous sequential machines, see References 403 and 619. The state assignment problem has been discussed in References 231,40,236,484,645,123, and 375. In References 32 and 34, genetic algorithms are applied to solve this problem. For low-power state assignment, see References 97,140, and 616. State assignment for easy testable implementations (44,45,126).

CHAPTER 8

HARDWARE IMPLEMENTATION OF SPECTRAL METHODS

In this chapter we discuss some methods for implementation of logic networks by using memories as basic modules.

In general, synthesis with memories has advantages that the design time and efforts are minimal, since design in this case is reduced to the programming of a memory structure (499). The optimization is possible in the case of two-level addressing of *Read-Only Memories* (ROM), and simplification of the related multiplexer network at the output. For more details, see Reference 41. This approach to the synthesis is efficient when a given system of functions f is represented by the truth vectors that are directly stored in the ROM, and there are no minimzation of f in the sense of reduction of the product terms in Sum-of-Product (SOP) expressions. Since the complete truth vectors are stored, it follows that the method is inefficient when f has many values 0 or 1, and unspecified values. In these cases, specification by cubes or analytical expressions may provide more compact representations. The method is efficient, if f has many product terms in SOP as the arithmetic functions. It is also efficient when it is required a frequent change of functionality (adaptivity) of the produced network.

In the case of representation of functions by spectral expressions, the memory, which is the core part of the implementations by spectral representations is used to store the spectral coefficients.

The considerations in this chapter can be viewed as an elaboration of the design methods discussed in Section 6.1 recalling further that present *Look-up-Table* (LUT)

Spectral Logic and Its Applications for the Design of Digital Devices by Mark G. Karpovsky, Radomiɪ S. Stanković and Jaakko T. Astola
Copyright © 2008 John Wiley & Sons, Inc.

FPGAs are suitable technology platforms for such implementations of logic functions, see References 41 and 394.

8.1 SPECTRAL METHODS OF SYNTHESIS WITH ROM

The presentation in this chapter will be mainly focussed on the implementations by the discrete Haar series of switching functions. The advantage is taken from the distinct feature of Haar functions that they take values in the set $\{-1, 0, 1\}$, which permits to avoid explicit generation of basis functions used in the series expansion for the function $f(z)$. Instead, values of basis functions for a given input z are viewed as signs associated to the Haar coefficients, the sum of which determines values of $f(z)$ for all possible values of z.

In this chapter, we present some complexity bounds that, although being approximative, allow to compare various spectral methods in logic networks synthesis.

The block diagrams of spectral implementations demonstrating an approach to the solution of the major technical problems that arise when spectral methods are employed will also be discussed in this chapter.

8.2 SERIAL IMPLEMENTATION OF SPECTRAL METHODS

We use the term *serial implementation* of spectral methods for the design technique in which the value of the function describing the operation of a network is obtained by a serial (i.e., sequential in time) summation of the appropriate spectral series.

When a state assignment has been selected, the implementation of a sequential network is reduced to the implementation of a suitable combinational network implementing excitation functions.

For this reason, the discussion of this chapter will be limited to the implementation of combinational networks for systems of switching functions, that is, we will consider logic networks with m inputs and k outputs.

As always in spectral implementations, a system of k switching functions of m variables in a fixed order is represented by a single step function $\Phi(z)$, which is then expanded into an orthogonal series. However, this system may also be viewed as 2^l ($0 \leq l < m$) systems of $m - l$ variables, obtained by fixing l arguments of the original system in all possible ways. Alternatively, we can speak of s ($0 < s \leq k$) systems of m variables, where the ith system contains p_i functions ($i = 1, 2, \ldots, s$), and $\sum_{i=1}^{k} p_i = k$. Yet another interpretation is to take some combination of these two cases.

Whatever the alternative chosen, each of the systems may be realized independently. It will become clear from the sequel that depending on the specific alternative, there are two possibilities

1. either the total number of nonzero expansion coefficients of the representative step functions is increased or
2. the total number of bits in the adders computing the values of the step functions is increased.

We shall therefore confine ourselves throughout the sequel to the case of a system of k switching functions of m variables represented by a single step function $\Phi(z)$ defined as in (1.2.4).

8.3 SEQUENTIAL HAAR NETWORKS

Figure 8.3.1 illustrates the block diagram for implementation of systems of switching functions by Haar series. The system operates as follows.

The binary encoded variable z is stored in an $(m + 1)$-bits shift register, whose rightmost bit is set to 1.

This register receives Clock Pulses (CL) that shift the code recorded therein. At consecutive instants, the portion of the shift register controlling the decoder will hold the code sequences $(1, 0, \ldots, 0), (z_0, 1, 0, \ldots, 0), (z_1, z_0, 1, 0, \ldots, 0), \cdots,$ $(z_{m-2}, z_{m-1}, \ldots, z_0, 1)$, where z_s is the sth digit of the binary code for z. Each of these sequences activates exactly one output of the decoder, depending on the code of z. If the decoder outputs are numbered from 0 through $2^m - 1$, the output activated at the lth time is the output corresponding to a number in the set $\{2^{l-1}, 2^{l-1} + 1, \ldots, 2^l - 1\}$, $l = 1, 2, \ldots, m$.

The decoder controls the operation of the memory storing binary codes of the expansion coefficients of $\Phi(z)$ in the corresponding Haar series.

When the δth input ($\delta = 1, 2, \ldots, 2^m - 1$) of the encoder is activated, the coefficient $c_l^{(q)}$ is fed from the output of the encoder to the input of the adder-accumulator Σ, where $l \in \{1, \ldots, m\}$ and $q \in \{1, \ldots, 2^l\}$ are uniquely determined by the condition

$$2^l + q - 1 = \delta. \tag{8.3.1}$$

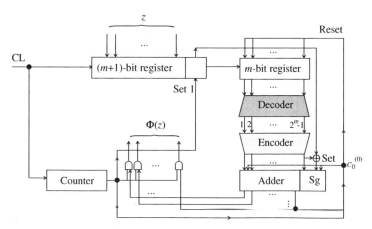

FIGURE 8.3.1 Block diagram for implementation of switching functions by Haar series with single dimensional ROM.

The sign of the coefficient is fed through an EXOR circuit into the sign bit Sg of the adder Σ.

To compute $\Phi(z)$ for any fixed z, it is required to sum up to $m + 1$ coefficients $c_l^{(q)}$, and so the value of $\Phi(z)$ is produced after m elementary addition operations. (Before summation begins, the adder Σ holds the code of the coefficient $c_0^{(0)}$, which is thus the initial state of Σ.) Upon each elementary addition, the number stored in the register is shifted.

We now consider the implementation of the encoder in detail.

If a coefficient $c_l^{(q)}$ is zero, there is no need to store it in the encoder or to realize the corresponding decoder output. Thus, the complexity of both encoder and decoder depends essentially on the number of nonzero coefficients.

We have already stated that the encoder is a memory, while the decoder computes the address for it. The memory can be organized as a single-coordinate device, or as a two-coordinate device. In the case of two coordinates (x, y), the set of m variables is split into subsets of $\lfloor m/2 \rfloor$ and $\lceil m/2 \rceil$ variables for the abscise x and the ordinate y of the coordinate (x, y). It will be shown below that this approach considerably reduces complexity of the decoder.

Figure 8.3.2 shows the block diagram of the implementation by spectral methods with two-coordinate ROM.

Each cell of the memory stores a coefficient $c_l^{(q)}$. The length of the binary code of this coefficient is at most $m + k + 1$.

At each instant of time, the code of a single coefficient should appear at the decoder output.

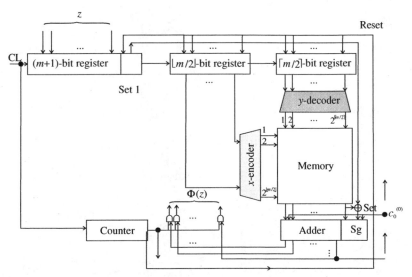

FIGURE 8.3.2 Block diagram for implementation of switching functions by Haar series with two-coordinate ROM.

We now consider generation of the sign digit Sg of the adder Σ, assuming as usual that 1 in the sign digit implies a negative value of the number stored in Σ, and 0 a positive value. Since,

$$H_l^{(q)}(z) = R_{l+1}(z) = (-1)^{z_l}, \qquad (8.3.2)$$

for $z \in ((q-1)2^{m-l}, q2^{m-l})$, it follows in view of the previously shown relation that the value of $H_l^{(q)}(z)$ is equal to the lth digit z_l of the argument code, and multiplication of the sign of the coefficient by the sign of $H^{(q)}(z)$ is thus accomplished by the EXOR circuit, whose output is fed to the sign digit of the adder Σ.

The computation of $\Phi(z)$ ends after m elementary additions, and a modulo m counter (see Fig. 8.3.1) sends a reading signal to a network of AND gates, a *reset* signal to the decoder address register, a *set* signal to the register bit controlling the sign in the adder Σ, and a signal restoring the code $c_0^{(0)}$ in Σ.

Example 8.3.1 *Let us design a network implementing the incompletely specified automaton of Example 7.3.1, with serial summation of the corresponding spectral series.*

The optimal completion of the state matrix is the matrix A_5' in Section 7.3, for which $n_a = 8$, $n_x = 8$. The state assignment is shown in Table 7.3.1, the order of variables in the excitation functions is $(x_0, a_0, a_1, x_1, x_2, a_2)$, and bounds on the number of nonzero coefficients are given in Table 7.3.2.

Using A_5' and the state assignment of Table 7.3.1, we construct a step function $\Phi(z)$ representing the system of excitation functions for the selected order of variables. This function and the nonzero coefficients $c_l^{(q)}$ of its expansion are given in Tables 8.3.1 and 8.4.1, respectively.

A network realizing this automaton as described above is illustrated in Fig. 8.4.1. The timing of the input signal coincides with the timing of signals at the counter output.

8.4 COMPLEXITY OF SERIAL REALIZATION BY HAAR SERIES

We now estimate the complexity (a number of two input gates and flip-flops) of a serial implementation of a combinational network by spectral methods. The block diagram in Fig. 8.3.1 contains the following components:

1. $(2m + 1)$-bit shift register,
2. decoder,
3. encoder,
4. adder,
5. modulo m counter,
6. AND networks.

TABLE 8.3.1 Function f Example 8.3.1.

z	$\Phi(z)$	z	$\Phi(z)$	z	$\Phi(z)$	z	$\Phi(z)$
0	0	16	4	32	5	48	0
1	0	17	4	33	5	49	0
2	0	18	6	34	5	50	0
3	0	19	6	35	5	51	5
4	2	20	6	36	1	52	2
5	2	21	6	37	1	53	2
6	2	22	6	38	7	54	2
7	2	23	6	39	7	55	2
8	0	24	3	40	2	56	4
9	0	25	3	41	2	57	4
10	0	26	3	42	2	58	4
11	0	27	3	43	2	59	4
12	0	28	7	44	1	60	1
13	0	29	7	45	5	61	1
14	0	30	7	46	7	62	1
15	0	31	7	47	7	63	1

TABLE 8.4.1 Nonzero Coefficients for the Function f in Example 8.3.1.

				Binary Representation of $c_l^{(q)}$							
$\delta = 2^l + q - 1$	(l, q)	$64c_l^{(q)}$	Sign	2^1	2^0	2^{-1}	2^{-2}	2^{-3}	2^{-4}	2^{-5}	2^{-6}
0	(0,0)	189	0	1	0	1	1	1	1	0	1
1	(0,1)	−5	1	0	0	0	0	0	1	0	1
2	(1,1)	−152	1	1	0	0	1	1	0	0	0
3	(1,2)	62	0	0	0	1	1	1	1	1	0
4	(2,1)	32	0	0	0	1	0	0	0	0	0
5	(2,2)	16	0	0	0	0	1	0	0	0	0
6	(2,3)	32	0	0	0	1	0	0	0	0	0
7	(2,4)	−28	1	0	0	0	1	1	1	0	0
8	(3,1)	−64	1	0	1	0	0	0	0	0	0
10	(3,3)	−32	1	0	1	1	0	0	0	0	0
11	(3,4)	−128	1	1	0	0	0	0	0	0	0
12	(3,5)	−32	1	0	0	1	0	0	0	0	0
13	(3,6)	96	0	0	1	1	0	0	0	0	0
14	(3,7)	−24	1	0	0	0	1	1	0	0	0
15	(3,8)	64	0	0	1	0	0	0	0	0	0
20	(4,5)	−64	1	0	1	0	0	0	0	0	0
25	(4,10)	−192	1	1	1	0	0	0	0	0	0
27	(4,12)	−128	1	1	0	0	0	0	0	0	0
28	(4,13)	−80	1	0	1	0	1	0	0	0	0
54	(5,23)	−128	1	1	0	0	0	0	0	0	0

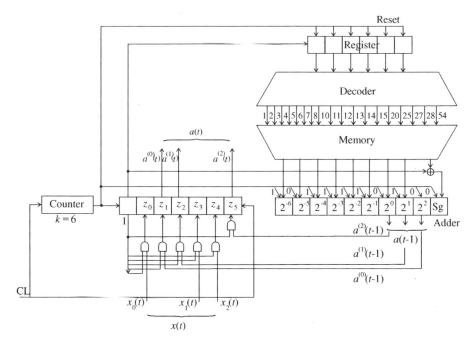

FIGURE 8.4.1 Block diagram for the implementation of the network in Example 8.3.1.

We now estimate the complexity of each block.

1. The complexity of the register L_{SR} is

$$L_{SR} = (2m + 1)L_{SR}^{(1)}, \tag{8.4.1}$$

where $L_{SR}^{(1)}$ is the complexity of one-bit register.

2. The complexity of the decoder is

$$
L_{Dc} \le L_{Dc}\left(\left\lfloor \frac{m}{2} \right\rfloor, 2^{\lfloor m/2 \rfloor}\right) + L_{Dc}\left(\left\lceil \frac{m}{2} \right\rceil, 2^{\lceil m/2 \rceil}\right)
$$
$$
\le (2^{\lfloor m/2 \rfloor + 1} + 2^{\lceil m/2 \rceil + 1} - 8)L_\wedge, \tag{8.4.2}
$$

where $L_{Dc}(p, q)$ is the complexity of a decoder with p inputs and q outputs, and $L_\wedge$ is that of a two-input AND gate.

To prove (8.4.2), we note that in a two-coordinate memory the decoder splits into two address decoders, with $\lfloor m/2 \rfloor$ and $\lceil m/2 \rceil$ inputs, respectively, and $2^{\lfloor m/2 \rfloor}$ and $2^{\lceil m/2 \rceil}$ outputs. Let us suppose that each of these decoders has the structure of a tree.

A tree decoder with λ inputs $z_0, \ldots, z_{\lambda-1}$ and 2^λ outputs is a network obtained by the serial connection of λ separate networks, the lth level receiving the output of the $(l-1)$th and the input variable z_{l-1}. The 0th level is a constant 1 signal, that is, a clock. In a tree decoder, each level, from the 0th to the $(l-1)$th inclusive, is a full decoder for the variables $z_0, \ldots, z_{l-1}$. It is readily shown by induction on λ that the complexity $L_{Dc}(\lambda, 2^\lambda)$ of a tree decoder with λ inputs and 2^λ outputs is

$$L_{Dc}(\lambda, 2^\lambda) = (2^{\lambda+1} - 4)L_\wedge.$$

The estimate (8.4.2) now follows easily.

If the encoder is a single-coordinate memory, the decoder has m inputs and L outputs, where L is the number of nonzero coefficients in the expansion. Reasoning as in the case of a two-coordinate ROM shows that its complexity is bounded by $2L \cdot L_\wedge$.

3. The encoder is a memory that stores the nonzero coefficients $c_l^{(q)}$. The complexity of the encoder is given approximately by

$$L_{En} \simeq \frac{1}{2} \sum_{l=1}^{m} L_{m-l}(k+1)L_1, \tag{8.4.3}$$

where L_{m-l} is the number of nonzero coefficients $c_{m-l}^{(q)}$, $q = 1, 2, \ldots, 2^{m-l}$ and L_1 is the complexity of the element (binary cell) necessary to store one bit of information in the memory. Indeed, if $\Phi(z)$ is the step function representing a system of k switching functions of m variables, then $\max_z \Phi(z) < 2^k$ and so $|c_{m-l}^{(q)}| = 2^{-l}\tilde{c}_{m-l}^{(q)}$, where $\lceil \log_2 \tilde{c}_{m-l}^{(q)} \rceil \leq k < l$.

In addition, it is assumed in (8.4.3) that the numbers of 1 and 0 values in the binary expansion of each nonzero coefficient $c_{m-l}^{(q)}$ are equal.

Remark 8.4.1 *Both in (8.4.3) and in further complexity estimates for encoders, if $l = m$, then $L_0 \leq 1$, since the coefficient $c_0^{(0)}$ is not produced in the encoder, but fed directly to the adder as an initial state.*

4. For serial summation of the terms of the series, it is used an adder accumulator containing at most $m + k + l$ bits. The complexity L_Σ of the adder accumulator is

$$L_\Sigma \leq (m + k + 1)L_\Sigma^{(1)}, \tag{8.4.4}$$

where L_Σ is the complexity of one-bit adder accumulator.

5. The complexity of a modulo m counter is

$$L_C = \lceil \log_2 m \rceil L_C^{(1)}, \tag{8.4.5}$$

where $L_C^{(1)}$ is the complexity of one-bit counter.

6. The complexity L_{AND} of the AND circuits is

$$L_{AND} = mL_{\wedge}. \tag{8.4.6}$$

Finally, the complexity L_{Sq} of the serial implementation of $\Phi(z)$ is obtained by setting $L_{SR}^{(1)} = L_{\Sigma}^{(1)} = L_{C}^{(1)} = L_{ff}$, where L_{ff} is the complexity of a flip-flop and $L_1 = L_{\wedge}$ for the case of a single-coordinate memory.
Noticing that $L = \sum_{l=1}^{m} L_{m-l}$, we have

$$
\begin{aligned}
L_{Sq} &= L_{SR} + L_{Dc} + L_{En} + L_{\Sigma} + L_C + L_{AND} \\
&\le (3m + k + \lceil \log_2 m \rceil + 2)L_{ff} \\
&\quad + \left(\left(\frac{1}{2}k + 2 \right) L + m + \frac{1}{2} \sum_{l=1}^{m} L_{m-l} \cdot l \right) L_{\wedge}.
\end{aligned}
\tag{8.4.7}
$$

For the case of a two-coordinate memory, we have

$$
\begin{aligned}
L_{Sq} &\le (3m + k + \lceil \log_2 m \rceil + 2)L_{ff} \\
&\quad + \left(\frac{1}{2}L \cdot k + \frac{1}{2} \sum_{l=1}^{m} L_{m-l} \cdot l + m + 2^{\lfloor m/2 \rfloor + 1} + 2^{\lceil m/2 \rceil + 1} - 8 \right) L_{\wedge}.
\end{aligned}
\tag{8.4.8}
$$

A comparison of estimates (8.4.7) and (8.4.8) shows that the use of single-coordinate memory is advisable when $L < 2^{m/2}$, while in other cases a two-coordinate memory should be used.

For example in Section 7.3, we have $m = 6$, $k = \lceil \log_2 n_a \rceil = 3$, $L_{S_q} = 26L_{ff} + 96L_{\wedge}$ when a single-coordinate ROM implemented with OR circuits is used, and $L_{S_q} = 26L_{ff} + 76L_{\wedge}$ for a two-coordinate ROM.

The upper bounds provided by formulas (8.4.7) and (8.4.8) in these cases are, by contrast,

$$L_{S_q} \le 26L_{ff} + 103L_{\wedge},$$

$$L_{S_q} \le 26L_{ff} + 89L_{\wedge}.$$

8.4.1 Optimization of Sequential Spectral Networks

To end this section, we outline a method whereby the complexity L_{S_q} of the above block diagrams for sequential implementation of spectral methods may be minimized.

Since by definition the step function $\Phi(z)$ being implemented takes integer values, it will suffice to compute another step function $\Psi(z)$ such that

$$\max_{z} |\Phi(z) - \Psi(z)| < \frac{1}{2}, \qquad (8.4.9)$$

and subsequently round off $\Psi(z)$ to the nearest integer (this approach may require a fairly simple automatic rounding-off network, but the implementation of $\Psi(z)$ may turn out to be substantially simpler than that of $\Phi(z)$). We consider two ways of doing this.

The first construction of $\Psi(z)$ involves deleting some of the expansion coefficients of $\Phi(z)$.

Note that if $c_{m-1}^{(q)} \neq 0$, then $|c_{m-1}^{(q)}| \geq 1/2$ and coefficients with the subscript $m - 1$ cannot be deleted.

Now, let $P_{m-l}, (l = 2, 3, \ldots, m)$ be a subset of coefficients $c_{m-l}^{(q)}$ for $\Phi(z)$ and P is the union of all the sets P_{m-l}. Then, the coefficients in P may be deleted in computing $\Phi(z)$ iff

$$\max_{z} \left| \sum_{c_{m-l}^{(q)} \in P} c_{m-l}^{(q)} H_{m-l}^{(q)}(z) \right| < \frac{1}{2}. \qquad (8.4.10)$$

If m is large, however, the use of this condition to determine a maximal set P of coefficients that may be deleted is not very practical. We, therefore, replace (8.4.10) by a somewhat weaker condition that is much easier to verify. Set

$$\hat{c}_{m-l} = \max_{c_{m-l}^{(q)} \in P_{m-l}} |c_{m-l}^{(q)}|. \qquad (8.4.11)$$

Then, the coefficients of P may be deleted if

$$\sum_{l=2}^{m} \hat{c}_{m-l} < \frac{1}{2}. \qquad (8.4.12)$$

Returning to Example 8.3.1 discussed in this section (see Table 8.4.1), we see that condition (8.4.10) allows to delete the coefficients $c_0^{(1)}$, $c_2^{(2)}$, $c_3^{(7)}$. The complexity of the encoder is thereby reduced by about 13%, and the complexity of the decoder is also reduced.

The second approach to minimization is based on deleting the least significant bits of the codes of $c_{m-l}^{(q)}$ for $\Phi(z)$. This reduces the length of the coefficient codes and thereby the necessary length of the adder.

Let $c_{m-l}^{(q)}(s)$ denote the value of the digit with the weight 2^{-s} in the binary expansion of $c_{m-l}^{(q)}$, ($s \leq m$, $c_{m-l}^{(q)}(s) \in \{0, 1\}$). For example, $c_{m-l}^{(q)}(m)$ is the value of the least significant bit in the binary expansion of $c_{m-l}^{(q)}$. Then, the bits in the binary representations of the coefficients $c_{m-l}^{(q)}$ with weights $-m, -m+1, \ldots, -m+r$ may be deleted from the expansion of $\Phi(z)$ if

$$\sum_{s=m-r}^{m} \sum_{l,q} c_{m-l}^{(q)}(s)2^{-s} < \frac{1}{2}. \tag{8.4.13}$$

This condition generates a simple procedure yielding the maximal number r of bits in the coefficients $c_{m-l}^{(q)}$ that can be deleted.

For the example of this section, the bits with weights $2^{-6}, 2^{-5}, 2^{-4}, (r = 3)$ can be deleted. The complexity of the adder is reduced by 30% and that of the encoder is also reduced.

8.5 PARALLEL REALIZATION OF SPECTRAL METHODS OF SYNTHESIS

The use of parallel summation to compute the series expansion of a step function $\Phi(z)$ representing a system of switching functions of m variables, yields an m-fold gain in speed. This advantage is achieved, however, at the cost of the corresponding increase in space (hardware) complexity, mainly due to the fact that the adder accumulator must be replaced by a parallel adder for m terms. In this section, we discuss the technical implementation of parallel summation and establish the corresponding complexity estimates.

A block diagram for parallel summation of series is shown in Fig. 8.5.1. Its operation is as follows.

The binary code $(z_0, z_1, \ldots, z_{m-1})$ of the variable z is loaded into m flip-flops. For any fixed $z = z^*$, there are exactly $m + 1$ Haar functions $H_l^{(q)}$ such that $H_l^{(q)}(z^*) \neq 0$ (in fact, of all functions with the same nonzero subscript, exactly one is not equal to zero), hence, only the coefficients of these functions have to be accessed from the encoder. This is ensured by using a decoder with the structure of a tree. At the output of the lth level of the decoder ($l = 0, 1, \ldots, m - 1$), one line is activated, corresponding to the coefficients $c_l^{(q)}$ such that $H_l^{(q)}(z) \neq 0$ for the z in question. Thus, at most m codes of coefficients $c_l^{(q)}$ (for different l) are produced simultaneously at the encoder output (the coefficient $c_0^{(0)}$ is fed directly to the adder Σ). These $m + 1$ coefficients are summed by the parallel adder Σ.

The decoder in this network has $m - 1$ levels (and correspondingly $m - 1$ inputs $z_0, \ldots, z_{m-2}$), since the output of the decoder corresponding to $c_0^{(0)}$ is taken directly from its input (see Fig. 8.5.1). Each of the m coefficients produced at the encoder output is multiplied by the values of the appropriate basis function, by means of EXOR circuits, and the process is precisely the same as in the serial architecture.

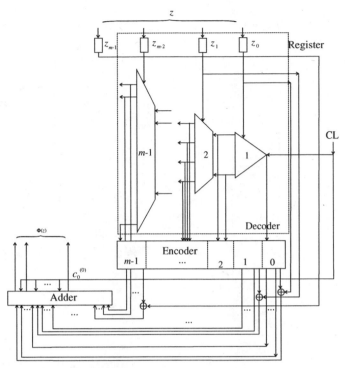

FIGURE 8.5.1 Block diagram for implementation of switching functions by Haar series with parallel summation of the coefficients.

The encoder is implemented by the same methods as in the serial architecture. Thus, for parallel summation, the encoder consists of m independent single-coordinate memory block, where the lth memory block ($l = 0, 1, \ldots, m - 1$) stores the codes of the coefficients $c_l^{(q)}$ ($q = 1, 2, \ldots, 2^l$) and the lth level of the tree decoder acts as the address decoder for the lth memory block.

Figure 8.5.2 is a block diagram of a parallel implementation of the automaton considered in Section 8.3.

8.6 COMPLEXITY OF PARALLEL REALIZATION

We now estimate the complexity L_{Pr} of a parallel implementation of an (m, k)-terminal network by spectral methods. The block diagram in Fig. 8.5.1 contains the following components:

1. Flip-flops to store the variables $(z_0, \ldots, z_{m-1})$
2. Decoder
3. Encoder

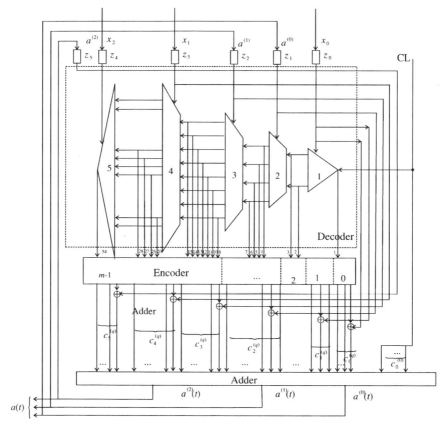

FIGURE 8.5.2 Block diagram of parallel implementation of the network in Example 8.3.1.

4. Sign-generation block (EXORs)
5. Adder.

We proceed to evaluate the complexity of each block.

1. The complexity of a block storing $(z_0, \ldots, z_{m-1})$ is

$$L_m = m \cdot L_{ff}, \tag{8.6.1}$$

with the notation as in the previous sections.

2. The decoder in Fig. 8.5.1 has $m - 1$ variables and the structure of a tree. The $(m - l)$th level has L_{m-1} outputs. Suppose that the decoder is designed so that the first $m - 1$ levels (for the first $(m - 2)$ variables) form a full tree decoder, while the $(m - 1)$th level consists of L_{m-1} two-input AND circuits whose

outputs correspond to the L_{m-1} nonzero coefficients $c_{m-1}^{(q)}$. Then, the complexity of the decoder satisfies the inequality (see Section 8.4)

$$L_{Dc} \leq (2^{m-1} + L_{m-1} - 4)L_{\wedge}. \tag{8.6.2}$$

Similarly, if the full tree decoder consists of the first $m - l$ levels, then

$$L_{Dc} \leq (2^{m-l+1} + L_{m-l+1} + 2L_{m-l+2} + 3L_{m-l+3} + \cdots$$
$$+ (l - 1)L_{m-1} - 4)L_{\wedge} \tag{8.6.3}$$
$$= \left(2^{m-l+1} - 4 + \sum_{s=1}^{l-1} sL_{m-l+s}\right) L_{\wedge}.$$

Since l may be chosen arbitrarily from the set $\{2, 3, \ldots, m - 1\}$, the final bound for the decoder complexity is

$$L_{Dc} \leq \min_{l \in \{2,3,\ldots,m-1\}} \left(2^{m-l+1} - 4 + \sum_{s=1}^{l-1} s \cdot L_{m-l+s}\right) L_{\wedge}. \tag{8.6.4}$$

For practical purposes, it is usually sufficient to examine the cases $l = 2, 3, 4$, thus obtaining the following rough estimate

$$L_{Dc} \leq \min(2^{m-1} + L_{m-1} - 4, 2^{m-2} + 2L_{m-1} - 4,$$
$$2^{m-3} + L_{m-3} + 2L_{m-2} + 3L_{m-1} - 4)L_{\wedge}. \tag{8.6.5}$$

3. The encoder consists of m independent encoders, of which the lth ($l = 0, 1, \ldots, m - 1$) is a single-coordinate memory storing binary representations of $c_l^{(q)}$, ($q = 1, 2, \ldots, 2^l$). Its complexity is the same as that of the encoder in Fig. 8.3.1 (see Section 8.3).

4. The sign block has complexity

$$L_{Sg} = m \cdot L_{\oplus}, \tag{8.6.6}$$

where $L_{\oplus}$ is the complexity of a two-input EXOR circuit.

5. In parallel implementation, summation is performed by a combinational parallel adder for m terms, each of which contains at most $m + k + 1$ bits. Thus, the complexity of the adder satisfies the inequality

$$L_{\Sigma} \leq (m - 1)(m + k + 1)L_{c\Sigma}^{(1)}, \tag{8.6.7}$$

where $L_{\Sigma}^{(1)}$ is the complexity of one-bit adder for two terms (the full adder) [247].

Finally, the complexity L_{Pr} of the entire network, assuming $L_1 = L_\oplus = L_\wedge$, $L_\Sigma^{(1)} = 9L_\wedge$ [247] and using the estimate $L_{D_c} \le (2^{m-1} + L_{m-1} - 4)L_\wedge$ is

$$L_{Pr} = L_m + L_{Dc} + L_{En} + L_{Sg} + L_{c\Sigma}$$

$$\le mL_{ff} + \left(2^{m-1} + 9m^2 + m(9k+1) + L_{m-1}\right.$$

$$\left. + \frac{1}{2}\sum_{l=1}^{m} l \cdot L_{m-1} + \left(\frac{1}{2}L_{m-1} - 9\right)k - 13\right)L_\wedge. \quad (8.6.8)$$

For the example in Section 7.3, it is $m = 6$, $k = \lceil \log_2 n_a \rceil = 3$ and $L_{Pr} = 6L_{ff} + 519L_\wedge$ (from (8.6.8) in this case we have $L_{Pr} \le 6L_{ff} + 544L_\wedge$).

A comparison of (8.4.7), (8.4.8), and (8.6.8) shows that the m-fold gain in speed over the serial architecture is achieved at the cost of an increase in the upper bound on the space complexity. When the serial architecture uses single-coordinate storage, the increase is

$$\Delta L - (2^{m-1} + 9m^2 + 9k(m-1) - 2I_1 + I_{m-1} - 13)L_\wedge$$

$$- (2m + k + \lceil \log_2 m \rceil + 2)L_{ff}, \quad (8.6.9)$$

and for two-coordinate storage

$$\Delta L = (2^{m-1} + 9m^2 + 9k(m-1) + L_{m-1} - 2^{\lceil m/2 \rceil + 1}$$

$$- 2^{\lfloor m/2 \rfloor + 1} - 5)L_\wedge \quad (8.6.10)$$

$$- (2m + k + \lceil \log_2 m \rceil + 2)L_{ff}.$$

Regarding the example in Section 7.3, we see that the increase in complexity over the serial implementation is $\Delta L = 423L_\wedge - 20L_{ff}$ for single-coordinate storage, $\Delta L = 443L_\wedge - 20L_{ff}$ for two-coordinate memory.

In most practical situations, the space complexity of the parallel implementation is increased by a factor of approximately m in comparison with the serial implementation.

Remark 8.6.1 *A parallel implementation of spectral methods of synthesis may be minimized by either of the two methods described in Section 8.4.1 (approximation of $\Phi(z)$ by a step function $\Psi(z)$ such that $max|\Phi(z) - \Psi(z)| < \frac{1}{2}$).*

8.7 REALIZATION BY EXPANSIONS OVER FINITE FIELDS

The techniques presented in Sections 8.2 and 8.5 will now be modified yielding a reduction in the number of bits of the adder Σ and in the lengths of the codes of the coefficients $c_l^{(q)}$ stored in the memory. The modification will be based on Haar expansions over finite fields (the Haar–Galois expansions, see Section 2.8.3).

As we know, the Haar expansion of a step function $\Phi(z)$ representing a system of switching functions of m variables has the form

$$\Phi(z) = c_0^{(0)} + \sum_{l=0}^{m-1} \sum_{q=1}^{2^l} c_l^{(q)} H_l^{(q)}(z), \tag{8.7.1}$$

where

$$c_l^{(q)} = 2^{-m+l} \left(\sum_{s=2^{m-l-1}+1}^{2^{m-l}} \Phi(2^{m-l}q - s) - \sum_{s=1}^{2^{m-l-1}-1} \Phi(2^{m-l}q - s) \right). \tag{8.7.2}$$

Assume now that all operations in (8.7.1) and (8.7.2) are performed modulo some prime number p. We refer to the result as a Haar expansion over the finite field $GF(p)$ (the field of residues modulo p).

We know that if

$$p > \max_z \Phi(z), \tag{8.7.3}$$

the Haar functions form a complete orthogonal system over $GF(p)$.

For any system of k switching functions,

$$\max_z \Phi(z) \le 2^k - 1, \tag{8.7.4}$$

and so condition (8.7.3) becomes simply

$$p > 2^k. \tag{8.7.5}$$

There is always at least one prime in the interval $(2^k, 2^{k+1})$, and so it follows from (8.7.5) that

$$\lceil \log_2 p \rceil = k + 1. \tag{8.7.6}$$

In general, there is a whole set of primes $\prod_k = \{p_1, p_2, \ldots, p_\theta\}$ such that $2^k < p_i < 2^{k+1}$, $(i = 1, 2, \ldots, \theta)$. Thus, we are faced with the problem how to select an optimal prime $p_{opt} \in \prod_k$ for a given $\Phi(z)$. If $\overline{L}_\Phi(p_i)$, $(p_i \in \prod_k)$ denotes the number of coefficients $c_l^{(q)}$ for $\Phi(z)$ such that $c_l^{(q)} \equiv 0 \pmod{p_i}$, a natural condition for p_{opt} is

$$\overline{L}_\Phi(p_{opt}) = \max_{p \in \prod_k} \overline{L}_\Phi(p).$$

For large values of k, however, the difference

$$\max_{p \in \prod_k} \overline{L}_\Phi(p) - \min_{p \in \prod_k} \overline{L}_\Phi(p)$$

is usually not too large, and so p may be selected from $\prod_k$ arbitrarily.

If the summation in (8.7.1) is performed over $GF(p)$, then $0 \le c_l^{(q)} \le p - 1$ for any l, q, and the upper bound on code length for $c_l^{(q)}$ is reduced (see (8.7.6)) from $m + k + 1$ to $k + 1$. There is a corresponding reduction in the number of bits for the adder.

For the example in Sections 8.2 and 8.5, $k = 3$, $\prod_k = \prod_3 = \{11, 13\}$, $\overline{L}_\Phi(11) = \overline{L}_\Phi(13) = 0$, and so we select $p = p_{opt} = 11$.

The nonzero expansion coefficients of the step function $\Phi(z)$ representing the system of excitation functions in this example, over the field $GF(11)$, are shown in Table 8.7.1. The length of the $c_l^{(q)}$ codes is reduced from 9 to 4 and the number of bits in the adder from 10 to 4, implying a substantial simplification of any implementation using the block diagram of either Fig. 8.3.1 or (in particular) Fig. 8.5.1.

The block diagrams in Figs. 8.3.1 and 8.5.1 in both serial and parallel versions remain essentially the same for implementation over finite fields, with the single difference that the adder is replaced by an adder modulo p.

TABLE 8.7.1 Nonzero Coefficients Over $GF(11)$ in the Expansion for f in Example 8.3.1.

			Binary Representation of $c_l^{(q)}$			
$\delta = 2^l + q - 1$	(l, q)	$c_l^{(q)}$	2^3	2^2	2^1	2^0
0	(0,0)	10	1	0	1	0
1	(0,1)	8	1	0	0	0
2	(1,1)	10	1	0	1	0
3	(1,2)	2	0	0	1	0
4	(2,1)	6	0	1	1	0
5	(2,2)	3	0	0	1	1
6	(2,3)	6	0	1	1	0
7	(2,4)	3	0	0	1	1
8	(3,1)	10	1	0	1	0
10	(3,3)	5	0	1	0	1
11	(3,4)	9	1	0	0	1
12	(3,5)	5	0	1	0	1
13	(3,6)	7	0	1	1	1
14	(3,7)	1	0	0	0	1
15	(3,8)	1	0	0	0	1
20	(1,5)	10	1	0	1	0
25	(4,10)	8	1	0	0	0
27	(4,12)	9	1	0	0	1
28	(4,13)	7	0	1	1	1
54	(5,23)	9	1	0	0	1

The complexity estimates for the encoder and the adder become, respectively,

$$L_{En} = \frac{1}{2}(k+1)L \cdot L_1, \tag{8.7.7}$$

$$L_\Sigma \le (k+1)\tilde{L}_\Sigma^{(1)} \tag{8.7.8}$$

in the serial case and

$$L_\Sigma \le (m-1)(k+1)\tilde{L}_\Sigma^{(1)} \tag{8.7.9}$$

in the parallel case, where $\tilde{L}_\Sigma^{(1)}$ and $\tilde{L}_\Sigma^{(1)}$ denote the complexity of one bit of a modulo p adder accumulator and of one bit of a combinational adder modulo p, respectively.

The number L of nonzero coefficients does not increase in calculations over a finite field. The complexity of all other components of the block diagrams in Figs. 8.3.1 and 8.5.1 (except the encoders and adders) remains unchanged. In addition, there is now no need for EXOR circuits to compute the sign digits. As a result, the upper bound on complexity is reduced by the amount

$$\Delta_p L_{Sq} = \frac{1}{2}\left(\sum_{l=1}^{m} L_{m-1}(k+l) - L(k+1)\right)L_1 + L_\oplus \tag{8.7.10}$$

$$+(m+k+1)L_\Sigma^{(1)} - (k+1)\tilde{L}_\Sigma^{(1)}$$

for the serial architecture and

$$\Delta_p L_{Pr} = \left(\sum_{l=1}^{m} L_{m-l}(k+l) - L(k+1)\right)L_1 + mL_\oplus \tag{8.7.11}$$

$$+(m-1)(m+k+1)L_\Sigma^{(1)} - (m-1)(k+1)\tilde{L}_\Sigma^{(1)}$$

for the parallel implementation.

Setting $\tilde{L}_\Sigma^{(1)} = L_{ff}$ for serial implementation, and $L_\Sigma^{(1)} = 9L_\wedge$ for parallel implementation, $L_1 = L_\oplus = L_\wedge$, we obtain the final estimates for the reduction in complexity

$$\Delta_p L_{Sq} = \left(\frac{1}{2}\left(\sum_{l=1}^{m} l \cdot L_{m-l} - L\right) + 1\right)L_\wedge + mL_{ff}, \tag{8.7.12}$$

$$\Delta_p L_{Pr} = \left(\frac{1}{2}\left(\sum_{l=1}^{m} l \cdot L_{m-l} - L\right) + 9m(m-1) + m\right)L_\wedge. \tag{8.7.13}$$

TABLE 8.7.2   Complexity of Blocks for Spectral Implementation with Calculations in R and $GF(p)$.

	Architecture	Modulo	Register	Counter	Decoder 1	Decoder 2
1	Serial	∞	$(2m+1)L_{ff}$	$\lceil \log_2 m \rceil \cdot L_{ff}$	$2L \cdot L_\wedge$	L_{Dc-1}
2	Serial	p	$(2m+1)L_{ff}$	$\lceil \log_2 m \rceil \cdot L_{ff}$	$2L \cdot L_\wedge$	L_{Dc-2}
3	Parallel	∞	mL_{ff}	0	L_{Dc-3}	L_{Dc-3}
4	Parallel	p	mL_{ff}	0	L_{Dc-4}	L_{Dc-4}
			Example			
1	Serial	∞	$13L_{ff}$	$3L_{ff}$	$44L_\wedge$	$24L_\wedge$
2	Serial	11	$13L_{ff}$	$3L_{ff}$	$44L_\wedge$	$24L_\wedge$
3	Parallel	∞	$6L_{ff}$	0	$18L_\wedge$	$18L_\wedge$
4	Parallel	11	$6L_{ff}$	0	$18L_\wedge$	$18L_\wedge$

An examination of estimations (8.7.10) through (8.7.13) shows that the transition to expansions over finite fields is justified when $L_\Sigma^{(1)}$ and $\tilde{L}_\Sigma^{(1)}$ are close to be equal each other, especially when parallel implementation is being employed.

For Example 8.3.1, the advantage of computation over $GF(11)$ is

$$\Delta_{11} L_{Sq} = 11L_\wedge + 6L_{ff}, \qquad \Delta_{11} L_{Pr} = 286L_\wedge.$$

Table 8.7.2 summarizes the various complexity estimates obtained for all blocks in the serial and parallel variants, for both ordinary expansions and expansions over finite fields.

Table 8.7.3 shows the total complexity for these implementations.

In these tables,

$$L_{Dc-1} = (2^{\lfloor m/2 \rfloor + 1} + 2^{\lceil m/2 \rceil + 1} - 8)L_\wedge,$$

TABLE 8.7.3   Total Complexity of the Implementation of the Network in Example 8.3.1.

Encoder	Adder	Circuits	Sign	Total Complexity 1-Coordinate	Total Complexity 2-Coordinates
E_R	Add_R	$mL_\wedge$	$1 \cdot L_\wedge$	R	S
E_Q	Add_Q	$mL_\wedge$	0	Q	V
E_W	Add_W	0	$mL_\wedge$	W	W
E_X	Add_X	0	0	X	X
		Example			
$46L_\wedge$	$10L_{ff}$	$6L_\wedge$	$1 \cdot L_\wedge$	R_{Ex}	S_{Ex}
$35L_\wedge$	$4L_{ff}$	$6L_\wedge$	0	Q_{Ex}	V_{Ex}
$45L_\wedge$	$450L_\wedge$	0	$6L_\wedge$	W_{Ex}	W_{Ex}
$35L_\wedge$	$180L_\wedge$	0	0	X_{Ex}	X_{Ex}

$$L_{DC-2} = (2^{\lfloor m/2 \rfloor + 1} + 2^{\lceil m/2 \rceil + 1} - 8)L_\wedge,$$

$$L_{Dc-3} = \left(\min_l \left(2^{m-l-1} + \sum_{s=1}^{l-1} s \cdot L_{m-l+s} - 4 \right) \right) L_\wedge,$$

$$L_{DC-4} = \left(\min_l \left(2^{m-l+1} + \sum_{s=1}^{l-1} s \cdot L_{m-l+s} - 4 \right) \right) L_\wedge,$$

and

$$R = (3m + k + \lceil \log_2 m \rceil + 2)L_{ff} + \left(\left(\frac{1}{2}k + 2 \right) L + m + \frac{1}{2} \sum_{l=1}^{m} L_{m-l} \cdot l \right) L_\wedge,$$

$$S = (3m + k + \lceil \log_2 m \rceil + 2)L_{ff}$$

$$+ \left(\frac{1}{2}k \cdot L + \frac{1}{2} \sum_{l=1}^{m} L_{m-l} + m + 2^{\lfloor m/2 \rfloor + 1} + 2^{\lceil m/2 \rceil + 1} - 8 \right) L_\wedge,$$

$$Q = (2m + k + \lceil \log_2 m \rceil + 2)L_{ff} + \left(\frac{1}{2}k \cdot L + 2.5L + m - 1 \right) L_\wedge,$$

$$V = (2m + k + \lceil \log_2 m \rceil + 2)L_{ff}$$

$$+ \left(\frac{1}{2}k \cdot L + \frac{1}{2}L + m + 2^{\lfloor m/2 \rfloor} + 2^{\lceil m/2 \rceil + 1} - 9 \right) L_\wedge,$$

$$W = mL_{ff} + (2^{m-1} + 9m^2 + m(9k + 1) + L_{m-1}$$

$$+ k \left(\left(\frac{1}{2}L - 9 \right) + \frac{1}{2} \sum_{l=1}^{m} L_{m-l} \cdot l - 13 \right) L_\wedge,$$

$$X = mL_{ff} + \left(2^{m-1} + 9(m - 1)(k + 1) + L_{m-1} + \frac{1}{2}k \cdot L + \frac{1}{2}L - 4 \right) L_\wedge,$$

$$R_{Ex} = 26L_{ff} + 96L_\wedge,$$

$$S_{Ex} = 26L_{ff} + 76L_\wedge,$$

$$Q_{Ex} = 20L_{ff} + 85L_\wedge,$$

$$V_{Ex} = 20L_{ff} + 65L_\wedge,$$

$$W_{Ex} = 6L_{ff} + 519L_\wedge,$$

$$X_{Ex} = 6L_{ff} + 233L_\wedge,$$

$$E_R = \frac{1}{2} \sum_{l=1}^{m} L_{m-l} \cdot (k+l) L_{\wedge},$$

$$E_Q = \frac{1}{2} L \cdot (k+1) L_{\wedge},$$

$$E_W = \frac{1}{2} \sum_{s=1}^{m} L_{m-l} \cdot (k+l) L_{\wedge},$$

$$E_X = \frac{1}{2} L_{m-l} \cdot (k+1) L_{\wedge},$$

$$Add_R = (m+k+1) L_{ff},$$

$$Add_Q = (k+1) L_{ff},$$

$$Add_W = 9(m-1)(k+m+1) L_{\wedge},$$

$$Add_X = 9(m-1)(k+1) L_{\wedge}.$$

All data in the table are subject to the assumptions $L_1 = L_{\oplus} = L_{\wedge}$, $L_{SR}^{(1)} = L_C^{(1)} = L_{\Sigma}^{(1)} = L_{ff}$, for serial implementation and $\tilde{L}_{\Sigma}^{(1)} = 9L_{\wedge}$ for parallel implementation.

The table also gives complexity estimates for all implementations of the automaton in the example considered. As regards the estimates for serial and parallel implementations over the field of real numbers, the possibility of minimization by approximating the function $\Phi(z)$ to within an error smaller than $\frac{1}{2}$ (see Section 8.4.1) is not taken into consideration.

It follows from our estimates that, given m and k, the complexity of the implementation depends only on the numbers $L_{m-1}, L_{m-2}, \ldots, L_0$ of nonzero coefficients $c_{m-l}^{(q)}$, $q = 1, 2, \ldots, 2^{m-l}$.

Thus, the methods of completion and linearization of systems of switching functions described in Section 6.1.6.1, and Section 6.2, as well as the methods of state-input assignment, completion of next-state functions and optimal ordering of arguments in the excitation functions, all of which successively minimize the numbers $L_{m-1}, L_{m-2}, \ldots, L_0$, are effective means for minimizing the complexity of network implementations. The various methods described in this chapter may also be used in the synthesis of reliable (fault-tolerant) digital devices (see Section 9.4) by spectral methods. If this is done, the block diagrams of Figs. 8.3.1 and 8.3.2 are left unchanged. Therefore, in Table 8.7.2, it should be introduced additional decoders for the error-correcting (or error-detecting) codes. The implementation of such decoders is considered. for example, in Reference 275. With slight modifications, the methods are also applicable when the basis system is the set of Walsh functions, or indeed any other orthogonal system of those considered in this book.

BIBLIOGRAPHIC NOTES

Synthesis with memories based on truth tables is a standard approach and has been discussed in many books, see References 121, 225, 395, and 491. The same implementation principles can be used in FPGAs with LUTs (121). Synthesis from spectral series is a generalization dealing with spectral coefficients instead of function values (278, 610, 624).

CHAPTER 9

SPECTRAL METHODS OF ANALYSIS AND SYNTHESIS OF RELIABLE DEVICES

The spectral approach developed in previous chapters will now be applied to the analysis of the reliability of digital devices and to the synthesis of reliable devices. These problems will be discussed both for digital devices including memory elements and for combinational (memoryless) networks. The analysis of correcting capability (Sections 9.1–9.3) will consider only "nonredundant" digital devices, that is, devices containing no special "redundant" logic elements or memory elements designed to increase reliability. The basic working tools in this chapter will be various correlation characteristics of the functions describing the operation of the digital devices.

9.1 SPECTRAL METHODS FOR ANALYSIS OF ERROR CORRECTING CAPABILITIES

9.1.1 Errors in Combinatorial Devices

We first analyze the types of errors that can be detected or corrected by switching (combinational) networks with no memory elements. The behavior of such networks is described by systems of logic functions.

In this context, the term "error" is reserved for errors at the input of a network realizing a given logic function (in particular, these may be owing to errors in previous logic networks or in communication channels). A knowledge of the types of errors

Spectral Logic and Its Applications for the Design of Digital Devices   by Mark G. Karpovsky, Radomir S. Stanković and Jaakko T. Astola
Copyright © 2008 John Wiley & Sons, Inc.

that a network is capable of correcting is of paramount importance, both to estimate its reliability and to use it for synthesis of another network realizing the same system of logic functions, but correcting errors of some prescribed type. We shall confine ourselves to the two most widespread types of errors: algebraic errors and arithmetic errors.

We begin with a descriptive outline of these errors and of the corresponding correcting capability of systems of logic functions. Formal definitions will be given later in this section.

An *algebraic error* is an error leading to an independent distortion of individual components of the input signal. In particular, an *l-fold error*, or the *error with multiplicity l*, is an error resulting in the distortion of exactly l components (bits) of the input signal.

An *arithmetic error* is an error that can spread from component to component of the input signal along the carry circuits. In particular, an *l-fold arithmetic error* in m digits of a p-ary input signal is an error that increases (or decreases) the input signal (mod p^m) by any number of the form $\alpha_0^{p_{i_0}} + \alpha_1^{p_{i_1}} + \cdots + \alpha_{l-1}^{p_{i_{l-1}}}$, where $\alpha_0, \ldots, \alpha_{l-1} \in, \{\pm 1, \pm 2, \ldots, \pm(p-1)\}, \quad 0 \leq i_0, \ldots, i_{l-1} \leq m - 1$. Arithmetic errors appear in a network if its input is the output of an arithmetic device (adder, counter, multiplier, etc.).

A system of logic functions *corrects* an error if the presence of the error does not change the values of all functions in the system. In other words, if a correctable error occurs at the input of any network (even a nonredundant network of minimal complexity) realizing the system (the network will correct the error automatically, with no need for any redundancy.

We reiterate that in general any nonredundant network will correct a certain class of errors. The determination of this class is extremely important for many practical situations. The rest of this section is devoted to this problem—determination of the correcting capability of systems of logic functions.

9.1.2 Analysis of Error-Correcting Capabilities

Consider a system of completely specified logic functions

$$y_s = f^{(s)}(z_0, \ldots, z_{m-1}), \tag{9.1.1}$$

where $z_0, \ldots, z_{m-1} \in \{0, 1, \ldots, p - 1\}$ and $s = 0, 1, \ldots, k - 1$.

We first consider the correction of algebraic errors, omitting the adjective "algebraic" whenever there is no danger of confusion.

In this chapter, we will slightly change the definition of errors. By an error we now mean an ordered pair (z, z') where z and z' are correct and distorted inputs of a device computing $f(z)$.

System (9.1.1) *corrects* a set of errors R if, for any $(z, z') \in R$,

$$f^{(s)}(z) = f^{(s)}(z'), \quad s = 0, \ldots, k - 1. \tag{9.1.2}$$

The *multiplicity of an error* (z, z') is the number $\|z \ominus z'\|$ modulo p, that is, the number of nonzero components of the (componentwise) difference modulo p between the vectors z and z'. This quantity is also known as the Hamming distance between z and z'.

The number of l-fold errors that can be corrected by a system f is denoted by $\eta_f(l)$. The function $\eta_f(l)$ is called the *correcting capability* (or *correcting power*) of the system f.

The problem is to construct the function $\eta_f(l)$ for a given system f.

We first construct a discrete function $y = f(z)$ representing system (9.1.1)

$$z = \sum_{s=0}^{m-1} z_s p^{m-1-s}, \tag{9.1.3}$$

$$y = \sum_{s=0}^{k-1} f^{(s)}(z) p^{k-1-s}. \tag{9.1.4}$$

The characteristic functions of $y = f(z)$ are defined, as usual, by

$$f_i(z) = \begin{cases} 1, & \text{if } f(z) = i, \\ 0, & \text{otherwise,} \end{cases} \tag{9.1.5}$$

for $i = 0, 1, \ldots, p^k - 1$.

The autocorrelation functions for $y = f(z)$ are defined in terms of the characteristic functions f_i as

$$B_i(\tau) = \sum_{z=0}^{p^m-1} f_i(z) f_i(z \ominus \tau), \quad i = 0, 1, \ldots, p^k - 1, \tag{9.1.6}$$

and the total autocorrelation function is

$$B_\Sigma(\tau) = \sum_{i=0}^{p^k-1} B_i(\tau). \tag{9.1.7}$$

The properties of autocorrelation functions $B_i(\tau)$ and their relationship to the Vilenkin–Chrestenson transforms were discussed in detail in Chapter 2.

Theorem 9.1.1 *For a given system f, the correcting capability of l-folded errors is*

$$\eta_f(l) = \sum_{\|\tau\|=l} B_\Sigma(\tau), \tag{9.1.8}$$

where $\|\tau\|$ denotes the number of nonzero components of the p-ary expansion of τ.

Proof. It follows from (9.1.5), (9.1.6), and the definition of the criterion $\eta_f(l)$ that $\sum_{\|\tau\|=l} B_i(\tau)$ is the number of l-fold errors corrected by the system at points z for which $f(z) = i$. Hence, summing over the characteristic functions and using (9.1.7), we obtain (9.1.8).

Theorem 9.1.1 provides a simple method for calculating the correcting capability of systems of logic functions in terms of their autocorrelation functions. The latter, in turn, may be evaluated using (9.1.6), or it is often more convenient to express them in terms of double Vilenkin–Chrestenson transforms. Recall that if $\chi^p(f_i)$ is the Vilenkin–Chrestenson transform of f_i, then

$$B_i = p^m (\chi^{(p)})^{-1} (\chi^{(p)}(f_i) \cdot \overline{\chi^{(p)}}(f_i)),$$

where $(\chi^{(p)})^{-1}$ and $\overline{\chi^{(p)}}$ are the inverse and the complex conjugate of the Vilenkin–Chrestenson transform $\chi^{(p)}$. The Vilenkin–Chrestenson transform and its inverse may be evaluated by the fast Vilenkin–Chrestenson transform algorithm, whose implementation requires $(p-1)mp^m$ elementary operations (see Sections 2.3, 2.5).

Another and in many cases more efficient method for computing B_i and B_Σ is based on decision diagrams (Section 3.5).

Computation of the correcting capability $\eta_f(l)$ for a given l may be simplified by the following observation.

Denote

$$\theta_l^{(p)}(z) = \sum_{\|w\|=l} \chi_w^{(p)}(z), \tag{9.1.9}$$

where $\chi_w^{(p)}(z)$ is the wth Vilenkin–Chrestenson function (see Section 2.5).

Notice that $\{\theta_i^{(p)}(z)\}$ is a system of orthogonal functions, but it is not complete.

Let $A_f(w)$ denote the total *amplitude spectrum* of the system of characteristic functions $\{f_i\}$, that is, the value of the function

$$A_f = \sum_{i=0}^{p^k-1} \chi^{(p)}(f_i)\overline{\chi^{(p)}}(f_i)$$

at the point w. In particular, if f is a system of switching functions ($p = 2$), then $A_f(w)$ is the value of the function $\sum_{i=0}^{2^k-1} (W(f_i))^2$, where $W(f_i)$ is the Walsh transform of f_i, since $W(f_i) = \chi^{(2)}(f_i) = \overline{\chi^{(2)}}(f_i)$.

Corollary 9.1.1 *The correcting capability can be expressed in terms of the amplitude spectrum as*

$$\eta_f(l) = p^m \sum_{w=0}^{p^m-1} A_f(w)\theta_i^{(p)}(w). \tag{9.1.10}$$

Proof. By using the definitions of $A_f(w)$, we deduce from (9.1.6) to (9.1.9) that

$$\eta_f(l) = \sum_{\|\tau\|=l} B_\Sigma(\tau) = \sum_{\|\tau\|=l} \sum_{i=0}^{p^k-1} B_i(\tau) = \sum_{\|\tau\|=l} p^m \sum_{w=0}^{p^k-1} A_f(w)\chi_\tau^{(p)}(w)$$

$$= p^m \sum_{w=0}^{p^k-1} A_f(w) \sum_{\|\tau\|=l} \chi_\tau^{(p)}(w) = p^m \sum_{w=0}^{p^k-1} A_f(w)\theta_l^{(p)}(w).$$

Thus, from Corollary 9.1.1, there is no need to evaluate the Vilenkin–Chrestenson spectrum of the function $A_f(w)$ when calculating $\eta_f(l)$. It suffices to evaluate the lth expansion coefficient of this function relative to the basis $\{\theta_l^{(p)}(z)\}$.

The computation of $B_\Sigma(\tau)$ by the formula (9.1.7) for $p > 2$ is facilitated by the "evenness" property

$$B_\Sigma(\tau) = B_\Sigma(\bar{\tau}), \quad \tau \oplus \bar{\tau} = 0, \quad \text{mod } p. \tag{9.1.11}$$

This relation follows directly from (9.1.6), (9.1.7), and halves the necessary computations.

Example 9.1.1   *Consider the ternary function of two variables ($p = 3$, $m = 2$, $k = 1$) defined by Table 9.1.1, where are also shown the characteristic functions f_1, f_2, and since $f_0 = 0$ it is omitted, the autocorrelation functions B_1, B_2, and the total autocorrelation function B_Σ.*

By using Theorem 9.1.1, we see that $\eta_f(1) = 20$, $\eta_f(2) = 12$. Notice that for $p = 3$, $m = 2$, $k = 1$, the total number of possible single errors is 36, and the number of double errors is also 36. Thus the above function corrects $5/9$ of all single errors and a third of all double errors.

TABLE 9.1.1   Ternary Function f in Example 9.1.1 and Its Autocorrelation Characteristics.

z, τ	$z_0 z_1$	$f(z)$	$f_1(z)$	$f_2(z)$	$B_1(\tau)$	$B_2(\tau)$	$B_\Sigma(\tau)$
0	00	1	1	0	5	4	9
1	01	2	0	1	2	1	3
2	02	1	1	0	2	1	3
3	10	1	1	0	4	3	7
4	11	2	0	1	2	1	3
5	12	2	0	1	2	1	3
6	20	1	1	0	4	3	7
7	21	2	0	1	2	1	3
8	22	1	1	0	2	1	3

Notice that according to our definition of errors as ordered pairs of correct and distorted inputs, there are $p \binom{m}{l} (p-1)^l$ errors with multiplicity l for an m-digit p-ary output .

We will now discuss properties of the function $\eta_f(l)$ characterizing the correcting capability of a system of logic functions.

First, the correcting capability is invariant under translations (componentwise addition modulo p of a constant vector) and permutations of the variables, and also under translations of the function itself. In other words, for any $0 \leq \tau < p^m$ and $0 \leq q < p^k$, and a permutation σ, it is true that

$$\eta_{f(z)}(l) = \eta_{f(z \oplus \tau)}(l) = \eta_{f(\sigma z)}(l) = \eta_{f(z) \oplus q}(l), \quad \text{mod } p, \qquad (9.1.12)$$

where σz is the number obtained by applying the permutation σ to the components of z. These invariance properties follow from the analogous invariance properties of the correlation functions.

A consequence of (9.1.12) is the following *duality property of the correcting capability of systems of switching functions* ($p = 2$).

If $f^*(z)$ is the switching function obtained from a switching function $f(z)$ by interchanging disjunction (OR) and conjunction (AND) in any formula expressing $f(z)$ as a superposition of disjunction, conjunction, negation, and addition modulo 2, then

$$\eta_{f(z)}(l) = \eta_{f^*(z)}(l),$$

for any l. This follows from (9.1.12) with $\tau = 2^m - 1$ and $q = 2^k - 1$ via De Morgan's laws (5.5.14) by reasoning similar to that proving the duality of spectral complexity (Corollary 5.5.4).

The next task is to establish a bound on the number $\eta_f = \sum_{l=1}^{m} \eta_f(l)$ of errors of all multiplicities corrected by the system f.

Theorem 9.1.2 *Let $\{f_{m,k}^{(p)}\}$ be the set of all systems of k p-valued logic functions of m variables. Then,*

$$\min_{f \in \{f_{m,k}^{(p)}\}} \eta_f = p^m (p^{m-k} - 1). \qquad (9.1.13)$$

Proof. By the definition of $B_i(\tau)$ (see (9.1.6))

$$\sum_{\tau=1}^{p^m - 1} B_i(\tau) = B_i(0)(B_i(0) - 1). \qquad (9.1.14)$$

Hence, from Theorem 9.1.1, it follows that for any $f \in \{f_{m,k}^{(p)}\}$,

$$\eta_f = \sum_{l=1}^{m} \eta_f(l) = \sum_{l=1}^{m} \sum_{\|\tau\|=l} B_{\Sigma}(\tau) = \sum_{\tau=1}^{p^m-1} B_{\Sigma}(\tau) \qquad (9.1.15)$$

$$= \sum_{\tau=1}^{p^m-1} \sum_{i=0}^{p^k-1} B_i(\tau) = \sum_{i=0}^{p^k-1} B_i(0)(B_i(0) - 1).$$

Minimizing the last expression in (9.1.15) over $B_i(0)$ $(i = 0, 1, \ldots, p^k - 1)$ under the constraint $\sum_{i=0}^{p^k-1} B_i(0) = p^m$, we see that the minimum of η_f is achieved when

$$B_i(0) = p^{m-k}, \quad i = 0, 1, \ldots, p^k - 1. \qquad (9.1.16)$$

Inserting (9.1.16) into (9.1.15), we obtain (9.1.13).

From (9.1.15), the total correcting capability η_f of a system f depends on the set of values $B_i(0) = \sum_{z=0}^{p^m-1} f_i(z)$ $(i = 0, 1, \ldots, p^k - 1)$ since $f_i(z) = f_i^2(z)$.

In other words, if we denote $\|f_i\| = \sum_{z=0}^{p^m-1} f_i(z)$ as the *power of* f_i, then η_f depends on the distribution of powers of the characteristic functions, and η_f is minimal when the functions f_i $(i = 0, 1, \ldots, p^k - 1)$ have equal powers.

We now specialize our results to the case of switching functions $(p = 2)$. The following proposition is a corollary of Theorem 9.1.2.

Corollary 9.1.2   *Let $f(z)$ be a switching function of m variables and power $\|f\| = \sum_z f(z)$. Then,*

$$\eta_f = 2\|f\|^2 - 2^{m+1}\|f\| + 2^{2m} - 2^m. \qquad (9.1.17)$$

Proof.   This follows from (9.1.15) with $p = 2$, $k = 1$, in view of the fact that in this case the power distribution of the characteristic functions is $\|f_1\| = \|f\|$, $\|f_0\| = 2^m - \|f\|$.

From (9.1.17), the total correcting capability of a switching function depends on its number of variables and its power. Since as the power increases, η_f decreases for $\|f\| < 2^{m-1}$ and increases for $\|f\| > 2^{m-1}$, with a minimum at $f = 2^{m-1}$,

$$\min_{f \in \{f_{m,1}^{(2)}\}} \eta_f = 2^{2m-1} - 2^m.$$

For a fixed number of variables m, all switching functions of the same power correct the same number of errors. However, the correcting capability of some functions is concentrated in the region of low-multiplicity errors, or the high-multiplicity errors, which depends on peculiar properties of the functions. Therefore, it is important to analyze the correcting capability of various different classes of switching functions, since for most applications errors with low multiplicity are more probable.

We first notice that for any single output switching function of m variables (thus, $p = 2, k = 1$)

$$f_1 = f, \quad f_0 = 1 - f,$$

and if $B_f(\tau)$ is the autocorrelation function of f, then by (9.1.7)

$$B_\Sigma(\tau) = 2^m - 2\|f\| + 2B(\tau), \quad (B(\tau) = B_1(\tau)). \tag{9.1.18}$$

Owing to that the autocorrelation functions of 21 classes of switching functions in the Appendix A may be used to analyze their correcting capabilities.

From the technical viewpoint, most interesting are the three classes of switching functions defined by the following distributions of correcting capability:

1. Concentrated in the region of low-multiplicity errors,
2. Uniformly distributed over multiplicities,
3. Concentrated in the region of errors of maximal multiplicity.

The reason for the prominence we give to these three classes is that devices realizing them possess high correcting capability with respect to three important classes of errors in the input signals:

1. Weakly correlated (independent) errors, and the most probable errors being those of low multiplicity,
2. Errors of all multiplicities having equal probabilities,
3. Strongly correlated errors, and the most probable errors being those of high multiplicity.

The distribution of correctable errors with respect to multiplicity l may be represented by the fraction $\hat{\eta}_f(f)$ of l-fold errors corrected by the function f.

The total number of l-fold errors for switching functions of m variables is $\binom{m}{l} \cdot 2^m$, and so

$$\hat{\eta}_f(l) = \frac{\eta_f(l)}{\binom{m}{l} \cdot 2^m}. \tag{9.1.19}$$

As an example of a class of switching functions with error-correcting capability concentrated mainly in the low-multiplicity region, we consider the class of *majority functions*.

A switching function $f(z)$ of m variables (where m is odd) is a *majority function* if its value is 1 iff $\|z\| \geq (m + 1)/2$.

For any majority function of m variables,

$$\|f\| = \sum_{z=0}^{2^m-1} f(z) = 2^{m-1},$$

and from (9.1.18), (9.1.8), (9.1.19),

$$B_\Sigma(\tau) = 2B_1(\tau) = 2B(\tau), \tag{9.1.20}$$

$$\hat{\eta}_f(l) = \binom{m}{l}^{-1} \cdot 2^{-m+1} \sum_{\|\tau\|=l} B(\tau). \tag{9.1.21}$$

A formula for the autocorrelation functions of majority functions is given in row 9 of Appendix A. The data in Appendix A, together with (9.1.21), imply the following formula for the fraction of errors corrected by majority functions

$$\hat{\eta}_f(l) = \begin{cases} 2^{-m+2} \sum_{i-0}^{\lfloor l/2 \rfloor} \binom{l}{i} \sum_{j=0}^{\lfloor m/2 \rfloor} \binom{m-l}{m-j-i}, & \text{if } l \text{ is odd,} \\[3mm] 2^{-m+1} \left(2 \sum_{i=0}^{l/2-1} \binom{l}{i} \sum_{j=0}^{\lfloor m/2 \rfloor} \binom{m-l}{m-j-i} \right. \\[3mm] \left. + \binom{l}{l/2} \sum_{j=0}^{\lfloor m/2 \rfloor} \binom{m-l}{m-l/2-j} \right), & \text{if } l \text{ is even.} \end{cases} \tag{9.1.22}$$

Here, $\binom{p}{q} = 0$ if $p < q$ and $\binom{p}{q} = 1$.

Figure 9.1.1 illustrates the functions $\hat{\eta}_f(l)$ for majority functions of $m = 3, 5, 7$ variables determined according to (9.1.22).

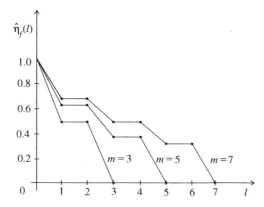

FIGURE 9.1.1 Distribution of correctable errors for majority functions for $m = 3, 5, 7$.

An analysis of (9.1.22) shows that if f is a majority function, $\hat{\eta}_f(l)$ is a monotone decreasing function of l, and

$$\hat{\eta}_f(2s-1) = \hat{\eta}_f(2s), \quad s = 1, \ldots, \lceil m/2 \rceil. \tag{9.1.23}$$

Therefore, the correcting capability of a majority function is concentrated primarily in the region of low-multiplicity errors.

An example of a class of switching functions with correcting capability uniformly distributed over multiplicities is provided by the nonrepetitive quadratic forms in $m = 2k$ variables.

We recall that a *nonrepetitive quadratic form* is a switching function such that

$$f(z) = f(z_0, \ldots, z_{2k-1}) = \bigoplus_{i,j=0, i<j}^{k-1} c_{ij} z_i z_j, \quad \text{mod } 2, \tag{9.1.24}$$

where each z_i appears exactly once.

It is shown in Section 5.1 that

$$\|f\| = 2^{2k-1} - 2^{k-1}, \tag{9.1.25}$$

and for any $\tau > 0$,

$$B(\tau) = 2^{2k-2} - 2^{k-1}, \tag{9.1.26}$$

$$B_\Sigma(\tau) = 2^{2k-1}. \tag{9.1.27}$$

It follows from (9.1.8), (9.1.18), (9.1.19), (9.1.25), and (9.1.26) that if f is a nonrepetitive quadratic form, then, for $l > 0$,

$$\hat{\eta}_f(l) = \frac{1}{2}. \tag{9.1.28}$$

Finally, as an example of a class of switching functions that correct mainly errors of maximal multiplicity, we consider the elementary symmetric switching functions of $m = 2k$ variables with operating number k.

A switching function $f(z)$ is an *elementary symmetric function with operating number k if $f(z) = 1$ iff $\|z\| = k$*. We then have

$$\|f\| = \binom{2k}{k}. \tag{9.1.29}$$

The autocorrelation function for an elementary symmetric switching function with the operating number k is (see Appendix A, row 8)

$$B(\tau) = \begin{cases} \begin{pmatrix} 2k - \|\tau\| \\ k - \|\tau\|/2 \end{pmatrix} \begin{pmatrix} \|\tau\| \\ \|\tau\|/2 \end{pmatrix}, & \text{if } \|\tau\| \text{ is even,} \\ 0, & \text{if } \|\tau\| \text{ is odd.} \end{cases} \qquad (9.1.30)$$

It follows from (9.1.7), (9.1.8), (9.1.18), (9.1.19), and (9.1.30) that if f is an elementary symmetric function, then

$$\hat\eta_f(l) = \begin{cases} \begin{pmatrix} 2k \\ l \end{pmatrix}^{-1} 2^{-2k} \left(2^{2k} - 2 \begin{pmatrix} 2k \\ k \end{pmatrix} \right. \\ \left. \quad +2 \begin{pmatrix} 2k - l \\ k - l/2 \end{pmatrix} \begin{pmatrix} l \\ l/2 \end{pmatrix} \begin{pmatrix} 2k \\ l \end{pmatrix} \right), & \text{if } l \text{ is even,} \\ \\ \begin{pmatrix} 2k \\ l \end{pmatrix}^{-1} 2^{-2k} \left(2^{2k} - 2 \begin{pmatrix} 2k \\ k \end{pmatrix} \right), & \text{if } l \text{ is odd.} \end{cases} \qquad (9.1.31)$$

Figure 9.1.2 illustrates the functions $\hat\eta_f(l)$ for elementary symmetric switching functions of $m = 2k$ variables with operating numbers $k = 2, 3, 4$.

An analysis of (9.1.31) shows that for any k the function $\hat\eta_f(l)$ goes through a maximum at $l = 2k$ and has local maxima at $l = 2i$ ($i = 1, 2, \ldots, k - 1$). Another conclusion from (9.1.31) is that $\hat\eta_f(l)$ is symmetric with respect to $l = k$; that is, if $l < k$, then

$$\hat\eta_f(l) = \hat\eta_f(k - l). \qquad (9.1.32)$$

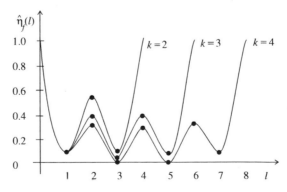

FIGURE 9.1.2 Distribution of correctable errors for the elementary symmetric switching functions of $2k$ variables with $k = 2, 3, 4$.

It follows from (9.1.31) that the asymptotic distribution of correctable errors for these functions is

$$\lim_{k\to\infty} \hat{\eta}_f(l) = 0, \quad l = 1, \ldots, 2k - 1. \tag{9.1.33}$$

Since

$$\hat{\eta}_f(2k) = 1, \tag{9.1.34}$$

for any k, it follows from (9.1.33) that the correcting capability of an elementary symmetric switching function of $2k$ variables with the operating number k is concentrated in the region of maximal multiplicity.

To summarize, devices realizing majority functions are reliable for weakly correlated (independent) errors, since the most probable errors in such cases are errors of low multiplicity. Devices realizing nonrepetitive quadratic forms display good correcting capability when errors of all multiplicities are equally probable, and devices realizing elementary symmetric switching functions of $2k$ variables with the operating numbers k are most reliable with respect to strongly correlated errors, since then errors of maximal multiplicity are most probable in this case.

There is an interesting relationship between correcting capability and complexity for completely specified switching functions.

Recall (see Section 5.3) that the complexity of a switching function may be measured by the number of unordered pairs of matched minterms or maxterms, and the complexity criterion $\bar{\eta}(f)$ for a switching function $f(z)$ is the number of pairs $\{z_1, z_2\}$ such that $f(z_1) = f(z_2)$ and $\|z_1 \oplus z_2\| = 1$, modulo 2 (see (5.3.10)).

As shown in Section 5.3, for almost all switching functions $f(z)$ of m variables ($m \to \infty$) the number of two-input logic elements necessary for a minimal network realizing $f(z)$ decreases with increasing $\bar{\eta}(f)$. A comparison of the definitions of the complexity criterion $\bar{\eta}(f)$, see (5.3.10), and of the correcting capability $\eta_f(l)$ reveals the simple relationship

$$\bar{\eta}(f) = \eta_f(1). \tag{9.1.35}$$

Thus, the higher the complexity criterion $\bar{\eta}(f)$ for the function (i.e., the simpler its implementation), the greater the number of single errors the function is capable of correcting, and vice versa.

9.1.3 Correction of Arithmetic Errors

We now consider the correction of arithmetic errors by systems of logic functions.

Given a system (9.1.1), we define an *arithmetic error*, as before, to be any ordered pair (z, z') of variable assignments. An error (z, z') is *corrected* if $f_i(z) = f_i(z')$ for $i = 0, 1, \ldots, k - 1$.

We consider two types of arithmetic errors: *symmetric* and *nonsymmetric* or *unidirectional*.

The multiplicity of a symmetric error (z, z'), denoted by $\|z \ominus z'\|^{(s)}$, is defined as the minimal number of terms in the representation of $z \ominus z'$ modulo p^m or $z' \ominus z$ modulo p^m as a linear combination of powers of p with exponents at most $m - 1$ and coefficients in $\{\pm 1, \pm 2, \ldots, \pm(p - 1)\}$.

For example, if $p = 2$, $m = 4$, and $z \ominus z' = 7$ (modulo 2^4), then $\|7\|^{(s)} = 2$, since $2^3 - 2^0 = 7$, but if $m = 3$ and $z \ominus z' = 7$ modulo 2^3, then $\|7\|^{(s)} = 1$, since $7 = -2^0$ modulo 2^3.

The multiplicity of a *nonsymmetric error* (z, z') is defined as the number of nonzero terms in the p-ary expansion of the number $z \ominus z'$ modulo p^m. For example, if $p = 2$, then $\|7\|^{(n)} = 3$ for any $m \geq 3$. (Note that $\|\tau\|^{(n)} = \|\tau\|$ for any $\|\tau\|$ and we nevertheless find it convenient to use the notation $\|\tau\|^{(n)}$ instead of $\|\tau\|$ throughout this section.)

It is easy to see that for any error (z, z') and any p, m,

$$\|z \ominus z'\|^{(s)} \leq \|z \ominus z'\|^{(n)}, \quad \text{mod } p^m \tag{9.1.36}$$

$$\|z \ominus z'\|^{(s)} = \|z' \ominus z\|^{(s)}. \tag{9.1.37}$$

In general, however,

$$\|z \ominus z'\|^{(n)} \neq \|z' \ominus z\|^{(n)}, \quad \text{mod } p^m.$$

An examination of the definition of multiplicity for symmetric and nonsymmetric errors reveals the following difference between the two types. In terms of a physical implementation of the system of logic functions, symmetric errors will both increase and decrease a value at the input to the device, whereas nonsymmetric errors will only increase (or only decrease) a value at the input. These two cases correspond to situations in which the input to the logic network is the output of a p-ary m-digit network implementing an arithmetical operation, and the additive noise produced by the network is two way or one way.

Any given system of logic functions corrects a certain class of algebraic errors (see Section 9.1.2) and certain classes of symmetric and nonsymmetric arithmetic errors. The latter are generally not the same, and the immediate task is therefore to find ways of constructing the classes of arithmetic errors corrected by a system.

We denote the number of l-fold symmetric (nonsymmetric) arithmetic errors corrected by a system f by $\lambda_f^{(s)}(l)$ $(\lambda_f^{(n)}(l))$. To calculate the correcting capabilities $\lambda_f^{(s)}(l)$ and $\lambda_f^{(n)}(l)$, we use a method similar to that used in Section 9.1.2 to calculate the correcting capability $\eta_f(l)$ for algebraic errors.

Let $\{f_i\}$ be the system of characteristic functions for f (see (9.1.5)). Now set

$$B_i(\tau) - \sum_{z=0}^{p^m-1} f_i(z) f_i(z \ominus \tau), \quad \text{mod } p^m \tag{9.1.38}$$

for $i = 0, 1, \ldots, p^k - 1$, $z, \tau = 0, 1, \ldots, p^m - 1$.

Reasoning as in the proof of Theorem 9.1.1, we can show that if $B_\Sigma(\tau) = \sum_{i=0}^{p^k-1} B_i(\tau)$, then

$$\lambda_f^{(s)}(l) = \sum_{\|\tau\|^{(s)}=l} B_\Sigma(\tau), \qquad (9.1.39)$$

$$\lambda_f^{(n)}(l) = \sum_{\|\tau\|^{(n)}=l} B_\Sigma(\tau). \qquad (9.1.40)$$

On the basis of formulas (9.1.39), (9.1.40), we have a simple computational procedure for computing the arithmetic error-correcting capabilities of systems of logic functions. The procedure is based on computing cyclic autocorrelation functions modulo p^m.

Example 9.1.2   *Table 9.1.2 defines a switching function of four variables ($m = 4$, $p = 2$, $k = 1$). Here, $f = f_1$ and $1 - f = f_0$. This table also shows the cyclic autocorrelation function $B(\tau) = B_1(\tau)$ of f, the total autocorrelation function*

$$B_\Sigma(\tau) = 2^m - 2\sum_z f(z) + 2B(\tau) = 4 + 2B(\tau),$$

(see (9.1.18)), and the values of $\|\tau\|^{(s)}$ and $\|\tau\|^{(n)}$.

For this example, the formulas (9.1.39) and (9.1.40) give $\lambda_f^{(s)}(1) = 40$, $\lambda_f^{(s)}(2) = 80$, $\lambda_f^{(s)}(3) = \lambda_f^{(s)}(4) = 0$, $\lambda_f^{(n)}(1) = 22$, $\lambda_f^{(n)}(2) = 60$, $\lambda_f^{(n)}(3) = 32$, $\lambda_f^{(n)}(4) = 6$.

TABLE 9.1.2   Function f in Example 9.1.2 and Its Cyclic Autocorrelation Characteristics.

z, τ	$\|\tau\|^{(s)}$	$\|\tau\|^{(n)}$	$z_0 z_1 z_2 z_3$	$f(z)$	$B(\tau)$	$B_\Sigma(\tau)$
0	0	0	0000	1	6	16
1	1	1	0001	0	1	6
2	1	1	0010	0	0	4
3	2	2	0011	1	5	14
4	1	1	0100	0	2	8
5	2	2	0101	0	0	4
6	2	2	0110	1	4	12
7	2	3	0111	0	3	10
8	1	1	1000	0	0	4
9	2	2	1001	1	3	10
10	2	2	1010	0	4	12
11	2	3	1011	0	0	4
12	1	2	1100	1	2	8
13	2	3	1101	0	5	14
14	1	3	1110	0	0	4
15	1	4	1111	1	1	6

The following theorem indicates the relationship between the numbers of correctable symmetric and nonsymmetric arithmetic errors for the case of most practical importance—single errors.

Theorem 9.1.3   *For any system f of p-valued logic functions of m*

$$\lambda_f^{(s)}(1) = \begin{cases} 2\lambda_f^{(n)}(1) - B_\Sigma(p^m/2), & \textit{if } p \textit{ is even,} \\ 2\lambda_f^{(n)}(1), & \textit{if } p \textit{ is odd.} \end{cases} \tag{9.1.41}$$

Proof. For any τ, $\|\tau\|^{(s)} = \|p^m \ominus \tau\|^{(s)}$ (modulo p^m). Hence, if $\|\tau\|^{(n)} = 1$, then $\|\tau\|^{(s)} = 1$ and $\|p^m \ominus \tau\|^{(s)} = 1$ (modulo p^m).

Moreover, for any τ and the functions $B_\Sigma(\tau)$ as defined before, we have the analogue of (9.1.11)

$$B_\Sigma(\tau) = B_\Sigma(p^m \ominus \tau), \quad \mathrm{mod}\ p^m. \tag{9.1.42}$$

If p is odd, then $\tau \neq p^m \ominus \tau$ (modulo p^m) for any τ. Therefore, by (9.1.39) and (9.1.42),

$$\lambda_f^{(s)}(1) = 2\lambda_f^{(n)}(1).$$

If p is even, then since $\tau = p^m \ominus \tau$ (modulo p^m) for any τ, we have $\|p^m/2\|^{(n)} = \|p^m/2\|^{(s)} = 1$, and hence, by (9.1.39), (9.1.40), and (9.1.42),

$$\lambda_f^{(s)}(1) = 2\lambda_f^{(n)}(1) - B_\Sigma(p^m/2),$$

proving (9.1.41).

Notice that the total correcting capabilities of any system of logic functions with respect to symmetric and nonsymmetric arithmetic errors are the same

$$\sum_{l=1}^{m} \lambda_f^{(s)}(l) = \sum_{l=1}^{m} \lambda_f^{(n)}(l) = \lambda_f. \tag{9.1.43}$$

This follows directly from (9.1.39) and (9.1.40). The quantity λ_f satisfies estimates analogous to those established for algebraic errors in Theorem 9.1.2 and Corollary 9.1.2.

The correcting capability of a system of logic functions with respect to arithmetic errors is not invariant under permutation of variables of the logic function, but it remains invariant under translation of variables of the functions itself.

For any $\leq \tau < p^m, 0 \leq q < p$,

$$\begin{cases} \lambda_{f(z)}^{(n)}(l) = \lambda_{f(z \oplus \tau)}^{(n)}(l), & \mod p^m, \\ \\ \lambda_{f(z)}^{(s)}(l) = \lambda_{f(z \oplus \tau)}^{(s)}(l), \end{cases}$$

(9.1.44)

and

$$\begin{cases} \lambda_{f(z)}^{(n)}(l) = \lambda_{f(z) \oplus q}^{(n)}(l) & \mod p^m, \\ \\ \lambda_{f(z)}^{(s)}(l) = \lambda_{f(z) \oplus q}^{(s)}(l). \end{cases}$$

(9.1.45)

The autocorrelation functions $B_i(\tau)$ modulo p^m may be calculated by using either (9.1.38) or the double Vilenkin–Chrestenson transforms $\chi^{(p^m)}$, which converts in this case into discrete Fourier transforms, with the interval of definition of the functions divided into p^m equal subintervals. The fast Fourier transform algorithm can be applied (193, 518), by using an analog of Corollary 9.1.1. If the formula (9.1.38) is employed, it is possible to use the symmetry relation (9.1.42) for $B_i(\tau)$, thus halving the computational labor involved, and in the case of symmetric errors, where $\|\tau\|^{(s)} = \|p^m \ominus \tau\|^{(s)}$, there is no need to evaluate $B_i(\tau)$ and $B_\Sigma(\tau)$ for $\tau > \lfloor p^m / 2 \rfloor$, since by using Theorem 9.1.3, we have from (9.1.39) and (9.1.40),

$$\lambda_f^{(s)}(l) = \begin{cases} 2 \sum_{\|\tau\|^{(s)}=1, 0 \leq \tau \leq p^m / 2} B_\Sigma(\tau) - B_\Sigma(p^m / 2), & \text{if } l = 1 \text{ and} \\ & p \text{ is even,} \\ \\ 2 \sum_{\|\tau\|^{(s)}=1, 0 \leq \tau \leq \lfloor p^m / 2 \rfloor} B_\Sigma(\tau), & \text{otherwise.} \end{cases}$$

(9.1.46)

We now analyze the correcting capability of systems of logic functions when the probabilities of individual errors are given. The correcting capability is measured by the expected number of corrected errors.

We now confine the attention to algebraic and symmetric arithmetic errors. Each error (z, z') is assigned a certain probability and the errors (z, z') and (z', z) are assumed to have the same probability.

Given a system of p-valued logic functions of m variables, we represent an algebraic error by $z \ominus z'$ (mod p) and an arithmetic error by $z \ominus z'$ (mod p^m). For each error $z \ominus z'$ (mod p), or $z \ominus z'$ (mod p^m), we assume given a probability $P(z \ominus z')$ (mod p) or $Q(z \ominus z')$ (mod p^m), such that

$$P(z \ominus z') = P(z' \ominus z), \quad \mod p, \tag{9.1.47}$$

$$Q(z \ominus z') = Q(z' \ominus z), \quad \mod p^m. \tag{9.1.48}$$

Thus, for any $\tau \in \{1, 2, \ldots, p^m - 1\}$, we can define functions $P(\tau)$ and $Q(\tau)$ giving the probabilities of algebraic and arithmetic errors (z, z') such that $\tau = z \ominus z'$ (mod p) and $\tau = z \ominus z'$ (mod p^m), respectively.

Formulas (9.1.8), (9.1.39), and (9.1.40) may be generalized to this case.

Let $M\{\eta_f(l)\}$ and $M\{\lambda_f^{(s)}(j)\}$ denote the numbers of *expected l-fold algebraic and symmetric arithmetic errors*, respectively, that can be corrected by a system f. Then,

$$M\{\eta_f(l)\} = \sum_{\|\tau\|=l} P(\tau) B_\Sigma(\tau), \qquad (9.1.49)$$

where $B_\Sigma(\tau)$ is the total autocorrelation function modulo p (see (9.1.7)), and

$$M\{\lambda_f^{(s)}(l)\} = \sum_{\|\tau\|^{(s)}=l} Q(\tau) B_\Sigma(\tau), \qquad (9.1.50)$$

where $B_\Sigma(\tau)$ is the total autocorrelation function modulo p^m.

Thus, the expected numbers of correctable errors may also be analyzed in terms of the corresponding autocorrelation functions.

9.2 SPECTRAL METHODS FOR SYNTHESIS OF RELIABLE DIGITAL DEVICES

The previous section was devoted to spectral methods for analysis of the error-correcting capability of systems of logical functions. We will use the results for the synthesis of reliable systems for the transmission and logical processing of information. We use binary signals throughout this section, though the results may be generalized to p-ary signals ($p > 2$).

9.2.1 Reliable Systems for Transmission and Logic Processing

The structure of the most general information transmission and processing system is shown in Fig. 9.2.1.

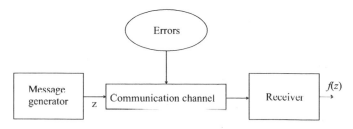

FIGURE 9.2.1   Digital system for transmission and processing of information.

We assume that the message generator produces information in the form of binary vectors $(q_0, \ldots, q_{m-1})$. This information may be distorted because of errors in the communication channel or in the message generator itself. It then proceeds to the input of the receiver. We consider parallel transmission; that is, all the components z_i, $i = 0, 1, \ldots, m - 1$ reach the receiver input simultaneously, and the receiver itself is a switching network with no memory elements. It should be noticed, however, that all the synthesis methods to be examined below may be extended to cases in which the information is transmitted in a serial code and the receiver includes memory elements (see Section 9.3).

We also assume that the errors appearing at the receiver input are algebraic, that is to say, an l-fold error will be an error distorting exactly l bits of the input signal.

If the receiver includes no memory elements, its operation may be described by a system of switching functions

$$y^{(s)} = f^{(s)}(z_0, \ldots, z_{m-1}), \quad s = 0, 1, \ldots, k - 1. \tag{9.2.1}$$

Note that the information processor realizing system (9.2.1) could have been combined with the message generator, however, combined are the results $\{y^{(s)}\}$, $s = 0, 1, \ldots, k - 1$ being transmitted along the communication channel. For many important applications this is, however, impossible as, for example, when the complexity of the message generator is restricted. Further, transmission of the result $\{y^{(s)}\}$, $s = 0, 1, \ldots, k - 1$ may prove to be no more reliable than that of the message $\{z_i\}$, $i = 0, 1, \ldots, m - 1$, for example, when $m \geq k$.

The reliability of the system illustrated in Fig. 9.2.1 may be increased by using the sophisticated methods of the theory of error-correcting codes (39, 55, 426, 437). The information $(z_0, \ldots, z_{m-1})$ is then transmitted in a redundant code (i.e., additional variables $z_m, \ldots, z_{m+r-1}$ are required) and quite complex encoders and decoders are needed. The system in Fig. 9.2.1 differs from those based on classical coding theory in that the information received is processed in the receiver that computes (9.2.1).

As shown in Section 9.1, the system of switching functions describing the operation of the receiver has a certain error-correcting capability. Therefore, instead of transmitting information in a redundant code and introducing encoders and decoders, we shall represent the information by a nonredundant code, trying at the same time to make full use of the correcting capability of the system of switching functions describing the operation of the receiver.

We assume that the errors in the communication channel are algebraic (see Section 9.1). For the sake of generality, we allow the probabilities of distortion of the individual transmitted symbols z_i, $i = 0, 1, \ldots, m - 1$ or of their combinations to be different. This will be the situation, for example, if the information is transmitted in parallel code along m channels with different statistical properties.

We consider the case in which the system (9.2.1) describing the receiver is completely specified. The problem is to minimize the expected number of uncorrected errors of the type in question at the output of the entire system of Fig. 9.2.1, that is, the output of the receiver.

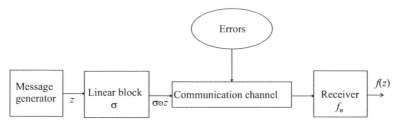

FIGURE 9.2.2   Linearized digital system for transmission and processing.

To increase the reliability of the entire transmission and processing system, we shall linearize the system of switching functions describing the receiver. As usual, we represent system (9.2.1) by a discrete function $f(z)$, $z = 0, 1, \ldots, 2^{m-1}$ and then express $f(z)$ as

$$f(z) = f_\sigma(\sigma \odot z), \qquad (9.2.2)$$

where σ is an $(m \times m)$ matrix nonsingular over $GF(2)$ and $\odot$ is the symbol for matrix multiplication over $GF(2)$.

We now replace the original system of Fig. 9.2.1 by that represented schematically in Fig. 9.2.2.

Here, we introduced an additional linear block implementing multiplication by the matrix σ (the complexity of this block is comparatively low, involving a number of two-input modulo 2 adders of the order of $m^2 / \log_2 m$, see Section 6.1.6.1). The modified receiver now realizes the function f_σ. Thus, on the basis of the superposition (9.2.2), we have a decomposition of the function f into blocks σ and f_σ, the task of correcting errors in the communication channel being assigned to f_σ.

The problem is now to determine a matrix σ minimizing the expected number of errors that are not corrected by f_σ. The solution of this problem for various classes of errors is the main topic of this section.

9.2.2 Correction of Single Errors

We start with a system of completely specified switching functions

$$y^{(s)} = f^{(s)}(z_0, \ldots, z_{m-1}), \quad s = 0, 1, \ldots, k - 1.$$

Let p_i for $i = 0, 1, \ldots, m - 1$ denote the probability of distortion of the transmitted symbol $z = \sigma \odot y$ and Θ the class of all nonsingular $(m \times m)$ matrices over $GF(2)$, that is, with elements in $\{0, 1\}$, and define f_σ by

$$f_\sigma(\sigma \odot z) = f(z), \quad \mod 2,$$

where $\sigma \in \Theta$ and $f(z)$ represents $\{f^{(s)}\}$.

Let $M\{\eta_{f_\sigma}(l)\}$ denote the number of expected errors with the multiplicity l that can be corrected by f_σ. Then, the problem is to find σ_1 such that

$$M\{\eta_{f_{\sigma_1}}(1)\} = \max_{\sigma \in \Theta} M\{\eta_{f_{\sigma_1}}(1)\}, \qquad (9.2.3)$$

where f_σ is defined by (9.2.2).

As usual, let $\{f_t(z)\}, t = 0, 1, \ldots, 2^k - 1$ denote the system of characteristic functions of $f(z)$ and $B_\Sigma(\tau)$ the total autocorrelation function of $\{f_t(z)\}$,

$$B_\Sigma(\tau) = \sum_{t=0}^{2^k-1} B_t(\tau) = \sum_{t=0}^{2^m-1} \sum_{z=0}^{2^m-1} f_t(z)f_t(z \oplus \tau), \quad \text{mod } 2. \qquad (9.2.4)$$

For a given system $(\tau_0, \ldots, \tau_{m-1})$ of m binary vectors of the length m, we define a matrix $\mathbf{T}$ whose columns are $\tau_0, \ldots, \tau_{m-1}$.

Theorem 9.2.1   *Let*

$$\max_{T \in \Theta} \sum_{i=0}^{m-1} p_i B_\Sigma(\tau_i) = \sum_{i=0}^{m-1} p_i B_\Sigma(\tilde{\tau}_i). \qquad (9.2.5)$$

Then,

$$\tilde{T} \odot \sigma_1 = \mathbf{I}_m, \quad \text{mod } 2, \qquad (9.2.6)$$

where $\mathbf{I}_m$ is the $(m \times m)$ identity matrix.

The proof follows immediately from the observation that

$$\sum_{i=0}^{m-1} p_i B_\Sigma(2^i) = M\{\eta_f(1)\}, \qquad (9.2.7)$$

after which Theorem 2.7.4 may be used.

Note that if $p_i = 1, i = 0, 1, \ldots, m - 1$, and $l = 1$, formula (9.2.7) follows from Theorem 9.1.1.

It follows from Theorem 9.2.1 that to find σ_1 we need to determine m vectors $\tilde{\tau}_0, \ldots, \tilde{\tau}_{m-1}$ linearly independent over $GF(2)$, which maximize $\sum_{i=0}^{m-1} p_i B_\Sigma(\tau_i)$. These vectors may be determined by the following simple algorithm.

Arrange the probabilities $p_i, i = 0, 1, \ldots, m - 1$ in decreasing order

$$p_{i_0} \geq p_{i_1} \geq \cdots \geq p_{i_{m-1}}, \quad i_s \neq i_r \text{ if } s \neq r. \qquad (9.2.8)$$

Now put

$$\max_{\tau \neq 0} B_\Sigma(\tau) = B_\Sigma(\tilde{\tau}_{i_0}). \tag{9.2.9}$$

Assuming that $\tilde{\tau}_{i_0}, \ldots, \tilde{\tau}_{i_s}$, for $s < m - 1$ have already been found, let $\tilde{\tau}_{i_{s+1}}$ be a vector satisfying the condition

$$\max_{\tau \notin L_s} B_\Sigma(\tau) = B_\Sigma(\tilde{\tau}_{i_{s+1}}), \tag{9.2.10}$$

where L_s is the set of all linear combinations of $\tilde{\tau}_0, \tilde{\tau}_1, \ldots, \tilde{\tau}_{m-1}$ over $GF(2)$.

Denote this algorithm by A. The output $\tilde{\tau}_0, \ldots, \tilde{\tau}_{m-1}$ of the algorithm A applied to $B_\Sigma(\tau)$ is independent of the probabilities p_i, $i = 0, 1, \ldots, m - 1$ and depends just on their ordering (9.2.8). If $p_i = 1$, $i = 0, 1, \ldots, m - 1$, algorithm A is simply the linearization algorithm for a system of switching functions with respect to $\eta(f)$ (see Section 5.4).

This provides yet another indication of the relationship between the concepts of complexity and the error-correcting capability of logic functions (see Section 9.1.2).

Example 9.2.1   *Table 9.2.1 defines two switching functions of three variables and also shows the discrete function $f(z)$ assigned to them, the characteristic functions $f_i(z)$, the autocorrelation functions $B_i(\tau)$, and the total autocorrelation function $B_\Sigma(\tau)$.*

Let the distortion probabilities be $p_0 = 0.7$, $p_1 = 0.8$, $p_2 = 0.9$. Then, by the algorithm A

$$\tilde{\tau}_2 = [1, 1, 1], \quad \tilde{\tau}_1 = [1, 0, 0], \quad \tilde{\tau}_0 = [0, 1, 0],$$

TABLE 9.2.1   Function f in Example 9.2.1, Its Autocorrelation and Cross-Correlation Functions.

z, τ	$z_0 z_1 z_2$	$f_0 f_1$	f	$f^0 f^1 f_2 f_3$	$B_0 B_1 B_2 B_3$	B_Σ	R	A_Σ
0	000	00	0	1000	1223	6	000000	0
1	001	11	3	0001	0000	0	002222	12
2	010	01	1	0100	0002	2	200202	8
3	011	10	2	0010	0000	0	020042	8
4	100	11	3	0001	0020	2	002040	8
5	101	01	1	0100	0002	2	200202	8
6	110	11	3	0001	0000	0	002222	12
7	111	10	2	0010	0202	4	020002	4

and

$$\tilde{\mathbf{T}} = \begin{bmatrix} 0 & 1 & 1 \\ 1 & 0 & 1 \\ 0 & 0 & 1 \end{bmatrix}$$

and by (9.2.6)

$$\sigma_1 = \tilde{\mathbf{T}}^{-1} = \begin{bmatrix} 0 & 1 & 1 \\ 1 & 0 & 1 \\ 0 & 0 & 1 \end{bmatrix}, \quad mod\ 2.$$

By using (9.2.7), we obtain the following expected values for the number of correctable errors

$$M\{\eta_f(1)\} = 0.7 \cdot 2 + 0.8 \cdot 2 + 0.9 \cdot 0 = 3,$$

$$M\{\eta_{f_{\sigma_1}}(1)\} = 0.9 \cdot 4 + 0.8 \cdot 2 + 0.7 \cdot 2 = 6.6.$$

To determine an optimal linear transformation σ_1, maximizing the expected number of correctable single errors, and to estimate the expected values themselves, it is possible to use the data collected in the Appendix A. In some cases, these data also yield analytical expressions for σ_1, $M\{\eta_f(1)\}$ and $M\{\eta_{f_{\sigma_1}}(1)\}$.

9.2.3 Correction of Burst Errors

A *burst of the length b* in a signal $(z_0, \ldots, z_{m-1})$ is defined as the simultaneous distortion of b variables $z_i, z_{i+1}, \ldots, z_{i+b-1}$ if $i \le m - 1 - b$ or $z_i, z_{i+1}, \ldots, z_{m-1}$ if $i > m - 1 - b$. Thus, if (z_1, z_2) is a burst of width b, then

$$z_1 \oplus z_2 \in \{\overbrace{1, 1, \ldots, 1}^{b}0, 0, \ldots, 0), (0, \overbrace{1, 1, \ldots, 1}^{b}, 0, 0, \ldots, 0), \ldots,$$

$$(0, 0, \ldots, 0, \overbrace{1, 1, \ldots, 1}^{b}), \ldots, (0, 0, \ldots, 0, 1, 1), (0, 0, \ldots, 0, 1)\}, \quad mod\ 2.$$

Example 9.2.2 *For example, if $b = 2$, $m = 4$, then*

$$z_1 \oplus z_2 \in \{(1, 1, 0, 0), (0, 1, 1, 0), (0, 0, 1, 1), (0, 0, 0, 1)\}, \quad mod\ 2.$$

As we have defined them, burst errors are "solid," in the sense that the distortion of a variable z_i invariably entails distortion of $z_{i+1}, \ldots, z_{i+b-1}$ if $i \le m - 1 - b$, or of $z_{i+1}, \ldots, z_{m-1}$ if $i > m - 1 - b$ (here z_i is assumed to be the leftmost erroneous bit). The concept of burst is a generalization of the single error. A burst of the length $b = 1$ is a single error.

Now let $p_i(b)$ be the probability of a burst of the length b for which the first distorted variable is z_i. We consider the parameters b and $p_i(b)$, for $i = 0, 1, \ldots, m - 1$ as given quantities, together with the system (9.2.1) of switching functions.

If $f(z)$ is the function representing the system (9.2.1) and $f_\sigma(z)$ is defined as in (9.2.2), we denote the expected numbers of corrected bursts of the length b by $M\{\eta_f^B(b)\}, M\{\eta_{f_\sigma}^B(b)\}$.

Let σ_b^B denote an optimal linear transformation of variables, maximizing $M\{\eta_{f_\sigma}^B(b)\}$.

The problem may be stated as follows: given $f(z)$, b and $p_i(b)$ for $i = 0, 1, \ldots, m - 1$, find a $(m \times m)$ matrix σ_b^B such that

$$\max_{\sigma \in \Theta} M\{\eta_{f_\sigma}^B(b)\} = M\{\eta_{f_{\sigma_b}^B}^B(b)\}. \tag{9.2.11}$$

Note that $M\{\eta_{f_\sigma}(1)\} = M\{\eta_f^B(1)\}$ and $\sigma_1^B = \sigma_1$.

Let $\mathbf{E}_m^{(b)}$ denote the $(m \times m)$ matrix whose columns are

$$(\overbrace{11\ldots1}^{b}0\ldots0), (0\overbrace{11\ldots1}^{b}0\ldots0), \ldots, (0\ldots\overbrace{11\ldots1}^{b}), (0\ldots0\overbrace{11\ldots1}^{b}), \ldots,$$

$$(00\ldots01).$$

Example 9.2.3   *For example, if $m = 3$, $b = 2$, then*

$$\mathbf{E}_3^{(2)} = \begin{bmatrix} 1 & 0 & 0 \\ 1 & 1 & 0 \\ 0 & 1 & 1 \end{bmatrix}.$$

For any b and m, the matrix $E_m^{(b)}$ is nonsingular over $GF(2)$ and $\mathbf{E}_m^{(1)} = \mathbf{I}_m$.

Theorem 9.2.2   *Let $B_\Sigma(\tau)$ be the total autocorrelation function of the system (9.2.1) (see (9.2.4)) and $\tilde{\tau}_0, \tilde{\tau}_1, \ldots, \tilde{\tau}_{m-1}$ linearly independent vectors of the length m over $GF(2)$ maximizing the function $\sum_{i=0}^{m-1} p_i(b)B_\Sigma(\tau_i)$.*

Let $\tilde{T}$ be the matrix with columns $\tilde{\tau}_0, \ldots, \tilde{\tau}_{m-1}$. Then,

$$\tilde{T} \odot \sigma_b^B = E_m^{(b)}, \quad mod\ 2. \tag{9.2.12}$$

The proof follows from the observation that

$$\sum_{i=0}^{m-1} p_i(b)B_\Sigma(e_{i,m}^{(b)}) = M\{\eta_f^B(b)\}, \tag{9.2.13}$$

where $e_{i,m}^{(b)}$ is the number whose binary expansion is the ith column of $E_m^{(b)}$, after which Theorem 2.7.4 can be applied.

Theorem 9.2.1 is the special case of the Theorem 9.2.2 with $b = 1$. Thus, to determine σ_b^B, we need to apply the algorithm A to $B_\Sigma(\tau)$ and then use (9.2.2).

Example 9.2.4 *As an example, consider the system of switching functions defined in Table 9.2.1 ($m = 3$). Set $b = 2$, $p_0(2) = 0.9$, $p_1(2) = 0.8$, $p_2(2) = 0.7$. (Thus, the probability of a simultaneous distortion of z_0 and z_1 is 0.9, for z_1 and z_2 the probability is 0.8, and for z_2 it is 0.7.) The function B_Σ is given in Table 9.2.1. Applying the algorithm A, we have*

$$
\tilde{T} = \begin{bmatrix} 1 & 0 & 1 \\ 1 & 1 & 0 \\ 1 & 0 & 0 \end{bmatrix}.
$$

Since

$$
\mathbf{E}_3^{(2)} = \begin{bmatrix} 1 & 0 & 0 \\ 1 & 1 & 0 \\ 0 & 1 & 1 \end{bmatrix},
$$

it follows from (9.2.12) that

$$
\sigma_2^B = \begin{bmatrix} 1 & 0 & 1 \\ 1 & 1 & 0 \\ 1 & 0 & 0 \end{bmatrix}^{-1} \odot \begin{bmatrix} 1 & 0 & 0 \\ 1 & 1 & 0 \\ 0 & 1 & 1 \end{bmatrix} = \begin{bmatrix} 0 & 0 & 1 \\ 1 & 1 & 1 \\ 1 & 0 & 1 \end{bmatrix}, \quad mod\ 2.
$$

Thus, by using (9.2.13), we obtain

$$
M\{\eta_f^B(2)\} = 0 \cdot 0.9 + 0 \cdot 0.8 + 0 \cdot 0.7 = 0,
$$

$$
M\{\eta_{f\sigma_2}^B(2)\} = 4 \cdot 0.9 + 2 \cdot 0.8 + 2 \cdot 0.7 = 6.6.
$$

9.2.4 Correction of Errors with Different Costs

We now characterize errors not only by their probabilities but also by their costs. In general, different errors that are not corrected will incur different costs. The *cost of an error* may be measured by its significance in a given system relative to other subsequent systems. The cost of an error leading to distortion of all the components of the output may usually be assumed to be larger than that of an error distorting only some of the components. Thus, all the results of this section will be generalizations of those in Sections 9.2.2 and 9.2.3. We proceed to the formal discussion.

Consider a system of k switching functions of m variables represented by the function $f(z)$.

Let $C(\alpha, \beta)$ be a given real-valued function for $\alpha, \beta \in \{0, 1, \ldots, 2^k - 1\}$. The *cost of an error* (z_1, z_2) for $z_1, z_2 \in \{0, 1, \ldots, 2^m - 1\}$ is defined as $C(f(z_1), f(z_2))$. The function $C(\alpha, \beta)$ is assumed to have the properties

$$C(\alpha, \alpha) = 0, \tag{9.2.14}$$

$$C(\alpha, \beta) = C(\beta, \alpha). \tag{9.2.15}$$

Formula (9.2.14) means that corrected errors cost nothing, and (9.2.15) means that errors (z_1, z_2) and (z_2, z_1) have equal costs.

We consider burst errors (and also single errors, since they are special cases of bursts, see Section 9.2.3). As before, every error is assigned a probability $p_i(b)$.

Let $M\{C_f^B(b)\}$ denote the expected cost of errors that are not corrected. The problem is now to find a nonsingular matrix $\tilde{\sigma}_b^B$ minimizing $M\{C_{f_{\tilde{\sigma}_b}^B}(b)\}$, where f_σ is defined by (9.2.2)

$$\min_{\sigma \in \Theta} M\{C_{f_\sigma}^B(b)\} = M\{C_{f_{\tilde{\sigma}_b}^B}^B(b)\}. \tag{9.2.16}$$

The previously considered problem (9.2.11) is a special case of (9.2.16). Set

$$C(\alpha, \beta) = \begin{cases} 1, & \text{if } \alpha \neq \beta, \\ 0, & \text{if } \alpha = \beta. \end{cases}$$

Instead of the autocorrelation functions for the solution of the problem (9.2.16), we will use the *cross-correlation functions* of the original system.

The *weighted total cross-correlation function* of the characteristic functions $\{f_t(z)\}$, for $t = 0, 1, \ldots, 2^k - 1$ is defined as

$$A_\Sigma(\tau) = \sum_{t_1 \neq t_2} C(t_1, t_2) A_{t_1, t_2}(\tau) \tag{9.2.17}$$

$$= \sum_{t_1 \neq t_2} C(t_1, t_2) \sum_{z=0}^{2^m - 1} f_{t_1}(z) f_{t_2}(z \oplus \tau), \quad \text{mod 2}. \tag{9.2.18}$$

Theorem 9.2.3 *Let*

$$\min_{T \in \Theta} \sum_{i=0}^{m-1} p_i(b) A_\Sigma(\tau_i) = \sum_{i=0}^{m-1} p_i(b) A_\Sigma(\tilde{\tau}_i). \tag{9.2.19}$$

Then,

$$\tilde{T} \odot \tilde{\sigma}_b^B = \mathbf{E}_m^{(b)}, \quad mod\ 2, \tag{9.2.20}$$

where τ_i and $\tilde{\tau}_i$ are the columns of the matrices T and $\tilde{T}$, respectively.

The proof is immediate, by Theorem 2.7.4, since

$$\sum_{i=0}^{m-1} p_i(b) A_\Sigma(e_{i,m}^{(b)}) = M\{C_f^B(b)\}, \tag{9.2.21}$$

where $e_{i,m}^{(b)}$ is the ith column of $\mathbf{E}_m^{(b)}$.

This theorem is a further generalization of Theorems 9.2.1 and 9.2.2, since for any $f(z)$ and any τ if the cost function is

$$C(\alpha, \beta) = \begin{cases} 1, & \text{if } \alpha \neq \beta, \\ 0, & \alpha = 0, \end{cases}$$

then

$$A_\Sigma(\tau) + B_\Sigma(\tau) = 2^m. \tag{9.2.22}$$

To determine $\tilde{T}$ from the condition (9.2.19), we can use a modified version of the basic algorithm A, with maximization of $B_\Sigma(\tau)$ in (9.2.9) and (9.2.10) replaced by the minimization of $A_\Sigma(\tau)$.

Example 9.2.5 *As an example, we determine the optimal linear transformation $\tilde{\sigma}_1$ for correction of single errors ($b = 1$) in Table 9.2.1, with the cost function defined by $C(\alpha, \beta) = \|\alpha \oplus \beta\|$.*

The functions $A_{t_1 t_2}(\tau)$ and $A_\Sigma(\tau)$ are also shown in Table 9.2.1, where $R = (2A_{01}, 2A_{02}, 2A_{03}, 2A_{12}, 2A_{13}, 2A_{23})$.

Since $A_{t_1 t_2}(\tau) = A_{t_2 t_1}(\tau)$, the table specifies the values of $2A_{t_1 t_2}(\tau)$ for $t_1 < t_2$.

Suppose that the distortion probabilities are $p_0(1) = 0.9$, $p_1(1) = 0.8$, and $p_2(1) = 0.7$. Then the modified algorithm A gives

$$\tilde{T} = \begin{bmatrix} 1 & 0 & 1 \\ 1 & 1 & 0 \\ 1 & 0 & 0 \end{bmatrix}$$

and

$$\tilde{\sigma}_1^B = \tilde{\sigma}_1 = \begin{bmatrix} 1 & 0 & 1 \\ 1 & 1 & 0 \\ 1 & 0 & 0 \end{bmatrix}^{-1} = \begin{bmatrix} 0 & 0 & 1 \\ 0 & 1 & 1 \\ 1 & 0 & 1 \end{bmatrix}, \quad mod\ 2,$$

and formula (9.2.21) yields the following expected single-error costs for the systems f and $f_{\tilde{\sigma}_1}$

$$M\{C_f(1)\} = 12 \cdot 0.9 + 8 \cdot 0.8 + 8 \cdot 0.7 = 22.8,$$

$$M\{C_{f_{\tilde{\sigma}_1}}(1)\} = 4 \cdot 0.9 + 8 \cdot 0.8 + 8 \cdot 0.7 = 15.6.$$

To minimize the expected error costs, the weighted total cross-correlation function A_Σ is constructed and applied to the modified algorithm A.

For large values of k, that is, for functions with many outputs, construction of the function A_Σ by (9.2.17) may become quite cumbersome. We therefore devote some attention to ways and means of simplifying the construction of it.

We first observe that since $C(t_1, t_2) = C(t_2, t_1)$ and $A_{t_1 t_2}(\tau) = A_{t_2 t_1}(\tau)$, it follows from (9.2.17) that

$$A_\Sigma(\tau) = 2 \sum_{t_1 < t_2} C(t_1, t_2) A_{t_1 t_2}(\tau) \tag{9.2.23}$$

$$= 2 \sum_{t_1 < t_2} C(t_1, t_2) \sum_{z=0}^{2^m - 1} f_{t_1}(z) f_{t_2}(z \oplus \tau), \quad \text{mod } 2. \tag{9.2.24}$$

Thus the functions $A_{t_1 t_2}(\tau)$ can be derived from the characteristic functions $f_t(z)$ in terms of double Walsh transforms, using the fast Walsh–Hadamard transform algorithm.

The cost of an error that is not corrected by a selected system of functions $y^{(s)} = f^{(s)}(z_0, \ldots, z_{m-1})$, for $s = 0, 1, \ldots, k - 1$ may be determined by the number of functions in the system that change value on appearance of the error.

If $y(z)$ is the value vector of the system, the cost of an error (z_1, z_2) is a function (usually monotone increasing) of $\| y(z_1) \oplus y(z_2) \|$. Then, $C(\alpha, \beta) = C(\| \alpha \oplus \beta \|)$ and A_Σ may be expressed as

$$A_\Sigma(\tau) = \sum_{z=0}^{2^m - 1} C(\| y(z) \oplus y(z \oplus \tau) \|), \quad \text{mod } 2. \tag{9.2.25}$$

This formula may be more convenient for large values of k.

9.2.5 Correction of Multiple Errors

In the previous sections, we studied the correction of single errors and bursts with different probabilities and error costs. We now consider correction of errors of arbitrary multiplicity.

Recall that the multiplicity of an error (z_1, z_2) is the number $\| z_1 \oplus z_2 \|$. Suppose that, given a system of switching functions (9.2.1), we want to correct all errors of a multiplicity not exceeding some number $l \geq 1$. The previous results (Theorems 9.2.1, 9.2.3) may be generalized to the case of arbitrary l, but the computational complexity of the algorithms is greatly increased.

As before, we assume that each error is assigned a probability and a cost. By the probability of an error (z_1, z_2), we mean the probability of simultaneous distortion of variables $(z_{i_1}, \ldots, z_{i_r})$ for which $(z_1 \oplus z_2)_{i_1} = \cdots = (z_1 \oplus z_2)_{i_r} = 1$. Thus, any two errors (z_1, z_2), (z_3, z_4) such that $z_1 \oplus z_2 = z_3 \oplus z_4$ have equal probabilities, so that we can consider the error probability as a function $p(z)$ defined for $z \in \{1, 2, \ldots,$ $2^m - 1\}$. If we are interested in errors of the multiplicity smaller or equal to l, then $p(z) = 0$ if $\|z\| > l$.

The cost of an error (z_1, z_2) will again be $C(f(z_1), f(z_2))$, where $C(\alpha, \beta)$ is a function satisfying (9.2.14) and (9.2.15).

Let $M\{C_{f_\sigma}(f)\}$ be the expected cost of errors of the multiplicity smaller or equal to l that are not corrected by f_σ. The problem is thus to determine a matrix $\tilde{\sigma}$ such that

$$\min_{\sigma \in \Theta} M\{C_{f_\sigma}(l)\} = M\{C_{f_{\tilde{\sigma}_l}}\}. \tag{9.2.26}$$

Let $\tau_0, \ldots, \tau_{m-1}$ be an m-tuple of vectors and T the matrix with columns $\tau_0, \ldots, \tau_{m-1}$, and $L_l(\tau, \ldots, \tau_{m-1})$ denote the set of all linear combinations $d_0 \tau_0 \oplus \cdots d_{m-1} \tau_{m-1}$ modulo 2, where $d_0, \ldots, d_{m-1} \in \{0, 1\}$ and the number $\|d\|$ of nonzero components of the vector $[d_0, \ldots, d_{m-1}]$ satisfies the inequality $0 < \|d\| \le l$.

As before, we denote the weighted total cross-correlation function of the characteristic functions by $A_\Sigma(\tau)$ (see(9.2.23)).

Theorem 9.2.4 *Let*

$$\min_{T \in \Theta} \sum_{q \in L_l(\tau_0, \ldots, \tau_{m-1})} p(q) A_\Sigma(q) = \sum_{q \in L_l(\tilde{\tau}_0, \ldots, \tilde{\tau}_{m-1})} p(q) A_\Sigma(q). \tag{9.2.27}$$

Then,

$$\tilde{T} \otimes \tilde{\sigma}_l = \mathbf{I}_m, \quad mod\ 2. \tag{9.2.28}$$

The proof is based on the relation

$$\sum_{q \in L_l(e_0, \ldots, e_{m-1})} p(q) A_\sigma(q) = M\{C_f(l)\}, \tag{9.2.29}$$

where $e_i = \{\underbrace{0, \ldots, 0}_{i}, 1, 0, \ldots, 0)$.

Setting $l = 1$ in Theorem 9.2.4 and using (9.2.22) we get Theorem 9.2.1 and also the case $b = 1$ in Theorem 9.2.3.

Example 9.2.6 *As an example, consider the correction of double errors by the system in Table 9.2.1,* *for $C(\alpha, \beta) = \|\alpha \oplus \beta\|$ and*

$$p(q) = \begin{cases} 0.9, & \text{if } \|q\| = 1, \\ 0.8, & \text{if } \|q\| = 2, \\ 0, & \text{otherwise.} \end{cases}$$

The function A_Σ is given in Table 9.2.1, and from this and the formula (9.2.27) we can set

$$\tilde{T} = \begin{bmatrix} 1 & 0 & 1 \\ 1 & 1 & 0 \\ 1 & 0 & 0 \end{bmatrix}.$$

Then,

$$\tilde{\sigma}_2 = \begin{bmatrix} 0 & 0 & 1 \\ 0 & 1 & 1 \\ 1 & 0 & 1 \end{bmatrix},$$

and by (9.2.29)

$$M\{C_f(2)\} = \sum_{q \in L_2(e_0, e_1, e_2)} p(q) A_\Sigma(q)$$

$$= 0.9(12 + 8 + 8) + 0.8(8 + 8 + 12) = 47.6$$

and

$$M\{C_{f_\sigma}(2)\} = \sum_{q \in L_2((111),(010),(100))} p(q) A_\Sigma(q)$$

$$= 0.9(4 + 8 + 8) + 0.8(8 + 8 + 12) = 40.4.$$

To summarize, in order to find the matrix $\tilde{\sigma}_l$ of an optimal linear transformation, minimizing the expected cost of errors of the multiplicity smaller or equal l that are not corrected, it is sufficient to construct $A_\Sigma(\tau)$ for f and to find $\tilde{T}$ from the condition (9.2.27). Notice, however, that in the general case $(l > 1)$ the determination of $\tilde{T}$ is a fairly complicated problem, which can no longer be solved by the basic algorithm A.

9.3 CORRECTING CAPABILITY OF SEQUENTIAL MACHINES

In this section, we assume that the mathematical model of a digital device with memory is the finite automaton defined as

$$M = \{X, A, Y, a_0, \phi(x, a), g(a)\},$$

where X is the set of input signals, A the set of (internal) states, Y the set of output signals, a_0 the initial state ($a_0 \in A$), $\phi(x, a)$ the next-state function ($X \times A \overset{\phi}{\to} A$), and $g(a)$ the output function ($A \overset{g}{\to} Y$).

We may assume without loss of generality that $Y = A$ and $g(a) = a$. Methods for specification and spectral implementation of finite automata were considered in Section 7.1.

9.3.1 Error Models for Finite Automata

Let $q = x_0 x_1, \ldots, x_{m-1}$ be an input word (i.e., a string of input signals) of the length m ($x_i \in X, i = 0, 1, \ldots, m - 1$), and set

$$\phi(q, a) = \phi(x_{m-1}, \ldots, \phi(x_2, \phi(x_1, \phi(x_0, a))) \ldots), \qquad (9.3.1)$$

$$\phi(q, a_0) = \phi(q). \qquad (9.3.2)$$

For example,

$$\phi(x_0 x_1 x_2, a) = \phi(x_2, \phi(x_1, \phi(x_0, a))).$$

We say that two states $a_i, a_j \in A$ are *equivalent* if, for any input word p,

$$\phi(p, a_i) = \phi(p, a_j).$$

Henceforth, we confine the attention to minimal automata, that is, to automata whose all states are pairwise inequivalent.

A standard theorem of automata theory states that for any automaton it is possible to construct a minimal automaton with minimal number of internal states implementing the same mapping of the set of input words into the set of output words, see References 247, 313.

An *error in a finite automaton* is defined as an arbitrary ordered pair (q, q') of input words where $q \neq q'$.

We say that the finite automaton *corrects an error* (q, q) if $\phi(q) = \phi(q')$. It will be shown below that every automaton corrects a certain (generally nonempty) set of errors.

9.3.2 Computing an Expected Number of Corrected Errors

Let Q be a set of errors for an automaton M. Suppose that each error $(q, q') \in Q$ is assigned a probability $p(q, q')$. The problem is to calculate the expected number $M\{\eta(Q)\}$ of errors from Q that are corrected by M.

We first construct a system of characteristic functions $\phi_i(q)$, defined on all input word

$$
\phi_i(q) = \begin{cases} 1, & \text{if } \phi(q) = a_i, \\ 0, & \text{otherwise}, \end{cases} \tag{9.3.3}
$$

for $i = 0, 1, \ldots, n_a - 1$, where n_a is the number of states.

We now define the total "two-dimensional" autocorrelation function of the characteristic functions

$$
B_\Sigma(q, q') = \sum_{i=0}^{n_a - 1} \phi_i(q)\phi_i(q'). \tag{9.3.4}
$$

The following theorem is a direct corollary from the above definitions.

Theorem 9.3.1

$$
M\{\eta(Q)\} = \sum_{(q,q')\in Q} p(q, q')B_\Sigma(q, q'). \tag{9.3.5}
$$

This theorem provides a formula for the expected number of errors in any set Q corrected by a given automaton. Its practical use, however, is limited by the fact that the computation of $M\{\eta(Q)\}$ is quite tedious even for relatively small values of n_a. The difficulties stem both from the need to calculate the characteristic functions $\phi_i(q)$ for $i = 0, 1, \ldots, n_a - 1$ by (9.3.1)–(9.3.3), and from the complexity of computation of the two-dimensional autocorrelation function by formula (9.3.4).

9.3.2.1 Simplified Calculation of Characteristic Functions   We first consider how to simplify calculation of the characteristic functions $\phi_i(q)$.

We assume that the original automaton M is defined by an $(n_a \times n_a)$ matrix $[M_{i,j}]$, where $M_{i,j} = \{x_{s_0}, x_{s_1}, \cdots, x_{s_\mu}\}$, for $x_{s_k} \in X$, and $k = 1, 2 \ldots, \mu$ iff

$$
\phi(x_{s_0}, a_i) = \phi(x_{s_1}, a_i) = \cdots = \phi(x_{s_\mu}, a_i) = a_j.
$$

If there is no $x_s \in X$ such that $\phi(x_s, a_i) = a_j$, we put $M_{i,j} = \emptyset$, where $\emptyset$ is the symbol for the empty set.

For two ($n_a \times n_a$) matrices $[M_{i,j}]$ and $[M'_{i,j}]$, we define their *logic product* $[M''_{i,j}]$ as the matrix with

$$M''_{i,j} = \bigcup_{s=0}^{n_a-1} M_{i,s} M'_{s,j}, \tag{9.3.6}$$

where, if $M_{i,s} = \{x_{\alpha_0}, x_{\alpha_1}, \cdots, x_{\alpha_\lambda}\}$ and $M'_{s,j} = \{x_{\beta_0}, x_{\beta_1}, \cdots, x_{\beta_\gamma}\}$, then

$$M_{i,s} M'_{i,j} = \bigcup_{g=0}^{\lambda} \bigcup_{q=0}^{\gamma} \{x_{\alpha_g} x_{\beta_q}\}, \tag{9.3.7}$$

where $\emptyset x = x \emptyset = \emptyset$ for any $x \in X$, $x_{\alpha_g} x_{\beta_q}$ is a word of the length 2 over X.

Thus, logic multiplication is analogous to the ordinary multiplication, except that summation is replaced by set-theoretic union and multiplication by concatenation of words.

If $(M''_{i,j}) = (M_{i,j})(M'_{i,j})$, the elements of $(M''_{i,j})$ are sets of input words of the length 2. Similarly, the elements of a logic product of m matrices are sets of input words of the length m.

Let $(M_{i,j})$ be a matrix defining an automaton and $(M^m_{i,j})$ its mth logic power. For a fixed m, let X^m denote the set of all input words of the length m.

Lemma 9.3.1 *Let $\{\phi_i(q)\}$ for $i = 0, 1, \ldots, n_a - 1$, $q \in X^m$ be the system of characteristic functions of the automaton defined by $(M_{i,j})$. Then,*

$$\phi_i(q) = \begin{cases} 1, & \text{if } q \in M^m_{0,i}, \\ 0, & \text{otherwise,} \end{cases} \tag{9.3.8}$$

for $i = 0, 1, \ldots, n_a - 1$.

The proof follows from the definition, of $(M_{i,j})$ and formulas (9.3.6), (9.3.7), by induction on m. Thus, we need to determine the 0th row of the mth logic power of the matrix $(M_{i,j})$ to construct the characteristic functions.

Example 9.3.1 *Let M be the automaton with the state diagram of Fig. 9.3.1. Here $A = \{a_0, a_1, a_2, a_3, a_4, a_5\}$, with $n_a = 6$ is the set of states, $X = \{0, 1\}$ the set of input signals, and a_0 is the initial state. (In the state diagram, an edge labeled by x_s, ($x_s \in X$) joins a_i to a_j, ($a_i, a_j \in A$) iff $\phi(x_s, a_i) = a_j$).*

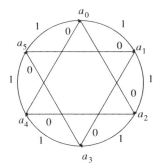

FIGURE 9.3.1   State diagram for the automaton in Example 9.3.1.

Construct the characteristic functions $\phi_i(q)$, $q \in X^m$, $i = 0, 1, 3, 4, 5$ of M for an arbitrary m. We have

$$[M_{i,j}] = \begin{bmatrix} \emptyset & 1 & 0 & \emptyset & \emptyset & \emptyset \\ \emptyset & \emptyset & 1 & 0 & \emptyset & \emptyset \\ \emptyset & \emptyset & \emptyset & 1 & 0 & \emptyset \\ \emptyset & \emptyset & \emptyset & \emptyset & 1 & 0 \\ 0 & \emptyset & \emptyset & \emptyset & \emptyset & 1 \\ 1 & 0 & \emptyset & \emptyset & \emptyset & \emptyset \end{bmatrix}.$$

This matrix satisfies the condition

$$M_{i,j} = \begin{cases} 1, & \text{if } i = j \ominus 1, \text{ modulo } 6, \\ 0, & \text{if } i = j \ominus 2, \text{ modulo } 6, \\ \emptyset, & \text{otherwise.} \end{cases} \tag{9.3.9}$$

We now determine the set $M_{0,i}^m$ for arbitrary m and i.
Let S_m^α denote the set of binary sequences of the length m containing α values 1. We claim that for any m

$$M_{0,i}^m = \bigcup_{\alpha = 2m \ominus i} S_m^\alpha, \quad \text{mod } 6, \tag{9.3.10}$$

for $i = 0, 1, 2, 3, 4, 5$.
We prove this by induction on m. Set

$$M_{0,t}^{m-1} = \bigcup_{\alpha = 2m \ominus t \ominus 2} S_{m-1}^\alpha, \quad \text{mod } 6 \tag{9.3.11}$$

for $t = 0, 1, 2, 3, 4, 5$.

Note that

$$S_{m-1}^{\alpha-1}1 \cup S_{m-1}^{\alpha}0 = S_m^{\alpha},\qquad(9.3.12)$$

where (see (9.3.7)) $S_{m-1}^{\alpha-1}1$ *and* $S_{m-1}^{\alpha}0$ *are the sets obtained by concatenating 1 and 0, respectively, to the right of vectors from* $S_{m-1}^{\alpha-1}$ *and* S_{m-1}^{α}.
  It now follows from (9.3.6), (9.3.7), (9.3.11), and (9.3.12) that

$$M_{0,i}^m = \bigcup_{t=0}^{5} M_{0,t}^{m-1} M_{t,i} = \bigcup_{t=0}^{5} \left(\bigcup_{\alpha=2m\ominus t\ominus 2} S_{m-1}^{\alpha} \right) M_{t,i}$$

$$= \left(\bigcup_{\alpha=2m\ominus i\ominus 2} S_{m-1}^{\alpha} \right) 1 \cup \left(\bigcup_{\alpha=2m\ominus i} S_{m-1}^{\alpha} \right) 0$$

$$= \bigcup_{\alpha=2m\ominus i} S_{m-1}^{\alpha-1}1 \cup \bigcup_{\alpha=2m\ominus i} S_{m-1}^{\alpha}0$$

$$= \bigcup_{\alpha=2m\ominus i} \left(S_{m-1}^{\alpha-1}1 \cup S_{m-1}^{\alpha}0 \right) = \bigcup_{\alpha=2m\ominus i} S_m^{\alpha}, \quad \text{mod } 6.$$

Example 9.3.2 *It follows from (9.3.11) and Lemma 9.3.1 that for the automaton in the Example 9.3.1* $\phi_i(q) = 1$ *iff the number of 1 values* $\|q\|$ *in the word q satisfies the condition* $\|q\| = 2m \ominus i$ *modulo 6, where m is the length of q, otherwise* $\phi_i(q) = 0$.

  Lemma 9.3.1 provides a method for calculating the number $\eta_{M,m}$ of errors in words of the length m corrected by an automaton M and a lower bound on this number for the set of all automata with given n_a and n_x.
  Let $|R|$ denote the number of elements of an arbitrary set R and $M(n_a, n_x)$ the set of all automata with n_a states and n_x input signals whose next-state functions $\phi(x, a)$ are defined for all $x \in X$, $a \in A$.

Corollary 9.3.1 *For any automaton* $M \in M(n_a, n_x)$ *defined by a matrix* $[M_{i,j}]$

$$\eta_{M,m} = \sum_{i=0}^{n_a-1} |M_{0,i}^m|(|M_{0,i}^m| - 1),\qquad(9.3.13)$$

and

$$\min_{M\in M(n_a,n_x)} \eta_{M,m} = n_x^m \left\lfloor \frac{n_x^m}{n_a} - 1 \right\rfloor.\qquad(9.3.14)$$

Proof. Formula (9.3.13) follows from Theorem 9.3.1 and Lemma 9.3.1 in view of the relation

$$\sum_{q \in X^m} \phi_i(q) = |M_{0,i}^m|.$$

To prove (9.3.14), we minimize (9.3.13) with respect to the variables $|M_{0,i}^m|$ for $i = 0, 1, \ldots, n_a - 1$, subject to the constraint

$$\sum_{i=0}^{n_a-1} |M_{0,i}^m| = n_x^m. \tag{9.3.15}$$

Example 9.3.3 *To illustrate the Corollary 9.3.1, we calculate the function $\eta_{M,m}$ for all m for the automaton M in Example 9.3.1.*
By (9.3.11),

$$|M_{0,i}^m| = |\bigcup_{\alpha = 2m \ominus i} S_m^\alpha|, \quad mod\ 6. \tag{9.3.16}$$

Since $S_m^{\alpha_1} \cap S_m^{\alpha_2} = \emptyset$, where $\cap$ is the set-theoretical intersection of two sets, if $\alpha_1 \neq \alpha_2$ by the definition of S_m^α and $|S_m^\alpha| = \binom{m}{\alpha}$, it follows from (9.3.16) that

$$|M_{0,i}^m| = \sum_{\alpha = 2m \ominus i} \binom{m}{\alpha}, \quad mod\ 6, \tag{9.3.17}$$

where $\binom{m}{\alpha} = 0$ if $\alpha > m$, and finally, by (9.3.13)

$$\eta_{M,m} = \sum_{i=0}^{5} \left(\sum_{\alpha = 2m \ominus i} \binom{m}{\alpha} \left(\sum_{\alpha = 2m \ominus i} \binom{m}{\alpha} - 1 \right) \right), \quad mod\ 6. \tag{9.3.18}$$

9.3.2.2 Calculation of Two-Dimensional Autocorrelation Functions

We now try to simplify calculation of the "two-dimensional" autocorrelation function $B_\sigma(q, q')$ defined by (9.3.4). To achieve this end, we impose certain restrictions on the set Q of errors.

First, as before, we fix the length m of the input words. We also assume that the set of input words of the length m is a commutative group G_m, whose structure is such that the class Q of errors may be described in terms of the group operation of G_m. It will be shown below that this can indeed be done for most cases of practical importance. In this setting, the "two-dimensional" autocorrelation function $B_\Sigma(q, q')$ may be replaced by the usual "one-dimensional" function $B_\Sigma(\tau)$, and the correcting capability of automata may be analyzed in exactly the same way as for systems of logic functions.

Let G_m be the group of input words, $\circ$ the group operation, and e the identity element of G_m. We assume that the set of errors Q is described by a subset Q_m of G_m with the following properties.

If $(q, q') \in Q$, then $q \circ q' \in Q_m$. In addition, we assume the existence of a function $p(q, q') = p(q', q) = p(\tau)$, where $\tau = q \circ q'$; that is, we assume that $p(q, q') = p(q_1, q_1')$ if $q \circ q' = q_1 \circ q_1'$. Thus, $p(q, q')$ is the probability of the error $(q, q') \in Q$.

Let $M\{\eta_m(Q)\}$ be the expected number of errors from the set Q in input words of length m that can be corrected by the automaton.

Corollary 9.3.2

$$M\{\eta_m(Q)\} = \sum_{\tau \in Q_m} p(\tau) B_\Sigma(\tau), \qquad (9.3.19)$$

where

$$B_\Sigma(\tau) = \sum_{i=0}^{n_a-1} B_i(\tau) = \sum_{i=0}^{n_a-1} \sum_{q \in G_m} \phi_i(q)\phi_i(q \circ \tau^{-1}), \qquad (9.3.20)$$

$\phi_i(q)$ *is the ith characteristic function of input words of the automaton (see (9.3.3) and $\tau \circ \tau^{-1} = e$.*

The Corollary 9.3.2 is the analog of formula (9.1.49) for systems of logic functions and permits calculation of $M\{\eta_n(Q)\}$ by a generalization of the Vilenkin–Chrestenson transform, since

$$B_i(\tau) = \sum_{q \in G_m} \phi_i(q)\phi_i(q \circ \tau^{-1}) \qquad (9.3.21)$$

is the autocorrelation function of $\phi_i(q)$ on the group G_m (see Section 2.8).

Generalized fast Vilenkin–Chrestenson transform algorithms for arbitrary finite commutative groups may be found in References 38 and 85.

We now consider four important classes of groups G_m of input words of a given length m. These classes correspond to serial or parallel input of data to the device, with algebraic or arithmetic errors (see Section 9.1) in the input data.

1. *Serial input, algebraic errors.* The set of input symbols X is $\{0, 1, \ldots, n_x - 1\}$. The group G_m is the group of all vectors $(x_0, \ldots, x_{m-1})$, with $x_i \in \{0, 1, \ldots, n_x - 1\}$ and with the group operation componentwise addition modulo n_x. The multiplicity of an error (q, q') is the number of nonzero components of $q \ominus q'$ modulo n_x.

2. *Serial input, arithmetic errors.* The set of input symbols X is as before. The group G_m is the set of all numbers $\{\sum_{i=0}^{m-1} x_i(n_x)^i\}$ for $x_i \in \{0, 1, \ldots, n_x - 1\}$, and the group operation is addition modulo n_x^m.

This situation corresponds to the finite automata receiving the input from an m-digit n_x-ary arithmetic device. For a symmetric error (q, q'), the multiplicity is defined as the minimal number of terms in the representation of $(q \ominus q')$ or $(q' \ominus q)$ modulo n_x^m as a linear combination of powers of n_x with exponents smaller or equal to $(m - 1)$ and coefficients in $\{\pm1, \pm2, \ldots, \pm(n_x - 1)\}$. The multiplicity of a nonsymmetric error is the number of terms in the n_x-ary representation of $(q \ominus q')$ modulo n_x (Section 9.1.3).

3. *Parallel input, algebraic errors.* The set of input symbols X is the set of all r-ary vectors of the length t, where $1 < r < n_x$, $n_x \leq r^t$, that is, $X = \{0, 1, \ldots, r - 1\}^t$. The group G_m is the set of all r-ary $(t \times m)$ matrices $[q_{i,j}]$, for $q_{i,j} \in \{0, 1, \ldots, r - 1\}$. The group operation is componentwise addition of matrices modulo r. The multiplicity of an error (q, q') is the number of nonzero components in the matrix $(q \ominus q')$ modulo r.

4. *Parallel input, arithmetic errors.* As before, $X = \{0, 1, \ldots, r - 1\}^t$. The group G_m is the set of all vectors

$$\left(\sum_{i=0}^{t-1} q_{0,i} r^i, \sum_{i=0}^{t-1} q_{1,i} r^i, \ldots, \sum_{i=0}^{t-1} q_{(m-1)i} r^i \right),$$

where $q_{i,j} \in \{0, 1, \ldots, r - 1\}$ and the group operation is componentwise addition modulo r^t.

This situation corresponds to parallel input of information to the sequential network from a t-digit r-ary arithmetic device. The multiplicities of symmetric and nonsymmetric errors are defined exactly as for serial input (case (2)), with t instead of m and r instead of n_x.

The methods for analysis of correcting capability described by (9.3.19)–(9.3.21) may be applied to each of these four groups of input words.

Note that if the input word is fed into the sequential network from a communication channel (in which algebraic errors may occur), the expected number of corrected errors in the channel may be increased by using linearization methods similar to those described in Section 9.2. The linearization procedure in such cases should be applied to the system $\{\phi_i(q)\}$ for $i = 0, 1, \ldots, n_a - 1$ of characteristic functions defined on the groups G_m in (2) and (4) above. These systems may be constructed with the aid of Lemma 9.3.1.

Example 9.3.4 *To illustrate the analysis of error-correcting capability of automata, we calculate $M\{\eta_5(l)\}$ for the automaton in Example 9.3.1, with input words of the length $m = 5$. We consider the case (1) of serial input and algebraic errors.*

Since $X = \{0, 1\}$, the group $G_m = G_5$ is the set of binary vectors of the length 5 under componentwise addition modulo 2.

It is shown in Section 9.3.2.1 that in this case, $\phi_i(q) = 1$ iff $\|q\| = 2m \ominus i = 4 \ominus i$ modulo 6, for $i = 0, 1, \ldots, 5$.

Recall that a switching function $\phi(q)$ is called an elementary symmetric function *with the operating number α if $\phi(q) = 1$ iff $\|q\| = \alpha$.*

Thus, each characteristic function $\phi_i(q)$ for $q = 0, 1, \ldots, 5$ of this automaton is an elementary symmetric function, with the operating number $4 \ominus i$ modulo 6 for $i = 0, 1, \ldots, 5$. To determine the autocorrelation functions

$$B_i(\tau) = \sum_{q \in G_5} \phi_i(q)\phi_i(q \oplus \tau), \quad mod\ 2, \tag{9.3.22}$$

we use the data in the row 8 of Appendix A. This gives

$$B_i(\tau) = \begin{cases} \left(\dfrac{5 - \|\tau\|}{(4 \ominus i) - \|\tau\|/2} \right) \left(\dfrac{\|\tau\|}{\|\tau\|/2} \right), & if\ \|\tau\|\ is\ even, \\ 0, & if\ \|\tau\|\ is\ odd, \end{cases} \tag{9.3.23}$$

with calculations modulo 6.

As usual, we put $\left(\begin{smallmatrix} t \\ q \end{smallmatrix} \right) = 0$ if $t < q$ or $q < 0$, and $\|\tau\|$ is the number of 1 values in the binary vector τ.

Assume that the probability of an l-fold error in the input words is p_l, that is, $p(\tau) = p_l$ for $\|\tau\| = l$.

Then, by Corollary 9.3.2, we have for the expected number of corrected l-fold errors

$$M\{\eta_5(l)\} = \sum_{\|\tau\|=l} p(\tau)B_\Sigma(\tau) = \sum_{\|\tau\|=l} p(\tau)\sum_{i=0}^{5} B_i(\tau). \tag{9.3.24}$$

Inserting (9.3.23) into (9.3.24), we finally obtain the result

$$M\{\eta_5(l)\} = 0, \tag{9.3.25}$$

if l is odd, and

$$M\{\eta_5(l)\} = \sum_{\|\tau\|=l} p(\tau)\sum_{i=0}^{5} \left(\frac{5 - \|\tau\|}{(4 \ominus i) - \|\tau\|/2} \right) \left(\frac{\|\tau\|}{\|\tau\|/2} \right), \tag{9.3.26}$$

$$= p_l \binom{5}{l}\binom{l}{l/2}\sum_{i=0}^{5} \left(\frac{5 - l}{(4 \ominus i) - l/2} \right)$$

$$= p_l \binom{5}{l}\binom{l}{l/2} 2^{5-l}, \quad mod\ 6,$$

if $l \in \{2, 4\}$.

9.3.3 Error-Correcting Capabilities of Linear Automata

We now estimate the correcting capability of several classes of automata that are important from the engineering standpoint. This will be done for the case of serial input and algebraic errors (case 1 in Section 9.3.2.2). Thus, the multiplicity of an error (q, q') is the number of noncoinciding components (letters) in the words q and q'.

We first consider the class of *linear automata* over an arbitrary finite field $GF(p)$ (where p is a prime).

We put $X = A = \{0, 1, \ldots, p - 1\}^t$ is the set of all p-ary vectors of the length t and

$$\phi(x_s, a_j) = T_1 \odot x_s \oplus T_2 \odot a_j, \quad \mod p, \tag{9.3.27}$$

where T_1 and T_2 are nonsingular $(t \times t)$ matrices over $GF(p)$ and $\odot$ is the symbol for matrix multiplication over $GF(p)$. Thus, the number of input signals is the same as the number of states $n_x = n_a = n = p^t$.

Let $\eta_{M,m}(l)$ denote the number of l-fold errors in the input words of length m corrected by the automaton M.

Theorem 9.3.2 *For any linear automaton M with n input signals and n states, we have for a number of corrected errors with the multiplicity l in the input words of the length m,*

$$\eta_{M,m}(l) = ((n - 1)^l + (-1)^l(n - 1))n^{m-1} \binom{m}{l}. \tag{9.3.28}$$

Proof. Let $q = x_0 x_1, \ldots, x_{m-1}$, with $(x_i \in X)$. Then, by (9.3.2), (9.3.27),

$$\phi(q) = T_2^m \odot a_0 \oplus T_2^{m-1} \odot T_1 \odot x_0 \oplus T_2^{m-2} \odot T_1 \odot x_1 \oplus \cdots \tag{9.3.29}$$

$$\oplus T_2^1 \odot T_1 \odot x_{m-2} \oplus T_2^0 \odot T_1 \odot x_{m-1}, \quad \mod p.$$

Let $q' = z_0 z_1, \cdots, z_{m-1}$ with $z_i \in X$. Then, the error (q, q') is corrected iff $\phi(q) = \phi(q')$, that is,

$$T_2^{m-1} \odot x_0 \oplus T_2^{m-2} \odot x_1 \oplus \cdots \oplus T_2^1 \odot x_{m-2} \oplus T_2^0 \odot x_{m-1} \tag{9.3.30}$$

$$= T_2^{m-1} \odot z_0 \oplus T_2^{m-2} \odot z_1 \oplus \cdots \oplus T_2^1 \odot z_{m-2} \oplus T_2^0 \odot z_{m-1}, \quad \mod p.$$

If (q, q') is an l-fold error, there exist l distinct numbers $i_0, i_1, \ldots, i_{l-1}$ with $0 \leq i_s \leq m - 1$, for $s = 0, 1, \ldots, l - 1$, such that $z_{i_s} \neq x_{i_s}$, $s = 0, 1, \ldots, l - 1$ and $z_j = x_j$ if there is no s such that $j = i_s$.

Then, from (9.3.30)

$$\bigoplus_{s=0}^{l-1}(T_2^{m-i_s-1} \odot x_{i_s}) = \bigoplus_{s=0}^{l-1}(T_2^{m-i_s-1} \odot z_{i_s}), \quad \text{mod } p. \tag{9.3.31}$$

We shall now calculate the number $N(l)$ of solutions of (9.3.31) for fixed $x_{i_0}, \ldots, x_{i_{l-1}}$ such that $z_{i_s} \neq x_{i_s}$ for $s = 0, 1, \ldots, l-1$.

Fix $z_{i_0}, \ldots, z_{i_{l-2}}$ arbitrarily so as to satisfy the conditions

$$\begin{cases} \bigoplus_{s=0}^{l-2}(T_2^{m-i_s-1} \odot x_{i_s}) \neq \bigoplus_{s=0}^{l-2}(T_2^{m-i_s-1} \odot z_{i_s}), \quad \text{mod } p \\ z_{i_s} \neq x_{i_s}, \quad s = 0, 1, \ldots, l-2. \end{cases} \tag{9.3.32}$$

The number of ways in which this can be done is $(n-1)^{l-1} - N(l-1)$, where $N(0) = 1$. For each choice of $z_{i_0}, \ldots, z_{i_{l-2}}$ satisfying (9.3.32), we can determine $z_{i_{l-1}}$, such that $z_{i_{l-1}} \neq x_{i_{l-1}}$ from (9.3.31), and conversely.

Thus,

$$N(l) = (n-1)^{l-1} - N(l-1). \tag{9.3.33}$$

By solving the difference equation (9.3.33), we get

$$N(l) = n^{-1}((n-1)^l + (-1)^l(n-1)). \tag{9.3.34}$$

Since the number of all possible choices of a word $x_0 x_1, \ldots, x_{m-1}$ and numbers $i_0, \ldots i_{l-1}$ as stipulated above is $n^m \binom{m}{l}$, it finally follows that

$$\eta_{M,m}(l) = n^m \binom{m}{l} N(l) \tag{9.3.35}$$

$$= ((n-1)^l + (-1)^l(n-1))n^{m-1} \binom{m}{l}.$$

Corollary 9.3.3 *Linear automata over $GF(p)$ do not correct single errors.*

Proof. For any n and m, by setting $l = 1$ in (9.3.28), we have

$$\eta_{M,m}(1) = 0. \tag{9.3.36}$$

Corollary 9.3.4 *For a linear automaton, the fraction $\tilde{\eta}_{M,m}(l)$ of corrected l-fold errors in input words of the length m is independent of m*

$$\tilde{\eta}_{M,m}(l) = n^{-1}(n-1)^{-l}((n-1)^l + (-1)^l(n-1)). \tag{9.3.37}$$

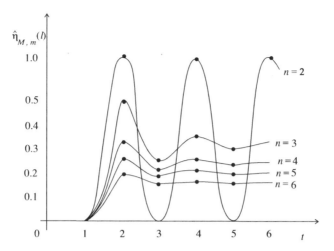

FIGURE 9.3.2   Fractions of corrected errors $\hat{\eta}_{M,m}(l)$ with multiplicity l for the linear automata with n inputs and n states.

Proof. Formula (9.3.37) follows from (9.3.28) in view of the fact that the total number of l-fold errors in input words of the length m for an automaton with n input signals is $n^m \begin{pmatrix} m \\ l \end{pmatrix} (n-1)^l$.

Figure 9.3.2 illustrates $\hat{\eta}_{M,m}(l)$ as a function of l for linear automata with $n = 2, 3, 4, 5, 6$.

Letting $n \to \infty$ in (9.3.37), we see that for any $l > 1$,

$$\lim_{n \to \infty} \hat{\eta}_{M,m}(l) = n^{-1}. \tag{9.3.38}$$

In other words, if the number n of input signals and states is sufficiently large, the correcting capability of a linear automaton for $l > 1$ is uniformly distributed with respect to multiplicities.

As we will see in Section 9.3.4, the results of this section may be generalized to other types of automata.

9.3.4 Error-Correcting Capability of Group Automata

A *group automaton* is an automaton M, whose sets of inputs and internal states are identical ($X = A$), and

$$\phi(x_s, a_j) = x_s \circ a_j \circ b, \tag{9.3.39}$$

where $\circ$ is some commutative group operation on X and b is independent of x_s and a_j.

For example, the linear automata considered above are group automata. Similarly, automata representing adders or multipliers in $GF(p)$ may be interpreted as group automata, for in these cases, respectively,

$$\phi(x_s, a_j) = x_s \oplus a_j \oplus b, \tag{9.3.40}$$

$$\phi(x_s, a_j) = x_s \odot a_j \odot b, \quad \mod R, \tag{9.3.41}$$

where $x_s, a_j, b \in \{0, 1, \ldots, R - 1\}$, and R is prime with b playing the role of the initial state.

Theorem 9.3.2 is also valid for arbitrary group automata with the proof analogous to this presented above. The same is true for Corollaries 9.3.3, 9.3.4, the asymptotic result (9.3.38), and the curves $\hat{\eta}_{M,m}(l)$ in Fig. 9.3.2.

The correcting capabilities $\eta_{M,m}(l)$ of linear and group automata may thus be determined (see the proof of Theorem 9.3.2) without actually constructing the characteristic functions $\phi_i(q)$ (see (9.3.3)) and the autocorrelation functions $B_i(\tau)$ (see (9.3.21), for $i = 0, 1, \ldots, n_a - 1$.

9.3.5 Error-Correcting Capabilities of Counting Automata

We now consider yet another important class of automata for which analytical calculation of the correcting capability is more conveniently done by using the characteristic functions $\phi_i(q)$ and the autocorrelation functions $B_i(\tau)$.

For a given automaton M with the input set $X = \{0, 1\}$, the numbers of 1 and 0 values in the input word q are $N_1(q)$ and $N_0(q)$. From the initial state, the automaton goes to the state $\phi(q)$ for the input word q.

An automaton M with $X = \{0, 1\}$, $A = \{0, 1, \ldots, n_a - 1\}$, where n_a is prime, and the initial state 0 is called a *counting automaton* if

$$\phi(q) \equiv C_1 N_1(q) + C_2 N_0(q), \quad \mod n_a, \tag{9.3.42}$$

where $C_1, C_2, (C_1 \neq C_2)$ are arbitrary (possibly even negative) integers. The notation $\alpha \equiv \beta$ (modulo γ) has the usual number-theoretical meaning of congruence modulo γ, that is, the numbers α and β have the same remainder upon division by γ.

For example, binary counters $(C_1 = 1, C_2 = 0)$ and reversible (up–down) counters $(C_1 = 1, C_2 = -1)$ are counting automata. The automaton in Example 9.3.1 is also a counting automaton with $C_1 = 1, C_2 = 2$.

Consider the correcting capability $\eta_{M,m}(l)$ and $\hat{\eta}_{m,m}(l)$, that is, the number and the fraction of corrected errors with the multiplicity l in input words of the length m of a counting automaton, assuming serial input and algebraic errors.

The group G_m of input words of the length m is the set of all binary vectors of the length m under componentwise addition modulo 2.

Theorem 9.3.3 *If M is a counting automaton, then for any C_1, C_2, and n_a, $m < n_a$,*

$$
\eta_{M,m}(l) =
\begin{cases}
2^{m-l} \dbinom{m}{l} \dbinom{l}{l/2}, & \text{if } l \text{ is even,} \\
0, & \text{if } l \text{ is odd,}
\end{cases}
\tag{9.3.43}
$$

and

$$
\hat{\eta}_{M,m}(l) =
\begin{cases}
2^{-l} \dbinom{l}{l/2}, & \text{if } l \text{ is even,} \\
0, & \text{if } l \text{ is odd.}
\end{cases}
\tag{9.3.44}
$$

Proof. For an input word q of the length m and any $i \in \{0, 1, \ldots, n_a - 1\}$, we have a system

$$
N_1(q) + N_0(q) = m,
\tag{9.3.45}
$$

$$
C_1 N_1(q) + C_2 N_0(q) \equiv i, \quad \bmod n_a.
\tag{9.3.46}
$$

Consequently, for fixed m and any $N_1(q) \in \{0, 1, \ldots, m\}$, there exists a unique $i \in \{0, 1, \ldots, n_a - 1\}$ satisfying (9.3.45) and (9.3.47). Moreover, these values for i are different for different $N_1(q)$, $(m < n_a)$. We may therefore write $N_1(q) = n(i, m)$. Then, in view of (9.3.1)–(9.3.3) and (9.3.42), it follows that if $i \in \{0, 1, \ldots, n_a - 1\}$, then $\phi(q)$ is an elementary symmetric switching function of m variables with the operating number $n(i, m)$. Since

$$
\eta_{M,m}(l) = \sum_{\|\tau\|=l} B_\Sigma(\tau) = \sum_{\|\tau\|=l} \sum_{i=0}^{n_a-1} B_i(\tau)
\tag{9.3.47}
$$

$$
= \sum_{\|\tau\|=l} \sum_{i=0}^{n_a-1} \sum_{q=0}^{2^m-1} \phi_i(q)\phi_i(q \oplus \tau), \quad \bmod 2,
\tag{9.3.48}
$$

where $\|\tau\| = N_1(\tau)$ is the number of 1 bits in the binary vector τ of the length m, we may use the data in the row 8 in Appendix A to evaluate $B_i(\tau)$, so that for odd l

$$
\eta_{M,m}(l) = 0,
\tag{9.3.49}
$$

and for even l,

$$
\eta_{M,m}(l) = \sum_{i=0}^{n_a-1} \sum_{\|\tau\|=l} \binom{m - \|\tau\|}{n(i,m) - \|\tau\|/2} \binom{\|\tau\|}{\|\tau\|/2}
$$

$$
= \sum_{i=0}^{n_a-1} \binom{m-l}{n(i,m)-l/2} \binom{l}{l/2} \binom{m}{l}
$$

$$
= \binom{l}{l/2} \binom{m}{l} \sum_{i=0}^{n_a-1} \binom{m-l}{n(i,m)-l/2}. \tag{9.3.50}
$$

Now it follows from (9.3.45) and (9.3.49) that for a fixed m, the function $n(i,m)$ runs through all values in $\{0, 1, \ldots, m\}$ as i runs over $\{0, 1, \ldots, n_a - 1\}$. Thus, for $m < n_a$, we have for even l

$$
\hat{\eta}_{M,m}(l) = \binom{l}{l/2} \binom{m}{l} \sum_{i=0}^{m-l} \binom{m-l}{i}
$$

$$
= 2^{m-l} \binom{l}{l/2} \binom{m}{l}. \tag{9.3.51}
$$

Using the definition of $\hat{\eta}_{M,m}(l)$ and formulas (9.3.49), (9.3.51), we obtain for a fraction of corrected errors with the multiplicity l in the input word of the length m for counting automata

$$
\hat{\hat{\eta}}_{M,m}(l) = \frac{\eta_{M,m}(l)}{2^m \binom{m}{l}} =
\begin{cases}
2^{-l} \binom{l}{l/2}, & \text{if } l \text{ is even,} \\
0, & \text{if } l \text{ is odd.}
\end{cases} \tag{9.3.52}
$$

The assertion of the theorem now follows from (9.3.49), (9.3.51), and (9.3.52).

Notice that by Theorem 9.3.3 the fraction $\hat{\hat{\eta}}_{M,m}(l)$ of errors corrected by a counting automaton is independent of the parameters C_1, C_2 of the number of states n_a and of the length m of input sequences (provided $m < n_a$).

Figure 9.3.3 illustrates the behavior of the function $\hat{\hat{\eta}}_{M,m}(l)$ for a counting automaton with $m < n_a$.

The asymptotic behavior of $\hat{\hat{\eta}}_{M,m}(l)$ for l is readily determined from (9.3.44), using the Stirling formula

$$
\lim_{s \to \infty} \hat{\hat{\eta}}_{M,m}(2s) = \sqrt{\frac{2}{\pi}}(2s)^{-1/2}. \tag{9.3.53}
$$

Thus, while the correcting capabilities of linear and group automata ($l > 1$) are approximatively uniformly distributed over the multiplicities (see (9.3.37), (9.3.38), and Fig. 9.3.2), the correcting capability of counting automata is concentrated mainly in the region of errors of low even multiplicity (see (9.3.44), (9.3.53), and Fig. 9.3.3).

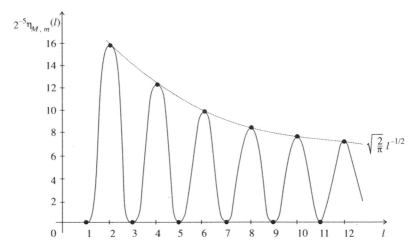

FIGURE 9.3.3   The fraction of corrected errors with the multiplicity l in the input words of the length m, $\hat{\eta}_{M,m}(l)$, for a counting automaton with $m < n_a$.

9.4   SYNTHESIS OF FAULT-TOLERANT AUTOMATA WITH SELF-ERROR CORRECTION

9.4.1   Fault-Tolerant Devices

In general, the requirement that a digital device be capable of correcting (or detecting) errors in a prescribed class implies the need for redundancy. By incorporating the error-correcting capability at the very earliest stages in design of the device one can usually lower the necessary redundancy (273, 274, 275). See also References 70, 126, 128, 328, 361, 414, 452 and references therein.

In this section, we confine the discussion for the most part to the case of error correction, but everything carries over without modification to error detection. We assume throughout that the excitation functions of the automaton A_0 to be synthesized are realized by expansion in orthogonal series (see Section 7.1) relative to the Walsh or Haar basis. The automaton A_0 itself need not be completely specified.

The automaton will be provided with error-correcting capability by the use of error-correcting codes for state assignment. There are two principal conditions to be met:

1. The parameters of the selected code should be matched in a flexible manner with the specific features of the next-state function. For example, this condition is not fulfilled in the familiar method of state redundancy based on replication codes. Indeed, in this case, the correction of l-fold errors in any automaton with n_a states, $2^{k-1} < n_a \le 2^k$, employs the same $((2l + 1)k, k)$-code (426) and the corresponding hardware implementation of the fault-tolerant device requires $2l + 1$ copies of the original device.

2. Low complexity of code selection and state assignment procedures. Underlying this condition is the increase in efficiency of error-correcting codes with increasing length of code words, and hence also with increasing number of states n_a.

The present section is devoted to methods for introducing redundancy in a finite automaton synthesized by spectral methods, assuming that the above two conditions are satisfied. A fairly complete description of error-correction methods for finite automata synthesized by classical methods may be found in References 273, 274, 275, 435. For recent development in this area see References 184, 249, 252, 442, 443, 533 and references therein.

9.4.2 Spectral Implementation of Fault-Tolerant Automata

In an automaton synthesized by spectral methods, the functions of memory are implemented by the adder–accumulator computing the sum of the series. We therefore use the arithmetic $(AN + B)$-codes (426) for error correction.

A binary m-digit $(AN + B)$-*code* is a set of numbers $N_1, N_2, \ldots, N_\theta$ such that

$$N_i \equiv B, \quad \mathrm{mod}\ A, \qquad (9.4.1)$$

$$0 \le N_i < 2^m,$$

for $i = 1, 2, \ldots, \theta$.

The binary expansions of the numbers $N_1, N_2, \ldots, N_\theta$ represents the codes of the internal states of the automata for error-correcting purposes.

The *arithmetic distance* $\rho(N_p, N_q)$ between numbers N_p, N_q is defined as the minimal number of terms in the representation of $|N_p - N_q|$ as a linear combination of powers of 2 with exponents smaller or equal $(m - 1)$ and the coefficients ± 1; that is, in this section, we restrict the considerations to *symmetric arithmetic errors*, see Section 9.1.3.

If the result of an error is to distort the number N_p into N_q, the multiplicity of the error is $\rho(N_p, N_q)$.

The *arithmetic code distance* $\rho(V)$ of an $(AN + B)$-*code* V is defined as

$$\rho(V) = \min_{N_p, N_q \in V} \rho(N_p, N_q). \qquad (9.4.2)$$

It can be shown that a code V detects (corrects) an l-fold error iff $\rho(V) \ge l + 1$ ($\rho(V) \ge 2l + 1$).

Methods for construction of optimal $(AN + B)$-codes are considered in Reference 426.

Notice that the $(AN + B)$-codes as defined here perform error detection and/or correction for symmetric errors in binary computing channels. Analogous $(AN + B)$-codes may be constructed for arithmetic nonsymmetric errors and bursts, and also for error correction in nonbinary channels (the latter should be used for digital devices synthesized from multistable elements) (153). All the error-correction methods described below carry over directly to any class of $(AN + B)$-codes.

9.4.3 Realization of Sequential Networks with Self-Error Correction

We now examine the problem of error correction for a sequential network realizing a given finite automaton, that is, correction of errors not in the input signals of the automaton (as before) but in the internal states (memory) of the automaton.

The definitions of errors and multiplicity in this case are entirely analogous to the definitions for input signals. As for the input signals themselves, we assume here that they are free of errors if the input to the finite automaton considered is the output of a preceding automaton, and error correction is implemented in the latter. We may also assume that the classical methods of error-correcting codes (55, 426) have been used to correct errors in the input signals.

Let A_0 be an automaton defined by a state table (state diagram) (see Section 7.1) and $\lambda = \{\lambda_0, \lambda_1, \ldots, \lambda_{n_\lambda - 1}\}$ a *partition* of its input set $X : \lambda_i \subseteq X$, $\lambda_i \cap \lambda_s = \emptyset$, $i \neq s$, $\bigcup_{i=0}^{n_\lambda - 1} \lambda_i = X$.

We call the subsets λ_s, for $s = 0, 1, \ldots, n_\lambda - 1$ the *blocks* of the partition λ.

We construct a redundant finite automaton A_λ, equivalent to A_0, in such a way that A_λ will be in any of its states only when input signals from the same block of the partition λ are applied.

To construct A_λ, we "split" each state a_i of A_0 into $n_\lambda(a_i)$ equivalent states of A_λ, where $n_\lambda(a_i)$ is the number of blocks of λ that contain input signals forcing A_0 into state a_i. To any state, $\tilde{a}_i$ of these $n_\lambda(a_i)$ states of A_λ corresponds the same output signal as for a_i in A_0. Moreover, if $\phi_0(x_s, a_i) = a_q$ in A_0, we put $\phi_\lambda(x_s, \tilde{a}_i) = \tilde{a}_q$ in A_λ, where $\tilde{a}_i$ and $\tilde{a}_q$ are states of A_λ obtained by "splitting" states a_i and a_q of A_0. The next-state functions of A_0 and A_λ are ϕ_0 and ϕ_λ, respectively.

In the state diagram for A_λ, all the directed edges coming to any given state are labeled by input signals from the same block of λ.

Example 9.4.1   *Consider a fragment of a state diagram for A_0 in Fig. 9.4.1. Let* $\lambda = \{\lambda_0, \lambda_1\}$, *where* $\lambda_0 = \{x_0, x_1\}$, $\lambda_1 = \{x_2\}$, $X = \{x_0, x_1, x_2\}$. *Then, the state a_4 is replaced by ("split" into) $n_\lambda(a_4) = 2$ states a'_4 and a''_4 in A_λ.*

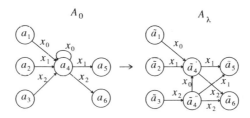

FIGURE 9.4.1   The fragment of a state diagram illustrating the "splitting" procedure for the state a_4 and the partition $\lambda = \{\lambda_0, \lambda_1\}$, $\lambda_0 = \{x_0, x_1\}$, $\lambda_1 = \{x_2\}$ for the finite automaton in Example 9.4.1.

A state of A_λ is λ_s-*reachable* if the input signals of the block λ_s force A_λ into this state.

To correct errors in A_λ, it is sufficient to assign to all the λ_s-reachable states of A_λ different elements of a suitable $(AN + s)$-code for $s = 0, 1, \ldots, n_\lambda - 1$ for which the modulus A ensures the desired correcting capability. The required redundancy for the modulus A then depends on the specific properties of the next-state function ϕ_0 of the automaton A_0, and for any multiplicity of corrected errors there exists a class of automata for which correction of errors of this multiplicity requires no redundant memory elements (see Example 9.4.2). A formal description of this error-correction method in the language of automata theory, including necessary and sufficient conditions for the existence of a digital device with the appropriate correcting capability implementing the given input–output mapping and having the stipulated number of memory elements, may be set up in the same way as for implementation of the combinational part by the usual methods of Boolean algebra, see References 273, 275, 491.

The algorithms computing an optimal partition λ, selecting a number A generating the appropriate code, and constructing decoders that define the error-correction procedure are analogous to those considered in detail in References 273, 275 and 276.

Example 9.4.2 *Consider an automaton A_0 defined by Table 9.4.1. Suppose that A_0 is realized by a network with binary gates, and it is required to detect single errors.*

An optimal partition for A_0 is $\lambda = \{\lambda_0, \lambda_1, \lambda_2\}$, where $\lambda_0 = \{x_0, x_3\}$, $\lambda_1 = \{x_1\}$, $\lambda_2 = \{x_3\}$, $(n_\lambda = 3)$.

The automaton A_λ coincides with A_0. To detect errors, we select the $AN + B$-codes, $(B = 0, 1, 2)$ with $A = 3$, which yield the state assignment in Table 9.4.2. Recall that $K^a(q) = r$ $(K^x(q) = r)$ if the code assigned to the state a_q, (input signal x_q) is the binary expansion of the number r.

The values of the function $\Phi(z)$ representing the excitation functions when the input assignment is $K^x(q) = q$ and the order of variables in the excitation functions defined by the permutation $T = (0, 1, 2, 3, 4)$ are given in Table 9.4.3. Shown are also the expansion coefficients $S(w)$ of $\Phi(z)$ relative to the Haar basis $\{H_l^{(q)}(z)\}$, where

TABLE 9.4.1 State Table for the Automaton in Example 9.4.2.

a/x	x_0	x_1	x_2	x_3
a_0	a_0	a_3	a_2	a_0
a_1	a_5	a_3	a_7	a_1
a_2	a_5	a_3	a_7	a_1
a_3	a_0	a_3	a_2	a_5
a_4	a_1	a_6	a_7	a_0
a_5	a_5	a_4	a_2	a_5
a_6	a_0	a_4	a_7	a_5
a_7	a_1	a_3	a_7	a_0

TABLE 9.4.2   State Assignment for Internal States in the Automaton in Example 9.4.2.

q	0	1	2	3	4	5	6	7
$K^a(q)$	0	3	2	1	4	6	7	5

$w = 2^p + q - 1$. *It is evident from Table 9.4.3 that the computation of the excitation functions for the finite automaton in Table 9.4.1 with single-error detection entails storage of* 13 *nonzero coefficients, of which six are distinct.*

The block diagram of a device whose excitation functions are realized by an expansion in orthogonal series involves a basis function generator, storage block for expansion coefficients, and an adder/accumulator computing the sum of the series.

The use of arithmetic codes makes it possible to correct (or detect) errors in the adder, in the storage block, and sometimes also in the basis function generator.

If the memory of the automaton is combined with the adder, errors may also be corrected or detected by methods not based on the use of arithmetic codes. Indeed, the binary codes of the expansion coefficients and the numbers stored in the adder during the summation procedure have integral and fractional parts. At the end of the computations, the fractional part of the number stored in the adder should be zero. This provides a fairly simple and efficient technique for detecting errors in the appropriate adder bits or for correcting them by rounding off the sum to the nearest integer. Thus, arithmetic codes should be used only to detect or correct errors in the

TABLE 9.4.3   Function $\Phi(z)$ Representing Excitation Functions of the Automaton in Example 9.4.2 and Its Haar Spectrum.

z, w	$\Phi(z)$	$4S(w)$	z, w	$\Phi(z)$	$4S(w)$
0	0	12	8	1	-12
1	0	-1	9	1	0
2	6	1	10	1	0
3	6	1	11	1	0
4	3	0	12	7	-6
5	3	-6	13	1	6
6	6	0	14	4	0
7	0	0	15	4	-12
z, w	$\Phi(z)$	$4S(w)$	z, w	$\Phi(z)$	$4S(w)$
16	2	0	24	0	0
17	2	0	25	6	0
18	5	0	26	3	0
19	5	12	27	3	-6
20	5	0	28	0	-12
21	5	0	29	0	0
22	2	12	30	6	0
23	5	0	31	6	0

digits of the integral part of the coefficient codes and in the corresponding bits of the adder. Errors in these digits can also be detected by using overflow signals in the adder and the value of the sign digit when the computation of the excitation functions has been completed.

In the implementation of automata by spectral methods combined with the use of $(AN + B)$-codes, a simultaneous detection and/or correction of errors in any system of automata containing arithmetic units can be efficiently organized.

9.5 COMPARISON OF SPECTRAL AND CLASSICAL METHODS

In this section, we briefly compare spectral methods for synthesis of combinational and sequential networks with the classical methods. By "classical" methods we mean those based on the use of switching algebra or many-valued logic and finite automata theory. A detailed account of the classical methods of synthesis may be found in References 231, 247, 258, 313, 604, 661.

The most important characteristic of these methods is that, generally speaking, they may lead to optimal solutions in the sense, say, of the complexity of the network being designed. However, they require an exhaustive search of all alternatives to tackle such important problems as minimization of systems of switching functions, optimal state and input assignment, optimal completion of incompletely specified switching functions and automata, and so on. Moreover, this limitation is apparently intrinsic (526, 652) to these problems. The amount of computational work involved in exhaustive search increases at an enormous rate with increase in the number of variables of the switching functions or in the number of states and input signals of the automaton. As a result, exact solution of the above-mentioned problems, even for a relatively small number of variables, usually presents even the most sophisticated computer with almost insurmountable difficulties. When the classical methods do yield an exact solution, the cost involved may completely outweigh the advantage of optimality. Moreover, in the classical framework, it is frequently difficult to estimate the minimal complexity of the synthesized network before the end of an extremely laborious synthesis process.

The classical methods usually depend essentially on the basis system of elements from which the device is designed. However, new and technologically economical basis systems are now being rapidly developed, integrated and homogeneous circuitry is extensively used. There is a need for the synthesis of networks with time-variable structure and networks capable of adapting themselves to the external medium, and this situation will in all probability become even more actual in the future. What we need are synthesis methods that depend only weakly on the specific features of the basis system of elements, suitable for application to integrated and homogeneous circuitry, and methods for the design of networks of variable structure and networks adaptable to changing environments. An additional factor is the applicability of synthesis methods to design devices with multistable elements, networks built from elements with different numbers of stable states, and digital–analog networks. This sufficiently requires general methods applicable to design of networks with any number of stable states.

Finally, the design of devices equipped with error-detecting and error-correcting abilities is a no less important and pressing task of synthesis methods.

Spectral methods meet all these requirements to a considerable degree. The main shortcoming of spectral methods is that they are approximate—the network implementations that they produce are not absolutely minimal. Nevertheless, they possess several advantages.

A major advantage is that spectral methods of synthesis are convenient for computer implementation and yield solutions to problems of quite high dimensions. Underlying this circumstance is the fact that in the spectral approach the structure of the device is rigidly fixed. Consequently, it is possible to perform algorithms related to the important problems involved in minimizing the complexity of networks realizing systems of logic functions (Section 6.1.1), optimal state–input assignment for automata (Section 7.2), optimal completion of incompletely specified logic functions (Section 6.2), and automata (Section 7.3) without having to resort to brute-force techniques.

In addition, the spectral methods provide an easy estimate of the complexity of the network being designed, based on the number of nonzero expansion coefficients. This in turn makes it possible to estimate the expected complexity of the network in terms of the number of components required for an implementation of the functions considered.

Another essential merit of spectral methods is their very weak dependence on the basis system of components. Indeed, the block diagram of a device synthesized by spectral methods contains standard components of computer technology as registers, adders, counters, decoders, and so on. Consequently, implementation is simplified.

Since the specific features of the functions realized by a network (given the number of variables or of states and input signals) have an effect only on the content of the memory, this makes for an easy adaptation of the network to the implementation of any system of functions. This adaptation may be implemented by erasing the information held in the memory and replacing it by the expansion coefficients of the step function representing the new system of logic or excitation functions. A similar principle may be employed to adapt the network to changes in its environment.

Yet another advantage of spectral methods, especially for the synthesis of combinational networks, is their weak dependence on the number of stable states of the basic components. This universal property makes spectral methods particularly suitable for the design of devices with elements having different numbers of stable states and for digital–analog devices. Indeed, in many cases the orthogonal expansions of step functions representing systems of logical functions or excitation functions in terms of the basis functions described in Sections 2.3 and 2.5 yield quite simple analog implementation of these step functions.

This approach may be extremely convenient for small numbers of nonzero spectral coefficients in the corresponding series and small numbers of variables of the original function or states and inputs of the automaton, especially in the synthesis of digital–analog devices.

In addition, as we saw in Section 9.4, the spectral approach provides for simple error detection and/or correction using systems of arithmetic codes, and it is also possible to organize simultaneous checking in any system of devices containing arithmetic units.

All the spectral methods of synthesis described in this book, as regard both systems of logical functions and automata, admit not only network interpretations but also program implementation. In other words, they may be utilized to simulate systems of logic functions and automata on a computer. In doing so, one is again presented with the problem of minimizing the number of nonzero expansion coefficients to be stored, and this may be done with the aid of methods set forth in this book.

To conclude this section, we also note that spectral methods provide for simple off-line testing procedures and design of devices with built-in self-testing when the functions implemented by the device have compact analytical representations (see, Chapter 9).

BIBLIOGRAPHIC NOTES

Theory of error-correcting codes that are often used in the design reliable devices are considered References 39,55,426,437.

CHAPTER 10

SPECTRAL METHODS FOR TESTING OF DIGITAL SYSTEMS

With the increasing complexity of semiconductor devices, the problem of hardware testing and diagnosis becomes one of the major bottlenecks in computer industry. As a result of a high density of components and limited numbers of input/output pins, *controllabilities* and *observabilities* of internal interconnections and gates are going down, which makes testing more and more costly. There are good reasons to believe that this trend will continue in the future (269).

The conventional approach to testing is to identify a subset of input vectors (the test set) such that correct behavior of the device-under-test for these input vectors ensures correct behavior of the device relative to the selected class of faults. The device is tested off-line by applying input test vectors and verifying test responses.

Testing of sequential devices is performed by breaking feedback loops in the testing mode and testing separately combinational part and memories (269).

In this chapter, we will present several approaches based on the Walsh transform and its generalizations for testing and diagnosis of combinational networks, *Random-Access Memories* (RAMs), *Read-Only Memories* (ROMs), and software computing numerical functions.

As we will see in the next few sections, spectral techniques provide in many cases for simple and analytical solutions of testing and diagnostic problems.

Spectral Logic and Its Applications for the Design of Digital Devices by Mark G. Karpovsky, Radomir S. Stanković and Jaakko T. Astola
Copyright © 2008 John Wiley & Sons, Inc.

Approaches to testing and diagnosis of computer hardware can be classified into

1. transistor-level,
2. gate-level,
3. functional-level,

testing depending on the level of description of the device-under-test.

Since transistor-level techniques are applicable to small devices only, we will concentrate in this chapter on the gate-level and the functional-level testing with the emphasis on functional testing.

For the systematic presentation of traditional nonspectral techniques for testing and diagnosis, we refer, to References 5 and 269.

10.1 TESTING AND DIAGNOSIS BY VERIFICATION OF WALSH COEFFICIENTS

10.1.1 Fault Models

The standard fault models for gate-level testing are single and multiple stuck-at faults.

We will denote *stuck-at-zero* and *stuck-at-one* faults at a line u as $u/0$ and $u/1$. The problem of constructing a minimal set of test patterns detecting even all single stuck-at faults in a given gate-level network is NP-complete (5), see also Reference 17.

Let $y^{(s)} = f^{(s)}(z_0, z_1, \ldots, z_{m-1})$, $s = 0, 1, \ldots, M - 1$, $y^{(s)}, z_s \in \{0, 1\}$, be a system of M switching functions of m variables and

$$F(z) = \sum_{s=0}^{M-1} y^{(s)}(z)2^{M-1-s},$$

is the corresponding integer function with the Walsh spectrum

$$S_F(w) = 2^{-m} \sum_{z=0}^{2^m-1} F(z)W_w(z),$$

where

$$W_w(z) = (-1)^{\sum_{s=0}^{m-1} w_s z_s}.$$

Suppose that a combinational device-under-test with m inputs $z_0, z_1, \ldots, z_{m-1}$ and M outputs $F(z) = (f^{(0)}(z), f^{(1)}(z), \ldots, f^{(M-1)}(z))$, as a result of a fault is computing $\tilde{f}(z)$ instead of $F(z)$.

Let $w = (w_0, \ldots, w_{m-1})$ be a fixed m-bit binary vector.

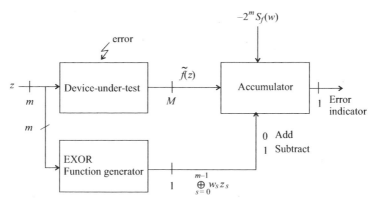

FIGURE 10.1.1   Block diagram for testing by verification of a spectral coefficient $S_F(w)$.

Definition 10.1.1   *We will say that a fault $f \rightarrow \tilde{f}$ is w-testable iff $S_F(w) \neq S_{\tilde{F}}(w)$.*

The block structure of testing by verification of spectral coefficients is given in Fig. 10.1.1.

The following theorem (see 398) provides for necessary and sufficient conditions for w-testability of input stuck-at faults.

Theorem 10.1.1   *(Testing of stuck-at faults)*

1. *Faults $z_s/0$ and $z_s/1$, replacing $f(z_0, \ldots, z_{s-1}, z_s, z_{s+1}, \ldots, z_{m-1})$ by $\tilde{f}(z_0, \ldots, z_{s-1}, 0, z_{s+1}, \ldots, z_{m-1})$ and $\tilde{f}(z_0, \ldots, z_{s-1}, 1, z_{s+1}, \ldots, z_{m-1})$, are $\mathbf{0}$ testable, where $\mathbf{0} = (0, 0, \ldots, 0)$, iff*

$$S_F(0, 0, \ldots, \overset{s}{1}, 0, \ldots, 0) \neq 0. \tag{10.1.1}$$

2. *Any input stuck-at fault, single or multiple, involving p or more inputs is w-testable if*

$$|S_F(w)| = t2^{-m+p}, \tag{10.1.2}$$

where t is an integer $(t > 0)$.

3. *Any multiple stuck-at fault involving input line z_s is w-testable for*

$$w = (w_0, \ldots, w_{s-1}, 1, w_{s+1}, \ldots, w_{m-1}),$$

iff

$$S_F(w_0, \ldots, w_{s-1}, 1, w_{s+1}, \ldots, w_{m-1}) \neq 0. \tag{10.1.3}$$

The proof of this theorem follows from the fact that for $z_s/0$ and $z_s/1$,

$$\tilde{f}(z_s = 0) = \tilde{f}(z_s = 1),$$

where

$$\tilde{f}(z_s = 0) = \tilde{f}(z_0, \ldots, z_{s-1}, 0, z_{s+1}, \ldots, z_{m-1})$$

$$\tilde{f}(z_s = 1) = \tilde{f}(z_0, \ldots, z_{s-1}, 1, z_{s+1}, \ldots, z_{m-1}),$$

for all $z_0, \ldots, z_{s-1}, z_{s+1}, \ldots, z_{m-1}$ and from formulas (3.1.2)–(3.1.4).

Example 10.1.1 *Table 10.1.1 presents the Walsh spectrum for a function f defined as $f(z_0, z_1, z_2, z_3) = z_0 z_1 z_2 \vee z_3(\overline{z_1} \vee z_2)$, $M = 1$, $m = 4$, and indicates w-testability conditions from Theorem 10.1.1 for stuck-at faults involving z_0, z_1, z_2, z_3. Faulty lines z_i are represented by the rightmost part of the Table 10.1.1. In Table 10.1.1, 1 on the right-hand side of the table in the row w and the column z_i indicates that all multiple stuck-at faults involving the line z_s are w-testable.*

The above results (Theorem 10.1.1) represent the characterization of testability by spectral coefficients for input stuck-at faults.

Testing by verification of Walsh coefficients provides for a simple technique for data compression of test responses.

Other approaches for compression of test responses (such as transition counting and signature analysis by linear feedback shift registers) can be found in References

TABLE 10.1.1   Spectrum and w-Testability Conditions for f in Example 10.1.1.

w_0	w_1	w_2	w_3	$16S_f(w)$	z_0	z_1	z_2	z_3
		w				w-testability Faults at		
0	0	0	0	8	1	0	0	1
0	0	0	1	−6	0	0	0	1
0	0	1	0	0	0	0	0	0
0	0	1	1	−2	0	0	1	1
0	1	0	0	0	0	0	0	0
0	1	0	1	−2	0	1	0	1
0	1	1	0	−2	0	1	1	0
0	1	1	1	2	0	1	1	1
1	0	0	0	−2	1	0	0	0
1	0	0	1	0	0	0	0	0
1	0	1	0	2	1	0	1	0
1	0	1	1	0	0	0	0	0
1	1	0	0	2	1	1	0	0
1	1	0	1	0	0	0	0	0
1	1	1	0	−2	1	1	1	0
1	1	1	1	0	0	0	0	0

5 and 269. Compression of test responses is required for built-in self-testing (269).

Testing by verification of spectral coefficients eliminates the very difficult problem of test pattern generation, but requires exhaustive application of all 2^m input patterns and can be applied only to networks with a relatively small number of inputs.

In the next section, we will extend spectral techniques to the cases when a small number of input patterns will be required for testing. We will also present a complete characterization of these devices.

Corollary 10.1.1 *(591)*
For a device implementing a system $\{f^{(s)}(z_0, \ldots, z_{m-1})\}$, $s = 0, 1, \ldots, M - 1$, *of switching functions*

1. If

$$S_F(\mathbf{1}) = S_F(1, 1, \ldots, 1) \neq 0, \tag{10.1.4}$$

then all single and multiple input stuck-at faults are **1**-*testable.*

2. If $\sum_z f(z)$ *is odd, then all single and multiple input faults are* **0**-*testable.*

10.1.2 Conditions for Testability

Theorem 10.1.1 and Corollary 10.1.1 provide conditions for w-testability for input faults.

The case of **0**-testability or *syndrome testing* was investigated in References 58, 152, 359, 398, 505, 506, and 517.

A generalization of these results to faults at the internal lines can be found in Reference 398. In this case, detection of faults at an internal line g may require computing of a spectral coefficient of the corresponding function of $m + 1$ variables $z_0, z_1, \ldots, z_{m-1}, g$, which makes it difficult to apply this approach for complex networks.

For any line g (input or internal) in a network computing a switching function $f(z) = f(z_0, z_1, \ldots, z_{m-1})$, there exist switching functions $A(z)$, $B(z)$, and $C(z)$ independent of $g(z)$, the function realized by the network line labeled g, such that

$$f(z) = A(z)g(z) \vee B(z)\overline{g(z)} \vee C(z). \tag{10.1.5}$$

Definition 10.1.2 *(Features of a line in the network)*

1. Line g is positive *if in (10.1.5), $B(z) = 0$ for all z.*
2. Line g is negative *if in (10.1.5), $A(z) = 0$ for all z.*
3. Line g is unate *if it is either positive or negative.*

Theorem 10.1.2 *(505)*
Any single stuck-at fault on a unate line is **0**-*testable.*

Proof. If g is positive, then from (10.1.5), we have for $g/0$

$$\tilde{f}(z) = C(z),$$

and for $g/1$

$$\tilde{f}(z) = A(z) \vee C(z).$$

If g is negative, then we have for $g/0$

$$\tilde{f}(z) = B(\tau) \vee C(z),$$

and for $g/1$

$$\tilde{f}(z) = C(z).$$

Theorem 10.1.2 follows now from the observations that functions $C(z)$, $A(z) \vee C(z)$, and $B(z) \vee C(z)$ have numbers of ones different from $f(z)$.

Corollary 10.1.2   *All single faults at input and internal lines in any fanout-free network containing AND, OR, NAND, NOR, NOT gates only are* **0**-*testable.*

It is shown in Reference 152 that any two-level network can be made **0**-testable by the addition of at most one control input and at most one gate.

Example 10.1.2   *Figure 10.1.2 shows a network implementing the function f from Example 10.1.1* $f(z_0, z_1, z_2, z_3) = z_0 z_1 z_2 \vee z_3(\overline{z_1} \vee z_2)$. *This network is* **0**-*testable for all single stuck-at faults except for faults at the input lines* z_1, z_2, *and internal line g.*

It is easy to check that by adding a control line c, as shown in Fig. 10.1.3, the network in Fig. 10.1.2 (due to Reference 398) can be modified into a network **0**-*testable for all single stuck-at faults at all inputs and internal lines.*

We note that the function $f_M(z_0, z_1, z_2, z_3, c)$ *implemented by the modified network is equal to the original function* $f(z_0, z_1, z_2, z_3)$ *for* $c = 1$.

The general problem of adding a minimal hardware to the existing network to make all single faults **0**-testable seems to be very difficult.

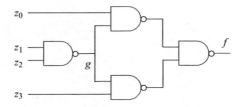

FIGURE 10.1.2   Network from Example 10.1.2.

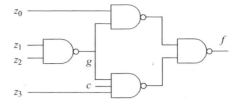

FIGURE 10.1.3   Networks from Example 10.1.2 with a control input c.

We will consider now the problem of *fault diagnosis (fault location)* by spectral techniques.

10.1.3 Conditions for Fault Diagnosis

Fault diagnosis will be implemented by analysis of distortions of spectral coefficients.

Let $F(z)$ be an integer function representing a system of M switching functions of m variables and E be a set of faults in a device implementing $F(z)$.

Denote by $\tilde{F}_i(z)$ a function implemented by the device in the presence of a fault $e_i \in E$.

Definition 10.1.3   *Set E of faults in a device implementing $f(z)$ is w-diagnosable if*

$$S_{\tilde{F}_i}(w) \neq S_{\tilde{F}_j}(w),$$

for all $e_i, e_j \in E$.

Theorem 10.1.3   *Set of single input stuck-at faults in a device implementing $f(z)$ is* **0**-*diagnosable iff*

$$S_F(2^i) \neq 0, \tag{10.1.6}$$
$$S_F(2^i) \neq S_F(2^j),$$
$$S_F(2^i) \neq S_F(0) - S_F(2^j),$$

for all $i, j \in \{0, 1, \ldots, m - 1\}, i \neq j$.

Proof.   Denote

$$N_0^{(s)} = \sum_{z|z_s=0} f(z),$$

$$N_1^{(s)} = \sum_{z|z_s=1} f(z),$$

$$N = \sum_{z} f(z).$$

Then for any s we have $N_1^{(s)} = N - N_0^{(s)}$, and

$$S_F(0) = 2^{-m} N,$$ (10.1.7)

$$S_F(2^s) = 2^{-m}(N_0^{(s)} - N_1^{(s)}) = 2^{-m}(2N_0^{(s)} - N).$$

For $z_s/0$, and $z_s/1$, we have respectively

$$S_{\bar{F}}(0) = 2^{-m+1} N_0^{(s)},$$ (10.1.8)

$$S_{\bar{F}}(0) = 2^{-m+1}(2N_0^{(s)} - N).$$

From (10.1.6) and (10.1.7),

$$N_0^{(i)} \neq N_0^{(j)}, \quad \text{and} \quad N_0^{(i)} \neq N - N_0^{(j)}.$$ (10.1.9)

Theorem 10.1.3 follows now from (10.1.8) and (10.1.9).

Example 10.1.3 *Consider a problem of **0**-diagnosability for single input stuck-at faults for a device with m inputs and 2m outputs computing $F(z) = z^2$, where $z = \sum_{s=0}^{m-1} z_s 2^{m-1-s}$.*

Since,

$$z_s = \frac{1 - W_{2^s}(z)}{2},$$

we have

$$z = \sum_{s=0}^{m-1} \frac{1 - W_{2^s}(z)}{2} \cdot 2^{m-1-s}$$ (10.1.10)

$$= \frac{1}{2}(2^m - 1) - \sum_{s=0}^{m-1} W_{2^s}(z) 2^{m-2-s}.$$

Thus, for $F(z) = z^2$,

$$S_F(2^s) = -(2^m - 1)2^{m-2-s}$$

and

$$S_F(0) = 2^{-m} \sum_{z=0}^{2^m - 1} z^2 = \frac{1}{6}(2^m - 1)(2^{m+1} - 1).$$ (10.1.11)

From (10.1.11),

$$S_F(2^i) \neq S_F(2^j),$$
$$S_F(2^i) \neq S_F(0) - S_F(2^j),$$

for $i \neq j$, and $i, j = 0, 1, \ldots, m - 1$, and by Theorem 10.1.3 all single input stuck-at faults are $\mathbf{0}$-diagnosable in any device computing $F(z) = z^2$.

The methods discussed in this section are applicable for exhaustive testing. For networks with large number of inputs, these tests may prove to be prohibitively long.

Hsiao and Seth (251) suggested an approach for the use of spectral coefficients in pseudorandom testing. For this approach, rather than applying all 2^m input vectors, only a pseudorandom sample is used. These pseudorandom vectors for *built-in self-testing* can be easily generated by Linear Feedback Shift Registers or Linear Cellular Automata (5, 269). The observed spectral coefficient normalized by dividing by the number of input vectors applied and compared to the precomputed reference value. In Reference 251, the guidelines for selection of the test length and the spectral coefficient are presented.

Savir (506), proposed constrained $\mathbf{0}$-testability method (constrained syndrome testing). For this approach certain inputs are held at constant values, while the remaining inputs are exhaustively exercised for verification of the sum of the corresponding subfunctions. The spectral characterization of constrained $\mathbf{0}$-testability method was presented in Reference 398. It was shown that constrained $\mathbf{0}$-testability method results in a drastic reduction of a number of input patterns required for detection of stuck-at faults. In the next section, we will present a generalization of the constrained $\mathbf{0}$-testability method, which will result in a further reduction of sizes of test sets. We will see, for example (Section 10.3), that for testing of hardware components computing basic microinstructions in most cases, only four input test patterns are sufficient.

Spectral techniques for memory testing have been investigated in References 244, 251, 260, 261, 263, and 276. We will discuss spectral techniques for memory testing in Section 10.9.

In addition to the Walsh transform, several other transforms have been used for fault detection. Testing by arithmetic transforms has been discussed in References 241 and 242, by Reed–Muller transforms in References 115, 116, 290, 305, 332, and 415, and both by arithmetic and Reed–Muller coefficients in Reference 397.

Spectral techniques for testing and diagnosis at the transistor level based on the Walsh and Haar transforms are described in References 480 and 481.

10.2 FUNCTIONAL TESTING, ERROR DETECTION, AND CORRECTION BY LINEAR CHECKS

10.2.1 Introduction to Linear Checks

Spectral methods based on verification of Walsh coefficients and described in the previous section require exhaustive application of all input patterns and can be used only for networks with small numbers of input lines.

In this section, we will develop another approach for testing and diagnosis (the linear checking approach), which will drastically reduce the time required for testing and diagnosis. This approach will be a generalization of the **0**-testability approach described in the previous section. The approach can be used for *functional testing* and diagnosis of combinational networks, memories, and software for numerical computations.

Conversely to the previous section, spectral techniques in the rest of this chapter will be used for minimization of complexities of testing and diagnostic procedures.

For any integer function $F(z)$, $z = 0, 1, \ldots, 2^m - 1$, representing a system of switching functions, or content of a memory with the address $z = (z_0, \ldots, z_{m-1})$, or an output of a program for the corresponding numerical computations, there exists a subgroup T of the group C_2^m of all binary m-vectors with respect to the operation $\oplus$ of componentwise addition mod 2 and a constant d such that

$$\sum_{\tau \in T} F(z \oplus \tau) - d = 0, \tag{10.2.1}$$

for any $z \in C_2^m$.

For example, take $T = C_2^m$. The verification of whether (10.2.1) is satisfied provides for the error detection (function verification) in any device or program computing F. The time required for this error detection is proportional to the size $|T|$ of T.

For the case $T = C_2^m$, the corresponding error detecting technique is known as the *check sum method*.

We will present in this section the spectral method based on the Walsh transform for constructing *optimal linear checks* with a *minimal cardinality $|T|$ of a check subgroup T*.

A generalization of this approach to functions defined on an arbitrary and not necessarily Abelian groups and for the case when summation in (10.2.1) is in a finite field can be found in References 280, 281, 300, and 302.

For a given $F(z)$, denote by $T(F)$ a minimal subgroup of C_2^m such that there exists a value d satisfying (10.2.1) for $T = T(F)$. We call $|T(F)|$ the *check complexity of* $F(z)$.

In the next section we will present the main properties of check complexities $|T(F)|$.

10.2.2 Check Complexities of Linear Checks

A linear check (10.2.1) can be represented as

$$\sum_{\tau \in C_2^m} \delta(\tau) F(z \oplus \tau) - d = 0, \tag{10.2.2}$$

where

$$\delta(\tau) = \begin{cases} 1, & \tau \in T, \\ 0, & \tau \notin T. \end{cases} \tag{10.2.3}$$

Recall the dyadic convolution defined by

$$(F_1 \circledast F_2)(y) = \sum_{z \in C_2^m} F_1(z) F_2(z \oplus y).$$

Thus, the linear check (10.2.1) can be represented as $\delta \circledast F - d = 0$.

Theorem 10.2.1 *(Check complexity)*

1. *Linear transform of arguments*
   Let σ be a $(m \times m)$ binary nonsingular over $GF(2)$ matrix, $y \in C_2^m$ and

$$V(z) = F(o \odot z \oplus y), \tag{10.2.4}$$

   for every $z \in C_2^m$.
   Then, $|T(V)| = |T(F)|$.

2. *Linear transform of functions*
   Let $V = \sum_{i=0}^{r-1} c_i F_i$, where $c_0, c_1, \dots, c_{r-1}$ are some nonzero constants.
   Then,

$$|T(V)| \leq |\bigoplus_{i=0}^{r-1} T(F_i)|,$$

   where

$$\bigoplus_{i=0}^{r-1} T(F_i) = \{\tau_0 \oplus \tau_1 \cdots \oplus \tau_{r-1}| \tag{10.2.5}$$

$$\tau_0 \in T(F_0), \tau_1 \in T(F_1), \dots \tau_{r-1} \in T(F_{r-1})\}.$$

3. *Convolution of functions over C_2^m*
   Let $V = F_0 \circledast \cdots \circledast F_{r-1}$, where $\circledast$ stands for the dyadic convolution (41),
   then

$$|T(V)| \leq \min_i |T(F_i)|. \tag{10.2.6}$$

4. *Necessary condition for nontrivial checks*
   If $F : C_2^m \to \{0, \pm 1, \pm 2, \dots\}$ and $|T(F)| < 2^m$, then there exist a constant

$d \in \{0, \pm1, \pm2, \ldots\}$ *and a value* $i \in \{1, \ldots, m-1\}$, *such that*

$$\sum_{z \in C_2^m} F(z) = d2^i. \tag{10.2.7}$$

5. *Lower bound for check complexity*
   If $F : C_2^m \to \{0, 1, \ldots\}$ *and* $F \neq 0$, *then*

$$|T(F)| \geq 2^m \left(\sum_{z \in C_2^m} F(z) \right)^{-1} \min_{\{z | F(z) \neq 0\}} F(z), \tag{10.2.8}$$

and there exists $F : C_2^m \to \{0, 1, 2, \ldots\}$ *such that the equality holds in (10.2.8).*

Proof.

1. By definition of $T(F)$, there exists d such that $\sum_{\tau \in T(F)} F(z \oplus \tau) = d$ for every $z \in C_2^m$.

   Then, we have from (10.2.4)

$$\sum_{\tau \in \sigma^{-1} T(F)} V(z \oplus \tau) = \sum_{\tau \in T(F)} V(z \oplus \sigma^{-1} \tau) = \sum_{\tau \in T(F)} F(\sigma z \oplus y \oplus \tau) = d,$$

   where σ^{-1} is the inverse of σ over $GF(2)$, $\sigma^{-1} T(F) = \{\sigma^{-1} \tau | \tau \in T(F)\}$ and $\sigma^{-1} T(F)$ is a check set for $V(z)$.

   Then, $\sigma^{-1} T(F)$ is a minimal check set for $V(z)$ because $|\sigma^{-1} T(F)| = |T(F)|$.

2. Let $T = \bigoplus_{i=0}^{r-1} T(F_i)$ and T_i be a subgroup isomorphic to the factor group $T/T(F_i)$. Then,

$$\sum_{\tau \in T} V(z \oplus \tau) = \sum_{\tau \in T_i} \sum_{\tau_i \in T(F_i)} V(z \oplus \tau_i \oplus \tau), \quad i = 0, \ldots, r-1,$$

   and because

$$\sum_{\tau_i \in T(F_i)} F_i(z \oplus \tau_i) = d_i, \quad i = 0, \ldots, r-1,$$

   for every $z \in C_2^m$, we have

$$\sum_{\tau \in T} V(z \oplus \tau) = \sum_{i=0}^{r-1} c_i \sum_{\tau \in T_i} \sum_{\tau_i \in T(F_i)} F_i(z \oplus \tau \oplus \tau_i) = \sum_{i=0}^{r-1} c_i d_i |T_i|,$$

and

$$T = \bigoplus_{i=0}^{r-1} T(F_i),$$

is the check set for V.

3. Let $\delta_i(z)$ be a characteristic function for $T(F_i)$,

$$\delta_i(z) = \begin{cases} 1, & z \in T(F_i), \\ 0, & z \notin T(F_i). \end{cases}$$

Then, by definition of $T(F_i)$, $(F_i \circledast \delta_i)(z) = d_i$ for all $z \in C_2^m$, and therefore there exists the constant d_i such that for every $i = 0, \ldots, r-1$,

$$V \circledast \delta_i = \left(\circledast_{s \neq i} F_s \right) \circledast F_i \circledast \delta_i = \circledast_{s \neq i} F_s \circledast d_i = d_V,$$

and $T(F_i)$ is a check set for V.

4. If H is isomorphic to $C_2^m / T(F)$, then

$$\sum_{z \in C_2^m} F(z) = \sum_{z \in H} \sum_{y \in T(F)} F(z \oplus y) = d|H| = d2^i.$$

5. Formula (10.2.8) follows from (10.2.7) because $|H| = 2^m |T(F)|^{-1}$ and $d \geq \min_{F(z) \neq 0} F(z)$.

   The lower bound (10.2.8) is reached, for example, for

$$F(z) = \begin{cases} 1, & 0 \leq z < 2^{m-1}, \\ 0, & 2^{m-1} \leq z < 2^m. \end{cases}$$

In this case,

$$\sum_{z \in C_2^m} F(z) = 2^{m-1},$$

and since $d = 1$, it follows $F(z) + F(z \oplus (1, 0, \ldots, 0)) = 1$ for every $z \in C_2^m$.

10.2.3 Spectral Methods for Construction of Optimal Linear Checks

In this section we will describe a simple spectral method for construction of *optimal linear equality checks* (10.2.1) minimizing testing time $|T|$ for numerical functions defined over C_2^m.

For a subgroup C of C_2^m, denote by $C^\perp$ the subgroup *orthogonal* to C, that is,

$$C^\perp = \{x \in C_2^m \mid \bigoplus_{i=0}^{m} x_i z_i = 0 \quad \text{for all} \quad z = (z_0, \ldots, z_{m-1}) \in C\}. \quad (10.2.9)$$

We note that $C^\perp$ is isomorphic to the factor group C_2^m / C.

For a given integer function $F(z)$ (where $z \in C_2^m$), we also denote by $T(F)$ a minimal subgroup of C_2^m satisfying (10.2.1) for some d and all $z \in C_2^m$.

Theorem 10.2.2 *Denote*

$$\Omega = \{w \mid S_F(w) = 0, w \neq \mathbf{0}\}, \quad (10.2.10)$$

and let C be a maximal subgroup of C_2^m such that $C \subseteq \Omega \cup \{\mathbf{0}\}$. Then, $T(F) = C^\perp$, $|T(F)| = 2^m / |C|$ and

$$d = \sum_{z \in C_2^m} F(z)/|C|.$$

Proof. From (10.2.1) and (10.2.2) we have by the convolution theorem (Theorem 2.6.4) for $\delta(\tau)$ defined by (10.2.3)

$$S_F(w) \cdot S_\delta(w) = \begin{cases} 2^{-m}d, & \text{for } w = \mathbf{0}, \\ 0, & \text{otherwise.} \end{cases} \quad (10.2.11)$$

Let

$$d = \frac{2^m}{|C|} S_F(\mathbf{0}) = \frac{1}{|C|} \sum_{z \in C_2^m} F(z), \quad (10.2.12)$$

and

$$S_\delta(w) = \begin{cases} |C|^{-1}, & \text{if } w \in C, \\ 0, & \text{if } w \notin C, \end{cases} \quad (10.2.13)$$

where C is the maximal subgroup of C_2^m contained in $\Omega \cup \{\mathbf{0}\} = \{w \mid S_F(w) = 0, w \neq \mathbf{0}\} \cup \{\mathbf{0}\}$.

Then (10.2.2) follows from (10.2.11).

From (10.2.13) we have

$$\delta(z) = \sum_{w \in C} S_\delta(w) W_z(w) = \frac{1}{|C|} \sum_{w \in C} W_z(w) = \begin{cases} 1, & z \in C^\perp, \\ 0, & z \notin C^\perp. \end{cases} \quad (10.2.14)$$

The proof of Theorem 10.2.2 generates a simple spectral method for construction of optimal linear equality checks (10.2.1), (10.2.2) for a given function $F(z)$. This method reduces to the following operations:

1. Compute the Walsh spectrum $S_F(w)$ for $F(z)$.
2. Construct a maximal subgroup C in $\Omega \cup \{0\}$.
3. Construct $C^\perp$ and take $T(F) = C^\perp$ and $d = \sum_{z \in C_2^m} \frac{F(z)}{|C|}$.

We note that construction of optimal linear checks in the original z-domain is very difficult.

We note also that any subgroup C in C_2^m can be represented as a *linear span* of the rows of its generating matrix $\mathbf{G}$ with $\log_2 |C|$ rows and m columns. (All elements of C can be obtained as linear combinations over $GF(2)$ of rows of $\mathbf{G}$.)

Matrix $\mathbf{G}$ can always be represented in the following standard equivalent form (see Reference 347)

$$\mathbf{G} = \left[\mathbf{I}_k \mid \mathbf{P} \right],$$

where $\mathbf{I}_k$ is the $(k \times k)$ identity matrix, $k = \log_2 |C|$, and $\mathbf{P}$ is a $(k \times (m - k))$ matrix. Then $C^\perp$ can be obtained as the linear span of the rows of

$$\mathbf{H} = \left[\mathbf{P}^T \mid \mathbf{I}_{m-k} \right], \tag{10.2.15}$$

where $\mathbf{P}^T$ is the $((m - k) \times k)$ matrix obtained by transposing $\mathbf{P}$ and $\mathbf{I}_{m-k}$ is the $((m - k) \times (m - k))$ identity matrix.

We note that for the nonbinary (p-ary, $p > 2$) case, (10.2.2) should be replaced by

$$\sum_{z \in C_p^m} \delta(\tau) f(z \ominus \tau) = d, \tag{10.2.16}$$

where $\ominus$ stands for componentwise subtraction modulo p of vectors from C_p^m, and (10.2.15) should be replaced by

$$\mathbf{H} = \left[\ominus \mathbf{P}^T \mid \mathbf{I}_{m-k} \right], \tag{10.2.17}$$

where $\ominus \mathbf{P}^T$ is the matrix $\mathbf{P}^T$ with all its elements multiplied by $-1 (\bmod p)$.

Example 10.2.1 *Consider error detection by linear equality checks for an n-bit binary adder. In this case, $m = 2n$ and*

$$f(x_0, \ldots, x_{n-1}, y_0, \ldots, y_{n-1}) = x + y.$$

Then,

$$F(x, y) = \sum_{s=0}^{n-1} x_s 2^{n-1-s} + \sum_{s=0}^{n-1} y_s 2^{n-1-s} \tag{10.2.18}$$

$$= \sum_{s=0}^{n-1} (0.5(1 - R_{s+1}) + 0.5(1 - R_{n+s+1})) 2^{n-1-s}$$

$$= 2^n - 1 - \sum_{s=0}^{n-1} (R_{s+1} + R_{n+s+1}) 2^{n-1-s},$$

where

$$R_{i+1}(x_0, \ldots, x_{n-1}, y_0, \ldots, y_{n-1}) = W_w(x_0, \ldots, x_{n-1}, y_0, \ldots, y_{n-1})$$

for $w = (\overbrace{0, \ldots, 0,}^{i-1} \overbrace{1}^{i}, 0, \ldots, 0)$ are the Rademacher functions.
It follows from (10.2.18) that

$$S_F(w) = S_{x+y}(w) = 0,$$

for all $w \in C_2^{2n}$ such that $\|w\| > 1$, where $\|w\|$ is the number of ones in $w = (w_0, \ldots, w_{2n-1})$.
Thus, by Theorem 10.2.2, we can take $C = \{w| \bigoplus_{s=0}^{2n-1} w_s = 0\}$ with $|C| = 2^{2n-1}$. The generating matrix for C can be taken as

$$\mathbf{G} = \left[\mathbf{I}_k \mid \mathbf{1}^T \right],$$

where $k = 2n - 1$ and $\mathbf{1}^T$ is the column of all ones, and

$$T(f) = T(x + y) = C^\perp = \{\mathbf{0}, \mathbf{1}\}.$$

Since

$$\sum_{x, y \in C_2^n} F(x, y) = 2^{2n}(2^n - 1),$$

it follows from (10.2.12) that $d = 2(2^n - 1)$ and we finally have the following linear check for adders

$$f(x_0, \ldots, x_{n-1}, y_0, \ldots, y_{n-1}) + f(x_0 \oplus 1, \ldots, x_{n-1} \oplus 1, y_0 \oplus 1, \ldots, y_{n-1} \oplus 1)$$

$$= F(x, y) + F(x \oplus \mathbf{1}, y \oplus \mathbf{1})$$

$$= F(x, y) + F(\bar{x}, \bar{y}) = 2(2^n - 1), \tag{10.2.19}$$

for all x, $y \in C_2^n$, *and the complexity* $|T(F)|$ *of the check for adders is equal to 2, that is,* $|T(x + y)| = 2$. *(Here,* $\bar{x}$ *and* $\bar{y}$ *are componentwise negations of x and y.)*

We note that the **0**-testability approach described in Section 10.2.1 is the special case of linear checks with $C = \{0\}$ and $T = C^{\perp} = C_2^m$.

Example 10.2.2 *We now consider linear equality checks for an n-bit binary multiplier.*

In this case, $m = 2n$ *and*

$$f(x_0, \ldots, x_{n-1}, y_0, \ldots, y_{n-1}) = x \cdot y \qquad (10.2.20)$$

$$= \left(\sum_{s=0}^{n-1} 0.5(1 - R_{s+1})2^{n-1-s} \right) \cdot \left(\sum_{s=0}^{n-1} 0.5(1 - R_{n+s+1})2^{n-1-s} \right).$$

It follows from (10.2.20) that

$$S_{x \cdot y}(w) = S_{x \cdot y}(w_0, \ldots, w_{n-1}, w_n, \ldots, w_{2n-1}) = 0$$

for all w such that

$$\sum_{s=0}^{n-1} w_s \geq 2, \quad and \quad \sum_{s=0}^{n-1} w_{n+s} \geq 2.$$

Thus, by Theorem 10.2.2 we can take

$$C = \{w | \sum_{s=0}^{n} w_s = 2k_1, \sum_{s=0}^{n-1} w_{n+s} = 2k_2, \quad k_1, k_2 = 0, 1, \ldots, \lfloor n/2 \rfloor \}.$$

with $|C| = 2^{2n-2}$.

The generating matrix **G** *for C can be selected as*

$$\mathbf{G} = \left[\begin{array}{ccccc} \mathbf{I}_{n-1} & \mathbf{1}^T & | & \mathbf{0} & \\ --- & --- & --- & --- & --- \\ \mathbf{0} & | & \mathbf{I}_{n-1} & \mathbf{1}^T \end{array} \right].$$

Then,

$$T(f) = T(x \cdot y) = \{\mathbf{00}, \mathbf{01}, \mathbf{10}, \mathbf{11}\},$$

where **0** *and* **1** *are n-bit vectors of all zeros and all ones.*

Since,

$$\sum_{x, y \in C_2^n} F(x, y) = \sum_{x, y = 0}^{2^n - 1} x \cdot y = 2^{2n-2}(2^n - 1)^2,$$

it follows from (10.2.12) that in this case $d = (2^n - 1)^2$.

Thus, we have the following linear equality check for the n-bit multipliers:

$$F(x, y) + F(x, \overline{y}) + F(\overline{x}, y) + F(\overline{x}, \overline{y}) = (2^n - 1)^2, \tag{10.2.21}$$

for all $x, y \in C_2^n$ and $|T(x \cdot y)| = 4$.

The lower bound on check complexity $|T(F)|$ is given by Theorem 10.2.1 (see (10.2.8)). We will now construct the exact upper bound for $|T(F)|$.

Theorem 10.2.3 *(The exact upper bound)*

1. *For any $F(z)$ with $z \in C_2^m$,*

$$|T(F)| \le \frac{1}{2}(2^m + 1 - |\Omega|), \tag{10.2.22}$$

   where Ω is defined by (10.2.10).
2. *For any m, there are functions $F(x)$ defined over C_2^m such that*

$$\log_2 |T(F)| = \lceil \log_2(2^m + 1 - |\Omega|) \rceil - 1. \tag{10.2.23}$$

Proof.

1. It was shown in Reference 285 that for any subset Q of $C_2^m - \{0\}$, the subset $Q \cup \{0\}$ contains a subgroup C of C_2^m such that

$$\log_2 C \ge m + 1 - \lfloor \log_2(2^m - |Q| + 1) \rfloor. \tag{10.2.24}$$

   The upper bound (10.2.22) follows now from (10.2.24) by Theorem 10.2.2 with $Q = \Omega$ since $|T(F)| \le |C^\perp| = \frac{2^m}{|C|}$.
2. It was also shown in Reference 285 that for any $k \in \{0, 1, \ldots, m\}$, there exists a set $Q^* \subseteq C_2^m - \{0\}$ with $|Q^*| = 2^m - 2^{m-k+1}$ such that $Q^* \cup \{0\}$ does not contain any subgroup C with $|C| = 2^k$. Then, for any function $F(x)$ such that $\{w | S_F(w) = 0, w \neq 0\} = Q^*$ equation (10.2.23) is satisfied.

To conclude this section, we note that the most suitable functions for testing by linear checks are functions with Walsh spectra containing sufficiently many zeros. (As we will see in the next sections, functions describing the basic computer instructions and software for numerical computations belong to this class.)

Another limitation on the use of linear checks is implied by the fact that they yield only solutions of (10.2.1) for which T is a subgroup of C_2^m.

The main advantage of linear checks lies in their simplicity and convenience from the computational point of view. Thus, if the initial function F is defined analytically, the solution $T(F)$ may often be found also analytically (see Examples 10.2.1 and 10.2.2 above). The tables which list the Walsh spectra for a large number of important classes of switching functions can be found in the Appendix A. Optimal linear checks for standard microinstructions will be given in the following section and for functions, computing polynomials in Section 10.4.

Another advantage of the proposed linear checks is their weak dependence on the structure of the original group C_2^m. The generalization of these checks to functions defined on any (not necessarily Abelian) finite group is straightforward (208,209,212). This generates a unified set of error-detecting methods for binary and nonbinary devices, devices implementing functions defined on the symmetric group of permutations, and so on.

10.2.4 Hardware Implementations of Linear Checks

We will consider now the problem of network implementation of linear checks starting with the following example.

Example 10.2.3 *Suppose that for a function $f(z) = f(z_0, \ldots, z_6)$, $m = 7$, the group C and $T = C^\perp$ are defined by the following matrices $\mathbf{G}$ and $\mathbf{H}$, where C is the set of all linear combinations of rows of $\mathbf{G}$ and $C^\perp$ is the set of all linear combinations of rows of $\mathbf{H}$ (see (10.2.15))*

$$\mathbf{G} = \begin{bmatrix} 1 & 0 & 0 & | & 0 & 1 & 1 & 1 \\ 0 & 1 & 0 & | & 1 & 0 & 1 & 1 \\ 0 & 0 & 1 & | & 1 & 1 & 0 & 1 \end{bmatrix},$$

and

$$\mathbf{H} = \begin{bmatrix} 0 & 1 & 1 & | & 1 & 0 & 0 & 0 \\ 1 & 0 & 1 & | & 0 & 1 & 0 & 0 \\ 1 & 1 & 0 & | & 0 & 0 & 1 & 0 \\ 1 & 1 & 1 & | & 0 & 0 & 0 & 1 \end{bmatrix}.$$

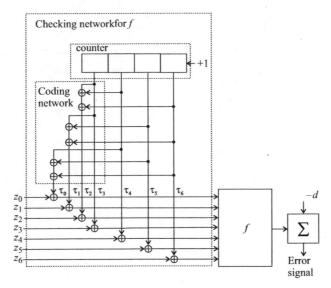

FIGURE 10.2.1   Network implementation of the check from Example 10.2.3.

Then, $|C^\perp| = |T| = 16$ and $\tau = (\tau_0, \ldots, \tau_6) \in C^\perp$ iff

$$\mathbf{G} \odot \tau = \begin{bmatrix} 0 \\ 0 \\ 0 \end{bmatrix},$$

or $\tau_0 = \tau_4 \oplus \tau_5 \oplus \tau_6$, $\tau_1 = \tau_3 \oplus \tau_5 \oplus \tau_6$ and $\tau_2 = \tau_3 \oplus \tau_4 \oplus \tau_6$.

The network implementation of this check is given in Fig. 10.2.1 and consists of a counter generating the information bits $\tau_3, \tau_4, \tau_5, \tau_6$ of $C^\perp$, a linear encoding network generating the check bits $\tau_0, \tau_1,$ and τ_2 of $C^\perp$, and a network for mod 2 summation of z and $\tau \in C^\perp$.

The general architecture for Built-In Self-Testing (BIST) by linear checks (10.2.1) is given in Fig. 10.2.2. In this figure, the linear encoding network computes check bits $\tau_0, \ldots, \tau_{k-1}$ by information bits $\tau_k, \ldots, \tau_{m-1}$ for $T = C^\perp$. The test pattern generator generates test patterns $(z_0, \ldots, z_{m-1})$, which may be either pseudorandom vector generated by a m-bit Linear Feedback Shit Register (269) or precomputed representatives of cosets of $C^\perp$ in C_2^m.

The complexity of an $(m - k)$-bit counter is proportional to $(m - k)$ and for the number $L(m, k)$ of two-input EXOR gates required for encoding network we have by (6.1.17) as $m - k \to \infty$

$$L(m, k) \lesssim \frac{(m - k)k}{\log_2(m - k)},$$

where $a(n) \lesssim b(n)$ iff $\lim_{n \to \infty} a(n)/b(n) = 1$.

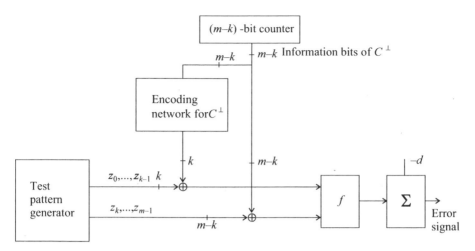

FIGURE 10.2.2 Built-in self-test architecture for testing by linear checks (10.2.1) $|T| = |C^\perp| = 2^{m-k}$.

10.2.5 Error-Detecting Capabilities of Linear Checks

In this section, we will analyze error-detecting capabilities of linear checks (10.2.1). These capabilities depend on a selected error model.

The simplest error model is the model of additive errors. In this case, by an error e with multiplicity l we mean any function $e(z) = e(z_0, \ldots, z_{m-1})$, which is not equal to 0 at l points (i.e., $F(z)$ is distorted at l points, $\|e\| = l$ and our device or program is computing $F(z) + e(z)$ instead of $F(z)$). This definition is natural if errors in computing $F(z)$ are independent for different z, as, for example, is the case where $F(z)$ is information stored in a memory cell which address is z. In this case, an error $e(z)$ has multiplicity $\|e\| = l$ iff exactly l cells contain a corrupted data.

It follows from (10.2.1) that $e(z)$ cannot be detected iff for every $z \in C_2^m$

$$\sum_{\tau \in T} e(z \oplus \tau) = 0. \tag{10.2.25}$$

It follows now from (10.2.25) that if $\hat\eta(l)$ is a fraction of errors with multiplicity l, which are not detected by the check (10.2.1), and M is a number of bits in the binary representation of $F(z)$ for every z, then

$$\hat\eta(1) = 0, \tag{10.2.26}$$

$$\hat\eta(l) \le (2^M - 1)^{-1} \tag{10.2.27}$$

for every $l > 1$.

Thus, for example, for the case of 32-bit computations ($m = M = 32$) even one linear check (10.2.1) provides for a very high error detecting capability for the case of additive errors.

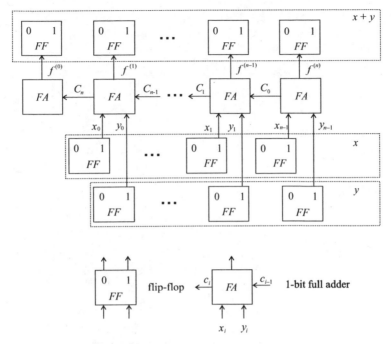

FIGURE 10.2.3   Block diagram of an n-bit adder.

In the case when errors at the output of the device are manifestations of faults in the internal components (such as stuck-at faults, bridging between lines), the error model depends on the selected model for internal faults.

Example 10.2.4 *To illustrate the error-detecting capability of linear checks with respect to internal, input, and output faults, we will consider the example of the n-bit adder (see Example 10.2.1) with block diagram shown in Fig. 10.2.3. In this case,* $f(x, y) = x + y$ *and*

$$f(x, y) + f(\overline{x}, \overline{y}) = 2(2^n - 1),$$

where $x, y \in \{0, 1, \ldots, 2^n - 1\}$.

We shall consider four classes of errors for the adder in Fig. 10.2.3, that is, input errors $e_{inp}(x, y)$, *output errors* $e_{out}(x, y)$ *carry errors* $e_c(x, y)$, *and shift errors* $e_{sh}(x, y)$.

An l-fold input (output) error, $0 < l \le 2n$, $(0 < l \le n + 1)$ *is said to occur if l bits of* $(x_0, \ldots, x_n, y_0, \ldots, y_{n-1})$ *(of* $(f^{(0)}(x, y), \ldots, f^{(n)}(x, y)))$ *are corrupted and converted into arbitrary binary constants (see Fig. 10.2.3).*

An l-fold carry error, $0 < l \le n$, *occurs if l components of the carry vector* $(C_0, \ldots, C_n)$ *(see Fig. 10.2.3) are replaced by binary constants.*

An l-fold shift error is a shift by l positions to the right or left in a vector recorded in any three registers $x, y, x + y$ *in Fig. 10.2.3.*

For a right (left) shift by l positions, the vector $(z_0, \ldots, z_{k-1})$ is changed into

$$(\underbrace{0, \ldots, 0}_{l} z_0, \ldots, z_{k-1-l}) \quad (z_l, \ldots, z_{k-1}, \underbrace{0, \ldots, 0}_{l}).$$

Shift errors are probable when the information is transferred to the x and y registers and from the x + y register in serial form.

We denote the fraction of errors with multiplicity l, which are detected for the above four classes by $\rho_{inp}(n, l)$, $\rho_{out}(n, l)$, $\rho_c(n, l)$, $\rho_{sh}(n, l)$, respectively.

Example 10.2.5 *(Example 10.2.4 continued)*
We will show now that for an n-bit adder

$$\rho_{inp}(n, l) = \begin{cases} 1 - \binom{n}{S}\binom{2n}{2S}^{-1} 2^{-S}, & \text{if } l = 2S, \\ 1, & \text{if } l = 2S - 1, \\ & S = 1, \ldots, n, \end{cases} \quad (10.2.28)$$

$$\rho_{out}(n, l) = 1 - \delta_{l,n+1} 2^{-n-1} \quad (10.2.29)$$

where $\delta_{l,n+1}$ - Kronecker symbol,

$$\rho_c(n, l) = \rho_{sh}(n, l) = 1, \quad (10.2.30)$$

for all n, l.
Any input error with multiplicity l may be expressed as

$$e_{inp}(x, y) = \sum_{i=1}^{S_1} (\alpha_{p_i} - x_{p_i}) 2^{n-1-p_i} \quad (10.2.31)$$

$$+ \sum_{i=1}^{S_2} (\beta_{r_i} - y_{r_i}) 2^{n-1-r_i},$$

where $S_1 + S_2 = l,$ $0 \le p_1 < \ldots < p_{S_1} \le n - 1,$ $0 \le r_1 < \ldots < r_{S_2} \le n - 1,$
$\alpha_{p_i}, \beta_{r_i} \in \{0, 1\}$.
Since

$$\sum_{x,y} (\alpha_{p_i} - x_{p_i}) = (-1)^{\alpha_{p_i}+1} 2^{2n-1}, \quad i = 1, \ldots S_1, \quad (10.2.32)$$

$$\sum_{x,y} (\beta_{r_i} - y_{r_i}) = (-1)^{\beta_{r_i}+1} 2^{2n-1}, \quad i = 1, \ldots, S_2,$$

it follows that

$$\sum_{x,y} e_{inp}(x, y) = 2^{2n-1} \left(\sum_{i=1}^{S_1} (-1)^{\alpha_{p_i}+1} 2^{n-1-p_i} \right. \tag{10.2.33}$$

$$\left. + \sum_{i=1}^{S_2} (-1)^{\beta_{r_i}+1} 2^{n-1-r_i} \right).$$

Set $E_{inp} = \{e_{inp} | S_1 = S_2 = S, p_i = r_i, \alpha_{p_i} = 1 - \beta_{r_i}, i = 1, \ldots, s\}$.
Then, if $e_{inp} \notin E_{inp}$, we see from (10.2.33) that $\sum_{x,y} e_{inp}(x, y) \neq 0$ and by (10.2.25) e_{inp} is detected for some x, y.
If $e_{inp} \in E_{inp}$, then by (10.2.33) $\sum_{x,y} e_{inp}(x, y) = 0$ and e_{inp} is not detected for all x, y.
Hence, in view of the fact that the total number of 2S-fold errors is equal to

$$\binom{2n}{2S} \cdot 2^{2S},$$

and the number of errors with multiplicity 2S, $e_{inp} \in E_{inp}$ is

$$\binom{n}{S} \cdot 2^S,$$

we obtain (10.2.28).
Any output error with the multiplicity l may be expressed as

$$e_{out}(x, y) = \sum_{i=1}^{l} (\alpha_{p_i} - f^{(p_i)}(x, y)) 2^{n-p_i}, \tag{10.2.34}$$

where ($\alpha_{p_i} \in \{0, 1\}, 0 \leq p_1 < \ldots < p_l \leq n$).
Since $x + y = \sum_{p=0}^{n} f^{(p)}(x, y) 2^{n-p}$, ($f^{(p)}(x, y) \in \{0, 1\}$), it is readily seen that for any $p_i \in \{0, \ldots, n\}$ and $\alpha_{p_i} \in \{0, 1\}$, $\sum_{x,y} f^{(p_i)}(x, y) = 2^{2n-1} - \delta_{p_i,0} \cdot 2^{n-1}$ and

$$\sum_{x,y} (\alpha_{p_i} - f^{(p_i)}(x, y)) = (-1)^{\alpha_{p_i}+1} 2^{2n-1} + (-1)^{\alpha_{p_i}} \cdot \delta_{p_i,0} \cdot 2^{n-1}. \tag{10.2.35}$$

Since $0 \leq p_1 < \ldots < p_l \leq n$, it follows from (10.2.34) and (10.2.35) that

$$\sum_{x,y} e_{out}(x, y) = 2^{2n-1} \left(\sum_{i=1}^{l} (-1)^{\alpha_{p_i}+1} 2^{n-p_i} + (-1)^{\alpha_{p_i}} \cdot \delta_{p_i,0} \right). \tag{10.2.36}$$

Denote

$$E_{out}(x, y) = -f^{(0)}(x, y)2^n + \sum_{p=1}^{n}(1 - f^{(p)}(x, y))2^{n-p}. \qquad (10.2.37)$$

Then, if $e_{out} \notin E_{out}$, it follows from (10.2.36) and (10.2.37) that $\sum_{x,y} e_{out}(x, y) \neq 0$, and e_{out} is detected.

If $e_{out} \in E_{out}$, then $\sum_{x,y} e_{out}(x, y) = 0$, and e_{out} is not detected.

Thus, the only undetected output error is the error E_{out} with multiplicity $(n + 1)$, and this implies (10.2.29).

Now, let $e_c(x, y) = e_c(x_0, \ldots, x_{n-1}, y_0, \ldots, y_{n-1})$ be a carry error with multiplicity l for which $C_{p_i} = \alpha_{p_i}$ (see Fig. 10.2.3) where the α_{p_i} are certain binary constants $(i = 1, \ldots, l, 0 \le p_l < \ldots < p_l \le n - 1)$.

Then, we have

$$e_c(\underbrace{0, \ldots 0}_{2n}) = \sum_{i=1}^{l} \alpha_{p_i} 2^{\alpha_{p_i}+1}, \qquad (10.2.38)$$

$$e_c(\underbrace{1, \ldots, 1}_{2n}) = \sum_{i=1}^{l} (\alpha_{p_i} - 1)2^{\alpha_{p_i}+1},$$

and

$$e_c(\underbrace{0, \ldots, 0}_{2n}) + e_c(\underbrace{1, \ldots, 1}_{2n}) = \sum_{i=1}^{l}(2\alpha_{p_i} - 1)2^{\alpha_{p_i}+1} \neq 0, \qquad (10.2.39)$$

for any $\alpha_{p_i} \in \{0, 1\}$, $i = 1, \ldots, l$.

Thus, it follows from (10.2.38) that $\rho_c(n, l) = 1$ for all l.

Similarly, for an arbitrary shift error

$$e_{sh}(x, y) = e_{sh}(x_0, \ldots, x_{n-1}, y_0, \ldots, y_{n-1}),$$

we have $\rho_{sh}(n, l) = 1$ for all $l \in \{1, \ldots, l\}$.

10.2.6 Detection and Correction of Errors by Systems of Orthogonal Linear Checks

As it was explained in the previous section for the additive errors, replacing $f(z)$ by $\tilde{f}(z) = f(z) + e(z)$, all single errors ($\|e\| = 1$) are detected and the fraction $\hat{\eta}(l)$ of multiple errors with multiplicity l ($\|e\| = l$), which are not detected, does not exceed $(2^M - 1)^{-1}$, where M is the number of bits in the binary representation of $f(z)$.

No errors can be corrected by verification of one linear check, and there are double errors that are not detected.

Let

$$\sum_{\tau \in T_i} f(z \oplus \tau) - d_i = 0, \quad i = 0, 1, \ldots, n - 1, \quad z, \tau \in G = C_2^m \quad (10.2.40)$$

be a system of n linear checks for $f(z)$.

We will say that these checks are *orthogonal* iff

$$T_i \cap T_j = \{\mathbf{0}\} = \{0^m\},$$

where $0^m = \mathbf{0} = \underbrace{(0, \ldots, 0)}_{m}$ for any $i \neq j$.

Pairs of orthogonal checks for several important classes of functions $f(z)$ are given in Tables 10.2.1.

Denote

$$\sum_{\tau \in T_i} \tilde{f}(z \oplus \tau) - d_i = \sum_{\tau \in T_i} e(z \oplus \tau) = S_i^{(e)}(z), \quad (10.2.41)$$

for $i = 0, 1, \ldots, n - 1$.

If $y, v \in z \oplus T_i$, then

$$S_i^{(e)}(y) = S_i^{(e)}(v). \quad (10.2.42)$$

We will call $S^{(e)}(z) = (S_0^{(e)}(z), \ldots, S_{n-1}^{(e)}(z))$ a *syndrome* for the error $e(z)$.

We will consider in this section, two classes of error-detecting and error-correcting procedures based on analysis of error syndromes,

1. Memoryless (combinational) decoding, and
2. Memory-aided (sequential) decoding.

We will see that the transition from the memoryless decoding to the memory-aided not only results in exponential increase of their error-detecting and error-correcting capabilities, but also requires a considerable increase in the complexity of decoding.

For *memoryless decoding*, error detection (verification of $e(z) \neq 0$) and error correction (computation of $e(z)$ for any given z) are implemented by a syndrome $S^{(e)}(z) = (S_0^{(e)}(z), \ldots, S_{n-1}^{(e)}(z))$ for any given z.

For *memory-aided decoding*, we first compute $S^{(e)}(z)$ for all z and then detect errors (decide whether z exists such that $e(z) \neq 0$) or correct the errors (compute $e(z)$ for all z).

We note that, as it follows from (10.2.42), $S_i^{(e)}(z)$ is a constant for all z that belong to the same coset of T_i in C_2^m.

TABLE 10.2.1   Orthogonal Checks for Some Numerical Functions ($|T_1| < |T_2|$).

N	Name	Function	T_1	d_1
1.	Multiplication	$f(X, Y) = XY$ $X, Y \in \{0, \dots, 2^m - 1\}$	$\{0^m, 1^m\}^2$ $= \{0^{2m}, 0^m 1^m,$ $1^m 0^m, 1^{2m}\}$	$(2^m - 1)^2$
2.	Conversion from the binary to the inverted code	$f(z) = z \oplus shr(z),$ $shr(z)$ $= (0, z_1, \dots, z_{m-2})$ $z = (z_0, \dots, z_{m-1})$	$\{0^m, 1010\dots\}$	$2^m - 1$
3.	Conversion from the inverted to the binary code	$f(z) = \oplus_{i=0}^{m-1} shr^i z$ $shr^0 z = z$ $shr^i z = shr(shr^{i-1} z)$ $z = (z_0, \dots, z_{m-1})$ $z_i \in \{0, 1\}$	$\{0^m, 10^{m-1}\}$	$2^m - 1$
4.	Conversion from the 2421 BCD code to the binary code	$f(z_1, \dots, z_m) =$ $\sum_{i=0}^{s-1} (z_{m-4i}$ $+ 2z_{m-4i-1}$ $+ 4z_{m-4i-2}$ $+ 2z_{m-4i-3})10^i$ $m = 4s, z_i \in \{0, 1\}$	$\{0^m, 1^m\}$	$10^s - 1$
5.	Conversion from the excess 3 BCD code to the binary code	$f(z_1, \dots, z_m) =$ $\sum_{i=0}^{s-1} (z_{m-4i}$ $+ 2z_{m-4i-1}$ $+ 4z_{m-4i-2}$ $+ 8z_{m-4i-3} - 3)10^i$	$\{0^m, 1^m\}$	$10^s - 1$
6.	Linear function	$f(z) = az + b$ $z \in \{0, \dots, 2^m - 1\}$	$\{0^m, 1^m\}$	$a(2^m - 1)$ $+ 2b$
7.	Scalar product	$f(x, y)$ $= \sum_{i=1}^n x_i y_i$ $x_i, y_i \in C_2^m$	$\{0^{nm}, 1^{nm}\}^2$	$n(2^m - 1)^2$
8.	Rademacher function	$f_i(z) = R_i(z) = (-1)^{z_{i-1}}$ $z = (z_0, \dots, z_{m-1})$	$\{0^m, 0^{i-1} 10^{m-i}\}$	0
9.	Walsh function	$W_{i_1, \dots, i_s}$ $= (-1)^{z_{i_1} + z_{i_2} + \dots + z_{i_s}}$ $1 \le s \le m$	$\{0^m, 0^{i_1-1} 10^{m-i_1}\}$	0

continued

TABLE 10.2.1   (Continued).

N	Name	T_2	d_2
1.	Multiplication	$\{0^m, 101^{m-2}, 011^{m-2}, 110^{m-2}\}^2$	$4(2^m-1)^2$
2.	Conversion from the binary to the inverted code	$\{0^m, 10101\ldots, 0101, \ldots, 10^{m-1}\}$	$2(2^m-1)$
3.	Conversion from the inverted to the binary code	$\{0^m, 1110^{m-3}, 010^{m-2}, 101^{m-3}\}$	$2(2^m-2)$
4.	Conversion from the 2421 BCD code to the binary code	$\{0^m, 1^40^41^{m-8}, 0^41^41^{m-8}, 1^80^{m-8}\}$	$2(10^s-1)$
5.	Conversion from the excess 3 BCD code to the binary code	$\{0^m, 1^40^41^{m-8}, 0^41^41^{m-8}, 1^80^{m-8}\}$	$2(10^s-1)$
6.	Linear function	$\{0^m, 101^{m-2}, 011^{m-2}, 110^{m-2}\}$	$2a(2^m-1)+4b$
7.	Scalar product	$\{0^{nm} \cup \{101^{m-2}\}^n \cup \{011^{m-2}\}^n$ $\cup\{110^{m-2}\}^n\}^2$	$4n(2^m-1)^2$
8.	Rademacher function	$\{0^m, 10^{i-2}10^{m-i}\}$	0
9.	Walsh function	$\{0^m, 0^{i_2}10^{m-i_2}\}$	0

Here $0^i = \underbrace{0\ldots0}_{i}$, $1^i = \underbrace{1,\ldots1}_{i}$, $A^2 = \{a_1a_2|a_1, a_2 \in A\}$,

$A^t = \{(a_1, \ldots, a_t)|a_i \in A\}$.

The following two theorems (Theorems 10.2.4 and 10.2.5) describe error-detecting and error-correcting capabilities of n orthogonal checks for memoryless and memory-aided decoding.

Let for any set E of errors, the error $e = 0^m$ belong to E.

Definition 10.2.1 *A set E of errors with checks (10.2.40) is detected by a memoryless decoding if, for any $e \in E$ and for every given $z \in G$, it follows from $e(z) \neq 0$ that there exists $j \in \{0, \ldots, n-1\}$ such that $S_j^{(e)}(z) \neq 0$, where $G = C_2^m$.*

Definition 10.2.2 *A set E of errors is corrected by a memoryless decoding, if for any $e_1, e_2 \in E$ and for every given $z \in G$, it follows from $e_1(z) \neq e_2(z)$ that there exists $j \in \{0, \ldots, n-1\}$ such that $S_j^{(e_1)}(z) \neq S_j^{(e_2)}(z)$.*

Definition 10.2.3 *A set E of errors with checks (10.2.40) is detected by a memory-aided decoding if, for any $e \in E$, it follows from $e \neq 0^m$ that there exist $j \in \{0, 1, \ldots, n-1\}$ and $z \in G$ such that $S_j^{(e)}(z) \neq 0$.*

Definition 10.2.4 *A set E of errors is corrected by a memory-aided decoding if for any $e_1, e_2 \in E$, it follows from $e_1 \neq e_2$ that there exist $j \subset \{0, 1, \ldots, n-1\}$ and $z \in G$ such that $S_j^{(e_1)}(z) \neq S_j^{(e_2)}(z)$.*

Theorem 10.2.4 *For any system of n orthogonal checks, we have for memoryless decoding*

1. *All errors with multiplicity at most n are detected and all those with multiplicity at most $\lfloor n/2 \rfloor$ are corrected.*
2. *There exist errors with multiplicity $n + 1$ and $\lfloor n/2 \rfloor + 1$, which are not detected and not corrected, respectively.*

Proof.

1. The error e is not detected by memoryless decoding if there exists $z \in G$ such that $e(z) \neq 0$ and from (10.2.41)

$$S_i^{(e)}(z) = \sum_{\tau \in T_i} e(z \oplus \tau) = e(z) + \sum_{\tau \in T_i - 0^m} e(z \oplus \tau) = 0, \quad (10.2.43)$$

for all $i = 0, 1, \ldots, n-1$.

By orthogonality of the checks, it follows from (10.2.43) that there exist at least n different $Z_0, Z_1, \ldots, Z_{n-1} \in G$ such that $Z_i \in T_i - 0^m$ and $e(Z_i) \neq 0$ for all $i = 0, 1, \ldots, n-1$. Thus, $\|e\| \geq n + 1$, and any error with multiplicity $\|e\| \leq n$, will be detected by n orthogonal checks.

Suppose that there exist $e_1(z)$, $e_2(z)$ such that $\|e_1\|$, $\|e_2\|$ are less or equal than $\lfloor n/2 \rfloor$, and $S^{(e_1)}(z) = S^{(e_2)}(z)$ for all z. Then, for $e(z) = e_1(z) - e_2(z)$, we have $\|e\| \leq n$, but if $S^{(e)}(z) = 0$ for all z, $e(z)$ is not detected.

2. We define e_0 as follows

$$e_0(\mathbf{0}) = 1,$$
$$e_0(Z_0) = \cdots = e_0(Z_{n-1}) = -1,$$
$$e(Z) = 0, \text{ if } \quad z \notin \{\mathbf{0}, Z_0, \ldots, Z_{n-1}\},$$

where $Z_i \in T_i$, $Z_i \neq \mathbf{0}$, $(i = 0, 1, \ldots, n-1)$, $\mathbf{0} = 0^m = \underbrace{0, \ldots 0}_{m}$.

Then, $\|e_0\| = n + 1$, but by (10.2.43) and orthogonality of the checks, $S_i^{(e_0)}(0) = 0$ for all $i = 0, 1, \ldots, n - 1$, and e_0 is not detected.

Defining

$$e_1(\mathbf{0}) = 1,$$
$$e_1(Z_0) = \cdots = e_1(Z_{\lfloor n/2 \rfloor - 1}) = -1,$$
$$e_1(z) = 0, \quad \text{if} \quad z \in \{\mathbf{0}, Z_0, \ldots, Z_{\lfloor n/2 \rfloor - 1}\},$$

and

$$e_2(Z_{\lfloor n/2 \rfloor}) = \cdots = e_2(Z_{n-1}) = 1,$$
$$e_2(z) = 0, \quad \text{if} \quad z \notin \{Z_{\lfloor n/2 \rfloor}, \ldots, Z_{n-1}\},$$

if $Z_i \in T_i$, $Z_i \neq \mathbf{0}$, $i = 0, 1, \ldots, n - 1$, we have

$$\|e_1\| = \lfloor n/2 \rfloor + 1,$$
$$\|e_2\| = n - \lfloor n/2 \rfloor \leq \lfloor n/2 \rfloor + 1,$$
$$e_1(\mathbf{0}) \neq e_2(\mathbf{0}),$$

but

$$S_i^{(e_1)}(0) = S_i^{(e_2)}(0) = \begin{cases} 0, & i = 0, 1, \ldots, \lfloor n/2 \rfloor - 1, \\ 1, & i = \lfloor n/2 \rfloor, \ldots, n - 1, \end{cases}$$

and errors e_1, e_2 cannot be corrected by memoryless decoding.

Note that for error correction with memoryless decoding, use may be made of a *majority decoding* (similar to majority decoding for error-correcting codes (347)).

Let $n = 2l + 1$ and $\|e\| \leq l$. Then, to correct an error e with the multiplicity at most l by $2l + 1$ orthogonal checks, we need that for any $z \in G = C_2^m$, there are at least $l + 1$ components with the same value $e(z)$ in a vector $S^{(e)}(z) = (S_0^{(e)}(z), \ldots, S_{2l}^{(e)}(z))$. Thus, we have a simple majority decoding method for computing $e(z)$ by $S^{(e)}(z)$.

We will consider now maximal multiplicities of errors detected or corrected with memory-aided decoding.

For any binary vector $\sigma = (\sigma_0, \ldots, \sigma_{n-1})$, we denote

$$M(\sigma) = \bigoplus_{i=0}^{n-1} \sigma_i(T_i - 0^m)$$

$$= \{\bigoplus_{i=0}^{n-1} \sigma_i \tau_i | \tau_i \in T_i - 0^m; \sigma_i \tau_i = \tau_i \text{ if } \sigma_i = 1, \text{ and } \sigma_i \tau_i = 0^m \text{ if } \sigma_i = 0\}.$$

For memory-aided decoding, we will require that for any $\sigma = (\sigma_0, \ldots, \sigma_{n-1})$ and $\sigma' = (\sigma'_0, \ldots, \sigma'_{n-1})$, $(\sigma \neq \sigma')$ we have

$$M(\sigma) \cap M(\sigma') = \emptyset. \tag{10.2.44}$$

Note that by setting $\sigma = (\underbrace{0, \ldots, 0}_{i}, 1, 0, \ldots, 0)$ and $\sigma' = (\underbrace{0, \ldots, 0}_{j}, 1, 0, \ldots, 0)$ we have from (10.2.44) the orthogonality condition $T_i \cap T_j = 0^m$, $(i, j = 0, 1, \ldots, n-1; i \neq j)$.

Condition (10.2.44) essentially implies that $\bigoplus_{i=0}^{n-1} T_i$ is a subgroup of $G = C_2^m$ and $n \leq m$.

Theorem 10.2.5 *For any system of n orthogonal checks (satisfying (10.2.44), we have for memory-aided decoding*

1. *All errors with the multiplicity at most $2^n - 1$ are detected, and all those with the multiplicity at most $2^{n-1} - 1$ are corrected.*

2. *There exist errors with the multiplicity 2^n and 2^{n-1}, which are not detected and not corrected, respectively.*

Proof.

1. Let $e(z) \neq 0$ for some $z \in C_2^m$. We shall show that if the error e is not detected by memory-aided decoding then, for any $\sigma = (\sigma_0, \ldots, \sigma_{n-1})$, $(\sigma_i \in \{0, 1\})$, there exists at least one $z_\sigma \in z \oplus M(\sigma)$ $(z \oplus M(\sigma) = \{t | t = z \oplus y, y \in M(\sigma)\})$ such that $e(z_\sigma) \neq 0$. Since from (10.2.43) $\bigcup_{\sigma \in \{0,1\}^n} M(\sigma) \geq 2^n$, it follows from the above that $\|e\| \geq 2^n$, which proves (1).

   The proof of (2) will be by induction on $\|\sigma\| = \sum_{i=0}^{n-1} \sigma_i$.

   Let $e(z) \neq 0$ and set $\sigma = (0, \ldots, 0)$. Then, $\|\sigma\| = 0$, and setting $z_\sigma = z$, we have $z \in z \oplus M(0)$ and $e(z_\sigma) = e(Z_0) \neq 0$.

   Let it further be assumed that $e(z) \neq 0$, e is not detected and for any $\sigma' \in C_2^n$ such that $\|\sigma'\| = l$, $(l \in \{0, 1, \ldots, n-1\})$, there exists $z_{\sigma'} \in z \oplus M(\sigma')$ such that $e(z_{\sigma'}) \neq 0$.

Select σ such that $\|\sigma\| = l + 1$. By the definition of $M(\sigma)$ (see (10.2.44), there exist σ' and some T_i ($T_i \neq \{\mathbf{0}\}$) such that $\|\sigma'\| = l$ and

$$M(\sigma) = \bigcup_{y \in T_i - \mathbf{0}} \{y \oplus M(\sigma')\}. \tag{10.2.45}$$

Since by the assumption $e(z_{\sigma'}) \neq 0$, and, if e is not detected, then

$$\sum_{\tau \in T_i} e(z_{\sigma'} \oplus \tau) = e(z_{\sigma'}) + \sum_{\tau \in T_i - \mathbf{0}} e(z_{\sigma'} \oplus \tau) = 0,$$

and there exists at least one $\tau \in T_i - \mathbf{0}$ such that, if we set $z_\sigma = z_{\sigma'} \oplus \tau$, then $e(z_\sigma) \neq 0$.

But $z_{\sigma'} \in z \oplus M(\sigma')$, and in view of (10.2.45), we have $z_\sigma = z_{\sigma'} \oplus \tau \in z \oplus M(\sigma)$. Consequently, all e such that $0 < \|e\| \leq 2^n - 1$ are detected.

Let now $\|e_1\| \leq 2^{n-1} - 1$, $\|e_2\| \leq 2^{n-1} - 1$, $e_1 \neq e_2$. Then, for $e = e_1 \oplus e_2$, we have $e \neq \mathbf{0}$, $\|e\| < 2^n$, e is detected and there exists $z \in C_2^m$ such that $S_j^{(e)}(z) = S_j^{(e_1)}(z) - S_j^{(e_2)}(z) \neq 0$. Thus, all errors with the multiplicity at most $2^{n-1} - 1$ are corrected.

2. We will now construct a nondetected error e_0 with the multiplicity 2^n.

Let us fix an arbitrary $Z_i \in T_i - \mathbf{0}$ for all $i = 0, 1, \ldots, n - 1$ and set

$$e_0(z) = \begin{cases} (-1)^{\|\sigma\|}, & \text{if there exists } \sigma = (\sigma_0, \ldots, \sigma_{n-1}) \\ & \text{such that } z = \bigoplus_{i=0}^{n-1} Z_i \sigma_i, \\ 0, & \text{otherwise.} \end{cases} \tag{10.2.46}$$

It follows by (10.2.46) that $\|e_0\| = 2^n$. We will show now that for any $z \in C_2^m$ and any $i \in \{0, 1, \ldots, n - 1\}$

$$S_i^{(e_0)}(z) = \sum_{\tau \in T_i} e_0(z \oplus \tau) = 0.$$

If for some $z \in C_2^m$ and some $\tau \in T_i$, $e_0(z \oplus \tau) \neq 0$, then in view of (10.2.46) there exists σ such that

$$z = \bigoplus_{i=0}^{n-1} Z_i \sigma_i,$$

and

$$S_j^{(e_0)}(z) = \sum_{\tau \in T_j} e_0(z \oplus \tau) = e_0 \left(\bigoplus_{i=0}^{n-1} Z_i \sigma_i \right) \tag{10.2.47}$$

$$+ \sum_{\tau \in T_i - \mathbf{0}} e_0 \left(\bigoplus_{i=0}^{j} Z_i \sigma_i \oplus \tau \oplus \bigoplus_{i=j+1}^{n-1} Z_i \sigma_i \right).$$

Now, if $\sigma_j = 0$, then in view of (10.2.44) and (10.2.47) we have

$$e_0 \left(\bigoplus_{i=0}^{j} Z_i \sigma_i \oplus \tau \oplus \bigoplus_{i=j+1}^{n-1} Z_i \sigma_i \right) \neq 0,$$

iff $\tau = Z_j$, and by (10.2.47)

$$\sum_{\tau \in T_j - \mathbf{0}} e_0 \left(\bigoplus_{i=0}^{j} Z_i \sigma_i \oplus \tau \oplus \bigoplus_{i=j+1}^{n-1} Z_i \sigma_i \right) = (-1)^{\|\sigma\|+1}.$$

Hence, in this case,

$$S_j^{(e_0)}(z) = (-1)^{\|\sigma\|} + (-1)^{\|\sigma\|+1} = 0.$$

Analogically, if $\sigma_j = 1$, then in view of (10.2.44) and (10.2.47) we have

$$e_0 \left(\sum_{i=0}^{j} Z_i \sigma_i \oplus \tau \oplus \bigoplus_{i=j+1}^{n-1} Z_i \sigma_i \right) \neq 0,$$

iff $\tau = \overline{Z}_j = 1 \oplus Z_j$, and

$$\sum_{\tau \in T_j - \mathbf{0}} e_0 \left(\bigoplus_{i=0}^{j} Z_i \sigma_i \oplus \tau \oplus \bigoplus_{i=j+1}^{n-1} Z_i \sigma_i \right) = (-1)^{\|\sigma\|-1}.$$

(Note that $\|\sigma\| \geq 1$ since $\sigma_j = 1$.) Thus, by (10.2.46) and (10.2.47) we have

$$S_j^{(e_0)}(z) = (-1)^{\|\sigma\|} + (-1)^{\|\sigma\|-1} = 0,$$

and e_0 is not detected.

To conclude this proof, we note that existence of errors with the multiplicity 2^{n-1}, which cannot be corrected, follows from the fact that otherwise any error with the multiplicity 2^n would be detected.

Thus, it follows from Theorems 10.2.4 and 10.2.5, that the error-detecting and error-correcting capabilities of a system of n orthogonal checks increase exponentially on transition from memoryless to memory-aided decoding.

Applications of the error-detecting and error-correcting techniques described in this section for testing of Read-Only Memories and Random-Access Memories by two orthogonal checks will be given in Section 10.9.

To conclude this section, we note that Theorems 10.2.4 and 10.2.5 can be generalized for the case of functions $f(z)$ defined over any finite Abelian and non-Abelian groups G and for the case when the verification of the check (10.2.40) is implemented in a finite field K (280, 281, 302). In this case f is a mapping from G to K and the summation in (10.2.40) is in K.

10.3 LINEAR CHECKS FOR PROCESSORS

It was shown in the previous section that there are very simple linear checks for addition and multiplication with complexities $|T(x + y)| = 2$ and $|T(x \cdot y)| = 4$. Optimal linear checks for basic computer components are given in Tables 10.3.1–10.3.3. (Here $0^i = \underbrace{00, \cdots 0}_{i}$ and $1^i = \underbrace{11 \ldots 1}_{i}$.)

If we view the arithmetic/logic instructions of an n-bit processor as functions of two variables over group C_2^m, where $m = 2n$, then it is easy to verify using the approach presented in Section 10.2.3 that for almost all arithmetical/logical instructions there exist integer constants d, such that for all pairs (x, y) of binary n-vectors

$$f(x, y) + f(x, \overline{y}) + f(\overline{x}, y) + f(\overline{x}, \overline{y}) = d. \tag{10.3.1}$$

The right-hand constant d depends only on the function f and the number n of bits in representations of operands. These rightmost constant are given in Table 10.3.4 for the basic arithmetic/logic instructions. In this table, we use the following conventions:

1. For instructions 13–19, the value is viewed as a binary $2n$-vector.
2. C_0, C_1, C_2, and C_3 are the carries before the evaluation of $f(x, y)$, $f(x, \overline{y})$, $f(\overline{x}, y)$, and $f(\overline{x}, \overline{y})$, respectively.
3. B_0, B_1, B_2, and B_3 are the borrows before the evaluation of $f(x, y)$, $f(x, \overline{y})$, $f(\overline{x}, y)$, and $f(\overline{x}, \overline{y})$, respectively.
4. We assume $n = 4s$, X is the decimal s-vector $(X_0, X_1, \ldots, X_{s-1})$, where $X_i \in \{0, 1, \ldots, 9\}$, for which x is the Binary Coded Decimal (BCD) representation (similarly for Y), $\overline{X}_i = 9 - X_i$, $i \in \{0, 1, \ldots, s - 1\}$, and $\overline{X} = (\overline{X}_0, \overline{X}_1, \ldots, \overline{X}_{s-1})$.

The testing procedure consists of verifying (10.3.1) for every instruction f for several pairs of operands (x, y).

For example, for verification of addition (x, y) can be selected as

$$(\mathbf{1}, 0 \cdots 001), (\mathbf{1}, 0 \cdots 010), \ldots, (\mathbf{1}, 10 \cdots 000)$$

TABLE 10.3.1 Optimal Linear Equality Checks for Some Basic Hardware Components.

N	Device	Function f Implemented by the Device
1.	AND	$f(z_1, \ldots, z_m) = \prod_{i=1}^{m} z_i$
2.	OR	$f(z_1, \ldots, z_m) = \bigvee_{i=1}^{m} z_i$
3.	Parity checker	$f(z_1, \ldots, z_m) = \bigoplus_{i=1}^{m} z_i$
4.	Majority voter	$f(z_1, \ldots, z_m) = \begin{cases} 0, & \|z\| \le 0.5(n-1), \\ 1, & \|z\| > 0.5(n-1) \end{cases}$ $m = 2s + 1, \|z\| = \sum_i z_i$
5.	Voter with the threshold equal to 2 ($m = 2^\alpha - 1$)	$f(z_1, \ldots, z_m) = \begin{cases} 0, & \|z\| \le 1, \\ 1, & \|z\| > 1 \end{cases}$
6.	PLA (product terms are orthogonal, AND circuits have at most t inputs)	$f(z_1, \ldots, z_m) = \bigvee_i f_i(z_1, \ldots, z_m)$ where $f_i(z_1, \ldots, z_m)$ is a product of at most t literals, and for any $z = (z_1, \ldots z_m)$, $f_i(z) f_j(z) = 0$
7.	Autonomous linear feedback register with initial state $(z_1, \ldots, z_m)$	$f_t(z_1, \ldots, z_m) = \mathbf{A}^t \begin{bmatrix} z_1, & \cdots & , z_m \end{bmatrix}^T$ $[z_1, \ldots, z_m]^T$ transpose of $[z_1, \ldots, z_m]$ $\mathbf{A} = \begin{bmatrix} 0 & 1 & 0 & \cdots & 0 & 0 \\ 0 & 0 & 1 & \cdots & 0 & 0 \\ \vdots & & & & & \\ 0 & 0 & 0 & \cdots & 1 & 0 \\ 0 & 0 & 0 & \cdots & 0 & 1 \\ a_1 & a_2 & a_3 & \cdots & a_{m-1} & a_m \end{bmatrix}$ $a_i \in \{0, 1\}$, $\mathbf{A}^t$ is a tth degree of $\mathbf{A}$ over $GF(2)$.

to verify that in each bit position a carry can be both generated and propagated.

Similarly, for subtraction verification, one can use

$$(\mathbf{0}, 0 \cdots 001), (\mathbf{0}, 0 \cdots 010), \ldots, (\mathbf{0}, 10 \cdots 000)$$

to test borrow generation and propagation.

Every general-purpose and data-address register should be used as a source register (for operands x and y) and as a destination register (for the result $f(x, y)$).

The number of reference values d required to be stored for testing by linear checks is equal to the number of instructions to be verified.

It is possible that different instructions have the same right-hand constant d for their linear checks. For example, for instructions *Clear* and *Subtract* this constant is equal to 0. Thus, linear checks will not detect some errors in instruction decoding, resulting in replacement of one instruction by another instruction, no instruction, multiple instructions, or an invalid instruction.

TABLE 10.3.2   Optimal Linear Equality Checks for Some Basic Hardware Components (Continued).

N	Device	Function f Implemented by the Device
8.	m-bit shifter	$f(C_l, C_r, z^{(1)}, \ldots, z^{(m)})$ $= \begin{cases} (z_1, z_2, \ldots, z_{m-1}, z_m), C_l = C_r = 0, \\ (z_2, z_3, \ldots, z_m, 0), C_l = 1, C_r = 0, \\ (0, z_1, \ldots, z_{m-2}, z_{m-1}), C_l = 0, C_r = 1, \\ (0, 0, \ldots, 0, 0), C_l = C_r = 1, \end{cases}$
9.	n-bit counter	$f(z_1, \ldots, z_m) = \sum_{i=1}^{m} z_i, m \le n$
10.	n-bit up and down counter	$f(x_1, \ldots, x_n, y_1, \ldots, y_n)$ $= \sum_{i=1}^{n} x_i - \sum_{i=1}^{n} y_i, n \le m$
11.	m by 1 multiplexer	$f(s_0, s_1, \ldots, s_\alpha, z_1, \ldots, z_m) = z_i$ iff $\sum_{j=0}^{m} s_j 2^{\alpha-1-j} = i, m = 2^\alpha$
12.	n-bit adder	$f(x, y) = x + y, x, y \in \{0, 1\}^n$
13.	n-bit subtractor	$f(x, y) = x - y, x, y \in \{0, 1\}^n$
14.	n-bit multiplier	$f(x, y) = xy, x, y \in \{0, 1\}^n$

To detect these errors, it is sufficient to execute all the instructions and verify the results for a pair of operands (x^*, y^*) such that for any two instructions f_1 and f_2 we have $f_1(x^*, y^*) \ne f_2(x^*, y^*)$. For most instruction sets one can choose x^* and y^* as $x^* = 1\underbrace{00\cdots0}_{n-4}101$ and $y^* = 1\underbrace{00\cdots0}_{n-4}011$.

Verification of instructions that are neither arithmetical nor logical (such as Branch, Skip) can be done by exhaustive exercising of all combination of internal states for status flip-flops.

To conclude this section, we note that for functions, describing basic hardware components and basic instruction sets, linear equality checks have very low check complexities.

The simple network implementation of the linear check for a device satisfying (10.3.1) (e.g., adder, subtractor, multiplier) is given in Fig. 10.3.1.

10.4   LINEAR CHECKS FOR ERROR DETECTION IN POLYNOMIAL COMPUTATIONS

In this section we apply the spectral techniques to construct linear checks (10.2.1) for devices or software computing polynomials of one or several variables.

We will see that complexities $|T(f)|$ of these checks are growing with increasing degrees of the polynomials.

We also note that the checks developed for polynomials can be used for error detection in software for numerical computations of analytical functions or for testing Read-Only Memories storing the values of these functions (see Section 10.9), since

TABLE 10.3.3 Optimal Linear Equality Checks for Some Basic Hardware Components, $T(f)$ and d.

N	Device	$T(f)$	d
1.	AND	$\{0, 1\}^m$	1
2.	OR	$\{0, 1\}^m$	$2^m - 1$
3.	Parity checker	$\{0^m, 0^{m-1}1\}$	1
4.	Majority voter	$\{0^m 1^m\}$	1
5.	Voter with the threshold equal to 2 ($m = 2^\alpha - 1$)	$(2^\alpha - 1, 2^\alpha - \alpha - 1)$ Hamming code (347)	$2^\alpha - \alpha - 2$
6.	PLA (product terms are orthogonal, AND circuits have at most t inputs)	$V^{\perp}(n, t + 1)$ dual code to a maximal code with the Hamming distance $t + 1$	$\sum_z f(z)\|V^{\perp}(n, t + 1)\|^{-1}$
7.	Autonomous linear feedback register with initial state $(z_1, \ldots, z_m)$	$\{0^m, \mathbf{A}^{-t}1^m\}$ $\mathbf{A}^{-t}$ is the inverse of $\mathbf{A}^t$ over $GF(2)$	$2^m - 1$
8.	m-bit shifter	$\{000^m, 001^m,$ $100^m, 101^m,$ $010^m, 011^m,$ $110^m, 111^m\}$	$5 \times 2^{m-1} - 4$
9.	n-bit counter	$\{0^m, 1^m\}$	m
10.	n-bit up and down counter	$\{0^m, 1^m\}$	0
11.	m by 1 multiplexer ($m = 2^\alpha$)	$\{0^\alpha 0^m, 0^\alpha 1^m\}$	1
12.	n-bit adder	$\{0^{2n}, 1^{2n}\}$	$2(2^n - 1)$
13.	n-nit subtractor	$\{0^{2n}, 1^{2n}\}$	0
14.	n-bit multiplier	$\{0^{2n}, 0^n 1^n, 1^n 0^n, 1^{2n}\}$	$(2^n - 1)^2$

in many cases analytical functions like $sin(x)$ are computed by their polynomial approximations.

We consider the problem of error detection in the process of computing polynomials

$$f(x_1, \ldots, x_m) = \sum_{i_1=0}^{s_1} \cdots \sum_{i_m=0}^{s_m} a(i_1, \ldots, i_m) x_1^{i_1} x_2^{i_2} \cdots x_m^{i_m}, \qquad (10.4.1)$$

TABLE 10.3.4 Linear Check Constants for Basic Instructions.

No.	Instruction (f)	$f(x, y)$	d
1.	Clear (CLR)	0	0
2.	Transfer (TRN)	x	$2(2^n - 1)$
3.	Complement (CMP)	$\bar{x}$	$2(2^n - 1)$
4.	Increase (INCR)	$x + 1$	$2(2^n + 1)$
5.	Decrease (DECR)	$x - 1$	$2(2^n - 3)$
6.	Twos complement (CMPL2)	$\bar{x} + 1$	$2(2^n + 1)$
7.	Shift left (SHL)	$(x_1, x_2, \ldots, x_{n-1}, 0)$	$2(2^n - 2)$
8.	Shift right (SHR)	$(0, x_0, x_1, \ldots, x_{n-2})$	$2(2^{n-1} - 1)$
9.	Rotate left (ROTL)	$(x_1, x_2, \ldots, x_{n-1}, x_0)$	$2(2^n - 1)$
10.	Rotate right (ROTR)	$(x_{n-1}, x_0, x_1, \ldots, x_{n-2})$	$2(2^n - 1)$
11.	4-bit shift left (SHL4)	$(x_4, x_5, \ldots, x_{n-1}, 0, 0, 0, 0)$	$2(2^n - 16)$
12.	4-bit shift right (SHR4)	$(0, 0, 0, 0, x_0, x_1, \ldots, x_{n-3})$	$2(2^{n-4} - 1)$
13[1].	Binary shift left (BSHL)	$(SHL(x), SHL(y))$	$2(2^{2n} - 2^n - 1)$
14.	Binary shift right (BSHR)	$(SHR(x), SHR(y))$	$2(2^{2n-1} - 2^{n-1} - 1)$
15.	Binary rotate left (BROTL)	$(ROTL(x), ROTL(y))$	$2(2^{2n} - 1)$
16.	Binary rotate right (BROTR)	$(ROTR(x), ROTR(y))$	$2(2^{2n} - 1)$
17.	Binary 4-bit shift left (BSHL4)	$(SHL4(x), SHL4(y))$	$2(2^{2n} - 15 \cdot 2^n - 16)$
18.	Binary 4-bit shift right (BSHR4)	$(SHR4(x), SHR4(y))$	$2(2^{2n} - 2^n + 2^{n-4} - 1)$
19.	Exchange (EXCH)	(y, x)	$2(2^{2n} - 1)$
20.	And (AND)	$x \wedge y$	$2^n - 1$
21.	Or (OR)	$x \vee y$	$3(2^n - 1)$
22.	Exclusive or (EXOR)	$x \oplus y$	$2(2^n - 1)$
23.	Add (ADD)	$x + y$	$4(2^n - 1)$
24[2].	Add with carry (ADDC)	$x + y + C$	$4(2^n - 1) + \sum_{i=0}^{3} C_i$
25.	Subtract (SUB)	$x - y$	0
26[3].	Subtract with borrow (SUBB)	$x - y - B$	$-\sum_{i=0}^{3} B_i$
27.	Multiply (MPY)	$x \cdot y$	$(2^n - 1)^2$
28[4].	BCD add (BCDADD)	$X + Y$	$4(10^s - 1)$
29.	BCD subtract (BCDSUB)	$X - Y$	0
30.	BCD multiply (BCDMPY)	$X \cdot Y$	$(10^s - 1)^2$

$f(x, y) = f(x_0, \ldots, x_{n-1}, y_0, \ldots, y_{n-1})$.

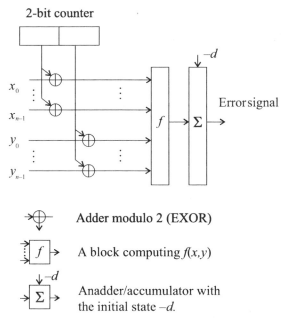

FIGURE 10.3.1   Network implementation of check (10.3.1) for basic computer components.

where $x_t \in \{0, \ldots, 2^{n_t} - 1\}$, $(t = 1, \ldots, m)$, and all the computations are in the field C of complex numbers or in a finite field $GF(p)$, ($p > 2$ is a prime). The set of all polynomials of this type we denote $K_{s_1, \ldots, s_m}[x_1, \ldots, x_m]$.

The errors to be detected are errors in the texts of the programs, in the case where f is calculated by a computer program, and they are catastrophic structural failures in the case where computations are carried out by a specialized digital device.

For practical reasons, we suppose that the variable x_t is represented in binary form, $x_t = (x_{t,0}, \ldots, x_{t,n_t-1})$. Notice that the generalization of the results presented below to the case when x_t is represented by q_t-ary vectors may be done without any difficulties.

Denote by C_2^n the group of binary vectors with n components, where $n = \sum_{t=1}^{m} n_t$, with respect to componentwise addition modulo 2. For error detection, we shall use linear checks over $GF(2)$

$$\sum_{\tau=(\tau_1,\ldots,\tau_m)\in T} f(x_1 \oplus \tau_1, \ldots, x_m \oplus \tau_m) = d, \qquad (10.4.2)$$

for every $x_1, \ldots, x_m$, when T (*check set for* f) is a subgroup of C_2^n, $n = \sum_{t=1}^{m} n_t$, $\tau_t \in C_2^{n_t}$, d — some constant, the symbol $\oplus$ stands for componentwise addition modulo 2 of binary vectors, and summation is carried out in the same field as in (10.4.1).

The verification of whether condition (10.4.2) is satisfied for the given assignment of variables $x_1, \ldots, x_m$ constitutes the error-detection method. It may be effectively used for the testing of manufacturing acceptance of the program or of the device computing the given polynomial. In the case of network implementation (see Section 10.6), the method may be used for testing during installation and maintenance of the corresponding devices.

We note also that although all the examples given below deal with computations in the field of real numbers, the same error-detecting technique may be used for the computations of polynomials with complex coefficients.

We shall denote by $T(f)$ a check set T with minimal cardinality. We shall use the cardinality $|T(f)|$ as a criterion for the *check complexity of the polynomial f*.

The first problem is to find for a given polynomial $f \in K_{s_1,\ldots,s_m}[x_1, \ldots, x_m]$ a minimal set $T(f)$.

The implementation of the check (10.4.2) and error-detecting capability of these checks will be considered in Sections 10.7 and 10.9. For the construction of $T(f)$ for a given f, we shall use the method proposed in Section 10.2.

We note also that there is another simple method of error detection for polynomial computations by linear checks based on the finite differences of orders $s_1, \ldots, s_m$ for polynomial (10.4.1). In this case we have the following check:

$$\sum_{\tau_1=0}^{s_1} \cdots \sum_{\tau_m=0}^{s_m} (-1)^{\tau_1+\ldots+\tau_m} \binom{s_1}{\tau_1} \cdots \binom{s_m}{\tau_m} \tag{10.4.3}$$

$$f(x_1 + s_1 - \tau_1, \ldots, x_m + s_m - \tau_m) = a(s_1, \ldots, s_m) \prod_{t=1}^{m} s_t!$$

The number of values of f involved in check (10.4.3) is $\prod_{t=1}^{m}(s_t + 1)$, and it is, generally speaking, smaller than the corresponding number $|T(f)|$ for the check (10.4.2), but there are at least three disadvantages of the check (10.4.3). These are as follows:

1. For implementation of (10.4.3) we need *arithmetical shifts* of variables x_i, whereas in (10.4.2) we need only componentwise additions mod 2.

2. For check (10.4.3) we need additional multiplications by the constants

$$(-1)^{\tau_1+\ldots+\tau_m} \prod_{t=1}^{m} \binom{s_t}{\tau_t}.$$

3. Check (10.4.3) cannot detect errors in coefficients $a(i_1, \ldots, i_m)$ resulting in the replacement of a given polynomial $f \in K_{s_1,\ldots,s_m}[x_1, \ldots, x_m]$ by another polynomial $\Phi \in K_{s_1,\ldots,s_m}[x_1, \ldots, x_m]$ with the same $a(s_1, \ldots, s_m)$. Almost all errors of this type are detected by (10.4.2), see Section 10.5.

Additional results on testing by checks with arithmetic shifts can be found in References 621 and 622.

10.5 CONSTRUCTION OF OPTIMAL LINEAR CHECKS FOR POLYNOMIAL COMPUTATIONS

Let for $f \in K_{s_1,\ldots,s_m}[x_1,\ldots,x_m]$,

$$f(x_1,\ldots,x_m) = \sum_{i_1=0}^{s_1} \cdots \sum_{i_m=0}^{s_m} a(i_1,\ldots,i_m)x_1^{i_1} \cdots x_m^{i_m},$$

where $x_t \in \{0,\ldots,2^{n_t}-1\}$, $x_t = (x_{t,0},\ldots,x_{t,n_t-1}) \in C_2^{n_t}$, $x_{t,j} \in \{0,1\}$, $s_t < n_t$, $t = 1,\ldots,m$.

Denote by $V(n_t, s_t+1)$ a maximal linear code in $C_2^{n_t}$ with the Hamming distance s_t+1, that is, $V(n_t, s_t+1)$ is a maximal subgroup in $C_2^{n_t}$ such that the Hamming distance between any two vectors from $V(n_t, s_t+1)$ is at least s_t+1. Methods for construction of maximal linear codes with given distances can be found in Reference 347.

Therefore,

$$V^{\perp}(n_t, s_t+1) = \{(\tau_{t,0},\ldots,\tau_{t,n_t-1}) | \bigoplus_{j=0}^{n_t-1} \tau_{t,j} y_{t,j} = 0,$$

where for every $(y_{t,0},\ldots,y_{t,n_t-1}) \in V(n_t, s_t+1)\}$ and

$$V^{\perp} = \prod_{t=1}^{m} V^{\perp}(n_t, s_t+1)$$

$$= \{\tau = (\tau_1,\ldots,\tau_m) | \tau_1 \in V^{\perp}(n_1, s_1+1),\ldots,\tau_m \in V^{\perp}(n_m, s_m+1)\}.$$

Theorem 10.5.1 *(Linear checks for polynomial computations)*

1. For every $f \in K_{s_1,\ldots,s_m}[x_1,\ldots,x_m]$

$$\sum_{\tau=(\tau_1,\ldots,\tau_m)\in V^{\perp}} f(x_1 \oplus \tau_1,\ldots,x_m \oplus \tau_m) = d, \qquad (10.5.1)$$

where

$$d = \prod_{t-1}^{m} |V(n_t, s_t+1)|^{-1} \sum_{x_1,\ldots,x_m} f(x_1,\ldots,x_m). \qquad (10.5.2)$$

2. For every $s = (s_1,\ldots,s_m)$, $(n_1,\ldots,n_m)$, $(s_t < n_t)$, there exists $f \in K_{s_1,\ldots,s_m}[x_1,\ldots,x_m]$ such that $T(f) = V^{\perp}$.

Proof.

1. Consider the Walsh spectrum S_f of $f \in K_{s_1,\ldots,s_m}[x_1,\ldots,x_m]$ over C_2^n, where $n = \sum_{t=1}^{m} n_t$.

   If for a given w there exits t such that

   $$\|w_t\| = \sum_{j=0}^{n_t-1} w_{t,j} \geq s_t + 1,$$

   then

   $$S_f(w) = 0, \quad w = (w_1,\ldots,w_m), \quad w_t \in C_2^{n_t}. \tag{10.5.3}$$

   Denote

   $$S_{\delta_V}(w) = \begin{cases} \prod_{t=1}^{m} |V(n_t, s_t + 1)|^{-1}, & \text{if } w \in V, \\ 0, & \text{if } w \notin V, \end{cases} \tag{10.5.4}$$

   where $V = \prod_{t=1}^{m} V(n_t, s_t + 1)$.

   Then,

   $$S_f(w)S_{\delta_V}(w) = \delta_{w,0} 2^{-n} \prod_{t=1}^{m} |V(n_t, s_t + 1)|^{-1} \tag{10.5.5}$$

   $$\times \sum_{x_1,\ldots,x_m} f(x_1,\ldots,x_m),$$

   where $\delta_{w,0}$ is the Kronecker symbol.

   From (10.5.2) and (10.5.5), we have

   $$f \circledast \delta_V = d, \tag{10.5.6}$$

   for every $x \in C_2^n$.

   For δ_V, we have, from (10.5.4) and the definition of $V^{\perp}(n_t, s_t + 1)$,

   $$\delta_V = \begin{cases} 1, & x \in V^{\perp}, \\ 0, & x \notin V^{\perp}, \end{cases} \tag{10.5.7}$$

   and (10.5.1) follows from (10.4.1) and (10.5.7).

2. Let

   $$f(x_1,\ldots,x_m) = \sum_{t=1}^{m} c(t) f_t(x_t), \quad c(t) > 0,$$

and

$$f_t(x_t) = a(t, 0) + a(t, 1)\overline{x}_t + \ldots + a(t, s_t)\overline{x}_t^{s_t}$$

for $t = 1, \ldots, m$, where

$$\overline{x}_t = x_t - \frac{1}{2}(2^{n_t} - 1),$$

and $a(t, j) > 0$ if $j = 2k$, and $a(t, j) < 0$ if $j = 2k + 1$.

Then, at it was shown in Section 6.4, we have

$$S_f(w_1, \ldots, w_m) > 0, \quad \|w_t\| \le s_t, (t = 1, \ldots, m), \tag{10.5.8}$$

and

$$S_f(w_1, \ldots, w_m) = 0,$$

if there exists t such that $\|w_t\| \ge s_t + 1$.

Now, let δ_T be the characteristic function of the subgroup T of C_2^n,

$$\delta_T(x) = \begin{cases} 1, & x \in T, \\ 0, & x \notin T. \end{cases}$$

Then,

$$T^\perp = \{w = (w_1, \ldots, w_m)|$$

for which $\bigoplus_{t=1}^m \bigoplus_{i=0}^{n_t} w_{t,i} x_{t,i} = 0$, for all $x = (x_1, \ldots, x_m) \in T \}$.

If T is a check set for f, then there exists the constant d such that

$$S_f(w)S_{\delta_V}(w) = \delta_{w,0} 2^{-m} d. \tag{10.5.9}$$

Since

$$V = \prod_{t=1}^m V(n_t, s_t + 1),$$

is a maximal subgroup in the set $\{(w_1, \ldots, w_m)|\exists t \|w_t\| \ge s_t + 1\}$, it follows from (10.5.8) and (10.5.9) that $T(f) = V^\perp$, and this completes the proof of Theorem 10.5.1.

Theorem 10.5.1 generates a simple method of constructing an optimal check (10.4.2) $T(f)$ with minimal $|T(f)|$ for a given polynomial $f \in K_{s_1,\ldots,s_m}[x_1, \ldots, x_m]$.

This method reduces to the following operations:

1. Choose maximal error correcting codes $V(n_t, s_t + 1)$ with the Hamming distances $s_t + 1$ in n_t-dimensional spaces of binary vectors ($t = 1, \ldots, m$).
2. Construct the corresponding orthogonal codes $V^\perp(n_t, s_t + 1)$, ($t = 1, \ldots, m$). Methods for constructing $V(n_t, s_t + 1)$ and $V^\perp(n_t, s_t + 1)$ may be found in Reference 347.
3. Construct the direct product

$$T(f) = V^\perp = \prod_{t=1}^{m} V^\perp(n_t, s_t + 1).$$

4. Compute by (10.5.2) the right-hand constant d.
    We note that the check set $V^\perp$ for $f \in K_{s_1, \ldots, s_m}[x_1, \ldots, x_m]$ depends only on degrees $s_1, \ldots, s_m$ of coefficients of f, but the right-hand constant d of the check depends on coefficients of f.

For estimation of the check complexity of polynomials from $K_{s_1, \ldots, s_m}[x_1, \ldots, x_m]$, one may use the following corollary from Theorem 10.5.1.
    Denote

$$\langle a \rangle = 2^i, \quad \text{iff} \quad 2^{i-1} \le a < 2^i \tag{10.5.10}$$

Corollary 10.5.1 *For every $f \in K_{s_1, \ldots, s_m}[x_1, \ldots, x_m]$,*

$$\log_2 |T(f)| \le \sum_{t=1}^{m} \langle \sum_{j=0}^{s_t-1} \binom{n_t - 1}{j} \rangle. \tag{10.5.11}$$

Proof. From Theorem 10.5.1, we have

$$|T(f)| \le |V^\perp| = 2^n \prod_{t=1}^{m} |V(n_t, s_t + 1)|^{-1},$$

and (10.5.11) follows from the Varshamov–Gilbert bound for $|V(n_t, s_t + 1)|$ (347). We note that lower bounds for

$$\max f \in K_{s_1, \ldots, s_m}[x_1, \ldots, x_m](\log_2 |T(f)|),$$

may be also obtained from Theorem 10.5.1 by the Hamming–Rao bound or from the Plotikin bound for $|V(n_t, s_t + 1)|$ (347).
    It follows from Theorem 10.5.1 and Corollary 10.5.1 that it is expedient to use linear checks in the case of relatively small number m of variables.

Example 10.5.1 *Consider a program computing a determinant $|\mathbf{X}|$ over the field of real numbers of a (3×3) matrix $\mathbf{X} = [x_{i,j}]$, where $x_{i,j} \in \{0, 1, \ldots, 2^{32} - 1\}$.*

In this case, $f = |\mathbf{X}|$, $m = 9$, $s_1 = s_2 = \cdots = s_9 = 1$, $n_1 = n_2 = \cdots = n_9 = 32$.

We construct a check set $T(f)$ for $f = |\mathbf{X}|$ by taking as $V(32, 2)$ the even parity code with $|V^{\perp}(32, 2)| = 2$ (347).

Then, we have

$$|T(f)| = |\prod_{t=1}^{9} V^{\perp}(n_t, s_t + 1)| = |(V^{\perp}(32, 2)^9| = 2^9.$$

We notice that for $f = |\mathbf{X}|$ where $\mathbf{X}$ is a $(t \times t)$ matrix, and $x_{i,j} \in \{0, 1, \ldots, 2^n - 1\}$, we have for any n, $\log_2(|T(f)|) = t^2$.

We also note that $V^{\perp}$ is a check set for every $f \in K_{s_1,\ldots,s_m}[x_1, \ldots, x_m]$, but, for some special f, checks may be considerably simplified. For example, it is easy to show that if f depends only on even (or only on odd) degrees of $\overline{x}_t = x_t - \frac{1}{2}(2^{n_t} - 1)$ for all t, then

$$f(\overline{x}_1, \ldots, \overline{x}_m) + (-1)^{\sum_{t=1}^{m} s_t} f(\overline{x}_1 \oplus 1, \ldots, \overline{x}_m \oplus 1) = 0, \qquad (10.5.12)$$

where $\mathbf{1} = (1, 1, \ldots, 1)$.

We now consider from the practical point of view, the important case of small-degree polynomials $s_t = 1, 2, 3$, and $t = 1, \ldots, m$.

Let

$$f(x_1, \ldots, x_m) = \sum_{i_1, \ldots, i_m \in \{0, \ldots, s\}} a(i_1, \ldots, i_m) x_1^{i_1} \cdots x_m^{i_m},$$

where $0 \leq x_t \leq 2^{n_t} - 1$.

We say that a given f depends on x_t^j if there exist $i_1, \ldots, i_{t-1}, j, i_{t+1}, \ldots, i_m \in \{0, \ldots, s\}$, such that

$$a(i_1, \ldots, i_{t-1}, j, i_{t+1}, \ldots, i_m) \neq 0.$$

The set of all polynomials, which depend on all x_t^j, $t = 1, \ldots, m$, $j = 1, \ldots, s$, we denote by $K_s[x_1, \ldots, x_m]$.

Corollary 10.5.2 *The following properties are satisfied:*

1. If $f \in K_1[x_1, \ldots, x_m]$, then

$$\log_2 |T(f)| = m. \qquad (10.5.13)$$

2. *If $f \in K_2[x_1, \ldots, x_m]$, then*

$$\log_2 |T(f)| = \sum_{t=1}^{m} \log_2 \langle n_t \rangle. \tag{10.5.14}$$

3. *If $f \in K_3[x_1, \ldots, x_m]$, then*

$$\log_2 |T(f)| = m + \sum_{t=1}^{m} \log_2 \langle n - 1 \rangle. \tag{10.5.15}$$

Proof. Note that, if $f \in K_s[x_1, \ldots, x_m]$, then

$$S_f(w_1, \ldots, w_m) = 0,$$

if $\|w_t\| > s$ for $t = 1, \ldots, m$.
Because

$$|T(f)| = |V^{\perp}| = 2^n \prod_{t=1}^{m} |V(n_t, s_t + 1)|^{-1}, \tag{10.5.16}$$

with $n = \sum_{t=1}^{m} n_t$, and (347)

$$\log_2 |V(n_t, 2)| = n_t - 1, \tag{10.5.17}$$

$$\log_2 |V(n_t, 3)| = n_t - \log_2 \langle n_t \rangle, \tag{10.5.18}$$

$$\log_2 |V(n_t, 4)| = n_t - \log_2 \langle n_t - 1 \rangle + 1, \tag{10.5.19}$$

we have (10.5.13)–(10.5.15) from (10.5.17)–(10.5.19).

For polynomials of one variable $f \in K_s[x]$, $x \in \{0, \ldots, 2^n - 1\}$, using the construction of Bose–Chaudhuri–Hocquenghem codes (BCH) (347), we have the following upper bound for the check complexity:

$$\log_2 |T(f)| \leq \log_2 |V^{\perp}(n, s + 1)| \tag{10.5.20}$$

$$\leq \begin{cases} \alpha \log_2 \langle n \rangle, & \text{if } s = 2\alpha, \\ \alpha \log_2 \langle n - 1 \rangle + 1, & \text{if } s = 2\alpha + 1. \end{cases}$$

Check complexities $|T(f)|$ and right-hand constants d for polynomials $f \in K_s[x]$ of one variable are given in Table 10.5.1, where B_v stands for Bernoulli numbers.

By the proof completely analogous to the proof of Theorem 10.5.1, one may obtain the following result.

TABLE 10.5.1   Parameters of the Optimal Checks for Polynomials of One Variable.

Degree of a Polynomial s	Check Complexity $\|T(F)\|$	Right-hand Constant d
1	2	$2a(0) + a(1)(2^n - 1)$
2	$\langle n \rangle$	$\langle n \rangle \left(a(0) + \frac{1}{2}a(1)(2^n - 1) \right.$ $\left. + \frac{1}{6}a(2)(2^n - 1)(2^{n+1} - 1) \right)$
3	$2\langle n \rangle$	$2\langle n - 1 \rangle \left(a(0) + \frac{1}{2}a(1)(2^n - 1) \right.$ $+ \frac{1}{6}a(2)(2^n - 1)(2^{n+1} - 1)$ $\left. + \frac{1}{4}a(3)2^n(2^n - 1)^2 \right)$
.	.	.
.	.	.
.	.	.
s	$2^n\|V(n, s+1)\|^{-1}$	$\|V(n, s+1)\|^{-1}$ $\times \sum_{i=0}^{s} a(i)\frac{1}{i+1} \sum_{v=0}^{i} \binom{i+1}{v} 2^{(i+1-v)n} B_v$

Theorem 10.5.2 *Let*

$$f(x_0, \ldots, x_{n-1}) = a(0) + \sum_{i_1=0}^{n-1} a(i_1)x_{i_1} \tag{10.5.21}$$

$$+ \sum_{0 \le i_1 < i_2 \le n-1} a(i_1, i_2)x_{i_1} x_{i_2}$$

$$+ \ldots + \sum_{0 \le i_1 < \ldots < i_s \le n-1} a(i_1, \ldots, i_s)x_{i_1} \ldots x_{i_s},$$

where $x_i \in \{0, 1\}$, $i = 0, \ldots, n-1$, $s < n$, and $a(0), a(i_1), a(i_1, i_2), \ldots, a(i_1, \ldots, i_s)$ are real or complex numbers.
    Then,

1. For every $x = (x_0, \ldots, x_{n-1})$

$$\sum_{\tau \in V^\perp(n, s+1)} f(x \oplus \tau) = \|V^\perp(n, s+1)\|2^{-s} \tag{10.5.22}$$

$$\times \left(2^s a(0) + 2^{s-1} \sum_{i_1=0}^{n-1} a(i_1) + \ldots + \sum_{0 \le i_1 < \ldots < i_s \le n-1} a(i_1, \ldots, i_s) \right).$$

2. If $a(0) \ne 0$, $a(i_1) \ne 0$, $\ldots$, $a(i_1, \ldots, i_s) \ne 0$ for all $i_1, \ldots, i_s$, then the check set $V^\perp(n, s+1)$ is minimal, that is, $T(f) = V^\perp(n, s+1)$.

We note that checks constructed by the Theorem 10.5.2 for polynomials of one variable coincide with checks constructed by the Theorem 10.5.1, but for polynomials of a small degree and of a large number of variables, checks constructed by Theorem 10.5.2 may be simpler. This may be the case when we are dealing with *matrix computations*.

For example, let $F(X) = AX$, where A, X are matrices of dimensions $(k \times m)$ and $(m \times r)$, and $X_{ij} \in \{0, \ldots, 2^n - 1\}$. Then, every $(F(X))_{ij}$ may be considered as a linear function of mn binary variables, and we have by Theorem 10.5.2

$$F(X) + F(\overline{X}) = (2^n - 1)A, \tag{10.5.23}$$

where $\overline{X}_{ij} = X_{ij} \oplus (1, 1, \ldots, 1)$.

We also note that Theorems 10.5.1 and 10.5.2 provide us with *multiplicative checks* for exponential functions, which are described by the following corollary.

Corollary 10.5.3 *Let*

$$f_i \in K_{s_1, \ldots, s_m}[x_1, \ldots, x_m], \quad i = 1, \ldots, r,$$

and

$$\phi(x_1, \ldots, x_m) = \prod_{i=1}^{r} a_i^{f_i(x_1, \ldots, x_m)}, \tag{10.5.24}$$

where $x_t \in \{0, \ldots, 2^{n_t} - 1\}$.
  Then, for every $x_1, \ldots, x_m$,

$$\prod_{(\tau_1, \ldots, \tau_m) \in V^\perp} \phi(x_1 \oplus \tau_1, \ldots, x_m \oplus \tau_m) = d, \tag{10.5.25}$$

where

$$d = \left\{ \prod_{x_1, \ldots, x_m} \phi(x_1, \ldots, x_m) \right\}^\lambda,$$

$$V^\perp = \prod_{t=1}^{m} V^\perp(n_t, s_t + 1),$$

$$\lambda = \prod_{t=1}^{m} |V(n_t, s_t + 1)|^{-1}.$$

Proof. From (10.5.24), we have

$$\log \phi(x_1, \ldots, x_m) = \sum_{i=1}^{r} f_i(x_1, \ldots, x_m) \cdot \log a_i \in K_{s_1, \ldots, s_m}[x_1, \ldots, x_m].$$

Then, by Theorem 10.4.2

$$\sum_{(\tau_1, \ldots, \tau_m) \in V^\perp} \log \phi(x_1 \oplus \tau_1, \ldots, x_m \oplus \tau_m) \tag{10.5.26}$$

$$= \lambda \sum_{x_1, \ldots, x_m} \log \phi(x_1, \ldots, x_m),$$

and (10.5.25) follows from (10.5.26).

The network implementation of a multiplicative check (10.5.25) may be obtained from the network implementations of an additive check (10.5.1), (10.5.2) (see Fig. 10.6.1) by the replacement of adder accumulations by multiplier accumulations.

So far we have supposed that every variable x_t, for $t = 1, \ldots, m$, is represented in the binary form

$$x_t = (x_{t,0}, \ldots, x_{t,n_t-1}), \quad x_{t,i} \in \{0, 1\}.$$

In the case, where x_t is represented in the q_t-ary form, $q_t \geq 2$, $t = 1, \ldots, m$, all the previous results remain valid, but the check set

$$\prod_{t=1}^{m} V^\perp(n_t, s_t + 1),$$

must be replaced by the set

$$\prod_{t=1}^{m} V_{q_t}^\perp(n_t, s_t + 1),$$

where $V_{q_t}(n_t, s_t + 1)$ is the maximal linear code in n_t-dimensional space of q_t-ary vectors, q_t is a prime, with the Hamming distance $s_t + 1$ (347), and

$$V_{q_t}^\perp(n_t, s_t + 1) = \left\{ (y_0, \ldots, y_{n_t-1}) \middle| \bigoplus_{i=0}^{n_t-1} x_i y_i = 0 \right\},$$

for $(x_0, \ldots, x_{n_t-1}) \in \{V_{q_t}(n_t, s_t + 1)\}$, where $x_i, y_i \in \{0, \ldots, q_t - 1\}$, and the symbol $\oplus$ stands for modulo q_t addition. (For the computations in a finite field $GF(p)$, we need the additional requirement that the least common multiple of $q_1, \ldots, q_m$ will be a divisor of $p - 1$, because only in this case we have the convolution theorem for the corresponding Fourier transform (see Section 2.8).

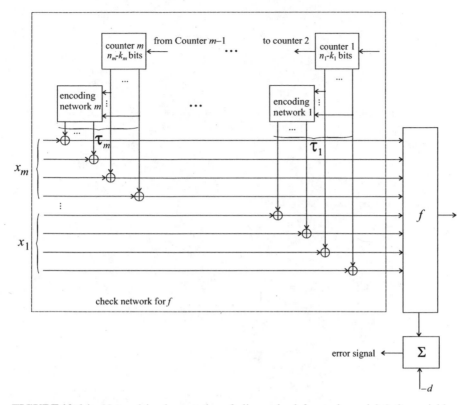

FIGURE 10.6.1 Network implementation of a linear check for a polynomial f of m variables.

10.6 IMPLEMENTATIONS AND ERROR-DETECTING CAPABILITIES OF LINEAR CHECKS

Network implementations of linear checks for polynomials $K_{s_1,\ldots,s_m}[x_1,\ldots,x_m]$ of m variables are similar to the implementations of checks (10.2.1) for functions of one variable (see Section 10.2.4 and Fig. 10.2.2).

The block diagram for a network implementing a linear check for a polynomial $f \in K_{s_1,\ldots,s_m}[x_1,\ldots,x_m]$ is given in Fig. 10.6.1.

Denote by $L(f)$ a minimal number of two-input gates in a check network for f. The asymptotic behavior of $L(f)$ is given by the following theorem.

Theorem 10.6.1 *If $n_t \to \infty$, and s_t is a constant for $t = 1, \ldots, m$, then for every $f \in K_{s_1,\ldots,s_m}[x_1,\ldots,x_m]$,*

$$L(f) \lesssim \sum_{t=1}^{m} \lfloor \frac{s_t}{2} \rfloor n_t \left(\log_2 n_t\right)(\log_2 \log_2 n_t)^{-1}, \qquad (10.6.1)$$

where $\lfloor c \rfloor$ is the greatest integer $\leq c$, and

$$a(n) \precsim b(n) \quad \text{iff} \quad \lim_{n \to \infty} a(n)b^{-1}(n) \leq 1,$$

$$a(n) \sim b(n) \quad \text{iff} \quad a(n) \precsim b(n) \quad \text{and} \quad b(n) \precsim a(n).$$

Proof. Denote $\log_2 |V(n_t, s_t + 1)| = K_t$. Then, $V^{\perp}(n_t, s_t + 1)$ is an $(n_t, n_t - K_t)$-linear code, and a check network for every $f \in K_{s_1, \ldots, s_m}[x_1, \ldots, x_m]$ may be implemented by the network in Fig. 10.6.1, where every encoding network t, for $t = 1, \ldots, m$, is a network linear over $GF(2)$ with $n_t - K_t$ inputs and K_t outputs.

If $s_t > 1$, then $n_t - K_t \to \infty$, as $n_t \to \infty$, and the encoding network t may be realized by the method described in Section 6.1.6 with the complexity

$$L_t \precsim \frac{(n_t - K_t)K_t}{\log_2(n_t - K_t)}. \tag{10.6.2}$$

If $s_t = 1$, then $n_t - K_t = 1$, $V^{\perp}(n_t, 2) = \{(0, \ldots, 0), (1, \ldots, 1)\}$ and $L_t = constant$. Because $n_t - K_t = \log_2 |V^{\perp}(n_t, s_t + 1)|$, $n_t \sim K_t$, and from the BCH bound (347) $(n_t - K_t) \precsim \lfloor s_t/2 \rfloor \log_2 n_t$, we finally have from (10.6.2)

$$L_t \precsim \frac{K_t \lfloor s_t/2 \rfloor \log_2 n_t}{\log_2(\lfloor s_t/2 \rfloor \log_2 n_t)} \sim \lfloor \frac{s_t}{2} \rfloor n_t(\log_2 n_t)(\log_2 \log_2 n_t)^{-1}.$$

We also note that there exists a constant C_t such that the complexity of the counter t with $n_t - K_t$ bits is no greater than

$$C_t(n_t - K_t) \precsim C_t \lfloor \frac{s_t}{2} \rfloor \log_2 n_t,$$

and we finally have

$$L(f) \precsim \sum_{t=1}^{m} \left(\lfloor s_t/2 \rfloor n_t(\log_2 n_t)(\log_2 \log_2 n_t)^{-1} + C_t \lfloor \frac{s_t}{2} \rfloor \log_2 n_t + n_t \right)$$

$$\sim \sum_{t=1}^{m} \lfloor s_t/2 \rfloor n_t(\log_2 n_t)(\log_2 \log_2 n_t)^{-1}.$$

Thus, for a polynomial f of degree s that is defined in 2^n points, the network complexity $L(f)$ of the optimal check increases almost linearly with increasing s or with increasing n.

We also note that upper bound (10.6.1) for complexity $L(f)$ may be decreased if $V(n_t, s_t + 1)$ and $V^{\perp}(n_t, s_t + 1)$ are cyclic codes, and the encoding network in Fig. 10.6.1 is implemented by linear sequential networks (347), but this results in an increase in the time required to implement the check.

We shall now describe the error-detecting capabilities of linear checks for polynomials.

We consider three classes of errors. These are errors in

1. Coefficients
2. Variables
3. Values of the polynomial.

We assume also that every coefficient $a(i_1, \ldots, i_m)$ (or the variable x_t, or the value $f(x_1, \ldots, x_m)$ of the polynomial) is represented by a M-bit binary vector ($M = n_1 = \cdots = n_m$).

By an *error with multiplicity l*, that is, an *l-fold error*, in coefficients (variables, values of the polynomial) we mean any error resulting in the replacement of l coefficients (variables, values of the polynomial) by some constants $C_1, \ldots, C_l$ (binary representation of $C_r, r = 1, \ldots, l$, contains M-bits).

We denote the fraction of l-fold errors that cannot be detected by our check for the above three classes by $\hat{\eta}_a(l)$, $\hat{\eta}_x(l)$, $\hat{\eta}_f(l)$, respectively.

The result of an error $e(x_1, \ldots, x_m)$ is to replace the given polynomial $f(x_1, \ldots, x_m)$ by $f(x_1, \ldots, x_m) + e(x_1, \ldots, x_m)$.

Corollary 10.6.1 *For every*

$$f(x_1, \ldots, x_m) = \sum_{t=1}^{m} \sum_{i_t=0}^{s_t} a(i_1, \ldots, i_m) x_1^{i_1} \cdots x_m^{i_m},$$

we have

$$\eta_a(l) \leq (1 - \delta_{l,1})(2^M - 1)^{-1} \quad \left(0 < l \leq \prod_{t=1}^{m} s_t\right), \tag{10.6.3}$$

$$\eta_x(l) \leq 2^{-M} \max_r s_r \leq M2^{-M}, \quad (0 < l \leq m), \tag{10.6.4}$$

$$\eta_f(l) \leq (1 - \delta_{l,1})(2^M - 1)^{-1}, \quad (0 < l \leq 2^{K_m}), \tag{10.6.5}$$

where $\delta_{l,1} = 1$, iff $l = 1$, and $\delta_{l,1} = 0$ if $l > 1$.

Proof. An error with multiplicity l in coefficients $e_a(x_1, \ldots, x_m)$ (in variables $e_x(x_1, \ldots, x_m)$ in values of f, $e_f(x_1, \ldots, x_m)$) may be represented as

$$e_a(x_1, \ldots, x_m) = \sum_{r=1}^{l} (C_r - a(i_{1,r}, \ldots, i_{m,r})) x_1^{i_{1,r}} \cdots x_m^{i_{m,r}}, \tag{10.6.6}$$

where $i_{t,r} \in \{0, \ldots, s_t\}$, $C_r \neq 0$, and

$$e_x(x_1, \ldots, x_m) = f(x_{i_1} = C_1, \ldots, x_{i_l} = C_l) - f(x_1, \ldots, x_m), \quad (10.6.7)$$

where $1 \leq i_1 < \cdots < i_l \leq m$ and $f(x_{i_1} = C_1, \ldots, x_{i_l} = C_l)$ is the function of $m - l$ variables obtained from $f(x_1, \ldots, x_m)$ by the replacement of x_{i_r} by C_r, $r = 1, \ldots, l$.

For an error in values of the polynomial, we have

$$\| e_f \| = l, \quad (10.6.8)$$

where $\| e_f \|$ is the number of nonzero values of $e_f(x_1, \ldots, x_m)$.

If an error e is not detected, then by (10.2.25),

$$\sum_{\tau \in V^\perp} (f(x \oplus \tau) + e(x \oplus \tau)) = d,$$

where $x = (x_1, \ldots, x_m)$, $\tau = (\tau_1, \ldots, \tau_m)$, and

$$\sum_{\tau \in V^\perp} e(x \oplus \tau) = \sum_{x_1 \cdots x_m} e(x_1, \ldots, x_m) = 0. \quad (10.6.9)$$

We have from (10.6.6), (10.6.7), and (10.6.9), $\eta_a(1) = \eta_f(1) = 0$. Next, from (10.6.6)–(10.6.8) for every $C_1, \ldots, C_{r-1}, C_{r+1}, \ldots, C_l$, there exists at most one C_r such that (10.6.9) is satisfied for errors in coefficients and values of the polynomial, and there exists at most s_r different values of C_r such that (10.6.9) is satisfied for errors in variables. This completes the proof of Corollary 10.6.1.

Thus, for every polynomial $f(x_1, \ldots, x_m)$ that is defined in $2^n = 2^M$ points, if M is large enough, then by a linear check we may detect almost all stuck-at errors in coefficients, variables, and values of the polynomial.

10.7   TESTING FOR NUMERICAL COMPUTATIONS

10.7.1   Linear Inequality Checks for Numerical Computations

In this section, we will consider the problem of error detection in programs or devices computing *real-valued* functions $f(z)$, where z is represented in the binary form $(z = (z_0, \ldots, z_{m-1}) \in C_2^m)$. By errors we mean errors in the texts of programs or the catastrophic failures in the corresponding devices.

In Sections 10.2–10.6, we described spectral methods for constructing linear equality checks (10.2.1), their complexities $|T(f)|$ for a given *integer-valued* function $f(z)$, and the *optimal equality checks* for basic computer instructions, standard hardware components, and optimal checks for polynomials of several variables. Notice that these tests can be effectively used in the case where $f(z)$ is an integer for every $z \in \{0, 1, \ldots, 2^m - 1\}$, and very few nonlinear functions have nontrivial checks.

In this section, we shall generalize linear check methods to the case of *noninteger* computations. These generalized checks will be constructed for such important noninteger computations as exponential, logarithmic, and trigonometric computations (see Table 10.8.1). For error detection in noninteger computations we shall use linear *inequality* checks.

The method described in this section may be effectively used for the testing of manufacturing acceptance of the program or the device computing the given numerical function $f(z)$. In the case of hardware implementation, this method may be used for maintenance testing of the corresponding devices or memories where values of these functions are stored.

10.7.2 Properties of Linear Inequality Checks

Let $f(z)$ be a real number for every $z \in \{0, 1, \ldots, 2^m - 1\}$, $z = (z_1, \ldots, z_m)$, and $z_i \in \{0, 1\}$, and let $\epsilon \geq 0$ be some small constant.

For error detection, we shall use linear *inequality* checks

$$|\sum_{\tau \in T} f(z \oplus \tau) - d| \leq \epsilon, \tag{10.7.1}$$

where d is a constant and T is a subgroup of the group C_2^m of binary m-vectors. (Check (10.2.1) is a special case of (10.7.1) discussed below with $\epsilon = 0$.)

We shall discuss in this section, the cardinality $|T(f, \epsilon)|$ of a minimal check subgroup $T = T(f, \epsilon)$ of C_2^m for a given function f and $\epsilon \geq 0$. These results will be the generalizations of the corresponding results from Section 10.2.2 ($T(f, 0) = T(f)$).

Linear transform of variables

Let σ be an $(m \times m)$ binary nonsingular over $GF(2)$ matrix, $y = (y_0, \ldots, y_{m-1})$ be a binary vector and

$$\phi(z) = f(\sigma z \oplus y) \tag{10.7.2}$$

for every $z = (z_0, \ldots, z_{m-1})$. Then, by definition of $T(f, \epsilon)$, there exists a constant d such that

$$|\sum_{\tau \in T(f, \epsilon)} f(z \oplus \tau) - d| \leq \epsilon,$$

for every z, and we have from (10.7.2) that

$$|\sum_{\tau \in \sigma^{-1} T(f, \epsilon)} \phi(z \oplus \tau) - d| = |\sum_{\tau \in T(f, \epsilon)} \phi(z \oplus \sigma^{-1} \tau) - d|$$

$$= |\sum_{\tau \in T(f, \epsilon)} f(\sigma z \oplus y \oplus \tau) - d| \leq \epsilon,$$

where σ^{-1} is the inverse of σ over $GF(2)$, $\sigma^{-1}T(t, \epsilon) = \{\sigma^{-1}\tau \mid \tau \in T(f, \epsilon)\}$, and $\sigma^{-1}T(f, \epsilon)$ is a check set for $\phi(z)$.

Notice that $\sigma^{-1}T(f, \epsilon)$ is a minimal check set for $\phi(z)$, since $|\sigma^{-1}T(f, \epsilon)| = |T(f, \epsilon)|$. Thus, we have, that for any $\phi(z)$ defined by (10.7.2)

$$T(\phi, \epsilon) = \sigma^{-1}T(f, \epsilon), \tag{10.7.3}$$

and check complexities are invariant under linear transforms of variables.
Linear transform of functions

Let $f_1, \ldots, f_r$ be some real-valued functions and $\epsilon_1 \geq 0, \ldots, \epsilon_r \geq 0$ be some small constants

$$\left| \sum_{\tau \in T(f_i, \epsilon_i)} f_i(z \oplus \tau) - d_i \right| \leq \epsilon_i, \quad i = 1, \ldots, r, \tag{10.7.4}$$

and

$$\phi(z) = \sum_{i=1}^{r} \alpha_i f_i(z). \tag{10.7.5}$$

Denote

$$T = \bigoplus_{i=1}^{r} T(f_i, \epsilon_i) \tag{10.7.6}$$

$$= \{\tau_1 \oplus \cdots \oplus \tau_r \mid \tau_1 \in T(f_1, \epsilon_1), \ldots, \tau_r \in T(f_r, \epsilon_r)\}. \tag{10.7.7}$$

Since $T(f_i, \epsilon_i)$ s, by definition, is a subgroup of the group C_2^m of binary m-vectors, T is also a subgroup of C_2^m.

Denote by T_i a subgroup isomorphic to the factor group $T/T(f_i, \epsilon_i)$. Then, we have from (10.7.4)–(10.7.6),

$$\left| \sum_{\tau \in T} \phi(z \oplus \tau) - \sum_{i=1}^{r} \alpha_i d_i \right| = \left| \sum_{i=1}^{r} \alpha_i \sum_{\tau \in T_i} \sum_{\tau_i \in T(f_i, \epsilon_i)} f_i(z \oplus \tau \oplus \tau_i) - \sum_{i=1}^{r} \alpha_i d_i \right|$$

$$= \left| \sum_{i=1}^{r} \alpha_i \sum_{\tau \in T_i} \left(\sum_{\tau_i \in T(f_i, \epsilon_i)} f(z \oplus \tau \oplus \tau_i) - d_i \right) \right|$$

$$\leq \sum_{i=1}^{r} \epsilon_i |\alpha_i| |T_i|. \tag{10.7.8}$$

It follows from (10.7.8) that for the function $\phi(z)$ defined by (10.7.5),

$$T = \bigoplus_{i=1}^{r} T(f_i, \epsilon_i)$$

is a check set and

$$\left|T\left(\phi, \sum_{i=1}^{r} \epsilon_i |\alpha_i| \|T_i\|\right)\right| \leq \left|\bigoplus_{i=1}^{r} T(f_i, \epsilon_i)\right| \leq \prod_{i=1}^{r} |T(f_i, \epsilon_i)|. \qquad (10.7.9)$$

Thus, a check complexity of a linear combination of functions does not exceed the product of check complexities of individual functions.

Convolution of functions

Denote

$$\phi(z) = \sum_{v \in G} f_1(v) f_2(z \oplus v), \quad G = C_2^m. \qquad (10.7.10)$$

If

$$\left| \sum_{\tau \in T(f_i, \epsilon_i)} f_i(z \oplus \tau) - d_i \right| \leq \epsilon_i, \quad (i = 1, 2),$$

then we have from (10.7.10),

$$\left| \sum_{\tau \in T(f_2, \epsilon_2)} \phi(z \oplus \tau) - d_2 \sum_{v \in G} f_1(v) \right|$$

$$= \left| \sum_{\tau \in T(f_2, \epsilon_2)} \sum_{v \in G} f_1(v) f_2(z \oplus \tau \oplus v) - d_2 \sum_{v \in G} f_1(v) \right|$$

$$= \left| \sum_{v \in G} f_1(v) \left(\sum_{\tau \in T(f_2, \epsilon_2)} f_2(z \oplus v \oplus \tau) - d_2 \right) \right|$$

$$\leq \epsilon_2 \sum_{v \in G} |f_1(v)|. \qquad (10.7.11)$$

It follows from (10.7.11) that $T(f_2, \epsilon_2)$ is a check set for $\phi(z)$ and

$$\left| T\left(\phi, \epsilon_2 \sum_{v \in G} |f_1(v)|\right) \right| \leq |T(f_2, \epsilon_2)|. \qquad (10.7.12)$$

By a similar proof, we can also show that

$$\left| T\left(\phi, \epsilon_1 \sum_{v \in G} |f_2(v)| \right) \right| \le |T(f_1, \epsilon_1)|. \tag{10.7.13}$$

Superposition of functions

Let $z = (z_0, \ldots, z_{m-1})$ and $f(z) = (f^{(0)}(z), \ldots, f^{(m-1)}(z))$ be a system of m Boolean functions of m variables.

We say that $\tau = (\tau_0, \ldots, \tau_{m-1})$ is a *self-duality point* for $f(z)$, that is, $f^{(i)}(z \oplus \tau) = 1 \oplus f^{(i)}(z)$ for all $i = 0, \ldots, m - 1$.

We denote by D_i the set of all self-duality points for $f^{(i)}$, $i = 1, \ldots, m$. (If $(1, \ldots, 1) \in D_i$, then $f^{(i)}$ is *self-dual*.)

Suppose

$$\psi(z) = \phi(f(z)), \tag{10.7.14}$$

and for $\phi(z)$ we have for every z

$$|\phi(z) + \phi(z \oplus (1, \ldots, 1)) - d| \le \epsilon, \tag{10.7.15}$$

where d and ϵ are some constants.

Then, we have for every $\tau \in \bigcap_{i=1}^{m} D_i$,

$$|\psi(z) + \psi(z \oplus \tau) - d| = |\phi((f(z)) + \phi(f(z \oplus \tau)) - d| \tag{10.7.16}$$

$$= |\phi(f(z)) + (\phi(f(z \oplus (1, \ldots, 1)))) - d| \le \epsilon.$$

It follows from (10.7.16) that, for $\psi(z)$ and every $\tau \in \bigcap_{i=1}^{m} D_i$,

$$T(\psi, \epsilon) = \{(0, \ldots, 0), \tau\}. \tag{10.7.17}$$

We also note that for any function $\phi(z)$, (10.7.15) is satisfied for every $\epsilon \ge 0.5(\max_z(\phi(z) + \phi(z \oplus (1, \ldots, 1))) - \min_z(\phi(z) + \phi(z \oplus (1, \ldots, 1))))$, if we choose $d = 0.5(\max_z(\phi(z) + \phi(z \oplus (1, \ldots, 1))) + \min_z(\phi(z) + \phi(z \oplus (1, \ldots, 1))))$.

Example 10.7.1 *Consider the following functions with $m = 3$, $f^{(0)}(z_0, z_1, z_2) = z_0$, $f^{(1)}(z_0, z_1, z_2) = Maj(z_0, z_1, z_2) = \bar{z}_0 z_1 z_2 \vee z_0 \bar{z}_1 z_2 \vee z_0 z_1 \bar{z}_2$, where $\vee$ denotes logical addition, $f^{(2)}(z_0, z_1, z_2) = EXOR(z_0, z_1, z_2) = z_0 \oplus z_1 \oplus z_2$, and $\phi(z) = az$, where $z = \sum_{i=1}^{3} z_i 2^{i-1}$.*

Then, $f^{(0)}, f^{(1)}, f^{(2)}$ are self-dual ($f^{(i)}(z \oplus (1, 1, 1)) = 1 \oplus f^{(i)}(z)$), since (10.7.15) is satisfied for $\epsilon = 0$, $d = 7a$, and from (10.7.16) and (10.7.17) for $\psi(z) = \phi(f(z))$ we have $\psi(z) + \psi(z \oplus (1, 1, 1)) = 7a$ for every $z = (z_0, z_1, z_2)$.

10.7.3 Check Complexities for Positive (Negative) Functions

Let $f(z)$ be a positive function ($f(z) \geq 0$ for every $z \in \{0, 1, \ldots, 2^m - 1\}$). By the definition of $T(f, \epsilon)$, there exists a constant d such that

$$| \sum_{\tau \in T(f, \epsilon)} f(z \oplus \tau) - d| \leq \epsilon, \qquad (10.7.18)$$

or

$$d - \epsilon \leq \sum_{\tau \in T(f, \epsilon)} f(z \oplus \tau) \leq d + \epsilon,$$

for every $z \in \{0, 1, \ldots, 2^m - 1\}$.

Then, we have from (10.7.18)

$$(d - \epsilon) 2^m |T(f, \epsilon)|^{-1} \leq \sum_{Y \in G} f(Y)$$

$$= \sum_{z \in G/T(f, \epsilon)} \sum_{\tau \in T(f, \epsilon)} f(z \oplus \tau) \qquad (10.7.19)$$

$$\leq (d + \epsilon) 2^m |T(f, \epsilon)|^{-1},$$

where G is C_2^m and $G/T(f, \epsilon)$ is a subgroup isomorphic to the factor group of G with respect to $T(f, \epsilon)$ and $|G/T(f, \epsilon)| = 2^m |T(f, \epsilon)|^{-1}$.

Since $\log_2 |T(f, \epsilon)|$ is an integer, we have from (10.7.19)

$$m + \lceil \log_2(d - \epsilon) - \log_2 \sum_{Y \in G} f(Y) \rceil \leq \log_2 |T(f, \epsilon)| \qquad (10.7.20)$$

$$\leq m + \lfloor \log_2(d + \epsilon) - \log_2 \sum_{Y \in G} f(Y) \rfloor,$$

where $\lceil \alpha \rceil$ ($\lfloor \alpha \rfloor$) is the smallest (greatest) integer $\geq \alpha$ ($\leq \alpha$).

For positive functions, $d \geq \min_{\{z | f(z) \neq 0\}} f(z)$, and we have from (10.7.20)

$$\log_2 |T(f, \epsilon)| \geq m + \lceil \log_2(\min_{\{z/f(z) \neq 0\}} f(z) - \epsilon) - \log_2 \sum_{Y \in G} f(Y) \rceil. \quad (10.7.21)$$

The bounds similar to (10.7.20) and (10.7.21) may be obtained also for negative functions ($f(z) \leq 0$ for every z).

We also note that the bounds in (10.7.20) and (10.7.21) are exact, and there exist positive functions such that these bounds are reached (see Example 10.7.2).

Example 10.7.2 Let $z = \sum_{i=0}^{m-1} z_i 2^i$, where $z_i \in \{0, 1\}$, $N = 2^m$, $\epsilon = 0.5(2^{0.5N} - 2^{-N+1})$, and $f(z) = z_{m-1}(a + 2^{-z})$, where $a \geq 1$.

Then,

$$\min_{\{z \mid f(z) \neq 0\}} f(z) = a + 2^{-N+1},$$

$$\sum_{Y \in G} f(Y) = \sum_{z=0.5N}^{N-1} (a + 2^{-z}) = 0.5aN + 2^{-0.5N+1} - 2^{-N+1},$$

and by (10.7.21), for every $a \geq 1$, $m > 1$,

$$\log_2 |T(f, \epsilon)| \geq m + \lceil \log_2(a + 2^{-N+1} - 0.5(2^{-0.5N} - 2^{-N+1}))$$
$$- \log_2(0.5aN + 2^{-0.5N+1} - 2^{-N+1}) \rceil = 1.$$

Choose

$$d = a + 0.5(2^{-0.5N} + 2^{-N+1}).$$

Then, it follows from (10.7.20) for every $a \geq 1$, $m > 1$,

$$m + \lceil \log_2(a + 2^{-N+1}) - \log_2(0.5aN + 2^{-0.5N+1} - 2^{-N+1}) \rceil$$
$$= m + \lfloor \log_2(a + 2^{-0.5N})$$
$$- \log_2(0.5aN + 2^{-0.5N+1} - 2^{-N+1}) \rfloor$$
$$= \log_2 |T(f, \epsilon)| = 1.$$

We note that for $f(z) = z_{m-1}(a + 2^{-z})$, $N = 2^m$,

$$|f(z) + f(z \oplus (0, 0, \ldots, 0, 1)) - (a + 0.5(2^{-0.5N} + 2^{-N+1}))|$$
$$\leq 0.5(2^{-0.5N} - 2^{-N+1}),$$

for every z, and the bounds (10.7.20) and (10.7.21) are reached.

10.8 OPTIMAL INEQUALITY CHECKS AND ERROR-CORRECTING CODES

The problem that we consider in this section is to construct, for a given function $f(z)$ and a given $\epsilon \geq 0$, nontrivial inequality checks (10.7.1). (For every function $f(z)$ there exists the trivial check with $|T| = |G| = |C_2^m|$, $d = \sum_{z \in G} f(z)$ and $\epsilon = 0$.)

Let $P_s(z) = \sum_{i=0}^{s} a_i z^i$ be a polynomial of the degree s, $(s < m)$, which is the *least-absolute-error approximation* for $f(z)$ over the set $\{0, 1, \ldots, 2^m - 1\}$, with maximum absolute error Δ_s

$$\Delta_s = \max_{z \in \{0, \ldots, 2^m - 1\}} |\Delta_s(z)| = \max_{z \in \{0, \ldots, 2^m - 1\}} |f(z) - P_s(z)|. \tag{10.8.1}$$

Methods for the construction of the optimal polynomial approximation $P_s(z)$ minimizing Δ_s and the estimations on the error Δ_s for the given $f(z)$ are well known (237, 344, p. 86).

Suppose that we have already found a check set T and a constant d such that $P_s(z)$ satisfies the equality check (10.2.1). Then, we have, for $f(z) = P_s(z) + \Delta_s(z)$, $(|\Delta_s(z)| \le \Delta_s)$ for every $z \in \{0, \ldots, 2^m - 1\}$

$$|\sum_{\tau \in T} f(z \oplus \tau) - d| = |\sum_{\tau \in T} P_s(z \oplus \tau) - d + \sum_{\tau \in T} \Delta_s(z \oplus \tau)| \qquad (10.8.2)$$

$$= |\sum_{\tau \in T} \Delta_s(z \oplus \tau)| \le \Delta_s |T|.$$

Thus, it follows from (10.8.2) that the check set T and constants d and ϵ satisfy the inequality check (10.7.1), if T and d satisfy the equality check (10.2.1) for the polynomial approximation $P_s(z)$, and

$$\Delta_s |T| \le \epsilon. \qquad (10.8.3)$$

For the construction of the check set T and the constant d satisfying linear equality check (10.2.1) for polynomials $P_s(z)$, we may use the results from the previous Section 10.4.

Let $V(m, t)$ be a maximal binary linear error-correcting code with code words of length m and distance t. Recall that code words of $V(m, t)$ are m-bit binary vectors and a Hamming distance between any two vectors from $V(m, t)$ is at least t.

If $V^\perp(m, t)$ is the dual (orthogonal) code to $V(m, t)$ (347), then,

$$V^\perp(m, t) = \{\tau = (\tau_0, \ldots, \tau_{m-1}) \in G \mid \bigoplus_{i=0}^{m-1} \tau_i z_i = 0,$$

$$\text{for every} \quad z = (z_0, \ldots z_{m-1}) \in V(m, t)\} \quad G = C_2^m.$$

Methods for constructing $V(m, t)$, $V^\perp(m, t)$, and for estimating their cardinalities may be found in Reference 347.

It has been shown in Section 10.7, (see Table 10.5.1) that if

$$P_s(z) = \sum_{i=0}^{s} a_i z^i, \quad a_s \ne 0,$$

and $z \in \{0, 1, \ldots, 2^m - 1\}$, then

$$\sum_{\tau \in V^\perp(m,s+1)} P_s(z \oplus \tau) - d = 0, \qquad (10.8.4)$$

and

$$d = |V(m, s + 1)|^{-1} \sum_{z \in G} P_s(z) = |V(m, s + 1)|^{-1} \sum_{i=0}^{s} a_i(i + 1)^{-1}$$
$$\times \sum_{v=0}^{i} \binom{i + 1}{v} 2^{(i+1-v)m} B_v,$$

where B_v stands for Bernoulli numbers.

Thus, we have from (10.8.2–10.8.4)

$$| \sum_{\tau \in V^{\perp}(m, s+1)} f(z \oplus \tau) - d \ | \leq \Delta_s |V^{\perp}(m, s + 1)|, \qquad (10.8.5)$$

and the dual code $V^{\perp}(m, s + 1)$ is the check set for $f(z)$ if $\Delta_s |V^{\perp}(m, s + 1)| \leq \epsilon$.

Thus, to construct the optimal inequality check

$$| \sum_{\tau \in T} f(z \oplus \tau) - d \ | \leq \epsilon, \qquad z \in G = C_2^m,$$

for a given function $f(z)$ and $\epsilon \geq 0$ minimizing $|T|$, we have to approximate $f(z)$ by a polynomial $P_s(z)$ of a minimal degree s, $(s \leq m)$, with the minimum absolute error Δ_s (see (10.8.1)) such that

$$\Delta_s |V^{\perp}(m, s + 1)| = 2^m (V(m, s + 1))^{-1} \Delta_s \leq \epsilon$$

and the best equality check for the approximating polynomial $P_s(z)$ is the best inequality check for $f(z)$.

Example 10.8.1   *Let $m = 24$, $z \in \{0, 1, \ldots, 2^{24} - 1\}$, $z = (z_0, \ldots, z_{23})$, and*

$$f(z) = \exp(-(\log_2 e)2^{-24} z),$$

where e is the base of natural logarithms, and $\epsilon = 10^{-6}$.

The function $f(z)$ may be approximated by the polynomial $P_7(z)$ of degree 7 with the maximum absolute error $\Delta_7 = 2 \times 10^{-10}$ (237).

Choose the (24, 12)-Golay code $V(24, 8)$ with the distance 8 as $V(m, s + 1) = V(24, 8)$ (347).

Then,

$$|V(24, 8)| = |V^{'}(24, 8)| = 2^{12}, \Delta_7 |V^{\perp}(24, 8)| \leq 2 \times 10^{-10} \times 2^{12} < 10^{-6},$$

and $T(f, 10^{-6}) = V(24, 8) = 2^{12}$.

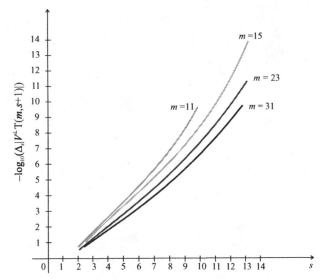

FIGURE 10.8.1   Function $\Delta_s |V^\perp(m, s+1)|$ for $f(y) = 10^{0.25y}$.

10.8.1   Error Detection in Computation of Numerical Functions

We note that for the great variety of analytical functions, $\Delta_s |V^\perp(m, s+1)|$ decreases very rapidly with the increase of the degree s, $(s < m)$ of an approximating polynomial.

Denoting $y = 2^{-m}z$, $0 \le y < 1$, an example of the behavior of $\Delta_s |V^\perp(m, s+1)|$ is given by Fig. 10.8.1 for $f(y) = 10^{0.25y}$. The maximum absolute errors Δ_s for this example are taken from Reference 237.

Using *Varshamov bound* (347) for $|T| = |V^\perp(m, s+1)|$, we have from (10.8.5), sufficient condition for the minimal degree s of the approximating polynomial $P_s(z)$

$$\Delta_s \sum_{j=0}^{s-1} \binom{m-1}{j} \le \epsilon. \tag{10.8.6}$$

For estimating Δ_s, we may use the Taylor expansion for $f(y)$, $(y = 2^{-m}z)$,

$$f(y) = \sum_{i=0}^{s}(i!)^{-1} f^{(i)}\left(\frac{1}{2}\right)\left(y - \frac{1}{2}\right)^i \tag{10.8.7}$$

$$+((s+1)!)^{-1} f^{(s+1)}(\theta(y))\left(y - \frac{1}{2}\right)^{s+1},$$

where $f^{(i+1)}(y)$ is the $(i+1)$th derivative of $f(y)$ and $0 \le \theta \le 1$. Then, we have from (10.8.7)

$$\Delta_s = \max_{y \in [0,1)} |\Delta_s(y)| \tag{10.8.8}$$

$$\le \max_{y \in [0,1)} |(s+1)!)^{-1} f^{(s+1)}(\theta(y)) \left(y - \frac{1}{2} \right)^{s+1}|$$

$$\le ((s+1)!)^{-1} 2^{-(s+1)} \max_{y \in [0,1)} |f^{(s+1)}(y)|.$$

Thus, from (10.8.6) and (10.8.8)

$$((s+1)!)^{-1} 2^{-(s+1)} (\max_{y \in [0,1)} |f^{(s+1)}(y)|) \sum_{j=0}^{s-1} \binom{m-1}{j} \le \epsilon, \tag{10.8.9}$$

and then there exists d such that

$$\left| \sum_{\tau \in V^{\perp}(m,s+1)} f(y \oplus \tau) - d \right| \le \epsilon.$$

Formula (10.8.9) provides us with a good upper bound for the cardinality $|T(f, \epsilon)|$ of the minimal check set for the given f, ϵ.

Let $s(f, \epsilon)$ be the minimal s satisfying (10.8.9). Then, by using the Varshamov–Gilbert bound, we have

$$|T(f, \epsilon)| \le \sum_{j=0}^{s(f,\epsilon)-1} \binom{m-1}{j}. \tag{10.8.10}$$

It follows, also, from (10.8.9) that simple inequality checks may be constructed only for "smooth" functions $f(y)$, such that $\max_{y \in [0,1)} |f^{(s+1)}(y)|$ increases very slowly (or not at all) with the increase of s.

In Table 10.8.1, the minimal s satisfying $\Delta_s |V^{\perp}(m, s+1)| \le \epsilon$ is given for several analytical functions for $m = 23$ and $\epsilon = 5 \times 10^{-3}$. The table also gives corresponding approximation errors Δ_s taken from Reference 344, the parameters (m, k, t) of the codes $V(m, s+1)$, and check complexities $|T|$. Thus, we see from Table 10.8.1 that many important analytical functions have very simple inequality checks of the type (10.7.1).

Example 10.8.2   *Consider an optimal inequality check for the function*

$$f(y) = y^{-0.5} \sin \frac{\pi}{2} y^{0.5},$$

TABLE 10.8.1   Optimal Inequality Checks for Some Numerical Computations for
$m = 23, \epsilon = 5 \times 10^{-3}, y = 2^{-23}z, z \in \{0, 1, \ldots, 2^{23} - 1\}.$

N	Function	s	$\Delta_s \times 10^{-7}$	$\log_2 \lvert T \rvert$	(m, k, t)
1.	e^y	7	2	12	$(23, 11, 8)$
2.	$10^{0.25y}$	5	17	10	$(23, 13, 6)$
3.	$y10^{0.25y}$	6	17	11	$(23, 12, 7)$
4.	$\ln(1 + y)$	6	15	11	$(23, 12, 7)$
5.	$\ln(1 - ay), a = 1 - 0.5\sqrt{2}$	5	4.1	10	$(23, 13, 6)$
6.	$y\ln(1 - ay), a = 1 - 0.5\sqrt{2}$	6	4.1	11	$(23, 13, 7)$
7.	$y^2\ln(1 - ay), a = 1 - 0.5\sqrt{2}$	7	4.1	12	$(23, 11, 8)$
8.	$\sin y$	7	10	12	$(23, 11, 8)$
9.	$\sin \frac{\pi}{2}y$	7	11	12	$(23, 11, 8)$
10.	$\sin \frac{\pi}{4}y$	5	5	10	$(23, 13, 6)$
11.	$y\sin \frac{\pi}{4}y$	6	5	11	$(23, 12, 7)$
12.	$y^2\sin \frac{\pi}{4}y$	7	5	12	$(23, 11, 8)$
13.	$y^{-1}\sin \frac{\pi}{4}y$	4	12	9	$(23, 14, 5)$
14.	$y^{-1/2}\sin \frac{\pi}{4}y^{1/2}$	1	31×10^2	1	$(23, 22, 2)$
15.	$\cos \frac{\pi}{4}y$	4	99	9	$(23, 14, 5)$
16.	$\cos \frac{\pi}{4}y^{1/2}$	1	1.92×10^4	1	$(23, 22, 2)$
17.	$\cos \frac{\pi}{2}y^{1/2}$	4	0.5	9	$(23, 14, 5)$
18.	$y\cos \frac{\pi}{2}y^{1/2}$	5	0.5	10	$(23, 13, 6)$
19.	$y^2\cos \frac{\pi}{2}y^{1/2}$	6	0.5	11	$(23, 12, 7)$
20.	$y^3\cos \frac{\pi}{2}y^{1/2}$	7	0.5	12	$(23, 11, 8)$
21.	$y^{1/2}\cot \frac{\pi}{4}y^{1/2}$	1	1.2×10^4	1	$(23, 22, 2)$
22.	$\left(\frac{\pi}{2} - \sin^{-1} y\right)\sqrt{1 - y}$	3	5×10^2	6	$(23, 17, 4)$
23.	$\cosh \sqrt{y}$	5	10^{-2}	10	$(23, 13, 6)$
24.	$y\cosh \sqrt{y}$	6	10^{-2}	10	$(23, 12, 7)$
25.	$y^2\cosh \sqrt{y}$	7	10^{-2}	12	$(23, 11, 8)$

s—Minimal degree of an approximating polynomial
$\Delta_s \times 10^{-7}$—Approximating error
$\log_2 \lvert T \rvert$—Complexity of a check
(m, k, t)—Parameters of the chosen code $V(m, s + 1)$
In this table, m is the length of the code, k is the number of information bits, and t is the distance for
$V(m, t = s + 1), \lvert V(m, s + 1) \rvert = 2^k.$

with $\epsilon = 5 \times 10^{-3}$, where $y = 2^{-23}z$, $z \in \{0, 1, \ldots, 2^{23} - 1\}$. *This function can be approximated by the polynomial* $P_2(y)$ *of the degree 2 (344)*

$$y^{-0.5} \sin \frac{\pi}{2} y^{0.5} = P_2(y) + \Delta_2(y),$$

where

$$P_2(y) = 0.07287y^2 - 0.64338y + 1.57064,$$

and

$$\max_y \Delta_2(y) = \Delta_2 \leq 14 \times 10^{-5}.$$

Choose (23, 18) *code with the distance 3 and the check matrix* **H** *with 5 rows as* $V(m, s + 1) = V(23, 3)$ *(347).*

Recall that code words of $V(23, 3)$ *form the null space for H and* $V^{\perp}(23, 3)$ *is the linear span of H.*

Then, $|V^{\perp}(23, 3)| = 2^5$ *and* $\Delta_2 |V^{\perp}(23, 3)| \leq \epsilon = 5 \times 10^{-3}.$

For the constant d, we have

$$d = 2^{-18} \sum_y P_2(y) = 40.74372.$$

Thus, we finally have the following optimal inequality check for the given function:

$$\left| \sum_{\tau \in T} (2^{-23}(z \oplus \tau))^{-0.5} \sin \left(\frac{\pi}{2} 2^{-3} (z \oplus \tau)^{0.5} \right) - 40.7437 \right| \leq 5 \times 10^{-3},$$

for every $z \in \{0, 1, \ldots, 2^{23} - 1\}$, *where* $T = V^{\perp}(23, 3)$ *is the set of all 32 linear mod 2 combinations of the rows of H.*

Notice also that all the results given above may be generalized to the case when z is represented in a nonbinary form. If z is represented as a q-ary m-vector $z = (z_0, \ldots, z_{m-1})$, $z_i \in \{0, 1, \ldots, q - 1\}$, the symbol $\oplus$ stands for mod q addition and $V_q(m, s + 1)$ is the maximal linear code in m-dimensional space of q-ary vectors with the Hamming distance $(s + 1)$ (347).

We conclude this section by noticing that all the checks considered above can be represented as a convolution over $GF(2)$

$$\left| \sum_{\tau} a(\tau) f(z \oplus \tau) - d \right| \leq \epsilon, \tag{10.8.11}$$

where $a(\tau) \in \{0, 1\}$ for every τ. We note that the check complexity (number of nonzero values of $a(\tau)$) may sometimes be essentially decreased if we use checks with $a(\tau) \in \{0, \pm 1\}$ for every τ.

For example, if

$$f(z) = \frac{z^t + b_1}{z^t + b_2}, \quad z \in \{0, 1, \ldots, 2^m - 1\}, \quad b_1 \geq b_2 > 0,$$

then we may construct the following check:

$$|f(z) - f(z \oplus (0, 0, \ldots, 0, 1))| \leq \frac{b_1 - b_2}{b_2(b_2 + 1)}. \tag{10.8.12}$$

The problem with constructing optimal checks (10.8.11) with $a(\tau) \in \{0, \pm 1\}$ for the given $f(z)$ seems to be difficult.

10.8.2 Estimations on Probabilities of Error Detection for Inequality Checks

As in the previous sections, we shall use the additive way of describing the influence of errors, that is, by the error e in a program or device computing $f(z) = f(z_0, \ldots, z_{m-1})$, $z_i \in \{0, 1\}$, we mean the function $e(z) = e(z_0, \ldots z_{m-1})$ such that as a result of the error a program or device computes $f(z) + e(z)$.

We also suppose that for every $T \subseteq \{0, \ldots, 2^m - 1\}$, either $\sum_{z \in T} e(z) = 0$ or $|\sum_{z \in T} e(z)| > 2\epsilon$. The last condition can be used for the choice of ϵ for practical applications.

The detecting capability of the linear inequality checks described in Sections 10.7.2 and 10.8.1 depends on a specific implementation of a computational process for $f(z)$. We shall consider below three widely used types of computational processes— polynomial approximations $f(z) \cong P(z)$, rational approximations $f(z) \cong P(z)/Q(z)$, and continued-fraction approximations

$$f(z) \cong P_1(z)/Q_1(z) + P_2(z)/Q_2(z) + \cdots + P_t(z)/Q_t(z), \qquad (10.8.13)$$

where $P_1, \ldots, P_t, Q_1, \ldots, Q_t$ represent polynomials (see 344).

By an error of multiplicity $l \geq 1$, we mean any error resulting in the replacement in a program computing $f(z)$ of l coefficients in some of these polynomials by constants $c_1, \ldots, c_l$. We assume that every coefficient of these polynomials is stored in the corresponding M-bit memory cell, thus, the binary representation of constants c_r, $r = 1, \ldots, l$ each contains M bits.

Suppose that (10.7.1) is satisfied for $f(z)$. Then, for the error e such that

$$|\sum_{\tau \in T} e(\tau)| > 2\epsilon,$$

we have $|\sum_{\tau \in T}(f(z \oplus \tau) + e(z \oplus \tau)) - d| > \epsilon$, and this error will be detected by the inequality check (10.7.18). Thus, if an error e cannot be detected, then $\sum_{\tau \in T} e(z \oplus \tau) = 0$ for every z. The last condition may be used for estimating the error-detecting capability of inequality checks. We may verify (10.7.1) for any given test pattern z.

We now describe the error-detecting capability in this case.

Denote the fraction of errors of the multiplicity l, which cannot be detected by $\hat{\eta}(l)$. (If the number of all possible errors of the multiplicity l tends to infinity, then $1 - \hat{\eta}(l)$ tends to the probability of the detection of errors with the multiplicity l.)

If the error e is a unidirectional error (i.e., $e(z) \geq 1$ for every z, or $e(z) \leq 0$ for every z), and for the given test pattern z, there exits $\tau \in T$ such that $e(z \oplus \tau) \neq 0$, then $\hat{\eta}(l) = 0$ for every l, since for unidirectional errors $\sum_{\tau \in T} e(z \oplus \tau) \neq 0$.

Since for polynomial, rational, or continued-fraction approximations, any single error is a unidirectional error, all single errors are detected.

For any error e of a multiplicity $l > 1$ and for any type of the approximation for every $c_1, \ldots, c_{r-1}, c_{r+1}, \ldots, c_l$, there exits at most one c_r, such that $\sum_{\tau \in T} e(z \oplus \tau) = 0$ for the given test pattern z.

Since the binary representation of c_r contains M-bits, we have for $\eta(l)$

$$\eta(l) \le (1 - \delta_{l,1})(2^M - 1)^{-1}, \tag{10.8.14}$$

where $\delta_{l,1}$ is the Kronecker symbol.

Formula (10.8.14) illustrates the good error-detecting capability of inequality checks for errors in coefficients in the case of polynomial, rational, or continued-fraction approximations.

As a disadvantage of these checks, we note that if we use for the computation of $f(z)$ an expansion in the orthogonal polynomials $P_i(z)$ (e.g., Chebyshev, Legendre, or Hermite polynomials), that is,

$$f(z) \cong \sum_{i=1}^{s} a_i P_i(z),$$

(where the degree of $P_i(z)$ is i), then for an error of the multiplicity l in coefficients $a_{i_1}, \ldots, a_{i_l}$ we have

$$e(z) = \sum_{r=1}^{l} (a_{i_r} - c_r) P_{i_r}(z), \qquad (a_{i_r} \ne c_r, r = 1, \ldots, l).$$

If $i_1 < i_2 < \cdots < i_l \le s$, we have from (10.8.4) for every given test z

$$\sum_{\tau \in T} e(z \oplus \tau) = \sum_{\tau \in V^\perp(m,s+1)} e(z \oplus \tau) = \sum_{r=1}^{l} (a_{i_r} - c_r) \sum_{\tau \in V^\perp(m,s+1)} P_{i_r}(z \oplus \tau) = 0,$$

and this error cannot be detected by (10.7.1). Thus, the inequality checks are inefficient for computations by expansions in orthogonal polynomials.

For a further improvement of the error-detecting capability of linear inequality checks, we may verify (10.7.1) for several test patterns z, which, however, causes increasing of the time required for testing.

By an output error e of the multiplicity l, we mean any function $e(z)$ different from 0 at l points (i.e., the multiplicity of the output error in computing the function f is the number of distorted values $f(z)$). This definition is natural if errors in computing $f(z)$ are independent for different z as, for example, in the case when $f(z)$ is information stored in a memory cell whose address is z.

An output error $e(z)$ cannot be detected by (10.7.1) if, for every z,

$$\sum_{\tau \in V^\perp(m,s+1)} e(z \oplus \tau) = \sum_{\tau \in G} e(\tau) = 0, \quad G = C_2^m.$$

Thus, if the computed values of $f(z) + e(z)$ are stored in M-bit memory cells, then we have, as before, for every $l > 1$,

$$\hat{\eta}(l) \le (2^M - 1)^{-1}.$$

We also note that all results in this section have been obtained for the case where fault-free programs or devices compute exact values of functions $f(z)$, but for many practical cases our program or devices computes $f(z)$ only with some finite accuracy δ. Hence, all the previous results remain valid only for $\delta \ll \epsilon$, and the proposed error-detection method may be effectively used for functions with good least-absolute-error polynomial approximations.

10.8.3 Construction of Optimal Systems of Orthogonal Inequality Checks

It follows from the previous section that with one inequality check, some multiple errors with $\|e\| > 1$ are not detected and even single errors with $\|e\| = 1$ are not located. (By error location we mean a procedure identifying all z such that $e(z) \ne 0$.)

Similarly, to the case of equality checks (Section 10.2.6), to improve an error-detecting capability and to provide for error location, we will introduce systems of orthogonal inequality checks.

The system

$$\left| \sum_{\tau \in T_i} f(z \oplus \tau) - d_i \right| \le \epsilon, \qquad (i = 0, \ldots, n - 1), \tag{10.8.15}$$

of n inequality checks is *orthogonal* iff for any $i, j \in \{0, 1, \ldots, n - 1\}$

$$T_i \cap T_j = (0, 0, \ldots, 0) = 0^m, (i \ne j). \tag{10.8.16}$$

Example 10.8.3 *Suppose that we have a ROM containing the value $f(z)$ in a cell whose address is z, where*

$$f(y) = \frac{\pi}{4} y \cot \frac{\pi}{4} y, \quad and \quad y = 2^{-23}z, z \in \{0, 1, \ldots, 2^{23} - 1\}, (m = 23).$$

Let us construct two orthogonal inequality checks with $e = 5 \times 10^{-3}$ for $f(y)$.

The function $f(y)$ can be approximated by the polynomial $P_1(y)$ of the degree 1 (344)

$$\frac{\pi}{4} y \cot \left(\frac{\pi}{4} y \right) = P_1(y) + \Delta_1(y),$$

where

$$P_1(y) = 1.0012 - 0.2146y,$$

and

$$\max_y \Delta_1(y) = \Delta_1 \leq 1.2 \times 10^{-3}.$$

Choose

$$T_1 = V_1^{\perp}(23, 2) = \{0^{23}, 1^{23}\}$$

and

$$T_2 = V_2^{\perp}(23, 2) = \{0^{23}, 101^{21}, 011^{21}, 110^{21}\}.$$

(We denote $a^i = \underbrace{aa \cdots a}_{i}$ for $a \in \{0, 1\}$).

Then, $T_1 \cap T_2 = 0^{23}$, the condition (10.8.3) is satisfied, and $d_1 = |T_1| 2^{-m} \sum_y P_1(y) = 1.7878$, $d_2 = |T_2| 2^{-m} \sum_y P_1(y) = 2d_1 = 3.5756$.

Thus, we finally have the following two orthogonality checks for function considered

$$\left| \frac{\pi}{4} 2^{-23} z \cdot \cot\left(\frac{\pi}{4} 2^{-23} z\right) + \frac{\pi}{4} 2^{-23} (z \oplus 1^{23}) \cdot \cot\left(\frac{\pi}{4} 2^{-23} (z \oplus 1^{23})\right) - 1.7878 \right| \leq 5 \times 10^{-3},$$

$$\left| \frac{\pi}{4} 2^{-23} z \cdot \cot\left(\frac{\pi}{4} 2^{-23} z\right) + \frac{\pi}{4} 2^{-23} (z \oplus 101^{21}) \cdot \cot\left(\frac{\pi}{4} 2^{-23} (z \oplus 101^{21})\right) \right.$$
$$+ \frac{\pi}{4} 2^{-23} (z \oplus 011^{21}) \cdot \cot\left(\frac{\pi}{4} 2^{-23} (z \oplus 011^{21})\right)$$
$$\left. + \frac{\pi}{4} 2^{-23} (z \oplus 110^{21}) \cdot \cot\left(\frac{\pi}{4} 2^{-23} (z \oplus 110^{21})\right) - 3.5756 \right| \leq 5 \times 10^{-3}.$$

Consider now the detection and location of errors by a system of n orthogonal inequality checks.

For an error e resulting in the replacement of $f(z)$ by $f(z) + e(z)$ for all z, the *syndrome* $S^{(e)}(z) = \{S_0^{(e)}(z), \ldots, S_{n-1}^{(e)}(z)\}$ is defined as a binary vector such that

$$S_i^{(e)}(z) = \begin{cases} 0, & \text{if } |\sum_{\tau \in T_i} \{f(z \oplus \tau) + e(z \oplus \tau)\} - d_i| \leq \epsilon, \\ 1, & \text{otherwise, } (i = 0, \ldots, n - 1). \end{cases} \tag{10.8.17}$$

From now on, we suppose that

$$\min_{\{z | e(z) \neq 0\}} |e(z)| > 2\epsilon. \tag{10.8.18}$$

For a single error, $e(z) = \delta_{z,t}e(t)$, where $t \in z \oplus T_i$ for some $z \in G = C_2^m$ and $i \in \{1, \dots, n\}$, $\delta_{z,t}$ is the Kronecker delta, $\|e\| = 1$, we have

$$|\sum_{\tau \in T_i} e(z \oplus \tau)| = |e(t)| > 2\epsilon. \qquad (10.8.19)$$

Thus, for a single error $e(z) = \delta_{z,t}e(t)$, $t \in z \oplus T_i$, we have from (10.8.16) and (10.8.17), $S_i^{(e)}(z) = 1$, and this error is detected.

Similarly, to detection and correction of errors by systems of orthogonal equality checks (see discussions in Section 10.2.6), we shall consider two methods of error detection and/or error location by the previously computed binary syndrome vector $S^{(e)}(z) = (S_0^{(e)}(z), \dots, S_{n-1}^{(e)}(z))$ in (10.8.17), that is, *memoryless* (combinational) and *memory-aided* (sequential) decoding.

In the case of memoryless decoding, for a given z, we first compute $S^{(e)}(z)$ and then by an analysis of $S^{(e)}(z)$, in the case of error detection, we decide whether there exists $\tau \in \cup_{i=0}^{n-1} T_i$, such that $e(z \oplus \tau) \neq 0$, and in the case of error location we decide whether $e(z) \neq 0$.

In the case of memory-aided decoding, for every given z, we first compute

$$S^{(e)}(z) = \left\{ S^{(e)}(z \oplus \tau) | \tau \in \bigoplus_{i=0}^{n-1} T_i \right\},$$

where

$$\bigoplus_{i=0}^{n-1} T_i = \{t_0 \oplus \cdots \oplus t_{n-1} | t_i \in T_i, i = 0, \dots, n-1\},$$

and, then, by the analysis of the set $S^{(e)}(z)$ of syndromes, in the case of error detection, we decide whether there exists $\tau \in \bigoplus_{i=0}^{n-1} T_i$, such that $e(z \oplus \tau) \neq 0$.

In the case of error location, we compute the *error locator*

$$l(t) = 1 - \delta_{0,e(t)}, \qquad (10.8.20)$$

for all $t \in z \oplus \bigoplus_{i=0}^{n-1} T_i$, where

$$\sum_{s \in G} l(s) = \|e\|, \quad G = C_2^m.$$

Notice that these definitions of error detection and error location by memoryless and memory-aided decoding are very similar to the corresponding definitions of error detection and error correction by systems of orthogonal equality checks (see Section 10.2.6).

The main difference is that in the case of inequality checks, for every z syndrome, $S^{(e)}(z)$ is a binary vector, and instead of computing the error $e(z)$, we compute the error locator $l(z)$ as in (10.8.20).

The following results have been proven in Section 10.2.6 for n orthogonal equality checks.

For memoryless decoding

1. All errors with the multiplicity at most n are detected, and there exist errors with the multiplicity $n + 1$ that cannot be detected.
2. All errors with the multiplicity at most $\lfloor n/2 \rfloor$ ($\lfloor a \rfloor$ is the greatest integer less or equal to a) are corrected, and there exist errors with the multiplicity $\lfloor n/2 \rfloor + 1$ that cannot be corrected.

For memory-aided decoding

1. All errors with the multiplicity at most $2^n - 1$ are detected, and there exist errors with the multiplicity 2^n that cannot be corrected.
2. All errors with the multiplicity at most $2^{n-1} - 1$ can be corrected, and there exist errors with the multiplicity 2^{n-1} that cannot be corrected.

We will see in the next section that for memoryless decoding, the error-detecting and the error-locating capabilities of equality and inequality checks are equal.

For memory-aided decoding, the error-detecting capabilities of equality and inequality checks are equal, but the error-locating capability of inequality checks is less than the error-correcting capability of equality checks.

10.8.4 Error-Detecting and Error-Correcting Capabilities of Systems of Orthogonal Inequality Checks

In this section, we will consider the error-detecting and error-locating capabilities of a system of n orthogonal inequality checks (10.8.15) for the cases of memoryless and memory-aided decoding.

Theorem 10.8.1   *For any system of n orthogonal inequality checks, we have for memoryless decoding*

1. *All errors with the multiplicity at most n are detected, and all those with the multiplicity at most $\lfloor n/2 \rfloor$ are located.*
2. *There exist errors with the multiplicity $n + 1$ and $\lfloor n/2 \rfloor + 1$, which are not detected and not located, respectively.*

The proof of this theorem is similar to the corresponding proof of Theorem 10.2.4 for systems of equality checks.

For error locator (10.8.20), we have for memoryless decoding

$$l(z) = \begin{cases} 0, & \text{if } \|S^{(e)}(z)\| \leq \lfloor n/2 \rfloor, \\ 1, & \text{if } \|S^{(e)}(z)\| > \lfloor n/2 \rfloor, \end{cases} \tag{10.8.21}$$

and the location of errors by memoryless decoding may be implemented by the following 1-*step majority decoding procedure*:

1. If $\|S^{(e)}(z)\| = 0$, then $e(t) = 0$ for all $t \in \bigcup_{i=1}^{n}(z \oplus T_i)$.
2. If $1 \leq \|S^{(e)}(z)\| \leq \lceil n/2 \rceil$, then $e(z) = 0$, but there exists $t \neq z$ such that $t \in \bigcup_{i=0}^{n-1}(z \oplus T_i)$ and $e(t) \neq 0$.
3. If $\|S^{(e)}(z)\| > \lceil n/2 \rceil$, then $e(z) \neq 0$.

We also note that for memoryless decoding, a high percentage of errors with the multiplicity greater than n, ($\lfloor n/2 \rfloor$) are detected (located). To illustrate this, we assume, as before, that for every $T \subseteq \{0, 1, \ldots, 2^m - 1\}$ either $\sum_{\tau \in T} e(t) = 0$ or $|\sum_{\tau \in T} e(t)| > 2\epsilon$.

For any error e with the multiplicity l, such that $e(z) \neq 0$, there exists $z_{ij} \in z \oplus T_i$, $i = 0, \ldots, n - 1$, such that $e(z_{ij}) \neq 0, (j = 1, \ldots, l_i, \sum_{i=0}^{n-1}(l_i - 1) \leq l - 1)$, and for any $e(z_{ij})$, $(i = 0, \ldots, n - 1, j = 1, \ldots l_i - 1)$, there exists at most one $e(z_i, l_i)$ such that

$$\sum_{\tau \in T_i} e(z \oplus \tau) = \sum_{j=1}^{l_i} e(z_{ij}) = \sum_{j=1}^{l_i-1} e(z_{i,j}) + e(z_{i,l_i}) = 0, \tag{10.8.22}$$

for $i = 0, \ldots, n - 1$.

If M is the number of bits in the binary representation of $f(z)$ (or $e(z) = 0$), then the fraction of errors satisfying (10.8.22) for any given $i \in \{0, \ldots n - 1\}$ is at most $(2^M - 1)^{-1}$.

Thus, in view of the orthogonality of checks and Theorem 10.8.1, we have for the fractions $\hat{\eta}_d(l)$ or $\hat{\eta}_L(l)$ of errors with the multiplicity l, which cannot be detected or located by n orthogonal checks for memoryless decoding

$$\hat{\eta}_d(l) \leq \begin{cases} 0, & l \leq n, \\ (2^M - 1)^{-n}, & l > n \end{cases} \tag{10.8.23}$$

$$\hat{\eta}_L(l) \leq \begin{cases} 0, & l \leq \lfloor n/2 \rfloor, \\ (2^M - 1)^{-\lfloor n/2 \rfloor}, & l > \lfloor n/2 \rfloor. \end{cases} \tag{10.8.24}$$

If the original function $f(z)$ is computed by a polynomial approximation $f(z) \cong P(z)$, or by a rational approximation $f(z) \cong P(z)/Q(z)$, or by a continued-fraction approximation $f(z) = P_1(z)/Q_1(z) + P_2(z)/Q_2(z) + \cdots + P_t(z)/Q_t(z)$, and an error with the multiplicity l results in the replacement of l coefficients in some of these polynomials by constants (see Section 10.8.2), then, using a similar proof, we have for errors in the coefficients in these polynomials

$$\hat{\eta}_d(l) < (2^M - 1)^{-n} \quad \text{for all } l > 1,$$
$$\hat{\eta}_L(l) \geq (2^M - 1)^{-\lfloor n/2 \rfloor}, \text{ for all } l > 1, \tag{10.8.25}$$
$$\hat{\eta}_d(1) = \eta_L(1) = 0,$$

where, in this case, M is the number of bits in the binary representation of the coefficients.

We shall now consider the error-detecting and error-locating capabilities of a system of n orthogonal inequality checks for the case of memory-aided decoding.

For any binary vector $\sigma = (\sigma_0, \ldots, \sigma_{n-1}) \in \{0, 1\}^n$, we denote

$$M(\sigma) = \bigoplus_{i=0}^{n-1} \sigma_i(T_i - 0^m) = \left\{ \bigoplus_{i=0}^{n-1} \sigma_i \tau_i \right\},$$

where $\tau_i \in T_i - 0^m$, $\sigma_i \tau_i = \tau_i$, if $\sigma_i = 1$, and $\sigma_i \tau_i = 0^m$, if $\sigma_i = 0$.

Utilizing conditions similar to those described in Section 10.2.6, we also require that for any $\alpha, \beta \in \{0, 1\}^n$, $(\alpha \neq \beta)$,

$$M(\alpha) \cap M(\beta) = \emptyset, \tag{10.8.26}$$

where $\emptyset$ is the empty set.

Theorem 10.8.2 *For any system of n inequality checks satisfying (10.8.26), we have for memory-aided decoding*

1. *All errors with the multiplicity at most $2^n - 1$ are detected.*
2. *There exist errors with the multiplicity 2^n that are not detected.*
3. *All errors with the multiplicity at most n are located.*
4. *There exist errors with the multiplicity $n + 1$ that are not located.*

Proof. Proofs for (1) and (2) are similar to the proof of Theorem 10.2.5.

To prove (3) we note that for any two errors e_1 and e_2 with different locators (see (10.8.20)), there exists $z \in C_2^m$ such that

$$e_1(z) = 0, \quad |e_2(z)| > 2\epsilon. \tag{10.8.27}$$

Denote

$$L_j(\sigma) = \begin{cases} 1, & \text{if there exists } \tau_\sigma \in z \oplus M(\sigma) \\ & \text{such that } |e_j(z \oplus \tau_\sigma)| > 2\epsilon, \\ 0, & \text{otherwise,} \end{cases} \qquad (10.8.28)$$

where $j = 1, 2$.

Since $\|e_1\|, \|e_2\| \leq n$, we have

$$|\{\sigma | L_1(\sigma) = L_2(\sigma) = 1\}| < n.$$

Thus, there exist $\alpha, \beta \in C_2^n$ and $i \in \{0, 1, \ldots, n-1\}$ such that

$$\begin{cases} M(\alpha) = M(\beta) \oplus \{T_i - 0^m\}, \\ L_1(\alpha) = L_2(\alpha) = 0, \\ L_1(\beta) \neq L_2(\beta). \end{cases} \qquad (10.8.29)$$

Then, by (10.8.28) and (10.8.29), there exists $\tau_\beta \in z \oplus M(\beta)$, such that we have for locators l_1 and l_2 of e_1 and e_2

$$l_1(z \oplus \tau_\beta) \neq l_2(z \oplus \tau_\beta). \qquad (10.8.30)$$

For any $\tau \in T_i - 0^m$, it follows from (10.8.29) that

$$e_1(z \oplus \tau_\beta \oplus \tau) = e_2(z \oplus \tau_\beta \oplus \tau) = 0, \qquad (10.8.31)$$

and we have from (10.8.29) and (10.8.31)

$$\sum_{\tau \in T_i} e_j(z \oplus \tau_\beta \oplus \tau) = e_j(z \oplus \tau_\beta), \quad j = 1, 2. \qquad (10.8.32)$$

Thus, we finally have from (10.8.30) and (10.8.32)

$$S_i^{(e_1)}(z \oplus \tau_\beta) \neq S_i^{(e_2)}(z \oplus \tau_\beta).$$

Consequently, all errors with the multiplicity at most n are located.

To prove (4), we now construct two errors e_1 and e_2 such that $\|e_1\| = n + 1$, $\|e_1\| \neq \|e_2\|$, but $S^{(e_1)}(z) = S^{(e_2)}(z)$ for all $z \in G = C_2^m$.

Let us fix arbitrarily $\tau_i \in T_i - 0^m$, $(i = 1, \ldots, n-1)$, and set

$$e_1(z) = \begin{cases} 3\epsilon, & z \in \{0^m, \tau_0, \ldots, \tau_{n-1}\}, \\ 0, & \text{otherwise,} \end{cases} \qquad (10.8.33)$$

$$e_2(z) = \begin{cases} 3\epsilon, & z \in \{\tau_0, \ldots, \tau_{n-1}\}, \\ 0, & \text{otherwise.} \end{cases}$$

Then, $l_1(0^m) = 1, l_2(0^m) = 0$, where $e_1(z)$ and $e_2(z)$ are locators of $e_1(z)$ and $e_2(z)$, $\|e_1\| = n + 1$, $\|e_2\| = n$, and we have

$$S^{(e_1)}(z) = S^{(e_2)}(z) \tag{10.8.34}$$

$$= \begin{cases} 1^m, & z \in \{0^m, \tau_0, \ldots, \tau_{n-1}\}, \\ 0^{i-1}10^{n-i}, & z \in \{T_i - 0^m - \tau_i\} \\ & \quad \cup \bigcup_{j \neq i}\{\tau_j \oplus \{T_i - 0^m - \tau_i\}\}, \\ 0^{i-1}10^{j-i-1}10^{n-i-j}, & z = \tau_i \oplus \tau j, \\ 0^n & \text{otherwise,} \end{cases}$$

and errors e_1 and e_2 defined by (10.8.33) cannot be located.

Theorems 10.8.1 and 10.8.2 and formulas (10.8.22–10.8.24) illustrate the very high error-detecting and error-locating capabilities of systems of orthogonal inequality checks.

We note that proofs of Theorems 10.8.1 and 10.8.2 may easily be generalized to the case when the group G of all inputs z is an arbitrary (not necessarily Abelian) finite group (e.g., z is represented in decimal form and $\oplus$ is the componentwise addition mod 10 of decimal numbers, or z is a permutation and $\oplus$ is the superposition of permutations).

The error-detecting and error-locating capabilities of a system of n orthogonal inequality checks do not depend on the group G or on the choice of the checking subgroups $T_0, \ldots, T_{n-1}$.

The error-detecting capability increases exponentially on transition from memoryless decoding to memory-aided decoding, as in the case of equality checks (see Section 10.2.6), whereas the error-locating capability of inequality checks increases only by the factor of two with this transition.

Note also that for inequality checks, the error-detecting capability of memoryless decoding is equal to the error-locating capability of memory-aided decoding.

Using the approach described in Sections 10.3 and 10.4, it can be shown that the hardware complexity of n inequality checks (defined as the minimum number of 2-input gates necessary to implement networks for the syndrome computation and for the decoding of the syndrome) increases about linearly with increasing n for memoryless decoding and exponentially for memory-aided decoding. For memory-aided decoding, n-bit memory cells are needed for storing a set of syndromes

$$\left\{ S^{(e)}(z \oplus \tau) | \tau \in \bigoplus_{i=0}^{n-1} T_i \right\},$$

where

$$S^{(e)}(z \oplus \tau) = (S_0^{(e)}(z \oplus \tau), \ldots, S_{n-1}^{(e)}(z \oplus \tau)), \quad S_i^{(e)}(z \oplus \tau) \in \{0, 1\}.$$

For error detection, the syndromes have to be computed for every $z \in G / \bigoplus_{i=0}^{n-1} T_i$, and for error location for all $z \in G$. Thus, for memory-aided decoding, the error-locating procedure is at least $\prod_{i=0}^{n-1} |T_i|$ times more complex than the error-detecting procedure.

Combining these results with Theorems 10.8.1 and 10.8.2, we note that it is expedient, from the practical point of view, to use memoryless decoding for error location (all errors with the multiplicity at most $\lfloor n/2 \rfloor$ are located, and $e(z) \neq 0$ iff $\|S^{(e)}(z)\| > \lfloor n/2 \rfloor$), and to use memory-aided decoding for error detection (all errors with the multiplicity at most $2^n - 1$ are detected, and $e(z \oplus \tau) = 0$, for all $\tau \in \bigoplus_{i=0}^{n-1} T_i$ iff $S^{(e)}(z \oplus \tau) = 0$ for all $\tau \in \bigoplus_{i=0}^{n-1} T_i$).

Consider now memoryless and memory-aided decoding for the special case of two orthogonal inequality check ($n = 2$), which is of a practical interest.

It follows from Theorems 10.8.1 and 10.8.2 that in this case

1. All single and double errors are detected and all single errors are located by the memoryless decoding.
2. All single, double, and triple errors are detected, and all single and double errors are located by the memory-aided decoding.

For memoryless decoding, we have in this case

1. If $\|S^{(e)}(z)\| = 0$, then $e(t) = 0$ for all $t \in \{z \oplus T_1\} \cup \{z \oplus T_2\}$.
2. If $\|S^{(e)}(z)\| = 1$, then $e(z) = 0$, but there exists $t \in \{z \oplus T_1\} \cup \{z \oplus T_2\}, t \neq z$, such that $l(t) = 1$.
3. If $\|S^{(e)}(z)\| = 2$, then $|e(z)| > 2\epsilon$ and $l(z) = 1$.

Suppose that $|T_1| \geq |T_2|$. Then, for detection of all single and double errors by memoryless decoding, it is sufficient to compute syndromes $S^{(e)}(z)$ only for all $z \in G/T_1$, where G/T_1 is the set of coset representatives of the subgroup T_1. Note also that if we compute $S^{(e)}(z)$ for all $z \in G$, then we can locate all single errors by memoryless decoding and detect all single, double, and triple errors by memory-aided decoding.

Applications of the error-detecting and error-locating techniques described in this section to memory testing will be discussed in Section 10.9.

10.9 ERROR DETECTION IN COMPUTER MEMORIES BY LINEAR CHECKS

10.9.1 Testing of Read-Only Memories

In this section we consider the problems of error detection, location, and correction for Read-Only Memories by systems of orthogonal checks. It is well known that memory testing is one of the bottlenecks in the computer industry.

The errors we shall consider may result from a wrong masking in ROM, faults in cells and the address decoder, and bridging between cells and wrong decoding of an address.

To solve these problems, we shall use the techniques developed in Sections 10.2 and 10.7. These techniques are based on error-correcting codes, Walsh transforms, and least-absolute-error polynomial approximations.

Let $z = (z_0, \ldots, z_{m-1})$, $(z_i \in \{0, 1\})$ be an address of the cell containing the data $f(z)$. We denote by G the set of all binary m-vectors, and we shall consider G as a group with respect to the operation $\oplus$ of componentwise addition mod 2.

In Section 10.2, the methods of error detection based on linear equality checks,

$$\sum_{\tau \in T_i} f(z \oplus \tau) - d_i = 0, \tag{10.9.1}$$

for every $z \in \{0, 1, \ldots, 2^m - 1\}$, $i = 0, 1, \ldots, n - 1$, have been developed.

In (10.9.1), T_i is a subgroup of G and d_i is a constant.

The verification of whether (10.9.1) is satisfied constitutes the error-detection method. In the case $T = G$, the check is the well known control-sum check (269).

Methods of error detection based on linear equality checks may be effectively used in the case where $f(z)$ is an integer for every $z \in \{0, 1, \ldots, 2^m - 1\}$, but very few noninteger functions have nontrivial checks of this type. To overcome this difficulty, we are going to use the following inequality checks for error detection in the case of noninteger computations

$$\left| \sum_{\tau \in T_i} f(z \oplus \tau) - d_i \right| \leq \epsilon \tag{10.9.2}$$

for every $z \in \{0, 1, \ldots, 2^m - 1\}$, $i = 0, 1, \ldots, n - 1$, where T_i is a subgroup of G, d_i is a constant, and $\epsilon \geq 0$ is a small constant. The general properties of a minimal check set $T = T(f, \epsilon)$ for a given function f and ϵ, methods of construction for these minimal check sets, the advantages and limitations of inequality checks, and their error-detecting capability were considered in Sections 10.7–10.8.4.

In this section we shall use systems of equality and inequality checks for error-detection, error-location, and error-correction in memories.

The testing methods proposed in this section may be used for manufacturing quality control and for maintenance testing of ROMs and RAMs.

We attribute an error $e(z)$ to our memory if the latter yields $f(z) + e(z)$ instead of $f(z)$, that is, as before, we are using an additive functional description of errors.

By the multiplicity of an error $e(z)$, we mean the number of nonzero values of the error function $e(z)$, which is a number of cells containing distorted data. Thus, an error with a multiplicity l appears in a memory as a result of a wrong masking or stuck-at faults in l cells, wrong decoding of l addresses, and so on.

10.9.2 Correction of Single and Double Errors in ROMs by Two Orthogonal Equality Checks

Syndromes of errors

Suppose we have a memory containing the value $f(z)$ in a cell with the address z, where f is the given integer function and z is a binary vector with m components.

Suppose we have a system of two linear orthogonal equality checks for f

$$\sum_{\tau \in T_i} f(z \oplus \tau) - d_i = 0, \quad i = 1, 2, \tag{10.9.3}$$

for all $z \in G = C_2^m$, where T_i is a subgroup of G, d_i is a constant, and

$$T_1 \cap T_2 = 0^m = \underbrace{(0, \ldots, 0)}_{m}.$$

Methods for the construction of optimal linear equality checks were described in Section 10.2.

Error detection and error correction are carried out by analyzing results of the check (10.9.3). We say that the result $S(z) = (S_1(z), S_2(z))$ of the check (10.9.3) is the syndrome of the error $e(z)$, where

$$S_i(z) = \sum_{\tau \in T_i} (f(z \oplus \tau) + e(z \oplus \tau)) - d_i = \sum_{\tau \in T_i} e(z \oplus \tau), \quad i = 1, 2. \tag{10.9.4}$$

By error correction, we mean computation of the error function $e(z)$ by the syndrome $S(z)$.

In this section, we shall discuss the techniques for the correction of single and double errors and the detection of multiple errors by the analysis of the syndrome $S(z) = (S_1(z), S_2(z))$.

It was proven in Section 10.2.6 that, theoretically, it is possible to detect all single, double, and triple errors, and correct all single errors by two orthogonal linear checks using a rather complicated memory-aided decoding technique. In this section, we shall describe a simple algorithm that will correct all single errors and almost all double errors by two orthogonal linear checks. We shall also discuss, in this section, the complexity of this algorithm (the number of READ operations required for its implementation) and its error-correcting capabilities.

Algorithm for correction of single and double errors

Now let us describe the algorithm for the correction of single and double errors by two orthogonal checks (10.9.3).

For a single error in a cell with the address z_1 and magnitude $e(z_1)$, we have

$$e(z) = \delta_{z,z_1} e(z_1), \tag{10.9.5}$$

where $\delta_{z,x}$ is the Kronecker delta. In this case, we have

$$S_1(z_1) = S_2(z_1) = e(z_1), \tag{10.9.6}$$

and for any $z \neq z_1$, at least one of the components of $(S_1(z), S_2(z))$ is equal to 0.

Let us consider now the problem of correction of double errors by the checks (10.9.3).

For a double error in cells with addresses z_1, and z_2

$$e(z) = \delta_{z,z_1} e(z_1) + \delta_{z,z_2} e(z_2), \tag{10.9.7}$$

we suppose that if

$$z_1, z_2 \in \tau \oplus T_1 \oplus T_2 = \{\tau \oplus t_1 \oplus t_2 | t_1 \in T_1, t_2 \in T_2\},$$

for some $\tau \in G$ (otherwise $e(z)$ may not be corrected), then

$$|e(z_1)| \neq |e(z_2)|. \tag{10.9.8}$$

At the first step in the error-correction procedure, we find $v \in G$ such that $S_1(v) \neq 0$ and $S_2(v) \neq 0$ (this v always exists in the case of double errors since we can choose $v = z_1$).

Denote by G/T_1 the set of coset representatives of the subgroup T_1 in G. To find $v \in G$ such that $S_1(v) \neq 0$ and $S_2(v) \neq 0$, we shall first find $x \in G/T_1$ such that $S_1(x) \neq 0$ and then find $v \in x \oplus T_1 = \{x \oplus t | t \in T_1\}$ such that $S_2(v) \neq 0$.

At the second step (after we have already found $v \in x \oplus T_1$ such that $S_1(v) = S_1(x) \neq 0$, $S_2(v) \neq 0$), we are looking for $w \in x \oplus T_1$ such that $S_2(w) \neq 0$, $(w \neq v)$.

1. If there is no such w, then the following two cases may occur:
   (a) If $S_1(v) = S_2(v)$, then there exists $v' \in y \oplus T_1$, $x \neq y$ such that $S_1(v') \neq 0$, $S_2(v') \neq 0$. In this case, $z_1 = v$, $e(z_1) = S_1(v)$, $S_1(v') = S_2(v')$ (if this condition is not satisfied, then there is an error with a multiplicity at least three), $z_2 = v'$ and $e(z_2) = S_1(v')$. This situation is illustrated by Fig. 10.9.1a and the cosets of T_1 and T_2 are represented by segments). Note that from the orthogonality of T_1 and T_2, we have for any $x \in G$ and any $v \in x \oplus T_1$ that $|x \oplus T_1 \cap v \oplus T_2| = 1$.
   (b) If $S_1(v) \neq S_2(v)$ (see Fig. 10.9.1b), then in view of (10.9.8), $z_1 = v$, $e(z_1) = S_1(v)$, and there exists $v' \oplus T_2$ such that $e(v') \neq 0$ and $z_2 = v'$. (This $v' = z_2$

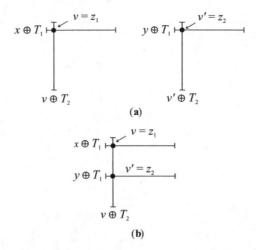

FIGURE 10.9.1 Correction of double errors $e(z) = \delta_{z,z_1} e(z_1) + \delta_{z,z_2} e(z_2)$, case 1, solid dots indicate error locations, horizontal and vertical lines represent cosets with respect to T_1 and T_2, respectively.

and $e(z_2)$ will be computed at a later step of the algorithm, since $S_1(v') \neq 0$, $S_2(v') \neq 0$, $S_1(v') \neq S_2(v')$, and $e(z_2) = S_1(v')$.)

2. If there exists $w \neq v$ such that $w \in x \oplus T_1$, and $S_2(w) \neq 0$, then in view of (10.9.8), only the following three cases may occur:

(a) If $S_1(v) = S_2(v) \neq S_2(w)$ (see Fig. 10.9.2a), then $z_1 = v$, $e(z_1) = S_1(v)$, and there exists $w' \in w \oplus T_2$, $(w \neq w')$ such that $e(w') \neq 0$, and $z_2 = w'$, and $e(z_2)$ will be computed at a later step of the algorithm.

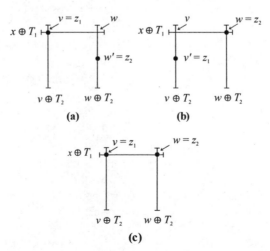

FIGURE 10.9.2 Correction of double error $e(z) = \delta_{z,z_1} e(z_1) + \delta_{z,z_2} e(z_2)$, case 2, solid dots indicate error locations.

(b) If $S_1(v) \neq S_2(v)$, $S_1(v) = S_2(w)$ (see Fig. 10.9.2b), then $z_2 = w$, $e(z_2) = S_1(w) = S_1(v)$, and there exists $v' \in v \oplus T_2(v' \neq v)$ such that $e(v') \neq 0$ and $z_1 = v'$.

(c) If $S_1(v) \neq S_2(v)$, $S_1(v) \neq S_2(w)$ (see Fig. 10.9.2c), then $z_1 = v$, $e(z_1) = S_2(v)$, $z_2 = w$, and $e(z_2) = S_2(w)$.

Complexity of error correction

We shall now estimate the time for correction of single and double errors by the number N of READ operations,

1. If there is no error, then

$$N = N_0 = |G| = 2^m. \tag{10.9.9}$$

2. If there is a single error, then

$$N = N_1 \leq 2^m + |T_1| \times |T_2| \leq 2 \times 2^m. \tag{10.9.10}$$

3. If there is a double error, then

$$N = N_2 \leq 2^m + 2|T_1| \times |T_2| \leq 3 \times 2^m. \tag{10.9.11}$$

The block diagram of the algorithm for corrections of single and double errors by two orthogonal equality checks is given in Fig. 10.9.3.

Denote by P_i the probability of an error with the multiplicity i ($P_0 + P_1 + P_2 = 1$, we suppose that for any $i > 2$, $P_i = 0$).

Thus, we have for the expected number N of READ operations

$$\overline{N} = P_0 N_0 + P_1 N_1 + P_2 N_2 \leq 2^m + |T_1| \times |T_2|(P_1 + 2P_2). \tag{10.9.12}$$

As a weaker upper bounder for $\overline{N}$, one can use the formula

$$\overline{N} \leq 2^m(1 + P_1 + 2P_2). \tag{10.9.13}$$

Error-correcting capability of two orthogonal checks

Let us describe now an error-correcting capability of two orthogonal linear equality checks.

First, we note that all single errors are corrected by the algorithm in Fig. 10.9.3. All double errors satisfying (10.9.8) are also corrected by this algorithm.

Denote by M the number of bits in a memory word. Then, for the large M, we have the following estimation of the probability $P^c(2)$ of the correction of double errors

$$P^c(2) \geq 1 - |T_1| \times |T_2| 2^{-m-M}. \tag{10.9.14}$$

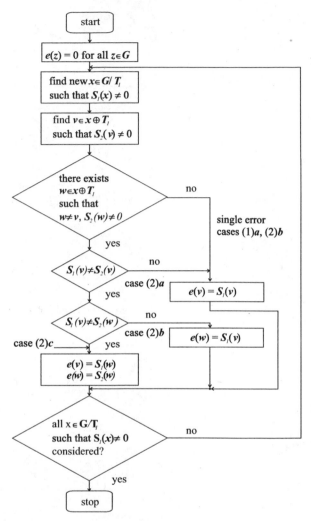

FIGURE 10.9.3 Block diagram of the algorithm for the correction of single and double errors by two orthogonal equality checks.

In the case when a double error results in a distortion of data in two binary cells (bitwise errors), we have to replace 2^m by $2m$ in (10.9.14).

Formula (10.9.14) illustrates the good error-capability of two orthogonal checks. It also follows from (10.9.14) that to maximize the error-correcting capability, we have to choose T_1 and T_2 for the given $f(z)$ with the minimal $|T_1| \times |T_2|$. This will also provide with the minimal complexity of the error-correcting procedure (see (10.9.9)–(10.9.14)).

Results of the computer experiments illustrating a high error correcting capability of this algorithm are given in Tables 10.9.1 and 10.9.2. Here, $P^c(l)$ is the percentage of errors with the multiplicity l corrected by the algorithm. In these experiments, first

TABLE 10.9.1   Error-Correcting Capability of Two Checks.

	$P^c(l)$				
Function $f(z) = f(z_1, z_2)$	$z_1 + z_2$	$z_1 - z_2$	$z_1 z_2$	$z - 1$	$z^2 - z - 1$
l					
2	100	100	100	100	100
3	99.90	99.90	97.00	99.93	58.06
4	99.90	99.90	88.86	99.90	23.46
5	99.33	99.26	76.43	99.56	6.36

Results of computer experiments on error-correcting capability of two orthogonal equality checks ($M = m = 8$), for every l and every $f(z)$, 3000 experiments have been made to estimate $P^c(l)$.

we write in the RAM $f(z)$ ($f(z)$ are the data written in a cell with the address z), then randomly generate locations and magnitudes of errors, distort correspondingly the data, and estimate the percentage of errors that are corrected by the algorithm.

Table 10.9.2 represents experimental results on error-correcting capability $P^c(l)$ for the special case when an error with the multiplicity l distorts data in l binary cells of the RAM (bitwise errors). For every $f(z)$ and every $l \in \{2, 3, 4, 5\}$, 3×10^3 computer experiments have been made to compute $P^c(l)$.

10.10 LOCATION OF ERRORS IN ROMs BY TWO ORTHOGONAL INEQUALITY CHECKS

Binary syndromes of errors

The error-correcting procedure described in Section 10.9.2 may be effectively used in the case where all values of a given function $f(z)$ that are stored in the memory are integers, since very few noninteger functions have nontrivial *equality* checks.

TABLE 10.9.2   Error-Correcting Capability of Two Checks for Bitwise Errors.

	$P^c(l)$				
Function $f(z) = f(z_1, z_2)$	$z_1 + z_2$	$z_1 - z_2$	$z_1 z_2$	$z - 1$	$z^2 - z - 1$
l					
2	99.93	99.83	99.13	99.83	98.50
3	99.70	99.53	94.93	99.46	54.63
4	99.43	99.13	84.96	99.08	20.96
5	98.70	98.60	71.43	98.43	6.26

Results of computer experiments on error-correcting capability of two orthogonal equality checks ($M = m = 8$), for every l and every $f(z)$, 3000 experiments have been made to estimate $P^c(l)$).

In this section, we shall use two orthogonal *inequality* checks,

$$|\sum_{\tau \in T_i} f(z \oplus \tau) - d_i| \le \epsilon, \quad i = 1, 2, \quad \text{for all } z \in G. \tag{10.10.1}$$

Here $T_1 \cap T_2 = 0^m$.

Denote by $l(z)$ the error-locating function (error locator) for the error $e(z)$, where

$$l(z) = 1 - \delta_{e(z),0}. \tag{10.10.2}$$

Thus, $l(z) = 1$ if there is an error in the cell with the address z.

By error location we mean computation of $l(z)$ by the binary syndrome $S(z) = (S_1(z), S_2(z))$, where

$$S_i(z) = \begin{cases} 0, & \text{if } |\sum_{\tau \in T_i}(f(z \oplus \tau) + e(z \oplus \tau)) - d_i| \le \epsilon, (i = 1, 2), \\ 1, & \text{otherwise.} \end{cases} \tag{10.10.3}$$

Error location is carried out by analysis of the syndrome $S(z)$ defined by (10.10.3).

Algorithm for error location

It was shown in Section 10.8.4 that using two orthogonal inequality checks and memory-aided decoding procedure, it is possible to detect all single, double, and triple errors, and locate all single errors. In this section, we shall describe a simple algorithm that will locate all single errors and almost all double errors by two orthogonal inequality checks. Again, we suppose that for the double errors, the condition (10.9.8) is satisfied.

First, as in the algorithm described in Section 10.9.2, we shall find $x \in G/T_1$ such that $S_1(x) = 1$, and $v \in x \oplus T_1$ such that $S_1(v) = S_2(v) = 1$ (this v always exists if there is at least one error).

Next, we check whether there exists $w \in x \oplus T_1$, such that $S_2(w) = 1$.

If there is no such w, (Fig. 10.9.1a, b), then there is an error in the cell with the address v and we set $l(v) = 1$.

If there exists $w \in x \oplus T_1$, $w \ne v$, $S_2(w) = 1$, then we check whether there exists $v' \in v \oplus T_2$, $(v' \ne v)$, such that $S_1(v') = 1$. If such a v' exists, (Fig. 10.9.2b), then we set $l(v') = 1, l(w) = 1$.

If there is no such v', then we check whether there exists $w' \in w \oplus T_2$, $w' \ne w$, such that $S_1(w') = 1$. If such a w' exists (Fig. 10.9.2a), then we set $l(v) = 1, l(w') = 1$.

If for any $v' \ne v$, $v' \in v \oplus T_2$, $w' \ne w$, $w' \in w \oplus T_2$, we have $S_1(v') = 0$ and $S_1(w') = 0$ (Fig. 10.9.2c), then we set $l(v) = 1, l(w) = 1$.

The block diagram of the algorithm for the location of single and double errors by inequality checks is shown in Fig. 10.10.1.

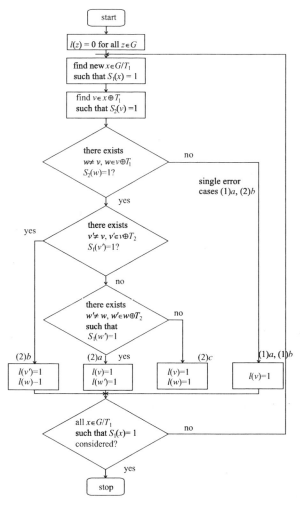

FIGURE 10.10.1 Block diagram of the algorithm for the location of single and double errors by two orthogonal inequality checks.

Complexity of error location

For the number N_i of READ operations in the case of errors with multiplicity i, $(i = 0, 1, 2)$, we have

$$N_0 = 2^m,$$
$$N_1 \leq 2^m + |T_1| \times |T_1|, \qquad (10.10.4)$$
$$N_2 \leq 2^m + 3|T_1| \times |T_2|,$$

and, for the expected number of $\overline{N}$ of READ operations,

$$\overline{N} \leq 2^m + |T_1| \times |T_2|(P_1 + 3P_2) \leq 2^m(1 + P_1 + 3P_2). \qquad (10.10.5)$$

TABLE 10.10.1   Error-Locating Capabilities of Two Orthogonal Inequality.

$f(y)$	m	q	$P^L(2)$	$P^L(3)$	$P^L(4)$	$P^L(5)$
$\frac{1}{\sqrt{y}} \sin\left(\frac{\pi}{2}\sqrt{y}\right)$	12	9	99.9	99.6	99.3	99.0
$\cos\left(\frac{\pi}{4}\sqrt{y}\right)$	12	4	97.0	84.0	72.5	56.0
$\left(\frac{\pi}{2} - \sin^{-1} y\right)\sqrt{1-y}$	15	3	94.4	66.8	42.3	22.0

$q = m - \log_2 |T_1| - \log_2 |T_2|$
Results of computer experiments on error-locating capabilities of two orthogonal inequality checks (an error with multiplicity l distorts data in l memory cells, $M = m$, $y = 2^{-m}z$, $z \in \{0, 1, \ldots, 2^m - 1\}$) for every l and every $f(y)$, 3000 experiments have been made to estimate $P_L(l)$).

Here P_1 and P_2 are probabilities of single and double errors.

Comparing (10.9.12), (10.9.13), and (10.10.4), we can see that the transition from equality to inequality checks results in an increase by $P_2|T_1| \times |T_2|$ of the expected number of READ operations.

To estimate the error-locating capability of two orthogonal inequality checks, we suppose that, as in Section 10.7, for every $T \subseteq \{0, 1, \ldots, 2^m - 1\}$ either

$$\sum_{z \in T} e(z) = 0,$$

or

$$\left|\sum_{z \in T} e(z)\right| > 2\epsilon.$$

Notice that the last condition may be used for the choice of ϵ for practical applications.

Then, all single errors are located by the algorithm illustrated by Fig. 10.10.1, and, similarly to the case of equality checks, the probability of the location of double errors is at least $1 - |T_1| \times |T_2|2^{-m-M}$.

Experimental estimations on probabilities $P^L(l)$ of location for errors with the multiplicity l by the algorithm of Fig. 10.10.1 are given in Table 10.10.1 for memories containing tables of several functions $f(y) = f(z \cdot 2^{-m})$.

In this table, $y = z2^{-m}$, $M = m$, $z \in \{0, 1, \ldots, 2^m - 1\}$ and 3×10^3 experiments with randomly generated locations and magnitudes of errors have been made to compute probabilities of correct location $P_L(l)$ of errors of the multiplicity l for every $l = 2, 3, 4, 5$ and every $f(z)$.

10.11 DETECTION AND LOCATION OF ERRORS IN RANDOM-ACCESS MEMORIES

Testing of a RAM

All the previous techniques based on linear checks can be used for error detection, location, or correction in a *Random-Access Memory*.

To implement this, we first have to choose the function $f(z)$ that we write in the RAM. Since the expected testing time $\overline{N}$ for linear equality or inequality checks increases linearly with the increase of $|T_1| \times |T_2|$ (see (10.9.12), (10.9.13)), or (10.10.5)), it is expedient for these checks to choose $f(z)$ in such a way that $|T_1| \times |T_2|$ will be minimal. This will provide also the maximal error-correcting (locating) capability of checks (see (10.9.14)).

After choosing $f(z)$, we have to construct the corresponding checks for this $f(z)$ using the techniques from Section 10.2 or 10.7. Next, for any $z \in \{0, 1, \ldots, 2^m - 1\}$, where m is the number of bits in an address, we write in a cell with an address z the value $f(z)$. After this we scan out the memory and compute a syndrome (see (10.9.4), (10.10.3)). Then we detect, locate, or correct errors by the analysis of a computed syndrome using the algorithms described in previous sections. If the implementation of a decoding algorithm analyzing a computed syndrome requires N READ operations, then the total number of READ and WRITE operations for a testing of a RAM is $N + 2^m$.

Complexity and error-detecting capability

Comparing the decoding algorithms represented in Figs. 10.9.3 and 10.10.1, we can see that both algorithms have about the same running time, but the linear equality checks algorithm (Fig. 10.9.3) have the maximal error-correcting capability. Thus, it is expedient to use orthogonal linear equality checks for RAMs testing.

The best choice of $f(z)$ to minimize $|T_1| \times |T_2|$ for equality checks is $f(z) = c$, where c is a constant for all $z \in G$, but in this case we cannot detect, locate or correct errors in the address decoder or bridgings between cells.

The next best choice to provide error correction for decoding errors is to choose $f(z)$ as a linear function, for example,

$$f(z) = f_1(z) = 2^{m-M} \left(\frac{2^m - 1}{2} - z \right),$$

where M is the number of bits in a memory word, $M \geq m$. In this case, we minimize $|T_1| \times |T_2|$, thus, minimizing the number of READ operations (see (10.9.10) and (10.9.12)) and maximizing the error-correcting capability of equality checks (see (10.9.14)). To correct all single stuck-at errors in memory cells, we have also to repeat our procedure for

$$f(z) = f_2(z) = 2^M - 1 - 2^{M-m} \left(\frac{2^m - 1}{2} - z \right),$$

(for any z, the binary representation of $f_2(z)$ is the componentwise negation of the corresponding representation for $f_1(z)$). For

$$f_1(z) = 2^{M-m} \left(\frac{2^m - 1}{2} - z \right),$$

it is expedient to use the following orthogonal equality checks with $|T_1| = 2$ and $|T_2| = 4$,

$$f_1(z) + f_1(z \oplus 1^m) = 0, \quad 1^m = (\underbrace{1, 1, \ldots, 1}_{m}), \tag{10.11.1}$$

$$f_1(z) + f_1(z \oplus 101^{m-2}) + f_1(z \oplus 011^{m-2}) + f_1(z \oplus 110^{m-2}) = 0.$$

For $f_2(z) = 2^M - 1 - f_1(z)$, we can use the same T_1 and T_2 as for $f_1(z)$, and we have the following two checks:

$$f_2(z) + f_2(z \oplus 1^m) = 2(2^m - 1), \tag{10.11.2}$$

and

$$f_2(z) + f_2(z \oplus 101^{m-2}) + f_2(z \oplus 011^{m-2}) + f_2(z \oplus 110^{m-2}) = 4(2^m - 1).$$

For the expected number N of READ and WRITE operations for the correction of single and double errors in a RAM, we have, from (10.9.12), (10.11.1), and (10.11.2)

$$\overline{N} \leq 2(2^{m+1} + 8(P_1 + 2P_2)) \simeq 2^{m+2}, \tag{10.11.3}$$

and for the probability $P^c(2)$ of the correction of double errors, we have, from (10.9.14),

$$P^c(2) \geq 1 - 2^{-M-m+3}. \tag{10.11.4}$$

If we are interested only in the error detection, but not the error correction, we again can use the same two orthogonal checks for $f_1(z)$ and $f_2(z)$. In this case, we have to check whether $S_1(z) \neq 0$ for at least one $z \in G/T_1$ or $S_2(z) \neq 0$ for at least one $z \in G/T_2$. This will require $N = 2^{m+2}$ READ and WRITE operations. By doing this we shall detect all single and double errors, and for a probability $P^d(l)$ of the detection of an error with the multiplicity $l \geq 3$, we have

$$P^d(l) \geq 1 - (2^M - 1)^{-2}. \tag{10.11.5}$$

For bitwise errors, all single and double errors are detected and for $l \geq 3$, we have

$$P^d(l) \geq 1 - (2M - 1)^{-2}. \tag{10.11.6}$$

We note that many stuck-at faults in cells of a RAM and at the outputs of the address decoder and bridging (short circuits) between output lines of the address decoder may result in *unidirectional errors* (269) such that $e(z) \geq 0$ for all z (or $e(z) \leq 0$ for all z). For example, all AND (or OR) bridging between rows in a RAM, errors in address decoders, and faults that affect power supply or READ/WRITE circuits in many cases result in unidirectional errors (269). (Each row in a RAM corresponds to a cell storing a value of $f(z)$.)

All unidirectional errors with any multiplicity will be detected.

Since any bridging between two rows results in a distortion of at most two values of $f(z)$, it follows from (10.11.4) that almost all the bridging will be corrected.

We also note that many errors in the address decoder may be detected and/or corrected by two orthogonal checks. We shall say that there exists an error with the multiplicity l in the address decoder if there exists $z_1 \ldots, z_l \in \{0, 1\}$ such that the output of the RAM is $f(y_i)$ for the address $z_i \neq y_i$, $(i = 1, \ldots, l)$. In this case,

$$e(z) = \sum_{i=1}^{l} \delta_{z,z_i}(f(y_i) - f(z_i)). \tag{10.11.7}$$

Thus, for errors in the address decoder, all single and double errors are detected, all single errors are corrected, and in view of (10.11.4)–(10.11.6), almost all multiple errors are detected and almost all double errors are corrected.

To conclude this section, we note that the complexity of testing (the testing time) for the presented approaches is about the same as the complexity of testing for such well known test procedures as Column bars, Checkboard, Marching 1s and 0s, and for our approaches the test complexity is less than for such procedures as Shifted diagonal, Galloping columns, Walkpat, Galwrec and Galpart (5, 269).

Linear equality checks are efficient for detection or correction of errors in a ROM, when $f(z)$ is an analytical function with integer values. For example, when a ROM is storing the multiplication table, $f(z) = a \cdot b$ is a number stored in a cell with the address $z = (a, b)$.

Equality checks may also be very efficient for detection or correction of errors in a RAM. This approach provides us with detection of all single, double, and triple errors and correction of all single errors. Moreover, almost all double errors and a high percentage of multiple errors can also be corrected. The lower bounds on the probability of the correction of double errors are given by (10.9.14) and (10.9.9). From the computer experiments (see Tables 10.9.1 and 10.9.2), we can see that at least 98.5 of all double errors have been corrected and a high percentage of errors with the multiplicities up to five have also been corrected by equality checks.

Linear inequality checks may be efficiently used for detection or location of errors in a ROM when $f(z)$ is an analytical function with noninteger values. For example, a ROM is storing tables of trigonometrical functions. In this case, it is possible to detect all single, double, and triple errors, and locate all single and almost all double errors. In computer experiments (see Table 10.10.1) at least 94.4% of all double errors also been located and a high percentage of multiple errors have also been located by two inequality checks.

We note that for all the approaches discussed above, probabilities of not detecting (or not locating, or not correcting) of multiple errors decrease exponentially with the increase of a number of bits in a memory word.

BIBLIOGRAPHIC NOTES

Fault models in logic networks are discussed in References 4,121,225, and 422. A very useful discussion of basic principles of testing digital devices can be found in Reference 269. For testable design, see Reference 5. Testing by using Walsh coefficients has been considered in References 398,251,260, and 276. For testing by the Reed–Muller transform, see References 115,116,290,305,332, and 415, and by the arithmetic transform See References 241,242, and 397. For testing by linear checks, see References 280 and 300.

CHAPTER 11

EXAMPLES OF APPLICATIONS AND GENERALIZATIONS OF SPECTRAL METHODS ON LOGIC FUNCTIONS

In preceding chapters, we discussed some particular applications of spectral logics in switching theory (including extensions to multiple-valued functions), circuit synthesis with emphasis to the optimization problems, design of devices with self-error-correction, and testing of digital systems. Main tools were several transforms on finite Abelian groups, primarily the groups were C_2^n and C_p^n and related operators.

Spectral techniques, however, are a more general theory and have interesting and important applications in many other areas, including, for instance, signal and image processing, communications, pattern recognition, system identification and design, as well as in solving certain problems in applied mathematics. These applications are mostly based on the fact that the Walsh transform is the Fourier transform on dyadic groups (6), which has simple implementations both in hardware and in software by binary digital circuits, since the basis functions take values 1 and -1.

In order to illustrate the power of spectral methods in various areas of computing and engineering, this chapter presents a few examples of applications of transforms that are considered in this book, as well as discusses some ways to the extensions and generalizations of spectral methods.

We make no attempt to comprehensively cover the vast field of applications of spectral methods in general. Instead, we try to convey the basic principles behind the power of the methods as well as indicate a few directions to which the standard approaches can be extended.

To compensate the necessary uncomplete coverage, we try to provide an extensive list of related references, where much more information about the considered topics can be found.

The applications of spectral techniques have been extensively reported in the literature, for instance, several monographs in this area used as references to clarify and support the discussions in this book, and references therein (7,8,16,21,22,43, 51,52,62,75,151,215,233,234,235,255,258,282,289,323,353,379,550,555,567,576, 584,587,604,611,617,658,661,663,671,673,675,676).

We start with discussion of transforms tailored to share properties of some other transform to suit better the needs in some particular applications. We use the Hadamard–Haar transform as an example.

This is also an example of application driven transforms, that is, transforms whose basis functions are constructed after analysis of the features of particular applications. The slant transforms, slant-Hadamard and slant-Haar transforms, are used as further examples. The latter has parameterised versions, which provides links to the wavelet transforms. These in turn have connections back to applications in switching theory and logic design through the discrete wavelet packet transforms. These transforms are used for compact representations of multiple-output functions and may be constructed separately for each function after gathering some information about the functions to be represented. We conclude this part with a discussion of Fibonacci transforms defined on Fibonacci interconnection topologies, that have been suggested as an alternative overcoming certain restrictions inherently imposed in Boolean interconnection topologies.

Then, we outline basic theoretical facts necessary for understanding application of spectral methods in image processing and coding as well as introduce a few transforms that have been found particularly efficient in these fields.

To conclude, we briefly discuss the use of the Walsh transform in *Code Division Multiple Access* (CDMA) communication systems.

11.1 TRANSFORMS DESIGNED FOR PARTICULAR APPLICATIONS

In this section, we will discuss examples of discrete spectral transforms that are designed intentionally to meet requirements of a particular application or to serve special purposes.

11.1.1 Hybrid Transforms

Every transform has some good features and certain less advantageous properties when used to solve a particular task. In order to utilize the good features of different transforms, various new transforms have been defined by combining existing transforms in such a way that the new one has their good features and hopefully does not have their less wanted properties.

We will discuss this approach by the example of the *Hadamard–Haar transform*.

11.1.2 Hadamard–Haar Transform

The Hadamard–Haar transform of order r, denoted as HHT_r has been defined recursively by the transform matrix $\mathbf{L}_r$ defined as in Reference 457.

$$\mathbf{L}_r = 2^{-m}\mathbf{HH}_r(m) = 2^{-m}\left(\mathbf{W}(r) \otimes \mathbf{H}(m-r)\right),$$

where $\mathbf{W}(r)$ and $\mathbf{H}(m-r)$ are the $(r \times r)$ Walsh and $(m-r \times m-r)$ nonnormalized Haar matrices, respectively. Different transforms can be obtained for different values of the parameter r, which allows to adapt a transform to the targeted application.

The inverse transform is defined by the transpose matrix $\mathbf{HH}_r^T$.

Example 11.1.1 *For $r = 1$ and $m = 3$, the Hadamard–Haar transform is*

$$\mathbf{L}_1(3) = 2^{-3}\mathbf{HH}_1(3) = 2^{-3}\mathbf{W}(1) \otimes \mathbf{H}(2)$$

$$= 2^{-3}\begin{bmatrix} 1 & 1 & 1 & 1 & 1 & 1 & 1 & 1 \\ 1 & 1 & -1 & -1 & 1 & 1 & -1 & -1 \\ \sqrt{2} & -\sqrt{2} & 0 & 0 & \sqrt{2} & -\sqrt{2} & 0 & 0 \\ 0 & 0 & \sqrt{2} & -\sqrt{2} & 0 & 0 & \sqrt{2} & -\sqrt{2} \\ 1 & 1 & 1 & 1 & -1 & -1 & -1 & -1 \\ 1 & 1 & -1 & -1 & -1 & -1 & 1 & 1 \\ \sqrt{2} & -\sqrt{2} & 0 & 0 & -\sqrt{2} & \sqrt{2} & 0 & 0 \\ 0 & 0 & \sqrt{2} & -\sqrt{2} & 0 & 0 & -\sqrt{2} & \sqrt{2} \end{bmatrix}.$$

It is obvious that rows of this matrix are obtained as linear combinations of rows of the Haar matrix of the same order and, at the same time, some of the rows are identical to the rows of the Walsh matrix. In this way, the transform shares features of both of original transforms.

Because of the factorization properties of these transforms, the Hadamard–Haar transform can be factorized in a similar way, which ensures existence of a fast calculation algorithm.

Example 11.1.2 *For r = 1, the Hadamard–Haar matrix can be factorized as*

$$\mathbf{HH}_1(n) = \mathbf{W} \otimes \mathbf{H}(m - 1)$$

$$= \begin{bmatrix} \mathbf{I}(m-1) & \mathbf{I}(m-1) \\ \mathbf{I}(m-1) & -\mathbf{I}(m-1) \end{bmatrix} \cdot \prod_{j=i}^{m-1} \begin{bmatrix} \mathbf{C}_j(m-1) & \mathbf{0}(m-1) \\ \mathbf{0}(m-1) & \mathbf{C}_j(m-1) \end{bmatrix},$$

where $\mathbf{I}(m - 1)$ *is the* $((m - 1) \times (m - 1))$ *identity matrix,* $\mathbf{C}_j(m - 1)$ *are the matrix factors in the factorization of the Haar matrix, and* $\mathbf{0}(m - 1)$ *is the* $((m - 1) \times (m - 1))$ *zero matrix.*

It is clear that the flow-graph of the corresponding fast algorithm consists of steps of the fast algorithms for the Walsh and Haar transforms.

The Hadamard–Haar transform has proved useful in feature selection in pattern recognition, Wiener filtering, and data compression in image processing. See References 16 and 587 for more information about this and some other related transforms. An excellent unified interpretation of a variety of these transforms has been developed by Leonid Yaroslavsky in a series of publications by exploiting matrix representations and using the characteristic common properties of transform matrices, see References 662–665, and references therein. In this context, see also References 180,214,631, and 670.

The above example of the Hadamard–Haar transform illustrates a trend in developing spectral techniques, that consists in combining different transforms and pooling their good features, or emphasizing features especially required in a concrete application. Such transforms are also called *hybrid transforms* (457), *composite transforms* (12,180), and so on.

Introducing some parameters, as the parameter r in the Hadamard–Haar transform, that can be tuned for different applications, provides flexibility in adapting transforms to target applications. This method leads to the class of the so-called *parameterized transforms*, that will be briefly illustrated by the example of the parameterization of the *slant-Haar transform* (12,13) in the following Section 11.1.3.

The majority of hybrid transforms consist of transforms derived by combining transforms on the same domain group, most often restricted to the finite dyadic group of order 2^m. A different step forward has been done in Reference 566 by introducing the *arithmetic-Haar transform* sharing properties of both the arithmetic and the Haar transforms on the Abelian finite dyadic groups of order 2^m and the Fourier transform on the non-Abelian quaternion groups that have been presented in Section 2.9. In this transform, instead of using parameters, the flexibility is provided by allowing extensions to higher dimensions either by repetition of the same (8×8) basic transform (given in the Example 11.1.3 below), or by selecting various basic matrices on constituent not necessarily Abelian subgroups of the domain group. In this way, a family of transforms can be generated in a straightforward way. For more details see Reference 567.

Example 11.1.3 *The basic arithmetic-Haar transform matrix is an* (8×8) *matrix, since the underlined domain group is the quaternion group that has an order 8. This* *matrix is given by*

$$
\mathbf{X}_q^{-1} = \frac{1}{2}
\begin{bmatrix}
1 & 0 & 1 & 0 & 0 & 0 & 0 & 0 \\
-1 & 1 & -1 & 1 & 0 & 0 & 0 & 0 \\
-1 & 0 & -1 & 0 & 1 & 0 & 1 & 0 \\
1 & -1 & 1 & -1 & -1 & 1 & -1 & 1 \\
1 & 0 & -1 & 0 & 0 & 0 & 0 & 0 \\
0 & 1 & 0 & -1 & 0 & 0 & 0 & 0 \\
0 & 0 & 0 & 0 & 1 & 0 & -1 & 0 \\
0 & 0 & 0 & 0 & 0 & 1 & 0 & -1
\end{bmatrix}.
$$

Its inverse matrix defines the set of basis functions in terms of which the arithmetic-Haar transform is defined. In Reference 566, these functions have been derived by expressing basis functions in Fourier transform on the quaternion group Q_2 in terms of binary valued variables. It is obvious that the same can be done with basis functions in the arithmetic-Haar transform. This allows to define *Fixed-polarity arithmetic-Haar* expressions (566), in the same way as Fixed-polarity arithmetic expressions are defined.

11.1.3 Slant Transform

In this section, we will briefly illustrate transforms driven by needs of particular applications by the example of the *Slant transform* (150).

The development of this particular class of transforms originates in 1971 (150), and as it is noticed in Reference 454, has been motivated by the following considerations.

Consider a random vector of length N and an ($N \times N$) transform matrix. In typical realizations, the random vector happen to be representable just with a few basis functions of the transform, so that the average error is small. We say that the transform packs the energy to the particular coefficients of the transform. If we need to transmit the random vector (representing, e.g., a segment of a line in an image), it is clear that we can transmit just the coefficients where energy is packed, without loosing much information. Each process has its optimal transform, the so-called Karhunen–Loève transform (KLT) that depends on the second error statistics of the process.

The *Discrete Cosine Transform* (DCT), to be discussed later in this chapter, approximates well the KLT for many natural processes. However, for processes that exhibit linear change, the DCT performs less well and for this reason the Slant transform with uniformly changing basis functions have been introduced (150).

In Reference 454, the slant transform has been generalized to arbitrary orders of the form 2^m and defined as follows

$$
S_{2^m} = \frac{1}{2^{1/2}}
\begin{bmatrix}
1 & 0 & & 1 & 0 & 0 \\
a_{2^m} & b_{2^m} & 0 & -a_{2^m} & b_{2^m} & \\
0 & & I_{2^{m-1}-2} & 0 & & I_{2^{m-1}-2} \\
0 & 1 & & 0 & -1 & \\
-b_{2^m} & a_{2^m} & 0 & b_{2^m} & a_{2^m} & 0 \\
0 & & I_{2^{m-1}-2} & 0 & & -I_{2^{m-1}-2}
\end{bmatrix}
$$

$$
\times
\begin{bmatrix}
S_{2^{m-1}} & 0_{2^{m-1}} \\
0_{2^{m-1}} & S_{2^{m-1}}
\end{bmatrix},
$$

where the scaling factors a_{2^m} and b_{2^m} can be computed from the recursive relation given in Reference 596

$$
a_2 = 1,
$$
$$
b_{2^m} = (1 + 4(a_{2^{m-1}}^2))^{-1/2},
$$
$$
a_{2^m} = 2b_{2^m}a_{2^{m-1}},
$$

or by the formulas (454)

$$
a_{2^{m+1}} = \left(\frac{3 \cdot 2^{2m}}{4 \cdot 2^{2m} - 1} \right)^{1/2},
$$

$$
b_{2^{m+1}} = \left(\frac{2^{2m} - 1}{4 \cdot 2^{m+1} - 1} \right).
$$

This transform is also called *slant-Hadamard transform*, see References 12 and 178, due to the obvious resemblance to the Walsh transform in Hadamard ordering.

Example 11.1.4 *For $n = 1$, the Slant transform matrix is*

$$
S_2 = \frac{1}{2^{1/2}}
\begin{bmatrix}
1 & 1 \\
1 & -1
\end{bmatrix}.
$$

For $n = 2$,

$$
S_4 = \frac{1}{2^{1/2}}
\begin{bmatrix}
1 & 0 & 1 & 0 \\
a_4 & b_4 & -a_4 & b_4 \\
0 & 1 & 0 & -1 \\
-b_4 & a_4 & b_4 & a_4
\end{bmatrix}
\cdot
\begin{bmatrix}
S_2 & 0_2 \\
0_2 & S_2
\end{bmatrix}
$$

$$= \frac{1}{2^{1/2}} \begin{bmatrix} 1 & 1 & 1 & 1 \\ a_4 + b_4 & a_4 - b_4 & -a_4 + b_4 & -a_4 - b_4 \\ 1 & -1 & -1 & 1 \\ a_4 - b_4 & -a_4 - b_4 & a_4 + b_4 & -a_4 + b_4 \end{bmatrix}$$

and, since $a_4 = 2b_4$ and $b_4 = \frac{1}{5^{1/2}}$, it follows

$$S_4 = \begin{bmatrix} 1 & 1 & 1 & 1 \\ \frac{3}{5^{1/2}} & \frac{1}{5^{1/2}} & \frac{-1}{5^{1/2}} & \frac{-3}{5^{1/2}} \\ 1 & -1 & -1 & 1 \\ \frac{1}{5^{1/2}} & \frac{-3}{5^{1/2}} & \frac{3}{5^{1/2}} & \frac{-1}{5^{1/2}} \end{bmatrix}. \tag{11.1.1}$$

Example 11.1.5   *Figure 11.1.1 compares waveforms of the Walsh in sequency ordering and slant functions for m = 4.*

Further generalizations of the slant transform are obtained in the same way as discussed in Section 11.1.2, by combining, for example, the Haar transform and the slant transform resulting in the *slant-Haar transform* (179), or another version of it in Reference 456, see also Reference 12.

11.1.4 Parameterised Transforms

The flexibility of a class of transforms driven by a certain application to the concrete particular application can be improved by allowing some parameters to be suitably tuned. The following example illustrates such transforms.

Example 11.1.6   *The parametric slant-Haar transform of order 2^m, $m = 3, 4, \ldots$, is defined by a transform matrix S_{2^m} defined recursively as (12)*

$$S_{2^m} = S_{2^m}(\beta_4, \beta_8, \ldots, \beta_{2^m})$$

$$= Q_{2^m} \cdot \begin{bmatrix} A_2 \otimes S_{2, 2^{m-1}} \\ \vdots \\ I_2 \otimes S_{2^m - 2, 2^{m-1}} \end{bmatrix},$$

for $-2^{2m-2} \leq \beta_{2^m} \leq 2^{2n-2}$ and $n \geq 3$, where $S_{2, 2^{m-1}}$ is a $(2 \times 2^{m-1})$ matrix comprised of the first two rows of $S_{2^{m-1}}$ and $S_{2^{m-1} - 2, 2^{m-1}}$ is a $((2^{m-1} - 2) \times (2^{m-1}))$ matrix comprised of the third to the (2^{m-1})th rows of $S_{2^{m-1}}$, and

$$A_2 = \frac{1}{\sqrt{2}} W(1) = \frac{1}{\sqrt{2}} \begin{bmatrix} 1 & 1 \\ 1 & -1 \end{bmatrix},$$

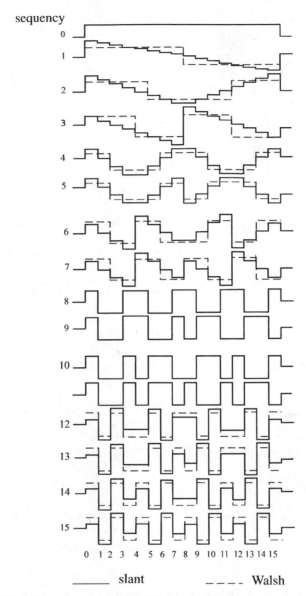

FIGURE 11.1.1   Slant functions and Walsh functions in sequency ordering for $m = 4$.

and S_4 is the 4-point slant-Hadamard transform in (11.1.1), and Q_{2^m} is a recursion kernel matrix defined as

$$
Q_{2^m} = \begin{bmatrix}
1 & & & & & & & \\
& b_{2^m} & a_{2^m} & & & & & \\
& a_{2^m} & -b_{2^m} & & & & & \\
& & & 1 & & & & \\
& & & & \ddots & & & \\
& & & & & 0 & & \\
& & & & & & \ddots & \\
& & & & & & & 1
\end{bmatrix},
$$

with

$$
a_{2^m} = \sqrt{\frac{3(2^{2m-2})}{4(2^{2m-2}) - \beta_{2^m}}}, \quad b_{2^m} = \sqrt{\frac{(2^{2m-2}) - \beta_{2^m}}{4(2^{2m-2}) - \beta_{2^m}}},
$$

for $-2^{2m-2} \le \beta_{2^m} \le 2^{2m-2}$ and $n \ge 3$.
The matrix S_{2^m} is a parametric matrix with parameters $\beta_2, \beta_4, \ldots, \beta_{2^m}$, which

1. *Reduces to the classical slant-Haar transform considered in Reference 179 for $\beta_i = 1, i = 4, 8, \ldots, 2^m$.*
2. *It is the* constant-β *slant-Haar transform, for $\beta_4 = \beta_8 = \beta$ and $\beta \le \|4\|$.*
3. *In general, it is called* multiple-β *slant-Haar transform.*

This transform does not preserve orthogonality if $\beta_{2^m} > \|2^{2m-2}\|$.

The parametric slant-Haar transform preserves all useful properties of the slant transform, including the parametric slant basis vector that appears as the second row in the transform matrix. This transform may be useful in signal and image compression and denoising (12).

It may be remarked that the application oriented basic features of the slant transform, extend to the generalizations of it, and have fulfilled a continuous interest in these transforms over the years as well as new applications (477). It is worth noticing that besides applications in the areas where spectral transforms are classical methods (681,682), the same transforms have been exploited in more recent research areas as, for example, watermarking (248,686).

Moreover, classical transforms may serve as models or prototypes in designing new transforms as it was the case, for instance, with the slant-Haar transform and the *slantlet transform* defined in Reference 514, which gives us a link to consider in the following Section the *wavelet transforms*.

11.2 WAVELET TRANSFORMS

As discussed in Section 2.3.3, the set of Haar functions can be split into packets, and functions within the same packet can be obtained form each other by sifting along the interval [0, 1]. Functions in a packet can be derived from functions in the preceding packet by scaling on the interval where these functions are different from zero followed by the multiplication with a power of $\sqrt{2}$.

Because of these properties, the Haar functions introduced in 1910 are related to the more recently developed wavelet theory, where the Haar wavelet (function) is viewed as the canonical example of an orthonormal wavelet and being at the same time the simplest possible wavelet.

Figure 11.2.1 shows the basic Haar wavelet. Disadvantage of the Haar wavelet is that it is not continuous and therefore not differentiable in the classical sense.

In general, in wavelet transforms basis functions are derived by scaling and translating copies of a finite length or fast decaying oscillating waveform that is called the *mother wavelet* (118).

A well known example of a mother wavelet is

$$\Psi(t) = 2\text{sinc}(2t) - \text{sinc}(t) = \frac{\sin(2\pi t) - \sin(\pi t)}{\pi t},$$

where the *sinc function* is $\text{sinc}(t) = \frac{\sin x}{x}$.

Figure 11.2.2 shows Meyer, Morlet, and Mexican hat wavelets.

The other wavelets,

$$\Psi_{a,b}(t) = \frac{1}{\sqrt{a}} \Psi\left(\frac{t-b}{a}\right),$$

obtained from the mother wavelet by scaling and shifting, are required to form either a complete orthonormal set of basis functions, or an overcomplete set of frame functions.

The feature that the mother wavelet is concentrated on a finite interval, makes essential difference with the classical Fourier analysis, where the basis, sine and cosine

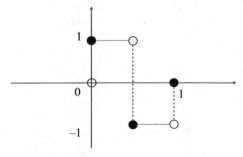

FIGURE 11.2.1   Haar wavelet.

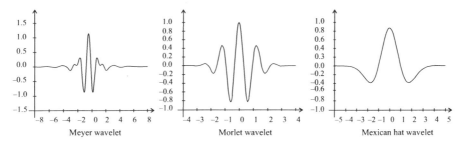

FIGURE 11.2.2 Meyer, Morlet, and Mexican hat wavelets.

functions, undulate infinitely in both directions. Due to that, in Fourier analysis, to represent a detail of a signal, a large number of infinitely many Fourier coefficients is needed. In wavelet transforms, the detail may be represented as a combination of few basic elements concentrated at the detail.

The *Discrete Wavelet Transform (DWT)* is a wavelet transform where the wavelets are discretely sampled.

The above mentioned Haar wavelet is usually viewed as the first DWT due to the following interpretation of the discrete Haar transform, that is obvious form either fast Haar algorithm or the computation of the Haar spectrum by decision diagrams.

For a signal defined in 2^m points, the Haar transform calculates the sum and the difference for each pair of input data. The difference is stored as the corresponding Haar coefficient, while the sum is forwarded to further processing as the input in another step of a recursive procedure (step in the fast Haar transform, or processing of nodes at the succeeding upper level in the decision diagram).

In general, we say that at each step of this recursive procedure, the previously obtained sequence is subjected to a high pass and low pass filters, the outputs of which are called the detail and the transform (approximation) coefficient, respectively.

In this way, for a signal defined in 2^m points, all the Haar spectral coefficients are calculated during m steps. It follows that the computational complexity is $O(2^m)$.

Since this transform examines a signal at different scales (Haar functions are nonzero at intervals of different length), it captures both the frequency content of the signal and the temporal content of it, meaning times at which these frequencies occur.

These two properties, computation complexity that approximates to $O(2^m)$ for a signal of length 2^m and simultaneous frequency and temporal analysis, are basic features of the *Fast Wavelet Transform (FWT)* that is often viewed as an alternative to the conventional Fast Fourier Transform (FFT).

In the *Wavelet Packet Transforms (WPT)*, both the detail and the approximation coefficient are further decomposed. In this way, in a *Wavelet Packet Decomposition (WPD)*, the related recursive procedure with m steps produces 2^m different sets of coefficients instead $(m + 1)$ sets in the discrete wavelet transform. Due to the downsampling (reducing the sampling rate, equivalently multiplying the sampling time),[1] the overall number of coefficients remains the same and there is no redundancy.

---

[1] If the downsampling factor is M, we pick up every Mth sample.

The *complex wavelet transform* is a complex-valued extension of the discrete wavelet transform intended primarily, but not restrictively, for applications in image processing.

Referring to the finite support of basis functions, as well as scaling of them, links between wavelet transforms and Reed-Muller and arithmetic transforms are obvious.

The following considerations motivated particular applications of wavelet packet analysis in representations of switching functions and circuit design.

Wavelets packets are a particular linear combination of wavelets. A *Discrete Wavelet Packet Analysis* (*DWPA*) is a transform of a given input signal into coefficients with respect to a collection of wavelet packets. Wavelet packet basis is any basis selected among the assumed collection of wavelet packets in a DWPA. Therefore, DWPA is a collection of Discrete Wavelet Packet Transforms (DWPT), each of them performed with respect to a particular basis. There may be many wavelet packet bases in a collection and, therefore, a DWPA should be specified by describing the chosen basis.

Similarly to classical discrete transforms and related series expressions, a DWPT performs a decomposition of the input signal with respect to the wavelet packet components. Since in a DWPA there are more wavelet packet components than is required for a basis, a DWPA is a class of transforms, allowing to choose the most suited transform for a given signal f. DWPA for a chosen basis is specified by the depth of the decomposition and two filters H and G used in the decomposition and determined by the chosen basis.

In Reference 146 the DWPA for the Walsh basis and the arithmetic transform basis has been considered for the derivation of compact word-level expressions for multiple-output switching functions. The corresponding filters are $H = [1, 0]$ and $G = [-1, 1]$ for the arithmetic transform basis, and $H = [1, 1]$ and $G = [1, -1]$ for the Walsh basis. The same method has been used in Reference 145 for the design of logic circuits based on these expressions.

Three-structured Haar transforms, see Reference 144 and references therein, are a related class of transforms, since are defined by referring to the decomposition trees. However, in this case, the tree structure is applied in the time domain.

11.3 FIBONACCI TRANSFORMS

In this section, we will return to the application driven transforms with applications in switching theory and logic design, and briefly present the *Fibonacci transforms* as an example of such transforms.

The adapted wavelet packet transforms discussed in the previous section, aim at exploiting properties of signals in their spectral processing. Fibonacci transforms contribute to this area, since extend the spectral methods to Fibonacci cubes and at the same time permit adaptation to the requirements of particular applications by choosing suitable values for the corresponding parameters.

Switching theory and logic design as implementation of it are greatly based on exploiting Boolean algebraic structures. However, in some applications, they express some inconvenience originating in their inherent features, as for example, restrictions to the power of two in the number of nodes or inputs, etc. For this reason, the Fibonacci interconnection topologies are offered as an alternative (9,142,143,141,535).

There are several reasons to consider the Fibonacci cubes as the algebraic structures suitable for applications in this area. We want to point out the following:

1. Boolean n-cube is included in the set of generalized Fibonacci cubes.
2. The order of a generalized Fibonacci cube that can be embedded into a Boolean n-cube with $k = 1, 2$ faulty nodes is greater than 2^{n-1}.
3. The k dimensional Fibonacci cube of the order $n + k$ is equivalent to a Boolean n-cube for $0 \leq n < k$.
4. It follows that the algorithms developed for a generalized Fibonacci cube are executable on the Boolean cube of the corresponding order.

Fibonacci topologies are defined from the generalized Fibonacci p-numbers and codes (143,142,147).

11.3.1 Fibonacci p-Numbers

Definition 11.3.1 *A sequence $\phi(n)$ is the Fibonacci sequence if for each $n \geq 1$,*

$$\phi(n) = \phi(n - 1) + \phi(n - 2),$$

with initial values $\phi(0) = 1, \phi(n) = 0, n < 0$. Elements of this sequence are the Fibonacci numbers.

A generalization of Fibonacci numbers is given in References 143, and 535 as follows.

Definition 11.3.2 *A sequence $\phi_p(i)$ is the generalized Fibonacci p-sequence if*

$$\phi_p(i) = \begin{cases} 0, & i < 0, \\ 1, & i = 0, \\ \phi_p(i - 1) + \phi_p(i - p - 1), & i > 0. \end{cases}$$

Elements of this sequence are the generalized Fibonacci p-numbers.

Example 11.3.1 *Table 11.3.1 shows the generalized Fibonacci p-numbers for $p = 0, 1, 2, 3,$ and $i = 0, 1, \ldots, 9$.*

TABLE 11.3.1   Generalized Fibonacci Numbers.

$\phi_p(i)$	$i = 0$	1	2	3	4	5	6	7	8	9
$p = 0$	1	2	4	8	16	32	64	128	256	512
1	1	1	2	3	5	8	13	21	34	55
2	1	1	1	2	3	4	6	9	13	19
3	1	1	1	1	2	3	4	5	7	10

11.3.2   Fibonacci p-Codes

The Fibonacci p-representation of a natural number B is defined as

$$B = \sum_{i=p}^{n-1} w_i \phi_p(i).$$

The sequence $\mathbf{w} = (w_{n-1}, \ldots, w_p)_p$ is the Fibonacci p-code for B (143). Since with thus defined weighting coefficients, a given number B may be represented by few different code sequences, the normal unique Fibonacci p-code is recursively introduced obtaining w_{n-1} from

$$B - w_{n-1}\psi_p(n-1) + m,$$

where $\phi(n-1)$ is the greatest Fibonacci p-number smaller or equal to B, and $0 \le m < \phi_p(n-p-1)$.

11.3.3   Contracted Fibonacci p-Codes

The following property of normal Fibonacci p-codes permit definition of the contracted Fibonacci p-codes.

Lemma 11.3.1 *(143)   In the normal Fibonacci p-code for a given number B, if $w_i = 1$, then $w_{i-1} = w_{i-2} = \cdots = w_{i-p} = 0$.*

Utilizing this property, the contracted Fibonacci p-code is defined by deleting p zeros after each 1 in the Fibonacci p-code for B.

In this section, we introduce the Fibonacci codes by the following example.

Example 11.3.2   *Table 11.3.2 shows encoding for the first 8 nonnegative integers in Boolean topology, the Fibonacci 1-codes and contracted Fibonacci 1-codes. The contracted Fibonacci codes are derived by deleting the underlined zeros in the Fibonacci code.*

Figure 11.3.1 compares the Boolean cube of the order $m = 3$ and the Fibonacci cube of the same order derived form these encodings.

Generalized Fibonacci transforms could be used to extend possibilities of adapted wavelet packet analysis (647). Classical Haar wavelet packets provide a class of

TABLE 11.3.2 Boolean Codes, Fibonacci 1-codes, Contracted Fibonacci 1-codes, and Fibonacci Minterms for $m = 3$.

i	Boolean $b_1b_2b_3b_4$	Fibonacci $k_1k_2k_3k_4$	Contracted Fibonacci $r_1r_2r_3r_4$	Fibonacci Minterms $w_1w_2w_3w_4$
0	000	0000	0000	$\overline{w}_1\overline{w}_2\overline{w}_3\overline{w}_4$
1	001	0001	0001	$\overline{w}_1\overline{w}_2\overline{w}_3 w_4$
2	010	0010	001	$\overline{w}_1\overline{w}_2 w_3$
3	011	0100	010	$\overline{w}_1 w_2\overline{w}_4$
4	100	0101	011	$\overline{w}_1 w_2 w_4$
5	101	1000	100	$w_1\overline{w}_3\overline{w}_4$
6	110	1001	101	$w_1\overline{w}_3 w_4$
7	111	1010	11	$w_1 w_3$

Haar-type transforms. Among them a transform can be chosen, which is the most adapted to peculiarities of a signal using some information cost function (e.g., entropy). This can be done by a tree pruning procedure known as a "best basis" selection algorithm (647). Generalized Fibonacci p- transforms (p-GFT) provide a parametric (on p) class of Haar-type transforms, defined on a tree structures—generalized Fibonacci trees. This class contains, as a particular case, the class of Haar wavelet packets. Thus, GFTs can be used for adapted generalized Fibonacci wavelet packet analysis that can be performed in the following two stage optimization procedure. First, for each p we define the corresponding Fibonacci p-tree (for $p = 0$, this is the complete binary tree, for $p = 1$ this is the classical Fibonacci tree, etc.), and apply a "best basis" selection algorithm for each of them. Then, among those "winner" bases for different p, we choose the final basis that is the best suited for spectral processing of a given signal with respect to the properties of it.

In References 142, and 143, definition of some discrete orthogonal transforms, as for example, the Walsh transform, the Haar transform, (8,258,278), is generalized into transforms defined by transform matrices whose orders are equal to the arbitrary Fibonacci p-numbers. These transforms are denoted as the generalized Fibonacci transforms.

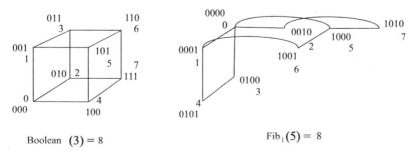

FIGURE 11.3.1 Boolean cube and Fibonacci cube for $m = 3$.

Let f be a function defined in $\phi_p(i)$ points. We assume that f is given by a sequence $\mathbf{F} = [f(0), \ldots, f(\phi_p(i) - 1)]^T$. We denote by $\mathbf{T}_p(i)$ a transform matrix defining a particular Fibonacci p-transform of order $\phi_p(i)$.

Definition 11.3.3 *The Fibonacci p-spectrum for f with respect to $\mathbf{T}_p(i)$ is defined as a sequence*

$$\mathbf{S}_{T,f} = \mathbf{T}_p(i)\mathbf{F}.$$

11.3.4 Fibonacci–Walsh Hadamard Transform

Definition 11.3.4 *The Fibonacci–Walsh p-transform in the Hadamard ordering (FW_pHT) is defined by the transform matrix determined as*

$$\mathbf{W}^{(p,n)} = \begin{bmatrix} \overset{(p,n-1)}{\overline{\mathbf{W}}} & \sqrt{2}\hat{\mathbf{W}}^{(p,n-1)} & \overset{(p,n-1)}{\overline{\mathbf{W}}} \\ (\sqrt{2})^p\mathbf{W}^{(p,n-p-1)} & \mathbf{0} & -(\sqrt{2})^p\mathbf{W}^{(p,n-p-1)} \end{bmatrix},$$

for $n > p$, and

$$\mathbf{W}^{(p,m)} = [1], \text{ for } m \le p, \ \mathbf{W}^{(p,p+1)} = \begin{bmatrix} 1 & 1 \\ 1 & -1 \end{bmatrix},$$

where $\overset{(p,n-1)}{\overline{\mathbf{W}}}$ and $\hat{\mathbf{W}}^{(p,n-1)}$ are the rectangular matrices formed from the matrix $\mathbf{W}^{(p,n-1)}$ by taking its first $\phi_p(n - p - 1)$ columns, and its last $\phi_p(n - 1) - \phi_p(n - p - 1)$ columns, respectively.

Example 11.3.3 *The FWHT for $\phi_1(5)$ is given by the matrix*

$$\mathbf{W}^{(1,5)} = \begin{bmatrix} 1 & \sqrt{2} & \sqrt{2} & \sqrt{2} & 2 & 1 & \sqrt{2} & \sqrt{2} \\ 1 & -\sqrt{2} & \sqrt{2} & \sqrt{2} & -2 & 1 & -\sqrt{2} & \sqrt{2} \\ \sqrt{2} & 0 & -2 & 2 & 0 & \sqrt{2} & 0 & -2 \\ \sqrt{2} & \sqrt{2} & 0 & -2 & -2 & \sqrt{2} & \sqrt{2} & 0 \\ \sqrt{2} & -\sqrt{2} & 0 & -2 & 2 & \sqrt{2} & -\sqrt{2} & 0 \\ \sqrt{2} & 2 & \sqrt{2} & 0 & 0 & -\sqrt{2} & -2 & -\sqrt{2} \\ \sqrt{2} & -2 & \sqrt{2} & 0 & 0 & -\sqrt{2} & 2 & -\sqrt{2} \\ 2 & 0 & -2 & 0 & 0 & -2 & 0 & 2 \end{bmatrix}.$$

For a function f given by the vector $\mathbf{F} = [1, 0, 1, 0, 1, 1, 1, 1]^T$, the FWHT spectrum for f is given by $\mathbf{S}_{FW,f} = [4 + 3\sqrt{2}, \sqrt{2}, -4 + 2\sqrt{2}, -2 + 3\sqrt{2}, 2 + \sqrt{2}, -2, 2, 0]^T$.

11.3.5 Fibonacci-Haar Transform

The Fibonacci–Haar p-transform in the Hadamard ordering (FH$_p$HT) is defined by the transform matrix determined as

$$\mathbf{H}^{(Had,p,n)} = \begin{bmatrix} \overset{-(Had,p,n-1)}{\mathbf{H}} & \sqrt{2}\hat{\mathbf{H}}^{(Had,p,n-1)} & \overset{-(Had,p,n-1)}{\mathbf{H}} \\ (\sqrt{2})^{n-p-1}\mathbf{I} & \mathbf{0} & -(\sqrt{2})^{n-p-1}\mathbf{I} \end{bmatrix},$$

for $n > p$, and the initial matrices are defined as in Definition 6, where $\overset{-(Had,p,n-1)}{\mathbf{H}}$ and $\hat{\mathbf{H}}^{(Had,p,n-1)}$ are the rectangular matrices formed from the matrix $\mathbf{H}^{(Had,p,n-1)}$ by taking its first $\phi_p(n-p-1)$ columns, and its last $\phi_p(n-1) - \phi_p(n-p-1)$ columns, respectively, and $\mathbf{I}$ is the identity matrix of order $\phi_p(n-p-1)$.

Note that in Reference 143, the FFT-like algorithm for the Fibonacci–Haar transform is derived from the Hadamard ordering. Therefore, it is assumed that the input sequences is given in the bit-reverse ordering with respect to the Fibonacci p-code, and the Fibonacci-Haar spectrum is obtained in the direct ordering. This convention will also be adapted in the further considerations of the Fibonacci-Haar spectrum in this paper.

Example 11.3.4 *The Fibonacci-Haar transform for $\phi_1(5)$ is given by the transform matrix determined as*

$$\mathbf{H}^{(Had,1,5)} = \begin{bmatrix} 1 & \sqrt{2} & \sqrt{2} & \sqrt{2} & 2 & 1 & \sqrt{2} & \sqrt{2} \\ 1 & -\sqrt{2} & \sqrt{2} & \sqrt{2} & -2 & 1 & -\sqrt{2} & \sqrt{2} \\ \sqrt{2} & 0 & -2 & 2 & 0 & \sqrt{2} & 0 & -2 \\ 2 & 0 & 0 & -2\sqrt{2} & 0 & 2 & 0 & 0 \\ 0 & 2 & 0 & 0 & -2\sqrt{2} & 0 & 2 & 0 \\ 2\sqrt{2} & 0 & 0 & 0 & 0 & -2\sqrt{2} & 0 & 0 \\ 0 & 2\sqrt{2} & 0 & 0 & 0 & 0 & -2\sqrt{2} & 0 \\ 0 & 0 & 2\sqrt{2} & 0 & 0 & 0 & 0 & -2\sqrt{2} \end{bmatrix}.$$

For f in Example 11.3.3, the vector $\mathbf{F}$ in the bit-reverse ordering with respect to the Fibonacci p-code is given by $\mathbf{F}' = [1, 1, 0, 1, 1, 0, 1, 1]^T$. The multiplication of $\mathbf{H}^{(Had,1,5)}$ with $\mathbf{F}'$ produces the Fibonacci-Haar spectrum in the direct ordering as $\mathbf{S}_{FH,f} = [3 + 4\sqrt{2}, -1, \sqrt{2}, 2 - 2\sqrt{2}, 4 - 2\sqrt{2}, 2\sqrt{2}, 0, -2\sqrt{2}]$.

11.3.6 Fibonacci SOP-Expressions

The previously discussed Fibonacci transforms are examples of word-level transforms. For applications to binary-valued functions on Fibonacci topologies, it may be useful to have defined bit-level Fibonacci transforms. That was the task in Reference 574 that has been accomplished by first defining Fibonacci minterms as illustrated in Table 11.3.2, and related Fibonacci Sum-of-Product (SOP) expressions. In matrix notation, the Fibonacci SOPs are defined as follows.

Definition 11.3.5 *Consider a function f defined on a Fibonacci cube for $m = 4$ by the vector $\mathbf{F} = [f(0), \ldots, f(\phi_p(i)]^T$. The Fibonacci canonic SOP for f is defined as*

$$f = \mathbf{Y}(p, i)\mathbf{B}(p, i)\mathbf{F},$$

where

$$\mathbf{Y}(p, i) = \bigotimes_{j=1}^{n} \left[\overline{w}_j \quad w_j \right],$$

where $\mathbf{B}(p, i)$ is the $(\phi_p(i) \times \phi_p(i))$ identity matrix, and $\otimes$ denotes the Kronecker product performed under the mentioned restrictions appreciating properties of Fibonacci p-codes.

The following example illustrates the application of this restricted Kronecker product and generations of Fibonacci SOPs.

Example 11.3.5 *For functions defined in $\phi_1(5) = 8$ points, the Fibonacci SOP is defined as*

$$f = \left(\left[\overline{w}_1 \quad w_1 \right] \otimes \left[\overline{w}_2 \quad w_2 \right] \otimes \left[\overline{w}_3 \quad w_3 \right] \otimes \left[\overline{w}_4 \quad w_4 \right] \right) \mathbf{B}(3)\mathbf{F}$$

$$= f_0 \overline{w}_1 \overline{w}_2 \overline{w}_3 \overline{w}_4 \oplus f_1 \overline{w}_1 \overline{w}_2 \overline{w}_3 w_4 \oplus f_2 \overline{w}_1 \overline{w}_2 w_3$$

$$\oplus f_3 \overline{w}_1 w_2 \overline{w}_4 \oplus f_4 \overline{w}_1 w_2 w_4 \oplus f_5 w_1 \overline{w}_3 \overline{w}_4$$

$$\oplus f_6 w_1 \overline{w}_3 w_4 \oplus f_7 w_1 w_3.$$

11.3.7 Fibonacci Reed–Muller Expressions

The Fibonacci positive-polarity Reed–Muller expressions (FibPPRMs) have been introduced in the matrix notation in the same way as that is done for Reed–Muller expressions for switching functions (574). The method will be introduced here by the following example.

Example 11.3.6 *The product terms appearing in a FibPPRM for functions defined in $\phi_1(5)$ points are generated as follows.*

$$\mathbf{Z}(1, 5) = \left[1 \quad w_1 \right] \otimes \left[1 \quad w_2 \right] \otimes \left[1 \quad w_3 \right] \otimes \left[1 \quad w_4 \right]$$

$$= [1, w_4, w_3, w_2, w_2 w_4, w_1, w_1 w_4, w_1 w_3].$$

The product terms appearing in a FibPPRM for functions defined in $\phi_p(i)$ points determine columns of the Fibonacci Reed–Muller matrix **FibR**(p, i).

Example 11.3.7   *For f defined in $\phi_1(5)$ points,*

$$\mathbf{FibR}(1, 5) = \begin{bmatrix} 1 & 0 & 0 & 0 & 0 & 0 & 0 & 0 \\ 1 & 1 & 0 & 0 & 0 & 0 & 0 & 0 \\ 1 & 0 & 1 & 0 & 0 & 0 & 0 & 0 \\ 1 & 0 & 0 & 1 & 0 & 0 & 0 & 0 \\ 1 & 1 & 0 & 1 & 1 & 0 & 0 & 0 \\ 1 & 0 & 0 & 0 & 0 & 1 & 0 & 0 \\ 1 & 1 & 0 & 0 & 0 & 1 & 1 & 0 \\ 1 & 0 & 1 & 0 & 0 & 1 & 0 & 1 \end{bmatrix}.$$

The Fibonacci Reed–Muller matrix is a self-inverse matrix over $GF(2)$. It satisfies the following recurrence relation

$$\mathbf{FibR}(p, i) = \begin{bmatrix} \mathbf{FibR}(p, i) & \mathbf{0}_{\phi_p(i-1) \times \phi_p(i-p-1)} & \\ \mathbf{FibR}(p, i - p - 1) & \mathbf{0}_{\phi_p(i-p-1) \times \phi_p(i-p-2)} & \mathbf{FibR}(i - p - 1) \end{bmatrix},$$

Extensions to fixed-polarity Fibonacci expressions are defined in the same way as fixed-polarity expressions on Boolean interconnection topologies.

When Fibonacci Reed–Muller expressions are defined, extension to arithmetic Fibonacci expressions was a matter of their proper interpretation and change of the algebraic structure for the range of basis functions (42).

Fibonacci decision diagrams have been defined as a tool to calculate efficiently in terms of space and time Fibonacci spectral transforms (575). Circuit implementations from these diagrams have been discussed in Reference 556. A summary of these research results in Fibonacci transforms can be found in Reference 571.

11.4 TWO-DIMENSIONAL SPECTRAL TRANSFORMS

Signals are mathematically modeled by functions whose domain and range, as well as number of variables are adopted to the space-time topology of mathematical representation of a particular phenomenon to be considered.

In this settings, two-dimensional signals, such as images, are represented by functions of two variables. Signals defined on finite sets can be represented by ($N_1 \times N_2$) matrices $\mathbf{f} = [f_{i,j}]$, $i \in \{0, 1, \ldots N_1 - 1\}$, $j \in \{0, 1, \ldots, N_2 - 1\}$, with entries $f_{i,j}$ in the field of complex numbers, real numbers, or some finite fields in the case of digital signals.

Thus, the spectrum for a discrete transform of a two-dimensional signal is also represented by a matrix $\mathbf{F} = \lfloor F_{u,v} \rfloor$, $u \in \{0, 1, \ldots, N_1 - 1\}$, $v \in \{0, 1, \ldots, N_2 - 1\}$, and expresses properties analogous to that of discrete spectral transforms for single dimensional signals.

In general, for a two-dimensional signal $[f(i, j)]$, the spectrum of a transform defined with respect to a complete set of two-dimensional functions $\{\phi(i, j, u, v)\}$ is defined as

$$F(u, v) = \sum_{i=0}^{N_1-1} \sum_{j=0}^{N_2-1} f(i, j)\phi(i, j, u, v).$$

The inverse transform is defined as

$$f(i, j) = \sum_{u=0}^{N_1-1} \sum_{v=0}^{N_2-1} F(u, v)\zeta(i, j, u, v),$$

looseness-1 where the set of functions $\zeta(i, j, u, v)$ is determined depending on the basis $\phi(i, j, u, v)$, such to satisfy the above relation between the signal and the spectrum.

The determination of the kernel $\zeta(i, j, u, v)$ of the inverse transform is simplified if the kernel of the transform is separable, that is, can be represented as

$$\phi(i, j, u, v) = \zeta_1(i, u)\zeta_2(j, v).$$

In this case the transform can be performed in two steps

$$F_1(j, u) = \frac{1}{N_1} \sum_{i=0}^{N_1-1} f(i, j)\zeta_1(u, i),$$

$$F_2(u, v) = \frac{1}{N_2} \sum_{j=0}^{N_2-1} F_1(u, j)\zeta_2(j, u),$$

which can be interpreted as the application of the corresponding one-dimensional transform to rows and columns of the two-dimensional signal $f(i, j)$, $i \in \{0, 1, \ldots, N_1 - 1\}$, $j \in \{0, 1, \ldots, N_2 - 1\}$.

This requirement for separable transform kernels is easily satisfied if the two-dimensional transform basis is defined as a product of orthogonal one-dimensional functions, for example, as the product of a vector $\phi^T(u)$ and the vector $\phi(v)$, that is,

$$\phi(u, v) = \phi^T(u)\phi(v),$$

where T denotes the transpose.

For this approach, a two-dimensional transform can be assigned to each orthogonal single-dimensional transform, that is, there can be defined two-dimensional Walsh, Haar, Vilenkin–Chrestenson, etc. transforms.

It follows that in the matrix notation, the two-dimensional transform with respect to a separable kernel and its inverse can be defined respectively as

$$\mathbf{F} = \mathbf{T}_{N_1} \mathbf{f} \, \mathbf{T}_{N_2}^{-1},$$

$$\mathbf{f} = \mathbf{T}_{N_1}^{-1} \mathbf{F} \mathbf{T}_{N_2},$$

where $\mathbf{T}_{N_1}$ and $\mathbf{T}_{N_2}$ are $(N_1 \times N_1)$ and $(N_2 \times N_2)$ matrices whose columns are elements from the function sets of the cardinalities N_1 and N_2 selected to define the two-dimensional transform considered.

Example 11.4.1 *The two-dimensional Walsh transform for signals* **x** *represented by* (8×8) *matrices is defined as*

$$\mathbf{F}_W(3) = \mathbf{W}(3)\mathbf{f} \, \mathbf{W}^{-1},$$

where $\mathbf{W}(3)$ *is the Walsh transform matrix.*

In the same way, the two-dimensional Haar transform is defined as

$$\mathbf{F}_H(3) = \mathbf{H}(3)\mathbf{f} \, \mathbf{H}(3)^{-1},$$

where $\mathbf{H}(3)$ *is the Haar transform matrix.*

Figures 11.4.1–11.4.3 show the two-dimensional Walsh functions for different orderings discussed in Section 2.3.2.1. The function values 1 and −1 are represented by black and white colors, respectively. The function wal(q, x) × wal(r, y) is positioned at the crossing of the column and the row corresponding to wal(q, x) and wal(r, y), respectively. In these figures, it is assumed that $-1/2 \leq x, y \leq 1/2$, *and* $N_1, N_2 = 0, 1, \ldots, 7$.

FIGURE 11.4.1 Two-dimensional Walsh functions in sequency ordering, $-1/2 \leq x, y \leq 1/2$ and $N_1, N_2 = 0, 1, \ldots, 7$.

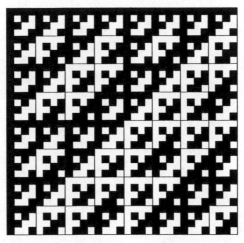

FIGURE 11.4.2 Two-dimensional Walsh functions in natural ordering, $-1/2 \le x, y \le 1/2$ and $N_1, N_2 = 0, 1, \ldots, 7$.

These figures illustrate and visualize the impact of different orderings for Walsh functions.

Figure 11.4.4 shows two-dimensional Haar functions. The values 1, -1 an 0 are represented by the black, white, and gray colors respectively. The parameters take the same range as in the case of Walsh functions.

FIGURE 11.4.3 Two-dimensional Walsh functions in natural ordering, $-1/2 \le x, y \le 1/2$ and $N_1, N_2 = 0, 1, \ldots, 7$.

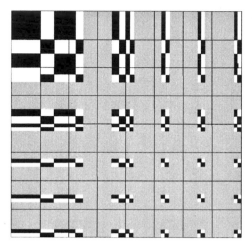

FIGURE 11.4.4 Two-dimensional Haar functions, $-1/2 \le x, y \le 1/2$ and $N_1, N_2 = 0,$ $1, \ldots, 7.$

11.4.1 Two-Dimensional Discrete Cosine Transform

To illustrate the construction of two-dimensional transforms, we will introduce the *Discrete Cosine Transform (DCT)* as used in image processing, which at the same time explains essential reasons for application of this transform in that area.

Some properties of this transform are based on the fact that the Fourier transform of a real symmetric function contains just Fourier coefficients whose indices are even numbers. Thus, these are coefficients corresponding to cosine terms in the Fourier transform. In the following, we derive the DCT from this point of view.

The same statement holds for the two-dimensional *Cosine transform* that has very important applications in image processing and it is accepted as a standard tool in this area within the recommendations for the *JPEG standard*.

For practical applications, the image is converted into a symmetric array by either of the two following approaches.

In the first approach, the $(N \times N)$ image array $[f(i, j)]$ is converted into a $(2N \times 2N)$ symmetric array $[f_s(j, k)]$ as

$$f_s(j, k) = \begin{cases} f(j, k), & j \ge 0, k \ge 0, \\ f(-1 - j, k), & j < 0, k \ge 0, \\ f(j, -1 - k), & j \ge 0, k < 0, \\ f(-1 - j, -1 - k), & j < 0, k < 0, \end{cases} \tag{11.4.1}$$

where $j, k \in \{-N, -N + 1, \ldots, N - 1\}$.

By the application of the Fourier transform, due to its properties, it follows that the Fourier transform of the two-dimensional signal (11.4.1) is given by

$$F_s(u, v) = \frac{2}{N} \sum_{j=0}^{N-1} \sum_{k=0}^{N-1} f_s(j, k) \cos\left(\frac{\pi}{N}u(j + \frac{1}{2})\right) \cos\left(\frac{\pi}{N}v(k - \frac{1}{2})\right). \quad (11.4.2)$$

The transform thus defined is called *Even symmetric transform* (69, 663).
The second approach converts the image array into a symmetric image array as

$$f_s(j, k) = \begin{cases} f(j, k), & j \geq 0, k \geq 0, \\ f(-j, k), & j < 0, k \geq 0, \\ f(j, -k), & j \geq 0, k < 0, \\ f(-j, -k), & j < 0, k < 0, \end{cases} \quad (11.4.3)$$

where $j, k \in \{-N, -N + 1, \ldots, N - 1\}$.
Because of the properties of the Fourier transform, it follows that to determine the Fourier spectrum of this symmetric two-dimensional signal, it is sufficient to calculate the Fourier coefficients $F_s(u, v)$ for the nonnegative values of u and v, that is,

$$F_s(u, v) = \frac{4}{2N - 1} \sum_{j=0}^{N-1} \sum_{k=0}^{n-1} \tilde{f}_s(j, k) \cos\left(\frac{2\pi}{2N - 1}ju\right) \cos\left(\frac{2\pi}{2N - 1}kv\right),$$

where

$$\tilde{f}_s(j, k) = \begin{cases} \frac{1}{4} f(j, k), & j = 0, k = 0, \\ \frac{1}{2} f(j, k), & j = 0, k \neq 0, \\ \frac{1}{2} f(j, k), & j \neq 0, k = 0, \\ f(j, k), & \text{for all other values of } j, k. \end{cases}$$

This consideration leads to the definition of the Cosine transform as follows

$$F(u, v) = \frac{1}{N} \sum_{j=0}^{N-1} \sum_{k=0}^{N-1} \tilde{f}(j, k), \quad u = 0, v = 0$$

and

$$F(u, v) = \frac{2}{N} \sum_{j=0}^{N-1} \sum_{k=0}^{N-1} \tilde{f}(j, k) \cos\left(\frac{2}{2N - 1}\right) \cos\left(\frac{2}{2N - 1}kv\right), \quad u, v \neq 0.$$

The corresponding inverse transform is given by

$$\tilde{f}(j, k) = \frac{1}{N} \sum_{u=0}^{N-1} \sum_{v=0}^{N-1} F(u, v), \quad u = 0, v = 0$$

and

$$\tilde{f}(j, k) = \frac{2}{N} \sum_{u=0}^{N-1} \sum_{v=0}^{N-1} F(u, v) \cos\left(\frac{2}{2N-1} ju\right) \cos\left(\frac{2}{2N-1} kv\right), \quad j, k \neq 0.$$

It is obvious that the original image can be reconstructed as

$$f(j, k) = \begin{cases} 4\tilde{f}(j, k), & j = 0, k = 0, \\ 2\tilde{f}(j, k), & j = 0, k \neq 0, \\ 2\tilde{f}(j, k), & j \neq 0, k = 0, \\ \tilde{f}(j, k), & \text{otherwise.} \end{cases}$$

Figure 11.4.5 shows the two-dimensional discrete Cosine functions for $N = 4$.

11.4.2 Related Applications of Spectral Methods in Image Processing

Spectral methods have found important applications in many aspects of image processing, including edge detection, image enhancement and restoration, denoising, filtering, compression, and so on. There is a voluminous literature on this subject, thus, we will avoid specific referencing for each particular subject, and point to couple of classical references in this area are References 8,483, and 663.

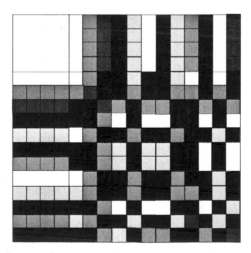

FIGURE 11.4.5   Two-dimensional discrete Cosine functions for (4×4) signals.

Watermarking and *steganography* are relatively recent new areas of application of spectral methods related to image processing (642).

Recall that digital watermarking is a procedure of hiding information into multimedia data, for instance, into images, in a robust and invisible manner. The hidden information should be imperceptible for an ordinary observer, but detectable from the host media when required.

The watermarking is intended to identify the source or ownership of the original data, the legitimacy of the usage of them, and some other accessory information that may be required for particular purposes.

Steganography is usually defined as the art and science of inserting hidden messages into a carrier, for example an image, in such a way that none except the intended recipient cannot observe it. Thus, steganography is opposite to cryptography, since in this case, the existence of an inserted message is known, but the contents is obscured.

Therefore, steganography implies an opposite procedure. *Steganalysis* is the procedure of detecting steganographically encoded messages into a carrier signal, for instance, an image.

Many of the algorithms used in these areas are based on manipulating with spectral coefficients, or by exploiting convolution and correlation, where the spectral transforms are often used for calculation purposes (73). Therefore, methods discussed in this book, especially the autocorrelation functions, as well as methods for efficient calculation of spectral transforms, can be directly applied or after some adaptations converted into convenient tools for performing various tasks in watermarking, steganography and steganalysis.

Some generalizations of Walsh–Hadamard transform (11) and Haar transform (10) have found interesting applications in steganogrpahy (10).

In particular, *tree-structured Haar transforms* (144) have also been advantageously used in this area (50,87).

11.5   APPLICATION OF THE WALSH TRANSFORM IN BROADBAND RADIO

This section is devoted to a particular application, the broad band radio, where the Walsh transform has proven useful in solving certain problems imposed by the technology and the desires therein for highly efficient exploiting resources in order to meet requirements from practice.

The current popularity of cell phones has prompted a large research and development effort to design more effective ways to utilize the limited radio frequency spectrum. A widely used scheme is *Code Division Multiple Access* (CDMA) in which a wideband in the spectrum is shared by many users simultaneously[2]. In this method of multiple access, the communication channel is not divided by time or frequency as in *Time Division Multiple Access* (TDMA) or *Frequency Division Multiple Access* (FDMA), but encodes data with a special code associated to each channel with codes

---

[2]This section has been written with the help by Dave Henderson of Coherent Logix Corp., Austin, Texas, USA.

TABLE 11.5.1   Walsh Codes for $n = 1, 2, 4$ and $k = 0, 1, \ldots n - 1$.

$W(0, 1) = 1$

$W(0, 2) = 1, 1$
$W(1, 2) = 1, -1$

$W(0, 4) = 1, 1, 1, 1$
$W(1, 4) = 1, -1, 1, -1$
$W(2, 4) = 1, 1, -1, -1$
$W(3, 4) = 1, -1, -1, 1$

selected in such a way that they permit multiplexing. CDMA is used in many communication systems, as cellular telephony, *Global Positioning Systems* (GPS), and the *OmniTRACS* satellite system for transportation logistics.

Currently, the most widely used system in cellular telephony is *the Global System for Mobile Telephony* (GSM) which uses narrowband time division multiple access.

CDMA provides a larger capacity for voice and data transmission thus allowing more subscribers to connect at the time. Therefore, it is a basic platform for $3G$ telephony.

In CDMA approach the shared signals will interfere with each other. CDMA solves this problem, for instance, by using Walsh functions, that are in this application usually called *Walsh codes*.

Example 11.5.1   *Table 11.5.1 shows the Walsh codes for $W(k, n)$ for $n = 2^m$, $m = 0, 1, 2$ where $k = 0, 1, \ldots, n - 1$.*

Other modulation schemes such as *Orthogonal Frequency Division Multiplexing* (OFDM) (48, 173) and *Frequency Hopping* can also make use of the orthogonal Walsh functions (685).

As an example, consider the standard IS-95 CDMA from 1993. It uses length 64 Walsh functions for modulation. If each transmitter is modulated by a different Walsh function, then the orthogonality of the functions provides a means of separating them at the receiver. In *Direct Sequence CDMA* the transmitted signal is multiplied by the same continuously repeating Walsh function that spreads the spectrum of the information carrying signal in a unique way. At the receiver, many such signals are present at once and appear noiselike. However by multiplying the combined signals by the same Walsh function used by a specific transmitter, the desired signal is recovered.

The Walsh functions act as unique identification codes for every transmitter. This is of course a highly simplified explanation, but it shows why Walsh functions are an important factor in CDMA.

The following example illustrates basic principles of application of Walsh functions in CDMA.

Example 11.5.2   *Assume that transition of the sequences 1001 and 1110 is required. For convenience, these sequences are written as vectors $[1, 0, 0, 1]$ and $[1, 1, 1, 0]$.*

From the basic Walsh matrix $\mathbf{W}(1) = \begin{bmatrix} 1 & 1 \\ 1 & -1 \end{bmatrix}$, *we derive two* chip codes *as* $\mathbf{v}_0 = (1, 1)$ *and* $\mathbf{v}_1 = (1, -1)$.

By using these codes, the initial sequences are encoded as $[1, 0, 0, 1] \otimes (1, 1) = [1, 1, -1, -1, -1, -1, 1, 1]$ *and* $[1, 1, 1, 0] \otimes (1, -1) = [1, -1, 1, -1, 1, -1, -1, 1]$. *The encoding can be formally interpreted as componentwise multiplication of the initial sequences by chip codes. After componentwise addition of encoded sequences, we get the transmission sequence* $[2, 0, 0, -2, 0, -2, 0, 2]$.

At the receiving side, the decoding is performed as follows by using the rule that negative and nonnegative values correspond to 0 and 1, respectively,

$$(2, 0)(1, 1) = 2 \cdot 1 + 0 \cdot 1 = 2 \to 1,$$

$$(0, -2)(1, 1) = 0 \cdot 1 + (-2) \cdot 1 = -2 \to 0,$$

$$(0, -2)(1, 1) = 0 \cdot 1 + (-2) \cdot 1 = -2 \to 0,$$

$$(0, 2)(1, 1) = 0 \cdot 1 + 2 \cdot 1 = 2 \to 1,$$

which produces the first sequence.

Similarly,

$$(2, 0)(1, -1) = 2 \cdot 1 + 0 \cdot (-1) = 2 \to 1,$$

$$(0, -2)(1, -1) = 0 \cdot 1 + (-2) \cdot (-1) = 2 \to 1,$$

$$(0, -2)(1, -1) = 0 \cdot 1 + (-2) \cdot (-1) = 2 \to 1,$$

$$(0, 2)(1, -1) = 0 \cdot 1 + 2 \cdot (-1) = -2 \to 0,$$

which reconstructs the second sequence.

This example shows how two users can be multiplexed together in a synchronous system. In general, a $(2^n \times 2^n)$ Walsh matrix can be used to multiplex 2^n users.

There are several technical problems faced by designers of CDMA systems. For example, Walsh functions are only orthogonal if they are synchronized. Since there is a finite delay between the transmitter and the receiver, which varies with location, the demodulating Walsh function must be adjusted to align with the transmitter. A correlation operation is done to determine the degree of misalignment of the transmitter and the receiver functions. Cross and autocorrelations were defined in Chapter 2. In this case, the sum of all the signals present in the frequency band is correlated against a single predetermined Walsh function.

Walsh functions are used due to orthogonality, but have multipeaked autocorrelations that make it difficult to build a circuit that can quickly and unambiguously determine the signal alignment. For this reason, the Walsh functions are used in conjunction with *Pseudo Noise* (PN) sequences that have good autocorrelations properties. This method is applied in the *Asynchronous CDMA* and related techniques.

Another problem in such applications is the optimization of the *Power to Average Power Ratio* (PAPR), where a direct application of Walsh and similar sequences allow room for improvements. Several attempts have been recently made to construct new orthogonal codes optimized for this application, see, recent work reported in References 439, and 440.

BIBLIOGRAPHIC NOTES

Reviews of various applications of spectral methods exploiting transforms discussed in this book, can be found, for example, in References 8,16,21,52,665,671, and 675.

APPENDIX A

This appendix presents 21 classes of switching functions (Table A.0.1) that often appear in engineering practice. For these functions, Walsh and the autocorrelation can be expressed analytically.

Table A.0.2, shows their Walsh spectra in Paley ordering (see Section 2.3.2.1).

The corresponding autocorrelation functions are shown in Tables A.0.3.

In Table A.0.4, we present complexities of functions (numbers of nonzero spectral coefficients) in terms of Walsh spectra.

Spectral complexities in terms of Haar series for the same functions are given in Table A.0.5.

Spectral Logic and Its Applications for the Design of Digital Devices by Mark G. Karpovsky, Radomir S. Stanković and Jaakko T. Astola
Copyright © 2008 John Wiley & Sons, Inc.

TABLE A.0.1   Switching Functions and Their Analytical Expressions.

	Name	Function $f(z_0, \ldots, z_{m-1})$
1	Constant	1
2	Elementary conjunction	$\bigwedge_{s=0}^{m-1} z_s$, $(n \leq m)$
3	Elementary disjunction	$\bigvee_{s=0}^{m-1} z_s$, $(n \leq m)$
4	Conjunction	$\bigwedge_{s=0}^{n-1} z_{i_s}$
5	Disjunction	$\bigvee_{s=0}^{n-1} z_{i_s}$
6	Linear function	$\bigoplus_{i=0}^{m-1} c_i z_i$, $(c_i \in \{0, 1\})$, mod 2
7.	Elementary symmetric function with operating number 1	$\begin{cases} 1, & \text{if } \|z\| = 1, \\ 0, & \text{otherwise.} \end{cases}$
8.	Elementary symmetric function with operating number i	$\begin{cases} 1, & \text{if } \|z\| = i, \\ & i \in \{0, 1, \ldots, m\}, \\ 0, & \text{if } \|z\| \neq i. \end{cases}$
9	Majority	$\begin{cases} 1, & \text{if } \|z\| \geq \lceil \frac{m}{2} \rceil, \\ 0, & \text{otherwise.} \end{cases}$
10.	Indicator of group code $\mathbf{V}$, $|\mathbf{V}| = 2^k$	$\begin{cases} 1, & \text{if } z \in \mathbf{V}, \\ 0, & \text{if } z \notin \mathbf{V}. \end{cases}$
11.	Equality indicator (indicator of repetition code) $(m = 2k)$	$\begin{cases} 1, & \text{if } z_i = z_{i+k}, \\ & i = 0, 1, \ldots, k-1, \\ 0, & \text{otherwise.} \end{cases}$
12.	Sum indicator $(m = (s+1)k)$	$\begin{cases} 1, & \text{if } z_i \oplus z_{i+k} \oplus \cdots \\ & \oplus z_{(s-1)k+i} = z_{sk+i}, \\ & i = 0, 1, \ldots, k-1, \\ & \text{mod } 2, \\ 0, & \text{otherwise.} \end{cases}$

TABLE A.0.1   (Continued).

Name	Function $f(z_0, \ldots, z_{m-1})$
13 Nonrepetitive quadratic form $(m = 2k)$	$\oplus_{i=0}^{k-1} z_i z_{i+k}, \quad \text{mod } 2$
14 Quadratic form	$\oplus_{i,q=0}^{m-1} c_i d_q z_i z_q \quad \text{mod } 2$ where $c_i, d_q \in \{0, 1\}$
15 k-ary form $(1 \leq k \leq m)$	$\prod_{i=1}^{k} \oplus_{s=0}^{m-1} a_{i_s} z_s, \quad \text{mod } 2$
16 Sign of sine $(0 < i < m)$	$sign(\sin(2^{-i} \pi z))^a$
17 Sign of cosine $(1 < i < m)$	$sign(\cos(2^{-i} \pi z))$
18 Sign of tangent (cotangent) $(1 < i < m)$	$sign(\tan(2^{-i} \pi z))$ $(= sign(\cot(2^{-i} \pi z)))$
19 Sign of logarithm	$sign(\log_2 z)^b$
20 Unit step function $A = 2^a(2k + 1)$	$f(z) = \begin{cases} 1, & \text{if } z < A, \\ 0, & \text{if } z \geq A. \end{cases}$
21 Unit impulse function	$f(z) = \begin{cases} 1, & \text{if } 2^i - A \leq z < 2^i + A, \\ & A < 2^i, \\ & i \in \{0, 1, \ldots, m-1\}, \\ 0, & \text{otherwise.} \end{cases}$

$^a sign(z) = \begin{cases} 1, & \text{if } z > 0, \\ 0, & \text{if } z \leq 0 \end{cases}$ $sign(f(z)) = sign(f(z + 0)), z \in \{0, 1, \ldots, 2^m - 1\}.$

$^b sign(\log_2 0) = 0.$

TABLE A.0.2   Functions and Their Walsh Spectra.

Function $f(z_0, \ldots, z_{m-1})$	Walsh transform $S(w) = S_f(w_0, \ldots, w_{m-1})$
1 Constant	$\begin{cases} 1, & \text{if } w = 0, \\ 0, & \text{if } w \neq 0. \end{cases}$
2 Elementary conjunction	$2^{-m} W_{2^m-1}(w)$
3 Elementary disjunction	$\begin{cases} 1 - 2^{-m}, & \text{if } w = 0, \\ -2^{-m}, & \text{if } w \neq 0. \end{cases}$
4 Conjunction	$\begin{cases} 0, & \text{if there exists } l \text{ such that } l \notin \{i_s\}, w_{m-1-l} = 1, \\ \frac{1}{2^n} W_\beta(w), \text{ where} \\ \beta = \sum_{s=0}^{n-1} 2^{m-1-i_s}, & \text{otherwise.} \end{cases}$
5 Disjunction	$\begin{cases} 1 - 2^{-n}, & \text{if } w = 0, \\ 0, & \text{if there exists } l \text{ such that } l \notin \{i_s\}, w_{m-1-l} = 1, \\ -2^{-n}, & \text{otherwise.} \end{cases}$
6 Linear function	$\begin{cases} 1/2, & \text{if } w = 0, \\ -1/2, & \text{if } w = \overleftarrow{c}, \ \overleftarrow{c} = \sum_{s=0}^{m-1} c_s 2^s, \\ 0, & \text{otherwise.} \end{cases}$
7 Elementary symmetric function with operating number 1	$2^{-m}(m - 2\|w\|),$
8 Elementary symmetric function with operating number i	$\frac{1}{2^m} \sum_{l=1}^{i} (-1)^l \begin{pmatrix} m - \|w\| \\ i - l \end{pmatrix} \begin{pmatrix} \|w\| \\ l \end{pmatrix},$

TABLE A.0.2   (Continued).

Function $f(z_0, \ldots, z_{m-1})$	Walsh transform $S(w) = S_f(w_0, \ldots, w_{m-1})$
9 Majority	$\frac{1}{2^m} \sum_{i=\lceil m/2 \rceil}^{m} \sum_{l=0}^{i} (-1)^l$ $\times \begin{pmatrix} m - \|w\| \\ i - l \end{pmatrix} \begin{pmatrix} \|w\| \\ l \end{pmatrix}$
10 Indicator of group code **V**	$2^{-m} \prod_{i=1}^{k} (W_{\overleftarrow{v}_i}(w) + 1)$, where $v_i = \sum_{s=0}^{m-1} v_{is} 2^s$. [a]
11 Equality indicator (indicator of code with repetition)	$\frac{1}{2^m} \prod_{i=1}^{k} (R_i(w) R_{i+k}(w) + 1)$ $= \begin{cases} 2^{-k}, & \text{if } w_i = w_{i+k}, \\ & i = 0, 1, \ldots, k-1, \\ 0, & \text{otherwise.} \end{cases}$
12 Sum indicator	$\begin{cases} 2^{-k}, & \text{if } w_i = w_{i+k} = \cdots, \\ & \cdots = w_{i+sk}, \\ & i = 0, 1, \ldots, k-1, \\ 0, & \text{otherwise.} \end{cases}$
13 Nonrepetitive quadratic form	$\begin{cases} \frac{1}{2^{k+1}}(2^k - 1), & \text{if } w = 0, \\ \frac{1}{2^{k+1}}, & \text{if } f(w) = 1, \\ & \text{and } w \neq 0, \\ -\frac{1}{2^{k+1}}, & \text{if } f(w) = 0, \\ & \text{and } w \neq 0. \end{cases}$
14 Quadratic form	$\begin{cases} \frac{1}{4}, & \text{if } w = 0, w = \overleftarrow{c} \oplus \overleftarrow{d}, \\ -\frac{1}{4}, & \text{if } w = \overleftarrow{c}, w = \overleftarrow{d}, \text{ [b]} \\ 0, & \text{otherwise.} \end{cases}$

TABLE A.0.2   (Further Continued).

Function $f(z_0, \ldots z_{m-1})$	Walsh transform $S(w) = S_f(w_0, \ldots, w_{m-1})$
15 k-ary form	$\begin{cases} (-1)^{\|c\|} 2^{-k}, & \text{if } w = c_1 \overleftarrow{a}_1 \oplus \\ & \quad c_2 \overleftarrow{a}_2 \oplus \cdots \oplus \\ & \quad c_k \overleftarrow{a}_k \pmod 2, \\ 0, & \text{otherwise.} \end{cases}$
16 Sign of sine	$\begin{cases} \frac{1}{2}, & w = 0, 2^{m-i-1}, \\ 0, & \text{otherwise.} \end{cases}$
17 Sign of cosine	$\begin{cases} \frac{1}{2}, & \text{if } w = 0, 2^{m-i} + 2^{m-i-1}, \\ 0, & \text{otherwise.} \end{cases}$
18 Sign of tangent (cotangent)	$\begin{cases} \frac{1}{2}, & \text{if } w = 0, 2^{m-i}, \\ 0, & \text{otherwise.} \end{cases}$
19 Sign of logarithm	$\begin{cases} 1 - 2^{-m}, & \text{if } w = 0, \\ -2^{-m}, & \text{if } w \neq 0. \end{cases}$
20 Unit step function	$2^{-m} J_w(A)^c$
21 Unit impulse function	$\begin{aligned} & 2^{-m}(J_w(2^i + A) - J_w(2^i - A))^d \\ & = 2^{-m}(1 + W_w(2^{i+1} - 1)) \\ & \quad \times (J_w(2^i) - J_w(2^i - A)). \end{aligned}$

$^a (v_{is})$, $i = 0, \ldots, k - 1$, $s = 0, \ldots, m - 1$ is the generating matrix of $\mathbf{V}$.

$^b \overleftarrow{c} = \sum_{i=0}^{m-1} c_i 2^i$, $\quad \overleftarrow{d} = \sum_{i=0}^{m-1} d_i 2^i$.

$^c J_w(y) = \sum_{i=0}^{y-1} W_w(z)$, $\qquad J_w(2^i) = \begin{cases} 2^i, & \text{if } w < 2^{m-i}, \\ 0, & \text{otherwise.} \end{cases}$

$^d f(z) = \begin{cases} 1, & \text{if } 2^i - A \leq z < 2^i + A, \\ 0, & \text{otherwise.} \end{cases}$

TABLE A.0.3   Functions and Their Autocorrelation Functions.

	Function $f(z_0, \ldots, z_{m-1})$	Autocorrelation $B_f(\tau) = B_f/(\tau_0, \ldots, \tau_{m-1})$
1	Constant	2^m
2	Elementary conjunction	$\begin{cases} 1, & \text{if } \tau = 0, \\ 0, & \text{if } \tau \neq 0. \end{cases}$
3	Elementary disjunction	$\begin{cases} 2^{-m} - 1, & \text{if } \tau = 0, \\ 2^{-m} - 2, & \text{if } \tau \neq 0. \end{cases}$
4	Conjunction	$\begin{cases} 2^{m-n}, & \text{if } \tau_{i_s} = 0, \\ & \quad s = 0, 1, \ldots, n-1, \\ 0, & \text{otherwise.} \end{cases}$
5	Disjunction	$\begin{cases} 2^m - 2^{m-n}, & \text{if } \tau_{i_s} = 0, \\ & \quad s = 0, \ldots, n-1, \\ 2^m - 2^{m-n+1}, & \text{otherwise.} \end{cases}$
6	Linear function	$2^{m-2}(W_{\widetilde{c}}(\tau) + 1)$
7	Elementary symmetric function with operating number 1	$\begin{cases} m, & \text{if } \tau = 0, \\ 2, & \text{if } \|\tau\| = 2, \\ 0, & \text{otherwise.} \end{cases}$
8	Elementary symmetric function with operating number i	$\begin{cases} \dbinom{m - \|\tau\|}{i - \|\tau\|/2} \dbinom{\|\tau\|}{\|\tau\|/2}, \\ \qquad \text{if } \|\tau\| \text{ is even,} \\ 0, \quad \text{otherwise,} \end{cases}$ $\left(\dbinom{p}{q} = 0, \text{if } p < q, \text{or } q < 0 \right).$

TABLE A.0.3 (Continued).

Function $f(z_0, \ldots, z_{m-1})$	Autocorrelation $B_f(\tau) = B_f(\tau_0, \ldots, \tau_{m-1})$
9 Majority	$\begin{cases} 2\sum_{i=0}^{\lfloor \|\tau\|/2 \rfloor} \binom{\|\tau\|}{i} \\ \qquad \times \sum_{j=0}^{\lfloor m/2 \rfloor} \binom{m - \|\tau\|}{m - j - i}, \\ \quad \text{if } \|\tau\| \text{ is odd}, \\ 2\sum_{i=0}^{\|\tau\|/2 - 1} \binom{\|\tau\|}{i} \sum_{j=0}^{\lfloor m/2 \rfloor} \binom{m - \|\tau\|}{m - j - i} \\ \quad + \binom{\|\tau\|}{\|\tau\|/2} \sum_{j=0}^{\lfloor m/2 \rfloor} \binom{m - \|\tau\|}{m - \|\tau\|/2 - j}, \\ \quad \text{if } \|\tau\| \text{ is even}, \\ \left(\binom{p}{q} = 0, \quad \text{if } p < q, \text{ or } q < 0 \right). \end{cases}$
10 Indicator of group code **V**	$\begin{cases} 2^k, & \text{if } \tau \in \mathbf{V}, \\ 0, & \text{if } \tau \notin \mathbf{V}. \end{cases}$
11 Equality indicator (indicator of code with repetition)	$\begin{cases} 2^k, & \text{if } \tau_i = \tau_{i+k}, \\ & i = 0, 1, \ldots, k - 1, \\ 0, & \text{otherwise}. \end{cases}$
12 Sum indicator	$\begin{cases} 2^{sk}, & \text{if } \tau_i \oplus \tau_{i+k} \oplus \cdots \\ & \quad \cdots \oplus \tau_{i+(s-1)k} = \tau_{i+sk}, \\ & i = 0, 1, \ldots, k - 1, \\ 0, & \text{otherwise}. \end{cases}$
13 Nonrepetitive quadratic form	$\begin{cases} 2^{2k-1} - 2^{k-1}, & \text{if } \tau = 0, \\ 2^{2k-2} - 2^{k-1}, & \text{if } \tau \neq 0, \end{cases}$
14 Quadratic form	$2^{m-4}(W_{\overleftarrow{c}}(\tau) + 1)(W_{\overleftarrow{d}}(\tau) + 1).$

TABLE A.0.3 (Further Continued).

Function $f(z_0, \ldots, m-1)$	Autocorrelation $B_f(\tau)$
15 k-ary form	$2^{m-2k} \prod_{i=1}^{k} (W_{\overleftarrow{a}_i}(\tau) + 1), \; (\overleftarrow{a}_i = \sum_{s=0}^{m-1} a_{is} 2^s)$
16 Sign of sine	$\begin{cases} 2^{m-1}, & \tau_{m-i-1} = 0, \\ 0, & \text{otherwise.} \end{cases}$
17 Sign of cosine	$2^{m-2}(W_{2^{m-i}+2^{m-i-1}}(\tau) + 1).$
18 Sign of tangent (cotangent)	$\begin{cases} 2^m - 1, & \text{if } \tau = 0, \\ 0, & \text{otherwise.} \end{cases}$
19 Sign of logarithm	$\begin{cases} 2^m - 1, & \text{if } \tau = 0, \\ 2^m - 2, & \text{if } \tau \neq 0. \end{cases}$
20 Unit step function	$\sum_{z=0}^{A-1} sign(A - (z \oplus \tau))$ $= \begin{cases} A, & \text{if } \tau = 0, \\ 2A_{m-t}(A - A^{(m-t)}) + A^{(m-t-1)}, \\ \quad \text{where } t = \lfloor \log_2 \tau \rfloor + 1,^a \\ \quad \text{if } \tau \geq 1. \end{cases}$
21 Unit impulse function	$\sum_{z=2^i-A}^{2^i+A-1} sign((2^i + A - (z \oplus \tau)))$ $\times ((z \oplus \tau) - (2^i - A) + 1)$ $= \begin{cases} 2A, & \text{if } \tau = 0, \tau = 2^{i+1} - 1, \\ 4A_{m-q}(A - A^{(m-q)}) + 2A^{(m-q-1)}, \\ \quad \text{where}^b \\ \quad q = \lfloor \log_2(\tau \oplus \tau_{m-1-i}(2^{i+1} - 1)) \rfloor + 1, \\ \quad \text{if } \tau \geq 1, \tau \neq 2^{i+1} - 1. \end{cases}$

$^a A = \sum_{s=0}^{m-1} A_s 2^{m-1-s}, \quad A^{(q)} = \sum_{s=0}^{q} A_s 2^{m-1-s}, \quad (A^{(m-1)} = A).$

$^b f(z) = \begin{cases} 1, & \text{if } 2^i - A \leq z < 2^i + A, \\ 0, & \text{otherwise.} \end{cases}$

TABLE A.0.4 Functions and Their Walsh Complexities.

Function $f(z_0, \ldots, z_{m-1})$	Spectral Complexity $L^W(f)$
1 Constant	1
2 Elementary conjunction	2^m
3 Elementary disjunction	2^m
4 Conjunction	2^n
5 Disjunction	2^n
6 Linear function	2
7 Elementary symmetric function with operating number 1	$\begin{cases} 2^m, & \text{if } m \text{ is odd,} \\ 2^m - \dbinom{m}{m/2}, & \\ & \text{if } m \text{ is even.} \end{cases}$
8 Elementary symmetric function with operating number i	$\begin{cases} 2^m, & \text{if } \dbinom{m}{i} \text{ is odd,} \\ 2^m - \sum_i \dbinom{m}{q_i}, & \\ & \text{otherwise,} \end{cases}$ where $\{q_i\}$ is the set of integer solutions x of $$\sum_{p=0}^{i}(-1)^p XY = 0, \quad X = \binom{m-x}{i-p}, \quad Y = \binom{x}{p}.$$

TABLE A.0.4   (Continued).

Function $f(z_0, \ldots, z_{m-1})$	Spectral Complexity $L^W(f)$
9 Majority	$2^m - \sum_l \binom{m}{q_l}$, where $\{q_l\}$ is the set of integer solutions x of $\sum_{i=\lceil m/2 \rceil}^{m} \sum_{l=0}^{i} (-1)^l XY = 0$, $X = \binom{m-x}{i-l}, Y = \binom{x}{l}$.
10 Indicator of group code **V**	2^{m-k}
11 Equality indicator (indicator of code with repetition)	2^k
12 Sum indicator	2^k
13 Nonrepetitive quadratic form	2^m
14 Quadratic form	4
15 k-Ary form	2^k
16 Sign of sine	2
17 Sign of cosine	2
18 Sign of tangent (cotangent)	2
19 Sign of logarithm	2^m
20 Unit step function	2^{m-a}, $A = 2^a(2k + 1)$
21 Unit impulse function	2^{m-a-1}, $A = 2^a(2k + 1)$

TABLE A.0.5 Functions and Their Haar Complexities.

	Function $f(z_0, \ldots, z_{m-1})$	Spectral Complexity $L^H(f)$
1	Constant	1
2	Elementary conjunction	$m + 1$
3	Elementary disjunction	$m + 1$
4	Conjunction	$n + 1$
5	Disjunction	$n + 1$
6	Linear function	$2^{\|c\| - 1} + 1$
7	Elementary symmetric function with operating number 1	$\dfrac{m(m+1)}{2}, \quad \text{if } m > 1$
8	Elementary symmetric function with operating number i	$\leq \max\left(\binom{m+1}{i} \cdot \binom{m+1}{i+1} + 1 \right)$
9	Majority	$\dfrac{3}{4} 2^m$
10	Indicator of group code **V**	$\leq 2^k(m - k) + 1$

TABLE A.0.5 (Continued).

Function $f(z_0, \ldots, z_{m-1})$	Spectral Complexity $L^H(f)$
11 Equality indicator (indicator of code with repetition)	$\leq 2^k k + 1$
12 Sum indicator	$\leq k 2^{m-k} + 1$
13 Nonrepetitive quadratic form	$\dfrac{1}{3}(2^{2k} - 1) + k + 1$
14 Quadratic form	$2^{m-2} + 2^{a-1} + 1$ where $a = \min(\|c\|, \|d\|)$
15 k-Ary form	$\leq L^H(F) 2^{\|a_q\|-1} + 1$ $\min_{1 \leq i \leq k} \|a_i\| = \|a_q\|,$ $F = f_q(z_{s_1} = 0, \ldots, z_{s_t} = 0)$ is the subfunction of $f_q(z) = \prod_{i=1, i \neq q}^{k} \bigoplus_{s=0}^{m-1} a_{i_s} z_s$ for $z_{s_1} = z_{s_2} = \cdots = z_{s_t} = 0.$
16 Sign of sine	2
17 Sign of cosine	3
18 Sign of tangent (cotangent)	2
19 Sign of logarithm	$m + 1$
20 Unit step function	$m - a + 1, A = 2^a(2k + 1)$
21 Unit impulse function	$2(m - a)(m - i)$

REFERENCES

1. Abbow, C.M., Brenner, J.L., Roots and canonical forms of circulant matrices, *Transactions of the American Mathematical Society*, 107(2), 1963, 360–373.

2. Abd-El-Barr, M., Hasan, M.N., New MVL-PLA structures based on current-mode CMOS circuits, *Proceedings of the 26th International Symposium on Multiple-Valued Logic*, Santiago de Campostela, Spain, May 19–21, 1996, 98–103.

3. Abd-El Barr, M.H., Zaky, S.G., Vranesic, Z.G., Synthesis of multivalued multithreshold functions for CCD implementation, *IEEE Transactions on Computers*, 35(2), 1986, 124–133.

4. Abraham, J.A., Fuchs, W.K., Fault and error models for VLSI, *Proceedings of IEEE*, 74(5), 1986, 639–654.

5. Abramovici, M., Breuer, M.A., Friedman, A.D., *Digital Systems Testing and Testable Design*, John Wiley & Sons, 1995.

6. Agaev, G.N., Vilenkin, N.Ya., Dzafarli, G.M., Rubinstein, A.I., *Multiplicative Systems of Functions and Harmonic Analysis on Zero-Dimensional Groups*, Elm Publisher, Baku, 1981.

7. Agaian, S.S., *Hadamard Matrices and Their Applications*, Springer-Verlag, Berlin, 1985.

8. Agaian, S., Astola, J., Egiazarian, K., *Binary Polynomial Transforms and Nonlinear Digital Filters*, Marcel Dekker, 1995.

9. Agaian, S., Astola, J., Egiazarian, K., Kuosmanen, P., Decompositional methods for stack filtering using Fibonacci *p*-codes, *Signal Processing*, 41(1), 1997, 101–110.

Spectral Logic and Its Applications for the Design of Digital Devices by Mark G. Karpovsky, Radomir S. Stanković and Jaakko T. Astola
Copyright © 2008 John Wiley & Sons, Inc.

10. Agaian, S., Caglayan, O., Perez, J., Sarukhanyan, H., Astola, J., Golden ration-Haar based steganography, *TICSP International Workshop on Spectral Transforms and Multirate Signal Processing, SMMSP 2006*, Florence, Italy, September 2–3. 2006, pp. 89–94.

11. Agaian, S., Sarukhanian, H. Astola, J., Golden-Hadamard transform matrices, *TICSP International Workshop on Spectral Transforms and Multirate Signal Processing, SMMSP 2006*, Florence, Italy, September 2–3, 2006, pp. 107–111.

12. Agaian, S., Tourshan, K., Noonan, J.P., Parametrisation of slant-Haar transforms, *IEE Proceedings of Vision Image and Signal Processing.*, 150(5), 2003, 306–311.

13. Agaian, S., Tourshan, K., Noonan, J.P., Performance of parametric slant-Haar transform, *Journal of Electronic Imaging*, 12(3), 2003, 539–550.

14. Ahmed, N., Rao, K.R., Discrete Fourier and Hadamard transforms, *Electronics Letters*, 6(7), 1970, 221–224.

15. Ahmed, N., Rao, K.R., Spectral analysis of linear digital systems using BIFORE, *Electronics Letters*, 6(2), 1970, 43–44.

16. Ahmed, N., Rao, K.R., *Orthogonal Transforms for Digital Signal Processing*, Springer, Heidelberg, 1975.

17. Ahmed, N., Rao, K.R., Abdusattar, A.L., BIFORE or Hadamard transform, *IEEE Transactions on Audio Electroacoustics*, AU-19(3), 1971, 225–234.

18. Ahmed, N., Rao, K.R., Abdusatar, A.L., On cyclic autocorrelation and Walsh-Hadamard transform, *IEEE Transactions on Electromagnetic Compatibility*, EMC-15, 1973, 141–146.

19. Ahmed, N., Rao, K.R., Schultz, R.B., The generalized transform, *Proceedings of the 1971 Symposium Application Walsh Functions*, AD-727-000 Washington, D.C., 1971, pp. 60–67. Also in *IEEE Transactions on Computers*, C-20(6), 1971, 695–698.

20. Ahmed, N., Schreiber, U.U., Lopresti, P.V., On notation and definition of terms related to a class of complete orthogonal functions, *IEEE Transactions on Electromagnetic Compatibility*, EMC-15, 1973, 75–80.

21. Aizenberg, I.N., Aizenberg, N.N., Vandewalle, J., *Multi-Valued and Universal Binary Neurons—Theory, Learning, Applications*, Kluwer Academic Publishers, Boston, Dordrecht, London, 2000.

22. Aizenberg, N.N., Ivaskiv, Yu.L., *Multivalued Threshold Logic* Naukova Dumka, Kiev, Ukraine, 1977 (in Russian).

23. Aizenberg, N.N., Ivaskiv, Yu.L., Pospelov, D.A., Khaidakov, U.A., Many-valued threshold functions, *Kibernetika*, (4), 1974 (in Russian).

24. Aizenberg, N.N., Kukharev, G.A., Pak, I.O., Shmerko, V.D., Methods of solution of logical equations by using fast orthogonal transforms and techniques of their realizations, *IX Vsesoyuznoe Sovetschanie Po Problemam Upravleniya*, Tezisy doklada, Moscow, 1983.

25. Aizenberg, N.N., Nutakov, V.D., Krenkelj, T.E., Harbat, Ya.G., Fresnel functions and Fresnel transforms for linear non-singular transforms, *Radiotehnika i Elektronika*, (4), 1984, 698–704.

26. Aizenberg, N.N., Rabinovich, Z.L., Some classes of functional systems of operations and canonical forms of many-valued logical functions, *Kibernetika*, (2), 1965, 37–45 (in Russian).

27. Aizenberg, N.N., Rudko, V.P., Sisuev, E.V., Haar functions and discrete mappings, *Tehn. Kibernetika*, 6, 1975, 86–94, (in Russian).

28. Aizenberg, N.N., Trofimljuk, O.T., Conjunctive transforms for discrete signals and their applications of tests and the detection of monotone functions, *Kibernetika*, (5), 1981, (in Russian).

29. Akers, S.B., On theory of Boolean functions, *Journal of the Society for Intustrial and Applied Mathematics*, 7(4), 1959, 487–498.

30. Akers, S.B., Binary decision diagrams, *IEEE Transactions on Computers*, C-27(6), 1978, 509–516.

31. Allen, C.M., Givone, D.D., A minimization technique for multiple valued logic systems, *IEEE Transactions Computers*, C-17(2), 1968, 182–194.

32. Almaini, A.E.A., Miller, J.F., Thomson, P., Billina, S., State assignment of finite state machines using a genetic algorithm, *IEE Proceedings E, Computer and Digital Techniques*, 142(4), 1995, 279–286.

33. Amaral, J.N., Cunha, W.C., State assignment algorithm for incompletely specified finite state machines, *Proceedings of 5th Congress of the Brazilian Society of Microelectronics*, July 1990, pp. 174–183.

34. Amaral, J.N., Turner, K., Ghosh, J., Designing genetic algorithms for the state assignment problem, *IEEE Transactions on Systems, Man, and Cybernetics*, 25(4), 1995, 686–694.

35. Andrews, H.C., Digital image transform processing, *Proceedings of 1971 Symposium Applications of Walsh Functions*, AD-727-000, Washington D.C., 1971, p. 26.

36. Andrews, H.C., Caspari, K.L., A generalized technique for spectral analysis, *IEEE Transactions on Computers*, C-19(1), 1969.

37. Antonenko, V.V., Ivanov, A., Shmerko, V., Linear arithmetic forms of k-valued logic functions and their realization on systolic arrays, *Avtomatika i Telemekhanika*, 56(3), 1995, 419–432.

38. Apple, G.G., Wintz, P.A., Calculation of Fourier transforms on finite Abelian groups, *IEEE Transactions on Information Theory*, IT-16, 1970, 233–234.

39. Arazi, B., *A Commonsense Approach to the Theory of Error-Correcting Codes*, The MIT Press, 1988.

40. Armstrong, B.D., A programmed aglorithm for assigning internal codes to sequential machines, *IEEE Transactions on Electronic Computers*, EC-11, 1962, 466–472.

41. Astola, J.T., Stanković, R.S., *Fundamentals of Switching Theory and Logic Design*, Springer, 2006.

42. Astola, J.T., Egiazarian, K., Stanković, M., Stanković, R.S., Fibonacci arithmetic expressions, *Avtomatika i Telemekhanika*, (6), 2004, 4–21. English translation, *Automation and Remote Control*, 65(6), 2004, 842–856.

43. Astola, J., Yaroslavsky, L. (eds.), *Advances in Signal Transforms—Theory and Applications, EURASIP Book Series on Signal Processing and Communications, Vol. 7*, Hindawi Publishing Corporation, 2007.

44. Avedillo, M.J., Quintana, J.M., Huertas, J.L., Easily testable PLA-based FSMs, *IEEE International Symposium on Circuits and Systems (ISCAS)*, Chicago, Illinois, USA, May 3–6, 1993, pp. 1603–1606.

45. Avedillo, M.J., Quintana, J.M., Huertas, J.L., Constrained state assignment of easily testable FSMs, *Journal of Electronic Testing: Theory and Applications*, 6(1), 1995, 133–138.

46. Baba, T., Uemura, T., Development of InGaAs-based multiple-junction surface tunnel transistors for multiple-valued logic circuits, *Proceedings of 28th International Symposium on Multiple-Valued Logic*, Fukuoka, Japan, May 27–29, 1998, 7–12.

47. Bader, D.A., Madduri, K., A parallel state assignment algorithm for finite state machines, *Proceedings of 11th International Conference on High Performance Computing (HiPC 2004)*, in: Bougé, L., Prasanna, V.K. (eds.), Springer-Verlag, LNCS 3296, 297–308, Bangalore, India, December 2004.

48. Bahai, A.R.S., Saltzberg, B.R., Ergen, M., *Multi Carries Digital Communications*, Springer, 2004.

49. Bartee, D.S., Schneider, G.F., Computation with finite fields, *Information and Control*, 6, 1963, 79–99.

50. Battisti, F., Carli, M., Egiazarian, K., Astola, J., Attack-resilient watermarking in the Haar wavelet domain, *TICSP International Workshop on Spectral Transforms and Multirate Signal Processing, SMMSP 2006*, Florence, Italy, September 2–3, 2006, pp. 121–126.

51. Beauchamp, K.G., *Walsh Functions and Their Applications*, Academic Press, Bristol, 1975.

52. Beauchamp, K.G., *Applications of Walsh and Related Functions with an Introduction to Sequency Theory*, Academic Press, Bristol, 1984.

53. Beiu, V., Quintana, J.M., Avedillo, M.J., VLSI implementations of threshold logic—a comprehensive survey, *IEEE Transactions on Neural Networks*, 14(5), 2003, 1217–1243.

54. Bennett, L.A.M., Synthesis of multi-output logic networks using spectral techniques, *IEE Proceedings Computers and Digital Techniques*, 142(4), 1995, 241–248.

55. Berlekamp, E.R., *Algebraic Coding Theory*, McGraw-Hill, New York, 1968.

56. Bern, J., Meinel, C., Slobodova, A., Efficient OBDD-based manipulation in CAD beyond current limits, *32nd Conference on Design Automation*, San Francisco, California, USA, June 12–16, 1995, pp. 408–413.

57. Bernasconi, A., Codendotti, B., Spectral analysis of Boolean functions as a graph eigenvalue problem, *IEEE Transactions on Computers*, 48(3), 1999, 345–351.

58. Berzilai, Z., Savir, J., Markowsky, G., Smith, M.G., Weighted syndrome sums approach to VLSI testing, *IEEE Transactions on Computers*, C-30(12), 1981, 996–1000.

59. Besslich, Ph.W., Determination of the irredundant forms of a Boolean function using Walsh-Hadamard analysis and dyadic groups, *IEE Journal of Computers and Digital Techniques*, 1, 1978, 143–151.

60. Besslich, Ph.W., Efficient computer method for XOR logic design, *IEE Proceedings, Part E, Computers and Digital Techniques*, 130, 1983, 203–206.

61. Besslich, Ph.W., Spectral processing of switching functions using signal flow transformations, in: Karpovsky, M.G. (ed.), *Spectral Techniques and Fault Detection*, Academic Press, Orlando, Florida, 1985.

62. Besslich, Ph.W., Lu, T., *Discrete Orthogonaltransformationen*, Springer-Verlag, Berlin, 1990.

63. Besslich, Ph.W., Trachtenberg, E.A., Sign transform, in: Moraga, C. (ed.), *Theory and Applications of Spectral Techniques*, Dortmund, 1988.

64. Besslich, Ph.W., Trachtenberg, E.A., The sign transform: an uniquely invertible nonlinear ternary transform, *Proceedings of International Conference on Signal Processing, Beijing'90*, Beijing, China, October 26–29, 1990, pp. 1195–1198.

65. Besslich, Ph.W., Trachtenberg, E.A., Binary input/ternary output switching circuits designed via the Sign transform, *Proceedings of 22nd International Symposium on Multiple-Valued Logic*, Sendai, Japan, May 27–29, 1992, pp. 348–354.

66. Beth, T., Jungnickel, D., Lenz, H., *Design Theory I, II*, 2nd edition, Cambridge University Press, 1999.

67. Blachman, N.M., Sinusoids versus Walsh functions, *Proceedings of IEEE*, 62(3), 1974, 346–354.

68. Bobwetter, C., The mutual spectral representation of trigonometric functions and Walsh functions, *Proceedings of 1971 Symposium Applications Walsh Functions*, AD-727-000, Washington D.C., 1971, pp. 43–46.

69. Bojković, Z., *Digital Image Processing*, Scientific Book, Belgrade, Serbia, 1989 (in Serbian).

70. Bolchini, C., Montandon, R., Salice, F., Sciuto, D., Design of VHDL-based totally self-checking finite-state machine and data-path descriptions, *IEEE Transactions on Very Large Scale Integration (VLSI) Systems*, 8(1), 2000, 98–103.

71. Bollig, B., Wegener, I., Improving the variable ordering of OBDDs is NP-complete, *IEEE Transactions on Computers*, C-45(9), 1996, 993–1002.

72. Booth, T.L., An analytical representation of signals in sequential networks, *Proceedings of Symposium on Mathematical Theory of Automata* (Microwave Research Inst. Symposia Series, Vol. XII), New York, Polytechnic Press, 1963, pp. 301–340.

73. Borodavka, N.V., Zadiraka, V.K., Steganographical algorithms based on the convolution theorem, *Cybernetics and System Analysis*, 40(1), 2004, 115–119.

74. Bracewell, R.N., The autocorrelation function, in: Bracewell, R.N. (ed.), *The Fourier Transform and Its Applications*, 3rd edition, McGraw-Hill, New York, 1999, pp. 40–45.

75. Bringham, O.E., *The Fast Fourier Transform*, Englewood Cliffs, N.J., Prentice Hall, 1974.

76. Bryant, R.E., Graph-based algorithms for Boolean functions manipulation, *IEEE Transactions on Computers*, C-35(8), 1986, 667–691.

77. Bryant, R.E., Chen, Y.A., Verification of arithmetic functions with binary moment decision diagrams, Technical Report No. CMU-CS-94-160, May 31, 1994.

78. Brayton, R.K., Hachtel, G.D., McMullen, C.T., Sangiovanni-Vincintelli, A.L., *Logic Minimization Algorithms for VLSI Synthesis*, Kluwer Academic Publishers, Boston, Massachusetts, 1984.

79. Bundalo, D., Djordjević, B., Bundalo, Z., Multiple-valued regenerative CMOS logic circuits with high-impedance output state, *Facta Universitatis, Series: Electrical Engineering* 19(1), 2006, 39–46.

80. Burrus, C.S., Gohinut, R.A., Guo, N., *Introduction to Wavelets and Wavelet Transforms*, Prentice-Hall, Upper Saddle River, 1998.

81. Bursenov, N.R., A ternary arithmetic machine, *Vestnik Moskov. Univ.*, 2, 39–48 (in Russian).

82. Butler, J.T., Nowlin, J.L., Sasao, T., Planarity in ROMDD's of Multiple-Valued Symmetric Functions, *26th International Symposium on Multiple-Valued Logic*, Santiago de Compostela, Spain, May 29–31, 1996, pp. 236–241.

83. Butson, A.T., Generalized Hadamard matrices, *Proceedings of American Mathematical Society*, 13(6), 1962, 894–898.

84. Butzer, P.L., Wagner, H.J., Approximation of Walsh polynomials and the concept of a derivative, *Proceedings of 1972 Symposium on Applications Walsh Functions*, Washington D.C., pp. 388–392.

85. Cairns, J.W., On the fast Fourier transform on finite abelian groups, *IEEE Transactions on Computers*, C-20(5), 1971, 569–572.

86. Calingaert, P., Switching function canonical form based on commutative and associative binary operations, *Transactions on American Institute Electrical Engineering*, Part I, 79, 1961, 808–814.

87. Cancellaro, M., Carli, M., Neri, A., Egiazarian, K., A robust data hiding scheme in tree-structured Haar transform, *TICSP International Workshop on Spectral Transforms and Multirate Signal Processing, SMMSP 2006*, Florence, Italy, September 2–3, 2006, pp. 113–120.

88. Canteaut, A., Carlet, C., Charpin, P., Fontaine, C., On cryptographic properties of the cosets of $R(1, m)$, *IEEE Transactions on Information Theory*, 47(4), 2001, 1494–1513.

89. Canteaut, A., Charpin, P., Decomposing bent functions, *IEEE Transactions on Information Theory*, 49(8), 2003, 2004–2019.

90. Carl, J.V., Swartwood, R.V., A hybrid Walsh transform computer, *IEEE Transactions on Computers*, C-22(7), 1973, 669–672.

91. Carlet, C., Ding, C., Highly non-linear mappings, *Journal of Complexity*, 20(2-3), 2004, 205–244.

92. Celinski, P., Cotofana, S.D., López, J.F., Al-Sarawi, S.F., Abbott, D., State of the art in CMOS threshold logic VLSI gate implementations and systems, in: Lopez, J.F., Montiel-Nelson, J.A., Pavlidis, D. (eds.), *VLSI Circuits and Systems, Proceedings of the SPIE*, Vol. 5117, 2003, pp. 53–64.

93. Chang, C.H., Falkowski, B.J., Generation of quasi-optimal FBDDs through paired Haar spectra, *Proceedings of IEEE International Symposium on Circuits and Systems, (31st ISCAS), Vol. VI*, Monterey, California, USA, May 31–June 3, 1998, pp. 167–170.

94. Chang, C.H., Falkowski, B.J., Haar spectra based entropy approach to quasi-minimization of FBDDs, *IEE Proceedings of Computers and Digital Techniques*, 146(1), 1999, 41–49.

95. Chang, S.H., Joseph, J., On ordering of a class of generalized Walsh functions, *Proceedings of 1972 Symposium Applications Walsh Functions*, Washington D.C., pp. 337–343.

96. Charmonman, S., Julius, R.S., Explicit inverses and condition numbers of certain circulants, *Mathematics and Computation*, 22(102), 1968, 428–430.

97. Chattopadhyay S., Low power state assignment flip-flop selection for finite state machine synthesis a Genetic algorithm approach, *IEE Proceedings of Computers and Digital Techniques*, 148(4–5), 2001, 147–151.

98. Chattopadhyay, S., Roy, S., Palchaudri, P., KGPMAP: library-based technology mapping technique for anti fuse based FPGAs, *IEE Proceedings of Computer and Digital Techniques*, 4(6), 1994, 361–368.

99. Chen, Y.-A., Bryant, R.E., An efficient graph representation for arithmetic circuit verification, *IEEE Transactions on Computer-Aided Design of Integrated Circuits and Systems*, 20(12), 2001, 1442–1454.

100. Chirikjian, G.S., Kyatkin, A.B., *Engineering Applications of Noncommutative Harmonic Analysis*, CRC Press, 2000.

101. Chow, C.K., On the characterization of threshold functions, *Proceedings of the Annals Symposium Switching Circuit Theory and Logical Design*, IEEE Special Publication S-134, September 1961, pp. 34–38.

102. Chrestenson, H.E., A class of generalized Walsh functions, *Pacific Journal of Math.*, 5(5), 1955, 17–31.

103. Clarke, E.M., Fujita, M., Zhao, X., Multi-terminal binary decision diagrams and hybrid decision diagrams, In: Sasao, T. Fujita. M. (eds.), *Representations of Discrete Functions*, Kluwer Academic Publishers, 1996, pp. 93–108.

104. Clarke, E.M., McMillan, K.L., Zhao, X., Fujita, M., Spectral transforms for extremely large Boolean functions, in: Kebschull, U., Schubert, E., Rosenstiel, W. (eds.), *Proceedings of IFIP WG 10.5 Workshop on Applications of the Reed–Muller Expansion in Circuit Design*, 1993, Hamburg, Germany, pp. 86–90.

105. Clarke, E.M., Zhao, X., Fujita, M., Matsunaga, Y., McGeer, R., Fast Walsh transform computation with Binary Decision Diagram, *Proceedings of IFIP WG 10.5 Workshop on Applications of the Reed-Muller Expansion in Circuit Design*, Hamburg, Germany, September 16–17, 1993, pp. 82–85.

106. Cohn, M., *Switching Function Canonical Form over Integer Fields*, PhD thesis, Harvard University, Cambridge, MA, December 1960.

107. Cohn, M., Walsh functions, sequency and Gray codes, *SIAM Journal of Applied Mathematics*, 21(3), 1971, 442–447.

108. Coleman, R.P., Orthogonal functions for the logical design of switching circuits, *IRE Transactions on Electronic Computers*, EC-10(3), 1961, 379–383.

109. Cooley, J.W., Tukey, J.W., An algorithm for the machine calculation of complex Fourier series, *Mathematics of Computation*, 19, 1965, 297–301.

110. Coudret, O., Madre, J.C., Implicit and incremental computation of primes and essential primes of Boolean functions, *Proceedings of the 29th Design Automation Conference*, Anaheim, California, USA, June 8–12, 1992, pp. 36–39.

111. Coudret, O., Sasao, T., Two-level logic minimization, In Hassoun,H., Sasao, T. (eds.), Brayton, R.K. (consulting editor), *Logic Synthesis and Verification*, Kluwer Academic Publishers, 2002, pp. 1–28.

112. Creutzburg, R., Recent results in image compression using the wavelet transform, *Proceedings of 5th International Workshop on Spectral Techniques*, Beijing, China, March 15–17, 1994, pp. 254–257.

113. Current, K.W., Current-mode CMOS multiple-valued logic circuits, *IEEE Journal of Solid-State Circuits*, 29(2), 1994, 95–107.

114. Cusic, C., Ding, C., Renvall, A., *Stream Ciphers and Number Theory*, North Holland Mathematical Library, 2004.

115. Damarla, T., Generalized transforms for multiple-valued circuits and fault detection, *IEEE Transactions on Computers*, C-48, 1992, 1101–1109.

116. Damarla, T.R., Karpovsky, M.G., Fault detection in combinational networks by Reed–Muller transform, *IEEE Transactions on Computers*, 38(6), 1989, 788–797.

117. Damarla, T., Karpovsky, M.G., Detection of stuck at and bridging faults in Reed–Muller canonical (RMC) network, *IEE Proceedings*, Part E, 136(5), 1989, 430–433.

118. Daubechies, I., Time-frequency localization operators—A geometric phase space approach, *IEEE Transactions on Information Theory*, 34(4), 1988, 605–612.

119. Davies, A.C., On the definition and generation of Walsh functions, *IEEE Transactions on Computers*, C-21(2), 1972, 187–189.

120. Debnath, D., Sasao, T., Exact minimization of FPRMs for incompletely specified functions by using MTBDDs, *IEICE Transactions on Fundamentals of Electronics, Communications and Computer Sciences*, E88-A(12), 2005, 3332–3341.

121. De Micheli, G., *Synthesis and Optimization of Digital Circuits*, McGraw Hill, 1994.

122. De Micheli, G., Brayton, R., Sangiovanni-Vincentelli, A., KISS, A program for optimal state assignment of finite state machines, *Proceedings of IEEE International Conference on Computers-Aided Design*, Santa Clara, CA, November 1984, pp. 209–211.

123. De Micheli, G., Brayton, R., Sangiovanni-Vincentelli, A., Optimal state assignment for finite state machines, *IEEE Transactions on Computer-Aided Design*, CAD-4(3), 1985, 269–284.

124. Dertouzos, M.L., *Threshold Logic—A Synthesis Approach*, Cambridge, MA, MIT Press, 1965.

125. Degtyaryov, A.N., Slyozkin, V.G., Conception of a generalized receiver in telecommunication systems, *Proceedings of the 11th International Conference on Microwave and Telecommunication Technology, CriMiCo'2001*, Sevastopol, Crimea, Ukraine, September 10–14, 2001, pp. 290–291.

126. Devadas, S., Ma, H.-K.T., Newton, A.R., A synthesis and optimization procedure for fully and easily testable sequential machines, *IEEE Transactions on Computer-Aided Design of Integrated Circuits and Systems*, CAD-8(10), 1989, 1100–1107.

127. Devdas, S., Ma, H., Newton, A.R., Sangiovanni-Vincentelli, A., MUSTANG: state assignment of finite state machines targeting multilevel logic implementations, *IEEE Transactions on Computer Aided Design of Integrated Circuits and Systems*, CAD-7(12), 1988, 1290–1300.

128. Dhawan, S., De Vries, R.C., Design of self-checking sequential machines, *IEEE Transactions on Computers*, C-37(10), 1988, 1280–1284.

129. Doetsch, G., *Anleitung zum praktischen Gebrauch der Laplace-Transformation und der Z-Transformation*, Oldenburg, Munchen, Wien, 1967.

130. Drechsler, R., Becker, B., *Binary Decision Diagrams—Theory and Implementations*, Kluwer Academic Publishers, 1998.

131. Du, X. Hachtel, G. Lin, B. Newton, A.R., MUSE: a multilevel symbolic encoding algorithm for state assignment, *IEEE Transactions on Computer-Aided Design of Integrated Circuits and Systems*, 10(1), 1991, 28–38.

132. Dubrova, E., Multiple-valued logic in VLSI, challenges and opportunities, *Proceedings of NORCHIP'99*, Oslo, Norway, November 9–12, 1999, pp. 340–350.

133. Dubrova, E.V., Miller, D.M., On disjunctive covers and ROBDD size, *Proceedings of Pacific Rim Conference on Communication, Computers and Signal Processing*, Victoria, B.C., Canada, August 23–25, 1999, pp. 162–164.

134. Dvortsin,. V.I., Ivanenko, V.I., Structural synthesis of controllers in automatic control systems on the basis of threshold element networks, *Kibernetika*, 5, 1966, 45–50 (in Russian).

135. Djoković, D.Ž., Two Hadamard matrices of order 956 of Goethals-Seidal type, *Combinatorica*, 14(3), 1994, 375–377.

136. Edmonds, J., Paths, trees and flowers, *Canadian Journal of Mathematics*, 17(3), 1965, 449–468.

137. Edmonds, J., Maximum matching and a polyhedron with 0, 1 vertices, *Journal of Research of the National Bureau of Standards*, 69B, 1965, 125–130.

138. Edwards, C.R., The application of Rademacher–Walsh transforms to digital circuit synthesis, *Proceedings of Symposium on Theory and Applications of Walsh and Other Nonsinusoidal Functions*, Hatfield Polytechnic Inst., United Kingdom, 1973.

139. Edwards, C.R., The application of Rademacher Walsh transform to Boolean function classification and threshold logic, *IEEE Transactions on Computers*, C-24(1), 1975, 48–62.

140. Eggermont, R., Cotofana, S., Lageweg, C., Profiling-based state assignment for low power dissipation, *Proceedings of ProRISC 2004*, ISBN 90-73461-43-X, Veldhoven, The Netherlands, November 25–26, 2004, pp. 377–384.

141. Egiazarian, K., Astola, J., Discrete orthogonal transforms based on Fibonacci-type recursion, *Proceedings of IEEE Digital Signal Processing Workshop (DSPWS-96)*, Loen, Norway, September 1–4, 1996, pp. 405–408.

142. Egiazarian, K., Astola, J., On generalized Fibonacci cubes and unitary transforms, *Applicable Algebra in Engineering, Communication and Computing*, AAECC-8, 1997, 371–377.

143. Egiazarian, K., Astola, J., Agaian, S., Orthogonal transforms based on generalized Fibonacci recursions, *Proceedings of the 2nd International Workshop on Spectral Techniques and Filter Banks*, Brandenburg, Germany, March 5–7, 1999, pp. 457–473.

144. Egiazarian, K., Astola, J.T., Tree-structured Haar transforms, *Journal of Mathematical Imaging and Vision*, 16(3), 2002, 269–279.

145. Egiazarian, K., Astola, J., Stanković, R.S., Stanković, M., Circuit design from optimal wavelet packet series expressions, *Proceedings of International Symposium on Circuits and Systems, ISCAS 2003*, Bangkok, Thailand, Vol. 5, May 25–28, 2003, pp. 597–600.

146. Egiazarian, K., Astola, J., Stanković, R.S., Stanković, M., Construction of compact word-level representations of multiple-output switching functions by wavelet packets, *Proceedings of 6th International Symposium on Representations and Methodology of Future Computing Technology (Reed–Muller Workshop)*, Trier, Germany, March 10–11, 2003, pp. 77–84.

147. Egizarian, K., Kuosmanen, P., Astola, J., Boolean derivatives, weighted Chow parameters and selection probabilities of stack filters, *IEEE Transactions on Signal Processing*, 44(7), 1996, 1634–1641.

148. *eInfochips* - Integrated Design Services Company Dashboard, *Speeding up Large FPGA Based Design Using One Hot State Machine Encoding*, Dashboard-March 2005 Issue, $http://www.einfochips.com/download/march_05_ip.pdf$

149. Elliot, D.F., Rao, K.R., *Orthogonal Transforms for Digital Signal Processing*, Academic Press, New York, 1982.

150. Enamoto, H., Shibata, K., Orthogonal transform coding system for television signals, *IEEE Transactions on Electromagnetic Compatibility*, EMC-13(3), 1971, 11–17.

151. Endow, Y., *Walsh Analysis*, Tokyo Denki University Press, Tokyo, 1993.

152. Eris, E., Miller, D.M., Syndrome-testable internally-unate combinational networks, *Electronic Letters*, 19(6), 1983, 637–638.

153. Erosh, I.L., Karpovsky, M.G., Error correction in arithmetic units based on multistable elements, *Teoriya Avtomatov*, 2, 1970, 73–79 (in Russian).

154. Falkowski, B.J., Generalized multi-polarity Hadamard-Walsh transform, *Recent Developments in Abstract Harmonic Analysis with Applications in Signal Processing*, Nauka, Belgrade, 1996, pp. 269–279.

155. Falkowski, B.J., Relationships between arithmetic and Haar wavelet transforms in the form of layered Kronecker matrices, *Electronic Letters*, 35(10), 1999, 799–800.

156. Falkowski, B.J., A note on the polynomial form of Boolean functions and related topics, *IEEE Transactions on Computers*, 48(8), 1999, 860–864.

157. Falkowski, B.J., Chang, C.H., A novel paired Haar transform: Algorithms and interpretations in Boolean domain, *Proceedings of IEEE Midwest Symposium on Circuits and Systems* (36th MWSCAS), Detroit, Michigan, USA, August 1993, pp. 1101–1104.

158. Falkowski, B.J., Chang, C.H., Efficient algorithm for forward and inverse transformations between Haar spectrum and Binary Decision Diagrams, *Proceedings of the 13th International Phoenix Conference on Computers and Communication*, Phoenix, Arizona, USA, April 1994, pp. 497–503.

159. Falkowski, B.J., Chang, C.H., Efficient algorithm for the calculation of arithmetic spectrum from OBDD and synthesis of OBDD from arithmetic spectrum for incompletely specified Boolean functions, *Proceedings of IEEE International of Symposium on Circuits and Systems ISCAS94*, Vol. 1, London, UK, May 30–June 2, 1994, pp. 197–200.

160. Falkowski, B.J., Chang, C.H., Forward and inverse transformations between Haar spectra and ordered binary decision diagrams of Boolean functions, *IEEE Transactions on Computers*, 46(11), 1997, 1272–1279.

161. Falkowski, B.J., Chang, C.H., Properties and applications of paired Haar transform, *Proceedings of IEEE International Conference on Information, Communications and Signal Processing, 1st ICICS*, Singapore, Vol. 1, September 1997, pp. 48–51.

162. Falkowski, B.J., Chang, C.H., Forward and inverse transformations between Haar spectra and ordered binary decision diagrams of Boolean functions, *IEEE Transactions on Computers*, 46(11), 1997, 1272–1279.

163. Falkowski, B.J., Chang, C.H., Calculation of paired Haar spectra for systems of incompletely specified Boolean functions, *Proceedings of IEEE International Symposium on Circuits and Systems, 31st ISCAS*, Monterey, California, USA, Vol. 6, May 31–June 3, 1998, 171–174.

164. Falkowski, B.J., Perkowski, M.A., One more way to compute the Hadamard-Walsh spectrum of completely and incompletely specified Boolean functions, *International Journal of Electronics*, 69(5), 1990, 595–602.

165. Falkowski, B.J., Perkowski, M.A., A family of all essential radix-2 addition/subtraction multi-polarity transforms: algorithms and interpretations in Boolean domain, *Proceedings of International Symposium on Circuits and Systems, 23rd ISCAS*, New Orleans, USA, Vol. 4, May 1–3, 1990, pp. 2913–2916.

166. Falkowski, B.J., Rahardja, S., Complex spectral decision diagrams, *Proceedings of the 26th International Symposium on Multiple-Valued Logic*, Santiago de Campostela, Spain, May 29-31, 1996, pp. 255–260.

167. Falkowski, B.J., Sasao, T., Unified algorithm to generate Walsh functions in four different orderings and its programmable hardware implementation, *IEE Proceedings of Vision, Image & Signal Processing*, 152(6), 2005, 819–826.

168. Falkowski, B.J., Shmerko, V.D., Yanushkevich, S.N., Arithmetic logic - its status and achievements, *Proceedings of 4th International Conference Application of Computer Systems, ACS'97*, Szczecin, Poland, November 1997, pp. 208–223.

169. Falkowski, B.J., Stanković, R.S., Janković, D., Minimization of circuit design using permutation of Haar wavelet series, *Journal of Circuits, Systems and Computers*, 14(3), 2005, 483–495.

170. Faradzhev, R.G., Analytical methods of computation in linear sequential machines, *Tekhnicheskaya Kiberntika*, 5, 1965, 93–102 (in Russian).

171. Faradzhev, R.G., On the spectral approach to problems of sequential machines, *Avtomatika i Telemekhanika*, 5, 1966, 50–55 (in Russian).

172. Faradzhev, R.G., Methods of sampled-data control systems in the theory of finite automata (sequential machines), *Izv. Akad. Nauk. Azerb. SSR*, Ser. Fiz.-Tekhn. i Mat. Nauk., 1, 1969 (in Russian).

173. Fazel, K., Kaiser, S., *Multi-Carrier and Spread Spectrum Systems*, Wiley, 2003.

174. Feinberg, V., *VLSI Planarization, Methods, Models, Implementation*, Kluwer Academic Publishers, 1997.

175. Ferel, S., Some Walsh function analysis techniques, *Proceedings of the 1971 Symposium on Application of Walsh Functions*, AD-727-000, Washington D.C., 1971, pp. 151–154.

176. Fine, N.J., On the Walsh functions, *Transactions of the American Society,* 3, 1949, 372–414.

177. Fino, B.J., Relations between Haar and Walsh/Hadamard transforms, *Proceedings of IEEE*, 60(5), 1972, 647–648.

178. Fino, B.J., Algazi, V.R., Slant Haar transform, *Proceedings of IEEE*, 62(5), 1974, 653–654.

179. Fino, B.J., Algazi, V.R., Unified matrix treatment of the Fast Walsh-Hadamard transform, *IEEE Transactions on Computers*, C-25(11), 1976, 1142–1146.

180. Fino, B.J., Algazi, V.R., A unified treatment of discrete Fast unitary transforms, *SIAM Journal on Computing*, 6(4), 1977, 700–717.

181. Fourier, J.B., *Théorie analytique de la chaleur*, Euvres 1, see also a paper by Fourier, J.B., form 1811 published in 1824 in *Mem. de l'Acad. des Sci.*, Paris, (2), 4, 1819/20, 135-155, published in 1824, and Fourier, J.B., Mémoire sur la propagation de la Chaleur dans les corps solides, *Nouveau Bulletin des sciences par la Societé philomathematique de Paris*, No. 6, Paris, Bernard, Mars 1808.

182. Frank, J., Implementation of dyadic correlation, *Proceedings of the 1971 Symposium on Application of Walsh Functions*, AD-727-000, Washington D.C., 1971, pp. 111–117.

183. Frankel, H.D., Applications of Walsh functions, *Proceedings of 1971 Symposium on Application of Walsh Functions*, AD-727-000, Washington D.C., 1971, pp. 134–136.

184. Fujita, M., Methods for automatic design error-correction in sequential circuits, *Proceeding of 41th European Design Automation Conference*, Paris, France, February 22–25, 1993, pp. 76–80.

185. Fujita, M., Kukimoto, Y., Brayton, R.K , BDD minimization by truth table permutation, *Proceedings of International Symposium on Circuits and Systems, ISCAS'96*, Vol. 4, Atlanta, Georgia, USA, May 12–15, 1996, pp. 596–599.

186. Fujita, M., Matsunaga, Y., Kukuda, T., On variable ordering of binary decision diagrams for the optimization in multi-level synthesis, *European Conference on Design Automation*, Amsterdam , Netherlands, February 25–28, 1991, pp. 50–54.

187. Fujita, M., Yang, J.C.-H., Clarke, E.M., Zhao, X., Geer, M.C., Fast spectrum computation for logic functions using binary decision diagrams, *Proceedings of International Symposium on Circuits and Systems, ISCAS-94*, Vol. 1, London, UK, May 30–June 2, 1994, pp. 275–278.

188. Fuhrer, R.M., Lin, B., Nowick, S.M., Algorithms for the optimal state assignment of asynchronous state machines, *Proceedings of 16th Conference Advanced Research in VLSI, ARVLSI'95*, Chapel Hill, NC, USA, March 27–29, 1995, pp. 59–5.

189. Fuhrer, R.M., Nowick, S.M., Theobald, M., Jha, N.K., Lin, B., Plana, L., *MINIMALIST: An environment for Synthesis, Verification and Testability of Burst-Mode Asynchronous Machines*, Technical Report, CUCS-020-99, Columbia University, Computer Science Department, 1999.

190. Garaev, M.U., Faradzhev, R.G., On an analogue of Fourier expansion over Galois fields and its applications to problem of generalized sequential machines, *Izv. Akad. Nauk Azerb. SSR*, Ser. Fiz. -Techn. i Math. Nauk, 6, 1965, 1–68.

191. Gelbaum, B.R., On the functions of Haar, *Annals of Mathematics*, 51(1), 1950, 26–36.

192. Gentleman, W.M., Matrix multiplication and fast Fourier transform, *Bell System Technical Journal*, 47, 1968, 1099–1103.

193. Gentleman, W.M., Sande, G., Fast Fourier transform for fun and profit, *AFIPS Proceedings of the 1966 Fall Joint Computer Conference*, Spartan, Washington, USA, Vol. 29, 1966, pp. 563–578.

194. Gerace, G.B., Gestri, G., State assignments for reducing the number of delay elements in sequential machines, *Information and Control*, 10(3), 1967, 223–253.

195. Gergov, J., Meinel, C., Efficient Boolean manipulation with OBDDs can be extended to FBDDs, *IEEE Trans. on Computers*, C-43(10), 1994, 1197–1209.

196. Gethoffer, H., Mutual mapping of generalized convolution systems, *Proceedings of the 1972 Symp. on Application Walsh Functions*, Washington D.C., pp. 310–316.

197. Gibbs, J.E., Walsh spectrometry a form of spectral analysis well suited to binary digital computation, *NPL DES Reports*, National Physical Lab., Teddington, Middlesex, England, 1967.

198. Gibbs, J.E., Harmonic analysis in the dyadic field regarded as a function space, Seminar, Royal Signals and Radar Establishment, 10.28.1976, pp. ii+24.

199. Gibbs, J.E., Instant Fourier transform, *Electronics Letters*, 13(5), 1997, 122–123.

200. Gibbs, J.E., Local and global views of differentiation, In: Butzer, P.L., Stanković, R.S. (eds), *Theory and Applications of Gibbs Derivatives and Applications*, Matematički institut, Beograd, 1990, pp. 1–19.

201. Gibbs, J.E., Ireland, B., Marshall, J.E., Generalization of the Gibbs derivative, *Proceedings of Colloquium on the Theory and Applications of Walsh Functions*, Hatfield, Hertfordshire, 6.28–29.1973, pp. ii+32.

202. Gibbs, J.E., Millard, M.J., Walsh functions as solutions of a logical differential equation, *NPL DES Reports*, National Physical Lab., Teddington, Middlesex, England, 1969.

203. Gibbs, J.E., Pichler, F.R., Comments on transformation of Fourier power spectra into Walsh power spectra, *Proceedings of 1971 Symposium on Applications on Walsh Functions*, Washington D. C., April 1971, pp. 51–54.

204. Gil, C., Ortega, J., Parallel test generation using circuit partitioning and spectral techniques, *Proceedings of the 6th Euromicro Workshop on Parallel and Distributed Processing*, January 21–23, 1998, pp. 264–270.

205. Givone, D.D., Snelsire, R.W., *Final Report on the Design of Multiple-Valued Logic Systems*, Digital Lab. Department of Electronic and Engineering, State University of New York, Buffalo, June, 1968.

206. Glukhov, Yu.I., Boikov, A.P., Spectral representations of Boolean functions, *Izv. Leningrad. Elektrotekhn. Inst. im. Lenina*, 91, 1969, 57–60 (in Russian).

207. Gobrunov, G.V., Moskalev, E.S., Application of spectral methods in minimization of combinational networks, *Avtomat. i Vychisl. Tekh.*, 3, 1971, 1–8, (in Russian).

208. Gobrunov, G.V., Moskalev, E.S., On a certain method for constructing digital generators for functions of three variables, in: Smolov, V.B. (ed.), *Vychislitel'naya Tekhnika*, Vol 1, Energiya, Moscow, 1970, pp. 195–206 (in Russian).

209. Gobrunov, G.V., Moskalev, E.S., Design of many-input digital function generators by the method of approximating functional lattices, *Kibernetika*, 2, 1971, 62–66 (in Russian).

210. Gobrunov, G.V., Moskalev, E.S., Application of Rademacher–Walsh polynomials to approximation of functions of several variables, *Kibernetika*, 3, 1971, 19–22 (in Russian).

211. Golomb, W., On the classification of Boolean functions, *IRE Transactions on Circuit Theory*, CT-6 (5), May 1959, 176–186.

212. Golomb, S.W., Baumert, L.D., The search for Hadamard matrices, *American Mathematics Monthly*, 70, 1963, 12–17.

213. Golomb, S.W., Gong, G., *Signal Design for Good Correlation for Wireless Communications, Cryptography and Radar*, Cambridge University Press, 2005.

214. Golubov, B.I., Efimov, A.V., Skvorcov, V.A., *Ryady i preobrazovaniya Uolsha, teoriya i primeneniya*, Nauka, Moskva, 1987.

215. Golubov, B., Efimov, A., Skvortsov, V.A., *Walsh Series and Transforms*, Kluwer Academic Publishers, Dordrecht, 1991.

216. Gongli, Z., Moraga, C., Orthogonal transforms on finite Abelian groups, In Stankovićc, R.S., Stojić, M.R., Stanković, M.S. (eds.), *Recent Developments in Abstract Harmonic Analysis with Applications in Signal Processing*, Nauka, Belgrade, 1996, pp. 293–304.

217. Good, I.J., The interaction algorithm and practical Fourier analysis, *Journal of the Royal Statistical Society*, series B, 20, 1958, 361–372, Addendum, 22, 1960, 372–375.

218. Good, I.J., The relationship between two fast Fourier transforms, *IEEE Transaction Computers*, C-20(3), 1971, 310–317.

219. Günther, W., Drechsler, R., BDD minimization by linear transforms, *Proceedings of International Conference on Advanced Computer Systems*, Szczecin, Poland, November 19–20, 1998, pp. 525–532.

220. Günther, W., Drechsler, R., Linear transformations and exact minimization of BDDs, *Proceeding of 8th Great Lake Symposium on VLSI*, February 19–21, 1998, pp. 325–330.

221. Günther, W., Drechsler, R., Efficient manipulation algorithms for linearly transformed BDDs, *Proceedings of 4th International Workshop on Applications of Reed–Muller Expansion in Circuit Design*, Victoria, Canada, May 20–21, 1999, pp. 225–232.

222. Günther, W., Drechsler, R., Minimization of BDDs using linear transformations based on evolutionary techniques, *Proceedings of International Symposium on Circuit and Systems, ISCAS '99*, Vol. 1, May 30 – June 2, 1999, 387–390.

223. Haar, A., Zur theorie der orthogonalen Funktionsysteme, *Mathematical Annalysis*, 69, 1910, 331–371.

224. Haas, G., *Fundamentals and Components of Electronic Digital Computer*, Philips Technical Library, 1963.

225. Hachtel, G.D., Somenzi, F., *Logic Synthesis and Verification Algorithms*, Springer, 1996.

226. Hadamard, M.J., Resolution d'une question relative aux determinants, *Bulletin Des Sciences and Mathematiques*, A17, 1893, 240–246.

227. Hammond, J.L., Jonson, L.B., Orthogonal square wave functions, *Journal of the Franklin Institute*, 273, 1962, 211–225.

228. Hansen, J.P., Sekine, M., Synthesis by spectral translation using Boolean decision diagrams, *Proceedings of Design Automation Conference*, June 1996, 248–253.

229. Hansen, J.P, Sekine, M., Decision diagrams based techniques for the Haar wavelet transform, *Proceedings of IEEE International Conference on Information, Communications and Signal Processing*, 1st ICICS, Vol. 1, Singapore, September 1997, pp. 59–63.

230. Hanyu, T., Challenge of a multiple-valued technology in recent deep-submicron VLSI, *Proceedings of the 31st IEEE International Symposium on Multiple-Valued Logic*, Warsaw, Poland, May 22–24, 2001, pp. 241–244.

231. Haring, D.R., *Sequential Circuit Synthesis, State Assignment Aspects*, MIT Press, Cambridge, MA, 1966.

232. Harking, B., Moraga, C., Efficient derivation of Reed–Muller expansions in multiple-valued logic systems, *Proceedings of 22nd International Symposium on Multiple-Valued Logic*, Sendai, Japan, May 27–29, 1992, pp. 436–441.

233. Harmuth, H.F., A generalized concept of frequency and some applications, *IEEE Transactions on Infromation Theory*, IT-14 (3), 1968, 375–382.

234. Harmuth, H.F., *Transmission of Information by Orthogonal Functions*, 2nd edition, Springer-Verlag, New York, 1972.

235. Harmuth, H.F., *Sequency Theory, Foundations and Application*, Academic Press, New York, 1977.

236. Harrison, M.A., On equivalence of state assignments, *IEEE Transactions on Computers*, C-17, 1968, 55–57.

237. Hastigns, C., *Approximations for Digital Computers*, Princeton, New Jersey, 1955.

238. Hasteer, G., Banerjee, P., A parallel algorithm for state assignment in finite state machines, *IEEE Transaction on Computers*, 47(2), 1998, 242--246.

239. Hawkins, J.K., *Circuit Design of Digital Computers*, Wiley, New York, 1968.

240. Heideman, M.T., Johnson, D.H., Burrus, C.S., Gauss and the history of the fast Fourier transform, *Archive for History of Exact Science*, Vol. 34(3), 1985, 265–277. Also in *IEEE ASSP Magazine*, 1(4), October 1984, 14–21.

241. Heidtmann, K.D., Arithmetic spectra applied to stuck-at-fault detection for combinatorial networks, *Proceedings of 2nd Technical Workshop New Directions in IC Testing*, Winnipeg, April 1987, pp. 4.1– 4.13.

242. Heidtmann, K.D., Arithmetic spectrum applied to fault detection for combinatorial networks, *IEEE Transactions on Computers*, 40(3), 1991, 320–324.

243. Helm, H.A., Group codes and Walsh functions, *Proceedings of the 1971 Symposium on Application of Walsh Functions*, AD-727-000, Washington, D.C., 1971.

244. Henderson, K.W., Some notes on the Walsh functions, *IEEE Transactions on Electronic Computers*, EC-13, 1962, 50–53.

245. Henderson, K.W., Comment on the fast Fourier transform, *IEEE Transactions on Computers*, C-19, 1970, 850.

246. Hewitt, E., Ross, K., *Abstract Harmonic Analysis*, Berlin, Springer, 1963.

247. Hill, F., Peterson, G.R., *Introduction to Switching Theory and Logical Design*, Wiley, New York, 1968.

248. Ho, A.T.S., Zhu, X., Guan, Y.L., Marziliano, P., Slant transform watermarking for textured images, *Proceedings of International Symposium on Circuits and Systems, ISCAS'04*, Vol. 5, Vancouver, Canada, May 23–26 2004, pp. V-700–V-703.

249. Hoffmann, D.W., Kropf, T., Efficient design error correction of digital circuits, *Proceedings of International Conference on Computer Design*, Austin, TX, USA, September 17–20, 2000, pp. 465–472.

250. Hopcraft, J.E., Karp, R.M., An $n^{5/2}$ algorithm for maximum matching bipartite graphs, *SIAM Journal of Computing*, 2(1), 1973, 225–232.

251. Hsiao, T.C., Seth, S.C., An analysis of the use of Rademacher–Walsh spectrum in compact testing, *IEEE Transactions on Computers*, 33 (10), 1984, 934–937.

252. Huang, S-Y., Cheng, K-T., Chen, K-C., Lu, J-Y., Fault-simulation based design error diagnosis for sequential circuits, *Proceedings of the 35th Design Automation Conference*, San Francisco, California, USA, 1998, pp. 632–637.

253. Hwa, H.R., Sheng, S.L., An approach for the realization of threshold functions of order r, *IEEE Transactions on Electronic Computers*, EC-18(10), 1969, 923–939.

254. Hurst, S.L., The application of Chow parameters and Rademacher–Walsh matrices in the synthesis of binary functions, *Computer Journal*, 16(2), 1973, 165–171.

255. Hurst, S.L., *Logical Processing of Digital Signals*, Crane Russak and Edward Arnold, London and Basel, 1978.

256. Hurst, S.L., The Haar transform in digital network synthesis, *Proceedings of the 11th International Symposium on Multiple-valued Logic*, Oklahoma City, Oklahoma, USA, May 1981, pp. 10–18.

257. Hurst, S.L., Use of linearization and spectral techniques in input and output compaction testing of digital networks, *IEE Proceedings*, Part 1, 136(1), 1989, 48–56.

258. Hurst, S.L., Miller, D.M., Muzio, J.C., *Spectral Techniques for Digital Logic*, Academic Press, 1985.

259. Iguchi, Y., Sasao, T., Hardware to compute Walsh coefficients, *Proceedings of the 35th International Symposium on Multiple-Valued Logic*, Calgary, Canada, May 19–21, 2005, pp. 75–81.

260. Iseno, A., Iguchi, Y., Sasao, T., Fault diagnosis of RAMs using Walsh spectrum, *Proceedings of International Workshop on Representations and Methodology of Future Computing Technologies, Reed–Muller Workshop, RM-03*, Trier, Germany, March 10–11, 2003, pp. 85–92.

261. Iseno, A., Iguchi, Y., Sasao, T., Fault diagnosis for RAMs using Walsh spectrum, *IEICE Transactions on Information and Systems*, E87-D, No. 3, 2004, 592–600.

262. Ito, T., A note on a general expansion of functions of binary variables, *Information and Control*, 12, 1968, 206–211.

263. Ito, T., The Applications of the Walsh functions to pattern recognition and switching theory, *Proceedings of 1970 Symposium Application of Walsh Functions*, Naval Research Lab., Cambridge, MA, 1970.

264. Jabir, A., Saul, J., Heuristic AND-OR-EXOR three-level minimisation algorithm for multiple-output incompletely-specified Boolean functions, *IEE Proceedings of Computers and Digital Techniques*, 147(6), 2000, 451–461.

265. Jackson, P., Pais, J., Computing prime implicants, *Proc of the 10th International Conference on Automated Deduction*, Kaiserslautern, West Germany, July 1990, *Lecture Notes in Artificial Intelligence*, Vol. 449, Springer-Verlag, pp. 543–557.

266. Jain, J., Arithmetic transform of Boolean functions, in: Sasao, T., Fujita, M. (eds.), *Representations of Discrete Functions*, Kluwer Academic Publishers, 1996, pp. 133–161.

267. Janković, D., Stanković, R.S., Drechsler, R., Decision diagram method for calculation of pruned Walsh transform, *IEEE Transactions on Computers*, 50(2), 2001, 147–151.

268. Jin, M., Zhang, Q., Copy feature of Walsh functions and its applications, *Proceedings of ISPC'93*, Nanjing, China, October 1993.

269. Jha, N., Gupta, S., *Testing of Digital Systems*, Cambridge University Press, 2003.

270. Jin, M., Zhang, Q., Copy theory of signals and its applications, *Recent Developments in Abstract Harmonic Analysis with Applications in Signal Processing*, Nauka, Belgrade, 1996, pp. 313–328.

271. Kaczmarz, S., Über ein orthogonal system, *Comptes Rendus du I Congres des mathematiciens des pays Slaves*, Warsaw, 1929, pp. 189–192.

272. Kaczmarz, S., Steinhaus, H., *Theorie der Orthogonalreihen*, Chelsea, New York, 1951.

273. Karpov, Yu. G., Karpovsky, M.G., On optimal methods of code redundancy implementation for error correction in finite automata, *Kibernetika*, 1, 1971, 62–67 (in Russian), English translation *Cybernetics*, 1971, 72–89.

274. Karpov, Yu.G., Karpovsky, M.G., Decomposition of algebras and synthesis of reliable discrete devices by integral moduli, *Kibernetika*, 3, 1973 (in Russian), English translation *Cybernetics*, 1975.

275. Karpovsky, M.G., Finite automata with error detection and correction, *Vychisltel'naya Tekhnika i Voprosy Kibetnetiki*, 5, 1968, 71–74 (in Russian).

276. Karpovsky, M.G., Error correction in automata whose combinational parts are realized by expansion in orthogonal series, *Avtomatika i Telemekhanika*, 9, 1971, 204–309 (in Russian), English translation *Automation and Remote Control*, 31, 1971, 1524–1527.

277. Karpovsky, M.G., Harmonic analysis over finite commutative groups in linearization problems for systems of logical functions, *Information and Control*, 33(2), 1977, 117–141.

278. Karpovsky, M.G., *Finite Orthogonal Series in the Design of Digital Devices*, John Wiley, 1976.

279. Karpovsky, M.G., Fast Fourier transform over finite non-Abelian group, *IEEE Transactions on Computers*, C-26(10), 1977, 1028–1031.

280. Karpovsky, M.G., Error detection in digital devices and computer programs with the aid of linear recurrent equations over finite groups, *IEEE Transactions on Computers*, Vol. C-26(3), 1977, 208–218.

281. Karpovsky, M.G., Recent developments in applications of spectral techniques in logic design and testing of computer hardware, *Proceedings of International Symposium on Multiple-Valued Logic*, Oklahoma City, Oklahoma, USA, May 1981, pp. 1–10.

282. Karpovsky, M.G. (ed.), *Spectral Techniques and Fault Detection*, Academic Press, Orlando, Florida, 1985.

283. Karpovsky, M.G., Spectral techniques for off-line testing and diagnosis of complex systems, *Proceedings of the 5th International Workshop on Spectral Techniques*, Beijing, China, March 15–17, 1994, pp. 8–18.

284. Karpovsky, M.G., Spectral techniques for off-line testing and diagnosis of computer systems, *Approximation Theory and Its Applications*, 1998, 55–72.

285. Karpovsky, M.G., Milman, V.D., On subspaces contained in subsets of finite homogeneous space, *Discrete Mathematics*, 22, 1978, 273–280.

286. Karpovsky, M.G., Moskalev, E.S., Realization of a system of logical functions by means of expansion in orthogonal series, *Avtomatika i Telemekhanika*, 12, 1967, 119–129, (in Russian), English translation *Automation and Remote Control*, 28 , 1967, 1921–1932.

287. Karpovsky, M.G., Moskalev, E.S., On a method for state assignment in automata, *Proceedings of the 3rd Conference on Theory of Transmission and Coding of Information*, USSR, sect. 3, Moscow, Nauka, 1967, pp. 32–42 (in Russian).

288. Karpovsky, M.G., Moskalev, E.S., Utilization of autocorrelation characteristics for the realization of systems of logical functions, *Avtomatika i Telmekhanika*, 2, 1970, 83–90, English translation *Automatic and Remote Control*, 31, 1970, 342–350.

289. Karpovsky, M.G., Moskalev, É.S., *Spektral'nye metody analiza i sintez diskretnykh ustroistv*, Energiya, Leningrad, 1973 (in Russian).

290. Karpovsky, M.G., Moskalev, E.S., Podkletnov, B.K., On a method for realization of an (m, k)-terminal logical network, *Voprosy Radioelektroniki*, Series 12, 28, 1966, 73–80, (in Russian).

291. Karpovsky, M.G., Nagvajara, P., Optimal time and space compression of test responses for VLSI devices, *Proceedings of International Test Conference*, 1987, 523–529.

292. Karpovsky, M.G., Nagvajara, P., Optimal robust compression of test responses, *IEEE Transactions on Computers*, 39(1), 1990, 138–141.

293. Karpovsky, M.G., Nagvajara, P., Optimal codes for the minimax criterion on error detection, *IEEE Transactions on Information Theory*, 35(6), 1989, 1299–1305.

294. Karpovsky, M.G., Nagvajara, P., Functions with flat autocorrelation and their generalizations, in: Moraga, C. (ed.), *Theory and Applications of Spectral Techniques*, Forschungbereicht 268, FB Informatik, Universitaet Dortmund, Dortmund, Germany, March 1988, ISSN 0933–6192.

295. Karpovsky, M.G., Roziner, T., Moraga, C., Error detection in multiprocessor systems and array processors, *IEEE Transactions on Computers*, 44(3), March 1995, 383–394.

296. Karpovsky, M.G., Shcherbakov, N.S., Automata with transition self-correction, *Kibernetika*, 7(6), 1971, 63–67, (in Russian), English translation *Cybernetics*, 1971, 1011–1015.

297. Karpovsky, M.G., Stanković, R.S., Astola, J.T., Spectral techniques for design and testing of computer hardware, *Proceedings of International Workshop on Spectral Techniques in Logic Design, SPECLOG-2000*, Tampere, Finland, June 2–3, 2000, pp. 1–34.

298. Karpovsky, M. G., Stanković, R. S., Astola, J. T., Construction of linearly transformed planar BDD by Walsh coefficients, *Proceedings of the 2004 IEEE International*

Symposium on Circuits and Systems, ISCAS 2004, Vancouver, Canada, May 23–25, 2004, pp. 517–520.

299. Karpovsky, M.G., Stanković, R.S. Moraga, C., Spectral transforms in the previous decade, *Proceedings of the 31st International Symposium on Multiple-Valued Logic*, Warszawa, Poland, May 22–24, 2001, pp. 41–46.

300. Karpovsky, M.G., Trachtenberg, E.A., Linear checking equations and error-correcting capability for computation channels, *Proceedings of the IFIP Congress*, 1977, North-Holland, 1977, pp. 619–624.

301. Karpovsky, M.G., Trachtenberg, E.A., Some optimization problems for convolution systems over finite groups, *Information and Control*, 34(3), 1977, 227–247.

302. Karpovsky, M.G., Trachtenberg, E.A., Fourier transform over finite groups for error detection and error corrections in computational channels, *Information and Control*, 1979, 40(3), 335–358.

303. Karpovsky, M.G., Trachtenberg, E.A., Statistical and computational performance of a class of generalized Wiener filters, *IEEE Transactions on Information Theory*, IT-32(2), 1986, 303–307.

304. Karpovsky, M.G., Trachtenberg, E.A., Roziner, T., Computation of discrete Fourier transforms over finite Abelian groups using pipelined and systolic array architectures, *Proceedings of the International Symposium on the Mathematical Theory of Networks and Systems*, Amsterdam, Netherlands, 1989.

305. Karpovsky, M.G., Troyanovsky, A.A., Analysis of error-correcting capability of logical functions, *Proceedings of the 5th Symposium on Use of Redundancy in Information Systems*, Leningrad, 1972 (in Russian).

306. Karpovsky, M.G., Troyanovsky, A.A., Methods for analyzing the correcting power of automata, *Avtomalika i Vychisietel'naya Tekhnika*, 1, 1974 (in Russian), English translation *Automatic Control and Computer Science*, 8(1), 1974, 22–27.

307. Kebschull, U., Schubert, E., Rosenstiel, W., Multilevel logic synthesis based on functional decision diagrams, *Proceedings of the European Conference on Design Automation, EURO-DAC'92*, Hamburg, Germany, September 7–10, 1992, pp. 43–47.

308. Kebschull, U., Schubert, E., Rosenstiel, W. (eds.), *Proceedings of IFIP WG 10.5 Workshop on Applications of the Reed–Muller Expansion in Circuit Design*, Hamburg, Germany, September 16-17, 1993.

309. Kelly, P.M., Thompson, C.J., McGinnity, T.M., Maguire, L.P., Investigation of a programmable threshold logic gate array, *Proceedings of the 9th International Conference on Electronics, Circuits and Systems*, September 15–18, 2002, 2, pp. 673–676.

310. Keren, O., Reduction of average path length in binary decision diagrams by spectral methods, accepted for publication in *IEEE-TC*, TC-0242-0606.

311. Keren, O., Levin, I., Reduction of the number of paths in Binary decision diagrams by linear transformation of variables, *Proceedings of the 7th International Workshop on Boolean Problems*, Freiberg, Germany, September 21–22, 2006.

312. Kitahashi, T., Tanaka, K., Orthogonal expansion of multi-valued logical functions and its application to the realization with a single threshold element, *IEEE Transactions on Computers*, C-21 (2), 1972, 211–218.

313. Kohavi, Z., *Switching and Finite Automata Theory*, New York, McGraw-Hill, 1972.

314. Kohonen, T., *Digital Circuits and Devices*, New Jersey, Prentice-Hall, 1972.

315. Komamiya, Y., Theory of relay networks for the transformation between the decimal and binary system, *Bulletin of E.T.L.*, 15(8), August 1951, 188–197.

316. Komamiya, Y., Theory of computing networks, *Researches of E.T.L.*, 526, November 1951, *Proceedings of the First National Congress for Applied Mathematics*, May 1952, pp. 527–532.

317. Komamiya, Y., *Theory of Computing Networks, Researches of the Applied Mathematics Section of Electrotechnical Laboratory in Japanese Government*, 2 Chome, Nagata-Cho, Chiyodaku, Tokyo, July 10, 1959, pages 40.

318. Kondratiev, V.N., Shalyto, A.A., Realizations of a system of the Boolean functions by using arithmetic polynomials, *Automatika and Telemekhanika*, 3, 1993.

319. Kondratiev, V.N., Shalyto, A.A., Realization of Boolean functions by a single arithmetic polynomial with masking, *Avtomatika i Telemekhanika*, 1996, 158–171.

320. Kremer, H., Algorithmen zur Berechnung der Haar-Funktionen und der schnellen Haar-Transformation, *ANT-Forschungsbericht*, Vol. 12, Institut für Allgemeine Nachrichtentechnik, Darmstadt, December, 1970.

321. Kuhn, H.W., The Hungarian method for the assignment problem, *Naval Research Logistics Quarterly*, 2, 1955, 83–97.

322. Kuhn, H.W., Variants of the Hungarian method for assignment problems, *Naval Research Logistics Quarterly*, 3, 1956, 253–258.

323. Kukharev, G.A., Shmerko, V.P., Yanushkevich, S.N., *Technique of Binary Data Parallel Processing for VLSI*, Vysheyshaja shcola, Minsk, Belarus, 1991.

324. Kukharev, G.A., Tropchenko, A.U., Shmerko, V.P., *Systolic Signal Processors*, Minsk, Belarus, 1988, p.125pp (in Russian).

325. Kuo, Y.S., Generating essential primes for a Boolean function with multiple-valued inputs, *IEEE Transactions on Computers*, 36(3), 1987, 356–359.

326. Lai, Y.F., Pedram, M., Vrudhula, S.B.K., EVBDD-based algorithms for integer linear programming, spectral transformation, and functional decomposition, *IEEE Transactions on CAD* 13(8), 1994, 959–975.

327. Lai Y.-T., Sastry, S., Edge-valued binary decision diagrams for multi-level hierarchical verification, *Proceedings of the 29th Design Automation Conference (DAC-92)*, Anaheim, California, USA, June 8–12, 1992, pp. 668–613.

328. Lala, P., *Self-Checking and Fault Tolerant Digital Design*, Academic Press, 2001.

329. Lang, S., *Algebra*, Addison-Wesley, Reading, MA, 1965.

330. Lange, F.H., *Correlation Techniques*, Van Nostrand, Princeton, NJ, 1967.

331. Lechner, R., A transform theory for functions of binary variables, *Theory of Switching*, Harvard Computation Lab., Cambridge, MA, Progress Report BL-30, Sec-X, November 1961, pp. 1–37.

332. Lechner, R.J., A transform approach to logic design, *Proceedings of the 9th Symposium on Switching and Automata Theory*, 1968, pp. 213–214, also *IEEE Transactions on Computers*, C-19(7), 1970, 627–640.

333. Lechner, R.J., Harmonic analysis of switching functions, in: Mukhopadhyay, A. (ed.), *Recent Developments in Switching Theory*, Academic Press, New York, 1971.

334. Lechner, R.J., Moezzi, A., Synthesis of encoded PLAs, in: Karpovsky, M.G. (ed.), *Spectral Techniques and Fault Detection*, Academic Press, Orlando, Florida, 1985.

335. Le Dinh, C.T., Le, P., Goulet, R., Sampling expansion in discrete and finite Walsh-Fourier analysis, *Proceeding of the 1972 Symposium Application Walsh Functions*, Washington D.C., 1972, pp. 265–271.

336. Le Dinh, C.T., Goulet, R., Time-sequency-limited signals in finite Walsh transforms, *IEEE Transactions on Information Theory*, IT-20 (2), 1974, 274–277.

337. Lee, G., Drechsler, R., ETDD-based synthesis of term-based FPGAs for incompletely specified Boolean functions, *Proceedings of the Asia and South Pacific Design Automation Conference, ASP-DAC*, Yokohama, Japan, February 10–13, 1998, pp. 75–80.

338. Lee, G., Drechsler, R., Perkowski, M.A., ETDD-based synthesis of two-dimensional cellular arrays for multi-output incompletely specified Boolean functions, *IEE Proceedings on Computers and Digital Techniques*, 146(6), 1999, 302–308.

339. Lee, J.R., Review of recent work on applications of Walsh functions in communications, *Proceedings of the 1970 Symposium on Application Walsh Functions*, Naval Research Lab., Cambridge, Massachusetts, USA, 1970, pp. 26–35.

340. Lindgren, P., Drechsler, R., Becker, B., Improved minimization methods for pseudo-Kronecker expressions for mutiple output functions, *Proceedings of the International Symposium on Circuits and Systems, ISCAS'98*, Monterey, California, USA, May 31–June 3, 1998, pp. VI-187–VL-190.

341. Liu, X.P., Recurrence relations for the spectrum of independent functions, in: Stanković, R.S., Stojić, M.R. Stanković, M.S. (eds.), *Recent Developments in Abstract Harmonic Analysis with Applications in Signal Processing*, Nauka, Belgrade, 1996, pp. 261–268.

342. Lupanov, O.B., On a method of network synthesis, *Izv. Vuzov, Radiofizika*, 1, 1958, 43–45 (in Russian).

343. Lupanov, O.B., On the possibilities of synthesis of networks from different types of elements, *Dokl. Akad. Nauk SSSR*, 103, 1955, 561–563 (in Russian).

344. Lysternik, L.A., Chezvonenkis, D.A., Yanpolskii, A.R., *Handbook for Computing Elementary Functions*, Pregamon Press, 1965.

345. Macii, E., Poncino, M., Predicting the functional complexity of combinatorial circuits by symbolic spectral analysis of Boolean functions, *Proceedings of the EURO-DAC95*, pp. 294–299.

346. Macii, E., Poncino, M., Using symbolic Rademacher–Walsh spectral transforms to evaluate the agreement between Boolean functions, *IEE Proceedings on Computers and Digital Techniques*, 143(1), 1996, 64–68.

347. MacWilliams, F.J., Sloane, N.J.A., *The Theory of Error-Correcting Codes*, North-Holland, Amsterdam, 1977.

348. Malyugin, V.D., Switching circuits reliability, *Automatics and Telemechanics*, 25(9), 1964, 1375–1383.

349. Malyugin, V.D., On a polynomial realization of a cortege of Boolean functions, *Reports of the USSR Academy of Sciences*, 265 (6), 1982.

350. Malyugin, V. D., Representation of Boolean functions by arithmetical polynomials, *Avtomatika i Telemekhanika*, 4, 1982, 84–93, English translation *Automation and Remote Control*, 43(4), Part 1, 1982, 496–504.

351. Malyugin, V. D., Realization of Boolean function corteges by means of linear arithmetical polynomials, *Avtomatika i Telemekhanika*, 2, 1984, 114–122, English translation *Automation and Remote Control*, 45(2), Part 1, 1984, 239–245.

352. Malyugin, V.D., *Elaboration of theoretical basis and methods for realization of parallel logical calculations through arithmetic polynomials*, PhD Thesis, Institute of Control, Russian Academy of Science, Moscow, 1988.

353. Malyugin, V.D., *Paralleled Calculations by Means of Arithmetic Polynomials*, Physical and Mathematical Publishing Company, Russian Academy of Sciences, Moscow, 1997 (in Russian).

354. Malyugin, V.D., Kukharev, G.A., Shmerko, V.P., Transforms of polynomial forms of Boolean functions, *Institute of Control Sciences*, Moscow, 1986, pp. 1–48.

355. Malyugin, V.D., Sokolov, V.V., Intensive logical calculations, *Avtomatika and Telemekhanika*, 4, 1993, 160–167.

356. Malyugin, V.D., Stanković, M., Stanković, R.S., Systolic realizations of discrete Haar transform, *Avtomatika i Telemekhanika*, 9, 1997, 138–145 (in Russian).

357. Malyugin, V.D., Veits, A.V., Intensive calculations in parallel logic, *Proceedings of the 5th International Workshop on Spectral Techniques*, Beijing, China, March 15–17, 1994, pp. 63–64.

358. Mar, H.Y.L., Sheng, C.L., Fast Hadamard transform using the *H*-Diagram, *IEEE Transactions on Computers*, C-22(10), 957–960.

359. Markowsky, G. Syndrome testability can be achieved by circuit modification, *IEEE Transactions on Computers*, C-30(8), 1981, 604–606.

360. Marshall, J.E., Ireland, B., On the prehistory of the Walsh-functions: circulants, bi-circulants and dyadic group, *Colloquium on the Theory and Applications of Walsh Functions*, Hatfield, Hertfordshire, 1975.

361. Matrosova, A., Ostanin, S., Levin, I., Survivable self-checking sequential circuits, *16th IEEE International Symposium on Defect and Fault-Tolerance in VLSI Systems (DFT 2001)*, San Francisco, CA, USA, October 24–26, 2001, 395–402.

362. McMullen, C., Shearer, J., Prime implicants, minimum covers, and the complexity of logic simplification, *IEEE Transactions on Computers*, 35(8), 1986, 761–762.

363. Megson, G.M., Systolic arrays for the Haar transform, *IEE Proceedings on Computers and Digital Techniques*, 145(6), 1998, 403–410.

364. Meinel, Ch., Somenzi, F., Theobald, T., Linear sifting of decision diagrams, *Proceedings of the 34th Design Automation Conference*, Anaheim, California, USA, June 9–13, 1997, pp. 202–207.

365. Meinel, Ch., Somenzi, F., Tehobald, T., Linear sifting of decision diagrams and its application in synthesis, *IEEE Transactions on CAD*, 19(5), 2000, 521–533.

366. Meinel, Ch., Theobald, T., *Algorithms and Data Structures in VLSI Design*, Springer, 1998.

367. Menger, K.S., A transform for logic networks, *IEEE Transactions on Computers*, C-18(3), 1969, 241–250.

368. Merekin, Y.V., Arithmetical forms of Boolean expressions and their applications in network reliability calculations, Institute of Mathematics, SOAN SSSR, 1963.

369. Miller, D.M., Spectral transformation of multiple-valued decision diagrams, *Proceedings of the 24th International Symposium on Multiple-valued Logic*, Boston, Massachusetts, USA, May 22–25, 1994, pp. 89 96.

370. Miller, D.M., A spectral method for Boolean function matching, *Proceedings of the European Design and Test Conference*, Paris, France, March 11–14, 1996, p. 602.

371. Miller, D.M., Drecshler, R., Dual edge operations in reduced ordered binary decision diagrams, *Proceedings of the International Symposium on Circuits and Systems, ISCAS 98*, Vol. 6, Monterey, California, USA, May 31–Jun 3, 1998, pp. 159–162.

372. Minato, S., Graph-based representations of discrete functions, in: Sasao, T., Fujita, M. (ed.), *Representations of Discrete Functions*, Kluwer Academic Publishers, 1996, pp. 1–28.

373. Mishchenko, A., Brayton, R.K., Sasao, T., Exploring multi-valued minimization using binary methods, *Proceedings of the 12th International Workshop on Logic and Synthesis*, Laguna Beach, California, USA, May 28–30, 2003, pp. 278–285.

374. Mister, S., Adams, C. Practical *s*-box design, *Workshop Record of the Workshop on Selected Areas in Cryptography (SAC '96)*, Queen's University, Kingston, Ontario, August 1996, pp. 61–76.

375. Monteiro, J., Kukula, J.H., Devadas, S., Neto, H.C., Bitwise encoding of finite state machines, *VLSI Design*, 1994, 379–382.

376. Moraga, C., A monograph on ternary threshold logic, In Rine, D.C. (ed.), *Computer Science and Multiple-Valued Logic*, North-Holland, New York, 1977.

377. Moraga, C., Systolic systems and multiple-valued logic, *Proceedings of the 14th International Symposium on Multiple-Valued Logic*, Winnipeg, Manitoba, Canada, May 29–31, 1984, pp. 98–108.

378. Moraga, C., Some applications of the Chrestenson functions in logic design and data processing, *Mathematics and Computers in Simulation*, 27(5–6), 1985, 431–439.

379. Moraga, C., *Spectral Techniques for Logic Design*, Dortmund Univeristy Press, Dortmund, Germany, 1986.

380. Moraga, C., A decade of spectral techniques, *Proceedings of the 21st International Symposium on Multiple-Valued Logic*, Victroia, Canada, May 1991, pp. 182–188.

381. Moraga, C., The two-dimensional Zhang-Watari orthogonal transform, Forschungsbericht Nr. 567, Fachbereich Informatik, Universität Dortmund, 1995.

382. Moraga, C. (ed.), *Theory and Applications of Spectral Techniques*, Forschungsbereicht 286, ISSN 0933-6192, Dortmund University, West Germany, 1988.

383. Moraga, C., *Advances in Spectral Techniques*, Berichte zur angewandten Informatik, Dortmund, Germany, 1998.2, ISSN 0946–2341.

384. Moraga, C., Improving the characterization of *p*-valued threshold functions, *Proceedings of the 332nd International Symposium on Multiple-Valued Logic*, Boston, Massachusetts, USA, May 15–18, 2002, pp. 28–34.

385. Moraga, C., Heider, R., Tutorial review on applications of the Walsh transform in switching theory, *Proceedings of the First International Workshop on Transforms and Filter Banks*, Tampere, Finland, February 23–25, 1998, Proceedings in TICSP Series # 1, June 1998, pp. 494–512.

386. Moraga, C., Heider, R., New lamps for old!, generalized multiple-valued neurons, *Proceedings of the 29th International Symposium on Multiple-Valued Logic*, Freiburg im Breisgau, Germany, May 20–22, 1999, pp. 36–41.

387. Moraga, C., Sasao, T. Stanković, R.S., A generalized approach to edge-valued decision diagrams for arithmetic transforms, *Avtomatika i Telemekhanika*, 1, 2002, 140–153 (in Russian).

388. Moraga, C., Salinas, L., On Hilbert and Chrestenson transforms on finite Abelian groups, *Scientia, Series A, Mathematical Sciences*, 2, 1988, 87–99.

389. Moraga, C., Zhang, Q. (eds.), *Proceedings of the 5th International Workshop on Spectral Techniques*, Beijing, China, March 15–17, 1994.

390. Motzkin, T.S., The assignment problem, *Proceedings of the 6th Symposium on Applied Mathematics*, New York, McGraw-Hill, 1956, pp. 109–125.

391. Muller, D.E., Application of Boolean algebra to switching circuits design and to error detection, *IRE Transactions on Electronic Computers*, EC-3, 1954, 6–12.

392. Muller, D.E., Boolean algebras in electric circuit design, *American Mathematical Monthly*, 61(7), Part 11, 1954, 27–28.

393. Munirul, H.M., Hasegawa, T., Kameyama, M., Implementation and evaluation of a fine-grain multiple-valued Field Programmable VLSI based on source-coupled logic, *Proceedings of the 35th IEEE International Symposium on Multiple-Valued Logic*, Calgary, Canada, May 18–21, 2005, pp. 120–125.

394. Murgai, R., Brayton, R.K., Sangiovanni-Vincentelli, A.L., *Logic Synthesis for Field-Programmable Gate Arrays*, Kluwer Academic Publishers, 1995.

395. Muroga, S., *Logic Design and Switching Theory*, John Wiley and Sons, 1979.

396. Muzio, J.C., Composite spectra and analysis of switching functions *IEEE Transactions on Computer*, C-29(8), 1980, 750–753.

397. Muzio, J.C., Stuck fault sensitivity of Reed–Muller and Arithmetic coefficients, in: Moraga, C. (ed.), *Theory and Applications of Spectral Techniques*, Dortmund, 1989, pp. 36–45.

398. Muzio, J.C., Miller, D.M., Spectral techniques for fault detection, in: Karpovsky, M.G. (ed.), *Spectral Techniques and Fault Detection*, Academic Press, 1985.

399. Muzio, J.C., Wesselkamper, T.C., *Multiple-Valued Switching Theory*, Adam Hilger, Bristol, 1986.

400. Nagvajara, P., Karpovsky, M.G., Signature analysis by quadratic compressors, *Proceedings of the Test and Instrumentation Conference*, Boston, 1988, pp. 751–758.

401. Nakajima, M., Kameyama, M., Design of highly parallel linear digital systems for ULSI processors, *IEICE Transactions*, 7 E76-C, 1993, 1119–1125.

402. Nambiar, K.K., A note on the Walsh functions, *IEEE Transactions on Electronic Computers*, EC-13(5), 1964, 631–632.

403. Nanya, T., Challenges to asynchronous processor design, in: Sasao, T. (ed.), *Logic Synthesis and Optimization*, Kluwer Academic Publishers, Boston, 1993, pp. 191–213.

404. Natsui, M., Homma, N., Aoki, T., Higuchi, T., Design of multiple-valued logic circuits using graph based evolutionary synthesis, *Multiple-Valued Logic & Soft Computing*, 11 (5–6), 2005, 519–544.

405. Nazarala, J., Moraga, C., Minimal realization of ternary threshold functions, *Proceedings of the 4th International Symposium on Multiple-Valued Logic*, 1974, 347–359.

406. Nechiporuk, E.I., On the synthesis of gate networks, *Problemy Kibernetiki*, 9, 1963 (in Russian).

407. Newton, N.J., Data synchronization and noisy environments, *IEEE Transactions on Information Theory*, 48(8), 2002, 2253–2262.

408. Nicholson, P.J.M., *Algebraic Theory of the Finite Fourier Transform*, PhD Thesis, Stanford University, Stanford, CA, 1969.

409. Ninomiya, I., A theory of the coordinate representation of switching functions, *Memoirs of Faculty of Engineering, Nagoya Univ.*, 10, 1958, 175–190, reviewed in *IEEE Trans. Electronic Computers*, Vol. EC-12, No. 2, 1963, 152.

410. Ninomiya, I., *A Study of the Structure of Boolean Functions and its Applications to the Synthesis of Switching Circuits*, PhD Thesis. University Tokyo, 1961.

411. Nussbaumer, H.J., *Fast Fourier Transform and Convolution Algorithms*, Springer-Verlag, Berlin, 1981.

412. Nyberg, K., Perfect non-linear S-boxes, *Advances in Cryptology, Eurocrypt 91*, Brighton, UK, April 8–11, 1991, *Lecture Notes in Computer Science*, Springer, 1992, Vol. 547, pp. 378–386.

413. Oenning, R., Moraga, C., Properties of the Zhang-Watari transform, *Proceedings of the 25th International Symposium on Multiple-Valued Logic*, Bloomington, Indiana, USA, May 22–25, 1995, pp. 44–49.

414. Omlin, C.W., Giles, C.L., *Fault-Tolerant Implementation of Finite-State Automata in Recurrent Neural Networks*, Technical Report 95–3, Computer Science Department, Rensselaer Polytechnic Institute, Troy, NY, 1995.

415. Ortega, S., Prierto, A., Lloris, A., Pelayo, F.J., Using Reed-Muller coefficients to synthesize optimal prediction modules for concurrent testing, *Electronics Letters*, 27(14), 1991, 1243–1245.

416. Ostapko, D.L., Yan, S.S., Realization of an arbitrary switching function with two-level network of threshold and parity elements, *IEEE Transactions on Computers*, C-19(3), 1970, 262–269.

417. Padure, M., Cotofana, S., Dan, C., Vassiliadis, S., Bodea, M., Compact delay modeling of latch-based threshold logic gates, *Proceedings of the International Semiconductor Conference, CAS 2002*, Sinaia, Romania, Vol. 2, October 8–12, 2002, pp. 317–320.

418. Padure, M., Cotofana, S., Vassiliadis, S., A low-power threshold logic family, *Proceedings of the 9th IEEE International Conference Electronics, Circuits and Systems ICECS 2002*, Dubrovnik, Croatia, Vol. 2, September 15–18, 2002, pp. 657–660.

419. Paley, R.E.A.C., A remarkable system of orthogonal functions, *Proceedings of the London Mathematical Societies*, Vol. 34, 1932, 241–279.

420. Panda, S., Somenzi, F., Who are the variables in your neighbourhood, *Proceedings of IEEE Internation Conference on Computer-Aided Design, ICCAD-95*, San José, California, USA, November 5–9, 1995, pp. 74–77.

421. Panda, S., Somenzi, F., Pleisser, B.F., Symmetry detection and dynamic variable ordering of decision diagrams, *Proceedings of IEEE International Conference on Computer-Aided Design, ICCAD-94*, San José, California, USA, November 6–10, 1994, pp. 628–631.

422. Patel, J.H., Stuck-at fault - A fault model for the next millennium, *Proceedings of the International Test Conference*, Washington D.C., USA, October 18–23, 1998 p. 1166.

423. Paull, M.C., Unger, S.H., Minimizing the number of states in incompletely specified sequential switching functions, *IRE Transactions on Electronic Computers*, EC-8(3), 1959, 356–366.

424. Perkowski, M.A., The generalized orthonormal expansions of functions with multiple-valued input and some of its applications, *Proceedings of the International Symposium on Multiple-Valued Logic*, Sendai, Japan, May 27–29, 1992, pp. 445–450.

425. Peter, F., Weyl, H., Vollstandingkeit der primitiven Darstellungen einer geschlossen kontinuierlichen Gruppe, *Mathematical Annalen*, 97, 1927, 737–755.

426. Peterson, W.W., *Error-Correcting Codes*, MIT Press, Cambridge, MA, 1961.

427. Pichler, F., *Das System der sal und cal Funktionen als Erweiterung des Systems der Walsh-Funktionen und die Theorie der sal- und cal-Fourier Transformationen*, PhD Thesis, Philosophische Fakultat, Innsbruck Univ., Innsbruck, Austria, 1967.

428. Pichler, F., *Some Aspects of Correlation Analysis with Respect to Walsh Harmonic Analysis*, Technical Research Report R-70 11, Department of Electrical Engineering, University of Maryland, Baltimore, MD, 1970.

429. Pichler, F., Walsh functions and linear system theory, *Proceedings of the 1970 Symposium on Application of Walsh Functions*, Washington D.C., 1970, 175–182.

430. Pichler, F., On discrete dyadic systems, *Proceedings of the 1971 Symposium on Theory and Applications of Walsh Functions*, Halfield Polytechnic, Hatfield. Herts. U.K., 1971.

431. Pichler, F., On state space description of linear dyadic invariant systems, *IEEE Transactions on Electromagnetic Compatibility*, EMC-13(3), 1971, 166–170.

432. Pichler, F., Some historical remarks on the theory of Walsh functions and their applications in information engineering, in: Butzer, P.L., Stanković, R.S. (eds.), *Theory and applications of Gibbs Derivatives and Applications*, Matematički institut, Beograd, 1990, pp. xxv–xxx.

433. Pichler, F., Realizations of Prigogine's Λ-transform by dyadic convolution, in: Trappl, R., Horn, W. (eds.), Austrian Society for Cybernetic Studies, ISBN 385206127X, 1992.

434. Picton, P.D., Higher order neural networks and the arithmetic transform, *Proceedings of the 2nd International Conference on Artificial Neural Networks*, Bournemouth, UK, November 18–20, 1991, pp. 290–294.

435. Pierce, W.H., *Failure-Tolerant Computer Design*, Academic Press, New York - London, 1965.

436. Pitassi, D.A., Fast convolution using the Walsh transform, *Proceedings of the 1971 Symposium on Applications Walsh Functions*, AD-727-000, Washington D.C., 1971, pp. 130–133.

437. Pless, V., *Introduction to the Theory of Error-Correcting Codes*, 3rd edition, Wiley, 1998.

438. Pless, V.S., Huffman, W.C. (eds.), *Handbook of Coding Theory*, Vol. 1, North Holland, Amsterdam, Netherlands, 1998.

439. Pogossova, E., Egiazarian, K., Astola, J., Spreading sequences for downlink MC-CDMA transmission, *Proceedings of IEEE Vehicular Technology Conference, VTC'2004*, Vol. 7, Los Angeles, California, September 26–29, 2004, pp. 4859–4863.

440. Pogossova, E., Egiazarian, K., Astola, J., Relation between Boolean functions and spreading sequences for MC-CDMA transmission, *Proceedings of the 6th International Workshop on Boolean Problems IWSBP-04*, Freiberg, Germany, September 23–24, 2004, pp. 97–102.

441. Polyak, B. Shreider, Yu., Application of Walsh functions in approximate computations, in Bazilevskii, Y.Y. (ed.), *Vaprosy Teorii Matematicheskikh Mashin*, Vol. 2, Moscow, Fizmatgiz, 1962, pp. 174–190.

442. Pomeranz, I., Reddy, S.M., A method for diagnosing implementation errors in synchronous sequential circuits and its implications on synthesis, *Proceedings of European Design Automation Conference, EURO-DAC-93*, Hamburg, Germany, September 20–24, 1993, pp. 252–258.

443. Pomeranz, I., Reddy, S.M., On correction of multiple design errors, *IEEE Transactions on Computer-Aided Design of Integrated Circuits and Systems*, CAD-14(2), 1995, 255–264.

444. Pontryagin, L.S., *Neprerivnie grupi*, Ghostehizdat, 1954 (in Russian).

445. Poreckii, P.S., Solution of general tasks in probability theory through the mathematical logic, Izd-vo Kazanj Univ, Kazanj, Russia, 1887.

446. Bass, C.A. (ed.), *Proceedings of Symposium on Application of Walsh Functions*, 1970; Zeek, R.W., Schowalter, A.E. (eds.), *Proceedings of Symposium on Application of Walsh Functions*, 1971, 1972, 1973; Schreiber, H., Sandy, G.P. (eds.), *Proceedings of Symposium on Application of Walsh Functions*, 1974.

447. *Proceedings of International Symposium on Walsh and Other Non-sinusoidal Functions Applications*, Hatfield Polytechnic, England, 1971, 1973, 1975.

448. *Proceedings of International Conference on Signal Processing, Beijing/90*, Beijing, China, October 22–26, 1990.

449. *Proceedings of the 3rd International Conference on Applications of Computer Systems, ACS'96*, Szczecin, Poland, November 21–22, 1996.

450. Posner, E.C., Combinatorial structures for planetary reconnaissance, in: Mann, H.B. (ed.), *Proceedings of the 1968 Symposium on Error Correcting Codes*, New York, Wiley, 1968, pp. 15–46.

451. Pospelov, Yu. D., *Logical Methods for Network Analysis and Synthesis*, Moscow, Energiya, 1968 (in Russian).

452. Pradhan, D.K., *Fault Tolerant Computing: Theory and Techniques*, Vol 1 Prentice-Hall, Englewood Cliffs, NJ, 1986.

453. Pratt, W.K., Kane, J., Andrews, H.C., Hadamard transform image coding, *Proceedings of IEEE*, 57(1), 1969, 58–68.

454. Pratt, W.K., Chen, W.H., Welch, L.R., Slant transform image coding, *IEEE Transactions on Communications*, COM-22(8), 1075–1095.

455. Rademacher, H., Einige Sätze von allgemeinen Orthogonalfunktionen, *Mathematical Annalen*, 87, 1922, 122–138.

456. Rao, K.R., Kuo, J.G., Narasimhan, M.A., Slant-Haar transform, *International Journal of Computer Mathematics B*, 7, 1979, 73–83.

457. Rao, K.R., Narasimhan, M.A., Revuluri, K., Image data processing by Hadamard–Haar transform, *IEEE Transactions on Computers*, C-24, (9), 1975, 888–896.

458. Ray Liy, K.J., VLSI computing architectures for Haar transform, *Electronics Letters*, 26(23), 1990, 1962–1963.

459. Redinbo, G.R., An implementation technique for Walsh functions, *IEEE Transaction on Computers*, C-20(6), 1971, 706–707.

460. Reed, I.S., A class of multiple error correcting codes and their decoding scheme, *IEEE Transactions on Information Theory*, PGIT-4 (4) 1954, 38–49.

461. Rejchart, V.J., Signal flow graph and Fortran program for Haar–Fourier transform, *IEEE Transactions on Computers*, C-21 (9), 1972, 1026–1027.

462. Revuluri, K., Rao, K.R., Narsihan, M.A., Ahmed, N., Cyclic and dyadic shifts, Walsh–Hadamard transform and the H-diagram, *IEEE Transactions on Computers*, C-13(12), 1974, 1303–1306.

463. Rice, J.E., *Autocorrelation Coefficients in Representation and Classification of Switching Functions*, PhD Dissertation, University of Victoria, Victoria B.C., Canada, 2003.

464. Rice, J.E., Muzio, J.C., Serra, M., Methods for calculating autocorrelation coefficients, *Proceedings of the 4th International Workshop on Boolean Problems, (IWSBP2000)*, Freiberg, Germany, September 21–22, 2000, p. 69–76.

465. Rice, J.E., Muzio, J.C., Use of autocorrelation function in the classification of switching functions, *Euromicro Symposium on Digital System Design, Architectures, Methods and Tools (DSD)*, Dortmund, Germany, September 4–6, 2002, 244–251.

466. Rice, J.E., Muzio, J.C., Properties of autocorrelation coefficients, *Proceedings of IEEE Pacific Rim Conference on Communications, Computers and Signal Processing, PACRIM'03*, Victoria, British Columbia, Canada, August 28–30, 2003, pp. 577–580.

467. Rice, J.E., Muzio, J.C., On the use of autocorrelation coefficients in the identification of three-level decompositions, *Proceedings of the International Workshop on Logic Synthesis, (IWLS 2003)*, Laguna Beach, California, USA, 2003, pp. 187–191.

468. Rice, J., Serra, M., Muzio, J.C., The use of autocorrelation coefficients for variable ordering for ROBDDs, *Proceedings of the 4th International Workshop on Applications of Reed–Muller Expansion in Circuit Design*, Victoria, Canada, August 20–21, 1999, pp. 185–196.

469. Robinson, G., Discrete Walsh and Fourier power spectra, *Proceedings of the 1972 Symposium on Applications Walsh Functions*, Washington D.C., 1972, pp. 298–309.

470. Rodriguez-Villegas, E., Quintana, M.J., Avedillo, M.J., Rueda, A., Threshold logic based adders using floating-gate circuits, *Advances in Physics, Electronics and Signal Processing Application*, World Scientific and Engineering Society Press, 2000, pp. 54–58.

471. Rodriguez-Villegas, E., Huertas, G., Avedillo, M.J., Quintana, J.M., Rueda, A., A practical floating-gate Muller-C element using vMOS threshold gates, *IEEE Transactions on Circuits and Systems II, Analog and Digital Signal Processing*, 48(1), 2001, 102–106.

472. Ross, I., Kelly, J.J., A new method for representing Walsh functions, *Proceedings of the 1972 Symposium on Applications Walsh Functions*, Washington D.C., pp. 359–361.

473. Rosenkrantz, D.J., Half-hot state assignments for finite state machines, *IEEE Transactions on Computers*, 39(5) 1990, 700–702.

474. Rothaus, O.S., On bent functions, *Journal Combinatorial Theory*, 20(A), 1976, 300–305.

475. Roziner, T., Karpovsky, M.G., Multidimensional Fourier transforms by systolic architectures, *Journal of VLSI Signal Processing*, 4, 1992, 343–354.

476. Roziner, T.D., Karpovsky, M.G., Trachtenberg, L.A., Fast Fourier transform over finite groups by multiprocessor systems, *IEEE Transactions on Acoustics, Speech, Signal Processing*, ASSP-38(2), 1990, 226–240.

477. Ruckmongathan, T.N., Nadig, D.S., Ranjitha, P.R., Gray shades in RMS responding displays with wavelets based on the slant transform, *IEEE Transactions on Electron Devices*, 54(4), 2007, 663–670.

478. Rudell, R., Dynamic variable ordering for ordered binary decision diagrams, *Proceedings on IEEE Conference Computer Aided Design, ICCAD-93*, Santa Clara, CA, November 7–11, 1993, pp. 42–47.

479. Rudin, W., *Fourier Analysis on Groups*, Interscience Publisher, New York, 1960.

480. Ruiz, G., Michell, J.A., Buron, A., Fault detection and diagnosis for MOS circuits from Haar and Walsh spectrum analysis: on the fault coverage of Haar reduced analysis, in: Moraga, C. (ed.), *Theory and Application of Spectral Techniques*, University Dortmund Press, October 1988, pp. 97–106.

481. Ruiz, G., Michell, J.A., Buron, A., Switch-level fault detection and diagnosis environment for MOS digital circuits using spectral techniques, *IEE Proceedings on Digital Techniques and Computers*, July 1992, 139 (4), 293–307.

482. Rushforth, C.K., Fast Fourier–Hadamard decoding of orthogonal codes, *Information and Control*, 15, 1969, 37–39.

483. Russ, J.C., *Image Processing Handbook*, 5th edition, CRC Press, 2002.

484. Sagalovich, Yu. L., *State Assignment and Reliability of Automata*, Svyaz, Moscow, 1975, (in Russian).

485. Sasao, T., AND-EXOR expressions and their optimizations, in: Sasao, T. (ed.), *Logic Design and Optimization*, Kluwer Academic Publishers, 1993, pp. 287–312.

486. Sasao, T. (ed.), *Logic Design and Optimization*, Kluwer Academic Publishers, 1993.

487. Sasao, T., Debnath, D., An exact minimization algorithm for generalized Reed–Muller expansions, *Proceedings of IEEE Asia-Pacific Conference on Circuits and Systems*, Taipei, Taiwan, December 5–8, 1994, pp. 460–465.

488. Sasao, T., Representation of logic functions using EXOR operators, in: Sasao, T. Fujita, M. (eds.) *Proceedings of IFIP WG 10.5 Workshop on Applications of the Reed–Muller Expansion in Circuit Design, Reed–Muller'95*, Makuhari, Chiba, Japan, August 27–29, 1995, pp. 11–20.

489. Sasao, T., Representation of logic functions using EXOR operators, in Sasao, T. Fujita, M. (eds.), *Representations of Discrete Functions*, Kluwer Academic Publishers, 1996, pp. 29–54.

490. Sasao, T., Ternary decision diagrams and their applications, in: Sasao, T., Fujita, M., (eds.), *Representation of Discrete Functions*, Kluwer Academic Publishers, 1996, pp. 269–292.

491. Sasao, T., *Switching Theory for Logic Synthesis*, Kluwer Academic Publishers, 1999.

492. Sasao, T., On the number of dependent variables for incompletely specified multiple-valued functions, *Proceedings of the 30th International Symposium on Multiple-Valued Logic*, Portland, Oregon, USA, May 23–25, 2000, pp. 91–95.

493. Sasao, T., Besslich, Ph.W., On the complexity of MOD-2 sum PLA's, *IEEE Transactions Computers*, C-33, 2, 1990, 262–266.

494. Sasao, T., Butler, J.T., A design method for look-up table type FPGA by pseudo-Kronecker expansions, *Proceedings of the 24th International Symposium on Multiple-valued Logic*, Boston, Massachusetts, May 25–27, 1994, pp. 97–104.

495. Sasao, T., Butler, J.T., Planar Multiple-Valued Decision Diagrams, *25th IEEE International Symposium on Multiple-Valued Logic*, Bloomington, Indiana, May 23–25, 1995, 28–35.

496. Sasao, T., Butler, J.T., Planar Multiple-Valued Decision Diagrams, *Multiple-Valued Logic*, 1 (1), 1996, 39–46.

497. Sasao, T., Debnath, D., An exact minimization algorithm for generalized Reed-Muller expansions, *Proceedings of IEEE Asia-Pacific Conference on Circuits and Systems*, Taipei, Taiwan, December, 5–8, 1994, pp. 460–465.

498. Sasao, T., Fujita, M. (eds.), *Proceedings of the IFIP WG 10.5 Workshop on Application of the Reed–Muller Expansion in Circuit Design*, Makuhari, Chiba, Japan, August 27–29, 1995.

499. Sasao, T., Fujita, M. (eds.), *Representations of Discrete Functions*, Kluwer Academic Publishers, 1996.

500. Sasao, T., Matsuura, M., BDD representation for incompletely specified multiple-output logic functions and its applications to functional decomposition, *Proceedings of the 42nd Design Automation Conference*, San Diego, California, USA, 2005, pp. 373–378.

501. Sasao, T., Nagayama, S., Representations of elementary functions using binary moment diagrams, *Proceedings of the 36th International Symposium on Multiple-Valued Logic*, Singapore, May 17–20, 2006, paper No. 28.

502. Saucier, G., Encoding for asynchronous sequential networks, *IEEE TEC*, EC-16 (3), 1967, 365–369.

503. Saucier, G., Paulet, M.C., Sicard, P., Asyl: A rule-based system for controller synthesis, *IEEE Transactions on Computers-Aided Design*, CAD-6, (6), 1987, 1088–1097.

504. Sauerhoff, M., Wegener, I., Werchner, R., Optimal ordered binary decision diagrams for read-once formulas, *Discrete Applied Mathematics*, 103, 2000, 237–258.

505. Savir, J., Syndrome testable design of combinational circuits, *IEEE Transactions on Computers*, C-29, (6), 1980, 442–451.

506. Savir, J., Syndrome testing of syndrome-untestable combinational circuits, *IEEE Transactions on Computers*, C-30 (8), 1981, 606–608.

507. Schäfer, I., Falkowski, B.J., Perkowski, M.A., A fast computer implementation of adding and arithmetic multi-polarity transforms for logic design, *IEEE 34th Midwest Symposium on Circuit and Systems*, Monterey, California, USA, May 14–17, 1991, Vol. 2, pp. 1109–1112.

508. Schäfer, I., Perkowski, M.A., Extended spectral transforms for logic synthesis, *Recent Developments in Abstract Harmonic Analysis with Applications in Signal Processing*, Nauka, Belgrade, 1996, pp. 217–259.

509. Schebery, J., Mieko, Y., Hadamard matrices, sequences and block designs, in: Dinitz, J.H., Stinson, P.R. (eds.), *Contemporary Design Theory: A Collection of Surveys*, Wiley, New York, 1992, 431–560.

510. Schmidt, R.O., A collection of Walsh analysis programs, *Proceedings of the 1971 Symposium Application of Walsh Functions*, AD-727-000, Washington D.C., 1971, pp. 88–94.

511. Schrauder, J., Eine Eigenschaft des Haarschen Qithogonalsystems, *Mathematical Z.*, 28, 1928, 317–320.

512. Searle, N.H., A logical Walsh-Fourier transform, *Proceedings of the 1970 Applications of Walsh Functions*, Washington D.C., USA, April 1970.

513. Selfridge, R.E., Generalized Walsh transforms, *Pacific Journal of Mathematics*, 5, 1955, 451–480.

514. Selesnick, I.W., The slantlet transform, *IEEE Transactions on Singal Processing*, 47 (5), 1999, 1304–1313.

515. Sellers, F. Jr., Hsia, M.Y., Bearnson, L.W., Analyzing errors with the Boolean difference, *IEEE Transactions Computers*, C-17 (7), 1968, 676–683.

516. Scntovich, E.M., Singh, K.J., Lavagno, L., Moon, C., Murgai, R., Saldanha, A., Savoj, H., Stephan, P.R., Brayton, R.K., Sangiovanni-Vincentelli, A., *SIS: A system for sequential circuit synthesis*, Electronics Research Laboratory, University of California, Berkeley, ucb/erl m92/41 edition, May 1992.

517. Serra, M., Muzio, J.C., Testing programmable logic arrays by sum of syndromes, *IEEE Transactions on Computers*, C-36, (9), 1987, 1097–1101.

518. Shanks, J.R., Computation of the fast Fourier transform, *IEEE Transactions on Computers*, C-18 (5), 1969, 457–459.

519. Shannon, C.E., The synthesis of two-terminal switching circuits, *Bell System Technical Journal*, 28, (1), 1949.

520. Shapiro, H.S., Slotnick, D.L., On the Mathematical Theory of Error-Correcting Codes, *IBM Journal of Research and development*, 3 (1), 1959, 25–34.

521. Sheikholeslami, A., Look-up tables for multiple-valued, combinational logic, *Proceedings 28th International Symposium, Multiple-Valued Logic*, Fukuoka, Kyushu, Japan, May 26–29, 1998, pp. 264–269.

522. Sherman, H., Some optimal signals for time measurement, *Transactions on IRE*, IT-2 (1), 1956.

523. Shipp, F., Wade, W.R., Simon, P. (with assistance from Pal, J.,), *Walsh Series*, Adam Hilger, Bristol, 1990.

524. Shmerko, V.P., Synthesis of arithmetical forms of Boolean functions through the Fourier transforms, *Avtomatika i Telemekhanika*, 5, 1989, 134–142.

525. Shmerko, V.D., Mikhailov, S.V., Review of publications in the former Soviet Union on spectral methods of logic data processing and logic differential calculus, *Proceedings 5th International Workshop on Spectral Techniques*, Beijing, P.R. China, March 15–17, 1994, pp. 48–64.

526. Sholomov, L.A., Complexity criteria for Boolean functions, *Poblemy Kibernetiki*, 17, 1966 (in Russian).

527. Shore, J.E., On the application of Haar functions, *IEEE Transactions Communications*, Vol. COM-21, No. 3, 1973, 209–216.

528. Sieling, D., On the existence of polynomial time approximation schemes for OBDD minimization, *Proceedings STACS'98*, Lecture Notes in Computer Science, Vol. 1373, Springer, Berlin, 1998, pp. 205–215.

529. Siemens, K.H., Kitai, R., Walsh series to Fourier series conversion, *Proceedings of the 1972 Symposium Walsh Functions*, 295–297.

530. Sobol, I.M., *Multidimensional Quadrature Formulas and Haar Functions*, Moscow, Nauka, 1969 (in Russian).

531. Somenzi, F., *CUDD — Colorado University Decision Diagram Package*, 1996.

532. Song, N., Perkowski, M.A., Minimization of exclusive sum of products expressions for multi-output multiple-valued input, incompletely specified functions, *IEEE Transactions on Computer Aided Design*, (4), 1996, 385–395.

533. Souza, A.L., Hsiao, M.S., Error diagnosis of sequential circuits using region-based model, *Journal of Electronic Testing*, (2), 2005, 115–126.

534. Srinivasan, A., Kam, T., Malik, Sh., Brayant, R.K., Algorithms for discrete function manipulation, *Proceedings of Informations Conference on CAD, ICCAD-90*, Santa Clara, California, USA, November 11–15, 1990, pp. 92–95.

535. Stakhov, A.P., *Algorithmic Measurement Theory*, Vol. 6, Znanie, Moscow, 1979, 64 pages (in Russian).

536. Stanković, M., Janković, D., Stanković, R.S., Efficient algorithm for Haar spectrum calculation, *Scientific Review*, 21–22, 1996, 171–182.

537. Stanković, M., Janković, D., Stanković, R.S., Efficient algorithm for Haar spectrum calculation, *Proceedings of IEEE International Conference on Information, Communications and Signal Processing* (1st ICICS), Singapore, Vol. 4, September 1997, pp. 6–10.

538. Stanković, M., Janković, D., Stanković, R.S., Falkowski, B.J., Calculation of the paired Haar transform through shared binary decision diagrams, *Computers and Electrical Engineering*, 29 (1), 2003, 13–24.

539. Stanković, M., Stojković, S., Calculation of symmetric transform of Boolean functions represented by decision diagrams, *Proceedings of XLII Yugoslav Conference for ETRAN*, Vrnjačka Banja, June 3–5, 1998, pp. 63–66, (in Serbian).

540. Stanković, M.S., Aizenberg, N.N., Generalized discrete Gibbs derivatives and related linear equations, in: Butzer, P.L. Stanković, R.S. (eds.), *Theory and Applications of Gibbs Derivatives*, Mathematički institut, Beograd, 1990, pp. 249–268.

541. Stanković, R.S., A note on the relation between Reed–Muller expansions and Walsh transform, *IEEE Transactions on Electromagnetic Compatibility*, EMC-24(1), 1982, 68–70.

542. Stanković, R.S., Linear harmonic translation invariant systems on finite non-Abelian groups, in: Trappl, R. (ed.), *Cybernetics and Systems Research*, North-Holland, 1986, pp. 103–110.

543. Stanković, R.S., A note on differential operators on finite non-Abelian groups, *Applicable Analysis*, 21, 1986, 31–41.

544. Stanković, R.S., Matrix interpretation of the fast Fourier transforms on finite non-Abelian groups, *Proceedings of International Conference on Signal Processing, Beijing/90*, Beijing, China, October 22–26, 1990, pp. 1187–1190.

545. Stanković, R.S., Some remarks on Fourier transforms and differential operators for digital functions, *Proceedings of the 22nd International Symposium on Multiple-Valued Logic*, Sendai, Japan, May 27–29, 1992, pp. 365–370.

546. Stanković, R.S., Functional decision diagrams for multiple-valued functions, *Proceedings of the 25th International Symposium on Multiple-Valued Logic*, Bloomington, Indiana, USA, May 23–25, 1995, pp. 284–289.

547. Stanković, R.S., Some remarks about spectral transform interpretation of MTBDDs and EVBDDs, *ASP-DAC'95*, Makuhari Messe, Chiba, Japan, August 29 – September 1, 1995, pp. 385–390.

548. Stanković, R.S., Fourier decision diagrams for optimization of discrete functions representations, *Proceedings of the 1996 Workshop on Post-Binary Ultra-Large Scale Integration*, Santiago de Compostela, Spain, May 28, 1996, pp. 8–12, in conjunction with *The 1996 International Symposium on Multiple-Valued Logic*.

549. Stanković, R., Fourier decision diagrams on finite non-Abelian groups with preprocessing, *Proceedings of the 27th International Symposium on Multiple-Valued Logic*, Antigonish, Nowa Scottia, Canada, May 1997, pp. 281–286.

550. Stanković, R.S., *Spectral Transform Decision Diagrams in Simple Questions and Simple Answers*, Nauka, Belgrade, 1998.

551. Stanković, R.S., Some remarks on basic characteristics of decision diagrams, *Proceedings of the 4th International Workshop on Applications of Reed–Muller Expansion in Circuit Design*, August, 20–21, 1999, pp. 139–146.

552. Stanković, R.S., Non-Abelian groups in optimization of decision diagrams representations of discrete functions, *Formal Methods in System Design*, 18, 2001, 209–231.

553. Stanković, R.S., Unified view of decision diagrams for representation of discrete functions, *Multiple Value Logic*, 8, (2), 2002, 237–283.

554. Stanković, R.S., Astola, J.T., Design of decision diagrams with increased functionality of nodes through group theory, *IEICE Transactions Fundamentals*, E86-A, (3), 2003, 693–703.

555. Stanković, R.S., Astola, J.T., *Spectral Interpretation of Decision Diagrams*, Springer, 2003.

556. Stanković, R.S., Astola, J., Stanković, M., Egiazarian, K., Circuit synthesis from Fibonacci decision diagrams, *VLSI Design, Special Issue on Spectral Techniques and Decision Diagrams*, 14(1), 2002, 23–34.

557. Stanković, R.S., Astola, J.T., Moraga, C., Word-level expressions with matrix-valued co-efficients for the representation of discrete functions, *Proceedings of the 7th International Symposium on Representations and Methodology of Future Computing Technologies, RM-2005*, Tokyo, Japan, September 5–6, 2005, pp. 137–144.

558. Stanković, R.S., Bhattacharaya, M., Astola, J.T., Calculation of dyadic autocorrelation through decision diagrams, *Proceedings of European Conference on Circuit Theory and Design, ECCTD'01*, Espoo, Finland, August 28–31, 2001, pp. II-337 – II-340.

559. Stanković, R.S., Falkowski, B.J., Haar functions and transforms and their generalizations, *Proceedings of IEEE International Conference on Information, Communications and Signal Processing* (1st ICICS), Singapore, Vol. 4, September 1997, pp. 1–5.

560. Stanković, R.S., Janković, D., Falkowski, B.J., Minimization of Haar wavelet series and Haar spectral decision diagrams for discrete functions, *Computers and Electrical Engineering*, 31(3), 2005, 203–216.

561. Stanković, R.S., Karpovsky, M.G., Remarks on calculation of the autocorrealtion on finite dyadic groups by local transformations of decision daigrams, *Lecture Notes in Computer Science*, Vol. 3643/2005, Springer, Berlin/Heidelberg, Germany, 2005, pp. 301–310.

562. Stanković, R., S., Milenović, D., Some remarks on calculation complexity of Fourier transforms on finite groups, *Proceedings of the 14th European Meeting on Cybernetics and Systems Research, CMRS'98*, Vienna, Austria, April 15–17, 1998, pp. 59–64.

563. Stanković, R.S., Milenović, D., Janković, D., Quaternion groups versus dyadic groups in representations and processing of switching functions, *Proceedings of the 20th International Symposium on Multiple-Valued Logic*, Freiburg im Breisgau, Germany, May 20–22, 1999, pp. 19-23.

564. Stanković, R.S., Moraga, C., Reed–Muller-Fourier representations of multiple-valued functions over Galois fields of prime cardinality, in: Kebschull, U., Schubert, E., Rosentiel, W. (eds.), *Proceedings of IFIP WG 10.5 Workshop on Applications of the Reed–Muller Expansion in Circuit Design*, Hamburg, Germany, September 16–17, 1993, pp. 115–124.

565. Stanković, R.S., Moraga, C., Edge-valued functional decision diagrams, *Proceedings of the International Conference on Computer Aided Design of Discrete Devices*, vol. 2, Minsk, Belarus, November 15–17, 1995, pp. 69–73.

566. Stanković, R.S., Moraga, C., Astola, J.T., From Fourier expansions to arithmetic- Haar expressions on quaternion groups, *Applicable Algebra in Engineering, Communication and Computing*, AAECC 12, 2001, 227–253.

567. Stanković, R.S., Moraga, C., Astola, J.T., *Fourier Analysis on Finite Non-Abelian Groups with Applications in Signal Processing and System Design*, Wiley/IEEE Press, 2005.

568. Stanković, R.S., Sasao, T., Decision diagrams for discrete functions: classification and unified interpretation, *Proceedings of Asian and South Pacific Design Automation Conference, ASP-DAC'98* Yokohama, Japan, February 13–17, 1998, pp. 439–446.

569. Stanković, R.S., Sasao, T., Moraga, C., Spectral transform decision diagrams in: Sasao, T., Fujita, M., *Representations of Discrete Functions*, Kluwer Academic Publishers, 1996, pp. 55–92.

570. Stanković, R.S., Stanković, M., Calculation of the Gibbs derivatives on finite Abelian groups through decision diagrams, *Journal of Approximation Theory and Its Applications*, 14(4), 1998, 12–25.

571. Stanković, R.S., Stanković, M., Astola, J.T., Egiazarian, K., *Fibonacci Decision Diagrams*, TICSP Series # 8, ISBN 952-15-0385-8, ISSN 1456-2774, Tampere, 2000.

572. Stanković, R.S., Stanković, M., Astola, J.T., Egiazaraian, K., Haar spectral transform decision diagrams with exact algorithm for minimization of the number of paths, *Proceedings of the 4th International Workshop on Boolean Problems*, Freiberg, Germany, September 21–22, 2000, pp. 113–129.

573. Stanković, R.S., Stanković, M., Astola, J.T., Egiazarian, K., Karpovsky's old Haar spectrum theorem in a new light, *Proceedings of the 1st International Workshop on Spectral Techniques and Logic Design for Future Digital Systems*, Tampere, Finland, June 2–3, 2000, TICSP Series #10, December 2000, pp. 95–102.

574. Stanković, R.S., Stanković, M., Astola, J.T., Egiazarian, K., Boolean representations for functions in Fibonacci interconnection topologies, *Proceedings of the 4th International Workshop on Boolean Problems*, Freiberg, Germany, September 21–22, 2000.

575. Stanković, R.S., Stanković, M., Astola, J.T., Egiazarian, K., Fibonacci decision diagrams and spectral transform Fibonacci decision diagrams, *Proceedings of the 30th International Symposium on Multiple-Valued Logic*, Portland, Oregon, USA, May 23–25, 2000, pp. 206–211.

576. Stanković, R.S., Stanković, M., Janković, D., *Spectral Transforms in Switching Theory, Definitions and Calculations*, Nauka, Belgrade, 1998.

577. Stanković, R., Stanković, M., Janković, D., Calculation of the Fourier transform on finite non-Abelian group through decision diagrams, *Scientific Review*, 19–20, 1996, 249–264.

578. Stanković, R.S., Stanković, M., Janković, D., Shmerko, V., Yanushkevich, S., Optimizing the calculation of logic derivatives through decision diagrams, *Proceedings of the 6th International Workshop on Post Binary VLSI Systems*, May 1997, Antigonish, Nova Scotia, Canada.

579. Stanković, R.S., Stanković, M., Janković, D., Shmerko, V., Yanushkevich, S., Calculation of logic derivatives through decision diagrams, *Proceedings of the International Conference on Computer-Aided Design of Discrete Devices*, Minsk, Belarus, Vol. 1, 1997, pp. 46–53.

580. Stanković, R.S., Stanković, M., Moraga, C., Design of Haar wavelet transforms and Haar spectral transform decision diagrams for multiple-valued functions, *Proceedings of the 31st International Symposium on Multiple-Valued Logic*, Warszawa, Poland, May 22–24, 2001, 311–316.

581. Stanković, R.S., Stanković, M., Moraga, C., Sasao, T., Calculation of Vilenkin–Chrestenson transform coefficients of multiple-valued functions through multiple-place

decision diagrams, *Proceedings of the 5th International Workshop on Spectral Techniques*, Beijing, China, March 15–17, 1994, pp. 107–116.

582. Stanković, R.S., Stanković, M., Moraga, C., Sasao, T., Calculation of Reed–Muller-Fourier coefficients of multiple-valued functions through multiple-place decision diagrams, *Proceedings of the 24th International Symposium on Multiple-valued Logic*, Boston, Massachusetts, USA, May 22–25, 1994, pp. 82–88.

583. Stanković, R.S., Stojić, M.R., A note on the discrete generalized Haar derivative, *Automatika*, 28(3–4), 1987, 117–122.

584. Stanković, R.S., Stojić, M.R., Stanković, M.S., *Recent Developments in Abstract Harmonic Analysis with Applications in Signal Processing*, Nauka and Faculty of Electronics Niš, Belgrade, 1996.

585. Stanković, S., Astola, J., XSLT-based method for automatic generation of a graphical representation of a decision diagram represented using XML, *7th International Workshop on Boolean Problems*, Freiberg, Germany, September 21–22, 2006.

586. Stanković, S., Takala, J., Astola, J., Method for automatic generation of RTL in VHDL using decision diagrams, *Proceedings of the 2006 International TICSP Workshop on Spectral Methods and Multirate Signal Processing, SMMSP2006*, Florence, Italy, September 2–3, 2006, pp. 75–83.

587. Stojić, M.R., Stanković, M.S., Stanković, R.S., *Discrete Transforms in Applications*, Nauka, Beograd, 1985, 2nd updated edition 1993.

588. Stokman, A., *Implementation of Threshold Logic*, Technical Reports 1-68340-28 (1998)01, Delft University of Technology, January 1998.

589. Stokman, A., Cotofan, S., Vassiliadis, S., A versatile threshold logic gate, *Proceedings of the International Semiconductor Conference CAS'98*, Sinaia, Romania, 1998, pp. 163–166.

590. Su, S.Y.H., Cheung, P.T., Computer-oriented algorithms for minimizing multi-valued switching functions, *Proceedings of the 1971 symposium on Multi-valued Logic Design, University of New York at Buffalo*, pp. 140–152.

591. Suskind, A.K., Testing by verifying Walsh coefficients, *IEEE Transactions on Computers*, C-32, 1983, 198–201.

592. Swick, D.A., Walsh function generation, *IEEE Translations on Information Theory*, IT-I5 (1), 1969, 167.

593. Syuto, M., Shen, J., Tanno, K., Ishizuka, O., Multi-input variable-threshold circuits for multi-valued logic functions, *Proceedings of the 30th IEEE International Symposium on Multiple-Valued Logic*, Portland, Oregon, USA, May 23–25, 2000, pp. 27–32.

594. Sylvester, J.J., Thoughts on inverse orthogonal matrices, simulations sign-successions and tessellated parameters in two or more colors, with application to Newton's rule, ornamental tilework and the theory of numbers, *Philosophical Magazine*, 34–4, 1857, 461–475.

595. *Synthesis of electronic calculation and control networks*, translation from English under supervision by Shestakov, B.I. Izv. Inostranoi Literaturi, Moscow, 1954.

596. Tasto, M., Wintz, P.A., Image coding by adaptive block quantization, *IEEE Transactions on Communication Technology*, COM-19(6), 1971, 957–972.

597. Thayse, A., *Boolean Calculus of Differences*, Springer-Verlag, 1981.

598. Thayse, A., Davio, M., Boolean difference calculus and its applications to switching theory, *IEEE Transactions on Computers*, C-12(4), 1973, 409–420.

599. *The Annals of the Computation Laboratory of Harvard University*, Vol. XXVII, *Synthesis of Electronic Computing and Control Circuits*, Cambridge, Massachusetts, USA, 1951.

600. Thornton, M.A., Modified Haar transform calculation using digital circuit output probabilities, *Proceedings of the 1st International Conference on Information, Communications and Signal Processing, ICICSP'97*, Singapore, September 1997, pp. 117–123.

601. Thornton, M.A., Drechsler, R., Günther, Probabilistic equivalence checking using partial Haar spectral diagrams, *Proceedings of the 4th International Workshop on Applications of the Reed–Muller Expansion in Circuit Design*, August 20–21, 1999, Victoria B.C., Victoria, Canada, 123–132.

602. Thornton, M.A., Drechsler, R., Günther, W., A method for approximate equivalence checking, *Proceedings of the 30th International Symposium on Multiple-Valued Logic*, Portland, USA, May 23–25, 2000, pp. 447–452.

603. Thornton, M.A., Miller, D.M., Drechsler, R., Transformations amongst the Walsh, Haar, arithmetic and Reed-Muller spectral domain, *Proceedings of the 5th International Workshop on Applications of the Reed–Muller Expression in Circuit Design*, Starkville, Mississippi, USA, August 10–11, 2001, pp. 215–225.

604. Thornton, M.A., Drechsler, R., Miller, D.M., *Spectral Techniques in VLSI CAD*, Kulwer Academic Publishers, 2001.

605. Tomaszewska, A.M., Yanuskevich, S.N., Shmerko, V.P., The word-level models for efficient computation of multiple-valued functions, LWL based model, *Proceedings of the 32nd International Symposium on Multiple-Valued Logic*, Boston, Massachusetts, USA, May 15–18, 2003, pp. 209–215.

606. Tomczuk, R., *Autocorrelation and Decomposition Methods in Combinational Logic Design*, PhD thesis, University of Victoria, 1996.

607. Tošić, Ž., Arithmetical representations of linear functions, *Discrete Automata and Logical Networks*, Nauka, Moscow, 1970, pp. 131–136 (in Russian).

608. Trachtenberg, E.A., Systems over finite groups as suboptimal filters: a comparative study, in: Fuhrmann, P.A. (ed.), *Proceedings of the 5th International Symposium Mathematical Theory of Systems and Networks*, Springer-Verlag, Beer-Sheva, Israel, 1983, pp. 856–863.

609. Trachtenberg, E.A., SVD of Frobenius matrices for approximate and multiobjective signal processing tasks, in: Derettere, E.F. (ed.), *SVD and Signal Processing*, Elsevier, North-Holland, Amsterdam, New York, 1988, pp. 331–345.

610. Trachtenberg, E.A., Applications of Fourier analysis on groups in engineering practices, *Recent Developments in Abstract Harmonic Analysis with Applications in Signal Processing*, Nauka and Faculty of Electronics, Belgrade, 1996, pp. 331–403.

611. Trakhtman, A.M., *Introduction to Generalized Spectral Theory of Signals*, Sovetskoe Radio, Moscow, 1972 (in Russian).

612. Trakhtman, A.M., Fundamentals of the linear theory of signals defined on a finite set of points, *Avtomatika i Telemekhanika*, 4, 1974 (in Russian), English translation *Automation and Remote Control*, 35, 1974, Part 1. 521–612.

613. Trakhtman, V.A., Factorization of Walsh function matrix ordered according to Paley and by sequence frequencies, *Radiotekhnika i Elektronika*, 12, 1973 (in Russian).

614. Trakhtman, A.M., Trakhtman, V.A., The frequency of Walsh functions, *Telecommunications and Radio Engngineering*, USSR, 27, Vol. 12, 1973, 56–58.

615. Trakhtman, A.M., Trakthman, V.A., *Basis of the Theory of Discrete Signals on Finite Intervals*, Sovetskoe Radio. Moscow, 1975 (in Russian).

616. Tsui, C-Y., Pedram, M., Despain, A.M., Low-power state assignment targeting two- and multilevel logic implementations, *IEEE Transactions on Computer-Aided Design of Integrated Circuits and Systems*, CAD-17(12) 1998, 1281–1291.

617. Tzafestas, S.G., *Walsh Functions in Signals and Systems Analysis and Design*, Van Nostrand Reinhold, New York, 1985.

618. Ulman, L.J., Computation of the Hadamard transform and *R*-transform in ordered form, *IEEE Transactions on Computers*, C-19(4), 1970, 359–360.

619. Unger, S.H., *Asynchronous Sequential Switching Circuit*, Wiley, New York, 1969, reissued by Krieger Publishing Co., Inc., Melbourne, FL, 1983.

620. Unger, S.H., *The Essence of Logic Circuits*, 2nd edition, IEEE Press, 1997.

621. Vainstein, F.S., Error detections and corrections in numerical computations by algebraic methods, *Proceedings of the 9th International Symposium Applied Algebra, Algebraic Algorithms and Error-Correcting Codes, AAECC-9*, New Orleans, LA, USA, October 7–11, 1991, pp. 456–464.

622. Vainstein, F.S., Low redundancy polynomial checks for numerical computations, *Applicable Algebra in Engineering Communication and Computing*, 7(6), 1996, 439–449.

623. Varma, D., Trachtenberg, E. A., A fast algorithm for the optimal state assignment of large finite state machines, *Proceedings of the International Conference on Computer-Aided Design, ICCAD-88*, Santa Clara, California, USA, November 7–10, 1988, pp. 152–155.

624. Varma, D., Trachtenberg, L.A., Efficient spectral techniques for logic synthesis, in: Sasao, T. (ed.), *Logic Synthesis and Optimization*, Kluwer Academic Publishers, Boston, 1993, pp. 215–232.

625. Vetterli, M., Kovačević, J., *Wavelets and Subband Coding*, Prentice-Hall, Upper Saddle River, 1995.

626. Vilenkin, N.Ya., Concerning a class of complete orthogonal system, *Izvestiya. Akademi Nauk SSSR*, Seriya Mathematicheskaya, 11, 1947 (in Russian).

627. Vilenkin, N.Ya., Towards a theory of Fourier integrals on topological groups, *Mathematics Sb.*, 30(2), 1952, 245–252.

628. Vilenkin, N.Ya., Agaev, G.N., Džafarli, G.M., Towards a theory of multiplicative orthogonal systems of functions, *DAN Azerbajian SSR*, 18(9), 1962, 3–7.

629. Villa, T., Sangiovanni-Vincentelli, A., NOVA: state assignment of finite state machines for optimal two-level logic implementation, *IEEE Transactions on Computer-Aided Design of Integrated Circuits and Systems*, 9(9), 1990, 905–924.

630. Viterbi, A., *CDMA - Principles of Spread Spectrum Communication*, Addison Wesley, 1995.

631. Vlasenko, V.A., Lappa, Ya. M., Yaroslavski, L.P., *Methods of Synthesis of Fast Algorithms for Convolution and Spectral Analysis of Signals*, Nauka, Moscow, 1990.

632. Von Neumann, J., A certain zero-sum two-person game equivalent to the optimal assignment problem, *Contributions to the Theory of Games*, Vol. 2, *Annals of Mathematics Studies* 28, Princeton University Press, 1953, pp. 5–12.

633. Vranesic, Z.G., Lee, E.S., Smith, K.C., A many-valued algebra for switching systems, *IEEE Transactions on Computers*, C-19(10), 1970, 964–971.

634. Vrudhula, S.B.K., Lai, Y.T., Pedram, M., Efficient computation of the probability and Reed–Muller spectra of Boolean functions using edge-valued binary decision diagrams, in Sasao, T., Fujita, M. (eds.), *Proceedings of IFIP WG 10.5 Workshop on Applications of*

the *Reed–Muller Expansion in Circuit Design, Reed–Muller95*, Chiba, Japan, Makuhari, August 27–29, 1995, pp. 62–69.

635. Wade, W.R., Review of the book by Golubov, B., Efimov, A., Skvortsov, V.A., *Walsh Series and Transforms*, Kluwer Academic Publishers, Dordrecht, 1991, *Bulletin of American Mathematics and society*, 29(2), 1992, 348–359.

636. Waho, T., A novel multiple-valued logic gate using resonant tunneling devices, *Proceedings of the 29th International Symposium on Multiple-Valued Logic*, Freiburg im Breisgau, Germany, May 20–22, 1999, 2–8.

637. Waho, T., Hattori, K., Honda, K., Novel resonant-tunneling multiple-threshold logic circuit based on switching sequence detection, *Proceedings of the 30th International Symposium on Multiple-Valued Logic*, Portland, Oregon, USA, May 23–25, 2000, pp. 317–322.

638. Walsh, J.L., A closed set of orthogonal functions, *American Journal of Mathematics*, 55, 1923, 5–24.

639. Walsh, J.L., A property of Haar system of orthonormal functions, *Mathematische Annalen*, 90, 1923, 38–45.

640. Wan, W., Perkowski, M.A., A new approach to the decomposition of incompletely specified multi-output functions based on graph coloring and local transformations and its application to FPGA mapping, *Proceedings of the European Design Automation Conference*, November 1992, pp. 230–235.

641. Watari, C., A generalization of Haar functions, *Tohoky Mathamatical Journal*, 8, 1956, 286–290.

642. Wayner, P., *Dis apearing Cryptography, Information Hiding - Steganogrpahy and Watermarking*, Morgan Kaufmann Publishers, Inc., 2002.

643. Wegener, I., Worst case examples for operations over OBDDs, *Information Processing Letters*, 74, 2000, 91–94.

644. Wei, Y., Zhang, Q., *Common Waveform Analysis: A New and Practical Generalization of Fourier Analysis*, Kluwer Academic Publishers, 2000.

645. Weiner, F.R., Smith, E.J., On the number of distinct state assignments for synchronous sequential machines, *IEEE Transactions on Electronics Computers*, EC-16, 1967, 220–221.

646. Whelch, J.E., Jr., Guinn, D.F., The fast Fourier-Hadamard transform and its use in signal representation and classification, *IEEE Transactions on Aerospace and Electronic Systems*, 1968, 561–573.

647. Wickerhuser, M.V., *Adapted Wavelet Analysis from Theory to Software*, IEEE Press, 1994.

648. Wiener, N., Paley, R.E.A.C., Analytic properties of the characters of infinite Abelian groups, *Verhandlungen des International mathematical Kongresses* Zürich, Zweiter Band, Seite 1932, p. 95.

649. Winder, R.O., The status of threshold logic, *Proceedings of the 1st-Annual Conference on Information Science Systems*, Princeton Univ. Press, Princeton, N.J., 1967.

650. Winder, R.O., The status of threshold logic, *RCA Review* 30, 1969, 62–84.

651. Yablonskii, S.W., Functional constructions in k-valued logic, *Trudy Mathematical Institute of Steklov*, 1958, 5–142 (in Russian).

652. Yablonskii, S.W., On algorithmic obstacles to the synthesis of minimal contact networks, *Problemy Kibernetiki*, 2, 1959, 75–121 (in Russian).

653. Yamamoto, Y., Fujita, S., Relationship between p-valued majority functions and p-valued threshold functions´, *IEEE Transactions on Computers*, 37 (11), 1442–1445.

654. Yang, S., Cieselski, M.J., Optimum and suboptimum algorithms for input encoding and its relationship to logic minimization, *IEEE Transactions on Computer-Aided Design*, CAD-10(1), 1991, 4–12.

655. Yang, J., De Micheli, G., Spectral transforms for technology mapping, Technical Report CSL-TR-91-498, Stanford University, December 1991.

656. Yanushkevich, S.N., Spectral and differential methods to synthesize polynomial forms of MVL-functions on systolic arrays, *Proceedings of the 5th International Workshop on Spectral Techniques*, Beijing, China, March 15–17, 1994, pp. 78–83.

657. Yanushkevich, S.N., Developing Boolean differential calculus methods for arithmetical logic, *Automation and Remote Control*, 55, (5), Part 2, 1994, 715–729.

658. Yanushkevich, S.N., *Logic Differential Calculus in Multi-Valued Logic Design*, Technical University of Szczecin Academic Publishers, Poland, 1998.

659. Yanushkevich, S.N., Dziurzanski, P., Shmerko, V.P., The word-level models for efficient computation of multiple-valued functions, LAR based model, *Proceedings of the 32nd International Symposium on Multiple-Valued Logic*, Boston, Massachusetts, USA, May 15–18, 2003, pp. 202–208.

660. Yanushkevich, S.N., Shmerko, V.P., Guy, L., Lu, D.C., Three dimensional multiple valued circuits design based on single-electron logic, *Proceedings of the 34th International Symposium on Multiple-Valued Logic*, Toronto, Canada, May 19–22, 2004, pp. 275–280.

661. Yanushkevich, S.N., Miller, D.M., Shmerko, V.P., Stanković, R.S., *Decision Diagram Techniques for Micro- and Nanoelectronic Design Handbook*, CRC Press, Taylor & Francis, 2006.

662. Yaroslavsky, P.L., *Vvedenie v cifrovuyu obrabotku izobrazhenii*, Sovetskoe radio, Moskva, 1979.

663. Yaroslavsky, L.P., *Digital Picture Processing*, Springer, Berlin, Heidelberg, 1985.

664. Yaroslavsky, L.P., *Digital Signal Processing in Optics and Holography, Introduction to Digital Optics*, Radio i Svazi, Moscow, 1987.

665. Yaroslavsky, L.P., *Digtal Holography and Digital Image Processing, Principles, Methods, Algorithms*, Kluwer Academic Publishers, 2004.

666. Yu, N.Y., Gong, G., *Constructions of Quadratic Bent Functions*, CACR Technical Report, CACR 2005-32, University of Waterloo, Waterloo, Canada, September 2005.

667. Yuen, C.K., Walsh functions and Gray code, *IEEE Transactions*, EMC-13(3) 1971, 68–73.

668. Yuen, C.K., Approximation errors of a Walsh series, *Proceedings of the 1972 Symposium Walsh Functions*, Washington D.C., USA, 1972, pp. 289–292.

669. Yuen, C.K., Remarks on the ordering of Walsh functions, *IEEE Transactions Computers*, C-21(12), 1972, 1452.

670. Zadiraka, V.K., *Teoriya vychisleniya preobrazovaniya Fur'e*, Naukova dumka, Kiev, 1983.

671. Zalmanzon, L.A., *Fourier, Walsh, and Haar Transforms and Their Applications in Control, Communication and Other Fields*, Nauka, Moscow, 1989 (in Russian).

672. Zhang, G., Moraga, C., Orthogonal transforms on finite discrete Abelian groups, in: Stanković, R.S., Stojić, M.R., Stanković, M.S. (eds.), *Recent Developments in Abstract Harmonic Analysis with Applications in Signal Processing*, Nauka and Faculty of Electronics Niš, Belgrade, 1996, pp. 293–304.

673. Zhang, G., Pan Ailing, *Theory and Applications of Digital Spectral Techniques*, National Defence Industry Press, Beijing, 1992 (in Chinese).

674. Zhang, Q., A summary of bridge functions, *Proceedings of the 5th International Workshop on Spectral Techniques*, Beijing, China, March 15–17, 1994, pp. 128–135.

675. Zhang, Q.S., *New Methods of Signal Information Transfer*, Aeronautics and Astronautics Publisher, Beijing, P.R. China, 1989 (in Mandarin).

676. Zhang, Q.S., Zhang, Y.G., *Theory and Applications of Bridge Functions*, Defense Industry Publisher, Beijing, P.R. China, 1992 (in Mandarin).

677. Zhang, R., Gupta, P., Zhong, L., Jha, N.K., Threshold network synthesis and optimization and its application to nanotechnologies, *IEEE Transactions on Computer-Aided Design of Integrated Circuits and Systems*, 24(1), 2005, 107–118.

678. Zhegalkin, I.I., O tekhnyke vychyslenyi predlozhenyi v symbolytscheskoi logykye, *Mathematics Sb.*, 34, 1927, 9–28, (in Russian).

679. Zhegalkin, I.I., Arifmetizatiya symbolytscheskoi logyky, *Mathematics Sb.*, 35, 1928, 311–377, (in Russian).

680. Zhendong, S., Zhang, Q., The relation of Walsh functions and parts of bridge functions, *Journal of Beijing University of Aeronautics and Astronautics*, 1, 1989.

681. Zheng-Xin, H., Ni-Ni, X., Chen, H., Li, X.L., Fast slant transform with sequency increment and its application in image compression, *Proceedings of the International Conference on Machine Learning and Cybernetics*, Vol. 7, Shanghai, P.R. China, August 26–29, 2004, pp. 4085–4089.

682. Zhengxin, H., Nini, X., Hong, Ch., Xuelei, L., Fast slant transform with sequency increment and its application in image compression, *Proceedings of the 7th International Conference on Signal Processing, ICSP'04*, Vol. 1, August 31–September 4, 2004 pp. 65–68.

683. Zhihua, L., Zhang, Q., Ordering of Walsh functions, *IEEE Transaction on Electromagnetic Compatibility*, EMC-25(2), 1983, 115–119.

684. Zhihua, L., Zhang, Q., Introduction to bridge functions, *IEEE Transactions on Electromagnetic Compatibility*, EMC-25, 4, 1983, 459–464.

685. Zigangirov, K. Sh., *Theory of Code Division Multiple Access Communication*, Wiley, 2004.

686. Zhu, X., Ho, A.T.S., A slant transform watermarking for copyright protection of satellite images, *Proceedings of Joint Conference of the 4th International Conference on Information, Communications, and Signal Processing and the 4th Pacific Rim Conference on Multimedia*, December 15–18, 2003, 2, 1178–1181.

687. Zilić, Z., Vranesić, Z.G., Polynomial interpolation for Reed–Muller forms for incompletely specified functions, *Multiple-Valued Logic*, 2, 1997, 217–243.

INDEX

Abelian group, 32
Abstract automata, 308
Abstract harmonic analysis, 17
Abstract harmonic analysis on finite
  groups, 31
Accuracy of DFG, 299
Additive approximations, 249
Additive group, 87
Advanced Cryptography Standard, 211
Algebraic error, 371
Aliasing probability, 212
α-(Anti)-self-dual, 204
Amplitude spectrum, 373
$(AN + B)$-code, 415
Anti-self-dual, 203
Anti-self-duality group, 205
Approximated system, 245
Approximation of the system, 250
Arithmetic code distance, 415
Arithmetic distance, 415
Arithmetic error, 371

Arithmetic expressions, 61
Arithmetic transform, 61
Arithmetic-Haar transform, 515
Assignment, 309
Asynchronous CDMA, 539
(Anti-)self-duality point, 205
Autonomous automata, 342

Basic arithmetic transform
  matrix, 61
Basic Reed–Muller matrix, 20
Basic Walsh functions, 38
Basic Walsh matrix, 42
Bent functions, 211
Binary Decision Diagram, 13
Binary Decision Tree, 11
Bit-level expressions, 31
Bit-level transforms, xvi
Boolean functions, 2
Built-in self-testing, 430
Burst of the length b, 391

Cartesian product, 2
Character of a group, 87
Characteristic of a field, 99
Characteristic function, 206
Check complexity, 461
Check sum method, 431
Chip codes, 539
Circulant matrices, 42
Circulants, 143
Code Division Multiple Access, 537
Coefficient vector, 17
Combinational devices, 1
Combinational networks, 27
Compact groups, 99
Comparable functions, 214
Completely monotone, 214
Complex values, 66
Complex wavelet transform, 523
Complexity of logic functions, 222
Complexity of DFG, 298
Complexity criteria, 222
Composite transforms, 515
Conjugate element, 33
Conjunctive transform, 22
Constant nodes, 12
Constant-β slant-Haar
    transform, 520
Controllabilities, 422
Corrected error, 408
Correcting capability, 372
Correcting power, 372
Cosets, 33
Cosine transform, 516
Cost of an error, 393
Counting automaton, 411
Cover of minterms, 225
Cross-correlation functions, 79, 394
Cyclic group, 32

Decision diagrams, 10
Digital devices, 1
Digital function generator, 298
Direct Sequence CDMA, 538
Discrete Cosine Transform (DCT),
    516

Discrete Haar functions, 51
Discrete wavelet packet analysis
    (DWPA), 523
Discrete wavelet transform
    (DWT), 522
Disjunctions, 6
Distance functions, 316
Distance matrices, 317
Dual object, 100
Duality principle, 257
Duality property, 375
Dyadic groups, 36
Dyadic order, 41

Elementary symmetric function, 180
Elementary symmetric function with
    operating number k, 379
Elementary symmetric function with the
    operating number α, 407
Encoding, 309
Entropy function, 223
Equivalent automata, 334
Equivalent states, 337
Error in a finite automaton, 399
Error locator, 492
Error with multiplicity l, 371
Even symmetric transform, 535
Excitation functions, 311
Expected l-fold errors, 407

Factor group, 33
False, 6
Fast Fourier transform (FFT), 107
Fast Hadamard–Walsh transform, 109
Fast wavelet transform (FWT), 522
Fault diagnosis, 428
Fault location, 428
Fibonacci decision diagrams, 530
Fibonacci transforms, 523
Field, 32
Field Programmable Gate Arrays, 314
Finite automaton, 308
Finite discrete function, 2
Finite dyadic group, 36
Finite groups, xv

Finite Walsh series, 44
Fixed polarity Reed–Muller (FPRM)
  polynomials, 23
Fixed-polarity arithmetic-Haar, 516
Fourier series, 34
Free BDDs, 14
Frequency Division Multiple
  Access, 537
Frequency Hopping, 538
Function algebra, 34
Functional testing, xx, 431
Functionally complete, 7
Functionally separable, 224

Generator of a group, 32
Global Positioning Systems, 538
Group, 32
Group automaton, 410
Group characters, 41
Group characters of Abelian groups, xv
Group representations, xv

Haar functions, 51
Haar matrix, 53
Haar ordering, 51
Haar spectral diagrams, 198
Haar spectral transform decision
  diagrams, 192
Haar transform, xvi
Haar-Galois transform, 94
Hadamard-Haar transform, 514
Hadamard matrices, 42
Hadamard ordering, 41
Hamming code, 173
Homomorphism, 87
Hungarian algorithm, 321
Hybrid transforms, 515

Identical computation family, 54
Implementing a function 001
  inclusion, 32
Index of a function, 38
Inertia group, 205
Initial state, 309
Input signals, 309

Integral Walsh functions, 259
Internal states, 309
Inverse conjunctive transform, 61
Irreducible representation, 100
Isometric (unitary), 76
Isomorphic groups, 86

JPEG standard, 534

k-ary form, 257
k-comparable, 214
k-monotonicity, 214
Karhunen–Loève transform, 516
Kronecker product, 17
Kronecker spectral transforms, 127
Kronecker transforms, 25

l-fold arithmetic error, 371
l-fold error, 371
L_2-norm, 76
λ_s-reachable, 417
Least-absolute-error
  approximation, 480
Length of a switching function, 225
Levels in a decision diagram, 13
Linear (m, k)-code, 205
Linear functions, 47
Linear automata, 408
Linear combination, 19
Linear span, 436
Linear transform, 17
Linearity group, 187
Linearity point, 187
Linearization of logic
  functions, 227
Linearization problem, 228
Lipschitz class, 303
Literal function, 6
Local behavior, 56
Locally compact Abelian groups, 74
Logic *NAND*, 8
Logic *NOR*, 8
Logic ordering, 42
Logic product, 401
Look-up-table, 348

Majority decoding, 451
Majority function, 377
Matching of minterms, 226
Matching problem, 344
Maxterm, 6
Mealy model of automata, 309
Mean-square distance, 299
Minimal automata, 399
Minimal cardinality of a check
    subgroup, 431
Minimal complete set of
    implicants, 225
Minimal disjunctive form, 225
Minimal symmetric matching, 321
Minimum length code, 314
Minimum Reed–Muller expansion, 24
Minterm, 6
Moore model of automata, 309
Mother wavelet, 521
Multioutput function, 2
Multiple-β slant-Haar transform, 520
Multiple-Place Decision Diagrams, 16
Multiple-valued functions, 2
Multiplicative closure, 40
Multiplicative group, 86
Multiplicity of an error, 372
Multiterminal Binary Decision
    Diagrams, 14
Multiterminal decision
    diagrams, 103

n-monotone, 214
Natural ordering, 40
Negative Davio expansion, 23
Negative line, 427
Negative literal, 6
Netlists, 2
Next-state function, 309
Non-Abelian group, 98
Noninteger number, 475
Nonrepetitive quadratic form, 207
Nonsymmetric error, 382
Nonterminal nodes, 12
Normal subgroup, 33
Normalized transform, 51

Observabilities, 422
OmniTRACS, 538
1-hot bit encoding, 314
1-minterms, 6
1-step majority decoding
    procedure, 493
Optimal approximation, 250
Optimal equality checks, 474
Optimal linear checks, 431
Optimal linear equality checks, 434
Ordered BDT, 13
Orthogonal checks, 447
Orthogonal Frequency Division
    Multiplexing, 47
Orthogonal inequality, 489
Orthogonal series, 35
Orthogonal subgroup, 434
Output function of an
    automaton, 309
Output functions, 1
Output signals, 308

Packet, 40
Paley ordering, 40
Parametrized transforms, 515
Parity function, 48
Parseval theorem, 104
Partially anti-self-dual, 204
Partially linear, 237
Partially self-dual, 204
Partition, 416
Path, 13
Perfect code, 172
π-complexity, 223
Piecewise-linear, 259
Polynomial approximation,
    244–245, 252
Positive Davio expansion, 20
Positive literal, 6
Positive line, 426
Positive polarity Reed–Muller
    polynomial, 20
Positive polarity Reed–Muller
    expressions, 20
power of f_i, 376

Power to average power ratio, 540
Prime implicant, 225
Principle character, 104
Product-of-Sum, 8
Products, 6
Programmable Logic Array, 314
Proper subgroup, 33
Proper subset, 32
Pseudo Noise, 539

Quadratic form, 207
Quaternion group, 97
Quotient group, 33

Rademacher functions, 38
Random Access Memories, 422
Random Access Memory, 49
Read Only Memories, 49
Reducible representations, 100
Reduction rules, 13
Reed–Muller functions, 20
Reed–Muller matrix, 20
Reed–Muller spectrum, 22
Reed–Muller transform, 20
Representations of functions, 2
Ring, 33
Ring of integers, 2
Root node, 12

Schauder functions, 299
Self-dual functions, 204
Self-duality point, 478
Sequence generators, 304
Sequency, 40
Sequency order, 40
Sequential machines, 1
Sequential networks, 27
Serial implementation, 349
Shannon expansion, 9
Shared BDDs, 15
Simplicity of functions, 227
Sinc function, 521
Single-threshold switching
    functions, 213
Size of the BDD, 154

Slant transform, 516
Slant-Haar transform, 518
Slant-Hadamard transform, 517
Slantlet transform, 520
Span, 36
Spectral domain, 17
Spectral complexity, 255
Spectral decision diagram, 189
Spectral decision tree, 189
Spectral decomposition rule, 189
Spectral expansions, 28
Spectral representation, 17
Spectral Transform Decision
    Diagrams, 128
Spectral Transform Decision Trees, 128
Spectrum, 35
Speed of a DFG, 299
State diagram, 309
State encoding, 309
State functions, 1
State table, 309
State-input assignment, 309
Steganalysis, 537
Steganography, 537
Structural finite automata, 308
Stuck-at-one, 423
Stuck-at-zero, 423
Subset, 32
Sum-of-Product, 8
Switching functions, 2
Symmetric arithmetic errors, 415
Synthesis of the network, 27

Threshold elements, 212
Time Division Multiple Access, 537
Total autocorrelation functions, 228
Total cross-correlation functions, 281
Tree-structured Haar transforms, 537
True, 6
Truth tables, 10
Truth vectors, 10

Unate line, 426
Unidirectional arithmetic error, 381
Unidirectional errors, 509

Uniform approximation, 55
Uniform distance, 299
Unitary representations, 98
Unnormalized transform, 51

Varshamov bound, 483
Varshamov–Gilbert bound, 465
Vector space, 33
Vilenkin–Chrestenson transform, 72
Vilenkin–Chrestenson–Galois, 94

Walsh, 72
Walsh analysis, xv
Walsh coefficients, 44
Walsh functions, xv
Walsh functions of first order, 38
Walsh matrix, 45
Walsh ordering, 40

Walsh spectrum, 44
Walsh–Galois transform, 94
Walsh–Hadamard functions, 42
Walsh–Hadamard matrix, 42
Walsh–Kaczmarz ordering, 41
Watermarking, 537
Wavelet functions, 51
Wavelet packet decomposition
   (WPD), 522
Wavelet packet transforms (WPT), 522
Wavelet transforms, 520
Wavelets theory, xvi
Weight, 38
Weighted total cross-correlation
   function, 394
Wiener–Khinchin theorem, 104
Word-level expressions, 31
Word-level transforms, xvi